D1179537

CONTROVERSY AND DIALOGUE IN THE JEWISH TRADITION

Controversy is the main instrument by which Judaism develops and shapes its philosophy, theology, and law. The rabbinical literature speaks with many voices, debating virtually every subject, and failing to reach a consensus on many. However, this willingness to condone controversy is accompanied by much deliberation. Controversy, and its legal, philosophical, and social ramifications, was and remains of unparalleled concern to the rabbis. Today, we are also witness to a burgeoning academic interest in controversy and pluralism in Jewish law.

Controversy and Dialogue in the Jewish Tradition: A Reader is an anthology of passages from the rabbinical literature that address the phenomenon of controversy in Jewish law, affording the English-speaking reader the opportunity for a first-hand encounter with this fascinating material. An extensive analytic introduction contextualizes the material from a philosophical perspective.

The Institute of Jewish Law
Boston University School of Law
765 Commonwealth Avenue
Boston MA 02215
Publication No. 31

Controversy and Dialogue in the Jewish Tradition

A Reader

With an interpretive essay by
Hanina Ben-Menahem

Edited by
Hanina Ben-Menahem
Neil S. Hecht
Shai Wosner

Routledge
Taylor & Francis Group

LONDON AND NEW YORK

First published 2005
by Routledge
2 Park Square, Milton Park, Abingdon, Oxon OX14 4RN

Simultaneously published in the USA and Canada
by Routledge
270 Madison Ave, New York, NY 10016

Routledge is an imprint of the Taylor & Francis Group

© 2005 by the editors

Typeset in Baskerville MT by
Newgen Imaging Systems (P) Ltd, Chennai, India
Printed and bound in Great Britain by
MPG Books Ltd, Bodmin

British Library Cataloguing in Publication Data
A catalogue record for this book is available from the British Library

Library of Congress Cataloging in Publication Data
A catalog record for this book has been requested

ISBN 0–415–34003–9

FOR AARON FEUERSTEIN

TRANSLATION

Shmuel Wosner
Nessa Olshansky-Ashtar
Hanina Ben-Menahem

CONTENTS

CONTROVERSY AND DIALOGUE IN THE JEWISH TRADITION: AN INTERPRETIVE ESSAY

HANINA BEN-MENAHEM

1

1. The pervasiveness of controversy

The halakhic discourse documented in both the Rabbinic literature, that is, the Mishna, the Midreshei Halakha, and the Talmud, and the post-talmudic literature, is characterized by diversity of opinion, and frequent agreement to disagree. Some of these controversies are resolved, others consensually left unresolved. This diversity of opinion is one of the salient differences between the biblical outlook and the talmudic. While the Bible always speaks with one voice, and suppresses internal disputes – the few that do emerge address external challenges – the talmudic literature speaks with many voices, and is replete with debate on virtually every subject that comes up for discussion. The transition from the monolithic biblical outlook to the pluralistic orientation of the Talmud was not unconscious, but accompanied by much soul-searching and deliberation, as is evidenced by the very large number of talmudic sources in *Controversy and Dialogue in the Halakhic Sources.*[1] This anthology, a collection of passages from the entire range of rabbinical literature, focuses on rabbinical awareness of the centrality of controversy in halakhic discourse. The present work, *Controversy and Dialogue in the Jewish Tradition: An English Reader*, affords the English-speaking reader the opportunity for a first-hand encounter with this fascinating material, by presenting a significant selection of passages from the first part of *Controversy and Dialogue*, vol. 1. Readers should take into account that while the arrangement of the passages serves a methodological purpose, it is not categorical, and some passages can also be classed under different headings, and are of relevance to the material in other chapters.

The halakhic endeavor in which the rabbinical authorities have engaged throughout the generations can be characterized as the intellectual effort to interpret the divine will, and translate it into daily conduct. As we said, this enterprise has often been accompanied by vigorous debate and divergence of opinion. This phenomenon – the inability to reach a consensus on a matter of law – is of unparalleled concern to the rabbis, in every generation, and throughout the Jewish world. Undoubtedly, there is no aspect of their endeavor that engages the rabbis as does the problem of controversy and its myriad legal and philosophical ramifications. The attention accorded controversy far exceeds that paid to basic jurisprudential questions such as what constitutes the basic norm, or rule of recognition, in Jewish law; how we determine if a given norm is a halakhic norm; the nature of the law–morality nexus; and the taxonomy and individuation of laws. Moreover, several foundational issues in the philosophy of

---

1 Hanina Ben-Menahem, Neil Hecht, and Shai Wosner (eds.), *Controversy and Dialogue in the Halakhic Sources* (Hebrew), vols. 1–2, Boston and Jerusalem: 1991; vol. 3, Commentary, Jerusalem: 2002.

halakha, and in particular, questions of authority and interpretation, and of the validity, flexibility and authenticity of the halakhic tradition, that are almost never dealt with directly in the talmudic literature, are nonetheless addressed in the course of grappling with the question of controversy.

It seems that the pervasiveness of controversy, and its connection to these fundamental philosophical questions, may explain the intensity of the passions it generated, and the Sages' willingness to delve into sensitive and hitherto unaddressed issues. Indeed, the questions that controversy brings to the fore are of such consequence that the analysis of controversy is, from early on, often imbued with ideological bias, as a result of which scholarly positions on historical and interpretive questions are determined by ideological considerations. In addition to the jurisprudential creativity mandated by the phenomenon of controversy and the difficulties to which it gave rise, the rabbinical authorities were also called upon to respond to another challenge. External elements used the existence of controversy as a pretext for attacks on the authenticity of the rabbinical tradition, attacks that were in truth motivated by other agendas. In such cases, the Sages' engagement with the phenomenon of controversy was reactive, arising out of a need to protect the law from those who sought to impugn it. And indeed, the pervasiveness of controversy, of failure to reach agreement on legal questions, and the religious implications of this phenomenon, did not go unnoticed outside the world of Jewish law. Controversy was constantly adduced by the Karaites, for example, in their fight against the hegemony of Rabbinic Judaism. And during the Haskalah, there was a great deal of discussion of the famous Mishna in Eduyot that explains the perpetuation of dissenting views for future reference.[2] Today too, we are witness to a burgeoning interest in halakhic pluralism,[3] interest that is reflected in the proliferating contemporary literature on halakhic controversy.

The purpose of this introductory essay is to give the reader a conceptual handle on the material, by calling attention to the different themes

---

2 mEduyot 1:5.

3 Since the publication of *Controversy and Dialogue* in 1991, the following works have appeared: Z. Lampel, *The Dynamics of Dispute*, New York: 1992; M. Sokol (ed.), *Rabbinic Authority and Personal Autonomy*, London: 1995; M. Kellner, *Maimonides on the 'Decline of the Generations' and the Nature of Rabbinic Authority*, Albany, NY: 1996; A. Sagi, *'Elu va-Elu': A Study on the Meaning of Halakhic Discourse* (Hebrew), Tel Aviv: 1996; M. Fisch, *Rational Rabbis: Science and Talmudic Culture*, Bloomington, IN: 1997; S. Rosenberg, *Not in Heaven* (Hebrew), Alon Shvut: 1997; Y. Silman, *The Voice Heard at Sinai: Once or Ongoing?* (Hebrew), Jerusalem: 1999; M. Walzer et al., *The Jewish Political Tradition*, vol. 1, New Haven, CT: 2000. Prior to publication of *Controversy and Dialogue*, the following had appeared: Jeffrey I. Roth, "Responding to dissent in Jewish law: suppression versus self-restraint," 40 *Rutgers L. Rev.*, 31–99 (1987) and "The justification for controversy in Jewish law," 76 *California Law Review* (1988); D. Weiss Halivni, *Peshat and Derash: Plain and Applied Meaning in Rabbinic Exegesis*, London: 1990.

that run through the book, and suggesting parameters that may be useful in thinking about controversy in the halakhic context. The axes around which the material presented in this book is organized are conceptual and thematic. The discussion does not seek to anchor the ideas of the rabbis in their social milieu, or to contextualize their halakhic worldviews. That, I leave to the historians. My goal is to offer a synoptic conceptualization of the ideas themselves, that is, the rabbinical reflections on controversy and its ramifications, as they are expressed in the halakhic literature. In this introduction, I will also attempt to formulate, on the basis of these documents, some conjectures as to the halakhic authorities' underlying motivations.

2. The meaning of *mahloket*

There is a range of meanings associated with the term "controversy" (*mahloket*). Let us start by considering two distinct senses found in the talmudic literature. In one of them – perhaps the primary, though not necessarily the original sense – *mahloket* signifies the existence of an unresolved conflict between different opinions, that is, a stalemated debate over the law. In addition, the term *mahloket* also has another, pejorative, sense, that of an altercation or rift within a group. The fact that the same term is used for both contexts is telling, and suggests a critical attitude toward halakhic controversy. The negative connotation of social discord does carry over, to some extent, to the semantic field of halakhic discourse.

A third, less common meaning of the term *mahloket* is group or sect, both at the level of social organization, and in the halakhic context. An example of the former usage is Numbers Rabbah 3:12: "The tribe of Levi became four divisions (*mahlokot*) to circumscribe the four sides [of the Tabernacle]." And the latter usage is exemplified in the following talmudic passage:

> R. Joshua was asked, What is the law regarding the rival [wife] of one's daughter? He answered them, It is a [matter of] controversy (*mahloket*) between the house of Shammai and the house of Hillel. But, [he was asked,] in accordance with whose ruling is the established law? Why should you, he said to them, put my head between two great mountains, between groups (*mahlokot*) of disputants, between the house of Shammai and the house of Hillel?
> bJebamot 15b

Sometimes it is hard to determine which of the three senses is intended. Consider the following Mishna:

> Every controversy that is for the sake of heaven, its end is to be sustained. And every controversy that is not for the sake of

heaven, its end is not to be sustained. What controversy is for the sake of heaven? The controversy between Hillel and Shammai. And that which is not for the sake of heaven? The controversy of Korah and all his congregation.[4]

Here, all three senses may be in evidence. The house of Hillel–house of Shammai controversy may be intended in the first sense we spoke of, the Korah controversy, in the second. However, some have construed both cases to refer to controversy in the second sense, namely, that of a social rift,[5] and others have argued that controversy in the house of Hillel–house of Shammai case is intended in the third sense.[6]

Let us now clarify the concept of controversy in the first sense, namely, failure to reach agreement on a legal question. A distinction must be drawn between a discussion wherein the disputants have not yet reached a decision about some halakhic question, but are in the process of doing so, and a situation where, because the process of attempting to clarify a certain question was unsuccessful, the parties have adopted contrary positions, which they are intent on defending.

Now debate and dialogue with a study partner or group is the recommended approach to Torah study, and the technique most suitable for clarifying legal points. A classic passage that refers to this methodology describes the study habits of R. Johanan and Resh Lakish:

> R. Shimon b. Lakish's soul expired, and R. Johanan was greatly saddened on account of his death. Our Rabbis said: Who will go to ease his mind? Let R. Eleazar b. Pedat, whose legal teachings are very subtle, go. So he went and sat before him; and upon every dictum uttered by R. Johanan, he said: There is a baraita that supports you. He said, [Do you think] you are, then, like the son of Lakisha? When I stated the law, the son of Lakisha would raise twenty-four separate objections, to which I gave twenty-four answers, which led to a fuller understanding of the law. And [all] you say is: There is a baraita that supports you. Do I not know that my opinions are well-grounded?
>
> bBaba Metzia 84a

---

4 mAvot 5:17.
5 Shlomo Naeh, "Compartmentalize your heart: additional reflections on controversy in the teachings of the Sages" (Hebrew) in A. Sagi and Z. Zohar (eds.), *Renewing Jewish Commitment: The Work and Thought of David Hartman*, Tel Aviv: 2001, p. 851.
6 E.Z. Melamed, "On the language of the *Ethics of the Fathers*" (Hebrew), *Leshonenu* 20 (1957), p. 107. This interpretation was already suggested by R. Nathan, 'father of the yeshiva' (d. before 1102).

This process of debate and dialogue must not be confused with controversy, which is a possible, but not inevitable, outcome of the process. For the debate may well end in agreement between the study partners that one of their positions is in fact correct or more persuasive. But if it does not, that is, if neither side is able to convince the other of the correctness of its view, or if both views seem equally acceptable, the outcome of the study process is a state of dilemma, a state of unresolved controversy between the views. This outcome is known as *mahloket*, literally, division. Since there is an intimate connection between the process and any resulting controversy, both the debate and the stalemate are discussed in the sources, which sometimes deal explicitly with only one of the two, but often shift rapidly from one to the other and back again.

Note that *mahloket* in the sense of a stalemated legal debate can also have a slightly different meaning: it can refer to scholarly critique in general, that is, to a disagreement that is not the outcome of actual dialogue and debate in the course of group Torah study. Such a difference of opinion may be generated by the juxtaposition of the views of individuals who never debated the issue together – and may be separated by centuries or millennia – but merely voiced contrary opinions on a given question. It should be noted, however, that a controversy where one side has not had the opportunity to appeal to, and perhaps convince, the other, is usually regarded as a defective sort of controversy. Here, the classical method for resolving controversies – application of the 'follow the majority' rule – is not helpful. For there is always the chance that a seeming controversy of this type would not have proven a genuine controversy at all had the proponents of the minority view been able to discuss the matter directly, either face to face or through correspondence, with the proponents of the majority view, as they might have found a way to resolve the apparent difference of opinion. One of the earliest formulations of this sentiment, which later gained currency, is found in a responsum pertaining to the famous debate over the renewal of ordination (*semikha*):

> But when the consensus of the majority is established without deliberation in which all the parties are involved, it is not considered consensus at all, since perhaps had the majority heard the arguments of the minority, they might have conceded to them, and retracted their opinion.
>
> Ralbah,[7] *Responsa Kuntres Hasemikha*

Implicit in this assumption that only controversies generated in direct discussion are genuine, and all others essentially pseudo-controversies, is

---

7 R. Levi b. Jacob b. Haviv, Spain–Jerusalem, 16th c.

a very optimistic evaluation of the halakhic system's capacity for resolving disputes between different views.

3. Controversy is the way of the Torah

In the sources, controversy is frequently characterized as "the way of the Torah." This self-awareness encompasses both the diachronic and the synchronic dimensions of the halakhic enterprise. Whether we look at the rabbinical literature over time, or consider a cross-section at any given moment, in either case lack of a consensus will be the principal characteristic manifested. As we will see, overall, a positive attitude to controversy undoubtedly prevails in halakhic reflection on the subject. But alongside acceptance of the reality of controversy as positive, we also find, though to a far lesser degree, the opposite attitude, that is, a tendency to present halakhic activity as cohesive and free of disagreement, a tendency that can only be accommodated by disregarding evidence to the contrary. Such aversion to controversy is clearly evident in the passages in chapter 1 classed under the heading "Controversy is not to be multiplied," which we discuss in section (8) below, 'Opposition to controversy.'

The title of the first chapter, "Controversy is the way of the Torah," was chosen because the phrase is used very often in the rabbinical sources, and captures, we believe, the essence and conceptual complexity of the pluralistic approach. The first to use this phrase is R. Israel Isserlein,[8] author of *Trumat Hadeshen*, who states:

> With regard to your question about whether a student is permitted to disagree with his teacher over a given ruling, and – if he can support his view on the basis of the Talmud or the rulings of the Geonim – rule contrary to his teacher's opinion. It seems evident to me that if the rulings are reasonably clear, and the logical sequence of the talmudic passages appears to support the student, there is no reason why he should not disagree. This has been the way of the Torah from the days of the Tannaim. On a number of points, our holy R. Judah the Prince disagreed with his father and with his teacher R. Shimon b. Gamaliel. Among the Amoraim, in a number of places Rava disagrees with Rabbah, who was his teacher, as it says in the *Mordekhai*.[9] Among the great halakhic authorities, Asheri disagrees with R. Meir of Rothenburg, who was his mentor. I do not wish to enlarge on this further, as these things need to be discussed face to face.
>
> Thus spoke the youngest and most junior in Israel

8 Ashkenaz, 1390–1460.
9 *Mordekhai* commentary on bBaba Kama, chapter 3, section 15.

The context here is a dispute between a student and his teacher, but subsequently the phrase was applied to controversy in general.

The source of the phrase "the way of the Torah" is mAvot 6:4: "This is the way of the Torah: a morsel of bread with salt thou shalt eat, and rationed-out water thou shalt drink, and upon the ground thou shalt sleep, and a life of trouble thou shalt live, while thou toilest in [study of] the law." It is possible that the choice of this locution to describe controversy is influenced by the Mishna that follows almost immediately, mAvot 6:6, which states: "The Torah is acquired by forty-eight means," one of which is "discussion with students," which might be a reference to controversy. It should also be kept in mind that the Hebrew term "*derekh*," way, has another equally important meaning, namely, nature or essence. In saying that controversy is the way of the Torah, the Sages are really saying that controversy is a characteristic feature of the Torah – it is of the very nature of the Torah.

The assertion that controversy is the way of the Torah can be taken as either a descriptive or a normative statement. Let us first consider the former. As a descriptive statement, it can be interpreted as describing three different things. (1) It can be read as describing Torah study, as it actually took place in given historical contexts, as a learning experience characterized by numerous controversies. (2) It can be read as describing human nature, which, in pursuing the truth, is inherently questioning and argumentative, and therefore subjects teachings to intellectual scrutiny prior to accepting them. (3) Finally, it can also be read, not as a historical or psychological observation, but as describing the essence and substance of the Torah: the Torah, in and of itself, induces those who study it to engage in controversy.

Let us now consider 'controversy is an inherent characteristic of the Torah' as a normative statement. With respect to its deontic status, there are three possibilities: engaging in controversy can be either permitted, obligatory, or somewhere in between, for example, recommended. In terms of scope, controversy can be defined along three axes: the temporal, the institutional, and the functional. The location of rabbinical authorities on the temporal axis may determine whether one is permitted (obliged) to disagree with them. The body that issues an opinion may be similarly positioned on an institutional axis, so to speak, determining whether one is permitted (obliged) to dispute its view. Similarly, the functional status of the law under discussion – theoretical law or law intended for implementation – may be a determining factor with regard to whether dissenting views are permitted (obliged) to be voiced. Essentially, these three axes circumscribe the discussion of controversy in the halakhic literature.

Different arguments can be invoked to justify the assertion that controversy is the way of the Torah, taken as a normative statement. On the one hand, it can be justified by citing the empirical claim, mentioned above, that in point of fact, controversy has almost always been an integral part of Torah study, along with the principle that the Sages are role models whose conduct should be emulated. It can, however, also be justified by citing methodological principles, particularly the idea that controversy contributes to discovery of the truth, discussed below in (5a).

4. "The war of the Torah"

In many Tannaitic and Amoraic sources,[10] Torah study is described as "the war of the Torah":

> And Scripture states, "All of them valiant, wagers of war" (II Kings 24:16). Now what valor can people who are going into exile display? And what war can people wage when they are fettered in shackles and bound by chains? Rather, "valiant" refers to those who are valiant in Torah study. This is like the thrust of the verse, "Bless the Lord, O you his angels, valiant and mighty, who do His word..." (Ps. 103:20); "wagers of war" – who engaged in dialogue and debate [lit., give and take] in the war of the Torah, as it is said, "Wherefore it is said in the book of the Wars of the Lord" (Num. 21:14).
>
> Sifre Deuteronomy, Haazinu 321 (Finkelstein edition, p. 370)

This metaphor highlights the competitive aspect of Torah study, expressing a decidedly 'Darwinian' conception of it, on which controversy is a central means of identifying the correct interpretation of the Torah, much as physical competition serves to identify the stronger species.[11]

The war metaphor is suitable primarily for describing group rather than individual study of the Torah, and further, it is more appropriate for describing the synchronic aspect of Torah study than the diachronic. The metaphor also alludes to the idea that those who study the Torah safeguard the community from outside attack.[12] In marked contrast to the war metaphor, however, is another, much later metaphor, which compares the study of the Torah to an orchestral performance, the disparate opinions being analogized to different instruments that together generate a beautiful melody:

> Truly, for one who understands things properly, all the controversies among the Tannaim, Amoraim, the Geonim and the decisors, are the words of the living God, and all are grounded in the law. And futhermore, this is the glory of our pure and holy Torah, all

---

10 Sifre Deuteronomy, Haazinu 321; jTaanit 4:5 (69b); Numbers Rabbah 11:3; bMegila 15b; bHagiga 14a; bSanhedrin 93b.
11 See, e.g., the quotation from Maharal at note 40 below.
12 jHagiga 1:7 (76c).

of which is called a melody. And the glory of the melody, the essence of its delight, is that the tones differ from each other. And one who sails the sea of the Talmud will experience the diverse delights of all these distinct voices.

Arukh Hashulhan, HM, preface[13]

Unlike the war metaphor, this metaphor emphasizes peace and harmony. It may well have been put forward as a reaction to the bellicosity of the notion of "the war of the Torah," which was viewed, even as a metaphor, as harmful.

Indeed, the war metaphor implies rejection of the values of cooperation, collaborative effort, and harmony, suggesting in their stead that elimination of the opposed opinion is a worthy goal. Now metaphors not only give expression to our worldviews, but also help shape them.[14] Frequent reference to the war metaphor might have had a negative cumulative pedagogic impact, engendering violent power struggles rather than healthy, constructive competition. In extreme cases, upholding war as a model could have led to physical confrontations, and perhaps one such episode is related in the tradition about the violent exchange between the house of Shammai and the house of Hillel, which led to bloodshed.[15] However, the use of bellicose rhetoric may also have had a positive effect, in serving to safely release pent-up anger and animosity generated by heated study-hall debates, without any actual acting out.

Alongside the war analogy, the sources attest to the emergence of a highly sensitive code of conduct detailing specific rules of etiquette governing halakhic debate and disputation. This will be taken up in (7a) below.

5. Problematics ensuing from controversy, and rabbinical reflections thereon

Controversy gives rise to various kinds of difficulties, among them conceptual, pragmatic and social difficulties. Analysis of the sources suggests that these difficulties aroused much concern on the part of the halakhic authorities. Examination of the problems in question may shed light on the broader phenomenon of controversy.

Conceptual questions The primary conceptual difficulty raised by controversy is undoubtedly alethic: what is the relation between the different opinions that have been expressed on a particular halakhic

---

13 R. Jehiel Mechal b. Aaron Isaac Halevi Epstein, Russia, 1829–1908.
14 See G. Lakoff and M. Johnson, *Metaphors We Live By*, Chicago: 1980.
15 See jShabat 1:4 (3:3); bShabat 17a; Megilat Taanit at the end.

question, and 'the truth'? On the face of it, it would seem that only one opinion can be true, and thus the others must be false. A very clear expression of this attitude is the following statement:

> The commentators were faced with a problem that warrants examination: the two opposed views, granted their pious intent, nevertheless contradict each other, and have opposite truth values. It necessarily follows that if one of them is true, the other must be false.
>
> *Midrash Shmuel*[16]

This conclusion, however, seems problematic, in that the traditional view is that all opinions of Torah scholars have some merit.

Pragmatic difficulties   Quite apart from the question of their truth values, the existence of conflicting halakhic opinions presents pragmatic difficulties. According to which opinion should one act? Furthermore, what constitutes fulfilment of the obligation to study the Torah? Does study of any opinion suffice, or must the material studied be the opinion accepted as the law? This dilemma is already articulated in the Talmud:

> "Masters of assemblies" – these are the scholars (*talmidei hakhamim*) who sit in various assemblies and apply themselves to the Torah; some deem a matter impure, others deem it pure, some prohibit, others permit, some disqualify, others declare fit. Lest you say: Under these circumstances, how can I learn the Torah?, therefore Scripture says: All "were given from one shepherd" (Eccles. 12:11). One God gave them, one leader[17] uttered them from the mouth of the Master of all deeds, blessed be He, as it is written, "And God spake all these words" (Exod. 20:1). So let your ears be as funnels, and cultivate an understanding heart, to hear the words of those who deem a matter impure and those who deem it pure, those who prohibit and those who permit, those who disqualify and those who declare fit.
>
> bHagiga 3b

The question raised in this passage is "Under these circumstances, how can I learn the Torah?" In a parallel passage, the emphasis is on knowing which view is to be followed, and how one is to conduct himself:

> "Masters of assemblies" (Eccles. 12:11) are the Sanhedrin. Should one say: some permit and some forbid, some disqualify and others

16 R. Samuel Di Uzida, Safed, b. 1540.
17 I.e., Moses. The term 'shepherd' is applied in the Bible both to God (e.g., Gen. 48:15; Ps. 80:2) and to Moses (e.g., Isa. 63: 11) – Maharsha.

11

declare fit, some deem a matter impure and others deem it pure;
R. Eliezer deems the action liable, R. Joshua deems it exempt; the
house of Shammai forbid and the house of Hillel permit; whom
shall I heed?

Tanhuma, Behaalotkha 15

Social impact   Other difficulties pertain to the social impact of
controversy. If controversies proliferate, each individual, or even every
community, following the opinion of its own choice, the Torah will
become tantamount to many sets of laws. This will have deleterious results
with respect to the cohesiveness of the social fibre. It is against the background of this apprehension that the prohibition against forming factions,
discussed below, is raised.

Conflicting moral imperatives   Though controversy may foster the
search for truth, it may also be said to impede the pursuit of another cardinal
moral imperative, namely, peace. Zeal and partisanship in the study-hall are
likely to engender divisiveness and animosity. This apprehension is a central
theme in the writings of R. Isaac Hakohen Kook[18]:

> Some people erroneously think that universal peace can only
> be achieved by a uniform hue of opinions and qualities. Conse-
> quently, upon beholding scholars investigating the wisdom of the
> Torah, and by their study generating a multiplicity of perspectives
> and approaches, they imagine that these scholars are thereby
> engendering controversy and subverting peace.
>
> *Olat Reiya*, part 1, p. 330

The authenticity of the tradition   The existence of controversy
might be thought to undermine the authenticity of the tradition and cor-
roborate the claim, voiced from the outside, that the true tradition has been
lost. Maimonides, in restricting the number of laws that were transmitted
by tradition, is addressing this concern. The original tradition, he explains,
includes only laws that have never been the subject of controversy:

> But the view of one who thinks that laws that are subject to
> controversy are traditions originating from Moses, and they
> engendered controversy due to error in the tradition, or its having
> been forgotten, so that one side is right with regard to its tradition,
> and the other errs with regard to its tradition, or forgot it, or did
> not hear from his teacher all that he should have heard . . . as God
> lives, he presents a contemptible and very bizarre argument.

18 Latvia–Israel, 1865–1935.

And it is not correct and does not conform to the [foregoing] principles, for it expresses misgivings about the individuals in the masoretic chain from whom we received the Torah, and is completely invalid.

Commentary on the Mishna, Introduction

Theological difficulties The proliferation of opinions ascribed to God could be thought of as undermining the uniqueness of the divine voice, and calling into question His unity. This concern is reflected in the following interpretation offered by the eminent Spanish halakhist and philosopher R. Yomtov of Seville (Ritba)[19]:

"Ye are the children of the Lord your God" (Deut. 14:1); since you are the children of one father and one God, it is proper that you not form factions, as if there were two Torahs and two deities.

Hidushei Haritba, bJebamot 13b

The talmudic Sages and the scholars who followed them struggled, to varying degrees, with these diverse problems. It is impossible to identify a single, universal approach to the matter, but rather, a broad range of ideas, sentiments and perspectives, differing greatly in their comprehensiveness, were aired. The prevailing tendency was, however, almost always to defend the legitimacy of controversy, and uphold its ultimate contribution to the halakhic enterprise, despite the problems involved, though it cannot be denied that there were indeed some who thought the problems so weighty as to render controversy objectionable. These negative voices will be discussed in (8) below. In the next three sections (sec. 5a–c), however, we will take a closer look at some of the rabbinical reflections on several of the difficulties just outlined.

a. Alethic-interpretive

For the most part, the controversies discussed in this collection are not over existential questions, on the one hand, or issues of community policy, on the other, but over the meanings of specific texts. Hence the intimate connection between different accounts of controversy, and theories of meaning, interpretation and truth, which often focus on the role of the interpreter. The passages in Chapter 3 address hermeneutical issues, though readers should bear in mind that the concepts of text, author, interpreter, and meaning, are not referred to explicitly. Nevertheless, they clearly underlie the halakhic discussions in question. These concepts can be construed as related in many different ways. Consider the following

---

19 Spain, *c.*1250–1330.

schematic outline of four distinct theories of interpretation germane to the halakhic context:

1   The interpreter discovers the meaning of the text by trying to establish the author's intent. Here, the assumption is that the text is a vehicle for conveying the author's ideas, and plays no independent role. It is assumed that, ordinarily, the text mirrors the author's intent. Should external evidence indicate that the intent of the author is not in line with what the text suggests, that is, should there be a discrepancy between the plain meaning of the text and the external evidence, the external evidence prevails, and the text is read accordingly.

2   The meaning is in the text; the interpreter derives the meaning from the text by employing a given set of rules of interpretation. On this theory, the author is indeed the creator of the text, but the meaning of the text is not equivalent to the author's intent. The role of the interpreter is to establish the independent meaning of the text.

3   The text has no meaning prior to the act of interpretation. The interpreter examines the text and creates its meaning through his own reasoning. On this theory, the interpreter, and not the text itself, is the creator of the text's meaning. The act of interpretation generates an account of how the text affects a given interpreter. The meaning is generated from the text, but not via a well-defined set of rules of interpretation. On this theory, the crucial question is not the identity of the author, but the identity of the interpreter.

4   The text, or rather, the text as formulated, is regarded as normative. The interpreter imposes a meaning on the text by imputing to the text his own ideas, independently arrived at, motivated by awareness that only if his ideas are presented as grounded in the text will they be given credence. On this theory, neither the author nor the text plays a role in arriving at the ideas ascribed to it. At most, the text serves as a filter constraining the ascription to it of specific content. Though presented as such, the product of this endeavor is not, strictly speaking, an interpretation of the text. In fact, this theory scarcely describes an act of interpretation. Generally speaking, those who engage in this quasi interpretation are reluctant to admit that they are indeed imposing their own ideas on the text. Nevertheless, most Amoraic interpretations of the Mishna seem to reflect this model of interpretation.

There is a clear connection between the interpretive theory one adopts, and the account one provides of how a particular halakhic ruling comes to be championed. When we try to determine under which of the aforementioned theories halakhic interpretation should be subsumed, we are immediately confronted by the question of which theory of the four is compatible with, or entails, the thesis that there is always one uniquely-correct answer to a halakhic question. The first two theories square with the notion that the text has one uniquely-correct reading, and hence every halakhic question has one uniquely-correct answer. On either of the first two theories, the existence of an unresolved dispute over a legal question means that we have missed something. The matter could have been resolved, had we had the necessary legal knowledge or acumen. The last two theories deny that every text has one uniquely-correct reading, and can, therefore, anchor halakhic pluralism. The existence of a controversy does not, on these theories, signify that we missed something, that we could have resolved the matter conclusively had we studied the matter more assiduously.

In the case of texts of divine authorship, the intent of the author may not be constrained by human limitations, such as the law of contradiction, and consequently, contradictory statements, or statements otherwise unfathomable to human intelligence, may be assertable in this context. Even if we postulate that divine intention is coherent, though not necessarily accessible to us, some commentators take the position that the text has two meanings – an objective, divine meaning, and a meaning that can be established by human understanding. This two-tiered vision of meaning is only relevant on the last three theories of interpretation outlined above (that is, theories (2)–(4)). Once a distinction between divine meaning and meaning that can be established by human reason is introduced, we face a divide. There is no necessary correspondence between correctness and validity, and questions as to the correct interpretation of divinely-authored texts are not to be conflated with those that address the validity of a given interpretation.[20]

Some halakhic authorities maintain that validity is determined by following a specific set of rules of interpretation or decision rules; others, that it is a matter of convention, namely, of what is accepted by the majority of the sages of a given generation. On the conventionalist account, the validity of halakhic statements is time-dependent.

This analysis suggests that we must distinguish between three different modalities of halakhic statements: true halakhic statements, valid halakhic statements, and halakhic statements that are neither true nor valid (*divrei tora*, lit., Torah views). The truth conditions of a halakhic statement obviously depend on which theory of interpretation is adopted. Validity is determined using the criteria just mentioned. As for the third modality – *divrei tora* – here, the criterion is the interpreter's motivation. When one is seriously engaged in the study of the Torah, with no personal interests at

---

20 For a comprehensive discussion of the criterion of truth for legal statements, see A. Pintore, *Law without Truth*, Liverpool: 2000.

stake, his conclusions, even if untrue and invalid, are deemed *divrei tora*, and anyone who studies them fulfills the obligation to study the Torah.

> When one is engaged in coming up with novel ideas about the Torah, it should be without any desire for self-interest or self-glorification, or merely for argument's sake, and so on, but rather, it should be out of great passion for the truth. And in that case, even if one errs, his novel views will nevertheless be considered words of Torah and the words of the living God. For the Talmud mentions erroneous words and those that were rejected from the law. Because even flawed premises are considered to be words of the Torah. For God, may He be blessed, has set down that even an initial, as-yet imperfect conception is a precursor to true knowledge, and even such an early conception is divinely inspired, and constitutes the words of the living God.
>
> *Tzidkat Hatzadik*, 115[21]

One of the classic texts that deal with the conceptual issues pertaining to truth and controversy is bEruvin 13b, much cited and discussed in the literature.

> R. Abba stated in the name of Samuel: For three years there was a controversy between the house of Shammai and the house of Hillel, the former asserting: The law is in accordance with our views, and the latter asserting: The law is in accordance with our views. A heavenly voice (*bat kol*) went forth, announcing: Both [lit., 'these and those'] are the words of the living God, but the law is in accordance with the view of the house of Hillel. Since, however, both are the words of the living God, for what reason did the house of Hillel merit the law's being decided in accordance with their view? Because they were kindly and modest, they studied their own views and those of the house of Shammai, and not only that, but they quoted the words of the house of Shammai before their own.

The assertion made here, that both sides to a controversy are "the words of the living God," plainly calls for clarification. In rabbinical treatments of this passage, many different opinions are expressed. Upon analysis, they can be seen to reflect six basic claims, which in turn appear to be variants of two polar positions: at one extreme, the position, which we will refer to as the monolithic position, that God did not utter contradictory statements, and that therefore the dictum "both are the words of the living God" cannot mean what it seems to mean; and at the other, the position that the contradictory statements were indeed actually uttered by God, a position we will refer to as the pluralistic position. Let us begin with the former.

---

21 R. Tzadok Hakohen of Lublin, Poland, 1823–1900.

One such claim asserts that what the dictum really means is that both views are interpreting the words of the living God, but not that both views themselves are the word of God.[22] A second claim in this same vein is that the word of God is open-textured, and therefore, any interpretation of it, if based on the prescribed set of interpretive rules, is deemed "the words of the living God," even though it was not actually spoken by God. There is no fact of the matter as to what God really meant.[23] (A variant of this argument suggests that there is a fact of the matter regarding what God meant, but since it is not readily accessible, that is, since no suggested intent can be demonstrated to be correct, every interpretation is, if based on the prescribed set of interpretive rules, deemed "the words of the living God."[24]) Another claim suggests that the "both are the words" dictum merely asserts that each of the contradictory opinions is a sincere effort to discover the one and unique voice of God.[25] These three attempts to explain the problematic dictum, then, all reject the premise that contradictory statements can be attributed to God.

At the other end of the spectrum, as we said, is the position that contradictory statements can indeed be attributed to God. One variant of this approach straightforwardly claims that God is above consistency.[26] This solution is often put forward by Kabbalists, who claim that esoteric knowledge is implied here: the sublime transcends logic. A second variant argues that both views were actually uttered by God, but refer to different sets of circumstances. Since the same event can be described in many different ways, with different legal rules being suitable for the different characterizations, more than one view will be applicable to any event.[27] A third variant of this approach suggests that both contradictory statements were actually uttered by God, though only one of them is correct, the other having been provided by God to serve as a foil for the true view, given that truth can only, or best, be discovered by being juxtaposed to falsehood.[28]

b. Theological

In that the subject matter of halakhic controversy is the divine word, the notion of controversy in this context is particularly problematic. Controversy raises concerns not only from the external point of view, as, for example, when the Sages are criticized for their numerous disputes and

---

22 R. Solomon b. Abraham ibn Parhon, Spain–Italy, 12th c., *Mahberet Hearukh*, helek hadikduk 5:4.
23 R. Yomtov Lippmann Mühlhausen, Prague, 14–15th c., *Sefer Hanitzahon*, section 321.
24 R. Moses Feinstein, Lithuania–US, 1895–1986, *Responsa Igrot Moshe*, OH, 1, foreword.
25 bGitin 6b.
26 R. Yomtov of Seville, *Hidushei Haritba*, bEruvin 13b s.v. *eilu veeilu*.
27 R. Solomon b. Isaac (Rashi), France, 1040–1105, bKetubot 57a s.v. *ha ka mashma lan*.
28 *Meharerei Nemeirim* 17a, quoted below at note 34.

controversies by outside circles, such as the Sadducees, and later, the Karaites – the critique being that controversy is an indication that the true tradition has been lost – but from the internal perspective as well. From the internal perspective, there is always the fear that social cohesion will be adversely affected, as we will see below, but the impact of controversy on the community is not the sole concern. Controversy also brings to the fore such theological issues as the singularity of the Torah and the uniqueness of the divine voice.

This concern finds its expression in bHagiga 3b,[29] which succinctly encapsulates the tension between the static and the dynamic aspects of the law, a tension that can also be seen as reflecting the divine law/human understanding dichotomy. For the phenomenon of controversy poses a profound question. How can it be that the word of God, which is supposed to be clear-cut and unambiguous, is so contentious and so manifold in its interpretations? Can it be that there is no one uniquely-correct answer to any given halakhic question? The divine will was indeed initially expressed in unequivocal dicta, first via prophecy, and later, via the Sanhedrin, the high court. However, the literature on controversy was generated, and developed, in a reality in which there was neither prophecy nor a Sanhedrin. While it is understandably difficult to conceive of a substitute for the institution of prophecy, this is not so with regard to the Sanhedrin, an institution for which it is entirely plausible to devise various kinds of functional substitutes. The fact that throughout Jewish history there was no real attempt to establish such a surrogate institution is instructive, I would argue. It suggests that the lack of a single authoritative voice was not considered a liability, despite rhetoric expressing great longing for the re-establishment of the high court. However, it did mean that the rabbinical authorities had to cultivate the sentiment that God Himself was the source of all the controversies that would occupy them. Indeed, even God Himself is portrayed as engaged in controversy. The portrayal of God as taking part in halakhic controversy implies that controversy is an immanent aspect of the Torah, allaying any qualms that the existence of controversy might be evidence of some inadequacy or failing.

---

29 And he too began to expound: "The words of the wise are as goads, and as nails well planted are those of masters of assemblies; they were given from one shepherd" (Eccles. 12:11). Why are the words of the Torah likened to a goad? To teach that just as a goad directs the cow along the furrow in order to bring life to the world, so the words of the Torah direct those who study them from the paths of death to the paths of life. But [should you think] that just as a goad is movable, so the words of the Torah are movable, therefore Scripture says: "nails." But [should you think] that just as a nail diminishes by being driven in, and does not increase, so too the words of the Torah diminish, and do not increase, therefore Scripture says: "well planted"; just as a plant grows and increases, so the words of the Torah grow and increase.

Now they were debating in the heavenly academy thus: If the spot preceded the white hair, he is impure; if the reverse, he is pure.[30] If [the order is] in doubt, the Holy One, blessed be He, ruled, he is pure, whereas the entire heavenly academy maintained, he is impure. Who shall decide it?, they asked. Rabbah bar Nahmani will decide, for he has declared, I am pre-eminent in the laws of leprosy.... A messenger was sent for him, but the Angel of Death could not approach him, because he did not interrupt his study. In the meantime, a wind blew and caused a rustling in the bushes, which he imagined to be a troop of soldiers. Let me die, he said, rather than be delivered into the hands of the state. As he was dying, he said: Pure, pure! A heavenly voice went forth and said, Happy art thou, O Rabbah bar Nahmani, whose body is pure and whose soul hath departed in purity.

bBaba Metzia 86a

The depiction of God as engaged in controversy also has pragmatic value. If the law is decided in accordance with the Sages' view when they are clearly in disagreement with God's own position – as, for instance, Maimonides decides it in the *Code*[31] – there need be no fear of following them with respect to questions on which God's position is not known!

c. Social

In many discussions, we find controversy over theoretical issues contrasted with controversy over practice, that is, controversy as to how individuals, groups and communities are to conduct themselves. It can be said that while the rabbinical authorities are tolerant of theoretical pluralism – the notion of dogma is indeed generally absent from the Jewish tradition – this is by no means the case at the level of practice, where total subjection to rabbinical authority is required. The most pronounced expression of the fact that conduct based on non-standard understandings of the law is discouraged is the prohibition against forming factions – "do not form factions" (*lo titgodedu*). At its core, this anti-factionalism principle is a halakhic device that impacts social behavior. Though clothed in halakhic language, it is essentially motivated by social concerns, principally, the desire to maximize social cohesiveness.

In line with the rabbis' approaches to the alethic and interpretive issues raised by the phenomenon of controversy, the "do not form factions" principle can be regarded as rooted in either the monolithic or the pluralistic worldview.

---

30 The reference here is to the laws of leprosy, see Leviticus 13:10.
31 *Code*, Laws concerning the Uncleanness of Leprosy 2:9.

On the monolithic worldview, according to which there is but a single truth, it stands to reason that in the realm of conduct, too, there must be but a single correct mode of behavior, which all must follow. From the monolithic perspective, then, the anti-factionalism principle is merely a reflection of the claim that there is but a single correct divine voice.

On the other hand, from the pluralistic perspective, the anti-factionalism principle appears to constitute a very significant qualification of the "both are the words" principle, to the effect that it is valid in the realm of halakhic speculation, but not in that of practice. This duality between speculative law and law intended for implementation is also found in the case of the rebellious elder.[32] Here, the law is that if the elder taught his dissenting view, he is exempt, but if he acted or handed down a ruling in accordance with it, he is liable.

Whether considered from the monolithic or the pluralistic perspective, however, the anti-factionalism principle can be regarded either as laying the foundation for all the other decision-making rules, by establishing cohesiveness and uniformity as paramount concerns, or, as itself a decision-making rule, a rule of last resort should the others fail to yield a decision.

In what follows, we will analyze the anti-factionalism principle from the pluralistic perspective, that is, reading it as conflicting with the "both are the words" principle, and attempt to gain insight into the balance between the principles that nonetheless emerges from the sources. For if we assume that halakhic truth is non-monolithic, and on a given question both positions can be correct, the determination of the law in accordance with one particular view requires justification. From a purely halakhic standpoint, all positions are equally valid, and no particular view can claim precedence. And indeed, the various justifications for the anti-factionalism principle, and the corollary it entails, namely, that decision-making rules are necessary, are consequential rather than substantive. This thus constitutes a good illustration of an element of the halakha that is motivated by sociological considerations, though formulated and presented in terms of halakhic prohibitions (*isur veheter*).

Let us enumerate some of the principal justifications for the principle found in the sources. First, there is the concern that incorrect theological conclusions will be drawn from the existence of controversy. Controversy, it is feared, could give rise to a situation where the Torah is regarded by the people as two sets of laws, that is, as the law of any given faction within the community. Here, the concern is the image of the Torah and the image of the Deity in the eyes of the multitude, who might find it difficult to fathom why God would speak in multiple voices, and drawn the erroneous conclusion that the law is not universal. There is also the jurisprudential consideration of the law's image in the eyes of the people: the law ought

---

32 mSanhedrin 11:2.

not appear inconsistent, with one court affirming something, and a second denying it. Thirdly, there is the straightforwardly social consideration that dissent and factionalism within and between communities should be avoided. There is, of course, also an institutional consideration: the court's institutional efficacy must be secured by solidifying its authority and standing, to which end it must speak with a single voice. The court ought not affirm something in one case, and deny it in another case. And finally, there is a consideration having to do with maintaining the sovereignty of the halakha: provision must be made for invalidating aberrant customs and behaviors that cannot be uprooted by legal means. This last consideration is of paramount importance, in that it makes it possible for the courts to act where they would otherwise by unable to do so. This consideration thus legitimizes a broadening of the scope of actions available to the rabbis to combat the divisive impact of halakhic dissent, as opposed to the other considerations we mentioned, which limited the courts' ability to act by demanding of them inter- and intra-court consistency.

A second point about which there is much discussion is the question of who the prohibition against factionalism addresses. One possibility is that it addresses the rabbinical authorities as legislators. On this understanding, it regulates the Sages' legislative activities, charging them to create a unified legal system that ignores conditions peculiar to specific times and locales, on the assumption that uniformity is more important than taking into account any contingencies that might beset the various communities. The criticism leveled at the practice of permitting the reading of the Megilla at different times in different places should be seen as arising from this idea that uniformity is to be preferred to accommodating contingent differences. A more plausible approach sees the prohibition as addressing the judiciary, imposing upon it the obligation to be consistent in its rulings. A judiciary that generates different rulings on the same issue would be perceived as not having arrived at its decisions on the basis of the same sources, and this, in turn, would, over time, undermine the cohesiveness of the legal system. Yet another understanding of the prohibition views it as directed at individuals, requiring them to follow the practices accepted in their respective communities. Underlying the prohibition is the concern that idiosyncratic conduct with respect to matters regulated by the law will trigger conflict within and between communities. It should be noted that there is considerable discussion in the literature about the criteria in terms of which communities are defined. Is a community constituted by individuals or families who reside in the same town? Is it generated by being under the jurisdiction of the same court of law, membership in an ethnic community (*kahal*), or membership in a synagogue? These questions are addressed and returned to in the literature as demographic developments within the ever-widening Diaspora unfold, with the criteria proposed clearly mirroring these developments.

Yet another axis around which the discussion revolves is the nature of the excluded conduct: does the prohibition apply to conduct grounded in custom, or to conduct grounded in law? There are opposing considerations in favor of each possibility. On the one hand, it could be argued that the prohibition against factionalism applies only in the realm of custom. Here, the desideratum of uniformity takes precedence over that of allowing individuals to follow their own customs, since the violation of customs is not as serious a matter as violation of the law. With regard to law, uniformity can be achieved only at the cost of requiring those who believe that the law calls for a certain mode of conduct to act in a manner contrary to their convictions. On the other hand, it could be argued that since fragmentation with respect to legal questions is far more dangerous than that arising from diversity of customs, the prohibition applies to the legal sphere. Custom, by its very nature, embraces diversity, but law mandates universality.

In general, an examination of the various sources points to the conclusion that the prohibition against factionalism expresses an ideal to be aspired to, rather than a binding legal principle. In the entire corpus of the Babylonian and Jerusalem Talmuds, it is found in just one discussion. Given that controversies abound in the Talmud, the prohibition appears to be relatively peripheral. It is hardly found in the Geonic literature, and rarely mentioned in the works of the Early Authorities. Maimonides' *Code* does bring the injunction, but circumspectly, in the Laws concerning Idolatry. It is not found at all in the *Tur* or the *Shulhan Arukh*, and is cited by the Rema only with regard to the marginal question of shaving during the period of the Counting of the Omer. In the responsa literature, too, the prohibition is little discussed. It would seem that the halakhic authorities did not view the "do not form factions" injunction as amenable to implementation, but rather solely as a desideratum.

As a careful examination of the sources reveals, the prohibition against factionalism becomes relevant at a rather late stage in the history of the halakha. Only after the expulsion from Spain, when Iberian exiles began to build new communities in the towns of Turkey and the Balkans, and disputes arose between the newcomers and the established communities, does mention of the prohibition increase. In the context of these disputes, the argument began to be voiced that, on the strength of the prohibition against factionalism, communities were forbidden to act in a manner counter to that agreed upon by the other communities in the town. As a rule, the argument was put forward in a very partisan way when this was conducive to the interests of one or the other side to a dispute. But while the prohibition is indeed raised in the halakhic deliberations that these disputes engendered, it is usually dismissed as irrelevant to the issue at hand. In the responsa literature, there are almost no cases in which decisors based their rulings on the prohibition.

6. Controversy: epistemic justifications and pragmatic considerations

As a rule, those engaged in study of the law are encouraged to speak their mind and not repress their true convictions. As a result, controversies abound. The presence of controversy in the halakhic enterprise engaged many, if not most, of the rabbinical authorities, as we have said. Given that so many different individuals have voiced their views on the matter, the ongoing dialogue about controversy is rich and multi-faceted. We must therefore be very cautious not to present an overly schematic and one-dimensional account of the rabbinical views on controversy. For even among those who were receptive to controversy, many different shades of opinion were expressed with respect to the justification for controversy.

Now the approbation of controversy can reflect either toleration or halakhic pluralism. Toleration allows a proponent of a given view not only to express himself, but also to teach his view, even though it might be deemed erroneous from the perspective of the 'tolerator.' Halakhic pluralism, on the other hand, at its most extreme, sincerely regards all opposed views as equally true, although for practical purposes, only one of them is adopted.[33] Now there may well be certain halakhic pluralists who adopt a less extreme view, conceding that all the views may not be equally true, but insisting nevertheless that they are all true to some degree. Thus, the approbation of controversy on the part of the rabbinical authorities is sometimes limited, sometimes comprehensive, as is manifest in the range of interpretations offered for the dictum "both are the words of the living God," as we saw above. And there are those, of course, who take a mixed approach: with regard to some controversies, a tolerant approach is adopted, whereas with regard to others, a pluralistic attitude is taken.

Be that as it may, the positive attitude on the part of the rabbinical authorities calls for an explanation, especially in light of the aforementioned deleterious effects of controversy. What were the underlying reasons for their willingness to adopt a positive attitude nonetheless? When the rabbis address this specific issue – namely, the rationale for this positive attitude toward controversy – although not when they deal with the etiology of controversy, their argument is basically epistemic: controversy enhances the discovery of the truth. The classic formulation of this argument is found in a Spanish methodological treatise:

> They were all spoken by one shepherd, which means that most times we gain a good understanding of something by considering its negation, and we cannot understand the matter on its own so

33 On the distinction between toleration and pluralism generally, see, e.g., J. Raz, *The Morality of Freedom*, Oxford: 1986.

well as by considering its negation. Therefore the Holy One, blessed be He, sought to endow us with dissenting opinions, in order that when we arrive at the true opinion, we will understand it thoroughly.

Meharerei Nemeirim[34] 17a

Sometimes the rationale is couched in terms of the pluralistic approach, on which all opinions are manifestations of the multi-faceted nature of halakhic truth. This attitude is to some extent rooted in the Talmud, but far more frequently expressed by the Kabbalists. The following passage is a good illustration:

Attend well to how the three [pairs of] rankings[35] are to be understood. The Sages said: Seventy facets to the Torah, and these facets fluctuate from one to the other; to deem it impure, to deem it pure, to prohibit, to permit, as one of the colleagues said: I can bring forty nine arguments to purify a creeping thing.[36] All these different interpretations were included in a single utterance, as it is written, "with a great voice, and it went on no more" (Deut. 5:19). It included all the aspects, their various changing configurations and their opposites: to render impure and render pure, to prohibit and to permit, to disqualify and to declare fit, because it could not be believed that that voice lacked anything. And therefore, in that voice everything was constantly turning over on all sides, one thing opposite the other. And every one of the future Sages who might arise in each and every generation received his portion, as it is said, "not only did all the prophets receive their prophecy from Sinai, but also each of the Sages who arise in each and every generation – each and every one received his portion, as it is said, "These words the Lord spoke unto all your assembly" (Deut. 5:19)."[37] Hence their dictum: "both are the words of the living God,"[38] as it is said, "One God gave them all."

Peirushei Haagadot Lerabi Azriel, bHagiga 3b

What is the experiential context in which acquiescence in the likelihood of controversy emerges? The notion that truth is many-faceted arises out of encounters between individuals who are engaged in dialogue and discussion. It could hardly have developed from the lone individual's

34 R. Abraham Akra, *Meharerei Nemeirim*, Venice: 1599.
35 I.e., impure/pure, prohibited/permitted, disqualified/made fit.
36 bSanhedrin 17a.
37 Exodus Rabbah 28:6.
38 bEruvin 13b.

encounter with the world, for the world around us, and the experiences of the individual who confronts it, do not suggest the idea of truth as many-faceted. The pluralistic approach reflects a reality that emerges only in the context of dialogue between a number of individuals. In the course of such dialogue, different – and often incompatible – views and perspectives will be voiced. The question of how individuals arrive at their different views is important, but must be referred to psychologists and anthropologists. From our perspective, the fact that individuals hold different views is a given.

One way to deal with this situation is to claim that the truth is but one, and that the opinions held by most people are therefore false. Another, of course, is to cultivate a pluralistic theory of truth. Both responses are found in the rabbinical tradition, but we will be concerned mainly with the latter.

The positive attitude to controversy so evident in the halakhic sources is, it appears, a response to the meeting of ideas that arises out of the very nature of Torah study, as opposed to an a priori approach to truth, though a pluralistic conception might nonetheless be construed by those who have internalized it as true a priori.[39]

I want to argue that the pluralistic approach to truth, and the epistemic considerations in favor of controversy, were indeed invoked by the rabbis as rationales for permitting controversy, but the primary factor in the crystallization of this attitude lies in pragmatic considerations that were not fully articulated in the rabbinical writings. My contention is that the positive attitude was determined by, among other things, the rabbis' estimation of the danger controversy posed to both the community as a whole, and the authority of the rabbinical establishment itself. Now ensuring the preservation and strength of the juridical establishment is a legitimate and appropriate desideratum in any legal system, and Jewish law is by no means exceptional in this matter. Awareness of these pragmatic considerations is repeatedly expressed in the rabbinical literature. As we are about to see, although controversy indeed poses a threat to rabbinical authority, the adoption of a positive attitude to controversy may have served, paradoxically, to ensure that the threat did not become a reality, and perhaps even to strengthen the rabbis' authority.

In suggesting these pragmatic considerations, I do not wish to argue that the rabbis were constantly aware of them, but rather to point out different trends that inform the thinking of the rabbis, ultimately sculpting the contours of the halakhic discourse. These trends crystallized out of awareness of the role played by controversy in building up the authority and standing of participants in the halakhic dialogue. We now turn to a more detailed examination of these trends.

39 See David Stern, "Midrash and indeterminacy," *Critical Inquiry* 15 (1988), 132–61; Daniel Boyarin, *Carnal Israel: Reading Sex in Talmudic Culture*, Berkeley and Los Angeles: 1993.

a. The paradox of controversy

Reflecting on what I call 'the paradox of controversy' is helpful in clarifying the halakhic attitude to controversy. The extensive discussion of controversy in the sources is, by and large, an elaboration of, and struggle with, two seemingly antithetical consequences of controversy. The countenancing of dissenting views both challenges authority, and reinforces it. Indeed, in some circumstances the countenancing of dissenting views may even generate authority. Controversy challenges authority, in that one who engages in controversy challenges received opinions, and thereby endangers the authority of the halakhic establishment. For when dissenting opinions are voiced, the outcome – quite apart from the fact that we may now be closer to the truth – could be that the authority of one side to the dispute, possibly that of the establishment, is called into question or eroded. But at the same time, I would argue, the fact that controversy is legitimate, encouraging individuals to voice dissenting opinions, results, paradoxically, in the enhancement of the establishment's authority, regardless of whether it wins the argument. If the challengers are defeated, the standing of the establishment is obviously reinforced. Even if they win, however, the establishment, by having allowed itself to be challenged, has displayed confidence that it is sufficiently powerful and secure to share its jurisdiction with others. This display of authority itself generates authority, and indeed, more than counter-balances any inroads made by the challenger.

Consciousness of these pragmatic considerations is expressed in the following passage from the Maharal of Prague.[40] The Maharal wrote extensively on the phenomenon of controversy, focusing on its metaphysical dimension. On his view, all divergent opinions display different aspects of the divine truth. In the following passage, however, which deals with theological polemics with Gentile scholars, whose views cannot, in his opinion, represent divine truth, he stresses the pragmatic dimension of acceptance of controversy, an important element of which is the contribution made by the challenging of one's opinions to strengthening the rabbinical position vis-a-vis its opponents in the disputations.

> Therefore it is improper, on the grounds of love of inquiry and knowledge, to dismiss anything that contradicts your view, and in particular, if that idea was not meant as a provocation, but merely to convey [its utterer's] belief, even if these words run counter to your beliefs and your religion. One should not say to him, 'Do not speak; shut your mouth!' For otherwise, the true religion would be not be clarified. . . . for any fighter who wants to overcome another, in order to demonstrate his might, greatly desires that the person whom he challenges will fight to his utmost, so that if he does

40 R. Judah Loew b. Bezalel, Austria–Poland, c.1525–1609.

overcome him, he will have overcome a worthy opponent. But what might does one display if that person against whom he fights is not allowed to resist and fight back? .... And therefore one should not silence someone who speaks against [the true] religion, saying to him, 'Do not speak this way'; on the contrary, if one does so, he is displaying weakness.

Beer Hagola, end of well 7

Cultivation of a positive attitude to controversy involves a certain element of risk, but also an element of reward: while there is undoubtedly some risk to the authority of the establishment, the possibility of its being strengthened appears to have outweighed this concern. As we have said, the dominant attitude to controversy in the rabbinical mind is positive, which seems to indicate the rabbis believed that, on balance, it would enhance their authority. This is not to say, however, that they ignored the risks inherent in controversy. Indeed, in response to their perception of the risks, they developed mechanisms for monitoring expression of dissenting opinion. These will be discussed in (7) below.

b. Domestication of subversive forces

In addition to the challenge inherent in controversy, which could pose a threat to the rabbinical establishment, as we just explained, controversy also gives rise to another concern: the fear that it could adversely affect the stability and vigor of the halakhic community. For a controversy that leads to a bitter dispute could end up with one camp leaving or being expelled from the halakhic community. Since an overly-sharp response, silencing the dissenter, might drive him away, a cautious response to the dissenting side is always desirable.

Indeed, much of the reflection about controversy in the halakhic sources seems to be a post factum justification for a given human reality, confrontation with which the Sages perceive as far more dangerous than accepting controversy. Explicit encouragement of freedom of expression might have served, or even been intended, to neutralize forces that would otherwise have been propelled outward. By legitimizing controversy, we enable those who challenge and dispute received opinions to remain within the camp. It appears that the Sages' main motivation for adopting a tolerant approach to controversy is recognition of the aspect of human nature that is inclined to subject received views to scrutiny before endorsing them, to seek convincing arguments where they are lacking, to press ever further in the search for knowledge, and if need be, to challenge accepted teachings. The toleration of controversy is, I submit, more an attempt to domesticate this potentially subversive, though perfectly natural, inclination, than a pragmatic harnessing of the epistemic advantages of intellectual pluralism.

This strategy transcends the domain of the interpretation of the law proper, and is also adopted with respect to questions of theology and philosophy. The rationale underlying the decision to include Ecclesiastes in the biblical canon, for instance, reflects this same strategy. The qualms of Kohelet are unsettling, and yet there is no denying they might indeed be felt by many, leading to heretical thoughts, and consequently, to guilt and alienation from the community. Including the book in the canon legitimizes such qualms, and, while allowing him to contemplate his scruples, assures the individual who has entertained them that he has not thereby distanced himself from the community of believers.

c. *Striving for excellence*

The endorsement of controversy could also stem from the perspective of the dissenting scholar himself, which is a perspective shared by all members of the community. Excellence in one's studies is a central theme in the world of the halakha. The community, by legitimizing expression of views that take issue with those of accepted authorities, on the one hand, and insisting that the dissenting scholar make a sufficiently sound case for his own view, on the other, helps to establish the scholarly credibility of the young challenger, and encourages the development of original critical thought. "Scholars (*talmidei hakhamim*) engaged in debating the law with one another"[41] are, in fact, on the traditional path to participation in the halakhic discourse, and on their way to establishing an authoritative standing within the halakhic community. Striving for excellence, so understood, is also in the interest of the community at large, for it ensures the continuity of high-calibre, intellectually independent halakhic leadership that can meet the challenges of new realities, and hence, ensure the community's survival.

That establishing one's authority by way of argumentation and dissent indeed serves to motivate members of the halakhic community can be inferred from the numerous admonitions that restrict this activity on ethical grounds, and warn against engaging in controversy for the sake of enhancing one's personal status and status within the scholarly community. It is repeatedly asserted that those who are engaged in disputation "for the sake of heaven," are not motivated by the desire for personal aggrandizement. The following passage illustrates this sentiment:

> "Every controversy that is for the sake of heaven, its end is to be sustained." This is a controversy between scholars over matters of wisdom. It does not seek to establish which of them is greater, or to misdirect a colleague from truth to falsehood. They turn to the same path and follow it until they reach the truth, which is their

41 See., e.g., bBaba Metzia 59b.

objective. Truth cannot be found in two directions, only in one. Therefore, neither is jealous of his fellow or wishes him harm because a controversy has arisen between them, for this controversy is for the sake of heaven and not to gratify material needs, but to know wisdom and achieve truth.

Peirushei Mishnat Avot (Sefer Hamusar),[42] mAvot 5:17

d. Involvement in the ongoing evolution of the halakha

By making provision for the expression of dissenting views, we allow individuals to be part of the evolution of the law. Such participation, though limited to those actually engaged in Torah study, has a ripple effect, generating a sense in the community that the law is democratic, so to speak, being an ongoing enterprise rather than dictated from above.

Such a spirit is manifest in R. Haim of Volozhin's[43] description of the experience of group Torah study, in which fathers and sons, great and small in learning, participate on an equal footing, and halakhic creativity is found not necessarily in the academy, but also in the private dwelling:

Now learning is called war, as in the dictum, "the war of the Torah"; students, then, are warriors. And as our Sages of blessed memory said: " 'They shall not be ashamed when they speak with their enemies at the gate,' even father and son, teacher and student, who apply themselves to the Torah at the same gate, become enemies of each other, yet do not budge," and so on.[44] A student must not accept his teacher's words if he has any objection to them. Sometimes the student will be right, just as a small piece of wood can set a large one aflame. As it is stated, "Let your home be a meeting place for the wise and you shall wrestle,"[45] from the verse "and there wrestled a man with him" (Gen. 32:25), an allusion to struggle, for this is indeed a holy struggle (*milhemet mitzva*). We likewise grapple with our holy teachers, whose renowned works we study. Their bodies are interred, while their souls dwell above. By the presence of their books in our homes, our homes become meeting places for encounters with these wise scholars. We have also been admonished and given permission to wrestle and do battle with their words, and to resolve problems they raised. And not to adulate anyone, but to love only the truth.

Ruah Haim, mAvot 1:4

42 R. Joseph b. Judah, Maimonides' student.
43 Lithuania, 1749–1821.
44 bKidushin 30b.
45 The verb can also mean "gather dust."

7. **Controversy regulated**

Above, we saw that as well as being an opportunity to enhance the establishment's authority, controversy also has the potential to endanger it. To lessen this risk, two main devices are in place: on the one hand, rules that limit the range of legitimate controversies, and on the other, rules intended to neutralize the negative impact of controversy in those cases where it is allowed. The rules that limit the range of legitimate controversies apply primarily to disputes with scholars of past generations – "The views of the earlier authorities are not to be disputed"; "The earlier authorities are not to be defamed"; "The view of a great authority is not to be invalidated after his death," and so on. These rules seek to preserve the standing of a halakhic authority when he is unable to do so himself. But it seems that they have been used much more broadly, as, for example, when one of the disputants relies on a particular earlier authority, and argues that his opponent may not attack this position, citing one of the aforementioned rules. The second set of rules, those intended to neutralize the negative impact of controversy, seek to make a sharp demarcation between the substance of an argument, and its mode of presentation, in order to prevent a substantively acceptable argument from being put forward in a manner that undermines the standing of a halakhic authority. The apologetic rhetoric and demonstrative humility expressed by the disputants reduce the tension that would otherwise be associated with engaging in controversy. The emphasis on expressions of the amity and friendship that must obtain between the parties to the controversy is intended to ensure that the friendly relations between them will not be adversely impacted by the heated debate. We now turn to an elaboration of these rules.

a. *The code of conduct*

The rabbis' approbation of – or at least acquiescence in – controversy should not be understood as willingness to sanction any and all expressions of disagreement with the views of rabbinical authorities. On the contrary, the rabbis instituted a system of checks and balances to regulate the manner in which controversy was conducted. These regulatory mechanisms are not articulated in terms of restrictions on the content of the dissenting opinions: no principles, texts or issues were impervious to scholarly scrutiny and critique. Rather, procedural limitations – both general principles and highly specific rules of etiquette – are imposed. Just as wars are governed by formal and informal codes of conduct, so the war of the Torah is strictly regulated by a partly explicit, partly implicit, code of conduct. The code of conduct is designed to allow for controversy and the voicing of dissenting opinions, while at the same time safeguarding the legal system against chaos and disintegration. It thus represents a delicate balance between two opposed interests: the short-term interest of allowing individuals to speak their mind, and the long-term interest of preserving the system's integrity and overall stability.

The code of conduct for those engaged in the study of the Torah is formulated partly in terms of general principles, and partly in terms of specific rules of etiquette. The latter are mainly the work of the Later Authorities, who composed manuals for halakhic discourse, with lists of permissible and impermissible locutions. These principles and rules address two spheres – external behavior, which is readily observable, and mental disposition, which has no direct external manifestations. In the former sphere, the code of conduct sets out the modes of expression deemed legitimate, while in the latter, the focus is the motivation of the disputants. The end to which they should aspire is the discovery of truth, and not the furtherance of personal agendas and gratification of material needs.

The code of conduct has two distinct sources, intuition and convention. Rules that originate in an intuitive sense of respect follow naturally from the feelings of high regard and affection of students for their teachers, and teachers for their colleagues and predecessors. Such rules come naturally to the individuals involved in halakhic debate, and need not be imposed formally other than in the exceptional case of individuals who do not share these sentiments. Conventional rules, however, follow only from a common perception that it is advisable to have an agreed-upon framework for expressing this respect for the halakhic authorities. Hence they are, by consensus, explicitly imposed, and adopted, as a condition for participation in the halakhic dialogue.

Underlying the code of conduct are two major considerations, one moral, the other institutional. The moral consideration, the need to avoid offending one's interlocutor, is a concern that is operative generally, and is not peculiar to halakhic discourse. The institutional consideration is preservation of the status and standing of the rabbinical authorities, despite the fact that their views are being challenged. With respect to controversies over the views of earlier authorities, the institutional consideration is paramount, for the obvious reason that the departed cannot be offended. The two considerations may overlap, but there could be cases where one consideration is operative and the other is not, for instance, should a party to a scholarly dispute forgo the honor due him. The tension between the two considerations is well brought out in the Talmud's discussion of the validity of a Sage's renunciation of his honor (bKidushin 32a).

The importance and impact of this code of conduct should not be underestimated. By delimiting with great specificity rules that govern the expression of dissent and disagreement, a psychological barrier against more dramatic challenges to received opinions is created. This barrier, though occasionally broken, does serve to contain potentially divisive confrontations. It appears that the legitimacy of a dissenting opinion is not generally a function of its content, but a function of its mode of presentation, that is, of the degree to which its proponent observes the code of conduct. Failure to abide by the code may deprive the dissenter of his status as a legitimate member of the halakhic community, and in extreme cases, bring about his expulsion. Surprising though this may sound, to a very great extent the code of conduct is actually constitutive of the halakhic community. The underlying assumption here is that there is an empirical association, though not a logical link, between observance of the code of conduct, and substantively correct halakhic content. That is, there is apparently a connection between form and substance: though there is no necessary connection between conduct and content, we do find that observance of the code's general principles, and specific rules of etiquette, virtually guarantees that the opinions generated are acceptable in terms of their content. And the reverse is also true: when the code of conduct is not observed, this is projected onto the product of the halakhic discourse, a phenomenon reflected in the talmudic dictum, "Regarding two scholars who live in the same town and are not amiable to each other in discussing the law, of them Scripture says, "I gave them also laws that were not good and ordinances by which they could not live" (Ezek. 20:25)."[46]

With respect to the requirement that disputants have the correct mental disposition, the criterion that the controversy must be engaged in "for the sake of heaven" is frequently proposed. While it is easy to identify violations of well-defined rules of conduct, assessing whether the dispositional condition has been met is more problematic, leaving room for an additional means of suppressing opinions unacceptable to the rabbinical authorities – the claim that their proponent is not acting for the sake of heaven. Thus considerations of motivation can be used when focusing on procedural flaws is not an effective means of eliminating ideas deemed substantively threatening.

b. Benefits of properly-conducted controversy

The halakhic acceptance of controversy, properly conducted, as a positive phenomenon that does not adversely affect the integrity of the community and the halakhic system, reaches fruition in the idea that not only is ongoing controversy not harmful, but it is actually beneficial and desirable, inasmuch as it fosters harmonious intellectual creativity. This attitude is explored in Chapter 5, entitled "Controversy and Social Harmony." Indeed, this daring conception, articulated only by the Later Authorities, sees controversy as conducive to peace. In that it makes possible the clarification of an issue from every angle, taking into account the contribution of each side to the dispute, controversy, on this approach, actually

46 bMegila 32a.

promotes peace and amity. Theoretical clarity can emerge, it is argued, only by taking into account the input of the participants in the debate. The idea here is that of a harmony of opposites. Peace is not the culmination of unanimity and uniformity, but, on the contrary, results from dialogical juxtaposition of conflicting viewpoints. The conception that peace is achieved through controversy is also grounded in the notion that one is duty-bound to engage in controversy if doing so is conducive to arriving at the truth. Peace can only be built on a foundation of truth, and not the other way around. Avoiding controversy for the sake of peace is thus a grave error.

8. Opposition to controversy

To present the overall halakhic attitude to controversy as entirely positive would certainly be a distortion. There are rabbis who see failure to reach a consensus as a regrettable phenomenon, and voice qualms and reservations. These qualms are sometimes expressed directly, sometimes indirectly. In the Talmud itself, such qualms are indeed few, though they reverberate throughout the entire halakhic literature. An apt example is the following mishnaic passage:

> If the house collapsed upon someone [an only son] and on his [widowed] mother, [the house of Shammai] and [the house of Hillel] agree that [their heirs] should share equally [in the estate]. R. Akiva said, I maintain that [the house Hillel hold that] the property should be left in the hands of its present possessors [i.e., that the house of Hillel disagree with the house of Shammai here too, as in a case discussed earlier in the Mishna]. Ben Azai said to him: We grieve over the [explicitly articulated] disagreement, and you seek to introduce a disagreement on a point on which they [can be construed as] agree[ing].
>
> mBaba Batra 9:10

Similarly, another talmudic Sage, R. Jose, described the distant past as an ideal time free of controversy: "Said R. Jose: Initially there was no controversy in Israel."[47] And a mishnaic passage expresses the longing for a return to this ideal state as a vision for the end of days:

> R. Joshua said: I have received a tradition from Rabban Johanan b. Zakai, who heard it from his teacher, and his teacher from his teacher, as a law given to Moses at Sinai, that Elijah will not come

47 tSanhedrin 7:1.

to pronounce impure or to pronounce pure, to send away or to bring near. ... R. Judah says: to bring near, but not to send away. R. Shimon says: to reconcile controversy.

mEduyot 8:7

In the same vein, the controversies between the house of Shammai and the house of Hillel are portrayed as a punishment, or at least as a historical contingency, being described as having been caused by students' failure to sufficiently attend their masters. And the talmudic prohibition against factionalism, discussed above in (5c), though, as we saw, of limited scope, also reflects a longing for consensus. Essentially, these are the only negative things the Talmud has to say about controversy. In the Geonic period, however, disapproval of controversy is far more pronounced. Indeed, in the Geonic writings, unlike the talmudic literature, there is no explicit endorsement of the possibly beneficial dimension of controversy.

The dictum "both are the words of the living God," which over the centuries became the classic expression of the positive attitude to controversy, is not found anywhere in the Geonic corpus. Moreover, the Geonim strive to present the halakha as being as free of controversy as possible. This agenda is readily understandable against the background of the struggle against the Karaite challenge to the primacy of Rabbinic Judaism. The following comment, made by R. Samuel b. Eli Gaon, a contemporary of Maimonides, should be understood in this context. Articulated at a time when the authority of the Geonim was challenged by the Karaites, it alludes to external rather than internal controversies.

> The academy is the place of Moses our teacher, and in it the law of Israel is completed. And whoever disputes its rulings is like one who disputes the sovereign of the law, whose place it is, and one who disputes the rulings of Moses our teacher, of blessed memory, whose seat it is.[48]

This Geonic attitude requires further explanation. The great contribution of the Geonim was undoubtedly the fact that they established the authority of the Babylonian Talmud as universally binding. Despite this Geonic attitude, we should not lose sight of the fact that the Geonim took an independent position toward the Talmud. There was thus a certain tension in their approach to the Talmud. On the one hand, the Geonim were the direct successors of the Amoraim. Due to both spatial and temporal contiguity, the Geonim perceived themselves as direct heirs to the Amoraic legacy. This would lead one to expect that they would uphold the

---

48 Simha Assaf, "Collected letters of R. Samuel b. Eli" (Hebrew), *Tarbiz* 1 (1930), 64–5.

predominantly positive talmudic attitude to controversy. On the other hand, the Geonic approach to the halakha was very different from that of the Amoraim: to entrench the principle that halakhic determinations would be based solely on the Talmud, they felt it was incumbent upon them to unequivocally resolve halakhic disputes in the Talmud – a policy that contravenes the spirit of the Talmud itself! To achieve this objective, they developed a sophisticated set of principles, and even took the liberty of deciding which passages in the Talmud should be considered authoritative. In other words, they adopted a selective attitude to the Talmud: the Talmud is binding, but not everything contained in it.

After the Geonic period, the most outspoken opponent of controversy is Maimonides, who in this regard follows the path of the Geonim. The main motivation behind his opposition to controversy is a desire to liberate Torah study from argumentation and polemics, by eliminating controversy and dissenting views. One formative source for this attitude was Maimonides' profound commitment to philosophy, and in particular, his notion of truth.

A separate issue altogether is the place of controversy in the Kabbala and the Zohar. The Kabbala's world of images and symbols cannot be covered in the framework of the present study, but the few Kabbalistic passages that have been presented in the volume attest to the intensive preoccupation of the Kabbalists with the problem of controversy. We will see that the Kabbalists' reservations about controversy echo their critique of traditional talmudic discourse. But at the same time, the opposite tendency is also pronounced – the Kabbalists emphasize the myriad facets of the Torah, and the role of the individual in making halakhic determinations. This aspect of their approach, it seems, is intended to pave the way for their own antinomian religious path.

Another context in which the expression of opposition to controversy appears to be present is that of the numerous comments found throughout the halakhic literature to the effect that "the views of the earlier authorities are not to be disputed." However, such remarks do not negate the legitimacy of controversy itself, but rather, serve to establish a certain hierarchy among the generations. The objection to disagreeing with early authorities is not a matter of principle, but an ad hominem argument invoking the respective merits of different generations. Though subtle, this distinction between opposition to controversy that is a matter of principle, and opposition due to historical contingencies, must be kept in mind as we proceed with our analysis.

Let me mention one last area where opposition to controversy is discernable, namely, the interpretive principle that controversy is not to be multiplied. This rule directs the interpreter of texts to read them, where possible, not as contradicting each other, but rather, as compatible with each other. As such, it is not a rule of conduct prohibiting controversies.

Nevertheless, it clearly reflects a negative attitude to controversy. It is discussed in (8b) below.

a. The genealogy of controversy

The sources in chapter 6 deal with rabbinical attitudes to the emergence of controversy. Some attempt to anchor the emergence of controversy in the flow of historical events, linking it to specific past occurrences. Others explain the existence of controversy as inherent in the nature of law, or of man; see chapter 1. The importance of the different explanations for the emergence of controversy lies in the fact that they reflect different value judgments about controversy itself. The view that the emergence of controversy is related to the nature of the Torah reflects a positive attitude to controversy, seeing in it a fitting expression of the Torah's wisdom. Explanations that link the proliferation of controversy to human nature do not necessarily signal a positive attitude to controversy on the part of their proponents, but do imply some degree of tolerance and understanding. As opposed to these explanations, accounts of the emergence of controversy that cite such historical contingencies as the demise of the Sanhedrin,[49] the multiplication of "students of Shammai and Hillel who did not attend to their teachers sufficiently,"[50] Moses' striking the rock,[51] and the cessation of prophecy,[52] are indicative of reservations about controversy, as they contrast an ideal controversy-free past with the controversy-ridden present, and link the birth of controversy to these unfortunate events.

The line of thought that seeks historical explanations for the emergence of controversy merits our attention, since historical explanations are, as a rule, rare in the rabbinical tradition, which does not concern itself with historical reflection and speculation, an attitude manifested in the dictum – expressed apropos a different matter, but very apt here – "whatever was, was" (bKetubot 3a). It appears that recourse to historical conjecture in this particular context is motivated by a negative outlook on controversy.

The claim that controversy resulted from the demise of the Sanhedrin occupies a powerful place in the explanation of controversy. The decision of the high court in the Hall of Hewn Stone in Jerusalem is perceived as a decision that dissolves any controversy that comes before it, unlike a decision of any other court (including the high court in Yavne), which can determine the law, but can neither dissolve the controversy nor exclude any opinions from the tradition. Paradoxically, in linking the fact of controversy to the demise of a specific institution, which cannot be

49 Maimonides' *Code*, Laws concerning Rebels 1:3–4.
50 bSota 47b.
51 *Megale Amukot*, ofen 74.
52 *Beit Elohim*, Shaar hayesodot, chapter 36; *Beit Habehira*, mAvot, preface.

reconstituted, this explanation, though hostile to controversy, obviates any chance of its eradication, and guarantees its perpetuation.

We have already pointed out that in theory the integrity of the tradition can be achieved in two different ways: by including within the tradition all opinions that have been voiced, even if they were rejected, thereby preserving the notion of one Torah, but a Torah containing many voices; and by excluding the repudiated dissenting views, thereby preserving the notion of a coherent Torah that speaks in one voice. However, the latter approach risks the emergence of a new body of law – the rejected voices – paralleling the law of the establishment. The risk is that the Torah would then become, literally, "two sets of laws." It stands to reason that the Sages preferred the former option, fearing that were there an institution in place that had the power to reject opinions and thereby create disgruntled halakhists, bifurcation would indeed be the outcome. Hence, they insisted on virtually impossible conditions for (re)convening the Sanhedrin, forestalling exclusion of dissenting views.

b. "Controversy is not to be multiplied"

The principle that controversy should not be multiplied is not a directive to rabbinical authorities to abstain from engaging in controversies, but rather, an interpretive principle stating that one should, as far as possible, attempt to harmonize apparently incompatible views that have already been expressed, and avoid, to the extent possible, interpreting the words of the halakhic authorities to the effect that they disagree with each other. This understanding of the principle can be inferred from the fact that its many different formulations all address the way in which one is to read accounts of existing controversies, as opposed to the way in which a participant in an ongoing debate is to conduct himself. Even within this limited sphere, however, it is not a categorical prohibition against ascribing controversies to the rabbis, but a desideratum directing the commentator faced with two interpretative options, to adopt, as far as possible, that which eliminates the controversy, or reduces its scope, even if this interpretation is forced. The principle is also cited as a rationale for the self-evident principle that new controversies are not to be instigated: those engaged in an ongoing dispute ought not ascribe a dissenting view to an authority who did not express himself on the issue.

Very different presuppositions may underlie the principle that controversy ought not be multiplied. On the one hand, there may be a presupposition that in most cases rabbinical controversies are pseudo-controversies, since it is not plausible that any of the dissenting authorities, who are well versed in the law, could be wrong. On this presupposition, the principle seeks to ascertain historical truth by removing the distorting veil of apparent controversy that cloaks the opinions in question, directing the commentator to attempt to reveal their proponents' true intents. On the other hand, a contrary presupposition may be in place here, to the effect that the authorities do indeed disagree occasionally. Out of institutional considerations, namely, the desire to harmonize between the different sources of binding halakha, however, the principle stipulates that contradictory statements ought to be interpreted as compatible, even if this interpretation twists the original intents of their authors. It would seem that the fact that the principle is formulated as a directive aimed at the commentator, and not as a descriptive statement about the halakhic authorities, supports the latter presupposition.

What is the motivation underlying this ideal of harmonizing halakhic sources? Harmonization advances several important goals. First, given that the halakha is a normative system, and individuals have to conduct themselves according to its directives, it must be consistent. Thus the harmonization of various opinions advances an institutional goal, the smooth application of the law in daily life. Second, harmonization advances compliance with a formal desideratum: the cardinal methodological principle, known as the principle of charity, that any interpretive endeavor should seek to provide a contradiction-free exposition of the system being analyzed. Thirdly, harmonization serves a social goal, namely, the lessening of any societal tension that might arise as a result of the fact that controversy is sanctioned.

The principle that controversy should not be multiplied thus directs the commentator to eliminate controversies from the halakhic corpus by reconciling apparently incompatible views. In so doing, the corpus as a whole retains its coherence, and the various opinions are interpreted in a manner that allows them to remain within it. It should, however, be noted that this coherence could be achieved by means of the opposite strategy – recognition of the existence of a controversy, and repudiation of the dissenting view. This would maintain the controversy-free coherence of the corpus, but at the cost of rejecting one side to the dispute.

The principle of reconciling conflicting sources is already found in the Talmud, and might even be seen as one of the characteristic features of talmudic discourse. Attesting to this is the fact that there are very few cases in which the Talmud interprets contradictory statements as having been voiced by "two different authorities," and hence, inherently resistant to harmonization, in contrast to endless attempts to harmonize apparently conflicting views and resolve the contradiction. Nevertheless, this principle, though implicit, is not articulated in the Talmud itself. Employed frequently in the post-talmudic literature, it is articulated for the first time only by the Spanish scholars of the Expulsion period. From then on it is cited constantly in works by both Ashkenazic and Sefardic scholars. More precisely, it seems that we can trace the crystallization of the principle to the circle of the students of R. Isaac Canpanton (Castile, d. 1463), one of the founders of the 'Sefardic speculative method.' This connection, which eluded earlier scholars, is borne out by a number of arguments that will not be detailed here, but just remarked on briefly.[53] It is possible to identify a conceptual affinity between the Sefardic method and the principle that controversy is not to be multiplied. One of the method's fundamental goals is to demonstrate that the views of both sides to a halakhic debate can be argued for convincingly. By establishing the plausibility of the views, this process, by its very nature, diminishes the gap between the two sides. Following this line of reasoning to its logical conclusion would suggest that apparent contradictions can be dissolved, as the opposed opinions can be shown to be compatible.

9. Final remarks

The controversy between the house of Shammai and the house of Hillel is a unique phenomenon in the history of the halakha. Two schools of thought arose and were perceived as such not only by their members, but also by the community at large. A distinction between the internal point of view and the external is instructive here. The latter identifies a number of rabbinical authorities who share the same outlook and methodology, either globally or with respect to a particular issue, without assuming that the individuals involved would so describe themselves. In the Talmud, the external characterization is manifested in those places where it is stated that a number of Sages constitute a "*shita*" (pattern of thought)[54]: this talmudic assertion tells us nothing about the said Sages' self-image, or the way they were perceived by their contemporaries. Schools of thought in this external sense were certainly commonplace. The determination that schools of thought existed from an internal point of view, however, requires that the individuals involved declare themselves to be so affiliated. Here, the decisive element is not so much identity of outlook or methodology, for there will certainly be numerous points of disagreement between them, but rather, consciousness of membership in a given group.

Belonging to a group has two motivations, one offensive, the other defensive. By affiliating ourselves with a group, we can define 'the other' very clearly. Having so categorized him, we are able to dismiss his views, should we wish to do so yet lack sound arguments against them. Such a perfunctory dismissal of the views held by an opposing group is evident in the following assertion: "The view of the house of Shammai, where it contradicts the view of the house of Hillel, is of no consequence" (bJebamot 9a). On the other hand, by adducing one's group affiliation as

---

53 The arguments are set out in *Controversy and Dialogue in the Halakhic Sources*, vol. 3 (2002).
54 bBaba Metzia 69a.

backing, one can defend oneself against critique from the outside. The disputes between the house of Shammai and the house of Hillel reflect a controversy between two schools of thought, and this determination can be made from the internal as well as the external point of view.[55]

This is what makes the phenomenon of the emergence of the house of Shammai and the house of Hillel as distinct schools of thought so very unique. In the entire history of the halakha, at least up to the time of the polemics between the Hasidim and the Mitnagdim, it is hard to point to another case where distinct schools of thought – from the internal perspective – can be said to have existed. Generally speaking, no halakhic opinion was rejected on the grounds that its author belonged to a certain school.

And indeed, the two schools of thought, the house of Shammai and the house of Hillel, flourished in the transitional period between the era in which, according to tradition, there were no disputes at all, and a later era, still upon us, in which controversy has been abundant. The importance of the schools in this transitional period reflects the fact that when controversy is not regarded favorably, the institution of schools of thought serves as a mechanism by means of which individuals can express nonconforming views. In a period when controversy is not yet welcome, any controversies that do arise have the potential to degenerate into violent conflict. The institution of schools of thought serves as a safety valve, so to speak, to prevent such an occurrence. This account of the contribution of the schools of Shammai and Hillel is close, though not identical, to that reflected in the following passage from the Maharal:

> And you should know that the Sages stated that both are the words of the living God only regarding the controversy between the house of Shammai and the house of Hillel. Because they were the first to engage in halakhic controversy, since prior to them there were no disputes at all about the Torah. And when the house of Shammai and the house of Hillel arose, their controversies were such that both views were the words of the living God, as we explained above. And it is inappropriate that Israel should descend [directly] from the lofty level of absence of controversy to a level where controversy occurs and one view is effaced. And therefore the controversy [between the house of Shammai and the house of Hillel] was such that both are the words of the living God. And after this, common controversy began to occur.
>
> *Beer Hagola*, well 1, p. 19

---

55 On the role of schools of thought in the history of philosophy generally, see Randall Collins, *The Sociology of Philosophy: A Global Theory of Intellectual Change*, Cambridge, MA: 1998.

The Maharal, who believes that history is a guided unfolding of the divine will, is saying that the two schools of thought played a visionary educational role in the community at the time. The dramatic transition from a controversy-free state to a situation where controversy is rampant is troubling. Introduction of an intermediate stage, a stage during which both schools represent halakhic truth, cushions the transition, softening its impact. According to the Maharal, the situation wherein the views of both schools represent the truth is unique in the history of the halakha, and has not recurred. In the period of the house of Shammai–house of Hillel debates, an important feature characteristic of the time prior to the emergence of controversy – the fact that every halakhic opinion expressed was true – is preserved, and, at the same time, a distinctive feature that will characterize future halakhic discourse – failure to reach agreement on legal questions – emerges.

Indeed, the implied legitimacy of controversy may explain the virtual absence of schools of thought in the halakhic world after the mishnaic period. Although obviously, schools of thought themselves originate in controversy, their persistence can usually be attributed to a situation where individuals seek to express their opinions yet feel reluctant to do so in the absence of some external backing, some intellectual home. But if controversy is condoned, the need for such schools of thought is greatly reduced, as individuals do not feel uncomfortable about voicing their true opinions. Nor do individuals who express dissenting views risk expulsion from the community. This conclusion is compatible with that reached by the historian Albert Baumgarten, who maintains that halakhic disputation did not engender sectarianism, and cannot be invoked to explain the emergence of the different sects of the mishnaic period.[56] The halakhic community was tolerant of significant halakhic differences, and proponents of different views were able to live in harmony side by side. I close this introduction with the hope that this spirit, the true spirit of the halakhic discourse, will continue to flourish, as will the time-honored halakhic code of conduct that has made its flourishing possible.

56 "The role of controversy as a factor in engendering sectarianism" (Hebrew), in G. Brin and B. Nitzan (eds.), *Fifty Years of Dead Sea Scrolls Research: Jacob Licht Festschrift* (Hebrew), Jerusalem: 2001, p. 155.

LIST OF PASSAGES

1. Controversy is the way of the Torah

1. Avot de-Rabbi Nathan, version A, chapter 1
2. Song of Songs Rabbah 6:14 (Dunsky edition, p. 146)
3. bKidushin 30a–b
4. bHagiga 3a–b
5. bBaba Metzia 84a
6. Midrash on Psalms 104 (22)
7. Responsa Rid, #1, pp. 6–7
8. Responsa Rid, #62
9. Responsa Trumat Hadeshen, Psakim ukhtavim, #238
10. Responsa Maharam Mintz, #99
11. Peirushei Rabbenu Avraham Farissol, mAvot 5:22
12. Responsa Beit Yosef, The law of boundless waters, #1 (p. 343)
13. Responsa Tashbetz, Hut Hameshulash, column 3, #35
14. Responsa Darkhei Noam, EH, #64
15. Responsa Noda Biyehuda, 2nd edition, OH, #54
16. Ruah Haim, mAvot 1:4
17. Responsa Hatam Sofer, EH 1, #151
18. Responsa Semikha Lehaim, EH, #9 (pp. 56–7)
19. Arukh Hashulhan, HM, preface
20. Responsa Sridei Esh 3, #9

1.1. Controversy is not to be multiplied

21. mBaba Batra 9:10
22. Hasagot Haraavad, bBerakhot 24a (Alfasi pagination)
23. Raavad, Katuv Sham, bBerakhot 49a (p. 12)
24. Nimukei Yosef, bBaba Metzia 65b (Alfasi pagination)
25. Responsa Maharik, #94 (p. 184)
26. Responsa Maharik, #176
27. Halikhot Olam, gate 2 (p. 16a)

2. The conduct of a controversy: etiquette and rules of debate

3. Controversy and truth

108. Lehem Mishne, mAvot 5:17
109. Yearot Dvash, part 2, sermon 8
110. Petah Einayim, bBaba Metzia 59b
111. Responsa Yosef Ometz, #51
112. Kedushat Levi, Likutim, s.v. *teiku*
113. Responsa Zivhei Tzedek, YD, #26
114. Vayaas Avraham, Kuntres pri haaretz, pp. 506–10
115. Ein Aiya, Berakhot, chapter 9, 68
116. Mikhtav Mieliahu, part 3, p. 353
117. Shiurei Daat, part 1, Darka shel tora, chapter 5
118. Pahad Yitzhak (Hutner), Hanuka, 3
119. Responsa Igrot Moshe, OH 1, foreword

3.1. *Seventy facets to the Torah*

120. Mekhilta Yitro, Masekhta de-bahodesh, 7 (Horowitz edition, p. 229)
121. bShabat 88b
122. bSanhedrin 34a
123. Numbers Rabbah 13:15
124. Zohar, Genesis 47:2
125. Zohar, Leviticus 20:1
126. Peirushei Haagadot Lerabi Azriel, bHagiga 3b
127. Sefer Hahinukh, precept 77
128. Responsa Radbaz, 3, #643
129. Baalei Brit Avram, foreword
130. Derekh Etz Haim, first paragraph

4. Controversy and uniformity of practice

4.1. The 'do not form factions' prohibition and its rationales

131. Sifre Deuteronomy 96 (Finkelstein edition, p. 158)
132. Sifre Deuteronomy 346 (Finkelstein edition, p. 403)
133. jPesahim 4:1 (30d)
134. bJebamot 13b–14a
135. Hidushei Haritba, bRosh Hashana 34a (responsum by R. Hai Gaon)
136. Rashi, bJebamot 13b s.v. *lo taasu*
137. Responsa Rashi, #128
138. Kuzari, III:49
139. Maimonides' Book of Precepts, Negative precepts, 45
140. Maimonides' *Code*, Laws concerning Idolatry 12:14

141. Responsa Maimonides, #329 (Freimann #111)
142. Responsa Maimonides, #262 (Freimann #33)
143. Hidushei Haramban, bMegila 2a
144. Hidushei Haritba, bJebamot 13b
145. Hagahot Harema, OH 493:3
146. Responsa Maharashdam, YD, #153
147. Responsa Piskei Uziel Besheeilot Hazman, #2

4.2. Who is bound by the prohibition?

148. Rabbenu Jeruham, Toldot Adam Vehava, path b (p. 23a)
149. Hidushei Haritba, bJebamot 14a s.v. *amar lei*
150. Piskei Riaz, Jebamot, chapter 1, halakha 1, letters 16–17 (p. 3)
151. Responsa Mabit, 1, #21
152. Responsa Maharashdam, YD, #153
153. Responsa Parashat Mordekhai, OH, #4
154. Responsa Maharshag, 2, #12
155. Responsa Sridei Esh, 2, #56 (p. 144)

4.3. The distinction between two courts and one court

156. bJebamot 14a
157. Raban, EH, Jebamot 118a
158. Maimonides' *Code*, Laws concerning Idolatry 12:14
159. Beit Habehira, bJebamot 14a s.v. *zo*
160. Sefer Mitzvot Gadol, Negative precepts, 62
161. Sefer Hahinukh, precept 467
162. Piskei Riaz, Jebamot, chapter 1, halakha 1, letters 16–17 (p. 3)
163. Responsa Binyamin Zeev, #303
164. Responsa Radbaz, 5, #1384
165. Responsa Radbaz, 8, #141

4.4. 'Do not form factions' as applied to different communities

166. Responsa Tashbetz, 3, #179
167. Responsa Radakh, house 11, chamber 1 (house 13, p. 104b in first edition)
168. Responsa Radakh, house 12, chambers 1–2 (house 14 in first edition)
169. Responsa Binyamin Zeev, #303
170. Responsa Avkat Rokhel, #32
171. Responsa Mahari Ben Lev, 3, #14

47

172. Responsa Mabit, 3, #77
173. Responsa Maharshag, 2, #12

4.5. The distinction between law and custom

174. Beit Habehira, bJebamot 14a s.v. *umegila*
175. Hidushei Haritba, bJebamot 14a s.v. *vehikshu batosafot*
176. Rosh, Jebamot, chapter 1, section 9

5. Controversy and social harmony

177. mPesahim 4:1
178. mJebamot 1:4
179. mEduyot 8:7
180. tJebamot 1:10–12
181. Genesis Rabbah 4:6
182. Leviticus Rabbah 9:9
183. bBerakhot 16b–17a
184. bBerakhot 39b
185. bBerakhot 64a
186. bKidushin 30b
187. Derekh Eretz Zuta 9:25
188. Sheiltot, Korah, #131
189. Kad Hakemah, 'Sinat hinam'
190. Yearot Dvash, part 2, sermon 8
191. Hidushei Agadot Maharam Shick, mAvot 5:17
192. Pri Tzadik, Numbers, Korah, 5
193. Olat Reiya, part 1, p. 330
194. Ein Aiya, Berakhot, chapter 6, 16
195. Responsa Igrot Moshe, OH 4, #25

6. The origins of halakhic controversy

196. tSanhedrin 7:1
197. jHagiga 2:2 (77d)
198. bSota 47b
199. bTemura 15b–16a
200. Exodus Rabbah 28:6
201. Emunot Vedeiot, introduction, p. 10
202. Peirushei R. Saadia Gaon on Genesis, preface, pp. 187–8
203. Mevo Hatalmud of R. Samuel b. Hofni Gaon, introduction
204. Mevo Hatalmud of R. Samuel b. Hofni Gaon, chapter 5
205. Igeret R. Sherira Gaon, pp. 8–11 (Spanish version)

TRANSLATORS' NOTE

It goes without saying that the problems inherent in translation, in general, made themselves felt in the course of preparing this volume. Particularly pressing was the dilemma of which desideratum to give precedence to: fidelity to the original language of the text, or idiomaticity of the target language. Nor need we mention the problems faced by the translator who attempts to translate a work not just from one tongue into another, but across millennia, cultures, and continents. We will, therefore, confine our remarks to clarifying what the reader should, and should not, expect of the translations in this volume.

First, readers should note that the present volume does not purport to provide a systematic translation in the mechanical sense – that is, to use the same English word to translate each occurrence of a given word in the Hebrew original. On the contrary, we are intentionally taking the liberty of not always translating even unambiguous terms with the same word. We prefer, rather, to be sensitive to the contexts in which the terms occur. In this regard, the translation is really a commentary. To overcome the limitations inherent in this approach, we are providing the original passages.

Second, readers should be aware that we do not seek to reproduce the stylistic differences that can be discerned, in the original texts, between the various genres of writing (talmudic, Geonic, early/middle/late medieval, Sefardic/Ashkenazic, and so on). Our objective is primarily to provide an accurate rendering of the substance of the passages, and not to mirror their literary style.

1

CONTROVERSY IS THE WAY OF THE TORAH

1. Avot de-Rabbi Nathan, version A, chapter 1

An incident that took place involving R. Joshia and R. Matia b. Heresh, who would both sit and occupy themselves with study of the Torah. R. Joshia withdrew [from learning] to a worldly occupation. Said R. Matia b. Heresh to him: My teacher, why do you forsake the words of the living God, and let yourself be swept away by a worldly occupation? Though you are my teacher and I am but your student, [I dare to tell you that] it is not good to forsake the words of the living God and be swept away by a worldly occupation.

They said: While they sat and applied themselves to [study of] the Torah, they would continually make each other jealous, but on parting they were like childhood friends.

2. Song of Songs Rabbah 6:14 (Dunsky edition, p. 146)

"There are threescore queens and fourscore concubines and maidens without number. My dove, my undefiled is but one" (Song of Songs 6:8–9).

R. Isaac explained these verses as referring to the sections of the Torah. "Threescore queens" – these are the sixty tractates of the laws [of the Talmud]; "and fourscore concubines" – these are the eighty sections in Torat Kohanim [Sifra]; "and maidens without number" – there is no end to the addenda. "But one" – even in disputing each other, they derive their positions from the same source, the same law, the same [logical principles:] inference from identical terms (*gzeira shava*) and a fortiori inference (*kal vahomer*).

R. Judan b. R. Ilai explained these verses as referring to the Tree of Life and to the Garden of Eden. "Threescore queens" – sixty groups of the pious sitting in the Garden of Eden under the Tree of Life and applying themselves to [study of] the Torah... "and fourscore concubines" – these are the eighty groups of lesser souls who sit and apply themselves to [study of] the Torah, but not under the Tree of Life. "And maidens without number" – there is no end to the students. Can it be that they dispute each other's views? The biblical verse teaches us: "My dove, my undefiled is but one" – they all derive their positions from the same source, the same law, the same [logical principles:] inference from identical terms and a fortiori inference.

3. bKidushin 30a–b

Our Rabbis taught: "And thou shalt teach them diligently[1]" (Deut. 6:7) [means] that the words of the Torah should be clear-cut in your mouth, so that should someone say something to you, you will not stammer before answering him, but answer him immediately, as it is said. ... It is also said, "Happy is the man who has his quiver full of them. They shall not be ashamed when they speak with their enemies at the gate" (Ps. 127:5).

What is meant by "with their enemies at the gate"? Said R. Hiya b. Abba: Even father and son, teacher and student, who apply themselves to [study of] the Torah at the same gate, become enemies of each other, yet do not budge from there until they come to love each other, as it is said, "Vaheb [love] in Suphah" (Num. 21:14); read not *besufa* [in Suphah] but *besofa* [in the end].

4. bHagiga 3a–b

Our Rabbis taught: Once R. Johanan b. Beroka and R. Eleazar Hisma went to pay their respects to R. Joshua at Pekiin. He said to them: What new teaching was there at the study hall today? They said to him: We are your students and thy waters do we drink. He said to them: Even so, it is impossible for a study hall session to pass without some novel teaching. Whose Sabbath was it? It was the Sabbath of R. Eleazar b. Azariah. And what was the sermon on today? They said to him: The Torah section that deals with [the commandment], Assemble the people (*hakhel*).[2] And what exposition did he give thereon? "Assemble the people, the men and the women and the little ones" (Deut. 31:12). If the men came to learn, and the women came to hear, why do the little ones come? In order to grant reward to those that bring them. He said to them: There was a fair jewel in your hand, and you sought to deprive me of it.

He further expounded: "Thou hast avouched the Lord this day ... and the Lord hath avouched thee this day" (Deut. 26:17–18). The Holy One, blessed be He, said to Israel: You have made me a unique entity in the world, and I shall make you a unique entity in the world. You have made me a unique entity, as it is written: "Hear, O Israel, the Lord our God, the Lord is One" (Deut. 6:4). And I shall make you a unique entity, as it is said: "And who is like unto Thy people Israel, a nation one in the earth" (I Chron. 17:21).

---

1 *Veshinantem*, from the root *sh"nn*, to sharpen.
2 Deuteronomy 31:10–13.

And he[3] too began to expound: "The words of the wise are as goads, and as nails well planted are those of masters of assemblies; they were given from one shepherd" (Eccles. 12:11). Why are the words of the Torah likened to a goad? To teach that just as a goad directs the cow along the furrow in order to bring life to the world, so the words of the Torah direct those who study them from the paths of death to the paths of life. But [should you think] that just as a goad is movable, so the words of the Torah are movable, therefore Scripture says: "nails." But [should you think] that just as a nail diminishes by being driven in, and does not increase, so too the words of the Torah diminish, and do not increase, therefore Scripture says: "well planted"; just as a plant grows and increases, so the words of the Torah grow and increase. "Masters of assemblies" – these are the scholars (*talmidei hakhamim*) who sit in various assemblies and apply themselves to the Torah; some deem a matter impure, others deem it pure, some prohibit, others permit, some disqualify, others declare fit. Lest you say, under these circumstances, how can I learn the Torah?, therefore Scripture says: All "were given from one shepherd."[4] One God gave them, one leader[5] uttered them from the mouth of the Master of all deeds, blessed be He, as it is written, "And God spake all these words" (Exod. 20:1). So let your ears be as funnels, and cultivate an understanding heart, to hear the words of those who deem a matter impure and those who deem it pure, those who prohibit and those who permit, those who disqualify and those who declare fit. He [then] spoke to them using this locution: The generation in which R. Eleazar b. Azariah lives is not an orphaned generation.

5. bBaba Metzia 84a

One day while R. Johanan was bathing in the Jordan, Resh Lakish saw him and leapt into the Jordan after him. He [R. Johanan] said to him: Your strength should be [used] for the Torah. He said to him: Your beauty should be for women. He said to him: If you will turn back [from your impious ways], I will give you [in marriage] my sister, who is more beautiful than I. He accepted this. He tried to go back and get his garments, but was not able to go back. [Subsequently, R. Johanan taught him] Bible and Mishnah, and made him a great man.

---

3 R. Eleazar b. Azariah, according to Rashi; R. Joshua, according to Maharsha.
4 Note that the verse in Ecclesiastes does not include the word "all" (*kulam*), which appears here, but reads simply, "they were given from one shepherd"; the "all" seems to be an interpolation made on the basis of Exodus 21:10, "And God spake **all** these words." From this point on, virtually all the sources that quote bHagiga 3b retain the interpolated "all" as if it were an integral part of the verse in Ecclesiastes.
5 I.e., Moses. More generally, sometimes the 'shepherd' metaphor is used to refer to God (e.g., Gen. 48:15; Ps. 80:2), sometimes to Moses (e.g., Isa. 63:11).

One day there was a disagreement in the study hall [between Resh Lakish and R. Johanan]: A sword, a knife, a dagger, a spear, a hand-saw and a scythe – at what stage do they become susceptible to impurity? When their manufacture is finished. And when is their manufacture finished? R. Johanan said, when they are tempered in a furnace. Resh Lakish said, when they have been polished in water. He said to him: A robber understands his trade.[6] He said to him: And in what have you benefitted me? There [i.e., as a robber] I was called Master, and here I am called Master. He said to him: By bringing you under the wings of the Divine Presence. R. Johanan felt deeply hurt, [as a result of which] Resh Lakish fell ill. His sister [R. Johanan's sister, married to Resh Lakish] came and wept before him. She said to him: Forgive him for the sake of my son. He said to her, "Leave thy fatherless children and I will preserve them alive" (Jer. 49:11). For the sake of my widowhood then. He said to her, "And let thy widows trust in me" (ibid.).

R. Shimon b. Lakish's soul expired, and R. Johanan was greatly saddened on account of his death. Our Rabbis said, Who will go to ease his mind? Let R. Eleazar b. Pedat, whose legal teachings are very subtle, go. So he went and sat before him; and upon every dictum uttered by R. Johanan, he said, There is a baraita that supports you. He said, [Do you think] you are, then, like the son of Lakisha? When I stated the law, the son of Lakisha would raise twenty-four separate objections, to which I gave twenty-four answers, which led to a fuller understanding of the law. And [all] you say is, There is a baraita that supports you. Do I not know that my opinions are well-grounded? He went on rending his garments and weeping, saying, Where are you, son of Lakisha, where are you, son of Lakisha? And he cried thus until his mind broke down. The scholars prayed that mercy be shown him, and his soul expired.

6. Midrash on Psalms 104:22

"Yonder sea, great and wide" (Ps. 104:25) is the Torah, of which it is said: "The measure thereof is longer than the earth, and wider than the sea" (Job 11:9). "Therein are creeping things innumerable" (Ps. ibid.): these are the tractates of the Talmud. Some say that these are the Mishna collections of Bar Kapara, of R. Hiya, of Rav, and of the Rabbis of Babylonia. "Beasts, small and great" (ibid.): these are the students, the small and the great (who sharpen one another).[7] "There go the ships" (Ps. 104:26): these are the children of the Torah, one saying, this is pure, and another saying, this is impure, thereby keeping the world on course as if it were a ship.

---

6 R. Johanan is alluding to Resh Lakish's impious past.
7 The parenthetical phrase is found in some manuscripts, and in the printed edition.

7. Responsa Rid, #1, pp. 6–7

And do not think that I invoke this interpretation in order to sustain the opinion of our teacher [Rashi], given that several of the most prominent authorities disagree with him. They say that [filling a ritual bath with] drawn water is biblically acceptable, and only Rabbinically prohibited. Furthermore, even if no great authority had disagreed with him on this point, I would write only what I think I can prove from the Talmud. And do not accuse me of being haughty of heart[8] because of this, as I am well aware that the fingernails of the righteous early authorities are greater than our bellies, and I do not compare myself even to their gatekeepers. But it is so. For anything that is not manifest to me in the Talmud, even if averred by Joshua the son of Nun, I do not heed. And I do not refrain from writing that which I consider correct. For this is the way of the Talmud. The later Amoraim did not refrain from discussing the views of the earlier Amoraim and even the Tannaim, and altogether refuted several Mishnayot. And in a number of places they rescinded the majority view, ruling in accordance with the minority view. Therefore, in the present case, over which great authorities are at odds, it is all the more necessary for us to explore and study the Talmud for clear evidence, so that we can see which way the law leans. For we do not have the power or intelligence to "weigh the mountains with a scale" (Isa. 40:12) to see which side is greater. Therefore, with all due respect, let us leave those masters, may they rest in peace, and return to expounding the Talmud, to see which way the law leans.

8. Responsa Rid, #62

First of all, let me respond to what you have written to me, that I am not to differ with our great authority R. Isaac, of blessed memory. Heaven forbid that I should do such a thing, and it never occurred to me to dispute his view, for compared to one of his students, I am but a single flea[9], in the sense of the Targum's explanation, and who am I to dispute the king?[10] Yet I say that a statement that I cannot accept, I do not heed, even if it was uttered by Joshua the son of Nun, and I do not refrain from speaking my mind about it as far as my limited wisdom permits. And in so doing I fulfil the verse: "I will speak of Your testimonies before kings and will not be ashamed" (Ps. 119:46).

And my witness is in heaven, that even when I think that I argue correctly against one of our early teachers, of blessed memory, heaven forbid that my heart should be so haughty as to say that "my wisdom stood me in stead" (Eccles. 2:9). Rather, I see my role in terms of a parable

---

8 Based on bSota 47b.
9 See I Samuel 24:15.
10 See Ecclesiastes 2:12.

of the philosophers. I learned the following from the wisdom of the philosophers. They asked the greatest among them: We obviously acknowledge that the ancients were wiser and more knowledgeable than we are, but also, that on numerous points we speak of them and contradict their views, and we are right. How can this be? He replied as follows: Who can see farther, a dwarf or a giant? Surely the giant, because his eyes are higher up than those of the dwarf. But if the giant carries the dwarf on his neck[11] – who can see farther? Surely the dwarf, whose eyes are now higher than the eyes of the giant. Thus we are dwarfs riding on the necks of giants, because, having digested their knowledge, we can transcend it. And it is by virtue of their wisdom that we have the wisdom to assert all that we assert, and not because we are greater than they were.

And nevertheless, should we say that we are not allowed to speak of the views of our early authorities even when we see that they disagree with each other, with one forbidding what the other permits – if so, on whom shall we rely? Can we "weigh the mountains with a scale and the hills with a balance" (Isa. 40:12), and declare that one is greater than the other, that we are overturning the opinions of one in favor of those of the other? We have no alternative but to inquire into what they said, because both are the words of the living God, and we must engage in incisive debate and penetrate the depths of their words, to ascertain which way the law leans. This was the practice of the Sages of the Mishna and Talmud, and later Sages never refrained from discussing their predecessors' views, deciding between them, or refuting them. And a number of mishnaic rulings were refuted by Amoraim, who declared that the law was not in accord with them. And wisdom is greater than the wise, and there is no wise man who is free of error, for perfect wisdom is the domain of God alone.

9. Responsa Trumat Hadeshen, Psakim ukhtavim, #238

With regard to what you wrote, [asking,] since a student is not permitted to take issue with his teacher over a given ruling or decision, whether he may rule contrary to his teacher's opinion, if he can support his view on the basis of the Talmud or the rulings of the Geonim: It seems evident to me that if the rulings are reasonably clear, and the logical sequence of the talmudic passages appears to support the student, why shouldn't he disagree? This has been the way of the Torah from the days of the Tannaim. On a number of points, our holy R. Judah the Prince disagreed with his father and teacher R. Shimon b. Gamaliel. Among the Amoraim, in a number of places Rava disagrees with Rabbah, who was his teacher,

---

11 The word "neck" may have been used here instead of the more idiomatic "shoulders" because the Hebrew word for giant, *anak*, also means "necklace."

as it says in the *Mordekhai*.[12] Among the great halakhic authorities, Asheri disagrees, in a number of places, with R. Meir of Rothenburg, who was his mentor. I do not wish to enlarge on this further, as these things need to be discussed face to face.

Thus spoke the youngest and most junior in Israel.

10. Responsa Maharam Mintz, #99

Concerning the contention and discord that arose between two men in Italy, the learned R. Kuzi and the honorable R. Katz, and their respective supporters. I saw how much ink had been spilled, how many nibs blunted, and how much paper blackened on both sides. And the matter was presented to the learned men of the time, each of whom rendered an opinion, in accordance with his understanding and opinion. Some support one side, some support the other, this one bringing a reasoned argument, and that one bringing a reasoned argument, each according to his comprehension, and both are the words of the living God.... And indeed, a number of laws can be understood and argued for in two different ways, and there is no compelling verdict as to which is correct. Yet every individual has sufficient intelligence, ultimately, to reach a concrete conclusion on the basis of that which is grasped abstractly.

... The Tannaim, Amoraim, Tosafists and great authorities were involved in many disagreements regarding both monetary law, and family law and other areas, some purely theoretical, others arising from actual cases they were adjudicating. We do not find one side holding the opposite side in contempt, or cursing and denouncing those who rule differently. In this country, too, there have been a number of controversies, in which some of the learned authorities ruled for Reuben while imposing harsh verdicts on [his adversary] Shimon, and others decided in favor of Shimon, imposing the harsh verdicts upon Reuben; yet all brought arguments in support of their decisions. And we have seen no contempt or imprecation for the other side in their words, or attempts to mollify those who supported the losing side. And this conclusion obtains, as any intelligent person can see, as I explained in my first letter.

11. Peirushei Rabbenu Avraham Farissol, mAvot 5:22

The controversy mentioned by the Tanna refers to that which arises in the course of study, where differences of opinion arise daily among the students and teachers of the Torah. Such quarrels and attempts to discredit the other's opinion in any way possible have always been

---

12 *Mordekhai* commentary on bBaba Kama, chapter 3, section 15.

customary. And for this reason, the Tanna emphasizes that when such a dispute between two sides arises in the course of examining Torah issues for the sake of heaven, in order to comprehend the law, it will be sustained in future study of the law, and in [future] scrutiny of the opposed views and the differences between them, since it is for the sake of heaven that scrutiny of Torah opinions should be undertaken, and conclusions derived from the Torah, in accordance with how it is comprehended. For as we know, the Torah has many divergent and disparate facets: "Is not My word like a fire?" (Jer. 23:29).

12. Responsa Beit Yosef, The law of boundless waters, #1 (p. 343)

And he wrote: "I wonder about the inner rectitude and integrity of this scholar: how could he permit himself to dispute the opinions of early authorities, rejecting them in favor of his own? It seems more fitting to maintain that he is not to dispute them."

For anyone versed in the law, this is not a valid argument, as this is the way of the Torah: the talmudic Sages and all succeeding generations of scholars, they and their students and their students' students, who eagerly absorb their every word, all contradict their predecessors, the students arguing against their teachers. And as this is very clear, it need not be discussed at length.

13. Responsa Tashbetz, Hut Hameshulash, column 3, #35

Your words in this responsum call for scrutiny. Firstly, you argued that because it was disputed by many learned men of Israel, the opinion of Maimonides, of blessed memory, on this matter, cannot be relied upon. But this is the way of our Talmud, the Tannaim and Amoraim disagreeing throughout. Likewise, the Geonim and decisors, of blessed memory, constantly disagree – some forbid where others permit, some declare impure, others, pure. But our holy Torah provides a solution for this, in its statement: "follow the majority" (*aharei rabim lehatot*)[13] (Exod. 23:2), and in stating, "If there arise a matter too hard for thee" (Deut. 17:8). For it having been apparent to the heavenly wisdom that the Sages would hold conflicting opinions regarding the interpretation of the details of the Torah's laws and precepts, it established that the decision would be in accordance with the majority view.

---

13 The verse reads: "Thou shalt not follow a multitude to do evil." The text follows the traditional Rabbinic interpretation of the verse.

14. Responsa Darkhei Noam, EH, #64

In permitting this chained woman (*aguna*) to marry, I concur with my colleague, the authority ruling on the matter, may God protect him, both in his statement of the law and in his reasoning. If my reasoning diverges slightly from his, it is not because I seek, heaven forbid, to dispute his opinion, but because this is the way of the Torah and "Vaheb [love] in Suphah" (Num. 21:14)."[14]

15. Responsa Noda Biyehuda, 2nd edition, OH, #54

Your letter has reached me, a tract replete with reservations about my work *Noda Biyehuda*. I was quite pleased, because I could see from it that you had studied my work tenaciously. Even if your arm is outstretched and your sword is a sharp one, I welcome your intentions, because I see that your questions have solid foundations, and you are not merely raising baseless objections for argument's sake. Your questions appear to be powerful and spoken with wisdom. To be frank, I can refute them all, but this is the way of the Torah, and the true meaning of the law is thereby clarified.

16. Ruah Haim, mAvot 1:4

"Let your home be a meeting place for the wise." It could be explained as follows. One of the forty-eight requirements for the acquisition of Torah, as explained in mAvot 6:6, is the ability to enhance one's teacher's acumen by sharp questions that enable the text's full meaning to be understood.[15] Now learning is called war, as in the dictum, "the war of the Torah"; students, then, are warriors. And as our Sages, of blessed memory, said: " 'They shall not be ashamed when they speak with their enemies at the gate,' even father and son, teacher and student, who apply themselves to [study of] the Torah at the same gate, become enemies of each other, yet do not budge from there until they come to love each other."[16] A student must not accept his teacher's words if he has any objection to them. Sometimes the student will be right, just as a small piece of wood can set a large one aflame. Hence it is stated, "Let your home be a meeting place for the wise and you shall wrestle,[17]" from the verse "and there wrestled a man with him" (Gen. 32:25), an allusion to struggle, for this is indeed an obligatory war (*milhemet mitzva*). We likewise grapple with our holy teachers, whose renowned works we study. Their bodies are interred,

---

14 See passage 3.
15 See passage 5.
16 bKidushin 30b.
17 The verb can also mean "gather dust."

while their souls dwell above. By the presence of their books in our homes, our homes become meeting places for encounters with these wise scholars. We have also been admonished and given permission to wrestle and do battle with their words, and to resolve problems they raised. And not to adulate anyone, but to love only the truth. Nevertheless, should one have occasion to dispute a point in such a work, he must be exceedingly wary of speaking haughtily or boastfully, and imagining himself a peer of his teacher or the author of the work he is criticizing, and must keep in mind that there are instances where he cannot begin to understand their words and intentions. He ought therefore remain very humble, saying, I am unworthy, but the Torah must be studied and clarified. This is the meaning of "wrestle (gather dust)" – the condition for such discussion is that one remain as the dust at their feet: humble and obedient.

17. Responsa Hatam Sofer, EH 1, #151

I will not refrain from letting your eminence know of my displeasure concerning your excessive apologies for seeking to refute my words. Am I really thus, God forbid, in your opinion? Has not the way of the Torah always been that one constructs arguments and another demolishes them, and who would demur?

18. Responsa Semikha Lehaim, EH, #9 (pp. 56–7)

And the obvious needs no proof. Since all the works of the decisors – the early as well the late – are replete with cases where the first decisor rules one way, and implements his ruling accordingly, and after him, a new court is convened, and examines the matter, and rules to the contrary on the basis of its own proofs, and nullifies the ruling of the first court. And all this is done for the sake of heaven. Even though the early authorities are like angels, we can attest that they themselves are pleased with this, and they have the attribute of their Creator, [namely,] to condone and to praise – "My sons have triumphed over Me" – that is, to seek the truth. And our eyes behold cases on a daily basis, in our locale and in every other place, of later rabbinical authorities ruling contrary to the rulings of earlier authorities....

And in my humble opinion, excusing my impudence and with all due respect, I cannot comprehend your position at all. How can it be proposed that a learned scholar and rabbinical authority who, knowing that a rabbinical colleague erred on a matter of law, or that there is an objection to his ruling, issued a contrary ruling, be subject to banning? God forbid that the leaders of the community should formulate and sign a bill to this effect. But I am utterly sure that this was not their intention at all. Nor does this situation fall under the category of 'one who challenges [authority],' which applies only to a challenge arising from the profligacy and scorn of one who does not obey the law, or doubts the law on the basis of ignorant, vacuous arguments and vain, deceptive imaginings. The case of a learned scholar who raises sensible and correct objections that are well-reasoned and knowledgeable, and based on Scripture, is, however, quite different. Praise, exaltation, greatness and respect should be lavished on him, that such learned men flourish in this generation. If a scholar can answer those who dispute his stance, this only elevates him and enhances his honor. And even if, on occasion, they defeat him, and he is forced to concede the truth and retract an erroneous opinion, he should be glad, for not only has a mishap due to this error been averted, but he now knows something of which he was previously ignorant. As the author of *Sefer Hasidim* wrote: "If you argue with a learned man, do not feel sorry if he triumphs over you, because you learn from him and gain wisdom. But if you triumph over him, what do you gain? But if he triumphs over you, you gain by acquiring knowledge of that regarding which you were previously ignorant."[18]

Moreover, we are charged with the lofty duty of emulating the Lord, as it is written, "and you should walk in His ways" (Deut. 28:9). He too was defeated – so to speak – in an argument, and was glad, as it says in the Talmud: "My sons have triumphed over Me."[19] Even though it is the nature of man to be sorrowful when defeated, this can by no means be applied to matters of the Torah, as we said.

Furthermore, the interchange in question is not an instance of 'one who challenges authority' and doubts the law. Besides, if the challenger bases his opposition to a ruling on the Torah, how can it be said of such a person, who bases his arguments on the Torah, that he is a challenger and doubter, merely to safeguard the honor of the incumbent authority, while ignoring the honor of the Torah and the honor of those authorities on whom the challenger relies? And this is an everyday occurrence for each generation and its own judges, from time immemorial, and from the days of yore: there have been numerous controversies among the halakhic authorities, with one demolishing his fellow's arguments and another building them up, whether the arguments are put forward in the opponent's presence, or in his absence, or one after the other. We have never heard of such behavior being regarded, God forbid, as contempt.

19. Arukh Hashulhan, HM, preface

Truly, for one who understands things properly, all the controversies among the Tannaim, Amoraim, the Geonim and the decisors, are the words of the

---

18 R. Judah the Pious (Ashkenaz, d. 1217), *Sefer Hasidim*, section 142.
19 bBaba Metzia 59b; bPesahim 119a.

living God, and all are grounded in the law. And furthermore, this is the glory of our pure and holy Torah, all of which is called a melody. And the glory of the melody, the essence of its delight, is that the tones differ from each other. And one who sails the sea of the Talmud will experience the diverse delights of all these distinct voices.

20. Responsa Sridei Esh 3, #9

Against my position on the issue of [decision-making based on a] majority versus [decision-making based on] legal presumption (*hazaka*), you cite the Pnei Yehoshua and the great R. Akiva Eger. I am not unaware that the greatest of the Later Authorities were unreservedly of the opinion that a decision made on the basis of a majority is preferable to [one made in] reliance on a legal presumption. But what does this matter? For this is the way of the Torah, to hone arguments ever sharper, and to formulate new ones, even against the greatest of the Later Authorities. Only with regard to rulings that are to be put into practice is it the case that we must not disregard the words of the great authorities, of blessed memory, whose understanding eclipses our own, and beside whom we all pale in comparison. But as far as reasoning and the clarification of concepts is concerned, we have the right to propose novel interpretations and put forward propositions that they did not grasp, for every person in Israel whose soul was present at the revelation of the Torah at Sinai received a share of the Torah and its ongoing interpretation, and this cannot be challenged.

I am wont to explain the passage in mAvot where the Sages, of blessed memory, enumerate the forty-eight requirements by which the Torah is acquired. One such requirement is "discussion with students," while another is "trust in the Sages." This appears to be a contradiction. Moreover, what is the relevance of "trust in the Sages" to the acquisition of Torah? I would explain it as follows: Those who do not trust in the Sages, frivolously dismiss their views with foolish insolence, superciliously claiming that the Sages failed to understand. The result is that they do not trouble to delve into and confirm the Sages' opinions, and in the end it turns out that it is we who have erred, and not the Sages. It is thus prudent to assume that they have not, heaven forbid, erred, but rather, that we are shortsighted and of limited intelligence. But simply to believe, without taxing the mind with study and reflection, but merely to say that they knew the law and we can rely on them without thinking, is equally mistaken. We must devise trenchant arguments, raising doubts and contradictions, as if the Sages were our peers, for this leads to a deeper and more penetrating theoretical understanding of the issues. Together, therefore, the two virtues, trust in the Sages and unrelenting analysis, lead to acquisition of the Torah. And the Holy One, blessed be He, himself rejoices over trenchant analysis of the Torah.

1.1. Controversy is not to be multiplied

21. mBaba Batra 9:10

If the house collapsed upon someone [an only son] and on his [widowed] mother, [the house of Shammai] and [the house of Hillel] agree that [their heirs] should share equally [in the estate]. R. Akiva said, I maintain that [the house Hillel hold that] the property should be left in the hands of its present possessors [i.e., that the house of Hillel disagree with the house of Shammai here too, as in a case discussed earlier in the Mishna]. Ben Azai said to him: We grieve over the [explicitly articulated] disagreement, and you seek to introduce a disagreement on a point on which [they can be construed as being] in agreement.

22. Hasagot Haraavad, bBerakhot 24a (Alfasi pagination)

Nevertheless, the words of Alfasi, of blessed memory, are more accurate and reasonable, for a number of reasons. First, as much as possible, controversies between two Amoraim should be minimized. Many endeavored to dispel controversies that arose between them, and this is well known and requires no deliberation.

23. Raavad, Katuv Sham, bBerakhot 49a (p. 12)

It is stated there: "And they disagree as to the New Moon: R. Huna holds the view that he has to repeat the benediction and R. Nahman holds that he does not have repeat the benediction."[20] Avraham said: This bald man (kireiah)[21] – why did he choose to perpetuate the controversy, and to impart controversy among all the Amoraim? And how great is the difference between him and R. Shalman,[22] who imparted peace among the scholars! Whereas he imparted non-existent controversy among them.

24. Nimukei Yosef, bBaba Metzia 65b (Alfasi pagination)

Furthermore, there is no justification for multiplying controversy between Rashi and the other commentators; on the contrary, it should be minimized.

---

20 The citation is from *Sefer Hamaor* of R. Zerahia Halevi, and the issue is whether one who says the Grace after Meals and forgets to mention the New Moon in his recitation has to repeat it.
21 See bBekhorot 58a. The allusion here is a pun on Korah and the word *kireiah* (bald).
22 See bBerakhot 39b.

25. Responsa Maharik, #94 (p. 184)

And we can bring proof for this point in what we learned in tractate Ketubot: Rav inserted [the following inquiry] between the lines [of a communication he sent] to Rabbi [Judah the Prince]: What is [the law] where the brothers have mortgaged [the estate they inherited from their father]?[23] and so on, and R. Johanan said, an estate may not be seized either to meet the one obligation [trousseau, *parnasa*], or the other [maintenance, *mezonot*]. The question was raised, did not R. Johanan hear the ruling of Rabbi? But had he heard it, would he have accepted it? Or is possible that he heard it, and did not accept it?"[24] After some deliberation, it is suggested that he heard it, but this suggestion is then rejected.[25]

And in a responsum, R. Hai Gaon wrote as follows:

> Now we examine the statement of R. Johanan, who is a later authority; do we therefore assume that he heard the statement of Rabbi [Judah the Prince]: 'authorize expenses for her trousseau,'[26] found it unacceptable, and rejected it, and since he is a later authority, we do not follow the opinion of Rabbi, or perhaps he did not know about the ruling of R. Judah [the Prince], because had he known, he would not have opposed his ruling. Come and hear, and so on. Hence, it cannot be resolved whether he heard it or did not hear it. Hence, on the basis of an uncertainty, we do not posit that there was a controversy between R. Johanan and Rabbi [Judah the Prince].

It is quite clear that R. Hai Gaon, of blessed memory, says that a controversy should not be posited. Therefore, we have to conclude that R. Johanan was not aware of the ruling of Rabbi [Judah the Prince], and that had he been aware of it, he would not have opposed it.

This must be so, since we do not find any baraita or statement attributed to Rabbi which expresses this view except for the correspondence with Rav. Therefore, we must surmise that R. Johanan was unaware of it. For this reason, R. Hai Gaon concludes that this is not a disputed issue.

26. Responsa Maharik, #176

It is apparent from your words that you assume that the Tanna who stated the baraita contradicts the Tanna who stated the Mishna.[27] With all due

---

23 The issue is, can it be seized from the holder of the mortgage on behalf of the brothers' orphaned sister, for her trousseau?
24 bKetubot 69a.
25 And thus, the question cannot be resolved.
26 bKetubot 69a.
27 mHulin 104.

respect, I cannot agree, because we do not assume a controversy between Tannaim unless this is explicitly stated. On the contrary, in every instance where a baraita and a Mishna do not agree, the Talmud notes the controversy, and makes an effort to resolve it, even if this entails implausible conjectures. Therefore we should not infer the existence of a controversy, unless explicitly stated, and this is obvious.

27. Halikhot Olam, gate 2 (p. 16a)

Occasionally the Amoraim disagree, yet the Gemara says that in fact, they do not disagree, but rather, one puts forward one point, and the other, another point, and there is no disagreement. That is, each concedes his interlocutor's point, see, for example, the first chapter of tractate Baba Metzia[28] . . . and there are many other examples. And wherever it is possible to explain such an apparent contradiction thus, rather than to posit controversies among the Sages, this is better.

28. Sheeirit Yosef, Netiv hapelugta, rule 1 (p. 60)

To the extent possible, whatever can be done to bring the sides closer together, so that the proliferation of controversy is avoided, is proper. The *Tosafot* comment on Rashi, regarding the Talmud's discussion of whether, in reciting the blessing over bread, a whole loaf takes precedence over slices, "it does not make sense for there to be a controversy where each side upholds a diametrically opposed position."[29] According to R. Huna, large slices are blessed first, while according to R. Johanan, a whole loaf takes precedence. And elsewhere it is stated, "we have never found Amoraic reasoning to be completely contrary."[30] More noteworthy still, sometimes the Gemara itself makes emendations, changing plural into singular so as to reduce the number of opposed views; for example, where the Talmud reads, "[The opinions of] which Sages have been stated here? R. Eliezer."[31] The *Tosafot* note: although the Tannaitic wording cites the plural "Sages," the opinion was attributed to R. Eliezer only, in order to reduce the conflicting views from three to two.

29. Sheeirit Yosef, Netiv hapelugta, rule 3 (p. 61)

When we come upon laconic statements of Amoraim, and they can be interpreted either as conflicting with each other or as compatible, we interpret them as compatible, even if this interpretation is quite forced.

---

28 bBaba Metzia 10b.
29 bBerakhot 39b.
30 bTemura 12a.
31 bNida 8b.

30. Klalei Shmuel, rule 324

One authority is referring to one thing, and the other, to another – this does not constitute a controversy. ... and whenever this conjecture is possible, avoiding controversy among the Sages, it is commendable. For this is the method of the Gemara; it takes pains to eliminate every instance of controversy between Mishnayot and baraitot, as well as between Mishnayot and baraitot and Amoraim. And this is the correct method – to harmonize views so that there is no controversy.

31. Responsa Radbaz, 2, #830

I agree with the students of the late R. Jonah. Further, I maintain that this is also the view of the Tur [R. Jacob b. Asher], and there is no controversy. For it is one of our fundamental principles that we do not multiply controversy.

32. Responsa Tashbetz, Hut Hameshulash, column 2, #14

Now in what we wrote in explaining the words of the Rama,[32] of blessed memory, we caused it to be the case that he disputes the view of Maimonides, of blessed memory.... But what can we do, since after all, the constraints of the language of the responsum compelled us to interpret it the way we did...to the point where we had to depart from the straight path, and to construe the Rama as disputing the view of Maimonides, of blessed memory. And this is exceedingly awkward, even more awkward than [reading] the responsum in a convoluted way [viz., against its plain meaning]. For we have a fundamental principle that controversy is not to be multiplied, and wherever it is possible to interpret the language – even if the interpretation is very forced – in a manner that reconciles the views of the decisors, we interpret it this way, even if it is forced. Therefore it is appropriate to resolve the words of the responsum differently than we did, even if it is forced, in order to bring about peace between these authorities, of blessed memory.

33. Responsa Ginat Vradim, OH, rule 1, #47

And if so, since the said decisors have written this rule explicitly, and it also appears to be so from the matter-of-fact tone of the decisors' words, we are duty-bound to interpret the words of any decisor who seems to dispute it as if he does not, even if our interpretation is somewhat far-fetched, in order to make peace between the decisors, since we do not cause controversy to be multiplied. If so, against our will we must force ourselves to interpret

32 R. Meir b. Todros Halevi Abulafia.

his words even in a far-fetched manner. Leave aside the verse, for it is convoluted and brings the forced interpretation upon itself.[33]

34. Pahad Yitzhak, Hatikha hareuya lehitkabed, p. 59d

Whenever we have the possibility of interpreting an author as not contradicting himself, we are bound to do so, even if it involves 'pulling an elephant through the eye of a needle.' If so, wherefore and why do you seek to interpret R. Caro according to your own reasoning, and to arrive at conclusions and meanings of your own, so as to generate a contradiction? It is agreed by the Talmud and all the commentators and all the prominent halakhists that we do not multiply controversies between different persons, how much more so ought we make every effort to reconcile statements made by the same decisor, so that he will not contradict his earlier statement.

35. Sdei Hemed, letter 'mem,' rule 16

We do not find controversies where one view is the polar opposite of the other (*mahloket min hakatze el hakatze*). We do not find a case in which, on one view, an action necessitates the bringing of a sin offering, while on another, it is permissible even *ab initio*. And see tractate Shabat: How is it possible that R. Eliezer permits this action outright, and the Sages require a sin-offering?[34] Denial [of the possibility of espousing diametrically opposed views] is only relevant in a case where the dispute is between two parties, one saying that the action demands a sin-offering and the other that it is permissible even *ab initio*; this is not possible. If, however, one says that the action necessitates the bringing of a sin-offering, and the other, that it does not [but is nonetheless prohibited], there may well be a third view, on which the action is indeed permitted *ab initio*, which is opposed to the second view, on which it is forbidden [but does not call for bringing a sin offering]....

This is true not only of controversies in which the views are diametrically opposed, but in general: where no explicit controversy is identified, it is not our job to come up with one, but to reconcile the positions as much as possible, even if we have to resort to subterfuge.

33 bPesahim 59b.
34 bShabat 138a.

2

THE CONDUCT OF
A CONTROVERSY: ETIQUETTE
AND RULES OF DEBATE

36. mAvot 5:7

Seven things are characteristic of a boor (*golem*), and seven of a wise man. A wise man does not speak before one who is greater in wisdom, and does not enter into the words of his fellow; he is not hasty to answer; he asks in accordance with the subject matter, and answers in terms of the accepted view; he speaks of the first point first, and of the last point last; of that about which he has not heard, he says, I have not heard; and he acknowledges the truth. And the opposite traits are characteristic of a boor.

37. mAvot 5:17

Every controversy that is for the sake of heaven, its end is to be sustained. And that which is not for the sake of heaven, its end is not to be sustained. What controversy is for the sake of heaven? The controversy between Hillel and Shammai. And that which is not for the sake of heaven? The controversy of Korah and all his congregation.

38. jSuka 2:8 (53b)

For what did the house of Hillel merit the law's being decided in accordance with their view? Said R. Judah b. Pazi: They quoted the words of the house of Shammai before their own. And not only that, but when they acknowledged [the correctness of] the view of the house of Shammai, they retracted their own. R. Simon b. Zavda asked R. Ila: Perhaps the Tanna[1] saw who was older and mentioned him first? But in the account of the incident related by the house of Hillel, it states: Did it not happen that the elders of the house of Shammai and the house of Hillel went to visit

---

1 Tanna here means either Rabbi Judah the Prince, redactor of the Mishna, or more likely, 'repeater.' The Sages' teachings were memorized and repeated in the academies by 'repeaters.'

R. Johanan b. Hahorani?[2] [Had the precedence of the house of Shammai been introduced solely by the Tanna, we would have expected to find that in the account of this visit, the house of Hillel would have said,] Our elders and your elders.

39. bEruvin 13b

R. Abba stated in the name of Samuel: For three years there was a controversy between the house of Shammai and the house of Hillel, the former asserting, The law is in accordance with our views, and the latter asserting: The law is in accordance with our views. A heavenly voice (*bat kol*) went forth and said: Both [lit., 'these and those'] are the words of the living God, but the law is in accordance with the view of the house of Hillel. Since, however, both are the words of the living God, for what reason did the house of Hillel merit the law's being decided in accordance with their view? Because they were kindly and modest, they studied their own views and those of the house of Shammai, and not only that, but they quoted the words of the house of Shammai before their own.

As may be seen from what we have learned: If a man had his head and the greater part of his body within the booth (*suka*) but his table in the house, the house of Shammai ruled it invalid but the house of Hillel ruled that it was valid. Said the house of Hillel to the house of Shammai: Did it not happen that the elders of the house of Shammai and the house of Hillel went to visit R. Johanan b. Hahoranit and found him sitting with his head and the greater part of his body within the booth while his table was in the house? The house of Shammai said to them: Does that constitute proof?! [lit., From there proof?] They indeed told him: If you have always acted in this manner you have never fulfilled the commandment of *suka*.[3] This teaches you that he who humbles himself, the Holy One, blessed be He, raises up, and he who exalts himself, the Holy One, blessed be He, humbles; from him who seeks greatness, greatness flees, but he who flees from greatness, greatness follows; he who forces time is forced back by time, but he who yields to time finds time standing at his side.

---

2 mSuka 2:7. Elsewhere "Hahoranit."

3 The story of R. Johanan b. Hahoranit quoted here by the Talmud appears in mSuka 2:7 (bSuka 28a); it is also found in bBerakhot 11a. The version that appears in these passages includes the words "and they said nothing to him" within the house of Hillel's report of the visit. On this account, the controversy between the house of Shammai and the house of Hillel is not simply about assessing the permissibility of R. Johanan b. Hahoranit's behavior, but also about the actual facts of the incident – what was said at the time. Textual analysis favors the version in bEruvin 13b, which is supported by the text of the Mishna as it appears in the Jerusalem Talmud.

40. bShabat 63a

R. Jeremiah said in the name of R. Shimon b. Lakish: When two scholars are amiable to each other in discussing the law, the Holy One, blessed be He, heeds them, for it is said, "Then they that feared the Lord spoke to one another" and so on (Mal. 3:16). Now speech (*dibur*) can only mean gentleness, for it is said: "He shall subdue (*yadber*) the peoples under us" (Ps. 47:4).[4] ...

R. Abba said in the name of Shimon b. Lakish: When two scholars listen to each other in discussing the law, the Holy One, blessed be He, listens to their voices, as it is said: "You, who dwell in the gardens, the companions hearken unto your voice: 'Cause me to hear it' " (Song of Songs 8:13).[5] But if they do not do so, they cause the Divine Presence to depart from Israel, as it is said: "Run away, my beloved," and so on (Song of Songs 8:14).

41. bTaanit 8a

Rava said: two scholars who live in the same town but are not amiable to each other in discussing the law, provoke anger, bringing it upon themselves, as it is said: "the cattle also concerning the storm that cometh up" (Job 36:33).[6]

42. bMegila 32a

This verse is to be applied as it was by R. Mesharshia, who said: Regarding two scholars who live in the same town and are not amiable to each other in discussing the law, of them Scripture says, "I gave them also laws that were not good and ordinances by which they could not live" (Ezek. 20:25).

43. bSota 49a

R. Elai b. Yevarkhiya also said: If two scholars live in the same town and are not amiable to each other in discussing the law, one dies and the other goes into exile[7]; as it is said: "That the manslayer might flee thither, that slayeth his neighbor without knowledge" (Deut. 4:42), and there is no knowledge but the Torah, as it is said, "My people are destroyed for lack of knowledge" (Hos. 4:6).

---

4 The idea being, one who has been subdued is docile.
5 In the allegorical interpretation of the Song of Songs as a dialogue between God and Israel, "garden" signifies 'academy.'
6 The verse reads: "The noise thereof telleth concerning it, the cattle also concerning the storm that cometh up" (*yagid alav reio, mikne af al ole*). Here Rava is alluding to the beginning of the verse, not quoted in the Talmud: "The noise thereof telleth concerning it." The Hebrew *reio* is obscure, but whatever it means, he interprets it to mean "his fellow," and slightly emends "the cattle also" (*mikne af*) to read "provoke anger" (*mitkane af*).
7 Being the cause of the other's death, he must flee to a city of refuge.

44. bTaanit 4a

Rava said: If a devoted scholar becomes enraged, it is because the Torah inflames him, as it is said, "Is not My word like a fire? declareth the Lord" (Jer. 23:29). And R. Ashi said, A scholar who is not as hard as iron is no scholar, as it is said, "And like a hammer that breaketh the rock in pieces" (ibid.). R. Abba said to R. Ashi, You have learned it from this verse, but we have learned it from the following verse: "A land whose stones are iron" (Deut. 8:9). Do not read, *avneha* (stones), but *boneha* (builders). Rabina said, Despite this, a man should train himself to be gentle, for it is said, "Therefore remove vexation from thy heart" (Eccles. 11:10).

45. bHagiga 22b

It is taught: R. Joshua said: I am ashamed of your words, O house of Shammai. Is it possible that if a woman kneads dough in a trough, the woman and the trough become impure for seven days, but the dough remains pure?!... [Thereupon] one of the students from the house of Shammai joined in the discussion and said to him: I will explain to you the reasoning of the house of Shammai. He said: Explain then. So he said to him: Does an impure vessel.... This, then, is the reasoning of the house of Shammai. Forthwith, R. Joshua went and prostrated himself upon the graves of the house of Shammai. He said: I humbly beg you to pardon me, bones of the house of Shammai. If your unexplained teachings are so [excellent], how much more so your explained teachings. They said: all his days his teeth were black because of his fasts.[8]

46. bJebamot 96b

R. Eleazar went and reported this statement at the house of study, but did not report it in the name of R. Johanan. When R. Johanan heard this he was annoyed. R. Ami and R. Asi came to see R. Johanan and said to him: Did it not happen at the synagogue in Tiberias that R. Eleazar and R. Jose argued so heatedly concerning a door bolt that had a knob at one end that they tore a Torah scroll in their excitement?! They tore it? Is this conceivable? Say, rather, that in their excitement a Torah scroll was torn. R. Jose b. Kisma, who was present, said, I will be surprised if this synagogue does not turn into a house of idolatry; and so it happened. [On hearing this] he [R. Johanan] was annoyed all the more. He said, Comradeship too!?[9]

---

8 That is, he fasted frequently to atone for not appreciating the view of the house of Shammai. See passage 68.
9 That is, he was annoyed that they compared the relationship between him and his student R. Eleazar to a relationship between two colleagues.

Thereupon R. Jacob b. Idi came and said to him: "As the Lord commanded Moses His servant, so did Moses command Joshua, and so did Joshua; he left nothing undone of all that the Lord commanded Moses" (Josh. 11:15); did Joshua, then, concerning every word he said, say to them, Thus did Moses tell me?! Rather, the fact is that Joshua sat and delivered his discourse without mentioning names, and all knew that it was the Torah of Moses. So your student R. Eleazar sat and delivered his discourse without mentioning names, and all knew that it was yours. He [R. Johanan] said to them, Why are you, unlike our friend the son of Idi, not capable of fostering a reconciliation?

47. bKidushin 52b

Our Rabbis taught: After R. Meir's demise, R. Judah said to his students, Let not R. Meir's students enter hither, because they are argumentative and do not come to learn Torah, but to overwhelm me with laws. Yet Symmachus forced his way through and entered. He said to them, R. Meir taught me as follows: If one betroths a woman with his portion [of the sacrifice], whether it is of higher or of lower sanctity, he has not betrothed her. Thereupon R. Judah became angry with them, and said to them, Did I not say to you, Let not R. Meir's students enter hither, because they are argumentative and do not come to learn Torah, but to overwhelm me with laws? How does a woman come to be in the Temple area?[10] Said R. Jose, Shall it be said: Meir is dead, Judah angry, and Jose silent? What is to become of the words of the Torah? Cannot a man accept betrothal on his daughter's behalf in the Temple? And cannot a woman authorize an agent to receive her betrothal in the Temple? And what if she forces her way in?

48. bSanhedrin 24a

R. Osheia said, What is the meaning of the verse, "And I took unto me the two staves[11]; the one I called *noam* (graciousness) and the other I called *hovlim* (ties)"[12] (Zech. 11:7). "Noam" denotes the scholars of Palestine, who treat each other graciously when engaged in halakhic debates; "*hovlim*," the scholars of Babylon, who injure each other's feelings when discussing the law.

[It is written] "Then said he, these are the two anointed ones (*bnei izhar*)[13] that stand," and so on (ibid. 4:14). [This is preceded by] "And two olive trees [stand] by it" (ibid. 4:3). R. Isaac said, "Clear oil (*yizhar*)" – (this

---

10 Sacrifices of the higher degree of sanctity could not be removed from the area of the Temple in which they were offered, not even into the women's area.
11 Plural of "staff."
12 Also, injuries.
13 Literally, "sons of *yizhar* (clear oil)."

denotes the scholars of Palestine, who are affable to each other when engaged in halakhic debates, like [soothing] olive oil; while "and two olive trees [stand] by it" denotes the scholars of Babylon, who are as bitter to each other in halakhic discussions as olive trees.[14]

49. bSanhedrin 110a

"And Moses rose up and went unto Dathan and Abiram" (Num. 16:25). Resh Lakish said: This teaches that one must not be obdurate in a quarrel, for Rav said: He who is unyielding in a dispute violates a negative precept, as it is said, "that he fare not as Korah, and as his company" (Num. 17:5). R. Ashi said: He deserves to be smitten with leprosy – here it is written "[as the Lord said unto him] by the hand of Moses" (ibid.); whereas elsewhere it is written, "And the Lord said furthermore unto him: Put now thine hand into thine bosom [. . . and when he took it out, behold his hand was leprous as snow]" (Exod. 4:6).[15] R. Joseph said: Whoever disputes the sovereignty of the House of David deserves to be bitten by a snake. Here it is written, "And Adonijah slew sheep and oxen and fat cattle by the stone of Zoheleth" (I Kings 1:9); while elsewhere it is written, "with the poison of serpents of (zohalei) the dust" (Deut. 32:24). R. Hisda said: Whoever takes issue with his teacher is as though he took issue with the Divine Presence, as it is said, "when they strove against the Lord" (Num. 26:9). R. Hama son of R. Hanina said: Whoever makes a quarrel with his teacher is as though he makes a quarrel with the Divine Presence, as it is said: "This is the water of Meribah, because the children of Israel strove with the Lord" (Num. 20:13). R. Hanina b. Papa said, Whoever complains about his teacher, it is as though he complained about the Divine Presence, as it is said: "Your murmurings are not against us, but against the Lord" (Exod. 16:8). R. Abbahu said, Whoever thinks ill of his teacher, it is as though he thought ill of the Divine Presence, as it said, "And the people spoke against God, and against Moses" (Num. 21:5).

50. Mahzor Vitry, commentary on mAvot 5:17

"Every controversy that is for the sake of heaven, its end is to be sustained."

"For the sake of heaven" means to establish the truth about some matter, or to admonish transgressors, as opposed to controversies engaged in for the sake of power or renown, or to be haughty with one's fellows for no reason. . . .

---

14 Olive wood is bitter to the taste.
15 To which "the hand of Moses" is taken to allude.

"The controversy of Korah" – Korah sought to gain power. Indeed, the controversy was not sustained, and did not last for any length of time, rather, devastation was visited upon him, as it is written, "and the earth opened," and so on (Num. 16:32). Thus, the controversy came to nothing.

51. Sefer Hasidim, 971

When two are engaged in a debate, one should not say to his fellow, 'Wise one, what say you?', for it sounds as if he is saying, 'Fool,' even though his fellow indeed has no adornments.

52. Teshuvot Ufsakim Raavad, p. 114

The God of Gods knows, and Israel knows, that were my words spoken in anger, in vexation, or in a quarrel or a battle, He should not now save me. But since I saw that you have chosen the style of the Spanish Jews, who are fond of each other, yet when they argue over matters pertaining to the Torah, appear to be enemies, I said to myself, I too will test you, to see if you indeed follow their custom. And I thus wrote to you a letter of affection with charming and enjoyable words, to engage you in a pleasant manner. And heaven forbid that they should be construed as belittlement.

53. Peirushei Mishnat Avot (Sefer Hamusar), mAvot 5:17

"Every controversy that is for the sake of heaven, its end is to be sustained." The interpretation of this is, a controversy between scholars over matters of wisdom. It does not seek to establish which of them is greater, or to misdirect a colleague from truth to falsehood. But they both turn to the same path and follow it until they reach the truth, which is their objective. And truth cannot be found in two directions, only in one. Therefore it is not the case that one of them is jealous of his fellow or wishes him harm because a controversy has arisen between them, for this controversy is for the sake of heaven and not to gratify material needs, but rather, both intend to know wisdom and achieve truth. As the Sages said there: "Nevertheless, though these declare unfit that which the others declare fit, these declare impure that which the others declare pure, these prohibit what the others permit, the house of Shammai did not refrain from marrying women of the house of Hillel, nor the house of Hillel from marrying women of the house of Shammai. And they did not refrain, in matters connected with purity, from making use of that which pertained to the others, to fulfill the scriptural dictum, "love truth and peace" (Zech. 8:19)."[16]

---

16 Paraphrase of mJebamot 1:4; the last phrase is from tJebamot 1:10. See passages 176 and 178.

But a controversy whose only aim is satisfaction of worldly desires – for power, esteem, riches and property – is not sustained. But the controversy and those who take part in it cease to exist, for it is a controversy for the sake of worldly desires that do not endure. But a controversy over matters of wisdom does not cease to be, as wisdom endures forever.

54. Beit Habehira, mAvot 5:19

"Every controversy that is for the sake of heaven, its end is to be sustained," and so on. This is puzzling: in what way is it apt to say of a controversy that it will be sustained? For in any event, only one of the two opposing views will ultimately be sustained. And the term 'controversy' covers two sides, and how can 'the controversy' [that is, both sides] be sustained? And anyway, it seems to me that the term 'controversy' refers only to the side challenging an existing view.[17] That is, when one party intends to do something, and says, It is proper for us to act thus, or else he is asked about something, and rules that it be carried out, there is [as yet] no controversy. But when the other responds, saying: That which you say it is proper for us to do, is not proper; or, [The law] on which you ruled is not as you ruled, but the reverse – then there is a controversy. It follows that 'controversy' does not encompass both sides, but only one, namely, that which challenges an existing view. The Mishna is saying that if this second party challenges [the other view] and disputes it, not as a provocation and out of competitiveness, but in order to reveal the truth, then its words will be sustained, since the truth will ultimately emerge. However, when the argument is not for the sake of heaven, but only to challenge and dispute [the first view] as a provocation and out of competitiveness, then it will not be sustained, but only that of the other side. And all the more so when the controversy is over other matters.

55. Hibur Hateshuva, maamar I, chapter 4, pp. 106–7

And also in the fifth class[18] are those who dissent from the words of the Sages. Now the term 'dissenter' refers to one whose intention is to disagree and to provoke and to speak words contrary to the truth in order to win

---

17 It is possible that Meiri's comments here echo the disputations that were held in the universities of his time. These disputations were subject to many detailed rules and procedures, one of which was the clear distinction between the proponent, the party who put forward a thesis, and the opponents, who argued against him, and attempted to refute it. See Anthony Kenny, "Medieval Philosophical Literature," in N. Kretzman and A. Kenny (eds.), *Cambridge History of Later Medieval Philosophy*, Cambridge: 1982, pp. 11–43.

18 The author is discussing the factors preventing or hampering repentance.

an argument. Such an individual is always referred to as a dissenter. As in the incident related by the Talmud, where one who held a [controversial] opinion and had this trait passed by two other Sages. Out of respect, one of them wished to rise, since Scripture commands "rise up before the hoary head" (Lev. 19:32), to which the other replied, shall we rise, then, before a dissenter?[19] Meaning, given that he is a dissenter, why should we be the ones to rise in his presence?! He wanted to demean and humble him so because his dissent was characterized by provocation and competitiveness.

The Mishna has the following to say about this: Every controversy that is for the sake of heaven, its end is to be sustained; and every controversy that is not for the sake of heaven, its end is not to be sustained. What controversy is for the sake of heaven? The controversy between Shammai and Hillel. And what controversy is not for the sake of heaven? The controversy of Korah and his congregation.[20] The controversy between Shammai and Hillel is called a "controversy that is for the sake of heaven," because neither sought simply to refute the opinion of his fellow, but rather, each sought to ascertain the truth. And in a few places the Mishna states that "the house of Hillel retracted their opinion and ruled in accordance with the view of the house of Shammai."[21] And the controversy of Korah and his congregation is called a "controversy that is not for the sake of heaven," since it is known to be motivated by his jealousy of the standing of Moses and Aaron, as is explicitly stated, "wherefore then lift ye up yourselves above the assembly of the Lord?" (Num. 16:3). And Scripture also said explicitly, "all the congregation are holy, every one of them" (ibid.), asserting that they were all of high standing and had no need of a leader. ... And since the controversy was motivated by jealousy and to provoke them, the Sages, of blessed memory, call it a controversy that is not for the sake of heaven.

So, whenever someone contradicts the halakhic authorities out of jealousy and as a provocation, but not in order to ascertain the truth, it is called a "controversy not for the sake of heaven." This trait is attributed to the boor, that is, he disputes their views in order to provoke them, and for this reason they said of him that he does not concede the truth, as the Sages, of blessed memory, said, "Seven things are characteristic of a boor, and seven of a wise man. A wise man does not speak before one who is greater in wisdom, and does not enter into the words of his fellow; he is not hasty to answer; he asks in accordance with the subject matter, and answers in terms of the accepted view; he speaks of the first point first, and of the last point last; of that about which he has not heard, he says,

19 bGitin 31b.
20 mAvot 5:17, see passage 37; the quotation is inexact.
21 mEduyot 1:12.

I have not heard; and he acknowledges the truth. And the opposite traits are characteristic of a boor."[22] The Mishna thus instructs us that if he challenges the truth, even a knowledgeable person is but a boor, if he will not admit the truth when it is known to him, but persists in arguing in order to be provocative and out of zeal to defeat the other side. For a boor is not necessarily one altogether without knowledge.

56. New Responsa Ribash, #33

And even in the case of controversy pertaining to Torah matters, we have found some of these controversies equated to the controversy of Korah, as I saw in a Spanish collection of laws concerning banning, regarding the case of R. Eliezer the Great. It stated:

> The strict law was applied to R. Eliezer, despite the fact that he was highly important, so that controversy would not be multiplied in Israel, because such conduct is unforgivable, even in one who is highly distinguished and the head of a court. And although R. Joseph said, In Usha it was enacted that a head of a court who acted disgracefully is not to be banned,[23] if the offender caused a controversy, the matter is different. And it was said, Gratuitous hatred is equivalent to three transgressions.[24] It appears that there is no greater desecration of God's Name than this. And the proof of this is the controversy concerning Korah and his entire congregation. Therefore, we indeed ought to impose bans and to excommunicate.

And if, to admonish against the proliferation of controversy in Israel, they treated thus one who was an angel of the Lord of Hosts, and all of whose acts were for the sake of heaven, and whose war was the war of the Torah, and on account of whom there was a great commotion in heaven and on earth, and whose words were agreed to, as is related in the Talmud,[25] and who was unlike us – [how much more so with respect to us], for we are but lowly humans, worse than animals, seeing that our evil inclination overcomes our better side, and all of our controversies are for the sake of earthly vanities, to be proud and to vanquish our peers, and many of us ordinary folk isolate ourselves,[26] each in his own corner, to destroy, to kill,

22 mAvot 5:7, passage 36.
23 bMoed Katan 17a.
24 jYoma 1:1.
25 bBaba Metzia 59b.
26 A pun on a phrase in Esther 8:17.

and to cause body and assets to perish[27] – then even more so should every God-fearing individual fight the war of [the Torah's] precepts, using banishments, excommunication and ostracism, and all manner of martial ruses against those who incite the controversy, and zealots should take the necessary steps against them.

57. Menorat Hamaor, candle II, rule 7, part 1, chapter 1

The seventh rule: not to persist in controversy. And it can be divided into two parts: the first part addressing controversy over questions arising in Torah study, the second addressing everyday quarrels.

Since the nature of human reality necessitates that people live together, serving and assisting each other in all their labors and needs, civilization is achieved through harmonization of opinions, love, and brotherhood among them, and through consensus and unity of outlook and law. Therefore, any discord that may arise among them is destructive for human society. Now study of the Torah should be undertaken by a group of students. If, in discussing a certain question, they are sincerely divided over how to understand it, for the sake of heaven – with a view to arriving at the truth, so that the law they arrive at will not be erroneous, but well-grounded – this is the service of God. And we learn in tractate Taanit: Said R. Aha b. Hanina: What is the meaning of the verse "as iron sharpens iron" (Prov. 27:17)?[28] It means that just as one piece of iron sharpens the other, so two scholars make each other sharper in their knowledge of the law. Said Rabbah b. Bar Hana: Why are the Torah's words likened to fire? As it is written, "Is not My word like a fire? declareth the Lord" (Jer. 23:29), meaning that just as fire does not burn on its own, so too the words of the Torah do not endure on their own. ...

Nevertheless, should a difference of opinion arise among the scholars, their intention ought to be for the sake of heaven, viz., to arrive at the truth regarding the law, and not simply to be contentious, as we learn in tractates Kidushin and Nazir: "Our Sages taught: After R. Meir's demise, R. Judah announced to his students, Let not R. Meir's students enter hither, because they are argumentative and do not come to learn Torah but to overwhelm us with laws."[29] But if their controversy over the law is for the sake of heaven, as it was in the case of the controversy between the students of Hillel and Shammai, it is good and commendable, as we learned in the Mishna: "Every controversy that is for the sake of heaven, its end is to be sustained. And that which is not for the sake of heaven, its end is not to be sustained. What controversy is for

---

27 Paraphrasing the language of Esther 8:11.
28 bTaanit 7a.
29 bKidushin 52b, bNazir 49b.

the sake of heaven? The controversy between Hillel and Shammai. And that which is not for the sake of heaven? The controversy of Korah and his congregation."[30] ...

So, all controversies similar to that between the house of Hillel and the house of Shammai or those of the Sages of the Mishna and the Talmud and succeeding authorities – all are similar in that they are offshoots, and all were for the sake of heaven. And such controversy is valuable, as it clarifies the truth regarding the law. But care should be taken to avoid jealousy and strife, as we learn in the Talmud, about the incident that occurred when R. Shimon bar Yohai left the cave. A certain old man said to him: The son of Yohai has purified a cemetery! Said he, Had you (not) been with us, or even had you been with us but not voted, you could have spoken thus. But as you were with us and voted with us, it will be said, Whores paint one another; how much more so scholars [ought help each other]. He cast his eye upon him, and he died.[31] We also learned, Rava said: two scholars who live in the same town but are not amiable to each other in discussing the law, provoke anger, bringing it upon themselves, as it is said: "the cattle also concerning the storm that cometh up" (Job 36:33).[32] But if they are amiable and pleasant with each other, they remove strife from the world, and the Holy One, blessed be He, listens to their prayers, as we learn in tractate Shabat: R. Jeremiah said in the name of R. Shimon b. Lakish: When two scholars are amiable to each other in discussing the law, the Holy One, blessed be He, heeds them, for it is said, "Then they that feared the Lord spoke to one another; and the Lord hearkened, and heard it" (Mal. 3:16).[33] ...

Thus, one should respect those who are greater in wisdom, and ought not regard them as his equal. We saw what happened to R. Anan and R. Huna, as related the Talmud.[34] ... Nevertheless, happy are the great who tolerate the small, and the small who defer to the great.

58. Commentary of the Preacher Rabbenu Yosef Yaavetz of the Spanish Exiles, on mAvot 5:19

He taught that the essence of study depends on motivation. For he whose motivation is for the sake of heaven, to discover the truth – even if he erred in his deliberations, it would be deemed as if he had arrived at the truth. And the reason is that it is not the exegesis that counts, but rather, the deed. And since his motivation was nothing other than to derive the

---

30 mAvot 5:17.
31 bShabat 34a.
32 bTaanit 8a.
33 bShabat 63a.
34 bKetubot 69a.

law to be applied, to be more alacritous in approaching God, may He be blessed, then this intention is deemed to [reflect] his soul.

59. Noam Vehovlim, p. 83

To be sure, I was much annoyed to hear from you that this individual[35] was gratified by the shaming of your honorable father-in-law,[36] of blessed memory, and for the life of me I seriously considered admonishing him privately in a letter. For although I did not know your father-in-law personally, his fame has indeed reached me, as the fragrance of his name has wafted far and wide, like that of a vial of perfume. I am intensely zealous about preventing the humiliation of Torah scholars, as it is said in the Talmud, "Jerusalem was not destroyed until her scholars became despised."[37] All the more so as it is the case that such aspersions were cast after your father-in-law's demise, and we may cite the verse, "As well their love, as their hatred [and their envy], is long ago perished" (Eccles. 9:6), which the Talmud applied in the incident involving R. Shimon the son of Rabbi, who said this about R. Meir and R. Nathan.[38]

However, we have here a student from Venice who saw the book. I questioned him closely and he attested, under oath, that it showed great respect for your father-in-law, esquire, referring to him by such superlative appellations as "Gaon" and "High Priest," and their like. I do not feel it is appropriate to bestow such titles upon our contemporaries, as we do not give the title "Gaon" even to our most monumental scholars, such pillars as Maimonides, Rashi, R. Abraham b. David, Rabbenu Tam, Nahmanides, R. Solomon b. Adret, and other such great decisors. And a fortiori, needless to say, we do not accord such titles to contemporary scholars. For it is analogous to extolling one who has not even a thousand silver dinar by saying that he has a million golden dinar, which mocks him, as is often cited in the Bahir and the Midrash. For this reason I do not accord these honors even to the greatest men of our generation, or to scholars of the preceding generations who certainly surpassed them. In any case, as the student from Venice reported to me, [the author] accords your father-in-law all this veneration, and it appears certain that his intention was simply to express great respect for him. Therefore, I refrained from rebuking him, but "I stand upon my watch" (Hab. 2:1). If the book is brought here and I see that your father-in-law was in fact taken lightly, I will definitely write him a personal letter rebuking him, for I "cannot look on mischief" (Hab. 1:13) and certainly will not suffer such jealousy,

35 R. Benjamin Zeev.
36 R. David Hakohen (Radakh).
37 bShabat 119b.
38 bHorayot 14a.

which is the undoing of this world. If scholars despise each other, the Torah is thereby discredited, to the glee of the ignorant and the evil. ...

Concerning your complaint that he referred to your father-in-law as "a priest from the house of Eli," I do not see this as an insult. On the contrary, it can be regarded as a compliment, for none of us are greater than the Sages of the Talmud, and some of them said of themselves that they were descendants of Eli.[39] It is also stated that Rabbah and Abbaye were of the house of Eli,[40] and the Talmud certainly did not intend this as an affront to them, but to exalt and praise them. And you surely remember the talmudic passage near the end of Kidushin: "R. Judah said in the name of Samuel: Pashur the son of Imer had four hundred slaves, some say four thousand, and they all assimilated into the priesthood."[41] Therefore, Sages of immaculate descent would praise themselves by citing their descent from Eli and other eminent priestly families, so as to declare to the world that they were not descendants of these assimilated priests, and there were no outsiders in their ancestry. And if the curse that was pronounced on the house of Eli disturbs you, you should take no heed, since Rava said, "With sacrifice and offering it cannot be expiated, but it can be expiated by studying the words of the Torah."[42] As your father-in-law was a prominent scholar, the decree is surely annulled for him and for his descendants. No evil will befall him and no mishap will come nigh to his dwelling.

And suppose he made, regarding your father-in-law, such remarks as: "his words are mangled"; "he erred"; "contemporary scholars have criticized him"; "examine your opinions and mine and see who is wrong"; "leave this confusion before your errors proliferate" and similar expressions that you mentioned. I do not regard them as insults, for this is the way debaters and those on opposed sides of a controversy speak in the heat of argument. He is not primarily interested in derogating your honorable father-in-law, but in enhancing his own stock by praising himself. The heat of the Torah may well arouse the anger of the debaters, as the Talmud states: Rava further said: If a devoted scholar becomes enraged, it is because the Torah inflames him, as it is said, "Is not My word like a fire? declareth the Lord" (Jer. 23:29).[43]

And who could possibly be free of all such slights? Even some of the greatest of the early teachers of eternal fame were criticized and confuted, sometimes honestly, sometimes fraudulently. A wise adage says, "ideas differ as do faces," this is all the truer with respect to the differences in the Talmud, which are wider than the sea. And you are surely aware that the

---

39 bSanhedrin 14a.
40 bRosh Hashana 18a.
41 bKidushin 70b.
42 bRosh Hashana 18a.
43 bTaanit 4a.

THE CONDUCT OF A CONTROVERSY

talmudic Sages, the Geonim and the decisors criticized each other, and there was criticism of our great master Maimonides, of blessed memory. Even if one is great beyond description, it does not necessarily follow that he never makes a small or even a big mistake. The Sages, of blessed memory, said: A man does not fully understand the words of the Torah until he has come to grief over them. As it is said, "This stumbling-block is under thy hand" (Isa. 3:6).[44]

Therefore, even if he did write that your father-in-law erred and was criticized by his peers, who corrected him, "do not marvel at the matter" (Eccles. 5:7), "but it has already been in the ages before us" (Eccles. 1:10); how much more so since he has no authority over us, and if he said about your father-in-law, esquire, that he erred and his contemporaries criticized him, your father-in-law can easily retort that he [the critic] was mistaken. And the great luminaries will chase him, and overtake him all the way "toward the sunrise" (Judges 20:43).[45] These and similar remarks are nothing but vain words drifting in the air. Take no heed of them and their like. King Solomon, of blessed memory, in his wisdom, asserted: "Also take no heed unto all the words that are spoken" (Eccles. 7:21).

60. Shnei Luhot Habrit, oral law, klal 'Pe kadosh'

We cannot but wonder that on numerous occasions the holy Talmud records disrespect in the exchanges between the Amoraim. This raises a question that is actually two questions; how could they speak to each other rudely, and why does the Talmud record this? And I will quote you some of these remarks: There is much to wonder about the following response – "Since you are Mamulai,[46] your words are frail"[47]; "it appears that he has no brains in his head"[48]; and the anecdote where Resh Lakish and R. Johanan called three Sages "cowherds" and "shepherds."[49]

You should understand that these remarks must be explained so as to show that they were uttered for good reason, or were instrumental in redressing some error. And, God be praised, I have always endeavored to show the good, whenever I encountered such [remarks] in the Talmud, and I have succeeded. Everything has to be explained in its context. Let me mention one [of the remarks]: "since you are Mamulai" – this was

---

44 bGitin 43a.
45 A pun on Judges 20:43 regarding the other tribes' fight with the tribe of Benjamin, the name of the critic in question, R. Benjamin Zeev.
46 "You are frail (*mamulai*)" can be understood as meaning either "you are frail," or, you are from Mamla. The author follows Rashi's interpretation that Mamulai refers to a frail family – the house of Eli.
47 bJebamot 76a.
48 bJebamot 9a.
49 bSanhedrin 26a.

84

not said to scorn, God forbid, but as words of wisdom and admonition, as the Sages said of the house of Eli, "[the curse] will not be atoned for by sacrificial offerings, but will be atoned for by study of the Torah and by loving-kindness."[50] So, the Sage was saying, 'since you are from the family of Eli and this is your atonement, you ought to take more care with your studies, so there will be no miserable consequences.' And all the other [seemingly objectionable] locutions should be similarly interpreted by the wise.

61. Responsa Pnei Yehoshua, 2, #34

The law has already become circulated in all communities that the new harvest (*hadash*), at the present, even of the Gentiles, is forbidden. And no one has ever challenged or attempted to rebut this prohibition. Because the prohibition came forth from the great scholar, the famed R. Isaac the Tosafist, of blessed memory, and all those who came after him agreed with him.... Until a certain authority arose, namely, the eminent author of *Bayit Hadash*, disputing the ruling of the Ri, the Tosafist, as is related in his book.[51] And behold, this authority will now be informed, just as he says in various places in his own book, that 'God [lit., his Master] will forgive him' for gratuitously disagreeing with the Ri and with those who concur with him.

And it is not about the dispute itself that I am angry, for certainly, there is no judge but "the judge that shall be in those days" (Deut. 17:9); and every individual is permitted to disagree – on the basis of clear evidence – even with early authorities, as was stated by Asheri, of blessed memory. But I am angry with him about the tone of his words and the haughtiness he manifested. For he concluded his analysis by saying that the prohibition against eating the new harvest of Gentiles is nothing but excessive piety, and one should not act in accordance with it in public. And in so doing, he rendered the words of the Ri, the Tosafist, null and void, and presents his own words, on the other hand, as if they were given at Sinai, to the point where the words of the Ri and all the other halakhic decisors are not to be heeded even by those seeking to be at the very least on the safe side. And instead of saying, 'though the words of the Ri are controversial, one ought not transgress them, since they were uttered by him,' which is the way of the Talmud and the Geonim of blessed memory, he said that his own opinion should be relied upon, and categorically stated that it is forbidden to follow the view of the Ri. And now I shall demonstrate publicly and openly, that there is no substance to his words, and in his entire analysis there is not even a single valid argument against the Ri.

50 bRosh Hashana 18a.
51 *Bayit Hadash* on *Tur*, YD 293.

62. Responsa Hut Hashani, #18

In response to a great man, my mentor and teacher, who took me to task for criticizing the great early scholars. You explicitly reproached me: Whence is the effrontery, you ask, to contradict the ancients who sat at the gates, whose fingernails were thicker than my waist, and more particularly, how could I say that some passages of the Talmud and earlier rulings have "escaped their attention"? I cannot help wondering about this accusation, since the very term "escaped their attention" is borrowed from the Talmud, where it is used on numerous occasions,[52] referring even to the greatest Amoraim. It is a pure expression, and a respectful way to say that a certain law has temporarily escaped someone's attention, since forgetfulness is human nature, and true of everyone, and people differ only with respect to the degree to which they suffer from it. Is there any-one greater than Moses our teacher, of blessed memory, the greatest of the prophets, yet in his anger two laws escaped his attention, as is stated by the Sages, of blessed memory, and Rashi,[53] and is there any greater scholar than Maimonides, who includes the entire oral law in his monumental work, and who prepared and composed a commentary on the six orders of the Mishna, based on the Talmud, and wrote in his foreword to the order Seeds, that the name of the Tanna Hanina b. Hakhinai appears but once in the entire Mishna, in Kilayim, and he overlooked that it appears once more, in Makot, chapter 3. ...

And Rashi, the repository of the Torah, wrote in his commentary on the Pentateuch that he did not know how R. Moses the Preacher's mode of interpreting "and called it Nobah" (Num. 32:42) could be applied to two verses in which the same grammatical anomaly appears. Nahmanides points out that Rashi must have overlooked the source used by R. Moses the Preacher.[54] Furthermore, in his commentary on the Pentateuch, in six places Rashi himself says 'I do not know,' and so on; 'I did not know,' and so on. ... And you can see with your own eyes that the Tosafists do not refrain from speaking out against Rashi, neither when Rashi says that he does not know the interpretation, nor when he says he does not know its sources. In addition, the great body of the *Tosafot* is replete with their reservations as to his interpretations of the laws and the various talmudic discussions.

63. Responsa Havat Yair, #152

Question: I was asked: Since "The words of the wise spoken in quiet are more acceptable" (Eccles. 9:17), and the Mishna says, "Let your friend's

---

52 bRosh Hashana 13b; bBaba Kama 76b; bHulin 107b; etc.
53 On Numbers 31:21.
54 Midrash Ruth.

honor be as dear to you as your own,"[55] why do we find expressions of provocation and discourtesy in the Talmud, such as, "Rav said this when he was dozing and lying down," which appears several times,[56] and similar expressions?

Answer: You ask well. Even though the scholars of Babylonia are called "injurers" (hovlim) in tractate Baba Batra,[57] it is not due to any propensity to wreak havoc by hopping about, shouting bitterly and clapping their hands as if they were fighting each other, or because of provocative discourse and scornful behavior, God forbid. For it is not with regard to this demeanor that the Talmud says, "They shall not be ashamed when they speak with their enemies at the gate" (Ps. 127:5).[58] For father and son, teacher and student, become enemies of each other, but only from the aspect of being adversaries in their opinions and proofs.... For surely, it is possible to engage in debate calmly and with good manners, listening to one's colleague without interrupting before answering – one of the seven attributes of the wise.[59] The importance of dialectics hardly needs emphasis. One of the questions asked in the world to come is whether the individual wisely engaged in debate when he was alive. This was the type of analysis used by R. Shimon bar Yohai and his son R. Eleazar,[60] and by R. Johanan and Resh Lakish.[61] It was also said of Rabbah[62] that he uprooted mountains, of Resh Lakish [sic, actually R. Meir], that he uprooted mountains of mountains,[63] and of Rava the son of R. Joseph b. Hama, that he was sharp as a knife.[64] This is the way of the Sages in their debates, and of the dialogues of the ancient philosophers....

Let us return to our subject. Rav said to Levi, "it appears that this man has no brains in his skull."[65] Were I not afraid to criticize the Lord's anointed – for Rav is none other than R. Abba, the most exemplary and distinguished student of R. Shimon bar Yohai...but due to my fear I dare not say that he mis-spoke and got his due when R. Sheshet said of him that he had taught while dozing and lying down.[66] Nevertheless, the truth is that this is not a derogatory expression, but on the contrary, constitutes

---

55 mAvot 2:10.
56 E.g., bJebamot 24b; bBaba Kama 47b; bNida 60a.
57 Actually bSanhedrin 24a.
58 bKidushin 30b.
59 Referring to mAvot 5:7.
60 bShabat 33b.
61 bBaba Metzia 84a.
62 bHorayot 14a.
63 bSanhedrin 24a.
64 bHulin 77a.
65 bJebamot 9a; bMenahot 80b. The remark is made by Rabbi, not Rav.
66 bJebamot 24b, 109b; bBaba Kama 47b, 65a, 67b; bNida 60a; bBekhorot 23b.

great praise, because it assumes that, given the outstanding stature of Rav, he could not have so erred had he been completely awake. Now the *Tosafot* distinguish two kinds of sleep.[67] One is dozing off before falling asleep, and the other the semi-conscious state before wakening. One is termed "dozing and lying down," the other "lying down and dozing." A person not yet fully awake, before regaining his senses, might make a mistake, but on awakening corrects himself, while one who is exhausted and about to fall sleep, does not.

And as to what Rav said, "it appears that," and so on, this means that a scholar may chastise his student even in harsh terms, in order to motivate him to study more rigorously and to avoid error. Levi was a student of Rabbi Judah the Prince, as the Talmud states.[68] In my humble opinion, this is the source for Maimonides' ruling that it is a teacher's duty to show resentment if he perceives that his students are inattentive in their studies. This ruling is accepted by the *Shulhan Arukh*.[69] Therefore, since Rabbi Judah the Prince knew that Levi was a great and outstanding individual, who was not likely to err unless he had studied something insufficiently, or had been careless, he spoke harshly to him, but not, heaven forbid, out of anger or arrogance. And indeed, tractate Sota states that when Rabbi died, modesty was extinguished.[70]

At other times rough language is used metaphorically or humorously, as when R. Johanan said to R. Hiya b. Abba, "While you were eating date-berries in Babylon..."[71]; or when Amoraim call each other "fool," as in the cases of Rabbah and R. Amram,[72] R. Hiya b. Abba and R. Zera,[73] and Abbaye and Abba b. Hanan.[74] And Rashi explains "fool" as "one without a heart," apropos Rava's words to R. Amram.[75] We have to say regarding all these instances that they [the derided] were greater in learning, and yet were not resentful at all. The expression "since you are frail," and so on,[76] was also intended humorously, and it should be noted that *Tosafot* ad loc. explain the expression as referring to a specific place, and so does the *Arukh*.[77] ...

Similarly, when R. Yanai said to his student R. Johanan, "what is the difference between mine and yours?"[78] it was not out of pride or in order

---

67 On bPesahim 119b s.v. *amar*.
68 bSanhedrin 17b.
69 YD 246:11.
70 bSota 49b.
71 bBaba Batra 107b; bBekhorot 18a.
72 bBaba Metzia 20b.
73 bZevahim 25b.
74 bKeritot 18b.
75 Rashi, bBaba Kama 105b.
76 bJebamot 76a.
77 Taking "you are frail (*mamulai*)" to mean, you are from Mamla. Cf. passage 60.
78 bShabat 140a.

to shame him, for a teacher is permitted to needle his student should he exhibit a lack of understanding or carelessness. However, it is possible that R. Johanan got what he deserved, for he used the same expression with Isi.[79] In both cases Rashi explains the remark as meaning, I can explain this Mishna better than you can. I find this enigmatic, since in both cases the teachers did not explain the Mishna, but referred to teachings of their teachers. If I would dare to contradict Rashi, I would say that these were expressions of humility, to boost [the confidence of] the student or colleague. And what he was saying to him was that he had received the tradition from his teacher, having served him very attentively, and as a result, had acquired a superior understanding of the tradition, but this was the only difference between them, and apart from this they were equals in comprehension, study and knowledge. Alternately, [another interpretation is that] between you and me certainly there is a lot of difference, however, the term "mine and yours" indicates acquisition, namely, absorbing something from someone else, and the meaning is that the teacher has received more than the student[80]; it is not intended to reflect on their personal stature, because in that case he would have said, "what is the difference between me and you?" And this is easy to understand.

There are many more examples of such difficult expressions, which I have explained in my book *Mar Kashisha*, so this will suffice as a short answer to your question; I hope you find my remarks agreeable.

64. Responsa Ginat Vradim, YD, rule 3, #3

It so happened that a devoted scholar,[81] inflamed by the zeal of the Torah, had written a work, entitled *Pri Hadash*, on *Tur* YD. It contains many original observations, and exhibits acute intelligence and erudition. Though we do not regard its conclusions as legally binding, nevertheless this book is useful to us, as it relieves us of the burden of looking up sources, which are set out for us, or at the very least, draws our attention to certain information, and we can then decide how to proceed. If we see that its words and judgments are true, we may support and adopt them, but if we do not admire them, we regard them as if they had never existed.

The book arrived in Egypt. Upon perusal of some of its content, it was discovered that the author had cast off the bridle of his tongue to say derogatory things about Israel's great authorities, whose words we drink thirstily and whose utterances we follow. He does not respect the rulings of

---

79 bHulin 137b.
80 On this interpretation, R. Yanai attributes his greater knowledge to the fact that his own teacher was more proficient than he is at teaching his student R. Johanan – or in other words, he is being modest.
81 R. Hezekiah di Silva (1657–1698).

89

venerable elders, and refers perfidiously to our great rabbi the Beit Yosef [R. Joseph Caro], whose work forms the basis of all our rulings and is the pillar of our study, as if he [Caro] were his inexperienced pupil, a fledgling who has not yet opened his eyes, in that "he has no qualms about forbidding what is permitted."

When this was made public, a group of brave men braced themselves and convened the scholars of Israel who dwelled in the city, and also some sojourners who are here from other countries, to call the author to order [lit., to destroy his egg[82]]. The local scholars agreed on a course of conciliation between the two sides, to avoid physical violence to the learned author or besmirching his honor, heaven forbid, by a public flogging or excommunication. Therefore they admonished him privately, and he apologized and became aware of his deeds, of which he was ashamed, like a thief caught red-handed. In order to appease the community, its leaders and officials, they agreed to bury all the books found here in Egypt in a building.

And it was most solemnly decreed, and a ban was imposed, invoking all possible admonitions, on the authority of the Omnipresent One, may He be blessed, that the said book must not be read casually or deeply by any member of the community. They put this agreement into writing, to make it stand forever, and it was signed by all the scholars of the city, and also those visiting from another land. It so happened that the rabbis of Hebron, may it be speedily rebuilt in our day, happened to be here, too, and they were asked to concur with what had been done. To satisfy the local community, they agreed to add their signatures to the document, but they would not be bound by it, and upon leaving the city, they would hold on to the said book and study it.

At present, two of the leading rabbis who used to reside in this land have gone back to their own country, and the learned author has been called upon to join the heavenly academy. Now several utterly wise scholars, and many others, are longing and eager to study the said book, to aid their studies, and they wish to know whether there might be found a remedy that would remedy their discomfiture, and as to the pomegranate that came their way – they will eat it selectively.[83] Furthermore, in the foreword to the book, the author himself cautioned his readers against accepting his opinions indiscriminately, and subsequently apologized for speaking out against his betters. Now, those fervent about [keeping] God's laws have come and asked whether or not it is possible to lift the said ban, since it concerned the dignity of great people. . . . When I, who am but junior, saw the city in this commotion, and the desire of numerous scholars to find a solution, I decided to occupy myself with this meritorious matter, and to

82 jAvoda Zara 44:1.
83 Alluding to bHagiga 16b, "he ate the insides of the pomegranate and threw away the rind."

examine it as much as my frail ability permits. All the more so, since I myself have for some time ardently sought a solution, but I would have preferred that clarification of such a serious matter be opened and concluded by eminent authorities. As it is, it will be opened up by lesser scholars, and concluded by eminent authorities, and they will choose, and not I. And may God grant us success in this endeavor, Amen, may it be His will.

First of all, let me reiterate that all that has been done is valid and in force. Next, I will examine whether or not the sin [of the author] can be atoned for, and finally, I will bring support for some of the arguments mentioned above. In my opinion, even if the aforementioned ban seems very strange – for how could they agree that this book, which contains numerous novel interpretations of the law, not be read, thereby denying academic sustenance to students? – in any event, we have found that greater precautions have been instituted, when this is required by the times, to serve as fences to safeguard the Torah. And as it is stated in the Gemara, sometimes the abrogation of the Torah serves for its firmer establishment. For instance, the Talmud[84] tells us about Hanania who intercalated a month in the year and fixed the time of the New Moon [abroad, without authority], and the Sages deemed his decisions invalid, going "out of their way to render pure what he declared impure and to permit what he had forbidden" [contrary to the usual halakhic principle that once an authority has rendered something impure, his colleague cannot render it pure], to discourage people from following him. And Moses, the faithful shepherd, who loved the people of Israel, broke the tablets made by God, causing grave hardship, by bringing it about that scholars would forget what they had learned, making it necessary for them to toil in studying the Torah. Indeed he did it due to the exigency of the times, as he said, let them be judged as [if their transgression were that of] a single rather than a married woman, and the Holy One, blessed be He, agreed with him, as the Talmud tells us.[85] In this light, a fortiori there is no doubt that the ban on the book is legally valid, for they were zealous for the honor of the early authorities, of blessed memory, and there is no exhortation to perform any action, but a call to abstain from acting, namely, to abstain from reading this book. Any [public] agreement, even if it is not really an exigency decision, even if made only by a local court, is perfectly valid. It is much more so, if we add the exigency, at that time, of saving the honor of the early authorities. Therefore, one who makes light of and abandons this covenant is like one who transgresses the complete Torah that was given to Moses by the Almighty, for it is the law that

---

84 bBerakhot 63a–b.
85 bShabat 87a; the relationship between God and Israel is conceived of as a marriage, consummated by accepting the law; transgression of the law is thus akin to adultery.

a court appointed in a town by its citizens is like the court of Moses our teacher, of blessed memory, as it is said by the Talmud, "any three persons appointed as a court over Israel is like the court of Moses our teacher, of blessed memory."[86] ... Generally speaking, a ruling by a court turns into permanent law, and as to those who scorn it, it is as if they were scorning the words of Moses our teacher, of blessed memory.

Now let us see if we can find a remedy for the injury of that scholar who tarnished and ridiculed the honor of Israel's great men. I say to this that we have learned in the Talmud[87] that four kinds of atonement were expounded upon by R. Ishmael, and even the great sin of profanation of God's Name is perfectly atoned for and cleansed by death. Now even if we treat this scholar very severely, since his offense is too great to bear, and he stumbled by profanation, by scorning the early authorities, setting a bad example and a precedent, that could have caused servants to rebel against the authority of their masters, and habituated the public to belittle and doubt the words of the early authorities; nevertheless, he has atoned for this sin by his death. Since his sin has been atoned for, the court may lift the ban that was made by general agreement.

Indeed, there is room for misgivings about this, because people could get into the habit of dishonoring early authorities. But since it is established that court rulings are widely circulated, the agreement and ban imposed for defamation are well known in Egypt, and the public will infer from them, a fortiori, that this is strictly forbidden, and will be extremely cautious from now on regarding the honor of the early authorities. Moreover, these qualms seem farfetched, since the work has been disseminated throughout all the Jewish communities, and there have been no misgivings anywhere. Nevertheless, the competent court of Egypt, may our city be speedily rebuilt, amen, has acted well in having scruples even regarding this far-fetched eventuality, since the honor of the early authorities has been enhanced, and what they did was the appropriate thing to do.

Furthermore, it is known that no reader will have any apprehension that the study of this book will teach him to scorn and dishonor the early authorities, since we see that readers of this kind of book are discriminating enough to take the insides and discard the rind, and the holy people of Israel harken to strictures and truly recognize the stature of the early authorities, of blessed memory, whose fingernails they respect far more the bellies of more recent scholars, and this truth has established itself, since there are numerous books that deserve to be taken out of circulation, and no one pays them any heed. Therefore, since we now know that his action did not bring about any mishap to the public, his sin may be forgiven.

---

86 bRosh Hashana 25a.
87 bYoma 86a.

Our opinion is well supported by an explicit talmudic passage,[88] the story of R. Meir and R. Nathan, who had wished to discredit the president (*nasi*), dishonor him, and take his place. When this was made known to the president, he expelled them from the academy, but because of their great wisdom and powerful intellect, R. Jose spoke up for them and enabled them to return to the academy. But the president decreed that they should not be credited for their teachings. This decree remained in place even after their deaths, until the grandson of the president recommended that since they were no longer alive, this offence ought to be forgiven them. The work *Ein Yaakov* quotes R. Meir b. Todros Halevi Abulafia (Rama), who explains that even after their deaths, they could be forgiven only because though their intention was to do harm, their action had no effect. It seems to me that according to the Rama, the fact that it had no effect does not suffice in itself, but only given that they had already died.

We deduce from this, regarding our case, that since the scholar is at eternal rest, and no harm has been done by his action, our earthly court may annul his punishment, the prohibition of his book. This is obvious in our case, because we must not assume, God forbid, that he had any evil intent to offend the early authorities. It was a matter of bad manners, and youthful inexperience.

65. Mishnat Hakhamim, §85–88

§85

A learned person must take care to avoid saying derogatory things about his fellow, or, God forbid, gaining honor at the expense of his fellow's shame – his punishment has already been recounted by scholars.[89] This must be heeded, particularly in recording legal decisions, for much ridicule and rebuke is due one who derides his fellow in speech, but even more if he does so in writing. And to those who print such things I exclaim, "and did that which is not good among his people" (Ezek. 18:18), lest the students drink[90] and God's Name is profaned, heaven forbid. Even if there was an exchange of insults, what is the use of printing it? And God, may He be blessed, is witness and judge as to how long I have refrained from printing what I have written against that snake and his faction,[91] may spirit

---

88 bHorayot 13b–14a.
89 See *Zohar*, part III, p. 167a.
90 An allusion to mAvot 1:11.
91 The reference is probably to the Sabbatean Shabtai Nehemiah Hayun (17th century), and to some of the scholars of Amsterdam who supported him. For a detailed account, see E. Carlebach, *The Pursuit of Heresy-Rabbi Moses Hagiz and the Sabbatian Controversies*, New York: 1990, esp. pp. 154, 307.

and soul depart from them, for I waited to see whether they might mend their sins against God and His Torah, and there would be no need to publish anything derogatory and contemptuous.

But when I considered my course of action and saw the publications of the opposing side, their acridity and defiance, and the audacity with which they persisted against all the sages of Israel, so as to sustain the error of heresy that they had fallen into, and what this snake, who has since expired, may his soul and spirit rot, had put into writing and printed, so that it would endure for a long time, I was personally bound to repay them without mercy, since they had shown no compassion for heaven, by not anticipating the injury that was inflicted on all Israel by the destructive venom of this viper, and his ilk, who come into being continuously. For our silence should not be regarded as acquiescence. Since I see all the great scholars of Israel burying their heads in the ground, and acting as though they need do nothing unless forced to [lit., "he who has a father, shall live, and he who has none, shall die?!"[92]], I have become zealous for the Lord of Hosts, His Torah and His people, and have resolved that "they shall both of them die" (Deut. 22:22) – for in a place where God's Name is profaned we may forgo respect for the public. Necessity calls for actions which may not be praiseworthy, but are not to be censured, particularly a necessity such as this, which was, and remains, mandated by both religion and reason. As it is written in the divine *Shela*, if denunciation serves as a punishment, it cannot be criticized for being uttered openly, because the law so mandates, and we frequently pronounce rulings in which evil persons are denounced, for according to the law, such punishment should be imposed on the sinner to induce him to repent, and so that the people will hear about it and fear, and so on,[93] see . . . . Therefore, in order that people, when they see that they have support, will not be induced to follow the snake and his ilk, I, heeding the Torah's example, have acted, as it is written, "She calleth at the head of the noisy streets, at the entrances of the gates [in the city] she uttereth her words" (Prov. 1:21).

God, who judges the world in righteousness, shall be my witness that they were first to breach the fence, and I have not overstepped the mark, and the Sages have taught us that the principle of measure for measure has not been overturned.[94] If the snake and his ilk had no respect for heaven or its creations, why should we have scruples about their dignity and keep this affair hidden as in night-time darkness?[95] They themselves have uncovered their shame before the sun and the moon by their adherence to heresy. Therefore I trust in God, may He be blessed, that He will not deem me a sinner, for my

---

92 bBaba Metzia 84b.
93 *Shnei Luhot Habrit*, p. 409, see passage 60 above.
94 See bSota 12a.
95 Alluding to bMoed Katan 17a, "a learned man should not be publicly chastised."

spirit is without cunning, and I do not take up arms and go to battle for my sake or for the sake of my father's house, or the like, but for the said reasons, which I have made public in my letters, both early on and of late, for all Israel to see. And may the good God pardon me and all Israel, and instil in the hearts of those distant from Him the desire that sin cease on earth, and let them harken to the wise and draw near. Amen, may it be Thy will.

§86

When you see your fellow taking pains and trouble to publish a book for the public good, you have no reason to attack it or write bitter things about it, not having toiled on it and not having nursed it. As long as it contains no material harmful to the people of Israel or to students, it must not be harshly criticized. And if you think yourself wiser than the author, let it be put to the test by debates, study, and sharp arguments, that give due respect to both sides. And you should think about this and give praise to the Creator of all things, who bestowed upon you a keener and deeper intellect than upon your fellow. This was the intention of Solomon the wise in saying, "Debate thy cause with thy neighbor, but reveal not the secret of another" (Prov. 25:9).

I found it very hard to understand how R. Abraham b. David (Raavad), of blessed memory, the most holy and pious man of his generation, great in scholarship and fear of the Lord – and it is said of him that at the time he critiqued Maimonides, he was already elderly and distinguished in learning and piety – contradicted with "contempt and wrath"[96] some of Maimonides' statements and criticized him in the harshest terms, whereas he could have done so with kindness and comradeship. He was surely aware of Maimonides' excellence, for he agrees with him almost all the time, since he does not contradict him. And the received rule is, wherever the Raavad, of blessed memory, does not contradict Maimonides, of blessed memory, the opinion of Maimonides is counted as two opinions. And Raavad must have seen what Maimonides, of blessed memory, wrote at the end of his *Commentary on the Mishna*, that anyone who wishes to criticize or contradict his work should not be censured for his point of view, as he will surely receive a reward from heaven, and will be much cherished by Maimonides for performing this divine labor. This being so, what is the reason for the great anger in his glosses, as if they were, God forbid, enemies, and as if he regards Maimonides, of blessed memory, as an ignorant wood-chopper?

§87

And I have seen that the divine Shela, of blessed memory, on the page noted above, states that he was perturbed by similar expressions, for in many

---

96 Alluding to Esther 1:18.

places in the Talmud we find unnecessary expressions in the discourse of the Amoraim, and he asks, how could an Amora utter anything degrading to his colleague, and how could the editors of the Talmud preserve it in this holy work? He quotes some such expressions: in tractate Eruvin, one says to the other, "Since you are frail,[97] your words are frail"[98]; in tractate Jebamot, "it appears that he has no brains in his head"[99]; and in tractate Sanhedrin the anecdote where R. Johanan called three Sages "cowherds" and "shepherds."[100] The Shela, of blessed memory, accounts for this, explaining that we must not, heaven forbid, think that these were said in scorn, but in a manner of wise admonishment and aphorism which can be understood in more than one sense. Please refer to it, for I do not have the text before me. For this divinely inspired author, in his great wisdom and piety, left nothing to be explained. He also cites the abduction of the daughters of Mar Samuel, and the meddling of R. Nahman's daughters in witchcraft, which is an accurate description of what happened, saying that perhaps their fathers had sinned by not educating them better, and hence the daughters reached this state, and it was written about as a means of punishment. When the denunciation serves as a punishment, it is not forbidden, for some benefit accrues from this publication, as I have written above.

§88

Furthermore, I was put at ease by what I heard explained by my grandfather, of blessed memory, quoting a valid and persuasive explanation proposed by my father, of blessed memory, about what the Talmud relates regarding Hanania, the nephew of R. Joshua,[101] whom the Sages put to shame by sending messengers after him to contradict what he had said, in order to discourage would-be followers. And similarly, in this case, too, it is certain that Raavad, of blessed memory, in his piety and wisdom, recognized the great work of Maimonides, which is very wonderful and well sustains scholars who render halakhic decisions, but is categorical and cites no references, as if it were law given to Moses at Sinai. But frankly, it has some points on which certain great scholars of Israel disagreed, and still disagree, as to the thrust of the teachings. And hence, the Raavad was afraid lest Maimonides would be followed by later generations, who would not dare to disagree with him, being under the impression that Maimonides had enjoyed the unanimous concurrence of all the scholars

---

97 Mamulai – the author follows Rashi's interpretation that Mamulai refers to a frail, short-lived family, the house of Eli.
98 bJebamot 76a.
99 bJebamot 9a.
100 bSanhedrin 26a.
101 bBerakhot 63a.

of Israel, who agreed to rule as he had pronounced regarding everything he had, in his vast learning, put in place. And thus they would not deviate or depart, in any direction, from his pronouncements. Therefore, to remove this obstacle from the path of future generations of scholars, the Raavad, while giving his full assent and validation to most of Maimonides' work, with which he concurred, crowning him with a coronet of glory, at the same time established that he loved the truth, and girding himself for the task at hand, valiantly took steps to loosen the restraints that kept his colleagues from disagreeing with Maimonides. And hence he did not mince words, but allowed himself to speak harshly, so that others would know that Maimonides was not right on every single point. And each soldier fighting the war of the Torah who has the capacity to hear and comprehend his rulings should indeed examine them. And should he discover that they are not concurred with by many of Israel's great scholars, it is permissible for him to disagree with Maimonides' rulings, as Maimonides himself did in admitting he had erred regarding some of their particulars, though such errors are few in number. Indeed, we see that his honorable defenders, his admirers and colleagues, and the divine and perfect Nahmanides, of blessed memory, and the author of the *Magid* [R. Vidal of Tolosa], of blessed memory, admit that some statements by Maimonides, of blessed memory, are somewhat indefensible. It is not out of place to say that he was mistaken, for joyful is he whose mistakes are few. And we also find clear statements in the Talmud itself acknowledging error, such as "this is a delusion"[102]; "he erred on two points"[103]; "Rav Papa went out and announced, the things I have said to you were in error"[104]; and "R. Safra revealed an error of three Sages."[105]

66. Tzidkat Hatzadik, 115

When one is engaged in coming up with novel ideas about the Torah, it should be without any desire for self-interest or self-glorification, or merely for argument's sake, and so on, but rather, it should be out of great passion for the truth. And in that case, even if one errs, his novel views will nevertheless be considered words of Torah and the words of the living God. For the Talmud mentions erroneous words and those that were rejected from the law. Because even prima facie arguments are considered to be words of the Torah. For God, may He be blessed, has set down that even an initial, as-yet imperfect conception is a precursor to true

---

102 bShabat 27a.
103 bSanhedrin 52b.
104 The author cites bGitin, but this reference, and the attribution to R. Papa, are erroneous; see bShabat 63b.
105 bGitin 29b.

knowledge, and even such an early conception is divinely inspired, and constitutes the words of the living God.

But when one is motivated by self-interest, then his views are not considered the words of the living God at all, as it is written regarding Jeroboam: "in the month which he had devised of his own heart" (I Kings 12:33), and certainly, he had formulated a certain exegetical inference that the Festival of the harvest (*asif*) is in Heshvan, but since this inference was motivated by self-interest, to act contrary to the authority of the court in Jerusalem, Scripture says, "which he had devised of his own heart," and does not say that these were the words of the living God. And so too Doeg[106] acted according to his understanding of the Torah, since he was the head of the Sanhedrin, and he taught, "an Ammonite and even an Ammonitess,"[107] according to his own understanding, and the Sages remained silent in the face of his argumentation. Consequently, it would follow that David could not be a king, and would be forbidden to enter the assembly of the Lord. Doeg was decreed a rebel. And likewise Ahimelech. And Saul, though he too was of that opinion, and was thus mistaken, was nonetheless called "the chosen of God." But in the case of Doeg, his interpretation was the outcome of jealousy, and had he not been acting out of self-interest, he would not have erred. In this way, the words of the Torah become an elixir of death, which means to say, that they are lost forever, for such views are not really the words of God at all, but only appear so on the surface.

67. Shlom Yehuda, 33 (p. 105), letter from the Hazon Ish

I would like to note that it is our duty to watch what we say in speaking against our teachers. And I was distressed by your eminence's, may you live long, use of the word "mistake" in arguing against the Maharaz,[108] of blessed memory. It is possible to clarify things in pure and respectful language that is suitable for speaking of our teachers. Furthermore, previous generations used to ask for forgiveness before writing anything against a talmudic authority, because respect for their teachers had been instilled in their hearts, and they spoke with fear and trembling. We, however, do not do the same; we, in asking for forgiveness, stress the correctness of our own view. And when expressing criticism, it is of the utmost importance to avoid taking pleasure in that which should not be pleasurable [viz., vindication], but rather, to take pleasure only in revealing the Torah. Even if this attitude is lacking in our hearts, it is nonetheless within our grasp to watch what we say.

---

106 See bSanhedrin 106b.
107 bJebamot 77a.
108 R. Ephraim Zalman Margaliot (Brody 1760–1828).

68. Responsa Igrot Moshe, YD 3, #88

Regarding a qualm you may have over establishing your residence in Bnei Brak, due to the fact that when you study the Torah you occasionally disagree with the words of the Hazon Ish, of blessed memory – such a qualm is groundless. On the contrary, this brings him honor, when his teaching on matters of the Torah is mentioned, and his words are discussed, even though the conclusion of the scholar studying [them] is not in accordance with his view. And it never occurred to the Hazon Ish, of blessed memory, that no scholars would disagree with him, and it is not reasonable that he would be perturbed by it. On the contrary, "therefore love truth and peace" (Zech. 8:19), as we find regarding the controversy between the house of Shammai and the house of Hillel.[109] And the dictum regarding "the lips that move gently"[110] also refers to reporting the words of a Sage, even in disagreeing with him.

But we certainly must refer to him respectfully, and regarding R. Joshua, whose teeth were black by reason of his fasts, this was not due to the fact that he questioned the words of the house of Shammai, but rather, because he did so contemptuously: "I am ashamed of your words, O house of Shammai."[111] But if polite language is used, certainly there is no criticism implied, neither in raising difficulties with his view, nor in disagreeing with it. On the contrary, it is explicitly stated in tractate Baba Batra that Rava told his students, R. Papa and R. Huna b. R. Joshua, that should they have any queries regarding his ruling, they should not rule as he did, because a judge must rely only on what his own eyes behold.[112] And this principle also applies to ritual law, but he said that they should not tear up his ruling and thereby nullify his opinion, for were he alive, he could, perhaps, have explained the reasoning behind his ruling. And the Rashbam interpreted this: And perhaps you too will find the solution to your query. And as long as the query remained unresolved, they were not to rule in accordance with Rava's view, even though he was their teacher. This being so, how much more so should one feel no qualms about questioning and disagreeing with the great authorities of our generation, even the greatest, but in a respectful manner. For this reason, there need be no qualms or uneasiness over your remaining in Bnei Brak and giving your classes; on the contrary, he [the Hazon Ish] would serve as advocate for you, because you consulted his works.

---

109 bJebamot 14b.
110 bJebamot 97a: "R. Johanan stated in the name of R. Shimon B. Yohai: the lips of a [deceased] scholar in whose name a traditional statement is reported in this world move gently in the grave."
111 bHagiga 22b, see passage 45 above.
112 bBaba Batra 131a.

3

CONTROVERSY AND TRUTH

69. tSota 7:11–12[1]

And he also expounded, "The words of the wise are as goads" (Eccles. 12:11). Why goads? Just as a goad directs the cow in order to bring life to the earth, so the words of the Torah bring life to earth. But [should you think] that just as a goad is movable, so the words of the Torah are movable, therefore Scripture says: "and as nails well planted" (ibid.). Do they not [like nails, being driven in and pulled out], diminish and increase? Therefore Scripture says, "well planted." The "masters of assemblies" are the scholars (*talmidei hakhamim*) who sit in assemblies and say of the impure, "this is impure," and of the pure, "this is pure."

One must not say: Since some forbid and others permit [the same thing], why should I study? Therefore Scripture says, "they were given from one shepherd." One shepherd received them, one God created them. So compartmentalize your heart and store there the words of those who deem a matter impure and the words of those who deem it pure. He said to them: The generation in which R. Eleazar b. Azariah lives is not an orphaned generation.

70. bHagiga 3b

And he too began to expound: The words of the wise are as goads, and as nails well planted are those of masters of assemblies; they were given from one shepherd (Eccles. 12:11). Why are the words of the Torah likened to a goad? To teach that just as a goad directs the cow along the furrow in order to bring life to the world, so the words of the Torah direct those who study them from the paths of death to the paths of life. But [should you think] that just as a goad is movable, so the words of the Torah are movable, therefore Scripture says: "nails." But [should you think] that just as a nail diminishes by being driven in, and does not increase, so too the words

---

1 Erfurt ms.

100

of the Torah diminish, and do not increase, therefore Scripture says: "well planted"; just as a plant grows and increases, so the words of the Torah grow and increase.

"Masters of assemblies" – these are the scholars (*talmidei hakhamim*) who sit in various assemblies and apply themselves to the Torah; some deem a matter impure, others deem it pure, some prohibit, others permit, some disqualify, others declare fit. Lest you say, Under these circumstances, how can I learn the Torah?, therefore Scripture says: All "were given from one shepherd."[2] One God gave them, one leader uttered them from the mouth of the Master of all deeds, blessed be He, as it is written, "And God spake all these words" (Exod. 20:1). So let your ears be as funnels, and cultivate an understanding heart, to hear the words of those who deem a matter impure and those who deem it pure, those who prohibit and those who permit, those who disqualify and those who declare fit.

71. Pesikta Rabati, parasha 3 (Ish-Shalom edition, p. 8a)

Another interpretation: What does "as goads" (Eccles. 12:11) mean? R. Berechiah said: A girls' ball, like the ball that little girls play catch with,[3] one tosses it here [to the other], and the other tosses it there. So too the Sages, who enter into their studies (*talmud*) and occupy themselves with the Torah: one gives his reasoning and the other his, one puts forward one account and the other another, but the words of all are from Moses, the shepherd, who received it from the Singular One of the world. Since one gives one account and the other another, perhaps their words merely fly about? Therefore Scripture says, "as nails well planted."

72. Midrash Tanhuma, Behaalotkha, 15

"Masters of assemblies" (Eccles. 12:11) – these are the Sanhedrin. Should you say: some permit and some forbid, some disqualify and others declare fit, some deem a matter impure and others deem it pure; R. Eliezer deems the action liable, R. Joshua deems it exempt; the house of Shammai forbids and the house of Hillel permit; whom shall I heed? [Hence] the Holy One, blessed be He, said: Nevertheless, all were given from one shepherd. This is Moses, of whom it is said, "And Moses was a shepherd" (Exod. 3:1), who received them from the Singular One of the world; and they are identical, but one states one rationale, and the other states another rationale. Therefore it is said, all were given from one shepherd.

---

2 See nn. to passage 4 above.

3 The phrase "as goads" is *ka-darbonot*. The exegesis, changing the vowel points slightly, reads it *kadur banot* – "girls' ball."

73. Numbers Rabbah 15:22

Scripture says: "Gather unto Me seventy men" (Num. 11:16). This is the explanation of the other verse: "The words of the wise are as goads, and as nails well planted are those of masters of assemblies; they were given from one shepherd" (Eccles. 12:11).... "Masters of assemblies" – these are the Sanhedrin. Should one say: some permit and some forbid, some disqualify and others declare fit, some deem a matter impure and others deem it pure; R. Eliezer deems the action liable, R. Joshua deems it exempt, the house of Shammai disqualifies it, the house of Hillel declares it fit – whom shall we heed? So the Holy One, blessed be He, said: Nevertheless, all were given from one shepherd.

74. jBerakhot 1:4 (3b)

It was taught: A heavenly voice went forth and declared: Both are the words of the living God, but the law is in accordance with the view of the house of Hillel.

75. bEruvin 13b

R. Abba stated in the name of Samuel: For three years there was a controversy between the house of Shammai and the house of Hillel, the former asserting: The law is in accordance with our views, and the latter asserting, The law is in accordance with our views. A heavenly voice (*bat kol*) went forth and said: Both [lit., these and those] are the words of the living God, but the law is in accordance with the view of the house of Hillel. Since, however, both are the words of the living God, for what reason did the house of Hillel merit the law's being decided in accordance with their view? Because they were kindly and modest, they studied their own words and those of the house of Shammai, and not only that, but they quoted the words of the house of Shammai before their own.

76. bGitin 6b

Commenting on the text, "And his concubine played the harlot against him," R. Eviatar said that the Levite found a fly [in food she prepared], and R. Jonathan said that he found a hair on her. Soon afterward R. Eviatar encountered Elijah and said to him: What is the Holy One, blessed be He, doing? and he answered, He is discussing the question of the concubine in Gibeah. What does He say? He said to him, My son Eviatar says this, and my son Jonathan says that. He [R. Eviatar] said to him: Heaven forbid. Can there possibly be uncertainty in the mind of the Heavenly One? He replied: Both are the words of the living God. He [the Levite] found a fly and excused it, he found a hair and did not excuse it.

77. jSanhedrin 4:2 (22a)

Said R. Yanai: Were the Torah to have been handed down in a clear-cut form, one would have had no solid ground to stand on. What is the basis for this statement? [Scripture says] "And the Lord spoke to Moses." [Moses] said to Him, Master of the Universe, tell me how the law is decided. He said to him, "follow the majority" (Exod. 23:2). If those who declare [the accused] exempt are in the majority, declare him exempt. If those who declare [the accused] liable are in the majority, declare him liable. This is so that the Torah may be expounded in forty-nine ways for a decision that something is impure and in forty-nine ways for a decision that it is pure. And forty-nine is the numerical equivalent of "and his banner (*vediglo*)" (Song of Songs 2:4).[4] Further, Scripture says: "The words of the Lord are pure words, as silver refined in a crucible upon the earth, purified seven times" (Ps. 12:7). And it says: "Sincerely do they love you" (Song of Songs 1:4).

78. Pesikta Rabati, parasha 21 (Ish-Shalom edition, p. 101a)

"The Lord spoke with you face to face[5]" (Deut. 5:4). R. Tanhum b. Hanilai said: Were the Torah to have been handed down in a clear-cut form, no judge would have had solid grounds for his ruling. But now, if he renders a thing impure, there are others who rendered it impure under similar circumstances. And if he renders it pure, there are others who rendered it pure under similar circumstances.

R. Yanai said: The Torah that the Holy One, blessed be He, gave to Moses, has forty-nine aspects of purity and forty-nine aspects of impurity, as it is written, "and his banner over me is love (*vediglo alai ahava*)" (Song of Songs 2:4), which has a numerical value of forty-nine.

He said to him: How shall I act? [God] said to him: If those who declare it impure are in the majority, it is impure. If those who declare it pure are in the majority, it is pure.

79. Midrash on Psalms 12

R. Yanai said: The words of the Torah were not given in a clear-cut form, but rather, for every word that the Holy One, blessed be He, spoke to Moses, He offered forty-nine arguments by which a thing might be proved pure, and forty-nine arguments by which it might be proved impure. He said to him: Master of the Universe, when will we grasp the precise sense of the law? [God] said to him: "follow the majority" (Exod. 23:2). If those

---

4 By adding the numerical values of the letters $(6 + 4 + 3 + 30 + 6)$. See passage 78.
5 Interpreted here "facet to facet."

who declare impure are in the majority, it is impure. If those who declare it pure are in the majority, it is pure.

R. Abbahu said in the name of R. Jonathan[6]: R. Akiva had a faithful disciple named R. Meir, who with forty-nine arguments from Scripture could prove even a reptile pure, and with forty-nine other arguments could prove it impure.

R. Joshua b. Levi said: Infants who lived during the time of Saul and David, and during the time of Samuel, knew how to expound the Torah with forty-nine arguments by which a thing might be proved pure, and forty-nine arguments by which it might be proved impure.

80. bBaba Metzia 59b

This is the oven of Akhnai. What is meant by Aknai? R. Judah said in the name of Samuel, it means that they encircled things in a snake-like way, and declared [the matter] impure.[7]

It has been taught: On that day R. Eliezer brought forward every imaginable argument, but they did not accept them. He said to them: If the law is in accordance with my view, let this carob-tree prove it! The carob-tree was torn a hundred cubits from its place – others say, four hundred cubits. They said to him: No proof can be brought from a carob-tree. Again he said to them: If the law is in accordance with my view, let the stream of water prove it! The stream of water flowed backwards. They said to him: No proof can be brought from a stream of water. Again he said to them: If the law is in accordance with my view, let the walls of the house of study prove it. The walls of the house of study started to tilt precariously. But R. Joshua rebuked them, saying to them: When scholars are engaged in debating the law with one another, what is it to you? They did not fall, out of respect for R. Joshua, nor did they revert to the upright position, out of respect for R. Eliezer; and though tilted they are still standing. Again he said to them: If the law is in accordance with my view, let it be proved from heaven! A heavenly voice went forth and said: What do you want from R. Eliezer, seeing that on all matters the law is in accordance with his view?! But R. Joshua rose to his feet and said: "It is not in heaven" (Deut. 30:12). What did he mean by, "It is not in heaven"? R. Jeremiah said: [it means that] the Torah has already been given at Mount Sinai; we pay no attention to a heavenly voice, because You have long ago written in the Torah at Mount Sinai, "Follow the majority" (Exod. 23:2). R. Nathan encountered Elijah and asked him: What did the Holy One, blessed be He, do at that hour? He said to him: He smiled and said, My sons have triumphed over Me, My sons have triumphed over Me.

6 It appears that the correct reading is R. Johanan.
7 See mEduyot 7:7; mKeilim 5:10; and tEduyot 2:1.

81. bBaba Metzia 84a

R. Shimon b. Lakish's soul expired, and R. Johanan was greatly saddened on account of his death. Our Rabbis said: Who will go to ease his mind? Let R. Eleazar b. Pedat, whose legal teachings are very subtle, go. So he went and sat before him; and upon every dictum uttered by R. Johanan, he said: There is a baraita that supports you. He said, [Do you think] you are, then, like the son of Lakisha? When I stated the law, the son of Lakisha would raise twenty-four separate objections, to which I gave twenty-four answers, which led to a fuller understanding of the law. And [all] you say is, There is a baraita that supports you. Do I not know that my opinions are well-grounded? He went on rending his garments and weeping, saying: Where are you, son of Lakisha, where are you, son of Lakisha? And he cried thus until his mind broke down. The scholars prayed that mercy be shown him, and his soul expired.

82. bBaba Metzia 86a

R. Kahana said: R. Hama, the son of the daughter of Hassa, related to me: As the result of persecution, Rabbah bar Nahmani's soul expired. Information against him had been leaked to the state. They [the informers] said: There is a certain man among the Jews who keeps twelve thousand Israelite men from paying the royal poll-tax one month in summer and one in winter. A royal officer was sent for him, but did not find him…and he went and fled to the marshland meadows. He sat on the trunk of a [fallen] palm and studied. Now in the heavenly academy they were debating thus: If the spot preceded the white hair, he is impure; if the white hair preceded the spot, he is pure.[8] If [the order is] in doubt, the Holy One, blessed be He, says he is pure, whereas the entire heavenly academy says he is impure. And they said: Who will decide it? Rabbah bar Nahmani will decide, for he has said, I am pre-eminent in the laws of leprosy, I am pre-eminent in the laws of tents. They sent out a messenger to get him, but the Angel of Death was not able to approach him, because he did not interrupt his study. In the meantime, a wind blew and caused a rustling in the reeds, which he imagined to be a troop of horsemen. He said: Let the soul of this man expire, rather than be delivered into the hands of the state. As his soul expired, he said: Pure, pure! A heavenly voice went forth and said, Happy are you, Rabbah bar Nahmani, as your body is pure and your soul has departed in purity.[9]

8 The reference here is to the laws of leprosy, see Leviticus 13:10.
9 See passage 96.

83. bBaba Batra 75a

"And I will make thy spires of *kadkhod*" (Isa. 54:12) – R. Samuel b. Nahmani said: There is a controversy [over the meaning of *kadkhod*] between two angels in heaven, Gabriel and Michael. Others say: The dispute is between two Amoraim in the West [the land of Israel]. And who are they? – Judah and Hezekiah, the sons of R. Hiya. One says [it means] onyx, and the other says, jasper. The Holy One, blessed be He, said to them: Let it be as this one says, and as that one says.

84. bMenahot 29b

R. Judah said in the name of Rav, When Moses ascended on high he found the Holy One, blessed be He, engaged in affixing coronets to the letters. He said, [standing] before Him: Master of the Universe, who is holding You back?[10] He said to him: There will arise a man, at the end of many generations, Akiva b. Joseph by name, who will expound upon each tittle heaps and heaps of laws. He said, [standing] before Him: Him, Master of the Universe, show him to me. He said, Turn thee round. Moses went and sat down behind eight rows [of R. Akiva's students] and did not know what they were saying. His strength faltered. But when, upon coming to a certain subject, the students said to [R. Akiva], Rabbi: Whence do you know it? and he said to them, It is a law given to Moses at Sinai, he regained his composure.

He then returned to the Holy One, blessed be He, and said, [standing] before Him, Master of the Universe, Thou hast such a man and Thou givest the Torah through me! He said to him: Be silent, for that is what occurred to Me. He said, [standing] before Him, Master of the Universe, Thou hast shown me his Torah, show me his reward. He said to him: Turn thee round. Moses turned around and saw them weighing out his flesh at the market-stalls.[11] He said, [standing] before Him, Master of the Universe, such Torah, and such a reward! He said to him: Be silent, for that is what occurred to Me.

85. Peirushei R. Saadia Gaon on Genesis, introduction, pp. 187–8

Should one ask, how did differences of opinion among those who received and transmitted the tradition find their way into the Mishna and the Talmud? We would answer: These are not genuine controversies. They

---

10 According to Rashi, this is a description of Moses' perplexity upon observing God affixing coronets to the letters of the completed Torah, that is, adding the small strokes (*tagin*) that serve as flourishes on certain letters. He questioned why the flourishes were needed, when all of mankind awaited the Torah.

11 R. Akiva died a martyr's death at the hands of the Romans during the Hadrianic persecution; see bBerakhot 61b.

only seem to be such when the listener first attends to them. And in truth, [controversies in the Talmud] are of three types.

1   A Sage pretended to disagree with his colleague and provoked him, in order to ascertain the nature of his colleague's opinion. And it is like the way in which Moses pretended to be angry at Aaron and his sons when they burned the goat of the sin-offering (Lev. 10:16), so that they would reveal their own opinion, because Moses could not believe that it had been burned out of ignorance.

2   The matter was heard from the prophet [Moses] in two different forms. In one form, the matter is permitted, in the other, it is forbidden. And one of the Sages preceded his colleague and mentioned the permitted aspect. And the other then followed and mentioned the forbidden. And the words of both are correct, since that matter is indeed permitted in one form and forbidden in another. And an example of this is what Scripture says: "Thou shalt not destroy the trees thereof" (Deut. 20:19), and later, it says, "Only the trees of which you knowest," and so on (Deut. 20:20). And it says, "And if a priest's daughter be married into a common man, she shall not eat of that which is set apart from the holy things" (Lev. 22:12), and later it says, "But if a priest's daughter be a widow...she may eat of her father's bread" (Lev. 22:13). And it makes no difference whether the deciding verse[12] is close to the two parallel verses, or far from them, and whether the two verses themselves are close to each other or not.

3   One of the Sages heard part of a matter, and thought that he had heard the entire matter, and others heard the continuation of the matter, and when the former mentioned to them what he thought about it, they argued against him, saying: We heard the continuation of the matter, and it qualifies your tradition. And an example of this: one finds in the third book of the Pentateuch: "neither shall there come upon thee a garment of two kinds of stuff mingled together" (Lev. 19:19), and he thinks that this prohibition applies to all mixtures. And when he relates this to someone who has read the entire Torah, the latter informs him that Scripture has qualified this rule in the fifth book of the Pentateuch, and limited it: "wool and linen together" (Deut. 22:11). And likewise, similar cases.

86. Otzar Hageonim, bRosh Hashana 34a, p. 60

Answer to the question addressed to our master Hai Gaon, of blessed memory, concerning the shofar [ram's horn] blasts enacted by

---

12 Referring to the last of the thirteen exegetical principles: "Similarly, if two biblical passages contradict each other, they can be harmonized only by a third passage."

R. Abbahu.[13][Question:]...Furthermore, this being a duty to be performed every year, what did they do before R. Abbahu? It cannot be that from the time of the early prophets to the time of R. Abbahu they omitted this for even a single year. And if this duty was known to them, what did R. Abbahu enact, since an enactment implies that the matter had been doubtful and confused. And it is our view that there cannot be two true modes: if the wailing blast (*terua*) is right, then the three brief groaning blasts (*shevarim*) are unimportant, and if the three brief groaning blasts are crucial, then the wailing blast is as naught....

Answer:...What you have written, 'And it is our view that there cannot be two true modes,' is surely right, but this is only so when the two are mutually exclusive. But in an instance where both are suitable, the truth can be manifested in two modes: the brief groans are true and *terua* can also be wailing blasts.

87. Rashi, bKetubot 57a s.v. *ha ka mashma lan*

When two Sages disagree concerning the view of a third, one saying, he said thus, and the other saying, he said so, one of the two must be uttering a falsehood; but when two Amoraim have a legal disagreement concerning monetary or ritual law, each adducing his own reasoning, there is no falsehood involved. Each of the two is putting forward his own argument, one providing a reason for permitting, the other a reason for prohibiting; one makes such an analogy, and the other makes a different analogy, and the principle of "both are the words of the living God" applies. Sometimes one reason is pertinent, and sometimes the other reason is pertinent, since the law's rationale changes according to variations in the circumstances, however minute.

88. Mahberet Hearukh, Helek hadikduk (5:4)

The Sages too use elliptical wording, for example, "both are the words of the living God," which means "both are interpreting the words of the living God," because it is impossible that the words of the living God should have contrary meanings. Rather, the law is in accordance with one of the views and the other is rejected, but incurs the reward for Torah study.

89. Sefer Hamanhig, introduction

And when time obstructed my paths and disturbed my slumber, [expelling me] from the land in which I resided, [impelling me] to leave my desired locale, inherited from my forefathers, and wander about, and journey hither and yon....And my heart resolved – with the permission of my teachers

13 bRosh Hashana 34a.

and mentors – to gird my intellectual loins, and the offspring of my thoughts, to comment upon and to examine the customs of each and every state and each and every town.[14] And I realized that their customs are very different, they are divided into seventy languages, being very numerous, and all are of different forms. And even so, all the rules of our Godly people and their customs and their law, and their fundamentals and their basis and their walls, in their courtyards and edifices – all are built on the foundations of truth. And these and those are the words of the living God, and all [these people] are solicitous about following the words of He who dwells on high, and they run with alacrity to fulfill His will, each and every state according to its writings, each and every community according to its language. Be he a grown man or a young man; one who is hairless or one who is hairy; one who sacrifices an ox, or one who sacrifices a goat; this one will consecrate his libation to his Creator in each and every town, and that one will burn his fat and blood offering with burning religious fervor; this one will arise at midnight and that one will be awoken by the dawn. All were given from one shepherd, and whether they say that it should be lit[15] or whether they say that it should not be lit, both intended but a single thing.

90. Responsa Min Hashamayim, #3

I also asked about the order of the passages in phylactery scrolls. My question was thus: I pray to You, great, mighty and awesome King, discerner of secrets, expounder of the recondite, guardian of the covenant and of loving-kindness, may Your loving-kindness toward us abound this day, and command Your holy angels to advise me regarding an uncertainty that has bewildered us with respect to the order of the passages in the phylacteries. For some scholars say that the existential verses[16] must be in the middle, and that if this order is changed, the phylacteries are invalid. Other scholars say that the passages should be in the order of their appearance in the Torah, and that if this order is changed the phylacteries are invalid. Now, King of Kings, command Your holy angels to advise me in accordance with which view the law is decided, and whose opinion You favor.

And they replied: Both are the words of the living God, and as there is controversy below, so there is above. The Holy One, blessed be He, says that the existential passages should be in the middle, while the entire heavenly entourage says that they should be in the order of their appearance in the Torah. This is the meaning of the verse, "Through them that are nigh unto

---

14 This passage is written in the style of the Book of Esther.

15 See bPesahim 53b, referring to the lighting of a candle on the eve of Yom Kipur.

16 That is, Exodus 13:11 and Deuteronomy 11:13, the verses traditionally known as 'existential,' *havaiot*, from the word "and it shall be" ("*vehaya*") with which they open.

me I will be sanctified, and before all the people I will be glorified" (Lev. 10:3). This is His glory, to mention first the passage that attests to divine sovereignty.

91. Tosafot R. Peretz, bEruvin 13b

"Both are the words of the living God." And should you ask: How is it relevant to say, "both are the words of the living God" regarding matters of ritual law, since if something is forbidden it is not permitted, and if it is permitted it is not forbidden? And our teacher Rabbenu Peretz, may he rest in peace, said that he found a Midrash quoted in the *Tosafot* of R. Yehiel, saying that the Holy One, blessed be He, had taught the Torah to Moses showing forty-nine aspects from which to permit, and forty-nine aspects from which to forbid. Moses said to the Holy One, blessed be He, What shall I do? The Holy One, blessed be He, said to him: Follow the majority view of the sages of the generation; if the majority of the sages of the generation agree on permitting something, it is permitted.

In any event, past events pose a difficulty: for example, the size of the Altar,[17] with one side proving from Scripture that the altar was sixty [*amot*], and the other proving from Scripture that it was twenty. And how can it be relevant to say "both are the words of the living God," as the dictum 'follow the view of the majority of the sages of the generation' is moot, since //there is but one fact of the matter// the Altar had but one size?[18]

But we have to say that all participants in a controversy over matters of fact admit that one of them is mistaken, but one argues from Scripture that the situation should have been in accordance with his particular view, and the other argues from Scripture that the situation should have been in accordance with his particular view, and the application of "both are the words of the living God" in this case means that each one can support his view on the basis of Scripture. But certainly the situation was but one.

Another translation:

But we have to say that all the controversies [that were thought to be over questions of law] were actually over the same question of fact [namely, what norm did God dictate?]. One argues from Scripture that the norm must have been in accordance with his particular view, and the other argues from Scripture that the norm must have been in accordance with his particular view, and the application of "both are the words of the living God" in this case means that each one can support his view on the basis of Scripture. But certainly the norm was but one.

---

17 bZevahim 62a.
18 Here, and below, the text can be interpreted in two ways, and it is not clear which is the intended meaning.

92. Commentary and Rulings of Rabbenu Avigdor, ruling 580, p. 473

"She is the only one of her mother" (Song of Songs 6:9). In the Talmud, it is explained that even though some forbid and others permit, "both are the words of the living God."[19] And it is puzzling how this is possible, for if it is forbidden it is not permitted, if it is pure it is not impure. It is understandable that in the case of the concubine in Gibeah, both views are possible: a fly that he found in his dish, and a hair found in that particular intimate place, but regarding prohibition and permission, it is puzzling. And the matter should be stated as follows: if the majority of the sages of Israel agree to forbid, the Holy One, blessed be He, would concur with them. For thus it is written in the Torah: "follow the majority" (Exod. 23:2), and when another generation arises, in which the majority agree to permit, then the Holy One, blessed be He, will also concur with them. And the proof: things forbidden by the Torah, if mixed with their own kind,[20] even if the forbidden element is of a minor quantity, render the mixture forbidden. This was the law in the generation of our master the eminent scholar Rashi, and now they have all agreed with the view of Rabbenu Tam that [the forbidden element] is nullified if it is a sixtieth part or less. It is a case of this one and that one are the words of the living God. Reported in the name of the saintly R. Vardimus.[21]

93. Milhamot Hashem, foreword

And after paying homage to the Almighty, respected and revered, with all my heart, soul and might, appealing for His willingness to lead me on the path of rectitude, and begging His forgiveness for my errors, I would like to say that my apology for undertaking this work is called for from two perspectives: first, in terms of our duty to inquire into matters of Torah and the precepts, and to bring to light cryptic enigmas, and we are not permitted to be dilatory in acquiring knowledge of the Torah, or negligent in its study. We must not fear any man in reaching legal decisions and in judgment, as it is written: "do not fear any man" (Deut. 1:17); and according to the meaning of this verse and other similar passages in the sayings of the Sages of Israel, of blessed memory. And secondly, because this book does not, overall, come up with any novel idea that has not been previously put forward....

And you who peruse my book, do not assume that I think that all my rejoinders to R. Zerahia [Halevi], of blessed memory, are decisive and

19 bEruvin 13b.
20 See bPesahim 30a.
21 The holy R. Menahem of Dreux, known as R. Vardimus, one of the Tosafists.

compel you to submit to them despite your resolve to reject them; and do not be proud when you succeed in casting doubt on one of my rejoinders in the eyes of those who study them, and do not bend over backwards to pass through the eye of the needle to resist the necessity of my proofs.

This is not the case, for every student of our Talmud knows that in a controversy between commentators, there are no incontrovertible arguments, and in most instances no absolute refutations. For in this discipline, there is no touchstone, as there is in the calculations of geometry and astronomy. But we must apply all our might; and in a controversy it is sufficient for us to eliminate one of the opinions by decisive reasoning, and by confronting it with what we have heard. This strengthens the other side, and supports it with legal explications, talmudic passages, and the endorsement of sound logic. This is the most we can do, and it is the goal of every God-fearing student of the Talmud's wisdom.

Sometimes we defend the opinions of our master [Alfasi] even if they are far from the definitive interpretation of the talmudic passage or passages in question, but our motivation here is to draw the students' attention to the points that favor Alfasi's view, and we do not try to conceal from the reader that which remains doubtful. We are permitted to do this because we are defending the great master and the words of earlier scholars. And this is our duty, as, indeed, the Sages of Israel, of blessed memory, instructed their students. They said: "When one of my rulings is presented to you [in written form] after my death, do not tear it up, and do not rely on it. Do not tear it up, because were I present I might have convinced you with my reasons; do not rely on it, because a judge must rely only on what his eyes behold."[22] We conclude from this that to be on the safe side we have to follow the words of our master strictly, not leniently. But this is in the minority of cases. In the majority of cases, however, it is evident from our book that we believe that, fundamentally, most issues are fully in accordance with the views of our master. Even if there is equal evidence for two possible positions, the law obliges us to follow his opinion, without deviating to the right or to the left. As the Sages taught, "where there are two, and one declares impure and the other, pure; one prohibits, and the other permits, if one of them is greater than his colleague in wisdom and in numbers, his view is to be followed."[23] All the more so since he was earlier, and thus one is precluded from controverting his view, since one would have to say, "the Elder has already handed down his ruling."[24] And this is the covenant that I have put into place regarding all our controversies on matters of halakha.

22 bBaba Batra 131a.
23 bAvoda Zara 7a.
24 bShabat 51a and parallels.

94. Sefer Harimon, p. 131

Indeed, you have already grasped that the Torah is called the Tree of Life…and indeed, trees have branches, and leaves, and bark, and pith, and roots, and each of these is referred to by the designation 'tree,' and there is no differentiation [in applying this term]. So too you will find that the Torah, has numerous internal and external subjects, and all are one Torah and one tree, with no differentiation [between the different parts]. And with regard to what we said, that in some places, you find a subject explained in the Torah in a certain manner, and later, the very same subject explained in a different manner, and further still, it might be explained in an entirely opposed manner: let this not perplex you, and let not your heart lead you astray to hold that these diverse explanations are indeed mutually exclusive and completely distinct. But rather, the entire Torah is made up of true teachings, and they are not differentiated. Because the subject-matter [of the Torah] is but one, as the Talmud interpreted the biblical verse, "And like a hammer that breaketh the rock in pieces" (Jer. 23:29),[25] and everything derives from one source, and all is one.

And even though you find in the words of the Sages, of blessed memory, that this one forbids and that one renders fit, this one rules strictly and that one permits, this one says one thing and that one says another, you should know that these [views] are one, and no one separates his view from the others. Because none of them spread outwards from the tree, and all the opinions are correct. And therefore, even though you might find one explanation for a given matter, and another interpretation, and another, and even more of them, everything is correct, and according to all these explanations was the matter given and constituted. And for this reason the Sages said: The voice issued forth at the time the Torah was given, and this voice was split into seven voices, and each of them was further split into ten facets, so that the original voice came out as seventy facets.[26] And that is the secret[27] of "one voice," and all the facets, which are seventy, come together in one secret, and, according to this secret, there are "seventy facets to the Torah," and all is one.

95. Hidushei Haritba, bEruvin 13b s.v. *eilu veeilu*

Both are the words of the living God. The rabbis of France, of blessed memory, asked, how is it possible that both are the words of the living God, when one forbids and another permits? And they answered: When Moses ascended to heaven to receive the Torah, on every issue he was

---

25 bShabat 88b.
26 Based on Exodus Rabbah 28:6.
27 The numerical value of the word for secret, *sod*, is 70 (60 + 6 + 4).

shown forty-nine aspects to forbid and forty-nine aspects to permit. He asked the Holy One, blessed be He, about this, and He said that it is delegated to the scholars of Israel of each and every generation, and the ruling will be made in accordance with their view. This is so in terms of exegesis, but with respect to truth, there is a secret reason for all this.[28]

96. Drashot Haran, #5 (version 2)

And even if an individual's view corresponds to the truth better than the majority opinion, he must rule out his own opinion in favor of theirs... and it was stated in tractate Baba Metzia concerning R. Eliezer and R. Joshua: R. Joshua arose and said, "It is not in heaven" (Deut. 30:12). What is the meaning of "It is not in heaven"? It had already been given to us by Moses at Mount Sinai, and in it is written, "follow the majority" (Exod. 23:2).[29] My interpretation of this is that the scholar solves the doubtful issues in the Torah – which is the basis of everything – and the prophet must listen to him even against his will. And if, on the strength of his prophecy, the prophet instructs the scholar about the laws of the Torah, he may be ignored altogether. The Sages all saw that R. Eliezer was closer to the truth than they had been, and his signs were genuine and correct, and that the heavenly decision had been as he said. Nonetheless, the Sages decided the matter according to their consensus. That is, since their reason told them to declare [the oven] impure, even though they were aware that their consensus was contrary to the truth, they did not want to declare it pure, and indeed they would have sinned against the Torah had they done so, since their reason compelled them to declare it impure, and the power to decide is delegated to the sages of the given generation, and whatever they decide is what God, may He be blessed, commands.

This point is clearly stated in tractate Hagiga, where they said: And he began to further expound: "The words of the wise are as goads, and as nails well planted are those of masters of assemblies; they were given from one shepherd" (Eccles. 12:11), to teach that just as a goad directs the cow along the furrow in order to bring life to the world, so the words of the Torah direct those who study them from the paths of death to the paths of life.[30] That is to say, that just as a goad keeps the cow in line so that it will not stray hither and thither, and its plowing will be straight, and from this straight path life comes to the world, namely, wheat and produce, so do the words of the Torah direct men's hearts and make them wiser. This is not the kind of wisdom that yields harm or misguided knowledge, but the acquisition of true wisdom, which guides human beings to their ultimate

---

28 Alluding to Kabbala.
29 bBaba Metzia 59b, passage 80.
30 See passage 4.

purpose. To be sure, there is learning that, though opening the human heart, diverts the individual from the path of life to the path of death, leading to wrong ideas that will trouble him. But the Torah does not leave its students with wrong ideas or ignoble attitudes.

And this is suggested in the Talmud,[31] where the Sages state "*vesamtem*" (Deut. 11:18): "*sam tam*"[32] – the Torah is likened to the elixir of life. And this is like one who inflicted a serious injury on his son, placed a dressing on the wound, and said: My son, as long as this dressing remains on your wound, you may eat and drink whatever you desire, and bathe in either hot or cold water, without fear. But if you remove the dressing, it will become infested with maggots. It has already been explained that while studying the Torah one need not fear attacks of lustful thoughts, because being occupied with the Torah will surely save him from all this. This is the meaning of 'the Torah directs the heart of its students.'

And they also said, "Masters of assemblies"[33] – these are the scholars (*talmidei hakhamim*) who sit in various assemblies and apply themselves to the Torah. Some deem a matter pure, others deem it impure, some permit, others prohibit, some declare fit and others disqualify. Lest you say, under these circumstances, how can I learn the Torah?, that is, I do not know which of them has arrived at the truth, Scripture teaches, "given from one shepherd" (Eccles. 12:11), one leader uttered all of them from the mouth of the Master of all deeds, blessed be He, as it is said, "And God spake all these words" (Exod. 20:1). And they interpreted the word "all" as including even the opinions of those who did not arrive at the truth.

Now this matter needs some study. How can we say that both sides of a controversy were spoken by the Almighty? For example, R. Eliezer and R. Joshua had a disagreement, and so one had arrived at the truth, and not the other – yet how could an untruth have been spoken by the Almighty? But this matter is as follows: It is already known that all the written and all the oral law was transmitted to Moses, as it is stated in tractate Megila: R. Hiya b. Abba said in the name of R. Johanan: What is the meaning of the verse "and on them was written according to all the words" (Deut. 9:10)? It teaches us that the Holy One, blessed be He, showed Moses the finer points of the Torah and the finer points of the Scribes and all the new points that the Scribes would formulate in the future. And what are they? Reading the Book of Esther. "Finer points of the Scribes" denotes the controversies and dissenting opinions among the scholars of Israel. And Moses learned all of them from the Almighty. And He gave Moses a rule

---

31 bKidushin 30b.

32 A play on words, taking a word from a biblical verse, *vesamtem*, dropping the initial conjunction (*ve*), and changing the spelling of the first of the remaining two syllables, and the vowelization of the second, to yield the phrase '*sam tam*,' pure elixir.

33 bHagiga 3b, which is paraphrased in the continuation of the paragraph.

for recognizing the truth, and it is "*aharei rabim lehatot*" – follow the majority (Exod. 23:2), and "do not deviate from the sentence which they shall declare unto thee" (Deut. 17:11).[34]

When dissent multiplied among the Sages, if it was one against many, the law was determined according to the view of the majority. If many against many, or one person against another, the law was decided according to what seemed proper to the sages of that generation, since the power to decide had been delegated to them. As it is said: "And thou shalt come unto the priests the Levites, and unto the judge that shall be in those days; and thou shalt inquire; and they shall declare unto thee the judgment" (Deut. 17:9). Furthermore, there is the injunction "do not deviate." For authorization was given to the sages of every generation to settle a scholarly controversy as they saw fit, even if their predecessors were greater and more numerous than they, for we were commanded to follow the consensus of the sages of a given generation, whether they assent to the truth or to its converse; and this point is explained in numerous places.

In like manner the [following] talmudic discussion can be explained: Rabbah bar Nahmani sat upon the trunk of a [fallen] palm and studied. He heard an argument in the heavenly academy. If the spot preceded the white hair, he is impure; if the reverse, he is pure. If [the order is] in doubt, the Holy One, blessed be He, ruled, he is pure; whereas the entire heavenly academy maintained, he is impure. They said: Who will decide for us? Rabbah bar Nahmani will decide, because he is pre-eminent in the laws of tents. But the Angel of Death could not approach him, because he did not interrupt his study. So the Angel of Death simulated the appearance of a squad of horsemen. Rabbah [who was a fugitive] exclaimed: Let him[35] die rather than be delivered into the hands of the state. He then was silenced and expired. As his soul departed, he called out, Pure, pure! A heavenly voice went forth and said: Happy art thou, O Rabbah bar Nahmani, whose body is pure and whose soul hath departed in purity.[36]

This narrative requires explanation. To be sure, no one doubted what had been imparted by God himself: He had declared it pure. They knew with certainty that this was the sole truth. If so, how could they argue that it was impure until they had no recourse but to seek the decision of Rabbah bar Nahmani? This narrative should be interpreted in accordance with what we have written. Although they knew that, according to the truth, "a doubtful spot is pure," they declared it impure, since the determination of the law, having been granted them when they were alive, was their province. And since their reasoning impelled them to declare it impure, it was fitting that it be declared impure, even though this contradicted the

---

34 bMegila 19b.
35 Referring to himself.
36 bBaba Metzia 86a, passage 82; the quotation is inexact.

truth, because this position is dictated by human cognition. Even if the other position constitutes the truth, in matters pertaining to the Torah, it is unseemly to act in accordance with it.

Similarly, the opponents of R. Eliezer did not declare the oven pure,[37] despite the fact that a heavenly voice had been sent to them proclaiming the law to be in accordance with the view of R. Eliezer. And as in this case, they did not doubt the veracity of the heavenly voice, yet they nonetheless declared: the law is not from heaven. For this reason it is stated, "Who will decide for us? Rabbah b. Nahmani." The decision of Rabbah b. Nahmani did not come to him from [privileged] access to the truth, because they had no doubt about that, as I said. Rather, he followed human understanding as dictated by the Torah and the exegetical principles for its interpretation. And their decision to declare it impure was merely the outcome of their limited human intelligence, or due to their having studied the law inattentively during their lifetimes.

97. Or Hashem, maamar 3, klal 5, chapter 2

The second chapter deals with the resolution of certain doubts that might be entertained with respect to this principle. And the puzzle is – regarding the part that is transmitted, namely, the oral law, it is conceivable that controversies and doubts will emerge, but even with regard to the written law, too, it is also possible that one or a number of issues will be controversial. And how can this be otherwise? And it has already happened with regard to this divine Torah that there was a controversy among different sects. Some acknowledge that it is divine, but disagree as to its principles; some believe that part of it is eternal and part not eternal; some disagree on the interpretation of some of the written law, and most of the oral law, and support their positions by saying that they have a tradition from the sages of their people and their elders, such as the Sadducees who are today referred to in the eastern and southern areas as Karaites – [given all this, the question is] Is there anything that the holder of the true belief could be strengthened by, and could confirm his belief? And this problem exists because each of the sectarians is fully committed to his own belief and is impervious to any doubts as to the truth of this belief and the falsity of the beliefs of others. And it must be apparent that the solution is not given to each individual according to his personal conception, for were the gate open to choose among the different beliefs, each doing what was right in his own eyes, no sect would be able to maintain its own faith, for personal conceptions are constantly changing. Given all this,

---

37 bBaba Metzia 59b, passage 80.

how can the holder of the true belief be certain of his convictions? If only I knew.

And indeed, the solution to this doubt is not too difficult, given what is stated in the written law and has been publicized in the tradition, namely, the principles [lit., roots] that we uphold. When an issue pertaining to the Torah is doubtful or controversial, the decision is granted to those who sit in judgment before God, may He be blessed, in the place that He will chose, saying: "If there arise a matter too hard for thee," and so on, "And thou shalt come unto the priests the Levites and unto the judge" (Deut. 17:8–9). But if there is no agreement we are bound to follow the majority. And this obligation exists, according to the tradition, "even if they tell you of right that it is left and of left that it is right."[38] And this teaching was based on the verse: "thou shalt not turn aside from the sentence which they shall declare unto thee, to the right hand, nor to the left" (Deut. 17:11). So much so that the Gemara tells us, regarding the controversy between R. Eliezer and the Sages over the oven of Akhnai,[39] that a heavenly voice went forth and declared, why do you debate with R. Eliezer? And R. Joshua rose to his feet and said, "It is not in heaven" (Deut. 30:12), which was interpreted as saying that the Torah has already been given at Mount Sinai, and in it is written, "Follow the majority" (Exod. 23:2). They explained this to mean, even if the Torah's true intention was in accordance with the view of R. Eliezer, nevertheless, since the majority of the Sages agreed to another view, although it was not the Torah's intention, their view is to be adhered to, since the Torah principle is to follow the majority even if they tell you that right is left.

And this policy really ought to be followed, for were the duty to follow the priests or the Sanhedrin of the contemporary generation conditional on and linked to their concurring with the law, then it would be open to whoever was adamant that the Sanhedrin's ruling was not in accordance with the halakha to dispute them and disobey them. And this would also bring about the proliferation of controversy in Israel, and the Torah would become like a thousand sets of laws [lit., a thousand Torahs]. But given this obligation to follow the judges of the current generation, it is impossible for controversies or doubts regarding any law of the Torah to remain, unless the issue is doubtful to all or most of them, which is very unlikely. And in the event of such an improbable contingency, there is a specific method for resolving this doubt according to the principles of tradition. Given all this, one who holds a belief that is in accordance with the view of the judges or the majority can be confident and is, to the greatest extent possible, spared misgivings and qualms.

38 Sifre Deuteronomy 154.
39 bBaba Metzia 59b, passage 80.

98. Sefer Hanitzahon, sec. 321 (p. 176)

"Masters of assemblies" (Eccles. 12:11) – The Sages explain in tractate Hagiga: These are the scholars who sit in various assemblies and apply themselves to the Torah; some deem a matter impure, others deem it pure. And the Talmud concludes, Lest someone say: Under these circumstances, how can I learn the Torah? They were given from one shepherd – one shepherd gave them, one leader uttered them, as it is written, "And God spake all these words," and so on (Exod. 20:1).[40] And we read in tractate Eruvin, "R. Abba stated in the name of Samuel: For three years there was a controversy between the house of Shammai and the house of Hillel, the former asserting: The law is in accordance with our views, and the latter asserting: The law is in accordance with our views. And a heavenly voice (*bat kol*) went forth and said: Both [lit., these and those] are the words of the living God, but the law is in accordance with the view of the house of Hillel. For what reason did the house of Hillel merit the law's being decided in accordance with their view? Because they were kindly and modest, and so on. This teaches you that he who humbles himself, the Holy One, blessed be He, raises up," and so on.[41]

Now this is difficult to understand. If the house of Shammai render a thing pure and the house of Hillel render it impure, how can both views be sustained as the words of the living God, and how could Moses, our teacher, may he rest in peace, receive both rulings from the Almighty? For surely if he received the ruling "pure," he did not receive "impure," and if he received "impure," he did not receive "pure." And if the intention is to claim that both views are correct, inasmuch as each side adduces the reasons for its view, but the view of the house of Hillel corresponds to that received by Moses our teacher, may he rest in peace, from the Almighty, how can the Talmud say that they were "given from one shepherd," and so on? Furthermore, why does the Talmud raise the question, "For what reason did the house of Hillel merit the law's being decided in accordance with their view?" Is it not because their opinion corresponds to the law? And what is the relevance of the claim: "because they were kindly and modest"? How does the kindness of their behavior have any bearing on the veracity of their words? Now it could be argued that God told Moses our teacher, may he rest in peace: in the future, the sages of Israel will differ over My words, A saying this and B saying that. But this is impossible, for were it true, what would be the significance of the question raised in the first chapter of tractate Gitin: My son Eviatar says this, and my son Jonathan says that. And he queries this: Can there possibly be uncertainty in the mind of the Holy One, blessed

40 bHagiga 3b, passage 4.
41 bEruvin 13b, passage 39.

be He?[42] Furthermore, were this so, then Moses our teacher, may he rest in peace, and all Israel, did not know whether the thing was pure or impure until the heavenly voice confirmed that the law was in accord with the view of the house of Hillel. And if Moses our teacher, may he rest in peace, had been told to act in accordance with the view of the house of Hillel, then we are again confronted with the problem of the relevance of inquiring: "For what reason did the house of Hillel merit the law's being decided in accordance with their view?"

Therefore, it appears that God, blessed be He, gave the Torah and the thirteen exegetical principles for its interpretation, [for the use of] every single sage according to his intellectual capacity, provided that he occupies himself with it and studies it with all his might, without dereliction. And if it appears to the Sanhedrin, on the basis of the Torah and the exegetical principles, that a thing is pure, it is pure. And should a future Sanhedrin arise, to whom it appears that according to the Torah and the exegetical principles that very thing is impure, it will be impure. Because God, blessed be He, who gave us the Torah, made it dependent on the sages' views, based on their perceptions. And concerning this it is said, "And from Zion shall go forth the Law" (Isa. 2:3), meaning, an understanding of the Torah will go forth today that did not go forth yesterday. This is the meaning of the verse, "Therefore, with joy shall ye draw water from the wells of salvation" (Isa. 12:3), which Jonathan[43] translated "a new Torah." This is to exclude the reading of the heretics, who interpret this verse as referring to the renewal effected by the birth of Jesus, which cannot be, for it is written, "with joy shall ye draw water," and still today, in the exile, due to our many sins, we have but grief from the renewal wrought by his teachings. The verse refers to innovative scholarly interpretations.

And we learn in tractate Sanhedrin: Scripture says: "with you in judgment" (II Chron. 19:6). The judge should be concerned only with what his own eyes behold.[44] Similarly, concerning the consecration of the new moon: Scripture says "you" three times, meaning: you – even inadvertently; you – even by error; you – even wilfully wrong.[45] The Talmud intends to say that if the court has decided about the new moon by error, even so, we have to fix the dates of the Festivals according to their erroneous computation. Furthermore, there is the case in which Rabban Gamaliel commanded R. Joshua to appear before him with his purse and stick on what was, according to R. Joshua's calculations, the Day of Atonement.[46]

---

42 bGitin 6b, passage 76.
43 Aramaic translation of Scriptures attributed to Jonathan b. Uziel.
44 bSanhedrin 6b.
45 bRosh Hashana 25a.
46 mRosh Hashana 2:9.

Furthermore, we always prevent the New Year from falling on Sunday, Wednesday or Friday, due to [burial of] dead persons and the willow-branches,[47] and were this not as I said, how would the scriptural mandate [Rosh Hashana] be uprooted for the sake of the Rabbinic willow branches? And it is written, "Thou shalt not turn aside from the sentence which they shall declare unto thee, to the right hand, nor to the left" (Deut. 17:11) and the Sages, of blessed memory, explain, "Even if they tell you of right that it is left" and so on,[48] and another example is, the Sages, of blessed memory, say, "That which cannot live is *treifa*."[49] [Nonetheless, Maimonides, in Laws concerning Shehita 10:12–13, says that if we know, on the basis of our tradition and medical knowledge that] an animal is about to die, and it does not have any of the defects enumerated by the Sages, it is permitted, as it is said, "according to the law which they shall teach thee" (Deut. 17:11). Similarly, the law of the rebellious elder.[50] He is put to death even though he claims to have a tradition and they argue [against it] based on their own reasoning, because the Torah was given to be implemented according to the interpretation of the majority, as it is said, "follow the majority" (Exod. 23:2).

And it is explicitly stated[51] that the law varies with the majority opinion, as we have learned, "R. Akabia b. Mehalalel said to his son as he was dying: My son, retract from four dicta that I have stated. [The son said:] Why did you not recant? He said: I heard them from the majority and they heard [the contrary opinion] from the majority. I adhered to my tradition and they adhered to theirs. But since you have only heard it from one individual and they heard it from the majority, it is better to abandon the opinion of one individual and adhere to that of the many." And for the same reason R. Joshua said, "it is not in heaven,"[52] as I have already explained.[53] And just as "this month shall be for you" (Exod. 12:2) is interpreted as meaning, it is up to your discretion, so it is possible to interpret "and I give you two tablets" (Exod. 24:12) and "I gave you my law" (Prov. 4:2).

99. Maase Efod, foreword (p. 6)

And to one who says that it is impossible that this work, the Talmud, was singled out as constituting mankind's utmost accomplishment, as it includes

47 Were the New Year, Rosh Hashana, to fall on either Wednesday or Friday, Yom Kipur would fall on Friday or Sunday, respectively, and burials would have to be postponed. Were Rosh Hashana to fall on Sunday, Hoshana Raba would fall on the Sabbath, precluding the rite of the willow branches (*arava*).
48 Sifre Deuteronomy 154.
49 mHulin 3:1.
50 bSanhedrin 88a.
51 mEduyot 5:7.
52 bBaba Metzia 59b, passage 80.
53 In sec. 148.

numerous things that cannot represent human accomplishment, such as many of the legends it contains and some of the stories. And who say that furthermore, this work contains the great controversies that arose among the Sages with regard to the laws of the Torah, in which only one of the two sides is correct and the other is groundless, and it is impossible to derive an everlasting achievement from something groundless. About these controversies it has already been stated: "When there multiplied students of Shammai and Hillel who did not attend to their teachers sufficiently, controversy multiplied in Israel, and the Torah became like two sets of laws [lit., two Torahs]."[54] And the said work is utterly replete with these and similar controversies.

The answer to him is that the concept of talmudic wisdom does not encompass all that is included in this work. For were this the case, how could the wisdom of David and Solomon and all the other Sages who lived before the redaction of the Talmud be complete? How could you think that the wisdom of Solomon was such as to encompass this entire work, written thirteen hundred years after his time? And it has been said of Rabban Johanan b. Zakai, who lived before the destruction of the Temple, that his knowledge omitted nothing from the written law, the Mishna, the Talmud, and the laws...[55] yet the Talmud was compiled more than four hundred years after the destruction. And the Talmud is mentioned in numerous places by Sages who lived years before it was compiled.

Therefore, the meaning of 'Talmud' must be something else. It is the true examination of the laws of the divine precepts by the force of reason, to infer one thing from another and to gain understanding by means of the thirteen exegetical principles, and to grasp the few Sinaitic legal rules received from Moses our teacher, may he rest in peace, that are not mentioned in the divine Torah, or are mentioned only by intimation (*remez*). And the master [Maimonides] has already explained this in the first chapter of his Laws concerning the Study of the Torah.

100. Akeidat Yitzhak, gate 12 (p. 90)

It is comparable to two wise men appearing before the king. One might cover his head, the other might remove his turban. Even if their actions differ in this respect, in line with what each of them considers respectful conduct, they are both in agreement on the point that it is fit and proper to pay homage to the king. Our Sages, of blessed memory, took pains to instruct us about this in their remarks in tractate Kidushin. What is meant by "when they speak with their enemies at the gate"? Said R. Hiya b. Abba: Even father and son, teacher and student, who apply themselves

54 bSota 47b, passage 198.
55 bSuka 28a.

to the Torah at the same gate, become enemies of each other, yet they do not budge from there until they come to love each other, as it is said, "Vaheb [love] in Suphah" (Num. 21:14); love at the end.[56] That is to say, at first when they conduct themselves differently or express independent opinions, it looks as if they are altogether opposed to each other, like the two wise men before the king, where it might appear that one seeks to pay respect to the king and the other does not. But when they discuss the matter and make their respective intentions known, it is clear that the very honor that the one would pay to the king is the intention of the other as well, and on this point they are united. For this reason it is said in the Talmud: "Some deem a matter pure, others deem it impure, some declare fit and others disqualify, some acquit, and others find liable, and both are the words of the living God."[57] For the intention of all of them is to establish the Torah and the precepts in the most perfect way, to gratify the will of God who bestowed them upon us. Therefore, all such opinions are within the framework of this constraint, and sustain it, as it is written, All of them "were given from one shepherd" (Eccles. 12:11). And for this reason they said, "Every controversy that is for the sake of heaven, its end is to be sustained," and so on.[58] That is, if it is like the controversy between the houses of Shammai and Hillel, namely, if it is such that the general intent of the one is the same as that of the other, the only differences being with respect to particular details.

101. Lev Avot, mAvot 5:17

In the same vein as the customary interpretations of the commentators, I would like to add a sound new interpretation of my own. It is known that debating all the conflicting sides of an issue in the course of study and learning will yield the truth about that matter, and clarify it beyond any doubt. Hence, doubts, comments and queries are the principal avenue for reaching this objective, and the philosopher himself[59] attests that doubting makes people wiser. Now this point should be kept in mind by all those who seek the truth in books and in wisdom. It is known that doubts cannot be allayed unless the two sides to the question confront each other, as querier and respondent, to bring the law to light. This point is hidden from those who ridicule what the Sages said, namely, that if the members of the Sanhedrin had, to a man, arrived at a unanimous death sentence, the accused was not to be executed, but if the majority was for the death

---

56 bKidushin 30b, passage 3; the quotation is inexact.
57 Paraphrasing bHagiga 3b, passage 4. The concluding "and both are the words of the living God" is from bEruvin 13b, passage 39.
58 mAvot 5:17, passage 37.
59 Aristotle, *Magna Moralia*, 1200b.

sentence while a minority called for acquittal, the sentence was carried out. Even though this is dictated by scriptural decree, as the Gemara states, I heard a very apt explanation for it attributed to Maimonides. It is, in fact, what I have said myself – to underscore the fact that in the absence of an opposing opinion that queries, argues and subjects a given view to rigorous investigation, it is impossible to arrive at the truth, and it is quite possible that all participants will err. This is close to the explanation offered by the Mishna [in Eduyot] as to why our holy master [R. Judah the Prince] includes the minority opinion along with the majority opinion even though he knows that the law is not in accordance with that minority opinion.

Therefore the Mishna [in Avot] says that when the argument is for the sake of heaven, that is, when the intention of the contending parties is to bring the truth to light, which would not occur otherwise, it is certain that this type of controversy is ultimately sustained. For even though the truth will be upheld and sustained by one party, all the opinions will be sustained, and will be cited together. Since their intention is to ascertain which alternative is correct, the opposing views both must be assessed, and the ensuing debate will then reveal the truth. Therefore the law mandates that all the contending sides should be mentioned and preserved together, even if only one of them is true.

102. Midrash Shmuel, mAvot 5:19

And afterwards he explains the question of controversy and says: "Every controversy that is for the sake of heaven, its end is to be sustained." The commentators were faced with a problem that warrants examination: the two opposed views, granted their pious intent, nevertheless contradict each other, and differ as to truth and falsity. It necessarily follows that if one of them is true, the other must be false. And how can it be asserted that any controversy is sustained, when only one of the two opinions can be sustained? Furthermore, given this, what is the difference between the controversy between Hillel and Shammai and that of Korah and his congregation, since in both controversies, one party is inevitably wrong?

I propose to explain it as follows. It is known that the controversy between Hillel and Shammai was for the sake of heaven, to elicit the true law, therefore, as far as their reward in the world to come is concerned, both sides are equal. Even if the house of Shammai were not right, and the law is not in accordance with their opinion, nevertheless, since their controversy was for the sake of heaven, their words are alive and persist, so that they will receive their reward for them. Hence the expression, "its end is to be sustained." But when the argument is not for the sake of heaven, like the dissent of Korah and his congregation, it will not be sustained in the end – the dissenters will descend alive to the netherworld.

And R. Menaham Hameiri wrote:

> It is puzzling: in what way is it apt to say of a controversy that it
> will be sustained? After all, only one of the two opposing views
> will ultimately be sustained. And the term 'controversy' covers
> two sides, and how can both be sustained? It seems to me that the
> term 'controversy' [here] refers only to the side challenging an
> existing view. That is, when one party intends to do something,
> and states that this action is proper, and rules that it be carried
> out, there is as yet no controversy. But when the other responds,
> saying that the proposed action is not proper, and the opposite
> course should be taken, then there is a controversy. Therefore,
> 'controversy' does not encompass both sides, but only one,
> namely, that which challenges an existing view. The Mishna
> intends to say that if this second party puts forward its arguments,
> not with the aim of provocation and competitiveness, but in order
> to reveal the truth, then its words will be sustained. However, if it
> argues only for the sake of provocation, then its words will not be
> sustained, but only those of the other side.[60]

In my opinion, the Meiri's response does not suffice and the problem
has not been resolved. It is possible that while the second party, who challenges the first, does so for the sake of heaven, nevertheless the opinion of
the first was correct and exact, whereas that of the challenger, who seeks
to refute him, is in error, and thus it transpires that the second opinion,
which challenges the first, is in fact wrong, and the first is right. Therefore
the 'controversy,' viz., the second opinion, is not sustained in the end, since
it is wrong. So the difficulty remains unresolved.

But it may be suggested that what the Mishna means in stating that a
controversy that is for the sake of heaven will be sustained in the end is
that the two parties will go on debating perpetually, for today they will
argue about one thing and tomorrow about another, and the controversy
will be sustained and perpetuated throughout their entire lives, and moreover, the number of their days and years may even be increased. But when
the dissent is not for the sake of heaven, it will not be sustained in the end;
the debate will somehow exhaust its participants. They will come to an
end, and then they will expire, as in the case of Korah.

It could also be said that the controversy between Hillel and Shammai,
and similar controversies, in which some disqualify and others render fit,
are both the words of the living God, as the Sages said. The meaning is
that all these opinions have heavenly roots that nourish them, and that
are nourished from above, and everything depends on the particular time

---

60 Commentary on mAvot 5:19.

and place indicated from above in *atzilut*.[61] Is it not the case that Abraham our forefather observed the entire Torah, even down to the laws permitting the preparation of food on Festivals for the Sabbath?; and yet Jacob, who was the chosen of the Patriarchs, married two sisters, which is forbidden by the Torah, and Judah cohabited with his daughter-in-law Tamar, which is forbidden by the Torah, and nevertheless, he is the progenitor of the entire royal House of David. But surely, all things descend from their roots above in accordance with the needs of the time and the place, and all in line with the truth. Hence every controversy that is for the sake of heaven is sustained in the end, because both opinions have roots and existence above. And these are ancient principles, and this suffices for the discerning mind.

103. Asara Maamarot, Maamar hikur hadin, part 2, 17–18

The Sages' dictum, "some of them forbid, some of them permit, but they are all the words of the living God"[62] is well known and poorly understood. The manifest truth of the matter is that any dissent that is for the sake of heaven – its end is to be sustained, and each aspect of it will prove true . . . but the Torah explicitly says to decide the law that is to be applied according to the majority, for "all its ways are peaceful" (Prov. 3:17). But this does not mean that the rejected minority view is regarded as false, for there is nothing close to falsehood, heaven forbid, in what was said at Sinai, and engraved on the Tablets, as we explained. On the contrary, by means of this comprehensive reflection, the eternal Guardian of truth judges men's actions, the proper and the improper, all according to one's actions at the given time. For what was proper before the sin, namely, Adam and his wife's being naked, became improper after the sin. Thus the assessment of what is proper and improper with respect to nakedness is a matter of context [lit., its time], and both are the words of the living God, Who rules over opposites and temporal changes. It never happened that any of the Sages argued for permitting the raven and forbidding the dove. What did they argue about? About things that have two true and justified facets; some explain the permissive facet, and some the prohibitive facet, according to the place and time. Hence, the permission and the prohibition are both true, and the discretion of the court decides which law is fitting to be deemed law to be applied. This implies that there is a law that is not to be applied, but this is as has been explained. . . .

Similarly, we find that eating meat was absolutely forbidden to Adam, except that which descended from heaven, that which the ministering

---

61 A Kabbalistic concept.
62 bHagiga 3b; the quotation is inexact.

angels would roast for him[63] or meat of an animal that he killed for the sake of its blood or hide.[64] But partaking of meat was unconditionally permitted to Noah and his descendants, and to the Israelites some of it was permitted because a new prohibition was imposed on some of it, but in the future, "The Almighty will loosen the bonds" by adding to some [of the animals] the marks of purity....

These are opposites and rulings that are changed, such as the permission to eat meat, and its prohibition, altogether or to some degree, as times change, and all of them are the words of the living God. As long as courts on earth had not been appointed, the Law was issued from the heavenly court, "And a word in due season, how good is it" (Prov. 15:23). But now the Torah has been given, and the law of following the majority has been instituted, so there is no authority but the judges of a given time, since one court may annul the rulings of another which preceded it by many years, and even a smaller court may contradict another, if the controversy arises regarding the understanding of the Torah, one interpreting and teaching on the basis of one exegetical principle, and the other, on the basis of another, for example, the inclusive rule and the exclusionary rule; or, the general and the particular. However, if a single judge in the first court were to hold the interpretation that the second court would eventually uphold, or, a single judge in the second court were to hold the interpretation of the first court, each one would be deemed a "rebellious elder" in his own generation if he ruled that his opinion should be implemented in practice, given that in each case the opposite opinion was upheld by the contemporary court.

We learn from this that the ruling of the court is true in both cases, and the desirable act is that which conforms to the view of the majority of the court at the given time and place, provided we are speaking about those who sit in the Hall of Hewn Stone and their followers thereafter, who orient their hearts toward the Omnipresent.

104. Yam Shel Shlomo, foreword to tractate Baba Kama

Solomon, of blessed memory, said in his wisdom, "And furthermore my son, be admonished: of making many books there is no end" (Eccles. 12:12). And the Sages explain this verse in the Talmud, saying that one is obliged to heed the Sages, who are also called Scribes, in all that they added and innovated with respect to the oral tradition, which is law given

---

63 bSanhedrin 59b.
64 *Asara Mamarot*, Maamar hikur hadin, part 4, 18. Disputing the position of the *Tosafot* on bSanhedrin 56b, that only meat from animals that had died from natural causes could be eaten by Adam, the author claims Adam could kill animals for either their hides or their blood, which would be used for medicinal purposes.

to Moses at Sinai, in addition to the written law, which is, in terms of quantity, the quintessence of brevity, yet contains a vast expanse of quality.[65] The Sages also added enactments to safeguard earlier enactments, as anticipated by the wise one [King Solomon], who affixed supports[66] to the Torah, as it is said, "pondered, and sought out" (Eccles. 12:9). And of what the Sages have said from the time of Moses, may he rest in peace, to this day, regarding all this, it is said, "The words of the wise are as goads, (all) were given from one shepherd" (Eccles. 12:11). So as to preempt any bewilderment about their controversies and widely diverging opinions, such as one rendering a thing impure, another rendering it pure, one forbidding what the other permits, one disqualifying and the other rendering fit, one exempting and the other holding liable, one casting away and one drawing close: as long as their intention is for the sake of heaven – and the early authorities even disregarded heavenly voices – they are all the words of the living God. It is as if it all have been received directly from the Almighty and from Moses. To be sure, Moses himself did never uttered two contradictory statements about the same subject, nevertheless, the Sage made this analogy due to the validity and strength of the positions [expressed], since in terms of validity there is no difference between a conclusion deduced logically, and a tradition transmitted orally from Moses at Sinai, even if the latter would not necessarily have been deduced by logic.

The Kabbalists explain this as follows. All souls were present at Mount Sinai and received the Torah through forty-nine channels – seven times seven, "refined seven times" (Ps. 12:7); these were the sounds that were both audible and visible, "And all Israel perceived the thunderings" (Exod. 20:15); and the differences are due to reception by different channels, each person according to his ability and according to the ability of his upper soul, according to its level, high or low. One individual is far from the other to such an extent that one concludes that a thing is pure, the other going to the opposite extreme, declaring it impure, while a third takes an intermediate position between these poles. It is all true, and this has to be understood.

Therefore, the wise one [King Solomon] says that since the words of the true Sages constitute the words of the living God even in their controversies, this is all the more so when they concur, if so, you should ponder why Moses did not write down from the Almighty everything in an unambiguous manner so that no doubts would arise regarding the law, and the Torah would have had but a single facet, and not forty-nine. Furthermore, everything else in need of a special enactment, should have been explicitly written down by Moses, so that should one find a gaping

---

65 bEruvin 21b.
66 Literally, affixed handles, *oznaim*, alluding, through its common root, to the verb "pondered" (*izen*).

lacuna, one could fence it in, and add to its structure that which ought to be added, or [remove] that which is not to be added, in line with the principle, "the public should not be subjected to decrees unless the majority of the public is able to endure them."[67]

And the response of the wise one to this question is, "of making many books there is no end," that is, it is impossible to write books that achieve this, because there is literally no end or point to it, and even were the heavens parchment and all the seas ink, nevertheless, because of [the Torah's] richness, they would not suffice for even one chapter, with all of its uncertainties and all the inferences that can be drawn from it, in addition to all that the scholars of Israel, by dint of their profound study, can deepen, change and augment it with. Furthermore, even were all this written in the Torah, how much more so would it still have required supplementation; what I mean to say is, there would be additions to the additions. What I mean to say is that it is impossible that there would be no uncertainties, changes and yet profounder insights resulting from the study of the first round of additions, until this second round of additions would be a thousand thousand times more numerous than the first. All in all, as the wise one said and informed us, there is no possibility of formulating and clarifying all the uncertainties regarding the Torah in such a way that human understanding will be able to grasp it, without unending differences of opinion. Therefore the Torah was given to the scholars who are embedded in every generation, each according to the cast of his intellect, and the measure of his intellectual ascendancy, to add whatever he will be shown by heaven. And if he thinks it correct to render a thing pure, he receives divine assistance in doing so. Blessed be the Merciful One who bestows wisdom on the wise.

105. Derekh Haim, mAvot 5:17

"Every controversy that is for the sake of heaven," and so on. We can ask, what is the relevance of this dictum to those preceding it? Furthermore, after stating, "every controversy that is for the sake of heaven," what is the point in asking, "what controversy is for the sake of heaven?" Indeed, every controversy intended by the parties for the sake of heaven qualifies. The controversy between R. Meir and R. Judah, and those of the other Sages – were they not for the sake of heaven? Furthermore, the Mishna seems to be contradicting itself. First it says "what controversy is for the sake of heaven? The controversy between Hillel and Shammai." It implies that any other controversy is not for the sake of heaven. But then it immediately goes on to say: "And that which is not for the sake of heaven?

67 bAvoda Zara 36a.

The controversy of Korah and his congregation." And it is known that Korah and his congregation took issue with God, may He be blessed. And this implies that any other controversy, in which there is no taking issue with God, may He be blessed, would be sustained in the end. And if so, then the first part contradicts the second.

Another difficulty is that it says, "Every controversy that is for the sake of heaven, its end is to be sustained." But it is impossible for two contradictory views to be true, and hence, conjointly upheld, for surely one must be repudiated and one upheld. If so, why does it say "its end is to be sustained"?

It should be explained why this particular dictum appears here. It is because earlier, [the Mishna] enumerates "four attributes of those who sit in the presence of Sages." And we explained that it refers to those who sit before the Sages, and hear the views of the Sages, and the whole dictum of the four attributes of students is as follows: Some students absorb both sides of a controversial matter, and they are called 'sponges'; and some do not accept even one view, and they are called 'funnels'; and some accept the opinions that are contrary to the law and discard the right opinion, and they are called 'strainers'. And some accept the received law and discard all other opinions, and they are called 'sieves.' And of this it is said that if the controversy of the Sages whose opinions the students accept is for the sake of heaven, it is sustained in the end. And the meaning of this is that at least during the lifetime of the parties to the controversy, it will not be negated.

And even should you say that sometimes a dissenting view is negated even during the lifetime of its proponent, indeed, the explanation given for "its end is to be sustained" does not imply that the controversy will certainly be sustained and must necessarily be sustained, but simply that it may possibly be sustained. The Mishna is saying that even though controversy is abhorrent to the Holy One, blessed be He, and because it is abhorrent, it is not sustained, nevertheless, when the controversy is for the sake of heaven it has a chance of survival. And God, may He be blessed, does not cause it to be effaced, as He does with controversies that are not for the sake of heaven, which He indeed effaces so that they no longer exist. For controversies are alien to God, may He be blessed, as it is said, "Love peace and loathe controversy."[68] Furthermore, when it is fully for the sake of heaven, God, may He be blessed, preserves the controversy. And it does not say, 'controversy that is for the sake of heaven is sustained,' to preclude reading this as saying that controversy for the sake of heaven is sustained only in the beginning but not in the end. Therefore it stresses that "its end is to be sustained." But though a controversy that is not for the sake of heaven may be sustained for some time – and indeed, several controversies

68 Derekh Eretz Zuta 9.

did persist for a time – nonetheless, in the end it will be effaced, because God, may He be blessed, causes the controversy to be effaced.

And we need not query the possibility of sustaining the two opposed sides of the controversy, as this presents no difficulty. For even if a controversy has been resolved from the perspective of the individuals who held the different opinions, given that the law was decided in accordance with one of those opinions, this does not mean that the controversy is "not to be sustained," as God, may He be blessed, has not negated this controversy. For the meaning of "not to be sustained" is that God, may He be blessed, ensures that it will not be sustained. And with regard to the controversy between the house of Shammai and the house of Hillel, even though a heavenly voice went forth [proclaiming] "the law is in accordance with the view of the house of Hillel," this heavenly voice did not efface the controversy because it was hated, for this dispute was indeed highly cherished. It went forth only to teach that law to those who wished to know what that law was. And indeed, the heavenly voice itself stated "both are the words of the living God," and hence it preserved the dissenters' view and did not efface the controversy. Therefore, this dictum follows the preceding one, to affirm that if the dissenters were arguing for the sake of heaven, their views would not be effaced, and the students who accepted their teachings did not accept opinions that would be effaced. But if their controversy was not for the sake of heaven, but only to promote rivalry, then their dispute would be effaced, and the views their students received from them would all be null and void. And this is the proper interpretation, and it will be further elaborated on below.

The Mishna says: "What controversy is for the sake of heaven? The controversy between Shammai and Hillel." For their controversy was completely for the sake of heaven – from no perspective can it be construed as not for the sake of heaven. For it cannot be said that had they taken greater pains to ascertain the law, by further reflection or by seeking the counsel of someone else, then the dispute could have been averted, and hence, was not purely for the sake of heaven – this is not so, since both are the words of the living God. And since both are the words of the living God, how could it even be claimed that it was possible for them to have arrived at the truth, as this would entail negation of words of the living God?! And a controversy such as this is certainly for the sake of heaven. But other controversies, even if they were for the sake of heaven, do have some aspect or element that is not completely for the sake of heaven. For it is possible that the parties in question could have ended their controversy by prodigious study, or by consulting numerous scholars, and so on. Even though the intention in such a case is for the sake of heaven, nevertheless it states that the controversy itself is not entirely for the sake of heaven, since it could have been otherwise. And this is unlike the controversy between Hillel and Shammai, which was certainly for the sake of heaven, and in fact, was a controversy that God, may He be blessed, desired, because [through it] each of the schools would reveal the words of the living God. Therefore, of all the controversies that have ever taken place, this controversy is the only one that is [totally] for the sake of heaven.

The Mishna goes on to ask, "And which controversy is not for the sake of heaven?" This means that it is totally not for the sake of heaven, to the point where it has no heavenward intent at all. For sometimes there are controversies that, while motivated by vain conceit, nevertheless the controversy itself has some element that is for the sake of heaven, in that it claims that it is fitting to act in a certain way, hence within the controversy there is some aspect that is for the sake of heaven and hence good, and each of the parties is asserting, I serve God. But in the dissent of Korah and his congregation there was no aspect whatsoever for the sake of heaven, as indeed it is written, "when they strove against the Lord" (Num. 26:9), for in taking issue with Moses and Aaron, their dispute was actually with God, may He be blessed. Thus this controversy was entirely not for the sake of heaven, and could not have any lasting existence at all.

And one should not raise a difficulty by juxtaposing the first dictum to the later dictum, since certainly there is no incompatibility here; it is certainly not a contradiction. For the dissent of Korah and his congregation, because it was entirely not for the sake of heaven, could not have any lasting existence at all, as is seen from the fact that the earth opened up and swallowed them alive. And to be so consumed is utterly fit for this type of controversy, which is altogether not for the sake of heaven. But as for other controversies, which are not entirely not for the sake of heaven, but do have an aspect that is for the sake of heaven – even though they certainly are not sustained in the end, they nevertheless are not negated in the same manner. To conclude, to the extent that the controversy is not for the sake of heaven, it is negated. And similarly, in the first statement, to the extent that it is for the sake of heaven, the controversy is sustained, for other controversies, that were not entirely for the sake of heaven, were not sustained to the extent that the controversy between the house of Shammai and the house of Hillel was. For certainly, God, may He be blessed, sustained this controversy because it was loved by Him, may He be blessed, as will be explained. And we have now resolved all the problems, and there is no doubt as to this explication; nor are contrived solutions required.

And another question arises. What is the reason that a controversy that is for the sake of heaven is sustained in the end, but one that is not for the sake of heaven is not sustained in the end? Even if it is certain that disputes are hated, this is still problematic, since there are other things hated by the Holy One, blessed be He, about which this is not said. And if you are to understand the words of the Sages, which will illuminate the connection between this mishnaic teaching and those preceding it, we must discuss this matter at some length, so that the teaching will be understood according to its inherent truth. You must know that controversy cannot be sustained, and this is because a controversy refers to two opposites. And the existence of fire utterly precludes that of its opposite, namely, water; similarly, the existence of water precludes the existence of its opposite, namely, fire. It is, therefore, impossible for two contrary things to exist together, because if so, there would be two opposites in the same thing. And should you argue that each of the two could exist separately, since fire and water, which are opposites, indeed exist on their own, and the two sides to a controversy could likewise each stand alone – this is definitely not comparable. To be sure, fire and water are two opposites in different things, and since they inhere in different things, there is a possibility of separate existence for each of them. But people, who are human, though divided into individuals, constitute a single whole. And this is particularly so in the case of Israel, which is absolutely a single people, and it is impossible for this single entity to be separated into two distinct bodies. If controversy, in which one side is the opposite of the other, could in fact be sustained, there would be two opposites in the same entity, and therefore, controversy cannot be sustained in the end.

Furthermore, it should be noted that fire and water are also in the same thing, namely, the world, which is one; indeed, this coexistence of fire and water, despite their being opposites, follows from the statement that every controversy that is for the sake of heaven, its end is to be sustained. And what this means is that the differentiation into fire and water is for the sake of heaven, for God, may He be blessed, created each one of them, and each one of them obeys His will: fire does so on its own, and water does so on its own. And this is certainly because it is a division that is for the sake of heaven and hence it is sustained, because such a controversy, when it is for the sake of heaven, can be sustained even though the sides are opposed, as God, may He be elevated and blessed, can unite two opposites. For even though, in themselves, they are separated and opposites, nevertheless, as far as God, may He be blessed, is concerned, they coalesce, as God, may He be blessed, who is one, is the cause of the two opposites. And in being the cause of the two opposites, this itself reflects His unity, may He be blessed, because were He the cause of only one of these things – were He, say, the cause of only the fire – then, God forbid, there would be another cause for the opposite of fire, which is water, the opposite of fire. Since He, may He be blessed, is the cause of the opposites, He is one, because there is none other than Him, as He is the cause of everything, even of opposites, and for the opposites that He is the cause of, He, may He be blessed, is one. And we have explained this in a number of places in the work *Gevurot Hashem*: that God, may He be blessed, who is one, is the cause of opposites, and therefore a controversy that is for the sake of heaven, even though it inherently constitutes a dichotomy of opposites which, by themselves, cannot coexist, nevertheless, from the perspective of God, may He be blessed, who is the cause of the opposites, the two opposites are one, since they incline toward God, may He be blessed, who is one, and He exercises His will upon them as He, may He be blessed, pleases. Therefore opposites that cannot exist together, nonetheless – from the perspective of God, may He be blessed, who is all-encompassing – coalesce, even if they are opposites. This is the sense of their dictum: "Every controversy that is for the sake of heaven, its end is to be sustained." And they said: What controversy is for the sake of heaven? The controversy between the house of Shammai and the house of Hillel, which was for the sake of heaven, for even though these positions, in themselves, are opposed, since one disqualifies and the other renders fit, and from the human aspect these are two distinct and opposed positions, nevertheless from the perspective of God, may He be blessed, for whose sake this controversy arose, who encompasses all opposites, and is their source, from this perspective they are one.

Turning to the meaning of the dictum from tractate Hagiga: "Masters of assemblies" (Eccles. 12:11) – these are the scholars (*talmidei hakhamim*) who sit in various assemblies, some deem a matter impure, others deem it pure, some prohibit, others permit, some disqualify, others declare fit. Lest someone say, since some deem a matter impure, others deem it pure, some prohibit, others permit, some disqualify, others declare fit, under these circumstances, how can I learn the Torah?, therefore Scripture says: "They were given from one shepherd." One God gave them all, one leader uttered them all from the mouth of the Master of all deeds; as it is said, "And God spake all these words" (Exod. 20:1).[69] This calls for examination. How is it possible to say that even if the views are entirely opposed to each other, it is said of them, they were "spoken by one God?" Furthermore, what need is there to say "from the mouth of the Master of all deeds"?, for this phrase is not relevant here. But the explication is that God, may He be blessed, is the only God, and since He is the only God, it is impossible that all deeds did not emanate from Him, including opposites, as we explained. And as He is the Master of all deeds, including opposites – for fire and water are, in themselves, opposites – nevertheless the existence of both is the will of God, may He be blessed, who desires the existence of both fire and water. So too with regard to the opinions of the Sages. Even though they contradict each other, since some declare a thing unfit while others declare it fit, nonetheless both are from God, may He be blessed. Because from one perspective, that is, on one rationale, it should be declared fit, and from another perspective, that is, on another rationale, it should be declared unfit. But both of these perspectives, both

---

69 bHagiga 3b; the quotation is inexact.

rationales, are from God, may He be blessed, since one side has a plausible rationale, and the other side has a plausible rationale, and both arguments are from God, may He be blessed. The meaning of their dictum, "all were spoken by one God" does not just relate to unfitness or fitness; rather, it refers to the rationale behind these rulings – for such and such a reason it is unfit, for such and such a reason it is fit. And both rationales are rooted in the truth from the Holy One, blessed be He, for there is one aspect which renders the thing unfit and another aspect which renders it fit, each such rationale standing on its own merits.

In this context, the query, "Can there possibly be uncertainty in the mind of the Heavenly One?"[70] is irrelevant. For it is only relevant concerning the concubine of Gibeah[71]; there, with regard to a certain act, it was relevant to comment: Can there possibly be uncertainty in the mind of the Heavenly One?, but in a debate concerning fit and unfit, impure and pure, both opinions are from God, may He be blessed, for the rationales underlying them are from Him, may He be blessed. And even though, as far as the law to be applied is concerned, they are opposites and it is impossible for both to be upheld, nevertheless both opinions and rationales are from God, may He be blessed, who embraces all opposites. And if someone has learned both opinions, he indeed has learned the Torah, which is from God, may He be blessed – both the opinion that renders a thing unfit and that which renders it fit. And when we decide the law, we are not simply deciding the law to be applied as to how the individual should act. For surely, even though the two opinions each have a good rationale, one may be more in line with the law. And it is similar in the case of created things that are opposites. Even though they are opposites that both derive from God, may He be blessed, nevertheless, one is nearer to God, may He be blessed, than the other. Nonetheless, there is a rationale for each one, and if they are opposed, they are from God, may He be blessed. And the legal decision is from the perspective of a level above that at which the controversy takes place. But everything is from God, may He be blessed, both the actual controversy itself, in which one side disqualifies and the other renders fit, each for its own reasons, and the clarification of the controversy, that is, determination of the law, which is carried out from the perspective of the unencumbered intellect, which is utterly pure and as such is not subject to any controversy. Even though unencumbered intellection is higher than ordinary intellection, nevertheless, everything is from God, may He be blessed, for everything comes from Him, and this is elementary.

If so, you might question why the heavenly voice said of the house of Shammai and the house of Hillel, in particular, "both are the words of the

70 bGitin 6b.
71 Judges 19.

living God," since every controversy of scholars in the world is like that, in that the two views both are the words of the Master of all deeds. This presents no difficulty, because there is a difference that becomes clear when one understands the phrase "both are the words of the living God"; what is said – "the living God" – alludes to something momentous. For in other controversies, even though both sides are from God, may He be blessed, nevertheless, when two scholars disagree as to the law, even though both views are inspired by God, may He be blessed, still, one is closer to God, may He be blessed, as we said, for even though [the other] one is also from God, may He be blessed, nevertheless, this one is closer to God than that one, much as among the creatures of God, sometimes some are closer to God, may He be blessed, than others. Even though all are His creatures, some are nonetheless closer. So it is with regard to rationales. Although both are from God, may He be blessed, nevertheless one is closer to God, may He be blessed, than the other. However, in the case of the house of Shammai and the house of Hillel, both are in exactly equal measure the words of the living God, hence, it is said, "words of the living God." And one who discerns, understands that the meaning of "the living God" is that both are close to the truth of God, may He be blessed, which is why it says "the living God," for aliveness is the touchstone of existence. For when it is said of something that it is alive, that means that it exists, but that which does not exist has no life. And so it says that both are close to the truth of God's existence.

Furthermore, you should understand that the term "living" (*haim*) is plural, referring to two entities, and it is in this context that you should understand the controversy between Hillel and Shammai. To refer to other scholars, another phrase, "from the mouth of the Master of all deeds" is used. For life may unfold in different directions, to the right and to the left, and this is how Hillel and Shammai received [their views]. And therefore, both are the words of the living God. And grasp this, for in my opinion it is clear and very wonderful. And what is so difficult about their dictum, "both are the words of the living God," that so many have sought to interpret it? And some have interpreted it by way of the hidden, but there is nothing concealed here. For when God, may He be blessed, renders a thing fit or unfit, it is not simply that a reason is put forward, for there is nothing in the Torah that has no reason. And when the reasons are equally good, for, say, declaring fit and disqualifying, to the point where they are equally balanced, they are termed "the words of the living God," as we explained, and there is no difficulty here. And this was the controversy between the house of Shammai and house of Hillel. But with regard to other controversies of the Sages, it is not so. Though they both have defensible reasons – each side arguing that it is inspired by God, may He be blessed, seeing as every defensible reason is inspired by God, may He be blessed – nevertheless, when subjected to pure intellection, one reason prevails over the other, and it determines the law. And in any event, both opinions are reasoned, and just as unencumbered intellection comes from God, may He be blessed, so ordinary, encumbered reasoning is also from God, may He be blessed; but unencumbered intellection is the higher level. In any case, it should now be clear to you why a controversy that is for the sake of heaven is sustained, and one that is not for the sake of heaven is not sustained, because opposites cannot coexist, since the one is contrary to the other.

106. Beer Hagola, well 1, p. 19

And you should know that it was stated that both are the words of the living God only regarding the controversy between the house of Shammai and the house of Hillel. Because they were the first to engage in halakhic controversy, since prior to them there were no disputes at all about the Torah. And when the house of Shammai and the house of Hillel arose, their controversies were such that both views were the words of the living God, as we explained above. And it is inappropriate that Israel should descend [directly] from the lofty level of absence of controversy to a level where controversy occurs and one view is effaced. And therefore the controversy [between the house of Shammai and the house of Hillel] was such that both are the words of the living God. And afterwards, common controversy began to occur. And understand this well.

107. Drashot Maharal, Drush al hatora (p. 41)

Perhaps it will occur to you that there is not a single teaching or law in the Torah that is not subject to controversy and different opinions of the Tannaim and the Amoraim or Geonim and others of elevated sanctity. One says one thing, the other a different thing. Perhaps those whose views are not accepted do not receive a reward for their Torah, or even, heaven forbid, become subject to punishment? And consider the house of Shammai, all of whose opinions are not accepted as law – do they, God forbid, fall into such a category?

But this is not a wise question. Regarding this the Talmud says,

> "Masters of assemblies," these are the scholars who sit in various assemblies and apply themselves to the Torah; some deem a matter impure, others deem it pure, some prohibit, others permit, some disqualify, others declare fit. Lest someone say, under these circumstances, how can I learn the Torah? Therefore Scripture says: All were given from one shepherd. One God gave them, one leader uttered them from the mouth of the Master of all deeds, blessed be He, as it is written, "And God spake all these

words" (Exod. 20:1). So let your ears be as funnels, and cultivate an understanding heart, to hear the words of those who deem a matter impure and those who deem it pure, the who prohibit and those who permit, those who disqualify and those who declare fit.[72]

One might wonder, what is the need to say "from the mouth of the Master of all deeds"; what is the relevance of this expression here? This is to prevent you from saying: Since their opinion is not accepted as law, how were they given from one shepherd? And what does that have to do with us? For this reason it is said that they are all from the mouth of the Master of all deeds, that is, all the deeds are from Him, blessed be He, as all creatures, though different, and some completely opposite to each other, are nevertheless all from God, may He be blessed, who is One, and they all possess some aspect of truth, as we state in the blessing of the New Moon, "The true Creator, whose deeds are true"; for water in terms of its elemental nature is true, and fire, which in terms of its elemental nature is the opposite of water, is also true. So it is with respect to the proliferation of opinions themselves; each is from Him, may He be blessed, even if they are contradictory, nevertheless each one has a true aspect, as can be attested to and verified by parable and analogy. And even if we find that each being is true from its own aspect, nevertheless, sometimes one is closer to truth than the other, and this is the complete truth. Just as man himself is closer to it [the truth] than all other living creatures, so too among the different opinions, one is far closer to truth and is the law, but the opinion that is not close enough to truth to be accepted as law should not be rejected because of this. Just as it is with the various creatures, all of which are in any event part of reality, as they are also complete and true from their own particular perspectives. Hence it is said, "even if one prohibits and the other permits, one disqualifies, the other declares fit, one God said them." For the Holy One, blessed be He, said that the law, from one aspect, is so, and in any event, the one opinion is completely true in itself, not only from its specific perspective. Thus similarly, just as we do not reject God's creatures, the other opinions must not be rejected as if they have no substance, even if some of them are more straightforward or veracious. Therefore each of the opinions is part of the Torah, and there is reward for its formulation, which is intended for the sake of heaven, for the one God who uttered them.

108. Lehem Mishne, mAvot 5:17

Because it is known that souls differ. Some are inclined to the perspective of law, and others to the perspective of kindness (*hesed*). And this was so

---

72 bHagiga 3b; the quotation is inexact.

regarding Shammai and Hillel. Because Shammai was rigid in terms of his spiritual core, and therefore was strict in every instance. And Hillel's humbleness, in terms of his spiritual core, inclined to kindness. And behold, the Torah can be expounded in forty-nine ways to render pure, from the perspective of kindness, and forty-nine ways to render impure and to forbid, from the perspective of law. And behold, throughout the Torah, there was a need for controversy, because no individual can expound it in both directions, for if his spiritual core is inclined toward the law, he is always disposed to strictness, to forbid, to render impure, and to impose liability, and his opponent must come up with a counter-argument, based on his spiritual core: to permit, to render pure, and to exempt, as was the case in the controversy between Shammai and Hillel.

109. Yearot Dvash, part 2, sermon 8

The Mishna says, "Every controversy that is for the sake of heaven, its end is to be sustained. What controversy is that? The controversy between Hillel and Shammai; and a controversy that is not for the sake of heaven, such as the controversy of Korah and his congregation, its end is not to be sustained."[73] The meaning of "its end is to be sustained" has to be understood. How can the opinions of the house of Shammai be sustained, when [the Talmud says that] where they contradict the house of Hillel, they are of no consequence?[74] And what is good about a controversy's being sustained in the end? ...

In fact, the explanation is in another Mishna, "Do not dismiss anything, because there is nothing that does not have its time and place"[75]; and they also said, "these forbid and the others permit"[76]; and "both the words of the living God."[77] On the surface, this seems strange, for how is it possible to make contrary statements about the same subject?

But it is so, for the world is a world of changes, and all is derived from the Tree of Knowledge of good and evil,[78] for the wheel of the world is constantly turning, round and round, as is the wheel in the Upper World, as it is explicitly explained in the *Book of Creation* 2:4 – the wheel[79] turns through two hundred and thirty-one stages until it returns to its starting

73 mAvot 5:17; the quotation is inexact.
74 bJebamot 9a.
75 mAvot 4:3.
76 bHagiga 3b.
77 bEruvin 13b.
78 In the Kabbalistic metaphor, the image of the Tree of Knowledge of good and evil conveys the idea of myriad controversies. The image of the Tree of Life, on the other hand, evokes the Torah as a unified body of knowledge.
79 Two concentric wheels, one of this world, and one of the Upper World, are inscribed with the letters of the alphabet, and at every stage a combination of one letter from each forms an anagram that influences the universe, for good or for evil.

point, sometimes good and sometimes bad. [Things become their opposites]: nothing is better than pleasure, and nothing worse than affliction [yet the letters in both words are the same, though read in different directions.] So too perfect and dead, abundance and evil. So the good and the bad alternate, sometimes one dominates, sometimes the other. Therefore everything depends on the way the two upper and lower wheels turn, round and round, and if so, that which is at one time impure, is pure at another time, and so it is regarding everything. And so therefore both are the words of the living God, for this time it may be impure, but at another time, according to the turn of the upper wheel, pure.

This is the meaning of "do not dismiss anything," as when one Sage says it is impure, and it is really pure, for there is nothing that does not have its appointed place and time when it really will be impure. We find this concerning the erection of pillars, which was beloved by God at the time of the Patriarchs; and it was regarded as a commanded and holy deed, but later became hated, as it was an impure sin. So everything changes, sometimes thus, and sometimes so, all according to the system of the wheels, and both are the words of the living God, for everything is from the root of good and evil. And therefore a person is not appointed to be among the members of the Sanhedrin unless he knows how to argue that the impure is pure, and vice versa.[80] It is not false and vain sophistry, as the *Tosafot* state,[81] but the truth; everything in its time, and we have to have a sophisticated understanding regarding the said Sage. That is, even if a thing is impure, it is not so categorically, for there is a time when it is pure, and everything is according to its time. There are numerous times that we find in the words of the Sages, of blessed memory, that they forbade something, and after a time permitted it, and then forbade it again, for everything is appropriate in its time, according to the two hundred and thirty-one configurations, as explained in the *Book of Creation*, and it has to be understood.

To conclude: do not dismiss anything, by saying 'this is false,' because as we explained, in its proper time it will be true, and there is no falsehood except that which is inherently false.... This is what the Sages of the Mishna, of blessed memory, meant by "the controversy between Shammai and Hillel, its end is to be sustained," for even if the law at present is in accordance with the view of the house of Hillel, that this thing is pure, a time will come when it will be impure, in accordance with the view of the house of Shammai, for there is nothing that does not have its place and time, and vice versa. And it is a controversy for the sake of heaven, for both opinions will be sustained, and both are true, as opposed to the controversy of Korah and his congregation, who disputed Moses' view

---

80 bSanhedrin 17a.
81 Ibid. s.v. *sheyodeia*.

regarding the completely blue prayer shawl, and the like, which were never true, and never will be true and they are absolute lies, and therefore they will not be sustained in the end at all, but will be as a withering leaf and a fading cloud. This is the controversy of Korah, and it is not for the sake of heaven. This must be understood.

110. Petah Einayim, bBaba Metzia 59b

"If the law is in accordance with my view, let the carob tree prove it."[82] One must understand these proofs brought by R. Eliezer: the carob tree, the stream of water, the walls of the house of study, and the additional proof of the heavenly voice, and understand the Sages' dictum, "no proof can be brought from a carob tree," and so on.

And we can discuss, by way of oratory and allusion, their dictum, "Both are the words of the living God." And early scholars pondered the question, how is it possible that both are the words of the living God, since the one whose opinion is not affirmed as law did not speak correctly? And the early scholars said that just as light cannot be discerned without darkness, and truth cannot be discerned without falsehood, so too in this matter the one cannot be understood and resolved on its own, but rather only from its opposite. Therefore God told Moses the opinions of those who acquit and those who find liable, and so on, for from the rejected opinion, the true opinion can be formulated and upheld. That is one answer. And another one we learn from Rashi: sometimes one reason is pertinent and sometimes the other reason is pertinent, since the law's rationale changes according to variations in the circumstances, however minute. And it turns out that in any event the rejected opinion will be pertinent, with minute variations, in a different reality.[83] And there is yet a third explanation, which will further explain it, from the mouth of our rabbis, the rabbis of France, that the Holy One, blessed be He, gave Moses forty-nine aspects from which a thing can be declared pure, and forty-nine aspects from which it can be declared impure, and so forth, and told him that the law would be in accordance with the consensus of the scholars of the given generation. Thus, all opinions are indeed the words of the living God.

And regarding this, it can be said, by way of allusion, that R. Eliezer said, "Let this carob tree prove it," that is, that it would be uprooted from its place, meaning, his view was true, and theirs, false, and the truth would be comprehended via the falsehood. And this would be indicated by the fact that the carob tree would be uprooted. That is to say, their view would be totally uprooted, for it had no truth to it whatsoever, and was not

82 bBaba Metzia 59b.
83 On bKetubot 57a s.v. *ha ka mashma lan.*

141

useful for anything other than explaining his view. And this is in line with the first explanation offered by the early scholars.

He further said, "Let the stream of water prove it." That is, even if you would maintain that your view is not false, in any event, it is only true in that sometimes one particular reason is pertinent – this is in line with the second aforementioned explanation. And hence he said: Let the stream of water prove it, so that it would flow backwards, meaning, that even though the view of his opponents is not in accordance with the law, and is not sustained, it is analogous to a stream of water flowing backwards, which remains a stream of water nonetheless, but its placement changes. And likewise, the view of the opponents is true, and is sustained in a different context, and its reason is correct and true, somewhere else.

And he went on to say, "Let the walls of the house of study prove it." Even if you would say that both opinions are true and the decision is in the hands of the scholars of the given generation, the walls of the house of study will prove that much of the time they were with me, for no one preceded me to the house of study, and when I left there was no one else there, as it is said in the Talmud.[84]

111. Responsa Yosef Ometz, #51

…and it could be said that the main reason for the enactment of our predecessors mandating recitation of Abbaye's recounting of the Temple service[85] in the morning prayers, is to gain merit for the whole nation by reciting a passage from the Mishna and Gemara. And they chose this passage, which deals with the Temple sacrifices. And it is known from what is stated in the discussion in tractate Eruvin that both are the words of the living God.[86] Relying on the rabbis of France, R. Yomtov of Seville writes in his novellae[87] that the two contrary opinions are true. And Moses our teacher, may he rest in peace, asked the Holy One, blessed be He: But in accordance with whom is the law decided?, and He answered that the decision is entrusted to the scholars of the given generation. Therefore, since such opinions are true, [their recitation] gives us the merit of studying the Talmud. Even if they entail something not accepted as law, it does not matter, because this opinion is also true, and both are the words of the living God.

As an example, I mention the enactment to recite a chapter of the Mishna, the fifth chapter of Zevahim, in the morning prayer. R. Joseph Caro writes in the name of R. Aaron Halevi that this chapter was chosen

---

84 bSuka 28a.
85 Despite the fact that his view, set out in bYoma 33a, is not accepted as the law.
86 bEruvin 13b.
87 *Hidushei Haritba* ad loc.

because it contains no controversy.[88] And the pre-eminent scholar of the generation, R. Haim Alfandari, of blessed memory, in his glosses on *Bnei Haye*,[89] notes that indeed, the chapter does not contain any controversy, but some of the laws mentioned there are disputed elsewhere by Sages of the Mishna. R. Yomtov of Seville, of blessed memory, goes even further:

> My teacher, may God protect and deliver him,[90] said that the choice of this chapter rests on the fact that it contains no controversy, though not all of it is accepted as law. For example, it is said there that the Passover sacrifice may be eaten until midnight, but we follow our teacher Nahmanides that the law is in accordance with the view of R. Akiva, who opines that it may be eaten all night, since his view is supported by an anonymous Mishna.[91] Nevertheless, since the whole chapter is presented without a dissenting view, it is more appropriate for recitation than any other.[92]

So this chapter is controversial; furthermore, not all of it is considered law.

Similarly, I saw the commentary of R. Shimon b. Zemah Duran,[93] of blessed memory, who says that some Sages of the Mishna disagree with R. Ishmael regarding some of his rules. Nevertheless, since we have the tradition that both are the words of the living God, it is all true Torah, and a person discharges his duty to study Scripture, Mishna and Gemara by reciting it. Although in the opinion of R. Jacob b. Asher (Tur) and R. Yomtov of Seville and their followers, the baraita of R. Ishmael is recited in place of Gemara, in any event, it is likely that the passage with Abbaye's account is for the same purpose, for which it is suitable even if not all of it represents the law, because his reasoning is also true, since both are the words of the living God, as explained.

Even though studying opinions that did not become law constitutes study of the Torah, since they are the words of the living God, nevertheless, the Mishna, in the first chapter of Eduyot, teaches, "Why do they mention the opinions of both Shammai and Hillel to no effect," and so on, "and why do they record the opinion of the individual against that of the majority to no effect" and so on.[94] Now, although opinions that are not legally binding are unreservedly part of the Torah, as both are the words of the living God, nevertheless, since the Holy One, blessed be He, wished that the decision be in the hands of the scholars of the given generation,

88 *Tur*, OH 50.
89 *Bnei Haye* by R. Haim b. Menahem Algazi.
90 R. Aaron Halevi.
91 mMegila chapter 2.
92 *Hidushei Haritba*, Avoda Zara 18.
93 On Zevahim 5 (Maamar Hametz) and on the baraita of R. Ishmael.
94 mEduyot 1:5–6.

and the law has already been disseminated everywhere and is accepted as law in line with one of the sides to the dispute, there is, in mentioning the rejected opinions, something that seems to smack of disrespect.[95] And [the Mishna] replied that the point is that, as has been explained, there is also a good side to this.

112. Kedushat Levi, Likutim, s.v. *teiku*

Teiku (the question remains undecided) is an acronym: the prophet Elijah will resolve difficulties and problems.[96] At first sight, it must be thoroughly examined, given that this event will take place after the coming of the redeemer speedily in our day, amen: why should Elijah resolve the difficulties and problems, when Moses our teacher, may he rest in peace, who gave us the Torah and the precepts, will be there? Why should he not resolve the difficulties and problems? And it seems that *The Book of Generations* (*Sefer Hadorot*) says, regarding the controversy between Rashi and Rabbenu Tam over phylacteries, that Rashi, of blessed memory, had Moses assisting him, but Rabbenu Tam did not pay attention to this, saying to him that the Torah had already been given to us, and it was in our hands to hand down rulings according to the way our intelligence tells us [to understand] the holy Torah. And in order that this be understood, I will explain it briefly. That is, with regard to the controversy between the house of Shammai and the house of Hillel: "both are the words of the living God." For there is a perspective according to which an individual studying the plain meaning of the holy Torah interprets it according to his own vantage point. If he is of the Sphere of Kindness,[97] his intellect is wont to interpret the Torah as deeming everything pure, permitted and fit. On the other hand, if he is connected to the Sphere of Might, the reverse is true. Now the house of Hillel is characterized by the attribute of kindness, and therefore it inclines to leniency, while the house of Shammai is characterized by might, and hence inclines to stringency. But in fact, each view, according to its own level, constitutes the words of the living God, and thus "both are the words of the living God."

And the Sages, of blessed memory, who lived after the generation of the house of Shammai and the house of Hillel, seeing that the world

---

95 Here, the Hida explains the question posed by the Mishna, viz., why they record the dissenting opinion, in the following manner: the very fact of mentioning a rejected opinion brings shame on the author of the opinion, and it might be preferable not to mention it at all. In so doing, he changes the plain meaning of the Mishna's query (namely, what is the point of mentioning a rejected opinion?), which is problematic in light of his position that rejected opinions are unequivocally considered Torah views, and it thus goes without saying that there is value in retaining them.

96 *tishbi yetaretz kushiyot uveayot*.

97 A Kabbalistic concept.

needed to conduct itself with kindness, decided the law in accordance with the view of the house of Hillel, which is in all matters lenient, in accordance with the view of the house of Hillel. Now who can discern the attribute in accord with which the world ought to be conducted, so that the law can be decided in a manner reflecting this? He who is living and is in this world, knows the appropriate attribute according to which the world should be conducted, but he who is not alive has no idea at all which attribute is required for the conduct of the world. Now Elijah is alive and exists, for he has not experienced death, and is eternally in our world. And therefore, he will straighten out all the difficulties and problems, as he knows the attributes according to which the world should be conducted. This explains what Rabbenu Tam said to Moses, our teacher, may he rest in peace: that he had already given the Torah to us, and we have the power to rule.

113. Responsa Zivhei Tzedek, YD, #26

Question: You asked about controversy between Sages, one forbidding, the other permitting – how could both views have been given to Moses at Sinai?

Answer: This is a very profound question, and we cannot get to the heart of it, for even the early scholars, of blessed memory, could not master it. This question was asked by the rabbis of France, of blessed memory, about the passage in tractate Eruvin:

> R. Abba stated in the name of Samuel: For three years there was a controversy between the house of Shammai and the house of Hillel, the former asserting, The law is in accordance with our views, and the latter asserting, The law is in accordance with our views. A heavenly voice (*bat kol*) went forth and said, Both are the words of the living God, but the law is in accordance with the view of the house of Hillel. Since, however, both are the words of the living God, for what reason did the house of Hillel merit the law's being decided in accordance with their view? Because they were kindly and modest.[98]

R. Yomtov of Seville, in his commentary on Eruvin, wrote as follows:

> The rabbis of France, of blessed memory, asked, how is it possible that both are the words of the living God, when one forbids

98 bEruvin 13b.

and another permits? And they answered: When Moses ascended to heaven to receive the Torah, on every issue he was shown forty nine aspects to forbid and forty nine aspects to permit. He asked the Holy One, blessed be He, about this, and He said that it is delegated to the scholars of Israel of each and every generation, and the decision will be made in accordance with their view. And this is so in terms of exegesis, but with respect to truth, there is a secret reason for all this.

That is what the Ritba, of blessed memory, wrote.

And a similar approach is taken by R. Nissim Solomon Elgazi in the work *Yavin Shmua*,[99] quoting *Mishpetei Shmuel*, which brings an interpretation in the name of Rabbenu Hananel, of blessed memory:

> What they said – "both are the words of the living God" – the interpretation is that the Holy One, blessed be He, related to Moses at Sinai forty nine aspects from which to render a matter pure and forty nine aspects from which to render it impure, and did not decide the matter, but left the decision to the consensus of the majority, as it is written in the Torah, "follow the majority," and so on (Exod. 23:2).

And so it appears from the Gemara in tractate Hagiga:

> "Masters of assemblies" – these are the scholars (*talmidei hakhamim*) who sit in various assemblies and apply themselves to the Torah; some deem a matter impure, others pure, some prohibit, and others permit, some disqualify and others declare fit. Lest someone say: Under these circumstances, how can I learn the Torah? Therefore Scripture says: All "were given from one shepherd." One God gave them, one leader uttered them from the mouth of the Master of all deeds, blessed be He, and so on.[100]

There is thus clear proof in the Talmud supporting the explanation of the rabbis of France and Rabbenu Hananel, of blessed memory, that both [the opposed opinions] were given to Moses at Sinai. And it is as the Shela [R. Isaiah Horowitz], of blessed memory, wrote. At the beginning he quotes R. Yomtov of Seville, then quotes the aforementioned rabbis of France, and then cites the aforesaid talmudic passage, and then states: "Those authorities, of blessed memory, attested that all the disputes and

99 p. 81b.
100 bHagiga 3b; the quotation is inexact.

the opinions that contradict each other – one God gave them, one leader uttered them."[101] And consult the text.

And in his work *Petah Einayim*, the Hida, of blessed memory, offers three explanations:

"Both are the words of the living God." And early scholars pondered the question, how is it possible that both are the words of the living God, since the one whose opinion is not affirmed as law did not speak correctly? And the early scholars said that just as light cannot be discerned without darkness, and truth cannot be discerned without falsehood, so too in this matter the one cannot be reconciled on its own but rather only from its opposite. Therefore God told Moses the opinions of those who acquit and those who find liable, and so on, for from the rejected opinion, the true opinion can be formulated and upheld. That is one answer. And another one we learn from Rashi[102]: sometimes one argument is pertinent and sometimes the other argument is pertinent, and it turns out that in any event the rejected opinion will be pertinent, with minute variations, in a different reality. The third explanation is according to our rabbis, the rabbis of France, namely, that the Holy One, blessed be He, gave Moses forty nine aspects from which a thing can be declared pure, and forty-nine aspects from which it can be declared impure, and so forth, and told him that the law would be in accordance with the consensus of the scholars of the given generation. Thus, all opinions are indeed the words of the living God.

And consult the text.

And what the Hida, of blessed memory, wrote in his second explanation, is based on what Rashi, of blessed memory, wrote in Ketubot, at the end of his comments:

When two Amoraim have a legal disagreement concerning monetary or ritual law, each adducing his own reasoning, there is no falsehood involved. Each of the two is putting forward his own argument, one providing reasons for permitting, the other reasons for prohibiting; one makes such an analogy, and the other makes a different analogy, and the principle of "both are the words of the living God" applies. Sometimes one reason is pertinent, and sometimes the other reason is pertinent, since the law's rationale changes according to variations in the circumstances, however minute.

---

101 *Shnei Luhot Habrit*, 25b.
102 On bKetubot 57a s.v. *ha ka mashma lan.*

That is what Rashi, of blessed memory, wrote.

From this we learn that the Sages, of blessed memory, were right in saying, "Both are the words of the living God," for even if one scholar says a matter is forbidden or permitted, and the law is not so, in any event the opinion is true and exists in the world, and was received by Moses at Sinai regarding a different situation. And it is correct to say that this opinion is the word of the living God.

There are more explanations of Later Authorities, of blessed memory, but nevertheless this inquiry has not proven very satisfactory, and we do not possess the understanding to pursue it to its essence, because even regarding the explanation of the rabbis of France, of blessed memory, the eminent scholar the Shela remarks: "This is very remote from human cognition, and beyond man's ability to grasp unless accompanied by the smooth path of divine guidance where the light of truth dwells." He also says: "The explanations of the rabbis of France, of blessed memory, do not give peace of mind, because they are not adequate. But the mind will have rest only through the reason and secret alluded to by the master [the Ritba]," and so on. Therefore we cannot delve any deeper into this question, or elaborate on it further. Regarding the plain meaning, to bring some peace of mind, and in particular, in order to answer the queries of ordinary people, we have brought the three explanations, and they more than suffice for the purpose of this investigation. Let the wise man answer the queries of the inquirers,[103] and in particular, cite the explanation of the rabbis of France, which is the most satisfying. But the essential explanation is arrived at by way of secrets, and none of us have any business delving into it.

114. Vayaas Avraham, Kuntres pri haaretz, pp. 506–10

And regarding the difference that we found between the Talmud and the decisors [on the one hand], and the Kabbalists [on the other], this is like that which is found in the passage in tractate Baba Metzia, "If the spot preceded the white hair, he is impure; if the reverse, he is pure. If [the order is] in doubt, the Holy One, blessed be He, ruled – he is pure; whereas the entire heavenly academy maintained – he is impure. Who shall decide it?, they asked. Rabbah bar Nahmani will decide," and so on. "As he was dying, he said, Pure, pure!"[104] Consult the passage. This point was the subject of a Tannaitic debate, with the first Tanna opining that it is impure, and the anonymous opinion concurring[105]; consult the passage.

---

103 The implication is negative, as this is a pun on Lamentations 5:18, and Maimonides, Laws concerning the Study of the Torah 5:4.
104 bBaba Metzia 86a.
105 mNegaim 4–5.

And we hold that the law is in accordance with the anonymous opinion. And this appears very strange – can it be conceivable to contradict the Holy One, blessed be He? For He says that it is pure, and He is the God of truth.

And it seems, according to what the Kabbalists, of blessed memory, said, that in heaven above the law is accordance with the view of the house of Shammai, and indeed, in the future the law will be in accordance with the view of the house of Shammai, whose members are [spiritually] elevated far above the house of Hillel, and only in the present is the law in accordance with the view of house of Hillel. And the matter is so because the Holy One, blessed be He, conducts this world according to the consensus of the majority of the scholars of Israel with respect to the interpretation of the precepts. For the Holy One, blessed be He, commanded in his Torah: "If there arise a matter too hard for thee in judgment," and so on, "...and thou shalt observe to do according to all that they shall teach thee" (Deut. 17:8–10). And when there are disagreements among the court itself, the Torah decrees, "follow the majority" (Exod. 23:2), and we follow the view of the majority. Even if it is not the consummate truth – for it is possible that the minority is more attuned to the truth than the majority – nevertheless the Torah decrees that we follow the majority view.

Since this is the decree of the Ultimate Creator and this is His will, may He be blessed, therefore the conduct of the world is, as regards the interpretation of this particular precept, only to be in accordance to the majority opinion of the scholars of the generation, even though as to its root [i.e., its true substance], the truth may be in accordance with the minority. It is also possible that afterwards a court of a succeeding generation will convene and a majority of that court will contradict the majority opinion of the court from the earlier generation, and its opinion will incline toward the minority opinion. And in this case the law will be in accordance with the opinion of the later court, as Maimonides, of blessed, memory writes,[106] and consult the passage. And so too the conduct above will also be in accordance with the opinion of the later court, since it is the decree and desire of God that the sole authority is the judge of one's own generation. And regarding these matters, an interpretation has been proffered, "Even if he tells you of right that it is left and left that it is right, listen to him."[107] Though there is but one truth, nevertheless it has been decreed by the Torah that explication of the precepts not thoroughly elucidated in the Torah is dependent on the views of the scholars of the given generation.

As to the rhetoric of the Sages, of blessed memory, that the Holy One, blessed be He, said "pure" – that is, according to the root of the law, this

106 *Code*, Laws concerning Rebels 2:1.
107 Sifre Deuteronomy 154.

case is pure, and this is the truth at the root of the matter. But the heavenly academy, which is a metaphor for the legal structures that regulate the world, declares it impure, because according to the majority of scholars of that generation, who accepted the law in accordance with the anonymous opinion in the Mishna, it is impure, and hence, this is the law in the world. And similarly with regard to the controversy between the house of Shammai and the house of Hillel. Even though the root of the truth corresponds to the view of the house of Shammai, and indeed, in the future the law will be as they aver, nevertheless, since now the scholars of the generation uphold the law according to the view of house of Hillel, one who conducts himself according to the view of house of Shammai rather than that of the house of Hillel is accountable with his life. As in the case of R. Tarfon, who inclined himself when reading the evening Shema prayer, in accordance with the opinion of the house of Shammai, and the Sages decreed: "The opinion of the house of Shammai, if it contradicts that of the house of Hillel, is of no consequence," as stated in tractate Berakhot.[108]

Hence, all the *tikunim*[109] made in the upper spheres by fulfilling the precepts are only valid if carried out in accordance with the view of the house of Hillel regarding the precept in question. For this is the will of God, may He be blessed, that we heed what the Sages determined concerning the law in question. So only one who follows the opinion of the house of Hillel inspires the divine will, and enables the worlds to adorn themselves, and the spheres to copulate in the order of this precept, but only if the precepts are observed as determined by the Sages at their discretion, as this is His will, may His Name be blessed. And one who transgresses their words reverses the divine channels and is accountable with his life.

This is also the point of the story in tractate Baba Metzia recounting the dispute between R. Eliezer and the Sages concerning the purity of the oven of Akhnai.[110] For after all the signs were sent down to indicate that in heaven the law is in accordance with the view of R. Eliezer, and even after the heavenly voice went forth affirming that the law was in accordance with the view of R. Eliezer, R. Joshua rose to his feet and said: We do not pay attention to a heavenly voice, for "it is not in heaven" (Deut. 30:12), because the Torah was already given at Sinai, and in the Torah it is written, "follow the majority" (Exod. 23:2). And consult the passage. Now this is perplexing: those acts occurred while they were having the disagreement, so the majority could still have retracted their view and agreed with R. Eliezer when they perceived the heavenly affirmation that the law was in accord with the view of R. Eliezer. Therefore we have to say that

---

108 mBerakhot 1:3, bBerakhot 36b.
109 A Kabbalistic term denoting cosmic restoration.
110 bBaba Metzia 59b.

since the directive of the Holy One, blessed be He, is that the law is to be decided according to the current majority scholarly opinion of the generation, according to its understanding and reasoning, if the scholars of that generation had retracted thier opinion, not on the strength of this conviction alone, but only because they had been so shown by heaven, they would have been acting against His will, may He be blessed, as He decreed and declared that the law would hinge on the will and conviction of the majority of the scholars of the generation, even if the root of the truth is not as they reason.

This is the meaning of the Sages' assertion in the Talmud that Elijah, who is remembered for beneficence, revealed to them that the Holy One, blessed by He, was pleased, so to speak, at that point, and said, "My sons have triumphed over Me, My sons have triumphed over me."[111] That is, that He was pleased that the Sages did not want to diverge from what their opinion and reasoning mandated regarding the laws of the Torah, for they thought that this alone was the will of God, may He be blessed, to heed them even should they say that right is left or vice versa. This is the import of "My sons have triumphed over Me" – for from then on, the conduct in heaven, too, has been only in accordance with the ruling decided on by the majority of the scholars of Israel regarding the oven, based on their reasoning.

Apparently this is the essence of the controversy between the Kabbalists and the decisors. The Kabbalists wrote in line with what seemed to them to be the substance [lit., root] of the law according to the 'combinations' and 'unities' known to them from the Kabbala and the structure of the worlds. But in any event, if the majority view on which the scholars of Israel agreed is the opposite, or if the custom has spread throughout that region, in accordance with the view of its most prominent decisor, to the point where it has become completely binding and a custom that is not to be deviated from, because we were admonished, "Ask thy father and he will declare unto thee" (Deut. 32:7) and "Forsake not the teachings of thy mother" (Prov. 1:8) – then all the *tikunim* are made only according to this ruling, which has been accepted among Israel. And all those who act in accordance with the views of the Kabbalists rather than the views of the decisors, are like those who act in accordance with the view of the house of Shammai against the view of the house of Hillel.

… Therefore, what they wrote was indeed right, that wherever there is a controversy between Kabbalists and decisors, only the view of the decisors is binding. But where there is no clear decision by the decisors, or if no custom has become widespread in accordance with the view of one particular decisor, the Kabbala is decisive, as is stated by R. David b. Zimra in

111 bBaba Metzia 59b.

a responsum, and consult it.[112] But if the people of Israel already conduct themselves in accordance with the view of a specific decisor, then all the cosmic restorations (*tikunim*) can be effected only in accordance with this opinion, and if they do not [so conduct themselves], the heavenly channels become reversed, as I wrote above.

And it is in line with what I wrote, that we are to understand the passage in tractate Eruvin about the controversy between the house of Shammai and the house of Hillel: "a heavenly voice (*bat kol*) went forth and said, Both are the words of the living God, but the law is in accordance with the view of the house of Hillel." And it is important to understand how two contrary opinions, one forbidding and the other permitting, can, with respect to the same matter, both be the words of the living God. And on this point see R. Yomtov of Seville's novellae ad loc. In the said talmudic passage, a difficulty is raised. "Since, however, both are the words of the living God, for what reason did the house of Hillel merit the law's being decided in accordance with their view?" They did not raise the difficulty, 'and is it possible for both opinions to be the words of the living God if the two are contrary?' A further difficulty is, even if we do not say that both are the words of the living God, it is still hard to understand why the house of Hillel merited having the law decided in accordance with their views, since they did not have an unqualified majority, as stated in tractate Jebamot – "since the house of Shammai were more incisive,"[113] and see the remarks of the *Tosafot*.[114] And why does the Talmud bring up this difficulty in the context of the two views both being the words of the living God?

But you must know and understand that halakhic truth is unlike the truth of arithmetic and geometry, wherein there is but a single correct solution. Rather, it is truth that is intelligible and based on reasoning, that is, it is as people understand and reason it out through their own comprehension. And the Holy One, blessed be He, commanded in His Torah that when a matter relating to the laws of the Torah is too perplexing, we obey the decision of the court of that generation, which will inform us of the solution that is in accord with what its own comprehension arrives at. And, as no two individuals have identical intellects, and opinions of necessity will differ most of the time, even within the very same court, God, may He be blessed, commanded that we follow the opinion of the majority. And since the majority view concurs in declaring something forbidden, it is the will of God, may He be blessed, that it be forbidden. However, should a court arise in a later generation wherein the majority are inclined toward the minority view of the earlier court, and toward permitting the matter, this

112 Cited in *Responsa Shaarei Teshuva* #25.
113 bJebamot 14a.
114 *Tosafot*, bBaba Metzia 59b s.v. *lo bashamayim*.

too would be the will of God, may He be blessed, for Scripture says, "unto the judge that shall be in those days" (Deut. 17:9). And as Maimonides, of blessed memory, wrote, "If the high court, applying one of the exegetical principles as it saw fit, determined that the law was thus, and rendered its ruling accordingly, and later on, another court arose and contradicted it, this [second court] may contradict it and rule as it sees fit, for Scripture says, "and unto the judge that shall be in those days," that is, the sole authority is the judge of one's own generation."[115]

And it is all for the same reason: the Torah chose a solution that is dependent on reasoned truth and variable opinion. For every single viewpoint has some hold on human opinion, and even within the same person, opinions will sometimes vary. And it is as the Talmud relates in tractate Eruvin regarding R. Meir, who was able to argue that an impure matter was pure and bring a variety of different arguments for it.[116] That is, he explained it using intellectual apprehension. And he was able to argue that a pure matter was impure and bring a variety of different arguments for it, giving this view, too, a grounding in opinion and in reason. And everything that can be grounded in opinion is termed "the words of the living God," since God commanded us to harken to the reasoning and the viewpoints of the court, in accordance with the way in which it understands the solution to the doubtful points that arise concerning the precepts of the Torah. But, since opinions vary, He commanded us to follow the majority view. Even though it is possible that the minority is more attuned to the truth than the majority, nevertheless, in order that Israel not become divided and have several sets of law, the scriptural decree (*gzeirat hakatuv*) was that we accept as truth apprehended by intellection that which the intellect of the majority will decide. And later, when a different court arises, and its majority understands the matter differently than the first court understood it, it will rule in accordance with its own reasoning at that time. And it will turn out that what was hitherto deemed impure by the will of the Holy One, blessed be He, who wished us to adjudicate the matter according to the opinion and reasoning of the previous court, is now rendered pure, in accordance with the will of the Holy One, blessed be He, who desires that we harken to the reasoning of the judge who presides in our own generation. And it thus turns out that both opinions are the words of the living God, and by scriptural decree (*gzeirat hakatuv*) we harken to the majority view of the court of our own times.

And as to the fact that the Sages of the Talmud do not ask and are not puzzled, 'If these forbid and those permit – how can both be the words of the living God?' – they take it for granted that every opinion arrived at by intellectual apprehension is the word of the living God, as I explained

115 *Code*, Laws concerning Rebels 2:1.
116 bEruvin 13b.

above. But they asked, since both are the words of the living God, and there is no unqualified majority, as we cited from the Talmud above,[117] then why did the house of Hillel merit the law's being decided in accordance with their view, so that the heavenly voice went forth and said, the law is in accordance with the view of the house of Hillel? Surely the matter is vouchsafed to the scholars of each generation, who will deliberate on the various opinions, and decide in accordance with the majority view? And the Talmud replies, "because they were kindly and modest," and so on.

To conclude the matter, since both the opinion forbidding and the opinion permitting have a place in human intellection, which God chose as the means by which the uncertainties in the Torah are to be resolved; if so, both are God's work, and thus both are called "words of the living God." But in practice, the Holy One, blessed be He, commanded us to follow the majority opinion of the court in any given generation, which may be changed by the court of a later generation. And if so, both opinions are true, not in the sense of geometrical truth, realistically speaking, but true in terms of human reasoning and intellectual apprehension.

And since all the precepts of the Torah were expressly chosen by God in accordance with His will, so that by means of our fulfilling them we will gain material and spiritual life, it was also His will that we solve uncertainties having to do with the details of our observance of the precepts in accordance with human reasoning and intellection, by the generation's Torah scholars. And however they resolve it, that is the will of God, may He be blessed. And as long as there has not arisen another court in a later generation that reversed this opinion, all who transgress their ruling transgress a negative commandment of the Torah, "do not deviate from the sentence which they shall declare unto thee, to the right hand, nor to the left" (Deut. 17:11) Although it is possible that they erred with regard to their judgment, nevertheless, the scriptural decree is that we must obey them "even if they say of right that it is left and left that it is right," as Sifre notes.[118] And this is the path beloved of the Omnipresent, blessed be He, in the observance of His precepts, may His Name be blessed. And if so, [such decisions] reflect the truth of reasoned intellection, for that is His desire, may His Name be blessed, in the observance of the precepts.

And in light of what I have written, we can clarify the rules set by the Sages in the Talmud for the law's being decided everywhere in favor of one of the disputants. For instance, "[in a controversy between] R. Meir and R. Judah, the law is in accordance with the view of R. Judah"[119]; "between R. Meir and R. Jose, the law is in accordance with the view of

---

117 bJebamot 14a.
118 Sifre Deuteronomy 154.
119 bEruvin 46b.

R. Jose"[120] and so too for disputes between Amoraim. And this is quite problematic: is it possible to declare that R. Meir's view were never attuned to the truth, while his opponents' views were always attuned to the truth? This is highly unlikely. And this has already been pointed out by the eminent author of *Responsa Havat Yair*, of blessed memory.

But as I wrote, halakhic truth is unlike geometric truth, in which there is only one solution. For anything that has a place in reasoning and among the views of those of profound comprehension, is truth by virtue of the intellect, and such truths may change in accordance with the views people hold at a given time. And it was the will of He who gave the Torah to delegate the matter to the scholars of the generation regarding all uncertainties that arise. For it was impossible to specify all of them in the Torah, and of necessity, new uncertainties come into being with the passage of time. And on all this, consult Nahmanides, of blessed memory, whose golden words well explain it.[121] And He commanded us and decreed that we are to follow the majority opinion. And since already at the time of the Sages of the Talmud, of blessed memory, differences of opinion had greatly proliferated on every single point of law, and the Sages were apprehensive lest, heaven forbid, Israel would split [and follow] several different sets of laws [lit., Torahs], and already during their time it was impossible to decide earlier controversies as to the laws themselves, and most of the laws had become ramified with respect to every single precept, and they did not feel themselves worthy of deciding between the opinions of their angelic predecessors, they relied on what is written in the Torah – that the resolution in [disputes about] the precepts hinges on the opinion of the high court. And the Torah gave permission to the pre-eminent court of each and every generation to determine the law in accordance with its opinion, for this would lessen the controversies, so that Israel would not follow several different sets of laws. And the Torah is indeed severe in sentencing the rebellious elder to death so that controversy will not proliferate; see Maimonides.[122]

And hence, the Sages formulated for themselves rules for decision making. And when they saw that one of the Tannaim or Amoraim had offered exceedingly sound arguments in almost every, or most, cases, they resolved that the law should be decided in accordance with his view everywhere. And even though there might be some detail with respect to which the true opinion seems to be the dissenting view, they were not concerned, since opinions change, and however correct it seems today it may look quite the opposite tomorrow. And as we cited above, in the passage from Eruvin, in which R. Meir would declare something impure and bring arguments

120 Ibid.
121 See Nahmanides' commentary on Deuteronomy 17:11.
122 *Code*, Laws concerning Rebels 3:4.

for it and then declare it pure and bring arguments for that. And so too the Sages determined that the law is in accordance with the view of Rav in matters of ritual law, and in accordance with that of Samuel in monetary matters,[123] because it seemed to them then that the view of Samuel, in monetary matters, was more cogent, and that that of Rav was more cogent in ritual law; except for a few cases in which the reasoning offered is patently untenable. And this is like the dictum, "Wherever the opinion of Rabban Shimon b. Gamaliel is mentioned in a Mishna, it is the law, except for *arev, tzidon, reiya aharona*."[124] And so too the law is everywhere in accordance with the view of Rava when it is opposed to that of Abbaye, except for *y"e"l k"g"m*,"[125] and there are many similar examples in the Talmud. And so too as to what they said, that up to [the generation of] Abbaye and Rava, the law is decided in accordance with the view of the earlier authority, but from Abbaye and Rava on, the law is in accordance with the view of the later authority. The reason for this is that the Sages saw that the discourse of Abbaye and Rava and the Amoraim after them was concerned mainly with clarification of earlier opinions, and since they derived the law from their deliberations, they thus constituted a later court, and the law is in accordance with their view, as we explained above, citing Maimonides, and consult the passage.[126]

115. Ein Aiya, Berakhot, chapter 9, 68

"R. Bisna b. Zabda said in the name of R. Ukba, who said it in the name of R. Panda, who said it in the name of R. Nahum, who said it in the name of R. Biryam, reporting a certain elder; and who was this? R. Banaa: There were twenty-four interpreters of dreams in Jerusalem. Once I dreamt a dream and went to consult all of them; the interpretation offered me by one, was not offered by the next, and all of them were fulfilled for me," and so on.[127] [From this] we learned that there are, on occasion, distinct views that do not really constitute a controversy, but rather, each individual addresses the problem from his own perspective on the matter, and no perspective precludes the other. And even with regard to the perspectives that seem to contradict each other, it is not to be concluded that they constitute a controversy, since it is possible that it looks like a controversy because the nature of the matter has not been sufficiently explored and elaborated on. But when one comes to know the matter thoroughly, he will discern that the different perspectives all have some value, even those that appear to contradict each other.

123 bBekhorot 49b.
124 bGitin 38a.
125 Six cases in which the law follows Abbaye; see Rif, bBerakhot 15a.
126 *Code*, Laws concerning Rebels 2:1.
127 bBerakhot 55b.

116. Mikhtav Mieliahu, part 3, p. 353

You ask me to clarify the talmudic passage, "All the prophets did not prophesy [foresee good] but for the repentant; as to the absolutely right-eous – 'Nor hath the eye seen a God other than Thee'[128] (Isa. 64:3). And this contradicts the view of R. Abbahu, who says that the repentant occupy a place unattainable by the absolutely righteous."[129] You note that this is not a contradiction, because the aspect of the grace of God, blessed be He, is revealed more in the penitent, which is not the case with respect to self-improvement, which is revealed more in those who have always been righteous. In saying this, you were absolutely right. And in truth, controversy is irrelevant except in legal matters, and even there, it is rele-vant only to questions of how we are to conduct ourselves in actual prac-tice. But controversy is irrelevant to the conceptual core of the issues, for the Sages, of blessed memory, said: Both are the words of the living God – meaning that both opinions are true perspectives, and both of them are true. For example, if we take a sheet of paper, and someone looks at its edge, its surface would be concealed from him. And if someone else sees only its surface, an argument would surely break out between them as to whether the paper had a broad surface or a sharp edge, and each would conceive of the other as completely mistaken. And what is the paper really like? Both see the very same sheet of paper, but from two perspectives, that is, two sides. And this too is analogous to what you mention in your letter about the controversy between the house of Shammai and the house of Hillel. For in the future the law will be in accordance with the view of the house of Shammai, as in the future the salient aspect of the law will be that of justice [whereas currently, the aspect of kindness is operative], and both are the words of the living God, and the nature of their controversy is that each saw the truth from the perspective of his own mode of serv-ing God. And see what my late great-grandfather, R. Israel Salanter, of blessed memory, wrote on this matter in *Or Yisrael*.[130]

And it is explicitly stated in *Tikunei Zohar* that controversy is not germane to matters of Aggada and Kabbala. The explanation is the same – both perspectives are true, each in terms of its own aspect, and there is no con-troversy as to actual practice. See *Even Shleima*[131] on the subject of the Messiah. It explains that there are two conceptions of the Messiah. The first is that of the Messiah who will bring about great spiritual revelation – the Messiah who is a descendant of David; the second, that of the Messiah who will bring only redemption from political bondage – the Messiah who is a descendant of Joseph. And the Sages' dicta about this that are

128 Their portion is so great that it is beyond description.
129 bBerakhot 34b.
130 Sec. 28.
131 By R. Elijah b. Solomon, the Vilna Gaon (1720–1797).

inconsistent with each other do not constitute a controversy. Now on the surface, this seems very strange, because there are several well-established talmudic passages – in tractates Berakhot, Sanhedrin, Shevuot, and elsewhere, I believe – which assert that "the prophecies of all the Prophets pertain only to the days of the Messiah," and so on. And "this is inconsistent with Samuel, who said that the sole difference between the present world and the time of the Messiah is freedom from political bondage." But we must of necessity say, as before, that 'inconsistent' means that there are two different aspects of redemption, one associated with the descendant of David and the other with the descendant of Joseph, and the meaning of 'inconsistent' in this context is 'to be separate and distinct.' And surely your distinction with respect to those who are repentant is quite true and clear, and I believe that I encountered this distinction some time ago in the holy books. And this is what the Sages, of blessed memory, mean in speaking of 'inconsistent' in this context.

117. Shiurei Daat, part 1, Darka shel tora, chapter 5

And what it is also important to realize in this regard, is that even among those privileged to have fathomed the truth of the Torah, there may well be controversies with regard to the law, some deeming a matter impure, others deeming it pure; some forbidding, others permitting; some holding liable and others exempting. Yet "both are the words of the living God."

The reason for this is that the Holy One, blessed be He, made the holy Torah, which is the foundation and root of creation, dependent on the chosen of His creatures, as it is said: "Thou hast made him have dominion over the works of Thy hand" (Ps. 8:7). And when the Torah was given to Israel, the laws on matters having to do with Israel were delegated to the Torah sages, so that, if only they fathomed the Torah's rationale and secrets, their thoughts would determine its reality and the reality of creation, which was contingent upon it. Therefore it is different from the other realms of wisdom, in which the investigators do not determine their reality, but discover it, as their thoughts and decisions can never change reality. It is not so with respect to knowledge of the Torah, in which the reality of impurity and purity, prohibition and permission, liability and exemption, is determined by the decisions of Torah scholars. For R. Joshua rose to his feet and exclaimed: "It is not in heaven" (Deut. 30:12) and we pay no attention to a heavenly voice . . . and the Holy One, blessed be He, smiled and said: My sons have triumphed over me, My sons have triumphed over me.[132] For with regard to the knowledge of the Torah, too, there are different aspects, and in every area of wisdom there are rationales pointing in a certain direction, and other rationales opposing it,

132 bBaba Metzia 59b.

for not only is wisdom deeper than the abyss, but it is wider than the sea. And the genuinely wise are not content to grasp wisdom from one side only, but seek to circumscribe it from every direction. Indeed we find that the house of Hillel had studied both its own opinions and those of the house of Shammai,[133] for both sides constitute the Torah. And the decision taken by considering all these various sides constitutes the binding determination of the law governing the reality of each of the sides, as long as no vote has been held to decide the law universally. Each individual comprehends the true law according to the elevation of his character, his disposition, his inner soul, and the influence of the thought and intellectual orientation imparted to him by his teachers. For teachers mold the intellectual bearings of their students, as it is said in the Talmud: "Anyone who teaches the son of his fellow, Scripture regards him as if he had sired him."[134] But all the various rationales and decisions are the words of the living God.

118. Pahad Yitzhak (Hutner), Hanuka, 3

Sometimes the abrogation of the Torah actually constitutes its observance, as it is written: "which thou didst break" (Exod. 34:1) – it is a credit to you that you broke them.[135] The act of breaking the tablets is an act of observing the Torah by abrogating it. And indeed, the Sages asserted that had the tablets not been broken, the Torah would not have been forgotten by Israel.[136] It follows, therefore, that breaking the tablets was, to some extent, an element in the Torah's having been forgotten. From this we learn a wonderful new idea, viz., that it is possible for the Torah to be augmented by its being forgotten, so that in this sense approbation is due even one who caused the Torah to be forgotten. And go out and see what the Sages said, that three hundred laws were forgotten in the period of mourning for Moses, but were recovered by Othniel b. Kenaz by means of his dialectics.[137] Now this dialectic analysis of the Torah, by which the laws were recovered, indeed constitutes an augmentation of the Torah solely because of its having been forgotten. Furthermore, the whole question of controversies as to the law is but a result of forgetting the Torah, and yet despite this the Sages say: "Even though some deem a matter pure, others deem it impure, some disqualify and others declare fit, some exempt and others find liable," and so on,[138] "both are the words of the

---

133 bEruvin 13b.
134 bSanhedrin 99b.
135 bJebamot 62a.
136 bEruvin 54a.
137 bTemura 16a.
138 bHagiga 3b; the quotation is inexact.

living God."[139] So it follows that all the differences of opinion and various approaches constitute an expansion of and tribute to the Torah, born precisely of its having been forgotten.

From this we also gain an even greater new insight: that the power of the oral law is better demonstrated in the espousal of contrary opinions than in consensus of opinion. For the dictum that both are the words of the living God contains the principle that the opinion rejected by the law, if advanced in the context of debating the oral law, is also an authoritative Torah view (*daat tora*). And thus, since the Torah was given subject to the understanding of its scholars,[140] if these scholars later decide by vote to uphold the rejected opinion, from then on the truth of the matter is that the law changes.[141] And it turns out that the disagreement of Torah scholars reveals the strength of the oral law much more than does their agreement. The war of the Torah is not [the discovery of] one of the many modes of expressing the words of the Torah, but rather, the war of the Torah is the actual creation of new Torah values, the likes of which are not found in plain Torah study. "Wherefore it is said in the book of the Wars of the Lord: Vaheb in Suphah" (Num. 21:14): the Sages explain that [in the heat of an argument], "even father and son, teacher and student, become enemies of each other, yet they do not budge from there until they come to love each other."[142] At first glance these words seem intended to inform us of the great significance of the amity inherently fostered by the words of the Torah, an affection so potent as to ensure devoted friendship even among those who had previously become enemies of each other. On this interpretation, the significance of the passage lies in showing that despite the enmity at the time of the controversy, ultimately companionship emerges and overtakes it, and the parties do not budge before they are friends. However, since the point that the war of the Torah constitutes a level of creativity surpassing that of plain Torah study has now become clear to us, this insight teaches us to appreciate that the issue here is not that friendship ultimately ensues despite the prior controversy, but rather, that this is the very means by which such friendship grows, as it was planted and cultivated precisely in the soil of the prior controversy. For all love reaches its zenith when the two sides are partners in creation, and the two contending sides in the halakhic dispute are partners in creating a new Torah value, the name of which is, the war of the Torah.

Let us now return to what was said earlier. The reality of controversy over matters of Torah, which has persisted to the present day, was indeed engendered by the darkness of Hellenism, but in any event this reality does not indicate that our redemption from Hellenism is incomplete.

139 bEruvin 13b.
140 Borrowing the words of Nahmanides on Deuteronomy 17:11.
141 See *Or Yisrael*, chapter 30, note.
142 bKidushin 30b; the quotation is inexact.

On the contrary, the Hanuka deliverance effected by the Hasmonean law courts is a victory over the Hellenistic darkness, by bringing forth light from within that very darkness. "To make the Torah great and glorious" (Isa. 42:21) – the Torah, by having been forgotten, was effaced, and this sustains it. While the fall of Babylonia and Media indeed brought relief from the oppression suffered by the congregation of Israel, the fall of Hellas, too, served as a balm for that injury, a balm compounded from the injury itself. For when the evil Hellenistic kingdom stood over Your people Israel, endeavoring to make it forget Your Torah, behold, within that very oblivion, new fountains of Torah sprang forth. This occurred through the burgeoning renewed dialectic that is emerging daily in order to reestablish the clarification of the Torah, which was increasingly forgotten. Hanuka was the last festival observance of which was mandated for generations to come. Since even in the thick of the darkness of oblivion itself it is possible to find sparks of the Torah's propagation, so it is possible that by virtue of this trait we will be able to proceed down the long road of forgetting – the Edomite exile – leading to the final days. "Then shall I complete in songs of praise the anointment of the altar."[143]

119. Responsa Igrot Moshe, OH 1, foreword

But the correct view, in my humble opinion, is that the scholars of later generations are permitted and required to hand down rulings, even if they would not have been considered worthy of handing down rulings in the generations of the talmudic Sages. To be sure, one certainly ought be apprehensive that he may not be able to reach the true legal conclusions – those that concur with the truth as known by heaven. But regarding truth in the context of legal rulings, it has already been declared that "it is not in heaven" (Deut. 30:12). Rather, the truth is as seems correct to the scholar after he has studied the law properly, to determine how it is explicated in the Talmud and the legal literature, according to his ability, with due solemnity and fear of God, may He be blessed. If it then seems to him that a certain conclusion is the law, this is indeed the true ruling, and he is required to proclaim it, even if in heaven it is really known that the true interpretation is otherwise. And regarding such instances it is said that his words, too, are the words of the living God, since he thinks that his ruling is the correct interpretation, and it has not been refuted, and he will be rewarded for his ruling even if the truth does not accord with the way he interpreted [the law].

And there is a good argument for this in the Talmud. "R. Isaac said: There was a town in the land of Israel in which they followed R. Eliezer, and the Holy One, blessed be He, rewarded them generously, so that they

---

143 From the Hanuka hymn "Maoz Tzur."

lived out their days, and when the evil monarchy forbade circumcision, this edict did not apply to that town."[144] Even though the truth, in terms of the law, is decided contrary to the opinion of R. Eliezer, and a transgressor is subject to stoning, if he transgressed intentionally, or must bring a sin-offering, if he transgressed unwittingly, nonetheless, we can see that as to handing down a ruling, the truth that must be handed down – and is rewarded by heaven – is that which the scholar, after deliberating with all his might, thinks to be the truth, even if the real truth is not as he decides. And this is the nature of all the controversies of our Rabbis and later scholars, one forbids and the other permits. As long as the law has not been determined to be in accordance with one of the views, each can, in his own jurisdiction, rule as he thinks correct, although the true law corresponds to only one of the views. And both scholars are rewarded for their rulings. And for this reason we find that there are numerous divergences even regarding serious prohibitions, between places in which they rule in accordance with the views of Maimonides and the Beit Yosef, and places where their custom is to follow the Tosafists and R. Moses Isserles, and both are the words of the living God, even though the true truth, as known in heaven, is in accordance with only one of the views.

And this is also stated explicitly in tractate Sanhedrin. After stating: And judges must be aware whom they judge, and before whom they pass judgment, and who will hold them responsible, lest the judge will say: Why do I need this burden? And Rashi explains, "if I am wrong, I will be punished" – Scripture teaches, "With you on the matters of judgment" (II Chron. 19:6) – [the talmudic text continues]: The judge must rely only on that which his eyes behold[145] – Rashi explains this as follows: "the judge need not fear, and refrain from rendering judgment, but rather must rule on the basis of what his eyes behold, with the intention of bringing what is right and true to light, and he will not be punished."[146] And consult the text. He means to say that even if it is not the real truth, the opinion of the judge is, for the purposes of deciding the law, the truth, which he is obliged to define and hand down.

This explains the passage from tractate Menahot, "R. Judah said in the name of Rav, When Moses ascended on high he found the Holy One, blessed be He, engaged in affixing coronets to the letters. He said, [standing] before Him, Master of the Universe, who is holding You back?[147] He answered, There will arise a man, at the end of many generations, Akiva

144 bShabat 130b.
145 bSanhedrin 6b; the quotation is inexact.
146 See Rashi ad loc.
147 This describes Moses' perplexity upon observing God affixing coronets, flourishes, to the letters of the completed Torah. He questioned why the flourishes were needed, when all of mankind awaited the Torah.

b. Joseph by name, who will expound upon each tittle heaps and heaps of laws."[148] Now the meaning of the term "coronets," used here, it is not immediately clear. Another difficulty is what Moses means in asking, "who is holding You back?" As to Rashi's explanation, 'Why do You need to add these coronets?' – if so, 'holding back' is the not the relevant concept, and even were it relevant, somehow, it is perplexing why He has to be bothered with all this. And if he wanted to ask: why did He not state [the additional laws] directly? – then the answer that R. Akiva will expound "heaps of laws" is unclear.

But given my explanation, this talk of coronets is indeed precise. For [by affixing coronets,] God, may He be blessed, makes the letters kings – that is, the scholar draws analogies from Scripture, and hands down his ruling according to his understanding of the arguments contained in the letters of the Torah. And when there is a controversy, they rule in accordance with the opinion of the majority of the Torah scholars, even if it is conceivable that they did not arrive at the truth, and the view of the Holy One, blessed be He, was not the same as theirs. For the Holy One, blessed be He, gave the Torah to Israel to act upon in accordance with their understanding of what is written and what was transmitted orally at Sinai, in accordance with their understanding. And God, may He be blessed, will provide no further interpretation or resolution of any matter pertaining to the laws of the Torah, for "it is not in heaven" (Deut. 30:12), but He agreed in advance with the way it would be understood and interpreted by the scholars. Thus it turns out that the letters of the Torah are like sovereigns, whom we obey by acting in accordance with the meaning scholars ascribe to the Torah, even if this is not in accordance with the way God, may He be blessed, understands it. And the expression "the Torah says," which we find in a number of places [in the Talmud], is fitting, because we only discuss what the Torah says. And also fitting is the passage regarding the house of Shammai and the house of Hillel in tractate Eruvin, "both are the words of the living God." Since the Torah can be interpreted in accordance with the views of both the house of Shammai and the house of Hillel, we find that the law was formulated in accordance with both views, as long as one of the opinions has not been invalidated by a majority view to the contrary. And this is the interpretation of "who is holding You back?" – Moses was asking why the Holy One, blessed be He, was making the letters of the Torah into sovereigns, meaning, that the people would have to follow the written and orally-transmitted text according to the scholars' interpretation, when there was no one to prevent God from writing it in such a way that it would be impossible for it to be interpreted in any way other than that in which He

---

148 bMenahot 29b; the quotation is inexact.

truly intended [it to be understood]. [Moses was asking] why God had given sovereign authority to the letters, making it likely that at times [the scholars] would interpret it in a manner contrary to His intended interpretation. And the Holy One, blessed be He, answered that this was so that from the little that had been written down or orally transmitted, R. Akiva and the Sages would be able to derive heaps of laws, which would constitute a magnification of the Torah, and to write copiously, explicating everything in infinite detail, for the Torah is without end or bounds.[149]

3.1. Seventy facets to the Torah

120. Mekhilta Yitro, Masekhta de-bahodesh, 7 (Horowitz edition, p. 229)

"Remember" (Exod. 20:8) and "observe" (Deut. 5:12) – both were spoken in a single utterance; "every one that profaneth it shall surely be put to death" (Exod. 31:14), and "on the Sabbath day two he-lambs" (Num. 28:9) – both were spoken in a single utterance; "the nakedness of thy brother's wife" (Lev. 18:16) and "her husband's brother shall go in unto her" (Deut. 25:5) – both were spoken in a single utterance; "thou shalt not wear a mingled stuff" (Deut. 22:11) and "thou shalt make thee twisted cords" (Deut. 22:12) – both were spoken in a single utterance; which cannot be done by a human being, as it is said, "God hath spoken once, twice have I heard this" (Ps. 62:12); and it says, "Is not My word like a fire? declareth the Lord. And like a hammer that breaketh the rock in pieces?" (Jer. 23:29).

121. bShabat 88b

R. Johanan said: What does Scripture mean by: "The Lord giveth the word; the women who proclaim the tidings are a great host" (Ps. 68:12)? Each and every word that leaves the mouth of the Almighty splits into seventy tongues. The school of R. Ishmael taught: "And like a hammer that breaketh the rock in pieces" (Jer. 23:29): just as a hammer breaks forth many sparks, so every each and every word that went forth from the Holy One, blessed be He, split into seventy languages.[150]

122. bSanhedrin 34a

As R. Asi asked R. Johanan, What if two [judges] derive the same teaching from two different verses? He said to him, they are only counted as

---

149 See bEruvin 21a.

150 The teaching of R. Ishmael here is far from clear. While the biblical verse speaks of a hammer that breaks up rock, the exegete focuses on a different aspect of the blow – the sparks it generates.

one. How do we know this? Abbaye said: Scripture says: "God hath spoken once, twice have I heard this: that strength belongeth unto God" (Ps. 62:12). One biblical verse may express several teachings, while one teaching is not deduced from several verses. The school of R. Ishmael taught: "And like a hammer that breaketh the rock in pieces" (Jer. 23:29): just as a hammer breaks forth many sparks, so a single biblical verse may express many teachings.

123. Numbers Rabbah 13:15

"One silver bowl of seventy shekels" (Num. 7:13) – this refers to the Torah, which is analogized to wine, as it is said, "and drink of the wine which I have mixed" (Prov. 9:5), and since it is the nature of wine to be drunk from a bowl, inasmuch as it is said, "who drink wine in bowls" (Amos 6:6), for this purpose, the bowl was invoked. "... seventy shekels, after the shekels of the sanctuary" (Num. 7:13). For what reason? Just as the numerical value of wine is seventy,[151] so there are seventy facets to the Torah.

124. Zohar, Genesis 47:2

"And all their hosts" (Gen. 2:1) – these are the minutiae of the Torah, the aspects of the Torah; there are seventy facets to the Torah.

125. Zohar, Leviticus 20:1

The members of the Sanhedrin knew seventy languages, for there are seventy facets to the Torah. For there are seventy languages from the side of the evil kingdom, and so on, each one distinct. As it is written "Of these were the isles of the nations divided in their lands, every one after his tongue" (Gen. 10:5). All seventy languages are different from each other. But in the case of the Torah – there are seventy facets to the Torah in one language.

126. Peirushei Haagadot Lerabi Azriel, bHagiga 3b

"The words of the wise are as goads, and as nails well planted are those of the masters of assemblies" (Eccles. 12:11), these are the scholars who sit in various assemblies and apply themselves to the Torah; some deem a matter impure, others deem it pure,

---

151 10 + 10 + 50 = 70.

some prohibit, others permit, some disqualify, others declare fit. Lest you say, since some deem a matter impure, and so on, under these circumstances, how can I learn the Torah?, therefore Scripture says: All "were given from one shepherd." One God gave them, one leader uttered them from the mouth of the Master of all deeds, blessed be He, as it is written, "And God spake all these words" (Exod. 20:1).[152]

Attend well to how the three [pairs of] rankings[153] are to be understood. The Sages said: Seventy facets to the Torah, and these facets fluctuate from one to the other; to deem it impure, to deem it pure, to prohibit, to permit, as one of the colleagues said: I can bring forty nine arguments to purify a creeping thing.[154] All these different interpretations were included in a single utterance, as it is written, "with a great voice, and it went on no more" (Deut. 5:19). It included all the aspects, their various changing configurations and their opposites: to render impure and render pure, to prohibit and to permit, to disqualify and to declare fit, because it could not be believed that that voice lacked anything. And therefore, in that voice everything was constantly turning over on all sides, one thing opposite the other. And every one of the future sages who might arise in each and every generation received his portion, as it is said, "not only did all the prophets receive their prophecy from Sinai, but also each of the Sages who arise in each and every generation – each and every one received his portion, as it is said, "These words the Lord spoke unto all your assembly" (Deut. 5:19)."[155] Hence their dictum: "both are the words of the living God,"[156] as it is said, "One God gave them all."[157]

127. Sefer Hahinukh, precept 77

All these matters we have learned from the verse, "neither shalt thou bear witness in a cause to turn aside" (Exod 23:2). This matter derives from the power of the wisdom of the Torah, in that from a single point in it we are to comprehend many points. And the Sages, of blessed memory, used to say: There are seventy facets to the Torah. And since God knows that the people who received the Torah, insofar as they behave the way they were commanded, will be open to wisdom and understanding, and they will understand everything in it that they need [to know] about the conduct of the world, He occasionally left things unspecified, and transmitted the

152 The quotation is inexact.
153 I.e., impure/pure, prohibited/permitted, disqualified/made fit.
154 bSanhedrin 17a.
155 Exodus Rabbah 28:6.
156 bEruvin 13b.
157 bHagiga 3b.

interpretation to them via the great mediator [Moses] between them and Him. And He did not give the Torah using more verbose locutions, since all its words are well-honed and essential, in their number and form, as they are. Because aside from the significance of the precious precepts that we comprehend in it, it also includes great and glorious wisdoms, so much so that our Rabbis, of blessed memory, elevated the greatness of the wisdom that God, blessed be He, set down in [the Torah], by saying of it that the Holy One, blessed is He, looked upon it and created the world.

128. Responsa Radbaz, 3, #643

You asked me to give you my opinion as to why, in view of the fact that all was given to Moses our teacher, may he rest in peace, at Sinai, the Torah scroll is written without vowel points, and it would have been appropriate to insert the cantillation signs too, so that the reader could read it smoothly, without blunder, since the cantillation signs sometimes clarify the meaning of Scripture.

Answer: Your question hinges on what the angels asked the Holy One, blessed be He, when Moses our teacher, may he rest in peace, ascended [to heaven] to receive the Torah: The attending angels said, What business has one who was born of a woman among us? The Holy One, blessed be He, said to them, He has come to receive the Torah. They said to Him: Give it to us, as it is written "whose majesty is rehearsed above the heavens" (Ps. 8:2). Moses said to them, What is written in the Torah? "Thou shalt not murder. Thou shalt not commit adultery," and so on (Exod. 20). Is there murder among you? Is there adultery among you? What do you need the Torah for? They conceded and said, "O Lord our God, how glorious is Thy Name in all the earth" (Ps. 8:2).[158] And here a question should be asked. Is it plausible that the angels were unaware of this answer? We must say, therefore, that they gave the Torah a different reading, a spiritual reading, not by means of separate words, but according to the Names of the Holy One, blessed be He. As the Rabbis, of blessed memory, said: the entire Torah consists of the Names of the Holy One, blessed be He.

So the Holy One, blessed be He, informed the angels that the Torah has another, material, reading, via its division into words pertinent to human matters – impurity and purity, matters prohibited and permitted, exemptions and liabilities, and all the other laws. And after you grasp this you will understand [the answer to] your question. For God, may He be exalted, commanded that the Torah be written without pointing and cantillation signs, as it was when it was in its infancy with Him, may He be blessed, so

158 bShabat 88b.

that it should have two readings, one spiritual and the other material, so that those capable of grasping it could grasp it. Indeed the Sages said: "Bezalel knew the art of joining the letters by which heaven and earth were created."[159] So He conveyed the pointing and cantillation signs as He did the rest of the oral law, which is a commentary on the written law, and thus the pointing and cantillation signs, too, constitute commentary on the written law. It is well known that the letters, without pointing and cantillation signs, have many meanings and different combinations, and contrary readings. And for this reason it was not permitted for the points and cantillation signs to be written in the Torah scrolls, but they are written in the printed editions of the Pentateuch on the basis of the dictum, "It is time to work for the Lord" (Ps. 119:126), so that the art of reading should not be forgotten, as is the case regarding the rest of the oral law.

And you can use what I have written you to answer a number of other uncertainties, such as the question asked by earlier scholars, namely, why the oral law was not written, or why some seemingly unnecessary stories are included in the Scriptures, and, why some of the important precepts were only hinted at with veiled hints. For you have to believe that there is not even one tiny word that does not contain deep secrets and permutations that are beyond our comprehension, and there is not a single letter in the Torah that is unnecessary. And these are not stylistic considerations, or *kaf rafa*,[160] as in Arabic, as many have surmised. And bear this in mind constantly and you are certain to succeed, and I guarantee it. And I have written that which seems right, in my humble opinion.

And here is something I found in a marginal annotation, and this is how it reads:

> I found this in a work by an earlier scholar, whose name is unknown to me. Know that since pointing is the form and soul of letters, therefore the Torah scroll is not pointed, because it contains every perspective and every profound direction. And all of them can be expounded from every single letter, perspectives and internal perspectives, and mysteries and internal mysteries, which have no boundaries known to us, as it is said, "the Deep saith it is not within me" (Job 28:14). If we were to point the Torah scroll, it would have, as does matter, a boundary and measure that assigns it a specific shape, and it would only be possible to interpret it according to the given pointing of each word. However, since the Torah mingles and intermingles all types of perfection, and each and every word of it supports mountains upon mountains

---

159 bBerakhot 55a.
160 A redundant letter inserted for stylistic reasons in Arabic.

[of significance], it is not pointed, so that it can be interpreted to reflect these perfections. Hence their dictum, "read it not thus, but so." Were it completely specified [by pointing], we would be unable to say that.

And behold, in a number of places the Sages, of blessed memory, were inspired to formulate exquisite interpretations. For instance, "And you shall have a spade among your weapons" (Deut. 23:14) – "read not 'weapons,' but 'ears,' to teach us that when one hears something uncouth, he should plug his ears with his fingers."[161] Here they draw our attention to the hidden reason that the Torah scroll is unpointed. And in the exegesis on this verse, simpletons are supplied with coarse bread, while the wise were given, in this very exegesis, choice loaves. And it all derives from the plain meaning of the text, and the whole Torah is conveyed in this manner. And therefore the Sages said: "There are seventy facets to the Torah." And seek to understood this.[162]

129. Baalei Brit Avram, foreword

So it should be clear to you that the ancient scholars, with the high level they attained, and their proximity to prophecy – as the Rabbis, of blessed memory, said in tractate Eruvin, "The hearts of the ancients were like the entrance to the *ulam* [20 cubits] and those of later generations, like the eye of a needle"; and also in tractate Shabat, and in tractate Demai of the Jerusalem Talmud, "If the earlier authorities were men, we are but sons of asses"; and in tractate Yoma, "The fingernails of the early authorities were greater than the bellies of the later authorities"[163] – And if the early authorities, with all their great wisdom, took care not to say anything they had not heard, as was mentioned above, as reflected in their expression, "I did not hear this, and I will not say it," all the more so should this be so for later authorities. And if so, it behooves us to investigate and ascertain who permitted the later authorities to offer new interpretations based on their own intellection, and to interpret the plain text of the Scriptures, each one [doing so] in line with the conjectures of his own understanding, though they had not received these interpretations from their teachers, nor had their teachers [received them] from their own teachers. And indeed this appears to be an instance of one who causes the law to have a meaning other than that

161 bKetubot 5a. The context is the injunction to ensure the sanitation of the Israelite camps, by mandating that spades be carried to cover excrement. The word for "your weapons" (*azeinekha*), differently pointed, reads "your ears" (*oznekha*).
162 This passage, with minor variants, has been found in the "Essay on the inner core of the Torah attributed to Nahmanides."
163 bEruvin 53a, bShabat 112b, jDemai 1:3, bYoma 9b.

which is in accordance with traditional law, as implied in the remarks of the Zohar, cited earlier, and it deserves a most severe punishment.

And here I would invoke the following parable: A king issued a royal proclamation, to be announced in the town, in his name and that of his nobles, declaring: All those who had served in the army were to gather together to defend themselves, everyone with his weapon in hand, and stand in readiness, lest the enemy approach the town without encountering risk, to annihilate, kill, and destroy it. Anyone who disobeyed the king's commandment would be subject to but one law – to be put to death. And this was written in the king's name and sealed with the king's ring. After the royal proclamation had been sounded, one of the town's elders and dignitaries came and secretly spoke thus to the townspeople: You have not understood the words read by the herald, and have not realized the meaning of the king's command. For his words were not comprehended, and his words constitute a cryptic enigma vouchsafed only to me. And the people sorely entreated the elder to reveal the king's intentions to them. And the elder told them: Know well, then, that the enemy lying in ambush is none other than the evil inclination in our hearts from the days of our youth. For a man's enemy comes from his own household, that is, his body. And the king's commandment is telling us to chastise it with penances and fasts, for these are the weapons that can counter it, and save our souls from the enemy waiting in ambush. And do not let the sleep of lassitude close your eyes. And what could be sweeter than the honey of the herald's oratory, and the allegory he related?

Now the words of the elder seemed very apt to the entire community, and they raised their voices in unison, and said to him, You have saved our lives, let us find favor in your eyes. And the people harkened to the words of the elder, and believed his words. So they removed their ornaments and declared a fast and prayer meeting; they dressed in sackcloth, and, overcoming their lascivious inclinations, as the elder had spoken, returned to God with all their hearts and all their might. But at night the enemy entered the city without hindrance and, as no one was standing guard to resist them, plundered and pillaged, then went on its way. And on the morrow, the king said to his subjects, Why did you not take steps in accordance with my directive? And why have you thrown me behind you? And the entire community raised their voices and cried, and begged the king for mercy, and fell at his feet and said to him, Let God investigate the old man, and He shall judge, for he caused this misfortune to befall us. They related to the king all that had befallen them due to the old man, and the king became vexed with them and also vexed with the old man.

And behold, I find the parable analogous to our discussion. For when there is a but a single certain divine intention in a given scriptural verse, and someone puts forward an interpretation contrary to that which He, may He be blessed, intended, without due caution lest he change its purpose, how very great is the punishment [that is warranted], for this has stripped the Torah of its regalia and dressed it in sackcloth. Therefore, I wish I knew[164] whence the licence for the early scholars of Israel, and even more surprisingly, the later scholars, to interpret the Torah, each straying in accordance with his own thinking, each going his own direction, one unlike the other.

But I will answer this as follows. For upon perusal of the works of our Rabbis, of blessed memory, we find that this is their way in exegesis and Aggada. And perhaps it is only the exception, for not all that the Rabbis, of blessed memory, say has been handed down by tradition, but some of it is what they, of blessed memory, newly arrived at by their pure study, yet is not to be regarded as tenets of faith. Indeed, their intention was to augment the meaning of Scripture and to expound upon it from every conceivable perspective. And certainly, most of the remarks made by these scholars on Scripture are not offered as an explanation of the text, in contrast to those commentators who intend to clarify the meaning of the text itself, as in the case of the said parable. Indeed, the aim of the Sages was to consider external matters and knowledge, either to demonstrate God's benevolence and greatness, to praise some virtue or deride some deficiency, or, to teach a moral in order to distance us from some folly. And they associated all these points with particular scriptural verses as a mnemonic aid. And indeed, note what our great and righteous halakhic authority, Maimonides, may his blessed memory be eternal, had to say on this subject:

> Regarding midrashic exegesis, people fall into two categories. In the first are those who believe that the exegeses are the true explanation of the verse and fight strenuously to confirm the exegetical interpretations and keep them within the parameters of traditional law. And those in the second mock them and consider them a joke, since it is clear and explicit that the verse does not mean what the said interpretation says. Neither of the two categories comprehends that midrashic exegesis adopted the literary and poetic forms that were current at the time, as in the exegesis: "Bar Kapara teaches, 'And you shall have a spade among your weapons' (Deut. 23:14) – read not 'weapons,' but 'ears,' to teach us that when one hears something uncouth he should plug his ears with his fingers."[165] And I wonder whether those fools believe that the Tanna here [Bar Kapara] indeed thought that this was the meaning of the verse, and the intended precept; that 'spade' means 'finger' and 'weapons' indeed denotes 'ears.' And I do not think anyone in his

164 Lit., "O that I knew...to come even to His seat," alluding to Job 23:3.
165 bKetubot 5a on Deuteronomy 23:14.

right mind would suppose this. However, the teaching [embodied in] this literary and poetic form is very good, admonishing us regarding a commendable trait, namely, that just as we are forbidden to utter vulgarities, so too it is forbidden to listen to them. And they associated this teaching with the verse in question by means of allegory and poetry. And in exegesis, whenever it says, 'read it not thus but read it so,' this is the intention.[166] . . .

. . . Hence, one cannot refute legal arguments on the basis of exegesis, nor is it subject to refutation. For the intention of such exegesis is not to offer an authoritative interpretation of the scriptural text, but to anchor [a homiletic teaching], as we said.

But with regard to their legal assertions, we must not deviate either to the right or to the left, and we must not contradict them, heaven forbid, for only a stubborn fool would put forward an interpretation contrary to theirs. For here the allegory we proposed about one who transgresses the king's commandment and thus undoubtedly forfeits his life is indeed apt; because in the determination of the law, the interpretation received by the Sages cannot be countered with an opposed interpretation, as discussed. And indeed Nahmanides, of blessed memory, formulated this rule, saying that if the Gemara's interpretation makes a difference in the law, we do not deviate from the Gemara.

The other type of textual interpretation, that is, midrashic exegesis, is where later authorities were permitted to interpret Scripture as each of them saw fit. And it does not serve even as a supporting allusion[167] (asmakhta), but is only in accordance with the second intended objective [i.e., it is a homiletic endeavor], as I have seen explained on the authority of Nahmanides, of blessed memory. And one can find examples of such interpretation in the Bible. And with respect to this second intended objective, it includes beautiful matters from the secrets of reality, to the extent that they can be discovered. And so it is possible to say that for this benefit, some of the enlightened members of our nation interpreted stories as alluding to these secrets, in line with the second intention.

And this approach is also warranted from the standpoint of reason. And the matter is thus: Just as the astronomers, in their wisdom, hypothesized that there are, in the heavens, concentric geocentric spheres [eccentrics], as well as spheres circumscribing the heavens [epicycles], and further, elliptical orbits [deferents], though they based their theory on premises refuted by nature, nevertheless we accept their theory, since it is attested to by the senses and by reasoning. Therefore when Ptolemy

---

166 *Guide for the Perplexed*, III:43.
167 Viz., a textual anchor.

assumed the existence of epicycles and eccentrics, he wrote in the third book of the *Almagest*, "Whether this is true or not, God alone knows, but we are satisfied that we have found a way to explain all that we observe in the motion of planets and stars in the heavens." And we can make an analogous assertion. Whether this interpretation is true or not only God knows, but we are satisfied that we have found a way to expound [Scripture] and to search for an axis on which can revolve resolution of the doubts with regard to the Scriptures or the dicta of the Sages, whether the solutions are in the same form or vary so as to be acceptable to reason. And all the more so since the Rabbis, of blessed memory, opened the gate for us in their adage, " 'And like a hammer that breaketh the rock in pieces' (Jer. 23:29): just as a hammer breaks forth many sparks,[168] so the words of the Torah may express many teachings." The Rabbis, of blessed memory, taught us that should you find various rationales and alternative meanings in words of the Torah, that is, words of prophecy or divine inspiration – a situation that does not arise in human discourse – this should not be rejected by the intellect. And the matter is analogous to the case of a single herb created by God, may He be blessed, to have various uses, much as in case of wine, which, as medical experts have made clear, has close to sixty medical uses, and one cannot ask which of these uses it was created for. Even more so, divine utterances can sustain a number of interpretations, and we do not purport to say what their true intent is. And this is what our Rabbis, of blessed memory, said: "Rabbah bar Abuha met Elijah, and asked him: Whose opinion guided Esther in her action? Elijah replied: The opinions of all the Tannaim and all the Amoraim."[169] And the intended meaning, as I mentioned, is that it is possible, even at the level of human discourse, to apprehend and grasp the various contradictions that can be conceived by human reason, and how much more so is this the case with regard to divine utterances.

In this context the Sages, of blessed memory, said, "Any new thing a seasoned scholar might say, was already declared to Moses at Sinai."[170] And they also said, "There are seventy facets to the Torah," and also said, "Inquire and receive your reward."[171] And I think that the meaning is that such a scholar adds power to the heavenly entourage, and demonstrates that every perfection is alluded to in the Torah. And it is for this reason that the oral law was not given together with the written law, to let us know that the written law was set down already prepared to accept any assumptions or perceptions with which it might be confronted. Just as

---

168 bShabat 88b.
169 bMegila 15b.
170 jPeia 2:4.
171 bSanhedrin 51b.

a burnished looking-glass mirrors the sights before it without any alteration, so does the Torah. And therefore: "Ben Bag Bag said: Turn it and turn it over again, for everything is in it."[172] This means that the assumptions and perfections are, without any doubt, alluded to in the Torah, for "everything is in it." And indeed, that which cannot be detected is due to lack of diligent scrutiny, hence, "turn it and turn it over again." And how apt are the words, "And see in it,"[173] as in the analogy we made. The meaning is that the Torah is like a looking-glass in which one sees his own face, and any face that is before it; the Torah is the same. And the Mishna concludes, "for you have no better principle than the Torah," meaning that one will not find this characteristic in any other legal doctrine, as mentioned above.

130. Derekh Etz Haim, first paragraph

About this, the Tanna said, "Turn it over and turn it over again, for everything is in it."[174] For those who are engaged [in study of the Torah] must turn it over and over, until it is virtually ignited, as an actual fire. Earlier, I noted that the burning flame comprises a variety of interwoven hues; similarly, many weighty matters are included in the flame of this light. But there is another matter as well. For the Torah has numerous aspects, and it was already accepted by our early authorities that at its root, every individual Israelite soul has a part in the Torah, so much so that there are six hundred thousand interpretations of the entire Torah found among the six hundred thousand Israelite souls. This is the meaning of the saying that the Torah brings forth many sparks, for in the beginning [the debate] heats up, and then all the lights that are relevant to the matter become visible, and these very lights enlighten in six hundred thousand ways the six hundred thousand Israelites, and this is the secret of the verse: "And like a hammer that breaketh the rock in pieces" (Jer. 23:29).

172 mAvot 5:22.
173 Ibid.
174 mAvot 5:22.

4

CONTROVERSY AND UNIFORMITY
OF PRACTICE

4.1. The 'do not form factions' prohibition
and its rationales

131. Sifre Deuteronomy 96 (Finkelstein edition, p. 158)

"Ye shall not cut yourselves" (*lo titgodedu*) (Deut. 14:1). Do not form factions, but be all bound together, as it is written, "It is He that buildeth His upper chambers in the heaven, and hath founded His binding[1] on earth" (Amos 9:6).

132. Sifre Deuteronomy 346 (Finkelstein edition, p. 403)

"[And there was a king in Jeshurun...] all the tribes of Israel together" (Deut. 33:5) – when they are all bound together, not when they are divided into factions, as it says: "It is He that buildeth His upper chamber in heaven, and hath founded His binding on earth" (Amos 9:6). R. Shimon b. Yohai says: A parable. A man brought two ships, anchored them and lashed them together with iron cable, securing them in the middle of the sea, and built a palace on them. As long as the two ships are tied together, the palace can stand. If the ships are separated, the palace cannot stand. Similarly with Israel. When Israel does the will of the Omnipresent, He builds His upper chamber in heaven, and when they do not do His will, He founds His binding on Earth, so to speak. Similarly, Scripture states: "This is my God and I will glorify Him" (Exod. 15:2) – when I acknowledge Him as my God, He is glorious, but if I do not acknowledge Him by His Name, He is glorious [only by virtue of] His Name, so to speak. Similarly regarding the verse, "For I will proclaim the Name of the Lord; ascribe ye greatness unto our God" (Deut. 32:3) – when I proclaim His Name He is great, and if not, so to speak, and so on. Similarly regarding the verse, "Therefore you are My witnesses, says the Lord, and I am God"

---

1 The term for binding, '*agudato*,' is in the singular.

(Isa. 43:12) – when you are My witnesses, I am God, and when you are not My witnesses, I am not God, so to speak. Similarly, "To You, enthroned in the heavens, I lift up my eyes" (Ps. 123:1) – were it not for me, so to speak, You would be not enthroned in the heavens, so to speak. And here too, you say: "[And there was a king in Jeshurun…] all the tribes of Israel together" (Deut. 33:5) – when they are all bound together, but not when they are divided into factions.

133. jPesahim 4:1 (30d)

> In a place where they are accustomed to work on the eve of Passover up to midday they do [work]; in a place where they are accustomed not to do work, they do not. Should someone go from a place where they do work to a place where they do not work, or from a place where they do not work to a place where they do work, the strictures of the place from which he came and the strictures of the place to which he has gone are applied to him. But one must not make any change due to[2] controversy.[3]

…R. Shimon b. Lakish asked R. Johanan: Is this not forbidden due to the prohibition against forming factions? He said to him: [The said prohibition applies only] when some act in accordance with the view of the house of Shammai and some act in accordance with the view of the house of Hillel. [But in case of a controversy between] the house of Shammai and the house of Hillel, is the law not in accordance with the view of the house of Hillel? [In which case the "do not form factions" prohibition is redundant.] He said to him: When some act in accordance with the view of R. Meir and others act in accordance with the view of R. Jose. [In a controversy between] R. Meir and R. Jose, is the law not in accordance with the views of R. Jose? He said to him: Two Tannaim argue over the words of R. Meir and two Tannaim argue over the words of R. Jose.

He said to him: But on the New Year and the Day of Atonement, in Judea, did people not conduct themselves in accordance with the views of R. Akiva, and in the Galilee, in accordance with those of R. Johanan b. Nuri?[4] He said to him: It is different, because one who moves to a different place, and follows the custom of the Judeans in the Galilee or the Galileans in Judea, has discharged his duty. But what about Purim, when some read the Book of Esther on the fourteenth [of Adar] and others on

---

2 The wording here is slightly ambiguous to reflect the Hebrew original: due to a past controversy, or a potential future controversy?

3 mPesahim 4:1.

4 This refers to the controversy over the order of the New Year prayer service; see mRosh Hashana 4:5.

the fifteenth? He said to him: The redactor of the Mishna relied on the verse, "every family, every province, and every city" (Esther 9:28).

134. bJebamot 13b–14a

We learned there: the Scroll [of Esther] is read on the eleventh, the twelfth, the thirteenth, the fourteenth or the fifteenth [of Adar], but not earlier or later.[5] Said Resh Lakish to R. Johanan: [Should we not] Apply here the admonition "ye shall not cut yourselves" (*lo titgodedu*) (Deut. 14:1), that is, do not form factions? Is not the injunction, "ye shall not cut yourselves" required in and of itself, the All-Merciful having said, You shall not inflict [upon yourselves] any bruise for the dead? If so, Scripture should have used the phrase, *lo tegodedu*; why then does it say *lo titgodedu*? So it can be inferred that this [the additional enjoinder against factionalism] is its object. Might it not then be suggested that the entire text refers to this latter point only? If so, Scripture should have said, *lo tagodu*, why then does it say *lo titgodedu*? So that the two injunctions can be inferred. He said to him, Do you not recall learning, In a place where they are accustomed to work on the eve of Passover up to midday, they do [work]; in a place where they are accustomed not to do work, they do not?[6] He said to him: I am speaking of a prohibition, for R. Shaman b. Abba said in the name of R. Johanan: [Scripture having said,] "To confirm these days of Purim in their appointed times" (Esther 9:31), the Sages have ordained many different times for them, and you speak to me of a custom! But is there no prohibition here? Surely we learned, The house of Shammai prohibit [work] during the night and the house of Hillel permit it.[7] He said to him: In that case, anyone seeing [someone abstaining from work] would suppose him to be out of work.[8] Yet "the house of Shammai permit the rival[-wive]s to the brothers, but the house of Hillel prohibit it,"[9] do they not? Do you suppose that the house of Shammai acted in accordance with their views? The house of Shammai did not act in accordance with their views! R. Johanan, however, said: They certainly did act thus.

Here they differ [on the same point as do Rav and Samuel]. For Rav maintains that the house of Shammai did not act in accordance with their views, while Samuel maintains that they certainly did. When?

---

5 mMegila 1:1.

6 mPesahim 4:1.

7 mPesahim 4:5.

8 And would not interpret it as pointing to the existence of a divergent practice. Hence, the question of factions would not arise.

9 mJebamot 1:4. The reference here is to rival-wives in the context of levirate marriage. When a husband has more than one wife, and dies childless, one of his brothers has to either marry the widow (levirate marriage), or perform the ritual of *halitza*. The debate between the houses refers to cases where, for some halakhic reason, one of the brothers is forbidden to marry one of the widows: is he permitted to marry a different one?

If it is suggested that this occurred prior to the decision of the heavenly voice,[10] for what reason could it be maintained that they did not act in accordance with their views? And if it was after the decision of the heavenly voice, for what reason could it be claimed that they did act in accordance with their views? If you wish, say it was prior to the decision of the heavenly voice; and if you wish, say, after the heavenly voice. If you wish, say it was prior to the heavenly voice, at the time when the house of Hillel were in the majority. It could be said that they did not act in accordance with their views since the house of Hillel were in the majority; and it could be said that they acted in accordance with their views because a majority is to be followed only when the sides are equally matched; in this case, however, the house of Shammai were more incisive.

If you wish, say it was after the heavenly voice, it could be said that they did not act in accordance with their views since the heavenly voice had already gone forth; while it could be said that they did act in accordance with their views, as they concurred with R. Joshua, who declared that a heavenly voice need not be attended to.[11]

Now as to those who say that they did act in accordance with their views, should not the admonition "ye shall not cut yourselves" (*lo titgodedu*) – do not form factions – be applied? Abbaye said: The admonition against forming factions is applicable to a case such as that of two courts of law in the same town, one of which rules in accordance with the view of the house of Shammai while the other rules in accordance with the view of the house of Hillel. However, in a case of two courts of law in two different towns, it is irrelevant. Rava said to him, surely the case of the house of Shammai and the house of Hillel is like that of two courts of law in the same town? But, Rava said, the dictum "do not form factions" is [only] applicable to a case such as that of a court of law in a given town, part of which rules in accordance with the view of the house of Shammai while the other part rules in accordance with the view of the house of Hillel. However, in a case of two courts of law in the same town, it is irrelevant.

Come and hear: In the locale of R. Eliezer, wood was chopped on the Sabbath to produce charcoal with which to forge the iron. In the locale of R. Jose the Galilean, the flesh of fowl was eaten with milk. In the locale of R. Eliezer only, but not in the locale of R. Akiva; as we learned: R. Akiva laid it down as a general rule that any labor that can be performed on the eve of the Sabbath does not supersede the Sabbath. What sort of an objection is that?[12] The case is surely different when the varied practices

---

10 See bEruvin 13a.
11 bBaba Metzia 59b.
12 From the perspective of the view that objects to creating different sects, it is difficult to understand why these variant practices were condoned.

take place in different locales. What did he who raised this point think? One might have assumed that owing to the exacting laws of the Sabbath, different locales are regarded as one, hence it was necessary to teach us that the law is not so.

Come and hear: R. Abbahu, when he happened to be in the locale of R. Joshua b. Levi, would carry a candle, but when he happened to be in the locale of R. Johanan, would not carry a candle.[13] What is the question here – have we not said that it is different when the varied practices are confined to different locales? We therefore say [that the question is,] how could R. Abbahu act one way in one place and otherwise in another? R. Abbahu shared the opinion of R. Joshua b. Levi, but, when he happened to be in R. Johanan's locale, did not carry [a candle] out of respect for R. Johanan. But surely his attendant was also there? He gave his attendant the necessary instructions.

135. Hidushei Haritba, bRosh Hashana 34a (responsum by R. Hai Gaon)

Our master [R. Hai Gaon] of blessed memory, was asked: Should we assume that before the time of R. Abbahu, Israel did not discharge the precept of blowing the shofar? Apparently, the sound of the *terua* was subject to doubt among them,[14] as it is said, "this is surely a matter of controversy," but there is no doubt that the issue must have been decided: is it conceivable that they did not know the true procedure for a precept that had to be observed every year? Had they not seen how it was observed, each generation showing the next, one hearing the tradition from another, back to Moses our teacher, of blessed memory?

And our master, of blessed memory, answered that the *terua* as prescribed by the Torah is certainly discharged with either a wailing or a groaning blast, because the Torah intended that the *terua* be composed of sounds and broken blasts. And in earlier times it was performed either as broken blasts or as wailing; it was a matter of individual judgment as to which was more apt, and the obligation was in any event discharged. This was known to the learned, but ordinary people mistakenly thought that there was a difference between them, and therefore that one or another group was not discharging its obligation with respect to the precept. So to dispel this view held by the ignorant, and in order to prevent the Torah from becoming like

---

13 According to R. Joshua b. Levi, a candle, though already lit when the Sabbath began, may be moved on the Sabbath after the flame has gone out. R. Johanan forbids this.

14 The Talmud relates that in Caesarea, R. Abbahu ordained, regarding the blowing of the shofar, that there should be a long blast, three short blasts, one wailing blast and another long blast. This was because R. Abbahu was in doubt over the *terua* – was it a kind of wailing or a kind of groaning?

two separate sets of laws [lit., two Torahs], R. Abbahu ordered that both customs be followed, and added one more *terua* blast at his own initiative, because he resolved to establish the *terua* in every possible customary broken sound. Since ordinary people thought that there was a controversy amongst them over this, the Talmud presents this in the style of a debate, that is, with objections raised and a resolution offered.

136. Rashi, bJebamot 13b s.v. *lo taasu*

Do not form factions, for it looks as if they observe two sets of laws [lit., two Torahs], when they read the Scroll in villages on the market day, and in the big towns on the fourteenth, and in walled [cities] on the fifteenth.

137. Responsa Rashi, #128

It once happened that Purim fell on Sunday, and they observed the Fast of Esther on the preceding Thursday, according to the common practice. And a certain woman, who had to ride to the [seat of the] government, came before our master [Rashi] and asked if she could fast the following day and eat on that day [Thursday], due to the hardship of the journey. And our master said: Even though this is not a prescribed public fast day, not by Torah law and not by Rabbinic law, it is just that the people behave thus . . . in any event, one must not separate himself from the community, as it is said in the first chapter of Jebamot,[15] "*lo titgodedu*, in observing the precepts, do not form factions."

And there are those who are ascetics (*prushim*), and even though they fast on Thursday, with the public, they still fast the following day, on Friday, in order to attach the fast to the feast [Purim], as is usually the case, but here, since they cannot do it [i.e., fast] on the Sabbath, they do it on Friday. And my teacher refers to such people with the verse, "But the fool walketh in darkness" (Eccles. 2:14), for the fast itself is nothing but a custom that is being observed in commemoration of the event, and they act strictly, observing it at the 'right' time, as if it had been prescribed by the Torah. And given that people have become accustomed to observe it on Thursday, this is sufficient. And that is why it is observed on Thursday, because we do not fast on the eve of the Sabbath.

138. Kuzari, III:49

And behold, if the Karaites would take upon themselves the precautions against the various impurities out of hygienic considerations, though not considering them to be precepts, there would be nothing wrong with that.

15 bJebamot 13b.

But, seeing as this is not the case, they become caught up in argumentation due to their ignorance, and change the Torah. And they reach [the point of] heresy, which is to say, they are divided into different sects, each with its own system, and this fragmentation is the primary cause of the disunity of the nation, and the basis for breaking away from the principle of "one law and one ordinance" (Num. 15:16).

139. Maimonides' Book of Precepts, Negative precepts, 45

Making cuttings in our flesh

...which admonishes us against making cuttings for souls in our flesh, as the idolaters do. And it is His dictum, may He be exalted, "Ye shall not cut yourselves (*lo titgodedu*)" (Deut. 14:1)....And behold they said that included in this prohibition is also the admonition against divergent customs among the townspeople and divisions between groups, and the Sages said, "*lo titgodedu* – do not form factions."[16] The meaning of the verse in itself, however, is, as we explained, 'Ye shall not inflict upon yourselves any bruise for the dead'; the [other interpretation] is essentially exegesis.

And behold, the Talmud says: One who fosters controversy transgresses a negative commandment, as it is said, "fare not as Korah, and as his company" (Num. 17:5) – this is also of an exegetical nature. The meaning of the verse itself is to deter. And as the Sages explain the verse, it contains a negation and not a prohibition, their interpretation being that God, may He be exalted, declares that whoever in the future disputes the authority of the priests and claims the priesthood for himself will not be visited with the punishment meted out to Korah – that is, will not be swallowed up by the earth – but will be punished "as the Lord spoke unto him by the hand of Moses" (Num. 17:5). [That is to say,] with leprosy, as when He said to Moses, "Put now thy hand into thy bosom [and he put his hand into his bosom; and when he took it out, behold, his hand was leprous]" (Exod. 4:6), and as is related of king Uziah.[17]

140. Maimonides' *Code*, Laws concerning Idolatry 12:14

And included in this admonition is the mandate that there not be two courts in one town, one following one custom and another following a different custom, for this leads to major controversies. As it is said: "ye shall not cut yourselves (*lo titgodedu*)" (Deut. 14:1) – do not form factions.

16 Sifre Deut. 96.
17 See II Chron. 26:19.

141. Responsa Maimonides, #329 (Freimann #111)

But it is forbidden for another reason, the injunction "ye shall not cut yourselves" (Deut. 14:1), which prohibits the formation of factions. For it is incumbent on the entire House of Israel, which is named after Jacob[18] and upholds the religion of Moses our teacher, may he rest in peace, that all Israel's communities and congregations be bound together, and there should be no controversy among them regarding anything at all. And you are wise and sagacious, and know well the punishment for controversy, and the evils it causes.

142. Responsa Maimonides, #262 (Freimann #33)

What would my esteemed lord, the light of the world, may his name live for ever, say concerning a town in which the scholars instituted the practice of remaining seated while reciting the Kedusha (sanctification) which occurs in the first blessing before the Shema prayer ('Kedushat hayotzer'). Some time later, someone new was appointed head of the town, and he was used to standing while reciting the 'Kedushat hayotzer.' And a few people followed him in this, and they started to stand. . . .

Answer: . . . This standing during the 'Kedushat hayotzer' in the first blessing before the Shema is without any doubt a custom of the ignorant, and the sitting that was instituted by the [previous] scholar is what ought to be done. But the standing instituted by this scholar, which is based on the custom of his former land, is a complete mistake. For even regarding matters on which a prohibition hinges, we said, one should not diverge, lest a controversy arise.[19] How much more so regarding a matter on which no prohibition whatsoever hinges. And he has violated the prohibition "*lo titgodedu* – do not form factions."

143. Hidushei Haramban, bMegila 2a

What we have learned in the Mishna: Cities that have been walled since the days of Joshua the son of Nun, read on the fifteenth; villages and large towns read on the fourteenth.[20]

I am greatly puzzled: what is the reason, and what struck them about this, that they made Israel factionalized in the observance of this precept? Although the prohibition of *lo titgodedu*, do not form factions, does not apply here, since this is a case of two courts in two towns, as we find in the first chapter of Jebamot, nevertheless, why did they divide the people into two

18 One name of the Jewish people is "the house of Jacob"; see, e.g., Isaiah 2:5.
19 bPesahim 50b.
20 mMegila 1:1.

sects from the outset? And furthermore, where else in the Torah have we found a similar factionalization of a precept? And the Torah says, "One law and one ordinance shall be for you" (Num. 15:16), and anything that the Rabbis enacted – in so doing, they followed the Torah.

144. Hidushei Haritba, bJebamot 13b

"Why then does it say *lo titgodedu?* So it can be inferred that this [the additional enjoinder against factionalism] is its object. Might it not then be suggested that the entire text refers to this latter point only?"

...Some of our authorities have questions about this – how can it be about factions only, since the verse refers to the prohibition against cutting oneself as a sign of mourning, and how can this meaning be uprooted?...I favor the explanation of Rashi, of blessed memory [viz., that the Talmud's query suggests that the verse in its entirety refers to factionalism.] And to those who ask, how can the context of mourning be uprooted, this is by no means difficult. It is simply the Talmud's method of dialectical analysis, so as to clarify these points as much as possible. And in addition, the verse can perhaps be read as follows: "Ye are the children of the Lord your God" (Deut. 14:1); since you are the children of one father and one God, it is proper that you not form factions, as if there were two Torahs and two deities. And it is also proper that "ye shall not cut yourselves, nor make any baldness between your eyes for the dead" (Deut. 14:1), "For thou art a holy people unto the Lord thy God" (Deut. 14:2).

145. Hagahot Harema, OH 493:3

However, in many localities the custom is that people cut their hair until the New Moon of Iyar, and they should not cut their hair from the 33rd day of the Omer (Lag Baomer) onwards, although it is permitted to cut one's hair on Lag Baomer itself. And in those localities where the custom is for people to get their hair cut from Lag Baomer onwards, they should not get their hair cut after Passover at all, until Lag Baomer. And people in the same town should not conduct themselves such that some follow one custom and some follow the other, due to the *lo titgodedu* prohibition. All the more so, one should not adopt the lenient aspect of both customs.

146. Responsa Maharashdam, YD, #153

Since the issue was raised, I think it is proper to record here a question asked by one of our outstanding colleagues at the yeshiva. It pertains to a passage from tractate Suka about the ritual 'taking' of the lulav, "And on the first day of the Festival, [the ritual 'taking' of the lulav] does not override [the Sabbath] for us, but does for them? And the answer was, It was said: For them too it does not override [the Sabbath]."[21] Rashi interprets this, "To avoid factions among Israel and so that the law should not appear to be two sets of laws [lit., two Torahs], since for us the lulav does not override the Sabbath." And it is puzzling, [as my colleague points out,] that even according to Abbaye, when there are two courts in two different towns, the "do not form factions" injunction does not apply, and a fortiori this is so according to Rava [who tolerates different opinions of two courts even in the same town].[22] I think that the same question can be raised with regard to the enactment of R. Abbahu concerning the shofar blasts.[23] The enactment is apparently uncalled for, since even though some acted in one way and some acted in another way, since they were in different locations, why is [the prohibition against factionalism] relevant? But it suddenly occurred to me that the prohibition against forming factions has two aspects: one a scriptural negative prohibition, and the second, though not a proscription, a directive as to praiseworthy conduct.

Therefore, with regard to the prohibition itself, on all opinions it is certain that there is no transgression in observing different practices in different locales, even according to Abbaye. Nevertheless it is unseemly, because it looks as if there is disparity among them over a precept that applies to all Israel. This being a case of 'sit and do nothing' (*shev veal taase*), they instructed all to refrain from acting, and said that the ritual 'taking' of the lulav was not to be carried out, even by those [in the land of Israel], who know the exact determination of [when] the month [begins]. And I stated that this is apparently the reason for the enactment of R. Abbahu concerning the blowing of the shofar.

147. Responsa Piskei Uziel Besheeilot Hazman, #2

It seems to me that this matter has to do with controversy over the main rationale for the injunction, "ye shall not cut yourselves – do not form factions." For Rashi explains, lest the law become like two sets of laws [lit., two Torahs]; on his view, the fact of divergent local customs is not perceived as the law's having split into two distinct sets of laws, while for Maimonides, the reason for the prohibition is that it leads to great controversy.[24] On this approach, all residents of a town, as well as groups residing there, though originally from other towns, must, with respect to every situation and every issue pertaining to the Torah and the precepts, abide by the very same custom. And there must not be controversy among them

---

21 bSuka 43b.
22 bJebamot 13b–14a.
23 bRosh Hashana 34b. See passages 86 and 135.
24 *Code*, Laws concerning Idolatry 12:14.

about anything at all, as Maimonides states in his responsum. And in his opinion, we have to say that when the Talmud states that the prohibition against factions does not apply to customs, the Talmud is noting the point that in every locale it is permissible to conduct oneself in accordance with the [local] custom, as exemplified by the controversy between R. Akiva and R. Johanan b. Nuri: for in the Galilee they conducted themselves as did R. Johanan b. Nuri, and in Judea, they conducted themselves as did R. Akiva. But to practice two different customs in the same locale is forbidden on the grounds of the "do not form factions" prohibition, even if the divergence is only over a matter of custom. This is so since the rationale for that prohibition is to avoid controversy, hence there is no point in distinguishing between prohibitions and customs. And so it is also written in the *Tosafot*, relying on the Jerusalem Talmud on the matter of the villagers who used to read the Book of Esther on the tenth, the twelfth, and so on, in their own place.[25]

4.2. Who is bound by the prohibition?

148. Rabbenu Jeruham, Toldot Adam Vehava, path b (p. 23a)

The Rama[26] writes: And even one court in one town – it applies only where some rule to permit and some to forbid. But if they do not rule, it is permitted [for each to act on his own view], since they do not issue a ruling explicitly. And likewise, those who permit it can, even when in the presence of those who forbid, conduct themselves as if it were permitted[27] – this does not constitute factionalism. And this can be confirmed from a number of sources.

149. Hidushei Haritba, bJebamot 14a s.v. *amar lei*

"Rava said to him: Surely the case of the house of Shammai and the house of Hillel is like that of two courts of law in the same town?"[28] This is the wording found in all the texts. I wonder why he said, "like that of two courts"; he should have said "that of two courts." Furthermore, how could Abbaye err on such a simple thing? We have to say, therefore, that Abbaye maintains that the prohibition against forming factions does not apply to the dissenting parties themselves, for each follows what he perceives to be the truth, and the Torah sanctions this. The issue of forming factions

---

25 On bJebamot 14 s.v. *ki amrinan*.
26 R. Meir b. Todros Halevi Abulafia.
27 Emending the text, which reads "forbidden," on the basis of *Responsa Mabit*, passage 151 below, which quotes Rabbenu Jeruham as here emended.
28 bJebamot 14a.

applies only to others, who seek to put the said teachings into practice. Although they could adopt either opinion, since both are equally sound, nevertheless, given the prohibition against forming factions, in any one town all must adopt one view for strictness. And this is the import of the language of the Talmud, "[Abbaye said, the admonition against forming factions is applicable to a case such as that of] two courts of law in the same town, one of which rules in accordance with the view of the house of Shammai while the other rules in accordance with the view of the house of Hillel." Against which Rava argues that if the two courts are deemed to be different factions, then the schools themselves should be regarded as two factions, that is, as two courts. Because Rava does not differentiate between scholars and those who follow them.

150. Piskei Riaz, Jebamot, chapter 1, halakha 1, letters 16–17 (p. 3)

And wherever there was a controversy among the Sages, the law was decided in accordance with the view of one of them, so that [the Torah] would not become like two sets of laws [lit., two Torahs]. And this was hinted at by the biblical verse, "Ye shall not cut yourselves, *lo titgodedu*" (Deut. 14:1) – do not form factions.

And also in the present, when in most places there are controversies among scholars and eminent halakhic authorities, the denizens of the city are forbidden to split into factions with regard to widespread customs, some in accordance with one [authority] and some in accordance with the other, but they should put the matter to a vote, and all should conduct themselves according to the majority.

151. Responsa Mabit, 1, #21

Therefore it is required that the scholars of the town assemble and, after due study and deliberation, take a vote so that they can lead the populace according to the majority view, whether it be strict or lenient. And until they do this, it will appear as though they belong to factions if some adopt the lenient view and others the strict.

However, in *The Book of Adam and Eve*,[29] I found the opinion of the Rama, of blessed memory, which is as follows: "And even one court in one town – it applies only where some rule to permit and some to forbid. But if they do not rule, it is permitted [for each to act on his own view], since they do not issue a ruling explicitly. And likewise, those who permit it can, even when in the presence of those who forbid, conduct themselves as if it

---

29 Path b; see passage 148 above.

were permitted – this does not constitute factionalism. And this can be confirmed from a number of sources." This suggests that if no vote has been taken, and it is not the case that some hand down rulings that permit, and some hand down rulings that forbid, everyone may conduct himself in accordance with his own mind, following either a strict or a lenient course. But if they hand down rulings for others, some permitting and others forbidding, on all accounts this constitutes factionalism.

And in his commentary on tractate Jebamot, our teacher R. Isaiah of Trani, of blessed memory, says that when the prohibition against factionalism does apply, they must not act in accordance with their respective [opposed] opinions, but debate the issue until they all agree on a certain opinion, or take a vote on the issue, coming to a final decision, either lenient or strict. And it should not be the case that some are lenient and some are strict. If they are unable to decide the law, they cannot rely on their respective views, but should adopt the stricter view on the matter until the law has finally been settled.

And even so we can still maintain that as long as they do not hand down rulings such that some permit and others forbid, but each one conducts himself in accordance with his own opinion, there is no [infraction of the prohibition against] factionalism. And even if people happen to see such a scholar acting strictly, or leniently, and they [follow and act] strictly or leniently as he does, this does not constitute factionalism, because no ruling for the general public has been handed down. All the more so if the view of the scholar in question does not have numerous followers, since the more numerous the followers, the more they might appear to be a different faction, as our teacher R. Isaiah, of blessed memory, wrote.

Nevertheless, I most certainly do not presume to rely on my own view here, even to adopt a stricture, until the majority of the scholars of the city reach an agreement, which I will follow after they take a vote – with the consent of our master, the eminence of his generation, the honorable R. Jacob Berab, in whose presence I sit on the ground of the land of Israel,[30] and discuss the law theoretically, but not as law to be applied, and so on.

152. Responsa Maharashdam, YD, #153

Since the issue was raised, I think it is proper to record here a question asked by one of our outstanding colleagues at the yeshiva. It pertains to a passage from tractate Suka about the ritual 'taking' of the lulav, "And on the first day of the Festival, [the ritual 'taking' of the lulav] does not override [the Sabbath] for us, but does for them?" And the answer was, "It was

---

30 An expression alluding to the fact that the scholars would be seated according to their stature.

said: For them too it does not override [the Sabbath]."[31] Rashi interprets this, "To avoid factions among Israel and so that the law should not appear to be two sets of laws [lit., two Torahs], since for us the ritual 'taking' of the lulav does not override the Sabbath." And it is puzzling [as my colleague points out,] that even according to Abbaye, when there are two courts in two different towns, the "do not form factions" injunction does not apply, and a fortiori this is so according to Rava [who tolerates different opinions of two courts even in the same town].[32] I think that the same question can be raised with regard to the enactment of R. Abbahu concerning the shofar blasts.[33] The enactment is apparently uncalled for, since even though some acted in one way and some acted in another way, since they were in different locations, why is [the prohibition against factionalism] relevant? . . .

Furthermore, he asked about the fact that we observe the Festivals for two days, whereas those living in the land of Israel observe only one. Now this is also not perplexing at all, since those living in the land of Israel never observed more than one day, and those living abroad observe two by force of law rather than by enactment, because of uncertainty [as to the correct date], and this reason was known to all. Things have remained as they were, even though nowadays we know the dates as well as they do.

I also said that what Rashi, of blessed memory, said regarding the prohibition against factions "*lo titgodedu* – ye shall not cut yourselves," viz., that it refers to the Sages who were about to issue an enactment that the ritual 'taking' of the lulav should not be observed [on the Sabbath]. They could not say "these persons shall take it" and "those persons shall not take it," because that would have looked like one court part of which [sometimes] ruled one way and the other part of which [sometimes] ruled otherwise. But with regard to the observance of the Festivals, there was no need for the Sages to so stipulate; but those who lived abroad observed, on their own, two days because of the uncertainty, while the others did not.

153. Responsa Parashat Mordekhai, OH, #4

We must say, therefore, that the "*lo titgodedu*" prohibition applies only if there are numerous people following various practices, but if it is just one individual, the "*lo titgodedu*" prohibition does not apply, because his action does not make the law look like two sets of laws [lit., two Torahs].[34] For it

31 bSuka 43b.
32 bJebamot 13b–14a.
33 See passages 86 and 135.
34 Cf. *Responsa Rashi*, #128, see passage 137 above.

can be assumed that this person is mistaken or has broken the law inadvertently. Although the rationale for [the principle] "one should not diverge from the local custom lest controversy be generated" applies even more so to a lone individual, still, the rationale underlying [the principle] of not making the Torah look like two sets of laws is less relevant with respect to the actions of an individual.... Nevertheless, this explanation is somehow forced.

154. Responsa Maharshag, 2, #12

My response is that it seems to me that this prohibition against forming factions applies only to one who calls upon others to act in accordance with his view, that is, were there, say, one court in a town, and one judge from this court hands down a ruling for everyone that phylacteries are to be donned on the intermediate days of Festivals, and another judge, from the same court, hands down a ruling for everyone that phylacteries are not be donned on the intermediate days of Festivals. Under such circumstances, the talmudic prohibition against forming factions, found in tractate Jebamot, is in force. The Talmud implies this in its conclusion there, because it says: "But, Rava said, the dictum "do not form factions" is [only] applicable to a case such as that of a court of law in a given town, part of which rules in accordance with the view of the house of Shammai while the other part rules in accordance with the view of the house of Hillel. However, in a case of two courts of law in the same town, it is irrelevant."[35] Why does it not say "two persons in the same town, one conducting himself in accordance with the view of the house of Shammai and the other in accordance with the view of the house of Hillel"? But certainly, as I see it, this implies that this prohibition does not apply at all to individuals acting only for themselves, and in no way seeking to direct others. For anyone may act in consonance with his own opinion with regard to the ways of the Torah and how God, may He be blessed, is to be served. And it is indeed stated in the Talmud, "Why is it that the top of the letter "*yud*" is curved? Because of the deeds of the righteous, which differ from each other."[36] And the said prohibition applies only to those who hand down rulings for others. For if, in a given town, three persons were elected to serve as a court that will hand down rulings for the town's citizens with regard to obligatory and voluntary observances, the forbidden and the permitted, and the impure and the pure, they must adopt a uniform policy, but an individual acting for himself is by no means subject to the prohibition against factions.

---

35 bJebamot 14a.
36 bMenahot 29b.

The Talmud furnishes support for this in a baraita: "The law is always in accordance with the view of the house of Hillel, but one who wishes to act in accordance with the view of the house of Shammai may do so, one who wishes to act in accordance with the view of the house of Hillel may do so," and so on.[37] The Talmud explains this baraita as referring first to times before the heavenly voice, then to times after the heavenly voice. Thus it follows from this baraita that prior to the heavenly voice, before it had been determined in accordance with which authority the law was, every individual had the right to act in accordance with the view of either the house of Shammai, provided he followed both its leniencies and its strictures, or the house of Hillel, provided he followed both its leniencies and its strictures. This implies that even if two such persons resided in the same town, one would still have the option available of acting in accordance with the view of the house of Hillel, for otherwise the Talmud would have said, "in a place where they wish to follow the house of Shammai they may do so, in a place where they wish to follow the house of Hillel they may do so." And since the Talmud says "as he wishes," it means that even an individual may decide for himself. This raises the difficulty of how individuals could have been granted the option of acting as they pleased – does this not constitute a violation of the prohibition against forming factions?...

We therefore must conclude that the baraita implies that the prohibition against factionalism applies only to those who hand down rulings for others, so that one should not hand down a ruling for others in accordance with the view of house of Shammai, while another hands down a ruling for others in accordance with the view of the house of Hillel. But as to each individual's personal conduct, where no rulings are being handed down to others, the prohibition does not apply at all.

This can also be proven, it seems, from the case of the phylacteries of Rabbenu Tam, as discussed in the *Shulhan Arukh*, OH 34:2, where it is recommended that those who conduct themselves with piety wear them. Why do we not say that the prohibition against factionalism is relevant here too? But unquestionably, it applies only to rulings handed down for others. There are a few individuals who also wear phylacteries according to *Shimusha Rabbah*,[38] and they do not have any qualms that this might be construed as factionalism. And also Maimonides, who wrote: "one following one custom and another following a different custom," and so on, was referring to one who hands down rulings for others to act thus. Even though in *Responsa Heshiv Moshe*, YD, #31, which the honorable Torah scholar cited, he did not write thus, and similarly *Teshurat Shai*, #89 disputes my reading, in any event, in my humble opinion, it is as I wrote.

---

37 bHulin 43.
38 A collection of laws relating to phylacteries attributed to the Geonim.

Furthermore, we can also deduce the law from popular conduct.[39] There are several points of law on which some are more particular than others: some do not eat from the new harvest [until Passover], while others do; some are careful not to eat the meat of an animal found to have had a pulmonary cyst that was readily removed, while others are not. And we have never heard of anyone, anywhere, objecting to this on the grounds of the prohibition against factionalism. For surely, as long as one observes such solicitudes for himself, there is no apprehension that this constitutes factionalism.

And the argument put forward in *Heshiv Moshe* against such an explanation, namely, that if we accept it, the prohibition against factionalism disappears into nothing – this is not a real argument, since indeed, it so disappears, and deserves to so disappear, and this is fitting! And this is the reason why people are not scrupulous about it, since it disappears, in most cases, into nothing. On the contrary, on this view we would have to be puzzled by the view of the *Tur* and the *Shulhan Arukh*, which clarify for us all the acts that we have to perform, and all the laws governing our daily conduct at present, yet these sources are very terse about the prohibition against factionalism – explicitly stated in the Talmud in the first chapter of tractate Jebamot referring to the courts, which are not to form factions – and do not explain it or the details governing it. And in fact, it is not mentioned at all, except in *Magen Avraham*, which presents a few of the laws related to the prohibition, and also did not explain it sufficiently.[40] From this, it seems that they concur with what I have written, that at present the "*lo titgodedu*" prohibition hardly applies at all, for every individual acts for himself, and it rarely happens that there are controversies within the courts themselves. It also seems to me that on their view [viz., that of the *Tur* and the *Shulhan Arukh*], the Talmud's teaching about not forming factions is not really exegesis, but is merely a supporting allusion (*asmakhta*), and not as the learned Torah scholar has written, relying on the authority of *Responsa Beit Yitzhak*, that it is real scriptural exegesis. Thus we do not scrupulously heed this prohibition.

155. Responsa Sridei Esh, 2, #56 (p. 144)

And on this basis we have found an opening allowing us to resolve the problem raised by the words of Maimonides,[41] that there are two different obligations, that of the townspeople, and that of the court and the leaders

---

39 Referring to bBerakhot 48a; bEruvin 14a.
40 *Magen Avraham*, OH 493:6.
41 *Code*, Laws concerning Idolatry 12:14, where Maimonides rules in accordance with the view of Abbaye, and not, as is customary, that of Rava.

of the town. For certainly, the townspeople are obligated in the first place to convene a court that will issue one ruling that applies to everyone in the town, and likewise, the court itself is obligated to deliberate until it reaches a consensus of opinion. But, in cases where the court cannot reach a consensus of opinion, and therefore, two different courts have been created, one ruling in one way and the other in a different way, each community is obliged to follow the opinions of its court, as was explained above, and this is the position of Rava. However, Maimonides does not speak of the townspeople, but rather, of the leaders of the town, who are obligated from the outset to convene a court [capable of] reaching a consensus, and likewise, the court itself is obligated to take the trouble to reach a single opinion. And Maimonides' formulation is meticulous, as he wrote: "that there not be two courts in one town, one following one custom and another following a different custom," and so on, as Maimonides speaks of the court's appointment by the heads of the townspeople, or, of the court's obligation [to seek a single opinion], and the Gemara in Jebamot speaks of the obligation of the townspeople.

4.3. The distinction between two courts and one court

156. bJebamot 14a

Now as to those who maintain that they did act in accordance with their views, should not the admonition, "ye shall not cut yourselves" (*lo titgodedu*) – do not form factions – be applied? Abbaye said: The admonition against forming factions is applicable to a case such as that of two courts of law in the same town, one of which rules in accordance with the view of the house of Shammai while the other rules in accordance with the view of the house of Hillel. However, in a case of two courts of law in two different towns, it is irrelevant. Rava said to him, surely the case of the house of Shammai and the house of Hillel is like that of two courts of law in the same town? But, Rava said, the dictum "do not form factions" is [only] applicable to a case such as that of a court of law in a given town, part of which rules in accordance with the view of the house of Shammai while the other part rules in accordance with the view of the house of Hillel. However, in a case of two courts of law in the same town, it is irrelevant.

    Come and hear: In the locale of R. Eliezer, wood was chopped on the Sabbath to produce charcoal with which to forge the iron.[42] In the locale of R. Jose the Galilean, the flesh of fowl was eaten with milk.[43] In the

---

42 To make the knife required for the performance of a circumcision.
43 R. Jose exempts the flesh of fowl from the prohibition against eating meat with milk, see bShabat 130a.

locale of R. Eliezer only, but not in the locale of R. Akiva; as we learned: R. Akiva laid it down as a general rule that any labor that can be performed on the eve of the Sabbath does not supersede the Sabbath.[44] What sort of an objection is that? The case is surely different when the varied practices are confined to different locales. What did he who raised this point think? One might have assumed that owing to the exacting laws of the Sabbath, different locales are regarded as one, hence it was necessary to teach us that the law is not so.

Come and hear: R. Abbahu, when he happened to be in the locale of R. Joshua b. Levi, would carry a candle, but when he happened to be in the locale of R. Johanan, would not carry a candle.[45] What is the question here – have we not said that it is different when the varied practices are confined to different locales? We therefore say [that the question is] how R. Abbahu could act one way in one place and otherwise in another. R. Abbahu shared the opinion of R. Joshua b. Levi, but, when he happened to be in R. Johanan's locale, did not carry [a candle] out of respect for R. Johanan. But surely his attendant was also there! He gave his attendant the necessary instructions.

157. Raban, EH, Jebamot 118a

We learned there: "The Book of Esther is read on the eleventh, the twelfth, the thirteenth," and so on.[46] The villagers advance the reading to the market day, when they come to the city on the market day, to appear in court or for the Torah reading, and sometimes the market day was on the eleventh and sometimes on the twelfth and sometimes on the thirteenth of Adar, as is explained there in the Mishna. "Said Resh Lakish to R. Johanan: [Should we not] Apply here the admonition "ye shall not cut yourselves (*lo titgodedu*)" (Deut. 14:1), that is, do not form factions,"[47] one group conducting itself one way, the other conducting itself differently? The Talmud goes on analyzing the question until it comes to the conclusion of Rava, "But, Rava said, the dictum "do not form factions" is [only] applicable to a case such as that of a court of law in a given town," that is, there is one teacher and his students, and the students form groups, some forbidding and others permitting. Since they have accepted one authority, they must not form factions. But if there are two scholars in the

---

44 E.g., cutting wood, preparing coal and forging the knife. In view of the undesirability of creating different sects, why were these variant practices condoned?
45 According to R. Joshua b. Levi, a candle, though already lit when the Sabbath began, may be moved on the Sabbath after the flame has gone out. R. Johanan forbids this.
46 bJebamot 13b.
47 Ibid.

same city and the students of one of them forbid and the students of the other permit, this is not forming factions, since they only assert that which they have received from their master, and all the more so if they lived in two towns, there is certainly no factionalism involved. But with regard to reading the Book of Esther, there is no factionalism, because there is no controversy regarding this matter, for it was an enactment of all the Sages to make it easier for the villagers to bring water and foodstuffs to their brothers in the cities on the fast-day, without having to worry about reading the Scroll, and there is no factionalism here.

From the talmudic discussion it follows that when two Sages reside in the same town, or in different places, and the followers of one forbid and of the other permit some matter, those who permit must inform those who forbid: "this thing you forbid and you must not partake of it." And therefore the inhabitants of Mainz forbid eating from an animal that had a cyst on the lower lobe of the lungs, and forbid eating fruit picked on both days of the Festivals, which are observed in the Diaspora, until after the end of the second day of the Festival, until enough time elapses to allow the fruit to be picked, and regard the aroma of the oven as influencing the food baked, and so forth, and in Worms they permit this. So when people from Mainz are in Worms, they must be informed, "this is meat from an animal that had a cyst on the lower lobe of the lung," or "this bread was baked in the oven together with meat, or with cheese," or "this fruit was picked on the first day of the Festival." And if, after being notified, the person is inclined to follow the scholars of Worms, he may do as they do, even though these things are forbidden in his own locale, as we have learned: "R. Abbahu, when he happened to be in the locale of R. Johanan, would not carry a candle, but when he happened to be in the locale of R. Joshua b. Levi, would carry a candle."[48] And the Talmud queries, "How could R. Abbahu act in one place in one way and in another place in another way?" The Talmud answers, R. Abbahu is of the same opinion as R. Joshua b. Levi about the law, but being a student of R. Johanan's, when he was in the locale of the latter he acted as he did, and informed his attendant that he agreed with R. Joshua b. Levi to prevent confusion.

158. Maimonides' *Code*, Laws concerning Idolatry 12:14

And included in this admonition is the mandate that there not be two courts in one town, one following one custom and another following a different custom, for this leads to major controversies. As it is said: "ye shall not cut yourselves (*lo titgodedu*)" (Deut. 14:1) – do not form factions.

---

48 bJebamot 14a; the quotation is inexact.

159. Beit Habehira, bJebamot 14a s.v. *zo*

As to the scriptural dictum "*lo titgodedu* – ye shall not cut yourselves" (Deut. 14:1), and so on – even though its primary meaning is to prohibit self-inflicted bruises for the dead, as it is understood in its context, it also suggests that the precepts should not be observed differentially by factions, that is, in one way by one group and in another way by another group, to the point where it seems that they observe two distinct sets of laws [lit., two Torahs]. What situation does this apply to? If there is only one court in the town, and within that very court they are divided among themselves, some ruling according to one outlook and others according to another. But as long as there are two courts, even if in the same town, one ruling according to one outlook and the other, according to another outlook, this does not constitute a case of factionalism, as it is never possible that all will assent to a single opinion. And all the more so when the matters at hand concern customs, for no concern is warranted if some act one way and others another way. Hence, "In a place where they are accustomed to work on the eve of Passover up to midday, they do [work]; in a place where they are accustomed not to do work, they do not." as we explained elsewhere,[49] for the locales differ, and doing or refraining from work is but a custom.

160. Sefer Mitzvot Gadol, Negative precepts, 62

And the Talmud[50] interprets the precept of "*lo titgodedu* – ye shall not cut yourselves" as including 'do not form factions' – there should not be two courts in the same town, one following one custom, and the other following another custom.

161. Sefer Hahinukh, precept 467

And Maimonides, of blessed memory, wrote that the Sages, of blessed memory, explain that this admonition includes the directive against two courts in the same town, one following one custom and the other following a different custom, for this leads to controversy. And the verse "ye shall not cut yourselves" (Deut. 14:1), that is, do not form factions, means that you should not divide yourselves into groups that disagree with each other. And I learned from my teacher, may God protect him, that this prohibition applies only within a single grouping in which scholars of equal wisdom disagree with each other. Each grouping is prohibited from following its own view, because this leads to controversy among them. But rather, they should

---

49 *Beit Habehira*, mPesahim 4:1.
50 bJebamot 13b–14a.

debate as long as necessary until they all reach a consensus. If they cannot [reach a consensus], they should all follow the more stringent view, if the controversy is over a matter of scriptural law. But with regard to controversy between two separate courts of equal wisdom, the "do not form factions" prohibition was not imposed. And they cite a proof from tractate bAvoda Zara: "A proclamation was issued by Rav saying that it was forbidden, and a proclamation was issued by Samuel saying that it was permitted."[51]

162. Piskei Riaz, Jebamot, chapter 1, halakha 1, letters 16–17 (p. 3)

In the days of the early Sages there was a great controversy between the Sages of the house of Shammai and the Sages of the house of Hillel over levirate marriage with rival[-wive]s. And the house of Shammai permitted marriage between [the deceased man's] brothers and the rivals, and in their great wisdom, presented excellent arguments for their position, and the Sages of the house of Hillel were not able to refute so many arguments, but relied on the tradition that their predecessors had received from the prophet Haggai, that if one rival is prohibited, all of them are, as we explained, and this prohibition became widespread. And wherever there was a controversy among the Sages, the law was decided in accordance with the view of one of them, so that [the Torah] would not become like two sets of laws [lit., two Torahs]. And this was hinted at by the biblical verse, "Ye shall not cut yourselves, *lo titgodedu*" (Deut. 14:1) – do not form factions.

And also in the present, when in most places there are controversies among scholars and eminent halakhic authorities, the denizens of the city are forbidden to split into factions with regard to widespread customs, some in accordance with one [authority] and some in accordance with the other, but they should put the matter to a vote, and all should conduct themselves according to the majority. To what does this apply? Where there is one court in a town, for example, if there was one talmudic academy, some of its scholars forbidding something, and some permitting it. But if there are two courts in a town, and one court diverges from the other, the prohibition against forming factions does not apply. And all the more so if the divergence is between two different towns.

163. Responsa Binyamin Zeev, #303

And therefore, on our understanding, the prohibition against forming factions does not apply to two courts in two towns, but the prohibition does

---

51 bAvoda Zara 40a and 57b. In the edition of the Talmud in use today, the reference is to a matter involving Rava and R. Huna b. Hinena.

apply to two courts in the same town, one following one custom and the other following another. And so it would seem from the words of Maimonides, of blessed memory, whom I quote, "And included in this admonition is the mandate that there not be two courts in one town, one following one custom and another following a different custom, for this leads to major controversies. As it is said: "ye shall not cut yourselves (*lo tit-godedu)*" (Deut. 14:1) – do not form factions."[52] And it is so in *Sefer Mitzvot Gadol* (*Semag*),[53] that is, they rule according to Abbaye. But I, Benjamin, find a difficulty in this ruling – that it is in accordance with the view of Abbaye, since we have a rule in the Talmud that in a controversy of Abbaye and Rava, we follow Rava, with the exception of the laws $y''e''l\ k''g''m$.[54] ...

And I would now like to explain why Maimonides and *Sefer Mitzvot Gadol* decided against the Talmud's $y''e''l\ k''g''m$ rule. What seems to me, in my humble opinion, to be the case, is that they decided contrary to the rule because the view of Abbaye seems to be more reasonable on this point than that of Rava. ... And we know that such a consideration can be legitimate from the following: "Said R. Abba in the name of R. Johanan: In a dispute between R. Judah and R. Shimon, the law is in accordance with the view of R. Judah."[55] Asheri ad loc. rules thus. But the Talmud goes on to quote R. Mesharshia: "These rules are to be disregarded." Rashi explains: "The rules of deciding disputes such as, 'In a dispute between A and B, the law is always in accordance with the view of A,' holds, but, when a particular view seems to be more reasonable, we decide the law accordingly, and if in another place his opponent's view is more reasonable, we follow him."

But, this explanation must be rejected, because, in my humble opinion, the $y''e''l\ k''g''m$ rule for deciding between Abbaye and Rava always applies. Maimonides and *Semag* decide in accordance with the view of Abbaye, though it is not one of the six cases mentioned by the Talmud, because this is not a dispute between Abbaye and Rava, but an account of the explanation of a Tannaitic dispute between Resh Lakish and R. Johanan over the Mishna: "the Scroll [of Esther] is read on the eleventh, the twelfth, the thirteenth, the fourteenth or the fifteenth [of Adar], but not earlier or later."[56]

And Resh Lakish said to R. Johanan: [Should we not] Apply here the admonition "ye shall not cut yourselves" (*lo titgodedu*) (Deut. 14:1), that is, do not form factions? Rashi explains: "and in the big towns on the fourteenth, and in walled [cities] on the fifteenth."[57] And another problem is raised

---

52 *Code*, Laws concerning Idolatry 12:14.
53 Negative precepts, 62.
54 bBaba Metzia 22b, bKidushin 52a.
55 bEruvin 46b.
56 bJebamot 13b.
57 Rashi, bJebamot 13b s.v. *lo taasu*.

there: "But is there no prohibition here? Surely we learned, "The house of Shammai prohibit [work] during the night," that is, to do work on the night of the search for leaven (*hametz*), "and the house of Hillel permit it" – and some act in accordance with the view of the house of Shammai and others act in accordance with the view of the house of Hillel. And is this, the Talmud asks, a case of factionalism!? And a further query is raised, "But do not the house of Shammai permit the rival[-wive]s to the other brothers and the house of Hillel forbid them?" On this Abbaye comments, "The admonition against forming factions (*lo titgodedu*) is applicable to a case such as that of two courts of law in the same town, one of which rules in accordance with the view of the house of Shammai while the other rules in accordance with the view of the house of Hillel. However, in a case of two courts of law in two different towns, it is irrelevant." On this Rava comments, "the dictum "do not form factions" is [only] applicable to a case such as that of a court of law in a given town, part of which rules in accordance with the view of the house of Shammai while the other part rules in accordance with the view of the house of Hillel. However, in a case of two courts of law in the same town, it is irrelevant." Since the opinion of Abbaye seems to be more reasonable than that of Rava, as I explained it, they ruled in accordance with it, and this does not constitute an exception to the six cases, because the dispute is over the explanation of an earlier Tannaitic controversy, as I explained it, and is not over a matter on which they themselves disagreed.

164. Responsa Radbaz, 5, #1384

You ask about what Maimonides, of blessed memory, wrote: And included in this admonition is the mandate that there not be two courts in one town, one following one custom and another following a different custom, for this leads to major controversies. As it is said: "ye shall not cut yourselves (*lo titgodedu*)" (Deut. 14:1) – do not form factions.[58] You ask how Maimonides could adopt the opinion of Abbaye against Rava, with respect to the following passage from the Talmud.

> Now as to those who maintain that they did act in accordance with their views, should not the admonition [*lo titgodedu* – ye shall not cut yourselves] do not form factions, be applied? Abbaye said: The admonition against forming factions is applicable to a case such as that of two courts of law in the same town, one of which rules in accordance with the view of the house of Shammai while the other rules in accordance with the view of the house of

---

58 *Code*, Laws concerning Idolatry 12:14.

Hillel. However, in a case of two courts of law in two different towns, it is irrelevant. Rava said to him, surely the case of the house of Shammai and the house of Hillel is like that of two courts of law in the same town? But, Rava said, the dictum "do not form factions" is [only] applicable to a case such as that of a court of law in a given town, part of which rules in accordance with the view of the house of Shammai while the other part rules in accordance with the view of the house of Hillel. However, in a case of two courts of law in the same town, it is irrelevant.[59]

And do we not rule that in any controversy between Abbaye and Rava, the law is in accordance with Rava's view, with the exception of *y"e"l k"g"m*?[60]

Answer: It is probable that our teacher, of blessed memory [Maimonides] ruled according to Abbaye on this matter on the grounds that his opinion, [namely,] that controversy should not proliferate among Israel, is more reasonable. For in a single town, even if they form two separate courts, it is impossible to avoid controversy, since the public is drawn after them, and one is lenient while the other is strict, one exempts while the other holds liable, one renders a thing impure, the other pure, and people "hop between two opinions" (I Kings 18:21). And hate and controversy will increase between them, and this can be plainly seen. But this does not apply to two courts in two different towns, for each town will follow its own court. With regard the question Rava posed to Abbaye, "surely the case of the house of Shammai and the house of Hillel is like that of two courts of law in the same town?" – this question is not difficult at all for Abbaye, since the situation with respect to the house of Shammai and the house of Hillel is quite different. Since there were many followers of each among Israel, it is analogous to two courts in two towns. And all the more so since their disputes were well known, and even if each group did in fact act on its own views, as the Gemara concludes, "they did not refrain from social contact," because they were completely pious and would inform their fellows,[61] as the Gemara relates regarding the rivals,[62] since all their controversy was for the sake of heaven. The proof of that is the question posed by Rava to Abbaye, "surely the case of the house of Shammai and the house of Hillel is like that of two courts of law in the same town?" as opposed to, "surely the case of the house of Shammai and the house of Hillel is that of two courts of law in the same town?" It follows that Abbaye

---

59 bJebamot 14a.
60 See bKidushin 52a.
61 Of their particular rulings, so as not to cause those holding the other view to transgress.
62 In the context of *halitza*.

himself did not so regard the controversy. We can also say that the houses of Shammai and Hillel indeed resided in two towns, but within the same town, the prohibition against factions applies even to courts such as theirs, and controversy is indeed a concern. And even though the rule that the law is decided in accordance with the view of Rava against Abbaye applies, the prohibition applies only where they differ as to their own opinions; but when they differ about the opinion of someone else, this rule does not apply. And in this passage they do not differ as to their own views, but rather on the resolution of a problem. Hence our teacher, of blessed memory [Maimonides], does not think that the rule applies here.

Alternatively, we can say that even according to Rava's view, "However, in a case of two courts of law in the same town, it is irrelevant" applies only if the two courts are of the stature of the house of Shammai and the house of Hillel, which would not foment controversy for the reasons I explained above. But with regard to two ordinary courts, even in the same town, Rava admits that controversy should be a concern, and the prohibition against forming factions applies. And now the question raised by the *Tosafot* regarding tractate Megila can also be resolved. The Talmud there relates that in towns, the Book of Esther was read on the fourteenth for townspeople, but for villagers they advanced the reading to the preceding market day. And on the strength of this difficulty [namely, that this appears to violate the "do not form factions" principle], the *Tosafot* say that the villagers read it in their place, and in their place they gather. But on the basis of what I have written, this is resolved, because it was known that villagers advanced the reading to the market day, and townspeople always read on the fourteenth, and this would not foment controversy, and the "do not form factions" prohibition does not apply, as we say with regard to the controversy between the house of Shammai and the house of Hillel.

165. Responsa Radbaz, 8, #141

And he[63] also wrote that, according to his opinion, [in the case under consideration] "the prohibition against factions, discussed in the Talmud,[64] does not apply, since it applies only to the case of a town in which there is one court, part of which rules in accordance with the view of the house of Shammai, and part of which rules in accordance with the view of the house of Hillel; but when there are two courts in the town, it does not apply." Now I heard this and found it odd, because if Samuel and his father are considered to be two courts, if so, then, the two sides to any controversy

---

63 This refers to a R. Isaac, with whom he had an ongoing argument regarding the laws of ritual immersion in rivers.
64 bJebamot 14a.

can be regarded as separate courts, and the prohibition against factionalism would never apply at all! Hence, the distinction applies only to disputes between the house of Shammai and the house of Hillel, for there were thousands who followed the view of the house of Shammai, and thousands, that of the house of Hillel. Likewise, two permanent courts that hand down rulings to the populace, some[65] ruling in accordance with the view of the house of Shammai and some ruling in accordance with the view of the house of Hillel. But two Amoraim who disagree are not considered to be separate courts. And if, in his opinion, some were in the habit of ruling leniently like Samuel and some were in the habit of ruling more stringently, the prohibition against factionalism does apply.

4.4. 'Do not form factions' as applied to different communities

166. Responsa Tashbetz, 3, #179

In those places where there are different communities whose enactments are at variance, and they are like two courts in one town, part ruling in accordance with the view of the house of Shammai and part in accordance with the view of the house of Hillel, the prohibition against forming factions, "lo titgodedu – ye shall not cut yourselves" (Deut. 14:1), does not apply, as it is said in the Talmud.[66] Now a man who was a member of one community married a woman who was a member of the other community. There is no doubt that the woman is counted with her husband in all his obligations, for one's wife is like oneself in every respect, and she is released from the obligations of the community to which her father's household belongs. And this is quite obvious, and it is beyond any doubt, for there should not be a couple dining at the same table, who cannot share the same bread, what is forbidden for one being permitted to the other.

167. Responsa Radakh, house 11, chamber 1 (house 13, p. 104b in first edition)

Question: Four communities settled in Meta Arta: from Corfu, from Sicily, from Calabria and from Foggia [Apulia]. And every community has its own synagogue, where they conduct the services as was customary in their places of origin. And the members of the Calabrian congregation had agreed among themselves, in the presence of their notables, that they would not permit anyone to separate himself from them and to go and

---

65 Emending the text, which reads "part," apparently due to the wording of bJebamot.
66 bJebamot 14a.

pray in any of the other synagogues, and that even if there were disagreements among them, between either individuals or groups, they would not be allowed to litigate [the matter] anywhere but before the elders of their own community, whose rulings would be accepted as final by the disputants, both individuals and groups, whatever the elders decreed for them. And now recently, some of them went to the Sicilian synagogue, and the elders of the holy community (*kahal kadosh*) of the Calabrians sent word to the elders of the holy community of the Sicilians, not to pray with those who had left their synagogue to pray with them, that is, in the synagogue of the Sicilians, because they [the Calabrian absconders] are sinners. And the Sicilians did not want to heed them. And also, some went from the synagogue of the holy community of Apulia to pray in the synagogue of the holy community of the Sicilians, and so too some from the holy community of Corfu also went to pray there.

When the leaders and patrons of the congregations saw this, they convened in the synagogue of the Corfiots, and sent for the leaders of the holy community of the Sicilians, who duly appeared. And the Corfiots said to them: Why do you not litigate the matter with them [the Corfiot judges]? And the Sicilians answered that the Corfiots were unfit to judge them, since some of their community had also gone to pray with them. Upon seeing this, the three holy communities – Corfu, Apulia and Calabria – agreed among themselves that no member of the said three communities would be permitted to pray in another synagogue on a permanent basis, but could do so only occasionally on a casual basis. And if the leaders of the synagogue from which there had been absconding would become angered by the fact that those who had prayed in their synagogues had left to pray in other synagogues, then the cantor and leaders of the other synagogues would not admit the absconders to pray there. And they did all this to minimize strife between the congregations. And the leaders of the Sicilian congregation did not want to enter into their agreement or to heed them.

And now instruct us, our master, as to whether the members of the holy community of Corfu and the holy community of Apulia are unfit to adjudicate between the holy communities of Sicily and Calabria about the decision already taken by the holy community of the Calabrians, as mentioned above, and also as to whether the holy community of the Sicilians, who are the minority, are bound to accept the customs of the other three communities, which are the majority, and must follow what they do, or not? Especially since, due to our increasingly many sins, we have many poor people among us, and taxes and local taxes, and if people do not return to their home regions and to their families, it may, God forbid, be the case that "Their heart is divided," and so on (Hoshea 10:2). Furthermore, some of the congregants among us are not quite respectable, and if they depart from the community, God forbid, they might cause the vineyard of the Lord of Hosts to be uprooted.

Answer: ...Concerning the agreement of the three congregations, it appears that the members of the fourth community are not obliged to join in your agreement, for one community is not subordinate to others, even if the others are in the majority, for in this context each and every community is like a town unto itself. And the members of one town are not subordinate to the members of another, nor are the members of one community subordinate to the members of another community, since because each community follows its own original customs, they are to be regarded as two courts in one town, and we rule according to the view of Rava that if there are two courts in the same town, one generally forbidding and the other generally permitting, the prohibition against forming factions does not apply, as is stated by the Talmud.[67]

Now, concerning what Maimonides, of blessed memory, and the Semag, of blessed memory, said,[68] that the prohibition against factionalism applies in the case of two courts in one town, one following one custom and the other following a different custom, it seems that they, of blessed memory, want to say that when there are differences in customs in the same town, with some acting according to one custom and the others acting according to a different custom, in so doing they become like two courts, but they are not fully two courts in every sense,[69] like the house of Shammai and the house of Hillel, or like the courts one can find today in the great city of Saloniki, a center of Jewish life, where the Sefardic Jews have their own court, and the Ashkenazic Jews have their own court, the former following their ancient customs, and latter following their own ancient customs. And everywhere this is indeed the case, they agree that this is not an instance of factionalism, since we follow Rava. It may very well be that for this reason they were careful not to use the formulation, "two courts in one town must not follow disparate customs" but instead wrote of the mandate "that there not be[come] two courts in one town," and so on, meaning, that where [one court] follows two distinct customs, this constitutes two courts. It is also possible that, the scribes having omitted the "like," there is an error in the text, the correct version of which is 'that there not be [a situation] **like** [that of] two courts,' etc. And in his short work, *The Book of Precepts*, Maimonides, of blessed memory, himself wrote the following: "and behold they said that included in this prohibition is also the admonition against divergent customs among the townspeople and divisions between groups."[70] And the master did not mention that there should not be two courts in one town.

---

67 bJebamot 14a.
68 *Code*, Laws concerning Idolatry 12:14; *Semag*, Negative precepts, 62.
69 And therefore, the disparate customs are, according to Maimonides, forbidden.
70 Negative precepts, 45.

168. Responsa Radakh, house 12, chambers 1–2 (house 14 in first edition)

Question: Instruct us, our master. Three synagogues in a city made a joint enactment pertaining to dancing with married women, because of the unseemly things that have become a daily occurrence at the dances, almost as if dances had become brothels, with young men telling the dance-master, "match me up with so-and-so, or else I won't dance," and women doing the same. One Sabbath a disturbance took place at the dancing. The husband of a certain girl had told his wife not to dance with someone, and later the husband found her dancing with him, and a disturbance ensued, and eventually the matter was taken up in the Gentile courts. The congregations, seeing the breach resulting from these dances, resolved to enact and impose a ban, upon which the majority agreed, with all possible severity, that no dancing take place, other than a man with his wife, and a father with his daughter, and a mother with her son, and a brother with his sisters. This enactment was upheld for nearly three years. Afterwards, due to a dispute in the aforementioned communities over taxes, the communities separated, and some of them gathered to put forward unsound claims: 'Since we are an independent community paying our own taxes, we want to revoke the joint agreement on dancing.' And the others replied: 'you cannot do such a thing, for such an agreement cannot be revoked, all the more so since you are the minority and we are the majority.' The others countered: 'the agreement was not in writing, and since it was not in writing, it is null,' and so on.

To conclude, they did not want to heed it and insolently rebelled, and broke the agreement, and danced. What shall be done with them? Can the minority annul [the majority's decision] without the concurrence of the majority, arguing that they constitute an independent community? They further argue that the agreement was general, and set no time-limits, therefore they are permitted to observe it for some time and then annul it afterwards, as they see fit.

Answer: ...And on becoming an independent community, they assumed the status of citizens of another town, and an independent community is not bound any more than the inhabitants of an independent town. Since each community conducts its affairs according to its own custom, they are like two courts in the same town, and the law is in accordance with the view of Rava[71] that when there are two courts in the same town, one that generally prohibits, and one that generally permits, the prohibition against forming faction does not apply....

---

71 bJebamot 14a.

Therefore, the members of one synagogue have no power to compel those of another synagogue to do anything, because they are a community of their own. But this only applies when the enactment is not a safeguard [against something prohibited] and is not for the general good; but when the enactment is a safeguard for the general good, then the enactment is compulsory, because [when it comes to matters of the general good,] the decision of the majority of the townspeople is binding. Even if they live in different quarters and have separate synagogues, the majority may compel the minority to accept their decision, since they live in the same town. How much more so in a case in which the decision had been accepted earlier – they obviously must adhere to it. And this law is unhindered.

169. Responsa Binyamin Zeev, #303

Four communities from the expulsion from the kingdom of Spain and Portugal had settled in the town of Arta. They came from Sicily, Calabria and Apulia, and there was also the indigenous community that had been settled there from ancient times in their castles and courts. And all their customs were in accordance with the custom of the holy community of Corfu. And they all followed the same customs in matters of ritual law, and were all in agreement on matters of taxes and local taxes and so on, aiding their fellows, in undivided unity. And then something happened in the said communities that originated in the expulsion: they found three betrothed women pregnant by their fiancés, without the proper canopy [that is, marriage ceremony], seven [marriage] benedictions, and purifying immersion [in the ritual bath]. And the matter had become known to the Gentile authorities, and some of them were taken to the magistrate of the city, who punished them according to their [Gentile] laws.

We were told of a second tribulation, that some of the lewd folks of our people had, while dancing, men and women together, fondled the bosoms of married women, which brought about a great and bitter outcry over this evil deed. And people came to the scholars of the town, and its leaders, and told them about this. And when the scholars of the town saw these indecent acts, they convened the officials of the communities and told them about the gravity of these transgressions, [namely,] having relations with one's fiancée without the purifying immersion and seven benedictions, which must not take place among Israel, and also the other bad thing as mentioned above. And the very pious scholars, wanting to enact a safeguard, agreed that after the betrothal benedictions and joint Sabbath meal, no betrothed woman should be allowed to enter the house of her fiancé before they had been led to the wedding canopy. They did this to prevent people from violating a prohibition, for they were apprehensive that they might have relations with their brides while they were menstrually impure, as had happened. They also decided that men and women should not dance together, because of the unseemly things that had happened. And the pious scholars of Arta, may God protect them, wrote to the eminent scholars in Constantinople and Salonika about the aforementioned happenings. However, some of our people protested against the safeguard enacted by these three scholars. But the eminent scholars of Salonika and Constantinople wrote that they agreed with the three scholars, and confirmed this by decreeing *n"h"sh* [bans, shaming and excommunication] against those who would transgress the enactment and safeguard [against sinning] instituted by these three scholars. And on the appointed day the three pious scholars of Arta called together the officials of the communities, the officials of Apulia too, and in a general assembly let them know of their enactment to safeguard people from violating prohibitions, and informed them of what had been written by the eminent scholars of Constantinople and Salonika, may God protect them. And they took out the Torah scroll and brought it to the pulpit (*dukhan*), and imposed the *n"h"sh* and a fine on anyone who would violate the said enactment. And while they were imposing the decrees with the Torah scroll, the Apulian officials noisily protested that they did not wish to be part of the enactment of the three scholars, but stood by their ancestral custom of the affianced man's entering the home of his betrothed to eat and drink together, and therefore they could not impose a ban on this custom. And they left the synagogue in a great hue and cry. And the pious scholars ordered them, by decreeing the *n"h"sh* sanctions, to subject themselves to the said ban and enactment that had been imposed as a safeguard for the law, and the officials took it upon themselves and their descendants to comply with the enactment of the pious scholars.

Though the community officials of the Apulians had left in a huff, nevertheless, they upheld that enactment and safeguard for four years, as did all the other communities. But now they suddenly came with made-up arguments purporting to rule that it was permitted, and were prepared to do battle with swords and shields in order to assert themselves, intending to rebel against the three pious scholars. And they made up and wrote a letter to the great crown of the rabbinate, R. Joseph Teitzak, that the congregation of Apulia did not wish to be part of the aforesaid enactment keeping them from the forbidden act, since they had not accepted it of their own free will, and though they conducted themselves as if it were forbidden, this was only because they could not abandon the other communities, may they be protected and guarded. Now instruct us, O master, if this community has the right to withdraw itself from this safeguard or not.

[Answer:]...It seems to me, in my humble opinion, that the said community of Apulia cannot free itself from a safeguard of that type, since the majority agreed, and imposed severe sanctions so that they would be kept from forbidden acts by instituting a precaution for a precaution, because on matters of ritual prohibitions we obviously follow the majority. All the more so since the scholars and eminent authorities of

Saloniki and Constantinople wrote that they assented to being part of the agreement regarding this enactment and safeguard, and those who transgress it transgress the law, and are to be excommunicated and banned from heaven and the community by decrees of *n"h"sh* sanctions....

Were it only a case of forming factions, it would be fitting for every scholar not to be involved or to permit it, even if it were a matter for voluntary compliance, and how much more so when it was instituted to safeguard the law, and permission might lead to infringement of a biblical prohibition. Since both [communities] are in the same town, they must not follow disparate customs, because in this case it would seem as if they were observing two different sets of laws [lit., two Torahs]. And here the following dictum of Rava does not apply: "But the dictum "do not form factions" is [only] applicable to a case such as that of a court of law in a given town, part of which rules in accordance with the view of the house of Shammai while the other part rules in accordance with the view of the house of Hillel. However, in a case of two courts of law in the same town, it is irrelevant."[72] And accordingly, my opponent could have an opening to argue against me. But this is not so. There are no scholars of any stature in the community of Apulia who could be deemed a court, even according to Rava, and be advised that Rava says "courts." Now only Torah scholars and halakhic experts can be called a court of law. All the more so according to Abbaye, who says: "The admonition against forming factions is applicable to a case such as that of two courts of law in the same town, one of which rules in accordance with the view of the house of Shammai while the other rules in accordance with the view of the house of Hillel. However, in a case of two courts of law in two different towns, it is irrelevant."

Now we have to deal with the apparent difficulty pertaining to the reading of the Book of Esther, which villagers may advance to the market day. This does not contradict the opinion of Rava, who says that the prohibition against forming factions applies to one court in a town, part of which rules in accordance with the view of the house of Shammai and part of which in accordance with the view of the house of Hillel, but two courts in the same town are permitted. On his opinion, since the villagers and the townspeople are like two courts in the same town, there is no difficulty. But it apparently contradicts the opinion of Abbaye, who says that the prohibition also applies to two courts in the same town, one ruling according to the view of the house of Shammai and the other according to the view of the house of Hillel – how do we permit the villagers to read the Scroll on the eleventh, twelfth or thirteenth, while the townspeople must read it on the fourteenth, the proper date? It is like two courts in the same town, and this poses a difficulty for Abbaye's view.

72 bJebamot 14a.

And we have to say that this is also analogous to two courts in two towns, since the villagers constitute a distinct community, and their intention is to return to their village. And the townspeople are a distinct community of their own, and it is like two courts in two towns. And it poses no problem. And it cannot be argued that if the reader is one of the townspeople, and in reading discharges their obligation, it is like the case of two courts in the same town. This is not so, as we cannot but hold that the reader who discharges their obligation is not one of the townspeople, but must be one of the villagers, since [at the advanced reading] the townspeople are not yet obligated to read the Scroll, and one who is not obligated cannot discharge the obligation of another, as the Jerusalem Talmud states.[73] Because of this, the villagers constitute one court, since their intention is to return to their homes, and the townspeople constitute another court, in their town, and it is like two courts in two towns, and is in harmony with the opinions of both Rava and Abbaye, for in such circumstances the prohibition against forming factions does not apply even according to Abbaye. And the reason why the villagers do not read in their own place is because they only gather together in the town.

Therefore, on our interpretation, the *lo titgodedu* prohibition does not apply in the case of two courts in two towns, but in the case of two courts in the same town, one conducting itself one way and the other conducting itself another way, the *lo titgodedu* prohibition does apply. And this is apparent in Maimonides' *Code*, which states: And included in the admonition is the mandate that there not be two courts in one town, one following one custom and another following a different custom, for this leads to major controversies. As it is said: "ye shall not cut yourselves (*lo titgodedu*)" (Deut. 14:1) – do not form factions"[74] and so too in *Sefer Mitzvot Gadol*, namely, that they rule in accordance with the view of Abbaye.[75] Yet I, Benjamin, find a difficulty in their ruling in accordance with the view of Abbaye,[76] since we hold that in a controversy between Abbaye and Rava the law is in accordance with the view of Rava, with the exception of the cases referred to as *y"e"l k"g"m*,[77] as is stated in the Talmud.

170. Responsa Avkat Rokhel, #32

Teach us, our master, regarding communities that follow the ways of Maimonides, of blessed memory, both in his leniencies and in his strictures, generation after generation. Could one coerce them to follow the

---

73 jMegila 4:7.
74 *Code*, Laws concerning Idolatry 12:14.
75 Negative precepts, 62.
76 For the solution to this difficulty, see passage 163 above.
77 bKidushin 52a.

authority of R. Jacob [author of the *Turim*], and other later authorities, who provide reasons for their positions, or ought one comply with the teaching, 'Follow your ancestors' customs,' even though the majority follows the other opinion?

Answer: Who conspires to coerce communities that follow Maimonides, of blessed memory, to follow another authority, early or late? And as to what we learned in the Talmud,

> It was taught: The law is always in accordance with the view of the house of Hillel, but he who wishes to act in accordance with the view of the house of Shammai may do so, and he who wishes to act in accordance with the view of the house of Hillel may do so. He who adopts the more lenient rulings of the house of Shammai and the more lenient rulings of the house of Hillel is a wicked man, while of one who adopts the strictures of the house of Shammai and the strictures of the house of Hillel, Scripture said: "the fool walketh in darkness" (Eccles. 2:14). But rather, if one adopts the views of the house of Shammai, one should adopt both their lenient and their strict rulings, and if one adopts the views of the house of Hillel, one should adopt both their lenient and their strict rulings.[78]

Now this is so a fortiori: if it is said of the views of the house of Shammai, which are not accepted as the law, that they can be followed, in both their lenient and their restrictive rulings, then so can those of Maimonides, of blessed memory, who is our greatest authority. And every community in the land of Israel, in Arabia and in the West [the Maghreb] has accepted him as its leader and conducts itself according to his teachings. Why should those who accept his rulings, both lenient and restrictive, be compelled to forsake him? And even more so considering that this may have been the practice of their fathers and their fathers' fathers, thus the sons must not deviate either to the right or to the left from following Maimonides, of blessed memory. Even if a majority in the town follow Asheri or others, they cannot force the few communities that follow Maimonides, of blessed memory, to adopt their ways. And the prohibition against factions does not apply here, since each community follows its original custom. This is like two courts in the same town, and we uphold the law in accordance with the view of Rava, who says that wherever there are two courts, one of which generally forbids and one of which generally permits, this is not an instance of factionalism, as it says in the Talmud.[79] And each and every community in the town is deemed

---

78 bEruvin 6b.
79 bJebamot 14a.

a town unto itself, and members of one cannot force members of another [to change]. And this is stated in the responsa of our teacher and rabbi R. David Hakohen,[80] of blessed memory. And I have written what appears correct to me, [Joseph] the junior.

171. Responsa Mahari Ben Lev, 3, #14

Regarding the practice in the great city of Constantinople, [where] the skilled porgers[81] follow Rashi, of blessed memory, who recommended leniency on the matter of fat covered by tough membranes[82] (hazak). And almost all, or all, the decisors disagree with him. The said porgers differentiate between lamb and beef, and say that the membrane in beef is tough and flesh-like, but in lamb this is not the case.

This calls for investigation of four issues. First, whether all the communities in Constantinople, the Romaniot and the Sefardic, may He save and redeem them, will unanimously agree to repudiate this custom, and abide by the stricter custom of porging the fat covered by the said membrane, in line with the opinion of the majority of the authorities. And all the communities we are aware of act strictly, with the exception of the Ashkenazic community, who from the days of yore have upheld Rashi's lenient opinion. Yet for several years now even some of the Ashkenazic community in Salonika have changed their custom, and inclined toward strictness. And there may well be room to inquire whether all the communities would agree to put an end to their custom of leniency, even though this would cast aspersions on the preceding authorities, who condoned leniency, and constitute an affront to the earlier scholars who permitted this custom and made no protest.

The second point that must be investigated is what would happen if the holy communities of the Romaniots do not agree to the stricture.[83] Would the Sefardic holy communities, whose forebears, in their own lands, were among those who were strict with regard to the said abdominal fat, be permitted to form their own faction, and if so, would this be a transgression of the dictum, 'lo titgodedu, do not form factions,' as specified in tractate Jebamot?[84] Furthermore, we have to explore whether, should we indeed say that this would not violate the prohibition against forming factions, were the Sefardic community to become divided, some of them choosing

---

80 See passages 167 and 168 above.
81 Butchers who 'clean' the meat by porging (nikur), that is, removing abdominal fat (helev). Unless covered by flesh, abdominal fat of oxen, sheep, and goats is forbidden (Lev. 3:17; 7:23–25).
82 There is controversy as to whether certain tough membranes are considered to be flesh.
83 The text here reads "leniency," but this is evidently a scribal error.
84 bJebamot 13b.

to uphold the custom of the Romaniot rabbis, and others to end the practice of this custom and to restore their ancestral custom, we would deem this 'forming factions' and deny them permission to do so....

In investigating this second point, we must ascertain whether the Romaniot and the Franco-German communities constitute two courts in one town, which is not considered factionalism, or are, perhaps, like one court in the town, part of which rules in accordance with the view of the house of Shammai and part in accordance with the view of the house of Hillel. In tractate Jebamot the Talmud states: Now as to those who maintain that the house of Shammai did act in accordance with their views, should not the admonition, do not form factions, be applied? Abbaye said: The admonition against forming factions is applicable to a case such as that of two courts of law in the same town, one of which rules in accordance with the view of the house of Shammai, while the other rules in accordance with the view of the house of Hillel. However, in a case of two courts of law in two different towns, it is irrelevant. Rava said to him, surely the case of the house of Shammai and the house of Hillel is like that of two courts of law in the same town? But, Rava said, the dictum "do not form factions" is [only] applicable to a case such as that of a court of law in a given town, part of which rules in accordance with the view of the house of Shammai while the other part rules in accordance with the view of the house of Hillel. However, in a case of two courts of law in the same town, it is irrelevant.[85]

And the Semag states, "there should not be two courts in the same town, one following one custom, and the other following another."[86] This implies that his ruling accords with the view of Abbaye, but we have a rule that where there is a disagreement between Abbaye and Rava, the law is in accordance with Rava's view, with the exception of *y"e"l k"g"m.*[87] And in his rulings, our teacher and rabbi R. David Hakohen, of blessed memory, raised this question, and explained that the thrust of what Maimonides and the Semag say is that there should not be two courts, and so on, in that, being a single court, they should not conduct themselves as if they were two courts, with some following one custom and others another. And the said rabbi wrote as follows: "It may very well be that for this reason Maimonides and Semag were careful not to use the formulation "two courts in one town must not follow disparate customs" but instead write of the mandate "that there not be two courts in one town," and so on, meaning, that where [one court] follows two distinct customs, this constitutes two courts. It is also possible that, the scribes having omitted the

---

85 bJebamot 14a.
86 *Sefer Mitzvot Gadol*, Negative precepts, 62.
87 bKidushin 52a.

"like," there is an error in the text, the correct version of which is 'that there not be [a situation] **like** [that of] two courts,' and so on.

And the same rabbi also wrote: "like [the courts one can find today in] the great city of Salonika, a center of Jewish life." And the truth is indeed thus: the Ashkenazic community has two customs that differ from the customs of the other communities, one being stricter and one more lenient. The Ashkenazic community's practice is strict with regard to perforations in the lung that do not render the animal non-kosher if the lung tissue has grown back together, except when located on the narrows of the chest, in accordance with the view of the majority of the decisors. And the Sefardic community relies on Rabbenu Tam and R. Zerahia Halevi and Maimonides, who considered such cases kosher if the lung could be inflated. And [the second custom is that of] the tough membrane, where the Ashkenazim follow the lenient view of Rashi, and the Sefardim follow the strict opinion of most of the other decisors. And they conduct themselves as two courts in one town. And what I have written about the first two points to be investigated should suffice.

172. Responsa Mabit, 3, #77

Concerning the matter of a town with three or four synagogues, whether the majority of the congregants and synagogues can compel the minority to accept its authority, even if the minority constitutes a separate community.[88] The learned sage, may God protect and deliver him,[89] discussed this at length in order to prove that the preponderance of communities in a town have the right to compel an individual community to comply with [their decisions] on any matter pertaining to safeguarding ritual law. I think that he is right about this.

And where, in their responsa, the Rashba and the Ribash write that one community cannot force another to accept their decisions, by "one community" they apparently mean the denizens of a given town, as the learned sage, may God protect and deliver him, wrote, and as is evident from the language of their responsa. But with regard to synagogues in a town, the majority may force the minority to take upon themselves [their decisions] on any matter pertaining to safeguarding ritual law, as it is plainly stated in the Talmud: "The townspeople are also at liberty to fix weights and measures, prices, and wages, and to inflict penalties for the infringement of their rules,"and so on.[90] All the authorities quote this – "The townspeople are also at liberty" – without any qualification, referring to denizens of a given

---

88 Referring to a controversy in Patras, Greece.
89 R. Joseph Formon.
90 bBaba Batra 8b.

town, whether the town is comprised of a single community, or several communities, because their division into two communities, or three, or four, is due solely to the fact that there is insufficient space in the synagogue, which cannot accommodate the multitude, as did the Temple, where people stood pressed together and yet had enough space to prostrate themselves freely. And in all the towns with a large Jewish population there is a need to establish houses of prayer, whether because one synagogue cannot contain them all, as I just said, or because the population is large and the town spread out, and not everyone who resides at the edge of town can attend synagogue services early in the morning and in the evening. For not everyone can merit the reward for making the effort [to reach the synagogue], and hence there is a need for a synagogue in each and every neighborhood. And this is not a justification for different ordinances, for, regarding any matter pertaining to safeguarding ritual law, they are all one group with one heart. ...And so too with respect to all civic issues, it should be thus: they should all be but one group, as they are united by one God, one Torah and one law, and so it should also be with regard to their enactments pertaining to safeguarding ritual law. For the minority must follow the majority on all these matters. Even if there are a number of synagogues in one town, the majority of the leading citizens, or the majority of the town's synagogues, can coerce the minority on matters that seem necessary to them at the time, issuing enactments and safeguards so that the Torah's prohibitions, or even Rabbinic prohibitions, will not be infringed, if they see that transgression is imminent or taking place. We do not say that the scriptural and Rabbinic prohibitions are sufficient for us, for agreements and ordinances support and sustain scriptural prohibitions and Rabbinic enactments.

173. Responsa Maharshag, 2, #12

It has also occurred to me to compare this issue with the prohibition against adding precepts, "thou shalt not add" (Deut. 13:1), which is surely an absolute scriptural prohibition. The Talmud states that one who wears two pairs of phylacteries transgresses this prohibition.[91] Nevertheless, the *Shulhan Arukh*[92] explains that due to the uncertainty [of the proper arrangement of the verses in the phylacteries], it is permitted to put on both those reflecting Rashi's view, and those of Rabbenu Tam, and there is no fear of transgressing "thou shalt not add." Since the two pairs are donned together only due to this uncertainty, and not due to any claim that indeed [the proper observance of the precept] does involve two pairs, the wearer does

91 bEruvin 96a.
92 OH 34.

not violate "thou shalt not add." And if so, the situation is similar with regard to the *lo titgodedu* prohibition. It too only applies if each of the parties assert that they conduct themselves as they do out of certitude [that they are right], as it is clear to them that the law is thus and the other view is totally wrong. But should one say that there is an element of uncertainty, because the decisors do not agree, and hence due to this concern one wishes to adopt the stricter view, for the law might be in accordance with it, even if others do not wish to be strict because of this uncertainty – in any event, since the one who acts thus [in accordance with the stricter position] does not do so due to certitude but rather is strict due to uncertainty, the prohibition against factions does not apply. If we do not say this, nobody would be allowed to adopt, regarding an even ever-so-slightly doubtful matter, a stricter position than that taken by his fellow. For example, some people eat cooked matza on Passover and others do not. Has it ever occurred to anyone that this constitutes factionalism? For even those who are careful about this do not say that partaking of cooked matza is prohibited by law, but say only that they wish to take precautions lest particles of unbaked flour are cooked, and for this reason they follow a stricter course. Thus, those who are strict only due to such doubts do not violate the prohibition against factions. And in fact, honorable Torah scholar, you said as much in your remarks, in stating that you do not recite the benediction when donning phylacteries on the intermediate days of Festivals, and for that reason the prohibition against factionalism does not apply; but the honorable Torah scholar did not fully explain the reason. But I have explained that since you do not say the benediction, it appears that you do not act on a certainty, but wish, due to uncertainty, to follow a stricter course, and hence, the prohibition against factionalism is not applicable.

R. Shneur Zalman of Lyadi, author of the Tanya, writes in his *Shulhan Arukh*:

> But if the local custom is known to him, it should not be changed. One must not be lenient on days when the locals are strict, or strict on the days when they are lenient, if this is not done as a self-imposed stricture due to a wish to follow the stricter opinion on the given days, but rather, one gives the impression that he acts thus because the stricter course should be followed by all, because the law is as the strict view claims – for then it looks as if there are two sets of laws [lit., two Torahs], since he is strict on a point where the locals are lenient, or vice versa. And this violates the prohibition against factionalism, "ye shall not cut yourselves," that is, do not form factions.[93]

93 *Shulhan Arukh Hatanya*, OH 493:7.

This implies that if one wishes to pursue a stricter course because he is concerned about uncertainties, this is not factionalism. And in my opinion, another indication that this must be so is the fact that the *Shulhan Arukh* is replete with laws that are somewhat questionable, and suggests following the stricter course, or says that those who do so will be blessed. If we do not maintain the position proposed above, it would seem that for fear of infringing the prohibition against factionalism, one would not be allowed, even for himself alone, to follow a stricter course. Therefore certainly, as long as one does not present his conduct as if it were the true law, it does not involve factionalism.

This solution should be read together with that which I provided above.[94] Now, how can we know whether the person's intention is to adopt a stricture, or if his intention is to be strict because he thinks that his conduct reflects the true law? This can be ascertained by his instructions to others: whether he exhorts them to follow his example, as otherwise they are transgressing a prohibition or violating the law. But in our case of the phylacteries on the intermediate days of the Festivals, according to what you have written, you state that you did not admonish others or accuse them of failing to observe a positive precept of the Torah by not donning phylacteries as you do, but that you are only acting for yourself. Evidently you do this as a stricture, and if so, the injunction against factionalism is not relevant, as stated above.

4.5. The distinction between law and custom

174. Beit Habehira, bJebamot 14a s.v. *umegila*

And as to the Book of Esther, which is read at different times in towns, villages and walled cities, as is explained in the appropriate place,[95] the issue of factions does not arise, as these are different locales, since the villagers too read it [in their own villages], as we determined in the appropriate place. And furthermore, even according to opinions which aver that the Scroll was read for the villagers in the [market] towns [on a different date than for the townspeople] – this is analogous to two courts in the same town, or it is as if one town was composed of two separate boroughs, because within the town the villagers maintain their own identity, and they reside in the town as if they were in a town unto itself.

Furthermore, I would also argue that the laws governing the reading of the Scroll are in no way related to the issue of factionalism, even according to those who maintain that two courts in the same town does constitute

---

94 See passage 154 above.
95 *Beit Habehira*, bMegila 2a.

factionalism, [the only case in which factionalism does not apply being] that of two courts in two different towns. And I interpret, "Abbaye said: The admonition against forming factions is applicable [to a case such as that of two courts in the same town]" as referring to a matter that is contested between two different courts in the same town – and the reference [namely, Resh Lakish's query to R. Johanan, Should we not apply here the admonition "ye shall not cut yourselves" (*lo titgodedu*) (Deut. 14:1), that is, do not form factions?] is to the mishnaic controversy regarding the rival[-wive]s. But the reading of the Scroll is not in any way included in the scope of this prohibition, because [the disparate conduct] is not due to controversy, with some conducting themselves in accordance with one opinion and others conducting themselves in accordance with a different opinion, for the townspeople acknowledge the date of the villagers' reading, and the villagers acknowledge the date of the townspeople's reading. And it is like the case of the reading of the Shema prayer at sunrise, where a concession was made for travelers, so they could recite the prayer [earlier,] at the crack of dawn. It is also possible that indeed the villagers' reading [of the Book of Esther on a different date] is not an instance of factionalism, and the focus of the debate [between Resh Lakish and R. Johanan] is something else: [the different dates on which the Scroll is read in open and walled cities] – the fourteenth and fifteenth of the month. These dates are definitive, and residents of the one must not read the Scroll on the dates set for residents of the other, as the passage states: the time set for the one is not the time set for the other. However, should the said villagers wish to read the Scroll on the fourteenth, they are welcome to do so, though they were given leeway to advance the reading [to the market day]. The problem arises only in the case of a prohibition, as indeed the Talmud says: "I am speaking of a prohibition … and you speak to me of a custom," and so on.

175. Hidushei Haritba, bJebamot 14a s.v. *vehikshu batosafot*

And the *Tosafot* ask: why does the Talmud not raise the issue of the villagers who advance the reading of the Book of Esther to the market-day, for they hold the reading in town, and this is analogous to two courts in one town, because they read it on the market-day while the others read it at the proper time? And many different solutions have been suggested. And it is implied in the reply of the *Tosafot* that the issue of factions does not arise in this case at all, because the problem of factions and the Torah splitting into two sets of laws only applies when there is a controversy where one side does not concede. But as to a matter on which they all concede each other's points, and each of them has a good reason for acting as he does, this is not factionalism. To what is the matter analogous? To the ritual 'taking' of the lulav, which was observed for seven days in the

Temple, but for one day elsewhere, or the blowing of the shofar, which was accompanied by trumpets in the Temple, but not elsewhere. And the Jerusalem Talmud discusses this problem along these lines, and provides a satisfactory account, and the matter is fully explained.[96]

But I have a problem with this, since Resh Lakish puts forward the case of the reading of the Scroll [as a case of factionalism], yet no one mentions this explanation in response; and Resh Lakish himself certainly did not accept this explanation. And on the above analysis, we have to say that R. Johanan and his colleagues for this very reason did not consider the Mishna about the reading of the Scroll to be a counterexample to the "*lo titgodedu*" prohibition, and for this very reason did not even mention it. And Resh Lakish, though aware that there is a good reason to make the distinction between villagers, townspeople, and residents of walled cities, each [group] reading the Scroll for itself [that is, on its own date], feels that it is not entirely decisive, and that since the Men of the Great Assembly had the authority to do so, they should have decided on a single time that would be the same for all, or [that it should be read] on the fourteenth and fifteenth. And this seems to be the correct way of interpreting the account put forward by the *Tosafot*.

176. Rosh, Jebamot, chapter 1, section 9

The Talmud raises a question about the teaching: "the house of Shammai permit the rival[-wive]s to the other brothers, and the house of Hillel forbid them"[97]; and about the teaching: "the Book of Esther is read on the eleventh, the twelfth, the thirteenth, the fourteenth and the fifteenth" – [Said Resh Lakish to R. Johanan:] [Should we not] Apply here the admonition "ye shall not cut yourselves (*lo titgodedu*)," that is, do not form factions? And Rava concluded: "But the dictum "do not form factions" is [only] applicable to a case such as that of a court of law in a given town, part of which rules in accordance with the view of the house of Shammai while the other part rules in accordance with the view of the house of Hillel. However, in a case of two courts of law in the same town, it is irrelevant."[98] And all the more so [is it inapplicable] in the case of two courts in two towns.

With regard to the Book of Esther, which is read for townspeople on the fourteenth but advanced to an earlier date for villagers, and this appears to be a case of one court in a town, part of which rules in accordance with the view of the house of Shammai and part of which in accordance with the view of the house of Hillel – this does not constitute factionalism,

---

96 See jPesahim 4:1 (30d).
97 With respect to levirate marriage.
98 bJebamot 14a.

because they do not act thus due to controversy, but it is a function of the place [where they reside]. And were someone from one place to move to another, he would do as they do, therefore it does not look as if there are two distinct sets of laws [lit., two Torahs]. Even though Resh Lakish posed his question regarding the Book of Esther to R. Johanan, R. Johanan did not think it necessary to refute it, since he did not think it could be construed as [a case where there was any fear that the law would become like] two sets of laws, for the reason outlined above, and [merely] said to him: Do you not recall learning, In place where they are accustomed...?[99] Your query should have been based on that [Mishna], because with regard to the Book of Esther, there is no real difficulty.

---

99 mPesahim 4:1.

5

CONTROVERSY AND SOCIAL HARMONY

177. mPesahim 4:1

In a place where they are accustomed to work on the eve of Passover up to midday they do [work]; in a place where they are accustomed not to do work, they do not. Should someone go from a place where they do work to a place where they do not work, or from a place where they do not work to a place where they do work, the strictures of the place from which he came and the strictures of the place to which he has gone are applied to him. But one must not make any change due to[1] controversy.

178. mJebamot 1:4

The house of Shammai permit the rival[-wive]s to the brothers, but the house of Hillel prohibit it. If they had performed the ceremony of *halitza* – the house of Shammai declare them unfit for [marriage to] the priesthood, but the house of Hillel declare them fit; if they had been taken in levirate marriage, the house of Shammai declare them fit, but the house of Hillel declare them unfit. Nevertheless, though these prohibit what the others permit, and these declare unfit that which the others declare fit, the house of Shammai did not refrain from marrying women of the house of Hillel, nor the house of Hillel from [marrying women of] the house of Shammai. [Despite] all the purities and impurities that these would declare pure and the others would declare impure – they did not refrain, in matters connected with purity, from making use of that which pertained to the others.

179. mEduyot 8:7

R. Joshua said: I have received a tradition from Rabban Johanan b. Zakai, who heard it from his teacher, and his teacher from his teacher, as a law

---

1 The wording here is slightly ambiguous to reflect the Hebrew original: due to a past controversy, or a potential future controversy?

given to Moses at Sinai, that Elijah will not come to declare impure or pure, to send away or to bring near, but to send away those brought near by force and to bring near those sent away by force. The family of Bet Zerephah was on the other side of the Jordan, and Ben Zion sent them away by force; and yet another family was there, and Ben Zion brought them near by force. Elijah will come to declare such cases impure or pure, to send away or to bring near. R. Judah says: to bring near, but not to send away. R. Shimon says: to reconcile controversy. And the Sages say: neither to send away nor to bring near, but to make peace to the world, as it is said, "Behold I send to you Elijah the prophet...and he shall turn the heart of the fathers to the children and the heart of the children to their fathers" (Mal. 3:23–24).

180. tJebamot 1:10–12

Even though the house of Shammai took issue with the view of the house of Hillel as to the rival[-wive]s,[2] as to the sisters, as to the doubtful married woman, as to a superannuated writ of divorce, as to one who betroths a woman with something valued at one *peruta*,[3] and as to one who divorces his wife and she spends a night with him at an inn, the house of Shammai did not refrain from marrying women of the house of Hillel, nor the house of Hillel from [marrying women of] the house of Shammai. Rather, they behaved toward one another truthfully, and there was peace between them, to fulfil the scriptural dictum: "love truth and peace" (Zech. 8:19).

And even though these prohibit what the others permit, they did not refrain, in matters connected with purity, from making use of that which pertained to the others, to fulfil the scriptural dictum: "Every way a man is pure in his own eyes, but the Lord weighs the hearts."[4]

181. Genesis Rabbah 4:6

Why is "that it was good" not written in connection with the second day?...R. Hanina said, Because on that day controversy was created, as it is written, "and let it divide[5] the waters" (Gen. 1:6). R. Tabyomi said: If a division made for the greater orderliness and stability of the world does not merit "that it was good," this applies all the more so to a division that mixes it up.

---

2 With respect to levirate marriage.
3 A coin of little value.
4 The verse cited is compounded from Proverbs 21:2 and 16:2.
5 The word for controversy, *mahloket*, comes from the root *hl"k*, "to divide."

182. Leviticus Rabbah 9:9

Hezekiah said: Great is peace, for with regard to all the journeyings it is written, "And the children of Israel journeyed [plural]…and encamped [plural]" (Num. 33:6), [the plural number implying that] they journeyed in dissension, and they encamped in dissension. Since, however, they all came before Mount Sinai, they all became one encampment: 'and there the children of Israel encamped [plural]' is not written here, but rather, "And there Israel encamped [sing.]" (Exod. 19:2). Said the Holy One, blessed be He: This is the [perfect] hour for Me to give the Torah to My children.

Bar Kapara said: Great is peace. Given that the uppermost ones amongst whom there is no jealousy, no hatred, no competition, no quarreling, no enmity, no controversy, and no evil eye, nonetheless need peace – "He maketh peace in his high places" (Job 25: 2), how much more so do the lower ones, who have all these traits.

183. bBerakhot 16b–17a

R. Safra, on concluding his prayer, said the following: May it be Thy will, O Lord our God, to establish peace among the heavenly entourage, and among the earthly entourage, and among the students who occupy themselves with Thy Torah, whether they so occupy themselves for its [the Torah's] own sake or not for its own sake; and as to those who so occupy themselves not for its own sake, may it be Thy will that they come to study it for its own sake.

184. bBerakhot 39b

It has been stated: If pieces and whole loaves are set before someone, R. Huna says: The benediction can be said over the pieces, and this exempts the whole loaves [from the requirement that a benediction be made over them], whereas R. Johanan says: The religious duty is better performed if the blessing is said over the whole [loaves].... A Tanna recited in the presence of R. Nahman b. Isaac: One should place the piece under the whole loaf and then take some and say the benediction. He said to him: What is your name? Shalman, he replied. He said to him: Thou art peace [*shalom*] and your Mishna is perfect [*shleima*], that you have placed peace between the students.

185. bBerakhot 64a

R. Eleazar said in the name of R. Hanina: The students of the scholars increase peace in the world, as it is said, "And all thy children shall be taught of the Lord, and manifold shall be the peace of thy children"

(Isa. 54:13). Read not *banayikh* (thy children) but *bonayikh* (thy builders). "Great peace have they who love thy law, and there is no stumbling for them" (Ps. 119:165). "Peace be within thy walls and tranquillity within thy palaces; For my brethren and companions' sake I will now say, Peace be within thee; For the sake of the house of the Lord our God I will seek thy good" (Ps. 122:7–9); "The Lord will give strength unto His people; the Lord will bless His people with peace" (Ps. 29:11).

186. bKidushin 30b

It is also said, "Happy is the man who has his quiver full of them. They shall not be ashamed when they speak with their enemies at the gate" (Ps. 127:5). What is meant by "with their enemies at the gate"? Said R. Hiya b. Abba: Even father and son, teacher and student, who apply themselves to [study of] the Torah at the same gate, become enemies of each other, yet do not budge from there until they come to love each other, as it is said, "Vaheb [love] in Suphah" (Num. 21:14); read not *besufa* [in Suphah] but *besofa* [in the end].

187. Derekh Eretz Zuta 9:25

And R. Eleazar Hakapar used to say, Love peace and hate controversy. Great is peace, for even were [Israel] to practice idolatry, if they maintained peace among themselves, the Divine Presence would be unable, as it were, to do them harm, as it is stated, "Ephraim is joined to idols; let him alone" (Hos. 4:17). But if there is controversy among them, what is said of them? "Their heart is divided; now shall they bear their guilt" (Hos. 10:2). How so? A house in which there is controversy will ultimately be destroyed. And the Sages say that a synagogue in which there is controversy will ultimately be split apart. If two scholars reside in the same town and constitute two courts of law, and there is controversy between them, they are destined to die prematurely. Abba Saul says, "controversy between courts of law is the ruination of the world."

188. Sheiltot, Korah, #131

Question: It is forbidden for the house of Israel to be involved in disputes, because the existence of disputes leads to general hatred, and the All-Merciful said, "Thou shalt not hate thy brother in thy heart" (Lev. 19:17). It is not only that the small should appease the great, but even the great should appease the small, so that there will be no controversy, as it is written, "And Moses rose up and went unto Dathan and Abiram," and so on (Num. 16:25). And Resh Lakish said: This teaches that one must not be unyielding in a dispute; and R. Judah said in the name of Rav: He who is unyielding in a dispute violates a negative precept, as it is written, "that he fare not as Korah, and as his company" (Num. 17:5). R. Asi said: He is to be smitten with leprosy; here it is written, "[as the Lord spoke] unto him (*lo*) by the hand of Moses" (ibid.), while there it is written, "And the Lord said furthermore unto him (*lo*), 'Put now thine hand,' " and so on (Exod. 4:6). R. Hama the son of R. Hanina said, Whoever makes a quarrel with his teacher is as one who makes a quarrel with the Divine Presence, as it is written, "These are the waters of Meribah (strife); where the children of Israel strove with the Lord" (Num. 20:13). And was it, then, with the Divine Presence that they made a quarrel? Rather, they made a quarrel with Moses, as it is said, "and the people strove with Moses" (Num. 20:3). This thus teaches us that whoever makes a quarrel with his teacher is as one who quarrels with the Divine Presence. R. Hanina b. Papa said: Whoever complains about his teacher, is as one who complains about the Divine Presence, as it is said, "your murmurings are not against us, but against the Lord" (Exod. 16:8). R. Abbahu said: He who thinks ill of his teacher is as one who thinks ill of the Divine Presence, as it is said, "And the people spoke against God, and against Moses" (Num. 21:5). R. Hisda said: Whoever takes issue with his teacher's view is as one who takes issue with the view of the Divine Presence, as it is said, "when they strove against the Lord" (Num. 26:9).[6]

189. Kad Hakemah, 'Sinat hinam'

Gratuitous hatred (*sinat hinam*) is a division of hearts, for people differ from one another as to their opinions, and they do not agree on a single view, and each and every one has his own opinion, and [in his eyes] his fellow's view is no better than his. And not one of them recognizes the worth of one who is greater than he is, but all wish to take precedence, and thus their opinions and hearts are divided. The Divine Presence does not abide among a people whose heart is divided, for the Sages, of blessed memory, expounded: "And there was a King in Jeshurun, when the heads of the people were gathered" (Deut. 33:5) – that is, when they were a single grouping.[7] And the prophet said, "Their heart is divided, now shall they bear their guilt" (Hos. 10:2), referring to the said division of hearts. It goes without saying that unity of hearts is beneficial in worshiping God, may He be blessed, for it is beneficial even for idolatry. And this is the meaning of the verse, "Ephraim is joined to the idols, let him alone" (Hos. 4:17), meaning that although it was fitting that they be cast out from the world because they worshiped idols, [nevertheless,] since they comprise one

6 The exegesis here is taken from bSanhedrin 110a; see passage 49 above.
7 Numbers Rabbah 15:14.

grouping and share one opinion, "let him alone," that is, I will defer My anger at them.

The cause and foundation of peace is unity, and the cause and foundation of controversy is dissension, that is, varied desires, and changes from one thing to another. And you will find this exemplified in the Creation [of the world]: on the first day, which alludes to His unity, you will find no discord, division or separation between one thing and another. But on the second day, which saw the onset of change, there was a division between the waters [under the firmament] and the waters [above the firmament],[8] and this was the beginning of controversy, departure from His will, and changes in things. And this division [between the waters] was the cause of all the controversy and varied desires in the upper realms, and the division of hearts in the lower realms. And this is the reason why it is not said of that day "that it was good," for the good was lacking because of the divisions.

And behold, the second day was the cause of all the dissensions that followed in its wake, due to its power, and therefore on all the [other days of Creation] we see fault-finding and departure from His will: on the third day, it says, "let the earth put forth fruit-tree bearing fruit," and the earth did not do this, but rather, "tree bearing fruit"; on the fourth day, the moon complained, on the fifth day He killed the female and castrated the male,[9] on the sixth day Adam and Eve sinned and were driven from the Garden of Eden. And what was the cause of this fault-finding and departure from His will on all these days? The second day, because it influenced those that followed in its wake, due to its power, and this was the beginning of [what transpired on] these days, and the cause of the fault-finding. And thus you find the trait of gratuitous hatred, which is the division of hearts, continuing from the second day – of which it is not said "that it was good" – onward.

And it is known that because of the sinfulness of this trait, the Second Temple was destroyed, as indeed the Sages, of blessed memory, expounded: Why was the First Temple destroyed? Because of idolatry. As to the Second Temple, since we know full well that they were pious and observed the precepts – why was it destroyed? Because of gratuitous hatred.[10] And the Midrash on Lamentations [Lamentations Rabbah] states: And not only that, but they rejoiced in each other's downfall, as it is said, "When thou doest evil, then thou rejoicest" (Jer. 11:15), and as it is written: "And he that is glad at calamity shall not be unpunished" (Prov. 17:5).

8 See Genesis 1:7.
9 Referring to the whale, see bBaba Batra 74b.
10 bYoma 9b.

190. Yearot Dvash, part 2, sermon 8

The Mishna states: Every controversy that is for the sake of heaven, its end is to be sustained. And which is that? The controversy between Hillel and Shammai. And the controversy that is not for the sake of heaven, such as the controversy of Korah and his congregation, its end is not to be sustained[11] .... And we ought to carefully analyze the statement, What controversy is for the sake of heaven? What sort of question is this! There are many controversies that are for the sake of heaven! And the inferences from this Mishna are likewise problematic. For the Mishna says, "such as the controversy between Shammai and Hillel," implying that any controversy other than this one is not for the sake of heaven, and further on it says, "And that which is not for the sake of heaven? The controversy of Korah and his congregation." This implies that any controversy other than this is for the sake of heaven. And these inferences are incompatible.

However, for us, due to our many sins, in every controversy, whatever it be, the evil inclination tempts us, saying that it is for the sake of heaven, and for a great precept, to prevail over traitors, and to break the high arm, and many similar things. All in all, there is no controversy in which the evil inclination does not tempt [the dissenter], saying that its whole intention is for the sake of heaven, and heaven forbid that we say of any controversy that it is not for the sake of heaven. But if this is so, how can we recognize whether or not it really is for the sake of heaven? This is how it can be known: if the disputants and the quarreling parties, are – aside from the matter over which the controversy has arisen, regarding which they oppose one another – intimate friends, heart and soul, this is a sign that their controversy is for sake of heaven; but if they are enemies who bear hatred for each other, manifested in the controversy, then it is not for the sake of heaven, and Satan has ensconced himself within them. And this is the sign that the Sages of the Mishna gave us: "What controversy is for the sake of heaven?" Since regarding any controversy people say it is for the sake of heaven, they said, "such as the controversy between Shammai and Hillel," who loved each other and respected each other, who were beloved and gentle; this is an indication that their controversy is for the sake of heaven. But a controversy such as that of Korah and his congregation, who bore hatred and animosity, and almost stoned Moses, and the like, this was not for the sake of heaven. For in heaven, love and ... and this is a reliable indication with respect to every controversy, allowing us to discern whether or not it is for the sake of heaven.

11 mAvot 5:17; the quotation is inexact.

191. Hidushei Agadot Maharam Shick, mAvot 5:17

"Every controversy that is for the sake of heaven," and so on. Apparently, the intention is to say that sometimes we have an obligation to enter into a controversy. That is, should one see that someone is saying of something non-kosher that it is kosher, he ought not say, 'Why should I tell him and bring about a controversy, perhaps the one who rules thus is right, and why should I bring about controversy? And peace is important.' One is forbidden to say this, but must disagree with what he said and tell him that, in his opinion, the thing is not kosher. It is quite possible that the one who issued the ruling reasoned correctly in reaching his decision, in which case one should listen to his reasoning and concede its truth. And some argue with their colleagues or with the town's halakhic authority only to show off their strength and power, to prevail over the authority in front of others and show that they know the law better than does the authority. Now this is a great sin, because such a person is not interested in the truth at all, and generates controversy and disturbs the peace only to show everyone his strength and power, mental acuity, his character, intelligence and wisdom. And so we are commanded to separate ourselves from these wicked people, physically and in our actions. And also for the sake of the truth, and the laws of the Torah, so that truth and Torah should not suffer a loss, as has been agreed upon by the great rabbis: if it is evident that the leaders of a group are wicked, one must separate himself from them. As it is written, "love truth and peace" (Zech. 8:19) – put truth first, and peace after it, because truth is the Torah, for there is no truth other than what the Torah says. And it is the great pillar upon which the world rests, and peace is nothing but the preservation of the world. So first the pillar must be strong, and after that it can be preserved. But if there is no pillar to support it, the world cannot exist in any event. Therefore, truth must come first, and afterwards, peace. And for the sake of truth not only are we permitted to engender controversy, but more than that, we are obligated to do so, because by engendering a controversy for the sake of the truth, this quarrel sustains the pillar of the world, and hence, sustains the world itself. And if so, the effect of controversy is the same as that of peace.

This, apparently, is the intention of the Tanna in this Mishna, "What controversy is for the sake of heaven?" That is, we have to understand and inquire into what kind of controversy is for the sake of heaven, and is sustained in the end, viz., ultimately sustains the world, since the quarrel is for the sake of the Torah. And the controversy between Hillel and Shammai was for the sake of heaven and to establish the truth. But a controversy that is not for the sake of heaven in the end does not help the world to be sustained, and on the contrary, by disturbing the peace, it disrupts the existence of the world, for it is through peace that the world is sustained. Sometimes, too, controversies are engendered in order to obscure the truth from people who follow the true path and desire truth, and will be frightened to do as they wish, and the controversy is instigated so as to prevent them from doing as they wish. This is surely a double sin, since not only do the instigators disturb the peace, which sustains the world, but they also disturb the truth, which is the great pillar of the world's existence. And falsehood does not endure, and in the end, "Truth springs up from the earth" (Ps. 85:12). And all those who are wicked will understand who was right, and grasp that the sole intent of the rabbis who decided on the separation was to benefit the wicked, so that they would mend their ways, and they too would abide by the truth, that is, the Torah, which is the eternal truth. May God grant that falsehood will disappear from the world and truth shall spring up from the earth. Amen.

192. Pri Tzadik, Numbers, Korah, 5

The holy Zohar says: "When the Holy One, blessed be He, created the world, it could not sustain its existence until He bestowed peace upon it. And what is this peace? It is the Sabbath, which is peace in the upper and the lower worlds, and so the world is able to exist," and so on.[12] ... And the holy Zohar also says, "Zelophad quarreled with the Sabbath because he gathered wood," and so on.[13] That is, as it is said in the holy Zohar elsewhere, "he inquired which of the trees was more important than the other," and so on, "he saw two trees, one of life and one of death," and so on.[14] That is, the written law is called the "tree of life," as it is stated at the beginning of *Tana Debei Eliahu* about the Tree of Life in the Garden of Eden: "There is no tree of life other than the Torah," and so on. And had the children of Israel not sinned, they would have received only the five books of Moses [and the Book of Joshua], as it is said in the Talmud, and this would have sufficed, and they would have known everything from the written law, as will indeed be the case in the future, as it is written, "And they shall teach no more every man his neighbor ... for they shall all know Me" (Jer. 31:34), and so on.[15] But the oral law has the aspect of the tree of knowledge of good and evil, what is forbidden and what is permitted, and so on, as it is said in the holy Zohar,[16] and they have forty nine aspects from which it can be declared pure, and forty-nine aspects from which it can be declared impure, and this constitutes controversy, but it is for the rectification (*tikun*) of the world. And Zelophad said that possibly the "Tree of Knowledge of good and evil" might be superior to the "Tree of Life," since it brings forth light from darkness, which constitutes the great wisdom

---

12 *Zohar*, Korah, 176b.
13 Ibid.
14 *Zohar*, Shelah, 157a.
15 bNedarim 22b.
16 *Raaya Mehemna*, Behaalotkha 153a.

that can put right the great strife, and therefore the Zohar says that he quarreled with the Sabbath, which is peace.

And later it says, "the Torah is peace, as it is written "and all its ways are peace" (Prov. 3:17),"[17] for it is written "and there Israel encamped before the mount" (Exod. 19:2) as one person with one heart,[18] and then they merited receiving the written law. Now the oral law, with all the controversies it contains, is for the rectification of the world and ultimately, for peace, as it is said, "Vaheb in Suphah" (Num. 21:14), as the Talmud states: "Even father and son...become enemies of each other, yet they do not budge from there until they come to love each other," and so on.[19]

And the holy Zohar says earlier: "Korah took the path of controversy," and so on, and "controversy is peaceable disagreement," and so on.[20] He erred, saying that there was no harm in the controversy, and thought that his intent was altogether for the sake of heaven, for he did not approve of his fellow's conduct, and disagreed with him, and felt that this sort of controversy would not be harmful. But in truth, "truth and peace are one,"[21] for "truth and peace are interrelated,"[22] and truth is impossible without peace. Now in the controversy between Shammai and Hillel, which was truly for the sake of heaven, even in the very hour of the debate itself they related to each other with affection and friendship, to fulfill the verse "love truth and peace" (Zech. 8:19), as it is said in the Talmud.[23] And also, scholars are called "friends," for they have between them a true bond, similar to that of the angels, who are also called "friends" because they know no enmity, jealousy, hatred or competition.[24] But if there is vexation in the heart and anger toward a colleague, this is a sign that the controversy is not intended to rectify the world, but to confound it. This was the error of Korah, that he quarreled with Aaron, who loved peace and pursued peace, who loved his fellow creatures and brought them close to the Torah. That is, he had the ability to imbue the hearts of Israel with the Torah's teachings, which is the main purpose of the oral law, as it is written, "for the lips of a priest guard knowledge, and men seek rulings from his mouth" (Mal. 2:7), and the Torah is peace.

193. Olat Reiya, part 1, p. 330

R. Eleazar said in the name of R. Hanina: The students of the scholars increase peace in the world, as it is said, "And all thy children shall be

17 *Zohar*, Korah, loc. cit.
18 As in the Mekhilta's exegesis.
19 bKidushin 30b.
20 *Zohar*, Korah, 176a.
21 *Sefer Habahir*.
22 *Zohar Hadash*, III, 12b.
23 bJebamot 14b.
24 Song of Songs Rabbah 8:9.

taught of the Lord, and manifold shall be the peace of thy children" (Isa. 54:13). Read not *banayikh* (thy children) but *bonayikh* (thy builders)."[25]

Some people erroneously think that universal peace can only be achieved by a uniform hue of opinions and qualities. Consequently, upon beholding scholars investigating the wisdom of the Torah, and by their study generating a multiplicity of perspectives and approaches, they imagine that these scholars are thereby engendering controversy and subverting peace. And in truth, it is not so, for only through the quality of multiplying itself does peace bring genuine peace to the world. Now peace multiplies by bringing to light all possible perspectives and approaches, and demonstrating how each such orientation has a legitimate place, each in accordance with its value, context and substantive focus. And on the contrary, even those matters that seem unwarranted or contradictory will be illuminated when true wisdom, in all its aspects, is revealed. For only by gathering all the distinctions and details, all the seemingly-different opinions, and all the distinct disciplines of knowledge, will truth and righteousness, and knowledge of God, love and fear of Him, and the elucidation of the true law, come to light. Therefore, scholars do increase peace, since in expanding upon, explicating, and begetting new words of wisdom, from various perspectives, which raise multiple and diverse issues – through all this they increase peace, as it is said, "And all thy children shall be taught of the Lord" (Isa. 54:13). For all will acknowledge that everything – even the apparent contradictions in their methods and in their different lines of thinking, is "taught of the Lord," and in each of them there is an aspect that reveals the knowledge of God and the light of his truth.

"And manifold shall be the peace of thy children." It does not say 'great shall be the peace of thy children,' which would describe a single large entity, to fit the delusion that peace requires uniformity of ideas and equivalence of opinions. This misconception truly detracts from the power of wisdom and the broadening of understanding, as the light of understanding must reflect every illuminating direction and facet present within. But the proliferation [of knowledge] is described thus – "manifold shall be the peace of thy children." Read not *banayikh* (thy children) but *bonayikh* (thy builders). For a building is constructed of various parts, and the truth of the universal light is built from different aspects and different approaches, all of them being the words of the living God. And there are different methods of service, teaching and education, each having its place and value. No talent or expertise should be squandered, but rather, each should be developed and accommodated. And should a contradiction between different concepts be discerned, it will serve as a base upon which wisdom will build its home. To find the inner logic of concepts, study is required – through

25 bBerakhot 64a.

study, they will be straightened out, and will no longer appear contradictory. The variety of opinions arising from diversity of personality and education is precisely what enriches wisdom and brings about its broadening, so that in the end everything will be properly understood. And it will be recognized that the edifice of peace cannot be erected other than by means of the various influences that appear to be doing battle with each other.

"Peace be within thy walls" (Ps. 122:7). Within the walls is the place of the workforce, whose members are blessed with the blessing of peace. But what is the nature of this peace? It surely is not a function of equality of abilities, for it is precisely their diversity of abilities and opposed propensities that endows its members with productive vitality. But the value of diversity and opposed inclinations lies in appropriate balance, so that the various forces are all directed toward a single goal. And therefore there will be "tranquility within thy palaces" (Ps. 122:7) – in the place where peace and tranquility are required to attain the central objective.

"For my brethren and companions' sake" (Ps. 122:8) – there will be a suitable place for the labor of every individual: intellectual work, and work requiring specific proclivities and sensitivities. "I will now say: Peace be within thee" (Ps. 122:8) – the state of unity that comes from the gathering of scattered forces and ideas. "For the sake of the house of the Lord our God" (Ps. 122:9) – the desirable objective for which all act, the goal of all labor. "I will seek thy good" – the good that accumulates in the vessel of peace, in which blessings inhere.

"The Lord will give strength unto His people" (Ps. 29:11) – He will grant them lives full of engaging interests, for this is strength. A life full of interest is one with a multitude of aspects, and it is built by the combination of many different capabilities. Thus, this is the true blessing of peace, which arises from strength. "The Lord will bless his people with peace" (Ps. 29:11). The blessing of peace, which accompanies strength, is peace constituted by the unification of all opposites. But opposites must exist if there is to be a workforce and something to unify. And then the blessing is manifested by the strength of the principle that both are the words of the living God. Accordingly, one of the Names of the Holy One, blessed be He, is "Peace," for He has every strength and is omnipotent and embraces everything. Let His great Name be blessed in the world forever.

194. Ein Aiya, Berakhot, chapter 6, 16

"Once R. Gamaliel and the elders were reclining in an upper chamber in Jericho, and dates were brought in, and they ate, and R. Gamaliel gave permission to R. Akiva to say grace, and with alacrity R. Akiva made one blessing that entailed three. Said R. Gamaliel to him: Akiva, how long will you risk becoming embroiled in controversies? He said to him: although you say one thing and your colleagues say another, you have taught us, our teacher: [in a controversy between] an individual and the majority, the law is in accordance with the majority view."[26]

The foundation for deciding the law is built on truth and peace. Sometimes the force of truth is decisive, and sometimes the force of peace is decisive. Here is the explanation for this. Certainly, in every controversy and case of doubt, the truth must be investigated, examining the views of all those whose words exhibit knowledge, logic and proofs. But when we reach a point where we are unable to decide on the basis of proofs, and we must nevertheless reach a decision, then we "follow the majority" (Exod. 23:2), that is, for the sake of peace, so that controversy will not proliferate in Israel.

This was the thrust of Rabban Gamaliel's dictum, "how long will you risk becoming embroiled in controversies?" – as if you are worthy of deciding which opinion is more plausible. He [R. Akiva] answered that indeed he did not possess this virtue, but had chosen to invoke the rule of following the majority, not because he was presuming to know that their opinion was more correct, but rather, because the love of peace, which is the foundation of the world, so required. And therefore, it was by no means a case of 'poking his nose,' that is, his own thinking, into the controversy, in a manner that could be perceived as dismissive of his teacher's thinking, for even if the truth of the matter was essentially in accordance with his teacher's opinion, nevertheless it was better to forego the [true] decision for the sake of peace.

And it must be noted that for this reason he did not say "follow the majority" (*aharei rabim lehatot*), quoting the scriptural verse. For here we have to say, as did the commentators, that this only applies to [decisions taken by a] forum convening proponents of all the views. To grasp the reason for this, the rationale of the scriptural verse has to be examined as well: is it because it makes sense that the majority is capable of reaching truth, or because the imperative of peace demands it? Now in a complete forum, it can be said that the majority can certainly reach the truth, because they have heard all the opposed views, but when the dissenters are not present, it may well be argued that had they heard the arguments of the dissenters, they would have retracted. And we therefore assert that it was established that the law is in accordance with the majority view even when the dissenters are not present, for the sake of peace, so that controversy will not proliferate in Israel. And we may therefore assert that this was the focus of the controversy between the house of Hillel and the house of Shammai.[27] The house of Shammai is of the opinion that the rationale for following the majority is [to enable us to arrive at the] truth, so that if those involved are intellectually sharper, the rule that the majority is to be

26 bBerakhot 37a.
27 bJebamot 14a.

followed may well be irrelevant, for those great in wisdom can grasp the truth more profoundly. And the house of Hillel is of the opinion that the rule that the majority is to be followed was established for the sake of peace, and hence, nothing should be taken into account aside from the number of the scholars, which can be ascertained empirically, and not the level of their erudition, the evaluation of which might itself engender controversy. In any event, when the matter was settled, namely, that [in a controversy between] an individual and the majority, the law is in accordance with the majority view, even when the dissenters are not present, it was for the sake of peace, and entails no disparagement of the opinion of the individual scholar that was rejected.

195. Responsa Igrot Moshe, OH 4, #25

An explanation of the question asked by Moses, "and they shall say to me: What is His name?" (Exod. 3:13) and of the answer of the Holy One, blessed be He.... For on the surface, it is difficult to understand why God, may He be blessed, answered Moses' query, "and they shall say to me, What is His name? what shall I say unto them?" with two assertions, the first assertion being, "I AM THAT I AM" (Exod. 3:14); and a second assertion in this same verse, "Thus shalt thou say unto the people of Israel, I AM hath sent me unto you." And this epithet is not mentioned again in the Torah....

And I must state that it is certain that every single individual, wherever he might be, is under divine providence, according to his deeds, and God, may He be blessed, bestows upon him all the benefits that He bestows upon him. But the redemption was not simply a matter of benefitting them by releasing them from enslavement and providing them with all kinds of good things, for God, may He be blessed, could have done this in Egypt as well, by instilling in the hearts of Pharaoh and his nobles the thought that from then on they should begin to honor them as they had been honored and had lacked for nothing during the time when Joseph and his brothers [lit., the tribes] were alive, and even more. But the substance of redemption, as understood by that time by all Israel, was the need for complete redemption from all the ways of the nations, whose conduct was based only on their lusts and base values, and [for taking up] an altogether different path that would be taught them by God, may He be blessed, as He did forthwith in giving the Torah. This made being mixed among the nations impossible, but rather, as God, may He be blessed, had promised the Patriarchs, they would become one nation, serving God, may He be blessed, and keeping His Torah in sanctity in a sanctified place, chosen for this end, that He had already given to them. So therefore, as soon as He told Moses that He was sending him to save them from the hand of the Egyptians, and to take [lit., elevate] them out of there, He immediately said to him that He was taking them to a good and spacious land, not to be with the Canaanites, but to the place of the Canaanites, for the people of Israel would itself inhabit that place in their stead after eradicating them from the world. There they would be a special people, a kingdom of priests and a holy nation, which would be the true redemption, to live in accordance with the way of the Torah and observance of the precepts, without jealousy, hatred, wars, robbery and violence, in accordance with the principal purpose [of the redemption] as understood by all Israel.

But what must be ascertained is how to achieve this. Even if all of Israel accept the Torah and the precepts, in connection with the Torah and the precepts there are far more differences of opinion than on any matter pertaining to the material world. For the material world has but a single focus, namely, to sustain physical existence, by satisfying needs that are essentially the same for every individual, as each and every person needs and wishes to enjoy the very same pleasures, and there is enough in the world to satisfy the needs of everyone, and in this regard there is but a single principle, namely, that God, may He be blessed, feeds and provides for all, and supplies food to all His creatures. So regarding these things, disagreements between an individual and his fellow, or between different nations, are absolutely uncalled for, and all rifts and controversies, hatred, jealousy, robbery and violence is due to a lack of faith in the true God. For indeed, regarding matters pertaining to the Torah and the precepts, every single individual in Israel has great faith and a great desire to know and comprehend the truth, not only for themselves, but to teach others and impel them too to know the truth and act in accordance with the will of God, may He be blessed, as expressed in the holy Torah. Here it is virtually impossible that all should share one approach and be of one mind. So we have to realize that while they will not, heaven forbid, suffer any lack of faith, and while they will not become embroiled in controversies due to carnal lust for robbery, violence, and waging wars, as is true of the nations, we do have to fear that there will be controversy among them over the laws of the Torah and how they are to be observed, and there will be distinct groups, every great rabbi and his students by themselves, as we see throughout the Talmud that there are differences of scholarly opinion on almost every law of the Torah, and so it has been in each and every era.

This is the meaning of the question asked by Moses, "What is His Name?" (Exod. 3:13). And see Nahmanides and R. Haim Ben-Atar,[28] who noted the impossibility of such a question.... But their question, "What is His Name?" specifically concerns this redemptive mission – how to bring into existence a redemption that would indeed be a true redemption,

---

28 Author of *Or Hahaim*.

characterized by peace, tranquility, fellowship and friendship. And God, may He be blessed, answered him, "I AM hath sent me unto you," that is, that God, may He be blessed, will be with all who apply themselves to the Torah, wishing to know the truth, but having no interest in winning arguments, being concerned only with knowing the truth. As is explained by tractate Jebamot in the baraita concerning the controversy between the house of Shammai and the house of Hillel: "This is to teach you that they showed love and friendship toward one another, fulfilling the scriptural dictum, 'love truth and peace' (Zech. 8:19)."[29] Because on the contrary, this actually increases love, peace, affection and friendship, as in the exegesis of the verse "Vaheb [love] in Suphah" (Num. 21:14) in tractate Kidushin: "Said R. Hiya b. Abba, Even father and son, teacher and student, who apply themselves to the Torah at the same gate, become enemies of each other; yet they do not budge from there until they come to love each other."[30] This is the second assertion that God, may He be blessed, spoke to Moses for him to relate to the children of Israel.

There is another important point. Already at the outset of the controversy, there are two opinions, and sometimes more; they are all consummately part of the Torah, as is stated in tractate Eruvin about the controversy between the house of Shammai and the house of Hillel: "A heavenly voice (*bat kol*) went forth, and said, Both [lit., 'these and those'] are the words of the living God, but the law is in accordance with the view of the house of Hillel."[31] Thus even though the law is in accordance with the view of the house of Hillel, nevertheless, the opinion of the house of Shammai is also the word of the living God. For this reason it is plain that one who rises in the morning and has decided that before the morning prayers he will study and clarify only the opinions of the house of Shammai, must [nonetheless] recite the benediction for studying the Torah, since they too are consummately part of the Torah and are true Torah. And this is so with respect to all the controversies in the Mishna, the baraitas, the two Talmuds – the Babylonian and the Jerusalem – as well as the words of the Geonim and even the great scholars of our own times, for there is a presumption that all study for the sake of heaven. This is the meaning of the first assertion, "I AM THAT I AM" – the house of Shammai know that "I AM" with the house of Hillel too, and the house of Hillel know that "I AM" with the house of Shammai too. And therefore the house of Hillel studied the opinions of the house of Shammai as well [as their own], and it is clear that the house of Shammai studied the opinions of the house of Hillel on a regular basis, the difference being that

---

29 bJebamot 14b.
30 bKidushin 30b.
31 bEruvin 13b.

the house of Hillel studied the opinions of the house of Shammai before studying their own opinions, as did the house of Shammai. And the first assertion He spoke only to Moses, since ordinary people would not understand such a notion, which would be perceived as a contradiction that could not possibly be attributed to the Heavenly One. But God, may He be blessed, told Moses to transmit this to Joshua, and to all great Torah scholars for eternity: the opinions of both are the words of the living God. So we can see that from the outset there was love, fellowship and friendship, and not for a moment were they ever like enemies of each other, for in fact both views are valid. For when a father studies with his son or a teacher with his student, one being much greater [in learning] than the other, it sometimes happens that the father becomes angry with his son or the teacher with his student. But in the end, upon seeing that the opinion of the son, or the student, is also correct, and may be equally plausible, then even when their difference of opinion remains, nevertheless, the father and many great scholars recognize that the opinion of the son or student is also fit to be asserted, and they come to love each other, just as the great Torah scholars loved each other from the outset of their debate on, despite their differences of opinion.

6

THE ORIGINS OF HALAKHIC CONTROVERSY

196. tSanhedrin 7:1[1]

Said R. Jose: At first there were no controversies in Israel; but there was the court of seventy in the Hall of Hewn Stone,[2] and the other courts of twenty three were in the towns of the land of Israel.... if someone needs a ruling, he turns to the court in his town; if there is no court in his town, he goes to a court near his town. If they [the court] had heard [a tradition], they told it to him [the litigant]; and if not, [the initiator of the action] and the most eminent member of the court go to the court on the Temple Mount. If they had heard, they told it to them; and if not, they [the litigants] and the most eminent of them go to the court on the Rampart. If they had heard, they told it to them; and if not, these and the others go to the court in the Hall of Hewn Stone.... If they had heard, they told it to them; and if not, they take for a vote; if the majority was for impurity, they declared it impure, if the majority was for purity, they declared it pure. From there the law originated and was disseminated in Israel. When there multiplied students of Shammai and Hillel who did not attend to their teachers sufficiently, controversies multiplied in Israel, and the law became like two sets of laws [lit., two Torahs].

197. jHagiga 2:2 (77d)

At first there was no controversy in Israel except regarding the laying on of hands, and Shammai and Hillel stood up [for their opinions] and made them four. When there multiplied students of the house of Shammai and students of the house of Hillel and they did not attend to their teachers sufficiently, controversies multiplied in Israel. And they were divided into

---

1 There are a number of variants of this passage: tHagiga 2:9, j Sanhedrin 1:4 (19c), bSanhedrin 88b.
2 This reading is based on the Vienna manuscript of the Tosefta, and the printed editions of the Jerusalem and Babylonian Talmuds.

two sects, these rendering impure, the others rendering pure, and it [the prior situation] will not be restored until the coming of the son of David.

198. bSota 47b

When the haughty of the heart multiplied, controversy multiplied in Israel. When there multiplied students of Shammai and Hillel who did not attend to their teachers sufficiently, controversy multiplied in Israel and the Torah became like two sets of laws [lit., two Torahs].

199. bTemura 15b–16a

We learned there: When Joseph b. Joezer of Zereda and Joseph b. Johanan of Jerusalem died, the grape-clusters came to an end.[3] [A grape-cluster is] one in whom all is found.[4] And R. Judah said in the name of Samuel: All the grape-clusters who arose in Israel from the days of Moses until the death of Joseph b. Joezer learned Torah as did Moses our teacher. From then on, they did not learn Torah as did Moses our teacher. And did not R. Judah say in the name of Samuel: Three thousand laws were forgotten during the period of mourning for Moses? Those laws that were forgotten were forgotten, but those that were learned they learned as did Moses our teacher. But has it not been taught: After the death of Moses, if those who declared something impure were in the majority, the Sages declared it impure, and if those who declared it pure in the majority, they declared it pure? Their faculties diminished, but what they learned they learned as did Moses our teacher.

It was taught in a *matnita*[5]: All the grape-clusters who arose in Israel from the days of Moses until the death of Joseph b. Joezer of Zereda were free of any taint. From that time on, they were tainted in some way. But has it not been taught: The story is told of a certain pious man (*hasid*) who groaned from pain in his heart, and they consulted physicians, who said that there was no remedy for him but to suck steaming hot milk each morning. And they brought a goat and tied it to the foot of his bed, and he would suck milk from it. On the morrow, his friends came to visit him. When they saw the goat they said: There are armed robbers in the house, shall we proceed to visit him? [They left him immediately. When he died] they sat down and investigated and found no other sin in him except that of [keeping] the goat. And even [the pious man], at the time of his death, said: I myself know that I am without sin, except for that goat, by which

---

3 mSota 9:9.
4 A play on words, reading *eshkol* (grape-cluster) as *ish shehakol bo*.
5 A Tannaitic teaching.

I transgressed the teachings of my colleagues. For the Sages taught: One must not rear small ruminants in the land of Israel. And we have an established principle that wherever the Talmud says, "The story is told of a certain pious man" it refers either to R. Judah b. Baba or R. Judah b. Ilai. Now did not these Sages live many many generations after Joseph b. Joezer of Zereda?! R. Joseph said: "Taint" here refers to the taint caused by controversy over the laying on of hands. And did not Joseph b. Joezer himself hold a dissenting view regarding the laying on of hands? He dissented in his later years, when his faculties declined.

The above-quoted dictum states: R. Judah said in the name of Samuel: Three thousand laws were forgotten during the period of mourning for Moses. They said to Joshua: Ask. He said to them: "It is not in heaven" (Deut. 30:12). They said to Samuel: Ask. He said to them: "These are the commandments" (Lev. 27:34). That is, henceforth no prophet has the right to introduce anything new. R. Isaac the blacksmith said: Even the law of a sin-offering whose owners died was forgotten during the period of mourning for Moses. They said to Phinehas: Ask. He said to them: "It is not in heaven." They said to Eleazar: Ask. He said to them: "These are the commandments." That is, henceforth no prophet has the right to introduce anything new.

R. Judah said in the name of Rav: When Moses our teacher was leaving this world for the Garden of Eden, he said to Joshua: Ask me concerning any doubts you may have. He said to him: My teacher, have I ever left you for even an hour and gone elsewhere? Did you not write of me: "But his minister Joshua, the son of Nun, a young man, departed not out of the Tent" (Exod. 33:11)? Immediately the strength of Joshua was spent, and he forgot three hundred laws, and seven hundred doubts were hatched in him, and all of Israel rose up to kill him. The Holy One, blessed be He, said to him: It is impossible to recount it to you; go and occupy them with war, as it is said: "After the death of Moses the servant of the Lord, the Lord spake," and so on (Josh. 1:1).

It was taught in our *matnita*: A thousand and seven hundred a fortiori (*kal vahomer*) arguments, inferences from identical terms (*gzeira shava*), and specifications of the Scribes were forgotten during the period of mourning for Moses. Said R. Abbahu: Despite this, Othniel, the son of Kenaz, restored them by way of his dialectics, as it is said: "And Othniel, the son of Kenaz, the brother of Caleb, captured it" (Josh. 15:17).

200. Exodus Rabbah 28:6

"And God spake all these words, saying" (Exod. 20:1) – R. Isaac said: That which the prophets were to prophesy in each and every future generation they received at Mount Sinai, for Moses says to them, to Israel: "but with him that standeth here with us this day before the Lord our God, and also with him that is not here with us this day" (Deut. 29:14). It is not written [in the second clause] 'standeth with us this day,' but "with us this day" – these are the souls to be created in the future but having no substantiality as yet; 'standing' is not said of them. For even though they were not in existence at that time, nevertheless each and every one of them received his share [of the Torah].

For it likewise says, "The burden of the word of the Lord to Israel by (*beyad*) [lit., by the hand of] Malachi" (Mal. 1:1). It does not say 'in the days of Malachi,' but "by [the hand of] Malachi," for prophecy had already been in his hands [so to speak,] since Sinai, but until that hour he had not been granted permission to prophesy.

So Isaiah said, "From the time that it was, there am I" (Isa. 48:16). Said Isaiah: I was present at the revelation in Sinai, whence I received this prophecy, only "And now the Lord God has sent me and His spirit" (ibid.); until now he was not given permission to prophesy. Not only did all the prophets receive their prophecy from Sinai, but also each of the sages that arose in every generation received his [wisdom] from Sinai, for so it says: "These words the Lord spoke unto all your assembly . . . with a great voice, and it went on no more" (Deut. 5:19). R. Johanan said: it was one voice that divided itself into seven voices, and these into seventy languages. R. Shimon b. Lakish said: [it was a voice] from which all the subsequent prophets received their prophecy.

201. Emunot Vedeiot, introduction, p. 10

The Sages of Israel said of those who did not fully complete their course their studies: "When there multiplied students of Shammai and Hillel who did not attend to their teachers sufficiently, controversy multiplied."[6] These words teach us that had the students fully completed their course of studies, there would not have been controversy or arguments among them. Therefore the impatient lout should not tender his sin to the Creator proudly and arrogantly, saying that it was He who instilled these doubts, for it is his loutishness or impatience that has brought them upon him, as we explained. For it is impossible that any single action on his part can eradicate all his doubts, as that would put him outside the laws governing the realm of the created, yet he is but a creature. And even one who does not reproach God for such doubts, but nevertheless yearns for God to grant him knowledge free of any doubts – this request amounts to asking God to make him like Him. Because only the Creator of all, may He be blessed and sanctified, has uncaused knowledge of everything, as will be explained below. But all those who were created can only comprehend by a causal process, that is, through

---

6 bSota 47b, passage 198.

study and learning, which, as we explained, takes time. And from its first moment to its very end, it is replete with doubts, as we discussed. But the choicest students are those who wait until they refine the silver from the dross, as it is said: "Take away the dross from the silver and there cometh forth a vessel for the refiner" (Prov. 25:4); or until they churn their studies long enough to obtain butter, as it is said, "For the churning of milk bringeth forth curd, and the wringing of the nose bringeth forth blood" (Prov. 30:33); or until their seeds germinate, so that they can later be harvested, as it is said, "Sow to yourselves according to righteousness, reap according to mercy" (Hos. 10:12); or until their fruits ripen on their trees and become edible, as it is said: "She is a tree of life to them that lay hold upon her" (Prov. 3:18).

202. Peirushei R. Saadia Gaon on Genesis, preface, pp. 187–8

Should one ask, how did differences of opinion among those who received and transmitted the tradition find their way into the Mishna and the Talmud? We would answer: These are not genuine controversies. They only seem to be such when the listener first hears of them. And in truth, [controversies in the Talmud] are of three types.

1   A Sage pretended to disagree with his colleague and provoked him, in order to ascertain the nature of his colleague's opinion. And it is like the way in which Moses pretended to be angry at Aaron and his sons when they burned the goat of the sin-offering (Lev. 10:16), so that they would reveal their own opinion to him, because Moses could not believe that it had been burned out of ignorance.

2   The matter was heard from the prophet [Moses] in two different forms. In one form, the matter is permitted, in the other, it is forbidden. And one of the Sages preceded his colleague and mentioned the permitted aspect, and then the other came and mentioned the forbidden. And the words of both are correct, since that matter is indeed permitted in one form and forbidden in another. And an example of this is what Scripture says: "Thou shalt not destroy the trees thereof" (Deut. 20:19), and then it says, "Only the trees of which thou knowest," and so on (Deut. 20:20). And it says, "And if a priest's daughter be married into a common man, she shall not eat [of that which is set apart from the holy things]" (Lev. 22:12), and after that it says, "But if a priest's daughter be a widow...she may eat of her father's bread" (Lev. 22:13). And it makes no difference whether the deciding verse[7] is close to the two parallel verses, or far from them, and the solution is apparent further on.

---

7 Referring to the last of the thirteen exegetical principles: "Similarly, if two biblical passages contradict each other, they can be harmonized only by a third passage."

3   One of the Sages heard part of a matter, and imagined that he had heard the entire matter, and others heard the continuation of the matter, and when the former mentioned to them what he thought about it, they argued against his view, saying: We heard the continuation of the matter, and it qualifies your tradition. And an example of this: one finds in the third book of the Pentateuch: "[neither shall there come upon thee] a garment of two kinds of stuff mingled together" (Lev. 19:19), and he thinks that this prohibition applies to all mixtures. And when he relates this to someone who has read the entire Torah, the latter informs him that Scripture has qualified this rule in the fifth book of the Pentateuch, and limited it: "wool and linen together" (Deut. 22:11). And likewise, all similar cases.

203. Mevo Hatalmud of R. Samuel b. Hofni Gaon, introduction

As to controversy on matters of the oral law – sometimes the controversy refers to two aspects [of a certain issue], one negating and the other affirming, one scholar having heard the law [explained] a certain way, and the other, a different way. And in such a case there is no contradiction, since each expounds a different aspect, as, for example, [in the case of] the Sages' statement, "Samuel said: a share-cropper may testify," and their statement, "but did we not learn, he may not testify?"[8] And the Talmud's solution is that the one who said a share-cropper may testify said so of a case where the field he is testifying about has no produce in it, and the one who said he may not testify, speaks of the case where the field contains produce and he occupies that field as a share-cropper. And in this way the two traditions about the matter were harmonized – they said, "there is no difficulty, in one case there is produce in the field, in the other there is no produce in the field."

Sometimes the two traditions [that reached us], one commending and the other condemning, refer to different aspects, as, for example, the Sages' dictum, "one who says Amen after his own blessings is [to be commended, but have we not learned, he is] to be condemned?"[9] And the Talmud's solution is that it is commendable to say Amen after the benediction "who builds Jerusalem," but to be condemned after the "who bringest forth [bread]" and similar benedictions.

Sometimes there is a difference of opinion between those who heard [a teaching] because they both heard the teaching from their teacher, but

---

8 bBaba Batra 46b.
9 bBerakhot 45b.

later the teacher retracted it, and one of them was aware of this retraction, while the other was unaware. For example, the Talmud states: "Fish are not caught," and so on. With regard to what are they permitted? Rav said: They are permitted to be received, and Levi said: They are permitted for eating.[10] Said Rav: A man should never absent himself from the study hall even for a single hour, for behold, Levi and I were both present in the study hall when Rabbi [Judah the Prince] taught this lesson. In the evening he said: They are permitted for eating; but in the morning, he retracted and said: They are permitted to be received. I, having been present in the study hall, retracted, but Levi, who was not present in the study hall, did not retract."[11]

Sometimes one of those who heard it heard the matter in a general way, and the other heard it in detail, and they disagree about the meaning [of the teaching], for example, the Talmud says, in general, "A Sabbath perimeter-marking (eruv) and a joint-property marking (shituf) can be effected with every kind of foodstuff, except for water and salt,"[12] but it also specifies, "Is there not another exception, truffles and mushrooms, which cannot effect an eruv?"[13] Of this R. Johanan said: "No inference may be drawn from general rulings, even where an exception was specified." Furthermore the Talmud says, in a general way: "All positive precepts the observance of which is time-dependent are incumbent upon men, and women are exempt," and it also says: "All positive precepts the observance of which is not time-dependent are incumbent upon men and women alike." But the Talmud brings exceptions to the first part of this Mishna: "And yet the precepts of unleavened bread, rejoicing on the Festivals and Assembly (hakhel) are positive precepts observance of which is time-dependent, and are they not incumbent upon women nonetheless?"[14] And the Talmud brings exceptions to the second part as well: "And yet the precepts of the study of the Torah, procreation and redemption of the [first-born] son are positive precepts the observance of which is not time-dependent, yet are not women nonetheless exempt?"

And sometimes students sat before their teacher and he had a tradition with which the law is not in accordance, and the teacher mentioned this tradition in a certain context. And he who heard it heard it and inferred from the general thrust of the teacher's words that it was the law, but another [student] heard the [full] explication of the matter, and therefore controversy ensues between them. And about this R. Judah said, "If so,

---

10 mBeitza 3:2. The Talmud states, regarding fish caught on a Festival and brought by a Gentile, that they are permitted.

11 bBeitza 24b.

12 mEruvin 3:1.

13 bEruvin 27a.

14 bKidushin 34a.

why do they record the opinion of the individual against that of the majority? So that if one should say, I have received such a tradition, they say to him, You have heard it only as the opinion of so-and-so.[15]

204. Mevo Hatalmud of R. Samuel b. Hofni Gaon, chapter 5

This fifth chapter discusses the reasons for the contradictions among those who hand down the traditions in the Mishna and the Talmud. Let me state that there are ten reasons for this.

The first reason is that the tradition was handed down so as to reflect two different aspects, one of them being negative and the other positive. And one of those who transmit it transmits its familiar aspect, and the other transmits its other aspect, and there is no contradiction between them if the act in question indeed has various aspects. As when the Talmud states, "Samuel said: a share-cropper may testify," and it states, "but did we not learn, a share-cropper may not testify?" And their response was, a share-cropper may testify if the field about which he testifies has no produce in it, and the one who says a share-cropper may not testify speaks of the case where the field contains produce and he occupies that field as a share-cropper. And in this way the two traditions on the matter were aligned, and they said, "there is no difficulty, in one case there is produce in the field, and in the other there is no produce in the field."[16]

And there are cases where two traditions have reached us, one of commendation and the other of condemnation, traditions with conflicting implications. As where the Talmud states, "one who says Amen after his own blessings is to be commended," yet it also states "one who says Amen after his own blessings is to be condemned."[17] And this is straightened out by the commendation's relating to the benediction "who builds Jerusalem," and the condemnation, to the rest of the benedictions. As the Talmud says, "there is no difficulty, one refers to the benediction, 'who builds Jerusalem,' the other to the rest of the benedictions."

Sometimes a tradition handed down by one teacher seems contradictory, as it implies two different injunctions, but they are not contradictory at all, as it is said in the Talmud: "The question was raised: What is the law in a case where a dying man has sold all his possessions [and having recovered, seeks to recant]?[18] R. Judah said in the name of R. Asi: If he recovered, he may withdraw. Sometimes, however, R. Judah said in the name of

---

15 mEduyot 1:6.
16 bBaba Batra 46b.
17 bBerakhot 45b.
18 That is, should he recover, can he cancel the sale as he can withdraw a gift?

Rav: he may not withdraw.[19] But there is no contradiction. The one refers to the case where the money is available; the other to the case where he spent it to pay a debt." This is reconciled in the manner in which two seemingly-contradictory scriptural verses are reconciled.

Now should someone argue, I can indeed accept what you said about two seemingly-contradictory scriptural verses, because I know that they are [both] correct, but this is not the case with regard to the mishnaic and talmudic traditions... the traditions of the Mishna and the Talmud are to be accepted only after we have acquired knowledge of their correctness. And I have already furnished proof of this in the foregoing, and what I have said should suffice to silence such a questioner.

The second reason is variations in the traditions of those who transmit the teachings, who did not hear both... but just a specific tradition... the other. As it is stated in the Talmud: For what are they permitted? Rav said: They are permitted to be received, and Levi says: They are permitted for eating. Said Rav: A man should never absent himself from the study hall even for a single hour, for Levi and I were both present in the study hall when Rabbi taught this lesson. In the evening he said: They are permitted for eating; but in the morning, he retracted and said: They are permitted to be received. I, having been present in the study hall, retracted, but Levi, who was not present in the study hall, did not retract."[20]

The third reason is that the transmitted tradition varies due to different interpretations, though the wording remains constant. One of those who transmitted the tradition in question interprets it... in accordance with what befalls him (what he sees fit). This is exemplified in the Talmud: "The question was raised: Are sales made during that year considered to be sales made by one who is under-age or of age? Rava said in the name of R. Nahman: the period is regarded as one during which he is under-age. Rava son of the son of R. Shila said in the name of R. Nahman: The period is regarded as one during which he is of age. Rava's view, however, was not stated explicitly, but arrived at inferentially. [For there was a certain youth,] who during his year of reaching maturity, went and sold the estate of his deceased father. And the case came before Rava. He said to them: He effected nothing by his action. An observer who saw what had happened thought that Rava decided thus because during the year of reaching maturity one is regarded as being under-age; but this is not so. In this particular case Rava observed excessive foolishness, for the youth was also manumitting his slaves."[21] For this reason, one often asks his colleague, "Did you hear this explicitly or did you infer this?" This is like the

19 bBaba Batra 149a.
20 bBeitza 24b.
21 bBaba Batra 155b.

talmudic discussion: "R. Zera said to R. Jacob b. Idi: "Did you hear this explicitly or did you infer this?" He said to him: "I heard it explicitly."[22]

The fourth reason is that one of those relaying the tradition heard the tradition in general, while another heard a particular element of the tradition, and they thus differ as to their interpretations of it. This is like the talmudic discussion regarding the Sabbath perimeter-marking (*eruv*): "A Sabbath perimeter-marking and a joint-property marking (*shituf*) can be effected with every kind of foodstuff, except for water and salt,"[23] and the Talmud states: "Now is there not another exception, that of truffles and mushrooms, which cannot effect an *eruv*?" And of this it is stated: "R. Johanan said: no inference may be drawn from general rulings, even where an exception was specified."[24] And also as the Talmud states as a general tradition: "All positive precepts the observance of which is time-dependent are incumbent upon men, and women are exempt,"[25] and the Talmud states in particular: "And yet the precepts of unleavened bread, rejoicing on the Festivals and Assembly (*hakhel*) are positive precepts observance of which is time-dependent, and are they not incumbent upon women nonetheless?"[26] And the Talmud says further: "All positive precepts the observance of which is not time-dependent are incumbent upon men and women alike."[27] And the Talmud states in particular: "And yet the precepts of the study of the Torah, procreation and redemption of the first-born son are positive precepts the observance of which is not time-dependent, yet are not women nonetheless exempt?"[28]

The fifth reason is that some of those relaying the tradition could recall it and some had forgotten it, and therefore had irrelevant notions about it. And indeed, consider what is said in the Talmud: "R. Safra went abroad from the land, and he had with him a barrel of wine of the Sabbatical year. Now, R. Kahana and R. [Hun]a [the son of R. Ik]a accompanied him. He asked them: Is there anyone who has heard from R. Abbahu whether the law is in accordance with the view of R. Shimon b. Eleazar or not? R. Huna the son of R. Ika said to him: Thus did R. Abbahu say: The law is not in accordance with the view of R. Shimon b. Eleazar. Said R. Safra: Accept this ruling of R. Huna b. Ika, because he is meticulously careful to learn the laws from his teacher, like Rehaba of Pumbedita."[29]

The sixth reason is that there was some confusion in the interpretation of the traditions, and they disagreed over their interpretations and

22 bEruvin 46a.
23 mEruvin 3:1.
24 bEruvin 27a.
25 mKidushin 1:7.
26 bKidushin 34a.
27 mKidushin 1:7.
28 bKidushin 34a.
29 bPesahim 52b.

complexities. For consider what is said in the Talmud: "R. Judah stated in the name of Rav: The Judeans, who were particular about their language, retained their Torah learning, but the Galileans, who were not careful about their language, did not retain their Torah learning."[30] The question is raised: "But does learning depend on being careful about language?" Rabina says: Those who are particular about their language, drew up mnemonics and retained their Torah learning. The Judeans, who were exact in their language, and who drew up mnemonics, retained their Torah learning; but the Galileans who were not exact in their language, did not retain their Torah learning." And also conducive to this was the fact that they constantly reminded one another, as the Talmud states there: "The Judeans, who made their studies accessible to the public, retained their Torah learning, but the Galileans, who did not make their studies accessible to the public, did not retain their Torah learning."[31]

And the seventh reason is that some of the transmitters of tradition paid attention to the dicta and remembered them well, and some did not pay attention due to some distraction, and interpreted the dicta in a manner that was not in accordance with what those who had transmitted them said. And this is like what the Talmud states: "The case of R. Kahana and R. Asi: when they left the lecture of Rav, one of them said, Rav said this, and the other said, Rav said that. When they would come before Rav, he would agree with one of them; the other would then say to him: Did I, then, lie, in saying what I did? He would reply to him, your heart deceived you."[32]

And the eighth reason is that some of the possessors of the tradition saw the one who transmitted it face to face, and comprehended him fully, but as for one who did not see (he who was conveying the tradition), that was not the case, as you can see from what one of the Sages said, "But I call heaven and earth to witness that upon this mortar sat the prophet Haggai and delivered the following three rulings: That a daughter's rival is forbidden, and so on.[33] And the allusion here is to the Talmud's dictum: "and the prophets handed it down to the Men of the Great Assembly."[34]

Should one say: "Those who disagree with you about the veracity of Rabbinic tradition, which they deny, demand proof of the tradition's veracity. And how can you bring evidence (to prove the truth of your tradition) from that tradition itself? You have to admit that any supportive argument based on the material to be proven is fallacious and incorrect." We answer him: "We do not rely on their [i.e., the Sages'] tradition's verifying itself,

---

30 bEruvin 53a.
31 Ibid.
32 bShevuot 26a.
33 bJebamot 16a.
34 mAvot 1:1.

but we prove its veracity by demonstrating that it was transmitted in ways that necessitate its veracity, namely, the tradition's being handed down continuously from person to person, and by many people, and reason necessitates that it is impossible that so many people are all lying. Therefore, this does not constitute adducing proof from the matter to be proven.

205. Igeret R. Sherira Gaon, pp. 8–11 (Spanish version)

The matter was as follows: the names of the early Sages were unknown, except for the names of the presidents and the heads of courts, because there were no controversies between them; rather, they had perfect knowledge of all the rationales of the written law, and they also knew the Talmud with great clarity, as well as the dialectics and finer points regarding every single issue in their teachings....

For as long as the Temple existed, each and every Sage taught his students the rationales of the Torah, the Mishna and the Talmud, putting it into his own words as he taught. And they instructed their students as they saw fit, and there was much wisdom, and they did not need to trouble themselves with other concerns. And the only controversy that existed between them was that over the issue of the laying on of hands. And even when the time of Shammai and Hillel came, there were only three points on which there was controversy, as it is said, "Said R. Huna: On three matters Shammai and Hillel disagreed."[35]

And as a result of the fact that the Temple was destroyed and they fled to Beitar, and Beitar was subsequently destroyed, the Sages dispersed in every direction. And because of the disturbances, persecutions and confusions, the students did not attend to their teachers sufficiently, and controversies proliferated.

206. Hidushei Haritba, bRosh Hashana 34a (responsum by R. Hai Gaon)

Our master [R. Hai Gaon] of blessed memory, was asked: Should we assume that before the time of R. Abbahu, Israel did not discharge the precept of blowing the shofar? Apparently, the sound of the *terua* was subject to doubt among them, as it is said, "this is surely a matter of controversy," but there is no doubt that the issue must have been decided: is it conceivable that they did not know the true procedure for a precept that had to be observed every year? Had they not seen how it was observed, each generation showing the next, one hearing the tradition from another, back to Moses our teacher, of blessed memory?

35 bShabat 14b.

And our master, of blessed memory, answered that the *terua* as prescribed by the Torah is certainly discharged with either a wailing or a groaning blast, because the Torah intended that the *terua* be composed of sounds and broken blasts. And in earlier times it was performed either as broken blasts or as wailing; it was a matter of individual judgment as to which was more apt, and the obligation was in any event discharged. This was known to the learned, but ordinary people mistakenly thought that there was a difference between them, and therefore that one or another group was not discharging its obligation with respect to the precept. So to dispel this view held by the ignorant, and in order to prevent the Torah from becoming like two separate sets of laws [lit., two Torahs], R. Abbahu ordered that both customs be followed, and added one more *terua* blast at his own initiative, because he resolved to establish the *terua* in every possible customary broken sound. Since ordinary people thought that there was a controversy amongst them over this, the Talmud presents this in the style of a debate, that is, with objections raised and a resolution offered.

207. Rashi, bBaba Metzia 33b s.v. *bimei rabi*

"This dictum was first formulated in the days of R. Judah the Prince" – this refers to what is stated: "Gemara – there is no greater virtue." Because when the number of students of Shammai and Hillel, who preceded [Rabbi] by three generations, increased, the number of controversies over the Torah increased, and the Torah became like two sets of laws [lit., two Torahs]. This took place due to the yoke of subjugation to foreign rule, and the decrees that were issued against them, and as a result they could not attend to the clarification of the disputed views, until the time of Rabbi [Judah the Prince], who the Holy One, blessed be He, caused to find favor in the eyes of Antoninus, king of the Romans, as is related by the Talmud.[36] And they found repose from their troubles, and Rabbi sent for all the scholars of the land of Israel, and convened them. And up to his day the tractates were unorganized, every student receiving a version from his superiors, learning it, and adding an attribution, "such-and-such a law I heard from so-and-so." Upon convening, each one related what he had heard, and attention was paid to clarifying the reasons for any controversies between them, and deciding which opinion merited being sustained. And they arranged the tractates, torts separately, the laws of levirate marriage separately, and the laws of sacrifices (*kodashim*) separately. And Rabbi stated some opinions of individuals anonymously (*stam*), because he preferred their views, and recorded them anonymously, so that the law would be established in accordance with them. Therefore they said

---

36 bAvoda Zara 10b.

that there is no greater virtue than Gemara – attending to the rationales underlying the Mishna.

208. Sefer Hakabala Leraavad, p. 47

This is the sequence of tradition, which we have committed to writing, so as to inform students that all the words of our teachers, of blessed memory, the Sages of the Mishna and the Talmud, were received by men of great wisdom and piety from men of great wisdom and piety, one academy head and his colleagues from another academy head and his colleagues, back to the time of the Men of the Great Assembly, who received the tradition from the prophets, all of blessed memory. And never did the Sages of the Talmud, and even more, the Sages of the Mishna, utter even the most minor word on their own, with the exception of enactments they enacted with the unanimous consent of all, instituted to safeguard the Torah. And should one with a heretical inclination whisper to you that because there are a number of controversies among them, he doubts their words, you may then refute him bluntly, informing him that he is rebelling against the court, and that our Rabbis, of blessed memory, never disagreed about the fundamentals of the precepts, but only about their ramifications, because they heard the fundaments from their teachers, and did not ask them about the ramifications, as they were insufficiently diligent. For example, there is no disagreement on whether Sabbath candles are to be lit or not. What did they disagree over? "What [material] can be kindled, and what cannot be kindled."[37] Similarly, they did not disagree over whether the Shema prayer must be recited evenings and mornings, or not. What did they disagree over? From what point on the evening Shema can be recited, and from what point on the morning Shema can be recited.[38] And it is so with regard to everything they said.

209. Maimonides' Commentary on the Mishna, Seeds, foreword

Before his death, Joshua handed over to the elders what he had received as interpretations, and all the novel interpretations that had been added in his time over which there was no controversy, and also, that which had been a matter of controversy, but had been decided in accordance with the majority view. This is what Scripture means by "[And Israel served the Lord all the days of Joshua] and all the days of the elders who outlived Joshua [and who had known all the works of the Lord]" (Josh. 24:31). And the elders handed over the tradition to the prophets, may they rest in peace, who handed it down from one to the next. And there was no

37 mShabat 2:1.
38 mBerakhot 1:1; 1:2.

generation that did not engage in inquiry and formulate new teachings. And each generation would regard the teachings of its predecessors as a fundamental principle, from which it learned and arrived at new teachings. And there was no controversy as to the received fundamental principles. This went on until the time of the Men of the Great Assembly, namely, Haggai, Zechariah, Malachi, Daniel, Hananiah, Mishael, Azariah, Ezra the Scribe, Nehemiah b. Hakalia, Mordekhai, Zerubabel b. Shaltiel. And along with these prophets were craftsmen, smiths and the like,[39] making up the full complement of one hundred and twenty elders. They too occupied themselves with their studies, as did their predecessors, and decreed decrees and enacted enactments. And the last of this pure company is the first of the Sages mentioned in the Mishna, he is Shimon the Just, who was the High Priest of that generation.

And after them time passed, until the age of our holy master, may he rest in peace, who was singular in his generation and distinguished in his epoch, a person God had endowed with virtues and piety to the extent that he merited being called "our holy Rabbi" by his contemporaries; and his name was Judah. He had the utmost wisdom and majesty, as the Talmud states: "from the days of Moses until Rabbi, we have not seen Torah and greatness in the same place." And he was perfectly humble, meek and removed from lust, as the Talmud states, "When Rabbi died, modesty and the fear of sin were extinguished."[40] And he was articulate and better versed in the Hebrew tongue than any other person, to the point where the Sages, may they rest in peace, learned the meanings of words in the Scriptures about which they had doubts from his slaves and servants, and this is well known in the Talmud.[41] And he had such riches and wealth that it was said of him: "Rabbi's equerry is richer than King Shapur." Therefore he was beneficent to scholars and students, and generated much Torah learning among Israel, and he gathered all the traditions, teachings and controversies that had been voiced from the time of Moses our teacher to his own day. And he himself was one of the recipients of the tradition, which he had received from his father Shimon, who received it from his father Gamaliel, who received it from his father Shimon, who received it from his father Gamaliel, who received it from his father Shimon, who received it from his father Hillel, who received it from his teachers Shemaiah and Avtalion, who received it from Judah b. Tabai and Shimon b. Shetah, who received it from Joshua b. Perahiah and Nitai the Arbelite, who received it from Jose b. Joezer and Jose b. Johanan, who received it from Antigonus of Sokho, who received it from Shimon the

---

39 Alluding to II Kings 24:14, and to bGitin 83a, where "craftsmen and smiths" are interpreted as "men of learning."
40 bSota 49b.
41 bRosh Hashana 28b.

Just, who received it from Ezra, because he was one of the last of the Great Assembly, and Ezra received it from his teacher Barukh b. Neriah, who received it from the prophet Jeremiah, and Jeremiah no doubt received it from the prophets who preceded him, from prophet to prophet back to the elders who received the tradition from Joshua, who received it from Moses.

And when he [R. Judah the Prince] had gathered all the opinions and traditions, he commenced upon the composition of the Mishna, which includes interpretations of all the precepts written in the Torah. Some of them are dicta received from Moses, may he rest in peace; some of them laws derived by exegesis over which there is no controversy; and some of them are laws that are subject to controversy [due to the use of different modes of exegesis]. He noted them as controversial: A says this and B says that. Even if there was but a single individual who held an opinion differing from that of the majority, he noted both the individual opinion and that of the majority. He did this for highly pragmatic reasons, as stated in the Mishna, tractate Eduyot,[42] and I shall mention them, but only after I explain an important basic principle that I feel is appropriate to mention here. And this is it. One might ask: If indeed all the explanations of the Torah were received from Moses, in accordance with the principles we spoke of in reference to the Talmud's dictum, "All of the Torah, its general rules and its details, and its finer points, were spoken at Sinai," why, then, are some laws characterized as "laws given to Moses at Sinai"? Here is a fundamental principle that you should grasp: there is no controversy at all in the explanations received from Moses. We have never encountered a controversy among the Sages at any point in time at all, from Moses our teacher to Rav Ashi, wherein one says that a man who blinded another is himself to be blinded, in line with the dictum of God, may He be exalted, "eye for eye" (Deut. 19:21), and the other says that he is only liable to pay compensation. And we also find no controversy in explaining the scriptural verse "fruit of a goodly tree" (Lev. 23:40) where one says it is a citron and another that it is a quince or a pomegranate or something else. And we also find no controversy in explaining the meaning of "boughs of thick trees" (ibid.) as myrtle. And we do not find any controversy over interpreting His statement, may He be exalted, "thou shalt cut off her hand" (Deut. 25:12) as monetary compensation, or over the verse, "And the daughter of any priest, if she profane herself...she shall be burnt with fire" (Lev. 21:9) – that this punishment is imposed only if she was a married woman. Similarly, from the time of Moses until today we have heard no dispute over the teaching that the punishment of stoning for a woman found not to be a virgin (Deut. 22:21) is applicable only if it turns out that,

42 mEduyot 1:5–6.

after being married, she committed adultery with someone other than her husband, there having been due forewarning and witnesses. And so too with regard to all similar instances of such interpretation of the precepts, there is no controversy, because they all are traditional interpretations received from Moses, and of them and similar teachings it is said, "All of the Torah, its general rules and its details, and its fine points, was spoken at Sinai." Even though these interpretations are transmitted by tradition, and there is no controversy over them, nevertheless, the wisdom of Scriptures is such that we are able to derive these interpretations from the written law by inference, supporting allusion (*asmakhtaot*), textual clues (*remazim*), and scriptural guidance.

When you see a debate in the Talmud, and there is a disagreement over some conjecture, and proofs are brought for one of these interpretations, or their like, as, for example, the Sages stated, regarding His dictum, may He be exalted, "fruit of goodly trees (*pri etz hadar*)" – that it might mean pomegranate or quince or other such fruits, until they brought conclusive proof [that this is not so], although it is not necessary, from the phrase "fruit [of goodly] trees" – trees such that both the wood and the fruit taste the same; and they made another suggestion, [that a "goodly" tree is] one on which fruit remains from year to year,[43] and yet another, that it is "a fruit that dwells (*hadar*) on all the water."[44] This is not because they had doubts about the matter until they gained knowledge of it through these proofs. But rather, we see, without any doubt, that from the time of Joshua until now, that it is the *etrog* (citron) that is ritually taken together with the lulav (palm frond), every year, and there is no controversy over this, but they were simply investigating the scriptural instructions that bear out this traditional interpretation. And so it is, too, regarding their analysis of the myrtle, and regarding their analysis that the punishment of monetary compensation is that which is to be paid by one who causes another to lose a bodily part, and their analysis that the "daughter of a priest" spoken of there refers to a married woman. And all similar things are on this basis, and this is the meaning of the Sages' dictum "its general rules and its details," that is, the matters which you observe us deriving by means of the interpretive rule, "a general term followed by a particular term," and by applying the rest of the thirteen exegetical principles – they are traditions received from Moses at Sinai. But even though they are traditions received from Moses, these laws are nonetheless not termed "law given to Moses at Sinai." We do not say that it is a law given to Moses at Sinai that the fruit of a goodly tree is the citron, or that it is a law given to Moses at Sinai that one who inflicts bodily harm on his fellow pays monetary compensation, for it has already been stated that it is axiomatic for us that all such

43 *hadar*=goodly; ha-dar=dwells.
44 Reading *hudor* (Greek for 'water') instead of *hadar*.

interpretations were received from Moses, and are hinted at, as we said, by scriptural clues, or can be derived by one of the exegetical principles, as we stated. But any matter that has no scriptural clue, and no supportive allusion, and cannot be derived by any of the exegetical principles, of these alone it is said that they are "law given to Moses at Sinai." Therefore, when the Talmud states, "measures are law given to Moses at Sinai,"[45] we questioned this statement, asking, How can you say of them that they are law given to Moses at Sinai when measures are hinted at by the verse "a land of wheat and barley" (Deut. 8:8)? And the answer to this was that they are law given to Moses at Sinai, and there are no grounds for deriving them by any of the exegetical principles, and there is no hint of them in all of the Torah, but rather, they were associated with the verse so that it would serve as a mnemonic sign to preserve them and call them to mind, but they are not the subject of the verse, and this is the import of the expression, "the verse is merely a supporting allusion (*asmakhta bealma*)," wherever it is found....

According to the preceding principles, then, all the laws set down in the Torah can be divided into five categories:

The first category consists of the traditional interpretations received from Moses that are hinted at in the Scriptures or can be derived by one of the exegetical principles; these are not subject to any controversy, but rather, whenever someone says, "I received such-and-such [a tradition]," all debate is irrelevant.

The second category consists of the laws of which it was said that they are "law given to Moses at Sinai," and for which there is no scriptural evidence, as we said. And they too are not subject to controversy.

The third category consists of the laws that are derived by one of the exegetical principles, and they may be subject to controversy, as we said. And here, the law is decided in accordance with the majority opinion, according to the principles we noted earlier. When is this applicable? When the arguments are of equal merit, hence the dictum, "if this is a traditional law, we accept it, if it is a conclusion based on reasoning, we can refute it."[46] Controversy and debate will only occur over matters regarding which there is no received tradition. And throughout the Talmud one can find examination of arguments over which controversy between the opposed opinions has ensued, in sayings such as: "what is the point of contention?" or "what are the reasons offered by Rabbi A?" or "what is the difference between their views?" For sometimes, in this type of context, this is the Talmud's way of clarifying the reasons for the controversy in question, and it concludes that A's position is based on one point, whereas B's is based on another, and so on.

45 bEruvin 4a.
46 mJebamot 8:3; mKritot 3:9.

But the view of one who thinks that laws that are subject to controversy are also traditions originating from Moses, and they engendered controversy due to error in the tradition, or its having been forgotten, so that one side is right with regard to its tradition, and the other errs with regard to its tradition, or forgot it, or did not hear from his teacher all that he needed to hear, and who cites in support of this the talmudic dictum, "When there multiplied students of Shammai and Hillel who did not attend to their teachers sufficiently, controversy multiplied in Israel, and the law became like two sets of laws [lit., two Torahs]"[47] – as God lives, he presents a contemptible and very bizarre argument. And it is not correct and does not conform to the [foregoing] principles, for it expresses misgivings about the individuals from whom we received the Torah, and is completely invalid. This worthless outlook is the result of a paucity of knowledge about what the Sages say in the Talmud. For while one who maintains this view has understood that the interpretations originate from Moses, which is indeed correct according to the principles we discussed earlier, nevertheless, he has failed to distinguish between the received laws and new laws arrived at by reasoning. But you, even should you have some doubts about this, will certainly have no doubts at all as to the controversy between the house of Shammai and the house of Hillel as [exemplified] by their respective dicta: "the floor is swept before they wash their hands[48]" and "they wash their hands and then the floor is swept." For neither of these opinions is a tradition received from Moses, and neither was heard at Sinai. And the reason for the disagreement is, as the Talmud states, that one of them forbids using ignorant servants, and the other permits it. And it is so in all similar controversies, which are offshoots of offshoots of offshoots.

As to the Talmud's statement, "When there multiplied students of Shammai and Hillel who did not attend to their teachers sufficiently, controversy multiplied in Israel" – this matter is quite clear. For two individuals of equal understanding, learning and knowledge of the exegetical principles, will not, under any circumstances, disagree over that which is derived by means of the exegetical principles. Should disagreement arise, it will be but minor. And indeed we do not find any disagreement between Shammai and Hillel except over a few laws, because their methods of deriving the law, with respect to all that they derived by means of one of the exegetical principles, were very similar, and the correct rules of inference that the one had mastered had also been mastered by the other. When the scholarship of their students diminished, and their facility in drawing legal conclusions weakened in comparison to that of their teachers Shammai and Hillel, controversies did arise between them over numerous points in the course of

---

47 bSanhedrin 88b.
48 Before the Grace after meals.

their dialogue and debate, as each argued according to his intellectual ability and his familiarity with the rules of inference. And they are not to be blamed for this, for we cannot force two people who are debating an issue to debate it at the intellectual level of Joshua and Phinehas. Nor are we permitted to be leery of their respective contentions because the scholars in question are not on a par with Shammai or Hillel, or superior to them, for God, may He be exalted, did not oblige us to do so, but rather, He obliged us to listen to the scholars of the given generation, whichever it be, as He said, "[or] unto the judge that shall be in those days" (Deut. 17:9). This, then, is how controversy arose, and it is not the case that they erred as to the tradition, the tradition of one side being true and of the other, null. And how clear these matters are to anyone who reflects upon them, and how great a cornerstone of the Torah.

And the fourth category consists of laws enacted by the prophets and sages of each and every generation in order to make a fence around the Torah and safeguard it. Their observance was commanded by God by way of a general dictum, in His utterance, "Therefore shall ye keep My charge" (Lev. 18:30), which tradition interprets as, "add a charge to My charge,"[49] and [these additional charges] are what the Sages, of blessed memory, call decrees (*gzeirot*). These too may be subject to controversy, for example, where one individual considers it appropriate to forbid something for some reason, and another does not. This is frequently the case in the Talmud – Rabbi A issued a decree for such-and-such a reason, while Rabbi B did not issue the decree – and this is one of the causes of controversy. You will observe, for instance, that eating fowl with milk is forbidden by Rabbinic decree in order to distance us from transgression, and is not forbidden by the scriptural prohibition, which pertains only to milk and meat of a pure animal. And the Sages forbade eating fowl with milk in order to distance us from that which is forbidden. But some of them did not consider this decree appropriate, because R. Jose the Galilean permitted eating fowl with milk, and the people in his area all did so, as is explained in the Talmud.[50] And when there is a consensus about one of these decrees, it is not to be transgressed under any circumstances. And as long as the prohibition is widespread in Israel, there is no way for the decree to be annulled, and even the prophets cannot render it permitted. And it is stated in the Talmud that not even Elijah can render permitted that which is forbidden by one of the eighteen decrees enacted by the house of Shammai and the house of Hillel.[51] And they gave a reason for this, namely, that it is because the prohibitions were widespread among all Israel.

---

49 I.e., add restrictive measures to safeguard the biblical precept, bJebamot 21a.
50 bShabat 130a.
51 bAvoda Zara 36a.

The fifth category consists of laws conceived in order to regulate relations between individuals, an enterprise that does not add to the words of the Torah, nor subtract from them; or laws regarding matters that have to do with rectification of the world (*tikun olam*) as to religious matters, and these the Sages call enactments and customs (*takanot* and *minhagot*).

210. Maimonides' Guide for the Perplexed, I:31

On the other hand, there are things for the apprehension of which man finds that he has great longing. The intellectual impulse to seek out and investigate the truth about them exists at every time and in every group of people engaged in intellectual speculation. With regard to such things, perspectives multiply and controversy arises among those engaged in such investigation, and doubts ensue. This is due to the fact that the intellect yearns to apprehend these things, that is, due to its longing for them; and also because everyone thinks that he has indeed found a way to ascertain the truth about these matters. And yet it is not within the power of the human intellect to provide demonstrations in these matters. For with respect to those things whose truth is known by means of demonstration, there is no controversy or argument or competitiveness – except on the part of the ignoramus whose stubborn resistance is known as incorrigibility vis-a-vis demonstration. Thus one finds people who stubbornly deny that the earth is a sphere, that celestial orbits are circular, and so on. Such folk will not be taken into account in our discussion. The points about which the said perplexity has arisen are very numerous in divine matters, few in matters pertaining to the natural, and nonexistent in matters of technical erudition.

Alexander of Aphrodisias said that there are three causes of controversy over such matters. One is love of hauteur and competitiveness, both of which turn man aside from the apprehension of the truth as it really is. The second cause is the subtlety of that which is to be grasped, in and of itself, and its profundity, and the difficulty of apprehending it. And the third cause is the ignorance of the individual who seeks to grasp it, and his inability to apprehend that which it is possible to apprehend. This is what Alexander said. And in our times there is a fourth cause that was not mentioned, as it did not then obtain, and it is habit and upbringing. For man has by nature a love of, and an inclination for, that to which he is habituated. Thus one sees that villagers – notwithstanding the harshness of their lives, the lack of pleasures, and the scarcity of food – detest the cities, and do not enjoy their pleasures, and prefer the wretched conditions they are used to over decent conditions they are not used to. Their souls thus find no comfort in living in palaces, nor in wearing silken clothing, or pampering themselves with baths, ointments or perfumes. This will transpire, too, with respect to the opinions an individual is used to and has been raised on: he is fond of them and defends them, eschewing all others.

And this too blinds man to the apprehension of the truth, inclining him toward the views he is used to . . . .

And do not suppose that what we have said about the insufficiency of the human intellect and the fact that there is a limit at which it is halted, is a statement grounded in the Torah. Rather, it is an assertion that was already made by the philosophers, who grasped it correctly without any connection to a particular religion or doctrine. And it is a correct notion, and will not be doubted except by an individual who ignores that which has been demonstrated.

211. Maimonides' Guide for the Perplexed, I:71

Know that the many sciences devoted to establishing the truth as to these matters, sciences which once existed in our nation, were lost over time, and also due to our having been governed by the backward nations, and because these matters were not imparted to everyone, as we explained. And these matters were not imparted to everyone, but only the written texts. And you are already aware that formerly, even the traditional oral law was not committed to writing, in line with this injunction, well-known in our nation: "Words that I have spoken to you orally, you are not permitted to state in writing."[52] Here the Torah is consummately wise, for it averted what ultimately came about, namely, the multiplicity of opinions, the proliferation of interpretive approaches, and the unclear statements that ensued when authors explained their opinions, and the lapses of memory that befell them. And controversies emerged among the people, who became factionalized and perplexed as to the proper way to conduct themselves. And all these matters were entrusted to the high court, as I explained in my legal works, and as is enjoined by the language of the Torah. Now if, regarding legal pronouncements, there was reluctance to set them down in a work that would be accessible to all, in view of the detrimental effect this would ultimately have, all the more so there could be no compilation of a work on the mysteries of the Torah that would be accessible to everyone. But rather, these mysteries were transmitted by an illustrious few to an illustrious few, as I made clear to you, citing the dictum: "The mysteries of the Torah may only be transmitted to one who is a counselor, a wise artificer."[53]

212. Maimonides' Code, Laws concerning Rebels 1:3–4

So far as traditional laws are concerned, there has never been any controversy over them. And on every matter where there has been

52 bGitin 60b.
53 bHagiga 13a; see Isaiah 3:3.

controversy, it is certain that it is not a tradition from Moses, our teacher. As for rules derived by means of the exegetical principles, if all the members of the high court agreed to them, then they agreed. And if there was a difference of opinion about them, they would follow the majority, and decide the law in accordance with the majority opinion. So too with regard to decrees, ordinances, and customs. If some felt that it was fitting to issue a decree, enact an ordinance, or to discontinue a certain custom, and others felt that it was not fitting to issue this decree, enact this ordinance, or abandon the custom, they deliberate and debate the matter, these against those, and they follow the majority opinion and resolve the matter in accord with the majority view.

So long as the high court was in existence, there were no controversies in Israel, but when a point of law arose concerning which someone was in doubt, he asked the court in his town. If the members thereof knew [the answer], they stated it; if not, the inquirer, together with the members of that court or their deputies went up to Jerusalem and posed the question to the court that sat at [the entrance to] the Temple Mount. If the members thereof knew the answer, they stated it; if not, they all went to the court that sat at the entrance to the Azara.[54] If its members knew the answer, they stated it, and if not, all proceeded to the Hall of Hewn Stone, seat of the high court, and put the question to that body. If the matter concerning which they were all in doubt was known to the high court, whether through tradition or through applying one of the principles by which Scripture is expounded, they stated it forthwith. If the matter was not clear to the high court, they commenced to consider it at that point, deliberating the matter until they either reached a consensus, or put it to a vote and decided in accordance with the majority opinion. They then said to the inquirers, 'This is the law,' and the latter departed.

After the high court became defunct, controversies multiplied in Israel: one declaring something impure, and giving a reason for his ruling, and another declaring it pure, and giving a reason for his ruling; one forbidding, the other permitting.

213. Beit Habehira, mAvot, preface (Havlin edition, p. 43)

And be aware that at all the times mentioned up to the end of the time of the prophets, which was the time of the destruction of the first Temple, they did not see a need to write down anything that it was fitting to transmit orally. They had nothing in writing save the Torah and the books of the prophesies, for all they needed regarding the talmudic clarification of

---

54 One of the Temple compounds, consisting of a number of chambers. Also referred to as the Temple Court.

the precepts was handed down orally from one person to another in its entirety.

And when a new matter arose that called for deliberation, due to changes in the circumstances, they had been given the basic tenets of the law and the exegetical principles with which to illuminate that which puzzled them and to clarify all the laws. And where analogy and reason did not suffice, they sometimes decided according to the majority, as it is said, "follow the majority" (Exod. 23:2). And at times prophecy would clarify all their perplexities for them, for we know from some of our perfect Sages that prophecy provides intellectual insight that cannot be achieved by study, much less by reasoning. For just as the imaginative faculty is able to conceive that which the senses cannot perceive, so the power of the mind is able to master that which cannot be arrived at via study, premises, analogy or reasoning. But nevertheless, they would deliberate and debate the matter on the basis of analogies and exegetical principles and reasoning, in order to resolve that which puzzled them, and all this generated no controversy whatsoever among them. Because at that time they would submit to the prophets, and accept their authority, and obey their instructions.

And sometimes they relied on matters traditionally accepted as law given to Moses at Sinai – namely, the matters that are not governed by study, reasoning, or by any of the exegetical principles by which the Torah is expounded. And at times they would also support these traditions with biblical verses, merely as a supporting allusion (*asmakhta bealma*), but everything continued to be a matter of oral tradition passed from one to another, along with what their leaders instituted as called for by the times, and as was required due to new conditions, without any controversy.

214. Beit Habehira, mAvot, preface (Havlin edition, p. 52)

And after him[55] came the time of Antigonus, who was the first [head] of the academy of the Sages at the time of the Second Temple, and he had no colleague [of that stature], and therefore no controversies arose in the academies during his time, but rather, all his colleagues and students and the wise men of his generation would follow his opinions, and hence virtually none of the multitude of the scholars of his day are mentioned by name. After him, there was an appointed president in every generation, and a head of the academy (*rosh yeshiva*), that is, the head of the court (*av beit din*), the pair being charged with the leadership of the academies and the rulings handed down by them, and at that point, the era of controversies dawned. The first appointees at the inception of this leadership structure, after Antigonus, were Jose b. Joezer and Joseph b. Hanan, who received the tradition from him together with many scholars of their generation. ...

55 R. Shimon the Just, one of the last of the Great Assembly.

And in their time controversy grew a little, as the president and the head of the academy would disagree with each other, and the students would follow them, some following the one, some the other. The only controversy between them that is related in the Talmud has to do with a sacrifice brought on a Festival – was the laying on of hands carried out, or not?[56] And also for all subsequent pairs, one of the two, and his followers, asserted that the laying on of hands was not to be carried out . . . and the other, along with his followers, permitted it.

215. Beit Habehira, mAvot, preface (Havlin edition, p. 62)

To conclude, after the demise of Hillel the Elder, the academies became divided; some of them were drawn to Hillel, and were called "the house of Hillel," and some to Shammai, and were called "the house of Shammai." Then the staff of controversy budded, and put forth buds, and bloomed blossoms[57]; it grew in stature and splendor and its branches multiplied, and opinions differed on most matters. This is what is stated in the baraita in tractate Hagiga: "At first there was no controversy in Israel. . . . When there multiplied students of Shammai and Hillel who did not attend to their teachers sufficiently, controversies multiplied in Israel, and the law became like two sets of laws [lit., two Torahs]."[58]

216. Magen Avot, foreword (p. 5)

And though the Torah reconciles and unifies opinions, all the more so when assisted by a prophet or wise leader in promulgating its ways and the modes of its secrets, until all those charged with instituting mores who follow God's perfect law indeed penetrate its very foundation, unifying and allying their hearts to hold a single belief. Notwithstanding all this, it does on occasion transpire that the Torah and its leadership do not encompass all the details so as to form a single opinion in every aspect, and not only that, but controversy may arise even in the interpretation of the ways of the Torah, and all the more so in the interpretation of the words of the ancient Sages, whose words and practices we long to follow, and constitute our guide to life and the abiding service of God, may His Name and memory be blessed. And even more so are there differences of opinion on some matters due to the power of different leaders, by virtue of the great distances between communities, and the great distances between the opinions of the more recent leaders, each leading his local community as he sees fit

56 mHagiga 2:2.
57 Based on Numbers 17:16–24.
58 tHagiga 2:9.

and deems right, and those who come after them adopt these customs and imagine that all who diverge from them have misunderstood the intention of the Torah or of the Sages, of blessed memory.

And it is known that there are four reasons for controversy. One is the competitive impulse; the second, the complexity of the questions involved, and their profundity; the third, obtuseness, rudeness and lack of comprehension; the fourth, society and upbringing, as it is human nature to admire our companions and those with whom we have grown up, and we thus imagine that their opinions and modes of comportment are set in stone, and find it very difficult to depart from them in any way whatever, whether on important or unimportant issues.

217. Sefer Haikarim, book 3, chapter 23

A thing is perfect if we cannot conceive of any addition to it or any subtraction from it. Now since [King] David characterizes God's Torah as perfect (Ps. 19:8) it follows that it cannot be deficient in the realization of its perfection and objective. Now every written document, of whatever nature, can be understood in two different ways, one corresponding to the intention of the writer and the other very far from it. Thus Maimonides, of blessed memory, writes in his epistle on resurrection that "Hear O Israel, the Lord our God, the Lord is One" [Deut. 6:4] is understood by the Jews as referring to absolute unity, whereas others interpret it as implying something different. For this reason, in order that the Torah of God, may He be blessed, be perfect and be correctly understood, it was essential that when God, may He be blessed, gave it to Moses in writing, He explained it to him as it was meant to be. Similarly, Moses explained it to Joshua, and Joshua to the elders, the elders to the prophets, and so on generation after generation, so that there would be no doubt as to the correct meaning of the written document.

This interpretation of the written law that Moses transmitted to Joshua and Joshua to his successors, is called the 'oral law,' for it is impossible for this interpretation to be committed to writing. For were it committed to writing, the same doubts that, as we said, befall the first written law, would befall it too, and this interpretation would require another interpretation, ad infinitum. As happened to the compilation of the Mishna, which is an interpretation of the written law, which gave rise to doubt and perplexity, to the point that it required another interpretation, namely, the Talmud compiled by Rav Ashi, to interpret the Mishna. And likewise the Gemara, that is, the commentary on the Mishna, itself required a commentary, and numerous commentaries and divergent opinions emerged, and the same happened to the commentaries themselves. It has thus become clear that the written Torah cannot be perfect unless it is accompanied by this oral commentary, which is called the 'oral law.' Regarding this, the Rabbis, of blessed memory, said: "The Holy One, blessed be He, made a covenant with Israel only for the sake of the oral law."[59] This is because there is no possibility of understanding the written law other than together with the oral law.

Furthermore, because the law of God, may He be blessed, cannot be so complete as to suffice for all times, since the ever-emerging particulars of mens' affairs, such as their litigation and their deeds, are too numerous to be embraced in a book, therefore general principles alluded to briefly in the Torah, by means of which the scholars of every generation could derive these ever-emerging particulars, were given to Moses orally at Sinai. These principles are mentioned in Torat Kohanim [Sifra], at the beginning, in the baraita which begins, "R. Ishmael says: Thirteen rules are applied in the interpretation of the Torah, inference from minor to major, inference from identical terms," and so on. By means of these modes, or any one of them, we can know that which is not explicit in the Torah. But if a thing is found in the Torah explicitly, or handed down by tradition, no derivation based on any of those principles is relevant or effective for uprooting that which is written or has been transmitted by tradition. Thus we often find in the Talmud the following remark, 'How do you know this?' and the answer is, 'It is a law given to Moses at Sinai.' We also find the expression used by a querier, 'If it is a traditional law, we accept it, if it is a conclusion based on reasoning, we can refute it.'

And since controversy may arise between the scholars of Israel regarding a matter that has not been transmitted by tradition, but is based on one of the thirteen exegetical principles or another mode of understanding, divine wisdom has resolved – in order to ensure the perfection of the Torah of God, may He be blessed – to eliminate controversy as much as possible. And for this it gave the ultimate decision in each and every generation to the majority of the sages, as it said, "Follow the majority" (Exod. 23:2); and as it also said, "Thou shalt not turn aside from the sentence which they shall declare unto thee, to the right hand, nor to the left" (Deut. 17:11). And the Rabbis, of blessed memory, explained: "Even if they tell you of right that it is left and left that it is right."[60] And in so saying their intent is to say that every person by nature thinks and attributes to himself more understanding, reasoning ability and intelligence than that possessed by anyone else, and thus you may find that even fools and women and ignorant persons speak disrespectfully of the learned and consider themselves more educated than they. Hence Scripture says that even if it appears to one who disagrees that the wise call the right left and the left right, he must never deviate from their decision, and the power to decide must always be delegated to the majority of the sages. And though it is'

---

59 bGitin 60b.
60 Sifre Deuteronomy 154.

possible that an individual may be wiser than every one of them, and his view more in accord with the truth than that of all the rest, nevertheless, the law is to be as the majority decide, and the individual is not permitted to disagree with them and to act upon his own view at all.

This was the issue that arose concerning R. Joshua and R. Eliezer.[61] For though R. Eliezer was more learned than all the rest, so much so that a heavenly voice went forth and said, Why do you debate with R. Eliezer, seeing that on all matters the law is in accordance with his view? R. Joshua rose to his feet and said, "It is not in heaven" (Deut. 30:12), that is, though the truth may be in accordance with the opinion of R. Eliezer, we ought not relinquish the opinion of the majority and follow an individual, for the Torah had already been given to us at Mount Sinai, and in it is written, "Follow the majority" (Exod. 23:2). And should we, on a particular matter, act in accordance with the opinion of an individual and relinquish that of the majority, great controversy will be generated anew in Israel in each and every generation. For every individual will come to think that his view is the truth and he will put his view into practice, and this will undermine the Torah altogether.

218. Beit Elohim, Shaar hayesodot, chapter 36

There may be room for people of little faith to ponder this essential tenet of faith[62] due to the controversies that have arisen among the Sages of Israel from ancient times, from the time when the laying on of hands controversy arose between the president and the head of the court. "This one said to lay on hands, the other said not to lay on hands,"[63] until the students of Shammai and Hillel multiplied, and the Torah, heaven forbid, became like two sets of laws [lit., two Torahs]. And the Amoraim, the Geonim, and the scholars who came after them, up to the present, have had disagreements: one permits, another forbids, one exempts, another holds liable, one declares a thing impure, another declares the same thing pure. If the truth is in accord with the one who permits or declares pure or exempts, the side that maintains the opposite view will be adding to what is written in the Torah; conversely, if the truth is in accord with the other side, then the former will transgress by diminishing what is written in the Torah, as they said to each other in the Mishna: "If so, you are adding to what is written in the Torah, if so you are diminishing," and so on.[64] And if we take a closer look, we find such controversy with respect to most of the laws of the Torah, and in view of what I wrote in the

---

61 bBaba Metzia 59b.
62 Namely, the principle, "Thou shalt not add thereto, nor diminish from it" (Deut. 13:1).
63 mHagiga 2:2.
64 Paraphrasing mZevahim 8:10.

previous chapter, namely, that the injunction against adding or diminishing applies primarily to the oral law, this problem will even be more severe, since most of the disagreements between the Sages arise in discussing the oral law.

The answer to this matter is, according to the principles of the Torah, that the Torah commanded that we "follow the majority" (Exod. 23:2). Because when God, may he be exalted, handed over to Moses our teacher at Sinai the rules for interpreting the Torah and its details, which the human mind cannot, by its very nature, possibly grasp, due to the Torah's comprehensiveness and profundity – as it is written, "the measure thereof is longer than the earth" (Job 11:9), referring to the extent and numerousness of the Torah's laws, and "broader than the sea," referring to the degree of profundity of the Torah's laws, which is as deep as the sea – Moses could not learn it but from the Almighty, who gave him the strength to receive the full extent and breadth of the laws of the Torah, down to the last detail, including even that which future students would say to their teachers. Moses could not teach Aaron and his sons and the elders of Israel and all of Israel what he had learned, for what he had learned from the Almighty in one day of the forty days, could not be taught in a year of the forty years that they tarried in the desert. Now even if he could teach them in a year what he himself had learned in a day, so that they could learn the entire Torah in forty years just as he, Moses, had learned it in forty days, that was only because Israel, in that generation, were well prepared, having all heard "I am" (Exod. 20:2) and "Thou shalt have no" (Exod. 20:3) from the Almighty. And it was a generation all of whom abounded in wisdom. And the Torah was not given in the complete way it had been learned by Moses our teacher from the mouth of the Almighty, except to those who had, in the desert, eaten manna, the bread of knights, the bread that nourishes the ministering angels. But from there on, in the generations thereafter, they transmitted, one to another, only the principles of the Torah along with some of its details, as the later generations were incapable of learning the entire Torah as it had been learned by those who left Egypt. But rather, they expounded the Torah using the exegetical principles for its interpretation which had been transmitted to them so that they could be used to learn the details of the laws of the Torah. Each individual, according to his intelligence and comprehension, so he could interpret and study much of the law of the Torah, without any controversy. For as long as prophecy continued in Israel, they were readily capable of learning the laws of the Torah by means of the exegetical principles, without any controversy, just as the laws had been given at Sinai.

After the time of the Men of the Great Assembly, when prophecy ceased, they were no longer capable of learning everything clearly, and doubts would arise regarding the subjects being studied, to the point where there were controversies about the tradition, one permitting and the other forbidding, and so on. The Mishna refers to this when it says: Moses received the Torah at Sinai,[65] for he had the strength and preparedness to grasp it only from the Almighty at Sinai. And he taught it to all Israel, as we explained. But since Joshua had entered the land of Israel and taught it, together with his court, to a different generation, which had not heard "I am" and "Thou shalt have no" at Sinai, and was not capable of learning it all, but only its principles and some of its details, therefore the Mishna says, "handed it down to Joshua," that is, handed it down to him to teach it by way of principles, through the exegetical principles. This method of transmission enabled them to learn the details from the principles. This was so until the times of the Men of the Great Assembly, who received it from the Prophets. But after them, with the cessation of prophecy, doubts and controversies emerged, as explained. And in reference to this, the Torah said, "follow the majority" (Exod. 23:2) about that which would be controversial regarding the laws of the Torah in the coming generations. And after they decide the law in accordance with the majority view, the law will be tantamount to law received by Moses at Sinai, which is not to be added to nor subtracted from. And the minority follows the majority, so that in the laws of the Torah there are no additions and no subtractions, for everything is in accordance with the majority view.

Now with regard to the talmudic passage about the controversy over the rival[-wive]s, "it might be said that the house of Shammai acted in accordance with their views, and it might be said that the house of Shammai did not act in accordance with their views," and so on,[66] even so, after the law was decided in accordance with the view of the house of Hillel, it became tantamount to law received by Moses at Sinai, which is not to be added to nor subtracted from. And this is also the case with respect to the other Tannaim and Amoraim who had disagreements regarding the laws of the Torah, once the law was decided in accordance with one of the opinions.

Now controversy was not the sole imprint left by the cessation of prophecy: another was the renunciation of the oral law by part of the people of Israel, namely, the Sadducees and their associates. They could not deny the written law, since it was written and sealed from the time it was given, and in the possession of every single tribe was a Torah scroll written by Moses our teacher, may he rest in peace. And as long as prophecy was alive in Israel, they could not deny the oral law either, for they could see the influence of prophecy on Israel; so too they also believed that the oral law was given to Moses as part of his prophecy, to interpret the Torah, even though it had not been committed to writing.

65 mAvot 1:1.
66 bJebamot 14a.

But when the influence of prophecy ceased, they denied even that which they had earlier accepted as the prophecy of Moses in interpreting the Torah, because it had not been explicitly committed to writing from the time it was given until that point.

219. Megale Amukot, ofen 74

And had Moses entered the land of Israel, there would never have been any controversy, but when Moses struck the rock, controversy multiplied in Israel, and this is the secret of the "rock of divisions,"[67] meaning, controversy among Israel originates from the rock. And this is the secret of "these are the waters of Meribah (strife), where the children of Israel strove" (Num. 20:13). That is to say, by striking the rock Moses caused it to be the case that the Torah trickles out slowly, drop by drop, and controversy ensues. And this is the secret of the verse, "Is not My word like a fire? declareth the Lord" (Jer. 23:29). What caused the sparks to break up into many hues? It is entailed by, "And like a hammer that breaketh the rock in pieces" (ibid.). The hammer with which Moses struck the rock caused an outburst and proliferation of controversy among Israel. The numerical value of 'hammer' equals that of 'the staff of Moses'[68] – the staff's striking it caused this. ...

For this reason, Moses wished to enter the land of Israel, so that the controversy between Shammai and Hillel would never take place, for their students would attend to their studies sufficiently, and there would be "one law and one ordinance" (Num. 15:16) for all Israel, and this is referred to by the verse, "for what god is there in heaven or on earth?" (Deut. 3:24) – as one God has created us, there can be only one Father. And had Moses entered the land of Israel, the verse "all were given from one shepherd" (Eccles. 12:11) would have been fulfilled. ... For this reason, Moses wanted to be in the land of Israel to bring it about that there be but one law for us, and to fulfill the verse "and who is like Your people Israel, a unique nation on the earth?" (II Sam. 7:23), and precisely so that there would be but one Father for all of us ... [but] the Holy One, blessed be He, answered, "You are overly [disputatious]" (Deut. 3:26) – you are the reason that disputes multiplied in Israel, because you struck the rock, whereas I told you to teach it a chapter or a law, and this is the secret of "speak no more unto Me of this matter" (ibid.), for you did damage regarding this matter, that is, by your [lack of] speaking,[69] as you did not speak to the rock.

---

67 See I Samuel 23:28.
68 Both *patish* (hammer) and *mate moshe* (the staff of Moses) add up to 399.
69 A pun on "matter" (*davar*) and "speech" (*dibur*).

220. Hakuzari Hasheini, third debate, letters 1–12

Said the Kuzari: I saw and am convinced that all that you have said in favor of the Sages, of blessed memory, and their veracity is true and certain. Yet those who deny this still have room to challenge it. For they will argue: if indeed all that was said by the Sages, of blessed memory, was transmitted by tradition, how is it that we see them holding diametrically opposed views, one saying a thing is fit and the other disqualifying it, one declaring a thing pure, and the other, impure, one forbidding and the other permitting, one holding liable and the other exempting; to conclude, one says this and the other says that.

Said the Rabbi: Know, your Majesty the king, that there has never been a controversy among the Sages, of blessed memory, over the received tenets, but only over the interpretation of some of them. For example, the sounding of the ram's horn on the New Year is only hinted at in the Torah, as in the statement, "it is a day of blowing the horn unto you" (Num. 29:1), yet it is mentioned in the Mishna as a matter well known to all Israel, as stated in tractate Rosh Hashana: "All types of shofar are fit except that made from [the horns of] a cow."[70] And even though the expressions "blowing" (*tekia*) and "wailing" (*terua*) are used in connection with trumpets, no Israelite ever entertained the thought that the "*terua*" on the New Year is to be performed using trumpets or any instrument other than the shofar. So too in tractate Suka, the *etrog* (citron) is mentioned as a well known thing, even though it is not found in the Torah, which mentions only "the fruit of goodly trees" (Lev. 23:40). The Mishna states: "R. Ishmael says: Three myrtles and two willows, one palm branch and one citron."[71] There is no controversy over this, because it is a received tenet among all Israel that "the fruit of goodly trees" spoken of in the Torah is the citron, and one who denies this is like one who denies the Torah of Moses, and so it is with the shofar.

Indeed, the controversy is over the interpretation of some of the received tenets. For example, R. Jose deems fit a shofar made of the horn of a cow, since he believes that it falls under the concept of "shofar." And this controversy does not impact the received tenets in any way whatsoever. And so too concerning "the boughs of thick trees" – no one disputes that it refers to myrtle, since this is a received tenet. What they will disagree about, however, is whether it is required that at least one [of the myrtle branches] be perfect, or we do not care if even all three of the myrtle branches are lopped off at the top. And this is not a controversy regarding a received tenet at all. So too regarding the labors prohibited on the Sabbath. No one disputes that there are thirty-nine such labors, as this

---

70 mRosh Hashana 3:2.
71 mSuka 3:4.

is the received tradition. And so too with regard to the signs that a [kosher] animal is not ritually fit for consumption. And so too with regard to almost all the laws, which are all received tenets, and no one disputes them.

. . .

Said the Rabbi: It is written in the Torah, "The choicest first fruits of thy land thou shalt bring into the house of the Lord thy God" (Exod. 23:19), and regarding the bringing of the first fruits it is written, "And thou shalt speak and say before the Lord thy God.... And now, behold, I have brought the first of the fruit of the land, which Thou, O Lord, hast given me" (Deut. 26:5–10). There is no doubt that the Holy One, blessed be He, taught Moses at Sinai all the fundamental laws that pertain to the first fruits. But the laws that are not fundamental, even those that are relevant, He left for the Sanhedrin, and they are included in the principle: "If there arise a matter too hard for thee in judgment" (Deut. 17:8). For example, regarding what is found in the fourth chapter of tractate Gitin: If a man sells his field with respect to the produce only[72] – Resh Lakish and R. Johanan disagree [as to the law]. R. Johanan said: [the buyer] brings the first fruits and recites [the declaration] over them, as possession of the produce is equivalent to possession of the land; Resh Lakish said: he brings them and does not recite it, as possession of the produce is not equivalent to possession of the land.[73]

. . .

Said the Kuzari: ... Indeed, since it is quite common for people to sell their land with respect to the produce only, how could the law have been forgotten to the point where it was necessary for Resh Lakish and R. Johanan to engage in a controversy over it?

Said the Rabbi: Know, your Majesty the king, that the offering of the first fruits was brought only when the Temple was in existence, and the Second Temple was destroyed, according to the calculation of the Tzemah David,[74] in the year 3828.[75] And R. Johanan and Resh Lakish lived in the year 3990. It follows have over 160 years had elapsed since the destruction. It follows that there is nothing astonishing about the fact that they had forgotten this law, since it was not practiced in their day, and when they sought to study the laws of the first fruits, they were in doubt as to what

72 I.e., on the understanding that the buyer is acquiring rights to the produce only, not to the land.
73 bGitin 47b.
74 A rabbinical chronology by R. David Ganz, a student of R. Moses Isserles.
75 68 CE.

the law would be regarding one who buys land with respect to its produce only. And they wanted to arrive at a ruling on the basis of reasoning. And I have no doubt whatsoever that this law was clear-cut during the time that the Temple stood, because at the time both the sale of land with respect to its produce alone, and the bringing of first fruits, were common.

221. Responsa Havat Yair, #192

Behold, the master [Maimonides] built a fortified wall around the oral law, in writing that it is not subject to being forgotten. Would that we could strengthen it and sustain it, but this is not possible, in my opinion. (Despite the merits of his idea, there is a drawback in what he says, for [it follows that] all other controversies of the Sages, of blessed memory, which constitute the greater part by far of the oral law, and almost all the orders of the Mishna – are not from Sinai at all.) I tend to agree with Nahmanides (*Reservations on Sefer Hamitzvot*, root 1) with respect to what the master wrote regarding the enumeration of the precepts. Maimonides wrote that the negative precept of "do not deviate" includes even moving a needle on the Sabbath, and every other Rabbinic enactment, and transgressors of this negative precept incur the scriptural punishment of lashes. For all his words are puzzling, and it is not possible, in my humble opinion, with my feeble intellect, to try and reconcile them with reason or draw them near to the view of the Torah as reflected in the Talmud. (My remarks are not intended as a critique or repudiation of what earlier scholars said, but merely to publicly declare my distress at not being able to penetrate the depths of the meditations and opinions of these holy men.)

Let us turn to examine that which was mentioned last – that regarding any controversy that is not over the interpretation of the Scriptures or derived by the thirteen exegetical principles, it cannot be said that one of the two opposed opinions is law given to Moses at Sinai. And it necessarily follows that on these points [viz, those not pertaining to the interpretation of Scripture or derived by the exegetical principles], the Rabbis, of blessed memory, said that there was no controversy among Israel until the time of the Pairs, and from then on, controversy steadily increased. Now how can reason accept this, for if they did not have a tradition originating in Moses our teacher, may he rest in peace, and transmitted from one [generation] to the next, how is it that all the Sages of Israel held the same opinion on matters grounded in reasoning alone, with respect to which valid considerations can be adduced in support of both sides?

Second, teachings derived by applying the thirteen exegetical principles originate from Sinai, as explained, and if so, are not subject to being forgotten. But the Talmud is replete with controversies on such points. Take, for example, the principle of inference from identical terms (*gzeira shava*), regarding which it is unanimously agreed that it could only have been acquired by tradition from Moses our teacher, may he rest in peace, and there is no doubt at all that Moses our teacher, may he rest in peace, explained it exceedingly thoroughly. Yet nonetheless, there are controversies over how a particular inference from identical terms is derived, whether from one thing or from another. For this was why they wrote that sometimes there was only a tradition about the words, but not the verses in which they are found, and sometimes the other way around, because the words or the verses in which they were found were forgotten. For we must not say, God forbid, that the tradition of Moses our teacher, may he rest in peace, from Sinai, or his transmission of it to Joshua, was in any way incomprehensible. And even one who says that the entire Torah is from heaven with the exception of the principle of a fortiori inference is a heretic (*apikoros*). And see what I wrote in volume four....

Third, the Talmud interprets the verse, "And I will give thee the tables of stone..." and so on (Exod. 24:12), as indicating that the Mishna and Talmud too were given to Moses our teacher, may he rest in peace, at Sinai.[76] But according to the master, all that was given was the interpretation of the scriptural texts and the matters derived by the thirteen exegetical principles, which constitute less than one percent of the laws mentioned in the Mishna and the Gemara, of all of which it is said, "Moses received the Torah at Sinai and handed it down to Joshua."[77] ...

Fourth, how does he explain the seven hundred – or by some accounts, one thousand and seven hundred, or three thousand – laws derived by a fortiori inference (*kal vahomer*) and inference from identical terms (*gzeira shava*) that were forgotten in the period of mourning for Moses our teacher, may he rest in peace?[78] How could they have been forgotten, since they are part of the tradition from Sinai?

Fifth, as to what the master wrote, namely, that there will not, under any circumstances, be controversy, and so on – in my humble opinion, it is altogether impossible to escape the fact that things are forgotten, with respect to the interpretation of Scriptures, with respect to the exegetical principles, with respect to that which the Sages, of blessed memory, called law given to Moses at Sinai, and with respect to the rest of the legal details in the *z"m"n n"k"t* [the acronym for the six orders of the Mishna], even though all of these are law given to Moses at Sinai....

And we had best stick to the well-trodden path – which is the Talmud – which relates that Jose b. Joezer said that the laying on of hands was not to be carried out [on Festivals],[79] and Rashi explains that this was the first

76 bBerakhot 5a.
77 mAvot 1:1.
78 bTemura 15b.
79 bHagiga 16a.

controversy among Israel.[80] And in tractate Temura the Talmud states: "from the days of Moses until the death of Joseph b. Joezer, they learned the Torah as did Moses our teacher, may he rest in peace"[81] and the expression "they learned as..." is explained there. It means that they did not agree to reconstruct the three thousand laws forgotten during the mourning for Moses by means of dialectics, but remained at odds over them. And it seems to me that, in any event, since there were not two opposed factions, but rather, different views were upheld as theory, though in practice the majority view was followed, [such disagreement] was not considered controversy, which began at the time of the said Jose [b. Joezer], when they began to have controversies, one grouping arrayed against the other, between the president and the head of the court. This also resolves the objection raised by the Tosafot that there had [already] been a controversy between Saul and David over betrothal by a loan and a *peruta* [a coin of little value].[82]

222. Mevo Hatalmud (Maharatz Chajes), chapter 14

And we also find there[83] that at the outset there were no controversies in Israel, for on any doubtful case on which there were different opinions, they took a vote and decided in accordance with the majority opinion. And there is controversy only since the time of Jose b. Joezer, who lived at the time of the Hasmoneans, when the Sages of the generation were scattered to many different lands during the persecutions of Antiochus, and were unable to assemble in one place, and unable to put matters to a vote so that they could be definitively tallied up and settled. And for this reason, the question of the laying on of hands was from then on a matter of controversy.[84] Nevertheless, later on the Lord was beneficent to His people, and the Sanhedrin returned to its place once more. We do not hear of controversies regarding matters other than that of the laying on of hands, because every president and every head of a court adhered to the opinion of his predecessor, and they did not seek to settle the matter by taking a vote. And in the days of Shammai and Hillel they were divided over three more issues, that are listed in the Talmud.[85] But we also find controversies among the Sages of a given generation even in ancient times. We saw, for example, that there was a controversy as far back as David and Saul over the validity of betrothal of a woman by a loan and a *peruta* [a coin of little

80 Ad loc.
81 bTemura 15b.
82 bHagiga 16a s.v. *yosi*.
83 bSanhedrin 87b.
84 See bHagiga 17b.
85 bShabat 15a.

value] – what is he who betroths thinking of, the loan or the coin?[86] And we saw that there was the controversy between Hezekiah, the king of Judah, and the Sages of his generation regarding intercalation in the month of Nissan,[87] and the Sages did not assent to his opinion. And there was another disagreement between two High Priests who survived the destruction of the First Temple, one saying, "I sprinkled the altar with my hands," the other saying, "I sprinkled the altar with my feet" [that is, by walking around it].[88] And indeed, this apparent contradiction was noticed by the *Tosafot*.[89] For in tractate Hagiga the Talmud does state that the first controversy that arose in Israel was indeed that which arose over the laying on of hands. And the same question is raised by the older *Tosafot* with regard to the two High Priests. But one who reflects closely will see that this is not a real difficulty, because the controversy over the laying on of hands is mentioned only due to the fact that it lasted for such a long time, remaining a matter of controversy among Israel and undecided in the early academies from the time of Jose b. Joezer to the time of the last students of Shammai and Hillel. But this is not the case regarding the other controversies we mentioned above, which did not last beyond the times at which they, on account of some cause, arose. And as soon as the cause abated, the effect was erased, and they took a vote, and the controversies were settled in accordance with the opinion of the majority, as I wrote in my *Mishpat Hahoraa*.

223. Or Yisrael, section 30 (p. 85, note)

This explains the phenomenon of the house of Shammai and the house of Hillel. We need not wonder about this, how it arose and what caused it, and why it came about that the students of the house of Shammai and the house of Hillel almost always agreed among themselves on a single view, and indeed, what is the relevance of group affiliation? For the cause of the controversies [between the two schools] was the differences in temperament and mental disposition, which the individual cannot separate from his intellect. And no scholar of God's Torah can follow anything but that which his own eyes behold, after having taken care to safeguard himself lest he exceed his limits, and after having ensured that he acts in purity of mind, as far as humans can achieve this. For in most cases those with a shared group affiliation march to the same beat with respect to temperament and mental disposition. And this is the meaning of the dictum of our Rabbis, of blessed memory, "both are the words of the living God."

---

86 See bSanhedrin 21b.
87 bSanhedrin 12a.
88 bYoma 59a.
89 bHagiga 17a.

For mental dispositions are not subject to refutation, and even though mental dispositions change constantly, the intellect of an individual will not be affected by these changes, since changes in mental disposition arise due to excitement over issues and ideas that come up. And this is man's essence and obligation – to strive with all his might to reach a point where his mental disposition is calm and at rest while he is engaged in intellectual endeavor. And when his disposition is calm, it is almost entirely steady at all times, and particularly so in the perfected individual, who guards himself against intense excitement, which will induce in him ever-changing emotions.

224. Resisei Laila, 16

Novel understandings of the Torah cannot be fully clarified to the point where there are no opposed subjective inclinations, as it is said in the Talmud, "some declare a matter impure..." and so on,[90] and "both are the words of the living God."[91] It means that God is the Master of all the distinct forces in the world, hence "God" (*el*) is in the plural (*elohim*). And "living" (*haim*) is in the plural too, since the words of the Torah are the very vitality of all Creation. And life too has several discrete aspects, and of this Scripture says, "The king's heart is in the hand of the Lord as the watercourses..." and so on (Prov. 21:1). And to whom does "the king" refer? – our Rabbis[92]; and "water" is none other than the Torah,[93] which [like water] divides into different springs, some forbidding, some permitting. We may think that it is all a matter of the scholar's opinion, but this is not the case, for this too in the hands of God, who enlightens the scholar and inclines his heart in accordance with His divine wish and will alone.

For this reason they are called "the words of the living God," because truly they are indeed the words of God, may He be blessed. And as the Talmud states, prophecy was not withdrawn from the Sages,[94] for in truth, it [viz., their learning] is all from God, just as is a prophecy. The only difference is that a prophecy takes the form of, "thus spake the Lord," that is, precisely thus, without any divergence or disagreement. Hence if two prophets contradict each other, one of them must be a false prophet. For "prophet," as Rashi explains in his commentary on the Torah,[95] comes from the root for "speech" (*niv*), that is, the speech of God, may He be blessed, for the words of God, may He be blessed, are literally coming from the prophet's throat. And speech is the actualization of a revelation,

---

90 bHagiga 3b.
91 bEruvin 13b.
92 bGitin 62a.
93 bBaba Kama 17a.
94 bBaba Batra 12a.
95 On Exodus 7:1.

and a revelation cannot ascribe two opposite characterizations to the same subject, as is well known, because the human mind rejects this, as is known to us from what Maimonides says.[96] But the Sage cleaves to the wisdom of God, may He be blessed, which is found in the thoughts in one's mind, which tolerates the existence of opposites applying to one subject. Indeed, it is almost inevitable, according to what God, may He be blessed, established. The whole of creation is such that everything has its opposite, as we know from *The Book of Creation*, and there is nothing in the world the opposite of which lacks reality too, and this surely stems from the wisdom of God, may He be blessed, who is the source of the will that actualizes being. But in actuality no two opposites inhere in the same subject: when it is day it is not night, and when it is night it is not day, which is not the case in the source, where everything is one. Therefore for every new interpretation of the words of the Torah that is brought into the world by a scholar, its opposite must necessarily emerge as well.

And this is the reasoning behind the verse, "the beginning of strife is as when one letteth out water" (Prov. 17:14). Water, that is, the Torah, is such that anyone who opens any gate, who initiates debate on any issue, unleashes strife and controversy. And the Sages, of blessed memory, said: "the beginning of a controversy inaugurates a hundred legal disputes."[97] The explanation is that there are fifty gates [degrees] of understanding, and this is the reason for "forty nine aspects from which it can be declared pure and forty-nine aspects from which it can be declared impure," because the fiftieth degree is unattainable.[98] And here "aspects" connotes 'revelations,' the forty-nine aspects in terms of which the scholar can formulate the reason for his opinion. And forty nine is seven times seven, as for the seven modes of the development of the powers of revelation, and the fiftieth gate is for the understanding in the heart, which cannot be revealed to another at all – the inner feeling that he senses in his heart to be the reason for the declaration [of purity or impurity], since a reason [lit., taste] is altogether impossible to explain or to reveal, as it is said in the Talmud, "What is in the heart, remains in the heart"[99] and cannot be expressed by way of the written word; and so too in speech it is impossible. For speech can only reflect the impression of this reason imprinted on the heart. The power of his speech is in accordance with the feeling in his heart as to the reason, and speech reveals an impression of what is felt in the heart. However, the truth as to the reason that he feels cannot be revealed.

---

96 *Guide for the Perplexed*, III:15.
97 bSanhedrin 7a; the numerical value of the term for strife in the verse from Proverbs, "*madon*," is 100 (40 + 4 + 6 + 50).
98 See bRosh Hashana 21b.
99 bSanhedrin 35a.

225. Mikhtav Mieliahu, part 4, pp. 56–7

It is standard talmudic phraseology to state, "Rabbi A said in the name of Rabbi B" or "some say it in the name of Rabbi A," and so forth. This purpose of this punctiliousness is to prevent the occurrence of changes and substitutions in the transmission of the oral law from generation to generation. And the Talmud states, "one is obliged to use the terminology of his teacher,"[100] for exceptional punctiliousness is indicative of exceptional appreciation. Illustration: when weighing diamonds, people are meticulous to a hair.

With the decline in character and the lessened inner esteem for the Torah, punctiliousness lessened and forgetfulness increased. And the Sages, of blessed memory, said that had Israel heard the entire Torah from the mouth of the Holy One, blessed be He, they would have experienced no forgetfulness,[101] as we just said. Indeed, for human beings, the learning process itself is tantamount to a miracle, since "You bestow sense upon man," but it is a concealed miracle. Learning directly from the mouth of the Almighty, however, is an open miracle, and the great significance of what is learned is clearly perceived, hence forgetfulness is not an issue. And if, in the Mishna, the Talmud and also newer scholarly expositions, such painstaking attention is paid to transmitting the tradition, how much more so is it the case regarding the masoretic text of the Bible, which is also a central component of the oral law received from Moses, who received it from the Almighty.

It did happen that some laws sank into oblivion over time, that is, the finer points lost their clarity, though some of the essentials of the laws, as well as certain details, still remained familiar to them, and they could reconstruct the forgotten parts by inference. In any event, in such cases the Sages turned to Scripture as an exegetical source, since if the exact recollection of the tradition about a given law has, to some degree, lapsed, it no longer has the status of oral law, and it cannot be relied upon in rendering a halakhic decision without corroboration from Scripture.

Even though surely they often still retained the customary practices of the earlier generations with regard to the matter at hand, nevertheless, these practices only had the status of custom and not that of oral law, and as such they are not to be relied upon as anything but customs, and they lack the status of law. And even though it is said that a custom of Israel is binding, this means binding as custom, but not binding as law.

And this is the proper explanation of all that pertains to the controversies among the Sages and the Early Authorities on issues of which they of

---

100 mEduyot 1:3; and see the comments of R. Elijah of Vilna ad loc. on why Hillel was meticulous about using the wording "a *hin* full of drawn water...."
101 Song of Songs Rabbah.

necessity must have had knowledge of how they had been carried out from time immemorial, for example, the controversy between the house of Shammai and the house of Hillel regarding the consanguineous rival[-wive]s, and the controversy between Rashi and Rabbenu Tam regarding phylacteries. For surely there had been an established practice that had been carried out generation after generation, but since they lacked a complete and exact tradition meeting the conditions of exactitude demanded of law, it was deemed to be custom only. For according to Torah law, it is necessary in such cases to revisit and clarify the law, using the authorized methodology, examining [the views of] the Tannaim and the Amoraim by means of exegesis of the written law, and [examining the views of] the Early Authorities [to determine which is best supported] by proofs from the Jerusalem and Babylonian Talmuds, and so on. And since this clarification revealed to them that the law was contrary to the conduct that was customary, they repudiated this customary conduct on the basis of the clarification of the law in accordance with the parameters set out by the Torah, for a judge has only what his own eyes behold.

The parameters of these modes of exegesis of the written law are defined with great exactitude, and in themselves constitute binding law, like all the law received at Sinai; and they were handed down with great exactitude. However, since then we have lost the exact details of the parameters governing what is to be learned by means of the thirty two rules of exegesis used in interpreting the Torah, and we are not permitted to produce our own exegeses and rely on them to in deciding legal matters. And even though, from the numerous examples offered by the Sages, of blessed memory, we seem to be familiar with the modes of exegesis and we might even be able to emulate them by reasoning similarly, nevertheless, should even the most gifted genius in Torah learning offer an exegesis arrived at by his own comparisons and the determinations of his own cognition, it would be regarded as an empty intellectual exercise bereft of any legal value. Sometimes we wonder about the Sages' certitude about a particular exegesis that they had offered for a scriptural passage, because by our lights it seems that the text would allow a number of other interpretations. But the explanation is that they had been handed down the exact method for scriptural exegesis and interpretation, and this method is the sole method of determining the law, to the exclusion of all others.

226. Mikhtav Mieliahu, part 4, p. 355

It should be understood that even according to R. David Kimhi (Radak), it is clear that variant readings did not proliferate by mere chance. Even in the material world, there is no chance, but everything happens according to His laws and righteousness, as He, may He be blessed, in His knowledge, revealed them. This being so, how much more so is it the case that when contending readings pertain to the words of the Torah, generating a controversy for the sake of heaven, it is certainly not by chance. For "God stands in the divine assembly" (Ps. 82:1), and could have made all of them tilt toward deciding in favor of one of the sides, but it was His will, may He be blessed, that there be such a controversy, and both are the words of the living God, and there is divine purpose in God's having brought it about that such controversy exists, and so on. So it is, necessarily, with respect to the variant readings in the Torah and the Prophets, since all transpires by the hand of God, and, as the pure principles of our faith aver, chance is irrelevant. Since it is so, while we may explain to those who are perplexed that a discrepancy between the written text and the way it is read [understood] echoes variants of the text, nonetheless, in any event it is thus by the hand of God, with much design, gravity and judgment (and we can also discern other advantages in this state of affairs), but having said this, we have arrived at the point where both the *keri* [the way the verse is read] and the *ketiv* [the way the verse is written] are true.

227. Shiurim Lezekher Aba Mari, "Two Kinds of Traditions," pp. 228–31

There are two traditions. (a) Tradition pertaining exclusively to the tradition of learning, argumentation, debate and intellectual edification; one says one thing and the other says another, one presents his reasons for his opinion, and the other presents his own, and they take a vote, as described by the Torah in the passage on the rebellious elder (Deut. 17:12); (b) Practical traditions as to the conduct of the entire nation in observing the precepts. And this is based on the verse, "Ask thy father and he will declare unto thee, thine elders and they will tell thee" (Deut. 32:7).

It is well known what transpired between my grandfather R. Joseph Dov Halevi and the Admor of Radzin with regard to the blue thread in the fringes (*tzitzit*). The Rebbe of Radzin introduced this usage and ordered all his followers to add a blue thread to their fringes. The Admor had tried to prove, on the basis of much evidence, that the particular color he used as dye was indeed the biblical purple. R. Joseph Dov argued against him, and said that no amount of evidence or reasoning can prove anything in the realm of the "ask thy father and he will declare unto thee" type of tradition. Here, it is not reason that is the decisive factor, but the tradition itself. This is what the fathers saw, and this is how they conducted themselves, and this is how the sons should conduct themselves.

. . .

Now controversy belongs only to the realm of learning-related tradition. If, for example, the law is transmitted by study and understanding, and it is put into practice only when the student grasps the law and his mind comprehends it, then controversy might be relevant. If one of the scholars does not understand one or another of the laws, and his intellect decides that the law is contrary to it, he is permitted to demur and say, 'I rule differently, for I do not agree.' This is on the basis of the principle that both are the words of the living God, which asserts that the existence of two different aspects of the law constitutes the very essence of the law, even though the law is decided in accordance with the view of only one of them. Disagreements are an integral part of received tradition, and are indeed embraced in the principle that 'the innovative insight that a seasoned scholar will formulate in the future was already told to Moses at Sinai by the Holy One, blessed be He.'

As to tradition regarding actual practice and received classifications, where intellectual judgments make no difference, here controversy is of absolutely no relevance. For example, if someone should come and say that matza is baked, not of wheat, but of rice, or that a certain color is not black but green, or say of what is acknowledged as the seventh day that it is not the Sabbath, his words are surely null and void, invalid and non-existent. And not only that, but furthermore, he would be regarded as a heretic who denied our traditions about practices transmitted to us from generation to generation. And therefore Maimonides states that there is no controversy among the Sages on the interpretations of the Torah that were given to Moses at Sinai – we do not find any controversy at any time from the days of Joshua until Rav Ashi where one side says that "eye for eye" is to be taken literally, or that the "fruit of goodly trees" is the apple – because the traditions on these matters have been handed down by our actual behavior and practices, not merely by study or abstract analysis (though the Gemara does deduce the relevant traditions from scriptural verses). The decisive element is traditional practice as handed down from generation to generation. And in his introduction, Maimonides states: "the proofs were not brought because they had doubts about the matter until they gained knowledge of it through these proofs. But rather, we see, without any doubt, that from the time of Joshua until now, the *etrog* (citron) is ritually taken together with the palm frond, every year, and there is no controversy over this."[102]

And the emphasis here is placed on seeing how the practice is actually carried out, and not on verbal accounts, however logical. And in this vein, explaining the verse "eye for eye" elsewhere in the *Code*, he writes: "Although these rules appear plausible from the context of the written law, and were all made clear by Moses, our teacher, from Mount Sinai, they have all come down to us as law to be applied. For thus did our forebears

---

102 *Commentary on the Mishna*, foreword; the quotation is inexact.

see the law administered in the court of Joshua and in the court of Samuel, the Ramathite, and in every court ever convened from the time of Moses up to the present day."[103] Maimonides emphasizes here that the interpretation is based on "law to be applied" (*halakha lemaase*): on an accepted tradition of actual behavior and practice; "thus have we seen it done in every court from the time of Moses up to the present day." Granted, the Talmud does take the trouble to ground this in the framework of learning-related tradition,[104] and to derive it from Scripture using the accepted modes of halakhic reasoning. But the validity of this law is based on practice, on law to be applied, and therefore it is not subject to controversy, for controversy would, on the contrary, entail denial of the authority of actual practice, which is a fundamental principle.

---

103 *Code*, Laws concerning Wounding and Damaging 1:6.
104 bBaba Kama 83b.

LIST OF SOURCES

Each entry is followed by the numbers of all passages taken from that source.

Akeidat Yitzhak, R. Isaac b. Moses Arama, philosophical commentary on the Torah (Spain–Italy, 1420?–1494), Warsaw 1883. [100]

Arukh Hashulhan, novellae and rulings on the laws of the *Shulhan Arukh*, R. Jehiel Mechal b. Aaron Isaac Halevi Epstein (Russia, 1829–1908), Pietrikov 1906. [19]

Asara Maamarot, Kabbalistic thought, R. Menaham Azariah da Fano (Rama of Fano) (Italy, 1548–1620), with the *Yad Yehuda* commentary, Jerusalem 1988. [103]

Avot de-Rabbi Nathan, tosefta on tractate Avot, Schechter edition, Vienna 1887. [1]

Baalei Brit Avram, Kabbalistic interpretations of the Bible, R. Abraham b. Mordekhai Azoulay (Morocco–Israel, 1570–1643), Vilna 1872. [129]

Babylonian Talmud, Vilna edition. [3, 4, 5, 39, 40, 41, 42, 43, 44, 45, 46, 47, 48, 49, 75, 76, 80, 81, 82, 83, 84, 121, 122, 134, 156, 183, 184, 185, 186, 198, 199]

Beer Hagola, commentary on the legends of the Sages, R. Judah Loew b. Bezalel (Maharal of Prague) (Austria–Poland, c.1525–1609), London 1964. [106]

Beit Elohim, ethics and religious principles, R. Moses b. Joseph di Trani (Mabit) (Salonika–Safed, 1500–1580), Warsaw 1913. [218]

Beit Habehira, commentary on the Talmud, and halakhic rulings, R. Menahem b. Solomon Hameiri (Provence, 1249–1316), Sofer edition, Jerusalem. [54, 159, 174, 213, 214, 215]

Commentary and Rulings of Rabbenu Avigdor, halakhic rulings arranged in the order of the weekly Torah portions, Rabbenu Avigdor (France, 13th c), one of the Tosafists, Jerusalem 1996. [92]

Commentary of the Preacher Rabbenu Yosef Yaavetz of the Spanish Exiles (Spain–Italy, 15th c), Warsaw 1880.[58]

Derekh Eretz Zuta, from the minor tractates of the Talmud, in the Vilna edition of the Talmud. [187]

Derekh Etz Haim, ethics, R. Moses Haim Luzzatto (Italy, 1707–1746), Warsaw 1926 (also found in many editions of *Mesilat Yesharim*). [130]

Derekh Haim, commentary on mAvot, R. Judah Loew b. Bezalel (the Maharal of Prague) (Austria–Poland, c.1525–1609), London 1961. [105]

Drashot Haran, sermons, R. Nissim b. Reuven Gerondi (Spain, 1310–1375?), Feldman edition, Jerusalem 1974. [96]

Drashot Maharal, sermons, R. Judah Loew b. Bezalel (the Maharal of Prague) (Austria–Poland, *c.*1525–1609), London 1964. [107]

Ein Aiya, Commentary on the talmudic legends in the *Ein Yaakov*, R. Abraham Isaac Hakohen Kook (Latvia–Israel, 1865–1935), Jerusalem 1987–1990. [115, 194]

Emunot Vedeiot (Beliefs and Opinions), fundamentals of faith and the Torah, R. Saadia Gaon (Egypt–Babylonia, 882–942), R. Joseph Kafih edition, Jerusalem 1970. [201]

Exodus Rabbah, Romm edition, Vilna 1878. [200]

Genesis Rabbah, Romm edition, Vilna 1878. [181]

Hagahot Harema (Glosses of the Rema), glosses on and additions to the *Shulhan Arukh*, R. Moses Isserles (Poland, 1530?–1572), in the *Shulhan Arukh*. [145]

Hakuzari Hasheini (*Mate Dan*), arguments for the veracity of the oral law, R. David Nieto (Italy–England, 1654–1728), Jerusalem 1958. [220]

Halikhot Olam, rules for interpreting the Talmud, R. Jeshua b. Joseph Halevi (Algiers–Spain, 15th c), Warsaw 1883. [27]

Hasagot Haraavad (Raavad's reservations about Alfasi's *Halakhot*), R. Abraham b. David of Posquières (Raavad) (Provence, *c.*1120–1198), in the Vilna Talmud. [22]

Hibur Hateshuva, halakha, exegesis and ethics pertaining to repentance, R. Menahem b. Solomon Hameiri (Provence, 1249–1316), Sofer edition, 1950. [55]

Hidushei Agadot Maharam Shick, commentary on mAvot, R. Moses Shick (Hungary, 1807–1879), Makhon Yerushalayim edition, Jerusalem 1981. [191]

Hidushei Haramban, novellae on the Talmud, R. Moses b. Nahman (Nahmanides) (Spain–Israel, 1194–1270), Jerusalem 1928. [143]

Hidushei Haritba, novellae on the Talmud, R. Yom Tov of Seville (Spain, *c.*1250–1330), Mosad Harav Kook edition, Jerusalem. [95, 135, 144, 149, 175, 206]

Igeret Rav Sherira Gaon, a responsum on the masoretic chain, from the Sages of the Mishna until the Geonim, R. Sherira Gaon (Babylonia, 906–1006), Levin edition, Haifa 1921. [205]

Jerusalem Talmud, Venice edition, 1523–1524. [38, 74, 77, 133, 197]

Kad Hakemah, sermons on law, ethics, and Kabbala, arranged alphabetically by topic, R. Bahya b. Asher (Spain, 13th c), in *Kitvei Rabeinu Bahya*, Chavel edition, Jerusalem 1970. [189]

Kedushat Levi, Likutim, sermons on the Torah and the Festivals, Haadmor R. Levi Isaac of Berditchev (Galicia–Russia, 1740?–1810), Munkacz 1939. [112]

Klalei Shmuel, rules for interpreting the Talmud, R. Samuel ibn Sid (Sirillio) (Spain–Egypt, 15th–16th c), Sofer edition, Jerusalem 1972. [30]

Kuzari, a defense of the Jewish religion, R. Judah b. Samuel Halevi (Spain, *c.*1075–1141), Even Shmuel edition, 1973. [138]

Lehem Mishne, clarificatory comments on Maimonides' *Code*, R. Abraham b. Moses di Boton (Salonika, 1545?–1588), in the *Code*. [108]

Lev Avot, commentary on tractate Avot, R. Solomon b. Isaac Beit-Halevi (Turkey, 16th c), Salonika 1565. [101]

Leviticus Rabbah, Margaliot edition, Jerusalem 1953–1954. [182]

Maase Efod, Hebrew grammar, R. Isaac b. Moses Profiat Duran (Spain, 14th–15th c), Vienna 1865. [99]

Magen Avot (responsa of Rabbenu Hameiri), a defense of the Provencal customs, R. Menahem b. Solomon Hameiri (Provence, 1249–1316), Jerusalem 1958. [216]

Mahberet Hearukh, biblical lexicon and rules of the Hebrew language, R. Solomon b. Abraham ibn Parhon (Spain–Italy, 12th c), Pressburg 1844. [88]

Mahzor Vitry, halakhic-liturgical compendium, R. Simha b. Samuel of Vitry, a student of Rashi (France, 11th c), Hurwitz edition, Nuremberg 1923. [50]

Maimonides' *Book of Precepts*, an enumeration of the 613 precepts, R. Moses b. Maimon (Spain–Egypt, 1138–1204), Warsaw 1891. [139]

Maimonides' *Code* (*Mishne Tora*), legal codex based on the Mishna and the Talmud, and some post-talmudic enactments and customs, R. Moses b. Maimon (Spain–Egypt, 1138–1204), various editions. [140, 158, 212]

Maimonides' *Commentary on the Mishna*, R. Moses b. Maimon (Spain–Egypt, 1138–1204), R. Joseph Kafih edition, Jerusalem 1963. [209]

Maimonides' *Guide for the Perplexed*, Jewish philosophy, R. Moses b. Maimon (Spain–Egypt, 1138–1204), R. Joseph Kafih edition, Jerusalem 1977. [210, 211]

Megale Amukot, Kabbalistic interpretations of Moses' prayer in the Torah portion "Vaethanan" (252 "*ofanim*"), R. Nathan Neta Shapiro (Poland, 1585–1633), Bnei Brak 1994. [219]

Mekhilta, Horowitz-Rabin edition. [120]

Menorat Hamaor, ethics, R. Isaac Aboab (Spain, 14th c), Mosad Harav Kook edition, Jerusalem 1961. [57]

Mevo Hatalmud (Maharatz Chajes), the foundations of the Talmuds and the comportment of the Sages with respect to halakha, Aggada and exegesis, R. Tzvi Hirsch Chajes (Poland, 1805-1855) in *Kol Sifrei Maharatz Hayut*, Jerusalem 1958. [222]

Mevo Hatalmud of R. Samuel b. Hofni Gaon, introduction to the study of the Mishna and the Talmud, R. Samuel b. Hofni Gaon (Babylonia, d. 1013), in "From the fifth chapter of *Mevo Hatalmud of R. Samuel b. Hofni*," S. Abramson, *Sinai* 88 (1981), pp. 193–218. [203, 204]

Midrash on Psalms, Midrash Shoher Tov on Psalms, Buber edition, Vilna 1891. [6, 79]

Midrash Shmuel, commentary on mAvot, R. Samuel di Uzida (Safed, b. 1540), R. Batzri edition, Makhon Haktav, Jerusalem 1989. [102]

Midrash Tanhuma, Midrash on the Torah, Eshkol edition, Jerusalem 1972. [72]

Mikhtav Mieliahu, reflections and ethics, R. Elijah Dessler (Russia–Israel, 1891–1954), revised seventh edition, Jerusalem 1992. [116, 225, 226]

Milhamot Hashem, defense of Alfasi against the reservations of R. Zerahiya Halevi, author of *Sefer Hamaor*, R. Moses b. Nahman (Ramban; Nahmanides) (Spain–Israel, 1194–1270), in the Vilna edition of the Talmud. [93]

Mishna, Albeck edition, Israel 1957–1958. [21, 36, 37, 177, 178, 179]

Mishnat Hakhamim, commentary on the chapter of the Mishna on the 48 qualifications for acquiring Torah (mAvot), R. Moses b. Jacob Hagiz (Israel, 1672–1751?), Lvov 1906. [65]

New Responsa Ribash, R. Isaac b. Sheshet (Spain–Algiers, 1326–1408), Frankel edition, Munkacz 1901. [56]

Nimukei Yosef, commentary on Alfasi, R. Joseph Habiba (Spain, 15th c), in the Vilna edition of the Talmud. [24]

Noam Vehovlim, responsum of R. Elijah Kapashali (Turkey, 16th c) on a work by R. David Vital, who sought to keep R. Benjamin of Arta, author of *Binyamin Zeev*, from issuing halakhic rulings. Published by Meir Benayahu under the title *Wolves Attacking Benjamin* (Hebrew), Tel-Aviv 1990. [59]

Numbers Rabbah, Romm edition, Vilna 1878. [73, 123]

Olat Reiya, commentary on the prayerbook, R. Abraham Isaac Hakohen Kook (Latvia–Israel, 1865–1935), Jerusalem 1939. [193]

Or Hashem, four essays on Judaism's foundations and principles of faith, R. Hasdai Crescas (Spain, d. 1412), Ferrara 1555. [97]

Or Yisrael, letters on ethical questions, R. Israel b. Zeev Wolf Salanter (Lipkin), (Lithuania–Germany, 1810–1883), compiled by his student R. Isaac Blaser (Lithuania, 1837–1907), Vilna 1900 (new edition in: *Kitvei R. Yisrael Misalant*, ed. Mordekhai Pacter, Jerusalem 1973). [223]

Otzar Hageonim, responsa and commentaries of the Geonim of Babylonia, arranged in the order of the Talmud, edited by R. Benjamin Manasseh Lewin, Haifa-Jerusalem 1928–1942. [86]

Pahad Yitzhak, talmudic encyclopedia, with responsa by Italian rabbinical authorities, R. Isaac Lampronti (Italy, 1679–1756), Venice–Reggio–Leghorn 1750–1840; Lyck–Koenigsburg–Pressburg–Berlin 1864–1888. [34]

Pahad Yitzhak (Hutner), reflections and ethics, R. Isaac Hutner (Lithuania–US, 1907–1980), volume on Hanuka, New York 1964. [118]

Peirushei Haagadot Lerabi Azriel, Kabbalistic commentary on talmudic legends, R. Azriel of Gerona (Spain, 13th c), 2nd Tishby edition, Jerusalem 1983. [126]

Peirushei Mishnat Avot (*Sefer Hamusar*), R. Joseph b. Judah, Maimonides' student (Spain–North Africa, 1140–1220), Berlin 1910. [53]

Peirushei Rabbenu Avraham b. Mordekhai Farissol, commentary on mAvot, R. Abraham Farissol (Provence–Italy, 1451–c.1525), Makhon Tora Shleima, Jerusalem 1969. [11]

Peirushei R. Saadia Gaon on Genesis, R. Saadia Gaon (Egypt–Babylonia, 882–942), Zucker edition, New York 1984. [85, 202]

Pesikta Rabati, Ish-Shalom edition, Vienna 1880. [71, 78]

Petah Einayim, novellae on the Talmud, R. Haim Joseph David Azoulay (Hida) (Israel–Italy, 1724–1806), Jerusalem 1959. [110]

Piskei Riaz, Isaiah b. Elijah di Trani the Younger (Riaz), (Italy, died c.1280), rabbinical scholar; grandson of Isaiah b. Mali di Trani (the Elder). [150, 162]

Pri Tzadik, sermons on the Torah, Haadmor R. Tzadok Hakohen of Lublin (Poland, 1823–1900), Lublin 1901–1934. [192]

Raavad, *Katuv Sham*, R. Abraham b. David of Posquières (Raavad) (Provence, 1120–1198), Raavad's reservations about R. Zerahiya Halevi's *Sefer Hamaor*, Jerusalem 1990. [23]

Raban, halakhic rulings, R. Eliezer b. Nathan of Mainz (Germany, c.1090–c.1170), Warsaw 1905. [157]

Rabbenu Jeruham, including *Toldot Adam Vehava*, rulings and laws, and *Sefer Meisharim*, monetary law, R. Jeruham b. Meshulam (Provence–Spain, c.1290–1350), Venice 1553. [148]

Rashi, Rashi's commentary on the Talmud, R. Solomon b. Isaac (France, 1040–1105), in the Vilna edition of the Talmud. [87, 136, 207]

Resisei Laila, Hasidic thought and reflections, Haadmor R. Tzadok Hakohen of Lublin (Poland, 1823–1900), Lublin 1903. [224]

Responsa Avkat Rokhel, R. Joseph b. Ephraim Caro (Israel, 1488–1575), Leipzig 1859. [170]

Responsa Beit Yosef, R. Joseph b. Ephraim Caro (Israel, 1488–1575), Jerusalem 1960. [12]

Responsa Binyamin Zeev, R. Benjamin b. Mattathias (Greece, 16th c), Jerusalem 1959. [163, 169]

Responsa Darkhei Noam, R. Mordekhai b. Judah Halevi (Egypt–Israel, d. 1684?), Venice 1697. [14]

Responsa Ginat Vradim, R. Abraham b. Mordekhai Halevi (Egypt, 17th c), Constantinople 1716–1717. [33, 64]

Responsa Hatam Sofer, R. Moses Sofer (Schreiber) (Germany–Hungary, 1762–1839), Jerusalem 1982. [17]

Responsa Havat Yair, R. Yair Haim b. Moses Samson Bacharach (Germany, 1638–1702), Lvov 1894. [63, 221]

Responsa Hut Hashani, responsa and reservations about the book *Nahlat Shiva*, R. Samuel b. Isaac and his son R. Moses Samson, and his grandson R. Yair Haim Bacharach (author of *Responsa Havat Yair*), (Germany, 1638–1702), Munkacz 1896. [62]

Responsa Igrot Moshe, R. Moses Feinstein (Lithuania–US, 1895–1986), New York 1959–1985. [68, 119, 195]

Responsa Mabit, R. Moses b. Joseph di Trani (Salonika–Safed, 1500–1580), Lvov 1861. [151, 172]

Responsa Maharam Mintz, responsa and addenda from mss, including the pamphlet "Three Branches," R. Moses Mintz (Ashkenaz, 1415?–1480?), Jerusalem 1991. [10]

Responsa Maharashdam, R. Samuel b. Moses di Modena (Salonika, 1506–1589), Lvov 1862. [146, 152]

Responsa Mahari Ben Lev, R. Joseph b. Lev (Turkey, 1505?–1580), Bnei Brak 1988. [171]

Responsa Maharik, R. Joseph b. Solomon Colon (France-Italy, c. 1420-1480), Jerusalem 1984. [25, 26]

Responsa Maharshag, R. Shimon Grunfeld (Hungary, d. 1930), Berdiov 1931. [154, 173]

Responsa Maimonides, R. Moses b. Maimon (Spain-Egypt, 1138-1204), Blau edition, Jerusalem 1986. [141, 142]

Responsa Min Hashamayim, R. Jacob of Marvège (France, late 12th–13th c), Margaliot edition, Jerusalem, n.d. [90]

Responsa Noda Biyehuda, R. Ezekiel b. Judah Landau (Prague, 1713–1793), [second ed.], Vilna 1928. [15]

Responsa Parashat Mordekhai, R. Mordekhai b. Abraham Benet (Hungary–Moravia, 1753–1829), Sighet 1889. [153]

Responsa Piskei Uziel Besheeilot Hazman, R. Ben Zion Meir Hai b. Joseph Rafael Uziel (Israel, 1880–1953), Jerusalem 1977. [147]

Responsa Pnei Yehoshua, R. Joshua b. Joseph of Cracow (Poland, 1578–1648), Lvov 1860. [61]

Responsa Radakh, R. David b. Haim Hakohen of Corfu (Corfu, d. 1530), Ostraha 1834. [167, 168]

Responsa Radbaz, R. David b. Solomon ibn Avi Zimra (Spain–Egypt–Israel, 1479–1573), Warsaw 1882. [31, 128, 164, 165]

Responsa Rashi, R. Solomon b. Isaac (France, 1040–1105), Elfenbein edition, New York 1943. [137]

Responsa Rid (Teshuvot Harid), R. Isaiah di Trani the Elder (Italy, 12–13th c), Jerusalem 1967. [7, 8]

Responsa Smikha Lehaim, R. Haim b. Jacob Palogi (Turkey, 1788–1868), Salonika 1826. [18]

Responsa Sridei Esh, R. Yehiel Jacob Weinberg (Lithuania–Germany–Switzerland, 1885–1966), Jerusalem 1977. [20, 155]

Responsa Tashbetz, R. Shimon b. Tzemah Duran (Rashbatz), (Spain–Algiers, 1361–1444), containing *Hut Hameshulash*, responsa of the halakhic authorities of Algiers (16th c). The work is divided into three columns, the first containing the responsa of R. Solomon Duran, the second, those of R. Solomon Seror, and the third, the responsa of R. Abraham ibn Tawa. Lvov 1891. [13, 32, 166]

Responsa Trumat Hadeshen, R. Israel b. Petahia Isserlein (Ashkenaz, 1390–1460), Warsaw 1882. [9]

Responsa Yosef Ometz, R. Haim Joseph David Azoulay (Hida) (Israel–Italy, 1724–1806), Jerusalem 1986. [111]

Responsa Zivhei Tzedek, R. Abdallah Abraham Joseph Somekh (Iraq, 1813–1889), Baghdad 1904. [113]

Rosh, rulings arranged in the order of the Talmud, R. Asher b. Yehiel (Ashkenaz–Spain, 1250?–1327), in the Vilna edition of the Talmud. [176]

Ruah Haim, commentary on mAvot, R. Haim of Volozhin (Lithuania, 1749–1821), Vilna 1859. [16]

Sdei Hemed, encyclopedia of halakha, Aggada, and halakhic decision-making rules, R. Haim Hezekiah b. Rafael Elijah Medini (Israel–Turkey–Crimea, 1832–1904), Warsaw 1891–1912. [35]

Sefer Hahinukh, on the 613 precepts, written anonymously by a student of the Rashba (Spain, 13th c), Eshkol edition, Jerusalem 1961. [127, 161]

Sefer Haikarim (The Book of Principles), an examination of the principles of Judaism, R. Joseph Albo (Spain, 15th c), Warsaw 1877. [217]

Sefer Hakabala, a history of the Sages from Adam to the author's generation, R. Abraham b. David ibn Daud Halevi (Spain, *c.*1100–*c.*1180), in *Seder Hahakhamim Vekorot Hayamim*, Oxford 1888. [208]

Sefer Hamanhig, rulings and customs, R. Avraham b. Nathan Hayarhi, (Provence–Spain, 1155–1215), Jerusalem 1978. [89]

Sefer Hanitzahon, replies to Christian polemics, R. Yomtov Lippmann Mühlhausen (Prague, 14th–15th c), Altdorf–Nuremberg 1644. [98]

Sefer Harimon, Kabbalistic rationales for the precepts, R. Moses b. Shem-Tov de Leon (Spain, 1240–1305), Dorit Cohen-Aloro edition, Jerusalem 1987. [94]

Sefer Hasidim, legal rulings and customs of the Hasidei Ashkenaz movement, R. Judah b. Samuel Hehasid (the Pious) of Regensburg (Ashkenaz, d. 1217), R. Reuben Margaliot edition, Jerusalem 1957. [51]

Sefer Mitzvot Gadol (*Semag*), on the 613 precepts, R. Moses b. Jacob of Coucy (France, 13th c), Venice 1547. [160]

Sheeirit Yosef, rules for interpreting the Mishna and the Talmud, R. Joseph ibn Verga (Spain–Turkey, d. 1559), Warsaw 1909. [28, 29]

Sheiltot, sermons on the halakha and Aggada of the weekly Torah potions, R. Aha of Shabha (Babylonia–Israel, 680?–752?), with the *Haamek Sheeila* commentary, Vilna 1861–1867. [188]

Shiurei Daat, ethics and contemplations, R. Joseph Judah Leib Bloch (Lithuania, 1860–1930), Jerusalem 1989. [117]

Shiurim Lezekher Aba Mari, lectures on various subjects, R. Joseph Dov Halevi Soloveitchik (United States, 1903–1993), Jerusalem 1983. [227]

Shlom Yehuda, novellae on Moed, R. Eliezer Manoah Polchinsky (Israel, 20th c), Jerusalem 1962. [67]

Shnei Luhot Habrit (*Shela*), ethics and Kabbala, R. Isaiah b. Abraham Halevi Horowitz (Poland–Israel, 1565?–1630), Warsaw 1863. [60]

Sifre Deuteronomy, Tannaitic Midrash on Deuteronomy, Finkelstein edition, Berlin 1940. [131, 132]

Song of Songs Rabbah, Dunsky edition, Jerusalem 1980. [2]

Teshuvot Ufsakim Raavaad, R. Abraham b. David of Posquières (Raavad) (Provence, *c.*1120–1198), R. Joseph Kapih edition, Jerusalem 1991. [52]

Tosafot R. Peretz, R. Peretz b. Elijah of Corbeil (France, 13th c). [91]

Tosefta, Zuckermandel edition, Vienna–Berlin 1877–1880. [69, 180, 196]

Tzidkat Hatzadik, contemplations and reflections, Haadmor R. Tzadok Hakohen of Lublin (Poland, 1823–1900), Lublin 1913. [66]

Vayaas Avraham, prayer customs of R. Abraham of Chechov, followed by *Kuntres Pri Haaretz* (responsa), R. Menahem Mendel Haim Landau (Poland, 1862–1935), Lodz 1936. [114]

Yam Shel Shlomo, novellae on the Talmud, R. Solomon Luria (Maharshal) (Poland, 1510–1574), Stettin 1861. [104]

Yearot Dvash, sermons, R. Jonathan Eibeschutz (Poland–Germany, d. 1764), Sulzbach 1779. [109, 190]

Zohar, Margaliot edition, Jerusalem 1956–1964. [124, 125]

APPENDIX OF HEBREW SOURCES

1. אבות דרבי נתן, נוסח א, א

מעשה שאירע ברבי יאשיה וברבי מתיא בן חרש, שהיו שניהם יושבים
ועוסקין בדברי תורה, פירש רבי יאשיה לדרך ארץ. אמר ליה רבי מתיא בן
חרש: רבי, מה לך לעזוב דברי אלהים חיים ולשטוף בדרך ארץ? ואף על פי
שאתה רבי ואני תלמידך, אין טוב לעזוב דברי אלהים חיים ולשטוף בדרך
ארץ. אמרו: כל זמן שיושבין ועוסקין בתורה היו עושין מקנאין זה לזה,
וכשנפטרין דומין כשהן אוהבים מנעוריהם.

2. שיר השירים רבה, פרשה ו, יד (עמ׳ קמו)

["ששים המה מלכות ושמונים פילגשים ועלמות אין מספר, אחת היא יונתי
תמתי" (שיר השירים ו, ח-ט)] רבי יצחק פתר קרייה בפרשיותיה של תורה:
"ששים המה מלכות" – אלו ששים מסכתות של הלכות; "ושמונים פלגשים"
– אלו שמונים פרשיות שבתורת כהנים; "ועלמות אין מספר" – אין קץ
לתוספות; "אחת היא" – הן חולקים אלו עם אלו, וכולהון דורשין מטעם
אחד, מהלכה אחת, מגזירה שוה, מקל וחומר.

רבי יודן ברבי אלעי פתר קרייה בעץ החיים ובגן עדן: "ששים המה מלכות"
– ששים חבורות של צדיקים שיושבות בגן עדן תחת עץ החיים ועוסקות
בתורה... "ושמונים פילגשים" – אלו שמונים חבורות בינוניות שיושבות
ועוסקות בתורה חוץ לעץ החיים; "ועלמות אין מספר" – אין קץ לתלמידים.
יכול שהן חלוקין זה עם זה? תלמוד לומר "אחת היא יונתי תמתי" – כולן
דורשין מטעם אחד, מהלכה אחת, מגזירה שוה אחת, מקל וחומר.

3. בבלי, קידושין ל, א-ב

תנו רבנן: "ושננתם" (דברים ו, ז) – שיהו דברי תורה מחודדים בפיך, שאם
יאמר לך אדם דבר – אל תגמגם ותאמר לו, אלא אמור לו מיד... ואומר
"אשרי הגבר אשר מלא את אשפתו מהם לא יבושו כי ידברו את אויבים
בשער" (תהלים קכז, ה). מאי "את אויבים בשער"? אמר רבי חייא בר אבא:
אפילו האב ובנו, הרב ותלמידו, שעוסקין בתורה בשער אחד, נעשים אויבים
זה את זה ואינם זזים משם עד שנעשים אוהבים זה את זה, שנאמר "את
והב בסופה" (במדבר כא, יד) – אל תקרי "בסופה" אלא "בסופה".

287

4. בבלי, חגיגה ג, א-ב

תנו רבנן: מעשה ברבי יוחנן בן ברוקה ורבי אלעזר (בן) חסמא שהלכו
להקביל פני רבי יהושע בפקיעין. אמר להם: מה חידוש היה בבית המדרש
היום? אמרו לו: תלמידיך אנו, ומימיך אנו שותין. אמר להם: אף על פי כן,
אי אפשר לבית המדרש בלא חידוש. שבת של מי היתה? שבת של רבי אלעזר
בן עזריה היתה. ובמה היתה הגדה היום? אמרו לו: בפרשת הקהל. ומה דרש
בה? "הקהל את העם האנשים והנשים והטף" (דברים לא, יב) – אם אנשים
באים ללמוד, נשים באות לשמוע, טף למה באין? כדי ליתן שכר למביאיהן.
אמר להם: מרגלית טובה היתה בידכם ובקשתם לאבדה ממני?!

ועוד דרש: "את ה' האמרת היום וה' האמירך היום" (דברים כו, יז) – אמר
להם הקדוש ברוך הוא לישראל: אתם עשיתוני חטיבה אחת בעולם, ואני
אעשה אתכם חטיבה אחת בעולם. אתם עשיתוני חטיבה אחת בעולם,
דכתיב "שמע ישראל ה' אלהינו ה' אחד" (דברים ו, ד); ואני אעשה אתכם
חטיבה אחת בעולם שנאמר: "ומי כעמך ישראל גוי אחד בארץ" (דברי הימים
א יז, כא).

ואף הוא פתח ודרש: "דברי חכמים כַּדָּרְבֹנוֹת וכמסמרות נטועים בעלי
אֲסֻפּוֹת נתנו מרועה אחד" (קהלת יב, יא) – למה נמשלו דברי תורה לדרבן?
לומר לך: מה דרבן זה מכוין את הפרה לתלמיה להוציא חיים לעולם, אף
דברי תורה מכוונין את לומדיהן מדרכי מיתה לדרכי חיים. אי מה דרבן זה
מטלטל אף דברי תורה מטלטלין? תלמוד לומר "מסמרות". אי מה מסמר
זה חסר ולא יתר אף דברי תורה חסירין ולא יתירין? תלמוד לומר "נטועים"
– מה נטיעה זו פרה ורבה אף דברי תורה פרין ורבין. "בעלי אסופות" – אלו
תלמידי חכמים שיושבין אסופות אסופות ועוסקין בתורה. הללו מטמאין
והללו מטהרין, הללו אוסרין והללו מתירין, הללו פוסלין והללו מכשירין.
שמא יאמר אדם היאך אני למד תורה מעתה? תלמוד לומר: כולם "נתנו
מרועה אחד" – אל אחד נתנן, פרנס אחד אמרן, מפי אדון כל המעשים ברוך
הוא, דכתיב "וידבר אלהים את כל הדברים האלה" (שמות כ, א). אף אתה
עשה אזניך כאפרכסת, וקנה לך לב מבין לשמוע את דברי מטמאים ואת
דברי מטהרים, את דברי אוסרין ואת דברי מתירין, את דברי פוסלין ואת
דברי מכשירין.

בלשון הזה אמר להם: אין דור יתום שרבי אלעזר בן עזריה שרוי בתוכו.

5. בבלי, בבא מציעא פד, א

יומא חד הוה קא סחי רבי יוחנן בירדנא, חזייה ריש לקיש ושוור לירדנא אבתריה, אמר ליה: "חילך לאורייתא". אמר ליה: "שופרך לנשי". אמר ליה: "אי הדרת בך יהיבנא לך אחותי, דשפירא מינאי". קביל עליה. בעי למיהדר לאתויי מאניה ולא מצי הדר. אקרייה ואתנייה, ושווייה גברא רבא.

יומא חד הוו מפלגי בי מדרשא: "הסייף והסכין והפגיון והרומח ומגל יד ומגל קציר, מאימתי מקבלין טומאה? משעת גמר מלאכתן". ומאימתי גמר מלאכתן? רבי יוחנן אומר "משיצרפם בכבשן", ריש לקיש אמר "משיצחצחן במים". אמר ליה: "לסטאה בלסטיותיה ידע". אמר ליה: "ומאי אהנת לי? התם רבי קרו לי, הכא רבי קרו לי". אמר ליה: "אהנאי לך דאקרבינך תחת כנפי השכינה". חלש דעתיה דרבי יוחנן. חלש ריש לקיש. אתאי אחתיה קא בכיא, אמרה ליה: "עשה בשביל בני"! אמר לה: "עָזְבָה יְתֹמֶיךָ אֲנִי אֲחַיֶּה" (ירמיה מט, יא). "עשה בשביל אלמנותי"! אמר לה: "וְאַלְמְנֹתֶיךָ עָלַי תִּבְטָחוּ" (שם).

נח נפשיה דרבי שמעון בן לקיש, והוה קא מצטער רבי יוחנן בתריה טובא. אמרו רבנן: מאן ליזיל ליתביה לדעתיה? ניזיל רבי אלעזר בן פדת דמחדדין שמעתתיה. אזל יתיב קמיה. כל מילתא דהוה אמר רבי יוחנן אמר ליה "תניא דמסייעא לך". אמר: את כבר לקישא? בר לקישא כי הוה אמינא מילתא, הוי מקשי לי עשרין וארבע קושייתא ומפרקינא ליה עשרין וארבעה פרוקי וממילא רווחא שמעתא, ואת אמרת "תניא דמסייע לך", אטו לא ידענא דשפיר קאמינא?! הוה קא אזיל וקרע מאניה וקא בכי ואמר: "היכא את בר לקישא?! היכא את בר לקישא?!". והוה קא צווח עד דשף דעתיה [מיניה]. בעו רבנן רחמי עליה ונח נפשיה.

6. מדרש תהלים, קד (כב)

"זה הים גדול ורחב ידים" (תהלים קד, כה), זו תורה, שנאמר "ארוכה מארץ מדה ורחבה מני ים" (איוב יא, ט). "שם רמש ואין מספר" (תהלים שם, שם), אלו המסכתות; ויש אומרים: אלו המשניות דבר קפרא ודרב חייא ודרבנן בבלאי. "חיות קטנות עם גדולות" (שם), אלו התלמידים הקטנים עם הגדולים. "שם אניות יהלכון" (שם שם, כו), אלו בני התלמידים, זה אומר טהור וזה אומר טמא, דמנהגין לעלמא כספינתא הדא.

7. שו״ת הרי״ד, א (עמ׳ ו-ז)

ואל תסברו מפני שאני חפץ לקיים דבר המורה אני נזקק לפרש כן, שהרי כמה עמודי עולם חולקים עליו ואומרים דכולה שאיבה כשירה מן התורה ואינה פסולה אלא מדרבנן. ואפילו אם לא היה אדם גדול חולק עליו בזה, אני מה שנראה לי להוכיח מתוך הספר אני כותב. ואל תחזיקוני בזה כזהוהי הלב, כי מכיר אני בעצמי שצפורנן של אותם הרבנים הראשונים הקדושים, יפה מכרסינן, ולא לשומרי פתח מדרשם. אך זה יש, כי כל דבר שאינו נראה לי מתוך הספר, אי אמרה יהושע בן נון לא צייתנא ליה, ואיני נמנע מלכתוב מה שנראה לי. כי כך דרך התלמוד, לא נמנעו דרך אחרוני האמוראים מלדבר על הראשונים וגם על התנאים, וכמה משניות סתרו מעיקרם וכמה דברי רבים בטלו ופסקו הלכה כיחיד. כל שכן שבדבר זה חולקים רבנים גדולים, ויש לנו לתור ולחקור מתוך הספר הראיות ברורות ולראות כמי ההלכה נוטה, ואין בנו כח ודעת לשקול בפלס הרים מי גדול מחבירו. הילכך נניח הרבנים ההמה, עליהם השלום, בכבודם, ונחזור לבינת הספרים לראות להיכן הדין נוטה.

8. שו״ת הרי״ד, סב

תחלת כל דבר אני משיב לאדוני על מה שכתבתה אלי, שלא אחלוק על הרב הגדול רבינו יצחק זצ״ל. חלילה לי מעשות זאת ולא עלתה במחשבה כחולק עליו, ומה אני נחשב, פרעוש אחד כתרגומו, כנגד תלמידו אף כי בדבר אחרי המלך. אך זאת אתי, כל דבר שאינו נראה בעיני אי אמרה יהושע בן נון לא צייתנא ליה, ואיני נמנע מלדבר עליו מה שייראה לי לפי מיעוט שכלי, ואני מקיים עלי מקרא זה ״ואדברה בעדותיך נגד מלכים ולא אבוש״ (תהלים קיט, מו).

ועדי בשחק נאמן סלה, שאף במקום שנראה לי שאני אומר יפה על כל אחד מדברי רבותינו הראשונים ז״ל, חלילה שיזיחתני לבי לומר ״אף חכמתי עמדה לי״, אלא אני דן בעצמי משל הפילוסופים. שמעתי מחכמי הפילוסופים: שאלו לגדול שבהם ואמרו לו: הלא אנחנו מודים שהראשונים חכמו והשכילו יותר ממנו, והלא אנחנו מודים שאנו מדברים עליהם וסותרים דבריהם בהרבה מקומות והאמת אתנו, היאך יכון הדבר הזה? השיבם אמר להם: מי צופה למרחוק הננס או הענק? הוי אומר הענק שעיניו עומדות במקום גבוה יותר מן הננס. ואם תרכיב הננס על צוארי הענק, מי צופה יותר למרחוק? הוי אומר הננס שעיניו גבוהות עכשיו יותר מעיני הענק. כך אנחנו ננסים רוכבים על צוארי הענקים מפני שראינו חכמתם ואנו

מעניקים עליה, ומכח חכמתם חכמנו לומר כל מה שאנו אומרים ולא שאנו גדולים מהם.

ואם זה באנו לומר שלא נדבר על דברי רבותינו הראשונים, אם כן במקום שאנו רואים שזה חולק על זה וזה אוסר וזה מתיר, אנו על מי נסמוך, הנוכל לשקול בפלס הרים וגבעות במאזנים ולומר שזה גדול מזה, שנבטל דברי זה מפני זה? הא אין לנו אלא לחקור אחרי דבריהם, שאילו ואילו דברי אלהים חיים הן, ולפלפל ולהעמיק מכח דבריהם להיכן הדין נוטה, שכך עשו חכמי המשנה והתלמוד, לא נמנעו מעולם האחרונים מלדבר על הראשונים ומלהכריע ביניהם ומלסתור דבריהם. וכמה משניות סתרו האמוראים לומר שאין הלכה כמותם. וגדולה החכמה מן החכם, ואין חכם שינקה מן השגיאות, שאין החכמה תמימה בלתי ליי'י לבדו.

9. שו"ת תרומת הדשן, פסקים וכתבים, רלח

אמנם מה שכתבת, אם אין לתלמיד רשות לחלוק על רבו באיזה פסק והוראה אם יש לו ראיות מן הספר ופסקי גאונים הפך מדעת הרב. נראה ודאי אם הוראות ברורות קצת וצורתא דשמעתא משמע כדברי התלמיד, למה לא יחלוק? כך היתה דרכה של תורה מימי התנאים, רבינו הקדוש חלק בכמה מקומות על אביו ועל רבי רשב"ג. באמוראים, רבא היה חולק בכמה דוכתי על רבה שהיה רבו, כדאיתא במרדכי פרק כיצד הרגל. בגאונים, אשירי חולק בכמה דוכתין אמהר"ם שהיה רבו מובהק. אין לי לבאר יותר מזה, כי דברים אלו צריכין תלמוד מפה אל פה. נאום הקטן והצעיר שבישראל.

10. שו"ת מהר"ם מינץ, צט

על דבר התעוררות מדנים ועסק ריב אשר נפל בין תרי גברי באיטליא, מהר"ר קוזי והנבחר ויץ כץ וצירופיהן. ראיתי כמה דיוטאות נשתפכו וקולמוסין נשתברו ונייירות הושחרו משני הצדדים, וכן באו הדברים לפני רבנן בארץ שיחיו, כל אחד כתב דעתו לפי שכלו ודעתו. יש מהן לחד גיסא ויש מהן לאידך גיסא, מר יהיב טעמא למלתיה ומר יהיב טעמא למילתיה, כל אחד ואחד לפי השגתו, ואלו ואלו דברי אלהים חיים. דתנו רבנן בפרק קמא דחגיגה (ג, ב): מעשה ברבי יוחנן בן ברוקא ורבי אליעזר בן חסמא כו'. אף הוא פתח ואמר "דברי חכמים כדרבונות" כו' כולם "נתנו מרועה אחד" למה נמשל דברי תורה כו' "בעלי אסופות" אסופים ועוסקים בדברי תורה, הללו מטהרין והללו מטמאין הללו פוסלין והללו מכשירין הללו אוסרין

והללו מתירין. ואם תאמר היאך אנו לומדין תורה מעתה תלמוד לומר כולם "נתנו מרועה אחד" כו' ופרנס אחד אמרן כו' מפי אדון כל המעשים, כאשר פירש רש"י הטעם בפרק אף על פי (כתובות נז, א). וכן יש כמה וכמה דינים שיש סברות וראיות לכאן ולכאן בלי הכרחה ומופת, אך כל אדם יש לו שכל העיוני להוציא לאור ההווים בדמיון מן הכח אל הפועל.

לכן כל תלמיד חכם דגמר וסבר ונקט רשותא מריש גלותא וניתן מקל ורצועה בידו, יש לו רשות לייסר מורדים ולהדריך פושעים לגזור ולהחרים ולנדויי למיגדר מילתא, לפי העניין וצורך שעה לפי דעתו, וכדי לקיים מצות עשה דהוכח תוכיח כו' המוטל עליו, וכדבעינן לפרושי לקמן אי"ה יתברך. וכדאמרינן בפרק קמא דסנהדרין (סנהדרין ו, ב): שמא יאמר הדיין מה לי בצער הזה, תלמוד לומר "וְעִמָּכֶם בדבר המשפט" (דברי הימים ב יט, ו), אין לדיין אלא מה שעיניו רואות. ואשרי לו שלא ישא פנים, ודינו דין היכא דלא טעה בדבר משנה או בשיקול הדעת.

וכן היה פלוגתא דתנאי או אמוראי ובעלי תוספות והגאונים אשר היה פלוגתא ביניהם, הן בדיני ממונות או בגיטין וקידושין ושאר מילי, הן על דינין בלא מעשה או על מעשה הבא לפניהם. ולא מצינו כת אחת שזלזל כת אחרת שכנגדו או מילט לייט מאן דכנגדו פסק. וכן היה במדינה בכהאי גוונא כמה מחלוקיות, אשר יש מרבותי שכתבו לזכות ראובן וכתבו גזירות ומרורות על שמעון, ויש שכתבו לזכות שמעון וכתבו מרורות על ראובן, וכל חד יהיב טעמא למלתייהו. ולא חזינא שום זילותא או לטותא שכתבו רבנן זה על זה או לפייס אותו שנכתב עליו מרורות. וכן הדין נותן מטעם גלויים וידועים לכל בעל שכל, וכאשר ביארתי במכתבי הראשון.

11. פירושי רבינו אברהם פריצול, אבות ה, כב

עניין המחלוקת הזה הנזכר הנה, ירצה בו התנא על מחלוקת למודי, שנופל בכל יום בין התלמידים ומלמדי התורה שתמיד נמשך המנהג להתקוטט יחדו ולכזב דברי חברו באי זה אופן שיהיה. ולזאת זכר התנא, כי כאשר יהיה המחלוקת זה עם זה בחקירת דברים התוריים לשם שמים להבין הדין, שסופו להתקיים בתוך המלמדים, ולהתבונן בחלוק והפרש דעותיהם, אחרי שהוא לשם שמים להתבונן בדעות התורה, לפי מה שיובן ממנה להוציא לאור משפט, כי יש בה תכונות חלוקות ונפרדות, כאמרו: "הֲלֹא כֹה דְבָרִי כָאֵשׁ" (ירמיה כג, כט).

12. שו"ת בית יוסף, דין מים שאין להם סוף, א (עמ' שמג)

כתב: "ואני תמה על צדקת לב החכם וישרות לבו איך התיר לעצמו להשיג
נגד דברי קדמונים ולבטל דבריהם לדעתו, כי היה ראוי לחשוב שלא יוכל
הוא להשיג עליהם". עד כאן.

טענה זו אינה טענה לפני יודעי דת ודין, כי כך היא דרכה של תורה בחכמי
התלמוד ובכל הדורות של החכמים הבאים אחריהם, והם ותלמידיהם
ותלמידי תלמידיהם השותים בצמא את דבריהם, להשיג האחרונים על
הראשונים ותלמידים על רבותיהם. ולהיות הדבר מבואר מאד אין להאריך
בו.

13. שו"ת התשב"ץ, חוט המשולש, הטור השלישי, לה

אלא שדבריו בתשובה זו עצמה איכא למידק. חדא, במה שנתן טעם שלא
לסמוך על הרמב"ם ז"ל מפני שחלקו עליו חכמי ישראל. והלא זה תלמודנו
תנאים ואמוראים חולקים בכל מקום, וכן הגאונים והפוסקים ז"ל תמיד
חולקים, הללו אוסרין והללו מתירין הללו מטמאין והללו מטהרין. ותורתינו
הקדושה הקדימה תקנה לזה במאמרה "אחרי רבים להטות" (שמות כג, ב),
ואמרה "כי יִפָּלֵא ממך דבר למשפט" וכו' (דברים יז, ח), דקמי שמיא גליא
שיחלקו החכמים בדעותיהם בהבנת פרטי הדינים ומצות התורה, שתהיה
ההכרעה על פי הרוב.

14. שו"ת דרכי נעם, אבן העזר, סד

והנה פִּי כְּפִיו בהיתר העגונה הזאת כהלכתיה דמר וכטעמיה, ואם בקצת
מהטעמים תטה אשורי מיני הדרך של הרב המורה השם ישמור אותו, לא
שרצוני חס ושלום לחלוק עליו, כי אם כך היא דרכה של תורה ו"את והב
בסופה" (במדבר כא, יד).

15. שו"ת נודע ביהודה, מהדורה תנינא, אורח חיים, נד

הגיעני מכתבו מלא השגות על חיבורי "נודע ביהודה". ודין הניין לי, כי
מתוכו ראיתי ששוקד על חיבורי בהתמדה. ואף כי ידו הדה וחרבו חרב חדה,
כוונתו רצויה אצלי, כי ראיתי שכל קושיותיו על אדני היושר בנוים, לא
כמבקש לקנתר בדברים דחויים, וכל קושיותיו לפום ריהטא קושיות
עצומות ופיו פתח החכמות. ואף כי באמת יש פירכא לכל דבריו, כך דרכה
של תורה, וממילא רוחא שמעתתא ויוצאת הלכה ברורה.

16. רוח חיים, אבות א, ד

יהי ביתך בית ועד כו'. יתכן לפרש, כי בארבעים ושמונה דברים שהתורה
נקנית בהם, כמבואר לקמן (אבות ו), אחד מהם הוא המחכים את רבותיו על
ידי שאלותיו החריפים וממילא רווחא שמעתתא. והנה הלימוד נקרא
מלחמה, כמו שאמרו "מלחמתה של תורה", אם כן גם התלמידים לוחמים
יקראו, וכמו שאמרו חז"ל (בבלי, קידושין ל, ב): "לא יבושו וגו' כי ידברו את
אויבים בשער", אפילו אב ובנו הרב ותלמידו נעשו אויבים זה את זה ואינם
זזים משם כו'. ואסור לו לתלמיד לקבל דברי רבו כשיש לו קושיות עליהם,
ולפעמים יהיה האמת עם התלמיד, וכמו שעץ קטן מדליק את הגדול. וזה
שאמר "יהי ביתך בית ועד לחכמים והוי מתאבק", מלשון "ויאבק איש עמו"
(בראשית לב, כה), שהוא ענין התאבקות מלחמה, כי מלחמת מצוה היא. וכן
אנו נגד רבותינו הקדושים אשר בארץ ונשמתם בשמי מרום, המחברים
המפורסמים, וספריהם אתנו, הנה על ידי הספרים אשר בבתינו, בתינו הוא
בית ועד לחכמים אלה, הוזהרנו גם כן וניתן לנו רשות להתאבק וללחום
בדבריהם ולתרץ קושייתם, ולא לישא פני איש רק לאהוב האמת. אבל עם
כל זה יזהר בנפשו מלדבר בגאוה וגודל לבב, באשר מצא מקום לחלוק
וידמה כי גדול הוא כרבו או כמחבר הספר אשר הוא משיג עליו, וידע בלבבו
כי כמה פעמים לא יבין דבריו וכוונתו, ולכן יהיה אך בענוה יתירה, באמרו
אם איני כדאי אך תורה היא וכו'. וזהו שאמר "הוי מתאבק" כנ"ל, אך
בתנאי, "בעפר רגליהם", רוצה לומר בענוה והכנעה ולדון לפניהם בקרקע.

17. שו"ת חתם סופר, אבן העזר א, קנא

ולא אמנע להודיע לפאר רום מעלתו שיש בלבי עליו על אשר האריך להתנצל
לפני על שבא להשיב על דברי. וכי כך אני בעיניו חס וחלילה? הלא כך היא
דרכה של תורה מעולם, וזה בונה וזה סותר, ומי יחוש לזה.

18. שו"ת סמיכה לחיים, אבן העזר, ט (נו ע"ד – נז ע"ד)

והמפורסמות אינן צריכות ראיה, שהרי כל ספרי הפוסקים הראשונים
והאחרונים מלאים מזה שהפוסק הראשון פוסק הדין ועושה מעשה, ואחריו
לו קם בית דין אחר ומדקדק בדבר ופוסק להפך על פי ראיותיו המספיקות,
וסותר פסק דין מבית דין הראשון, והכל לשם שמים. אף על פי שהראשונים
כמלאכים, אנן סהדי דאינהו גופייהו ניחא להו בהכי, ומידת קונם יש בהם
להודות ולשבח: "נצחוני בני" על דרך אמת. ועינינו הרואות מעשים בכל יום

במקומינו זה ובכל אתר ואתר, דפוסקים רבני האחרונים הפך פסק דינם של הראשונים...

ולעניות דעתי אחרי המחילה רבתי בנשיקת ידיו ורגלי קדשו, לא הבנתי דבריו כלל, דאיך יתכן לומר כן על מי שהוא תלמיד חכם ורב מומחה ופקיע ויודע שחביריו טעה בדין, או שיש עליו טענה על פסק דין ולכן הוא פוסק להפך ממה שפסק הרב שכנגדו, שיהיה חייב נדוי?! וחלילה וחס על טובי העיר שיכתבו ויחתמו בשטר הקבלה כדבר הזה, כי בודאי הגמור דלא כיוונו לזה כלל. וגם אינו נכנס זה במשמעות הלשון שכתבו "שיתריז כנגדו", כי אם דוקא למי שמתריז לנגדו באפיקירותא וזלזול ולא ציית דינא, ומפקפק בדינו בדברים רקים מבלי דעת, במשאות שוא ומדוחים. ברם אם הוא תלמיד חכם וטוען כנגדו בדברים טובים ונכונים בטוב טעם ודעת במילי דאורייתא, אדרבה שבח ויקר וגדולה וכבוד יתנו להרב, שיש תלמידי חכמים מבינים בדור. ואם המצא להם תשובה - יותר מעלה וכבוד יוסיפו לו. ואפילו אם לפעמים מוכרח לחזור בו ולהודות על האמת ונצחו אותו - יהיה שמח, כי מלבד דלא בא תקלה על ידו, זאת ועוד שיודע עכשיו מה שלא היה יודע מקודם, וכמו שכתב הרב בספר חסידים (סימן קמב) וזה לשונו : אם אתה מתווכח עם חכם, אל יהיה לך צער אם נצחך, כי ממנו תלמוד ותוסיף חכמה. אם תנצח אותו מה תרויח? אבל אם נצחך הרוחת אשר ידעת עתה מה שלא ידעת קודם לכן, עכ"ל.

ומה גם דחיובא רמיא ללכת בדרכי ה' כדכתיב "והלכת בדרכיו" (דברים כח, ט), וכביכול נוצחים אותו ושמח, כמו שאמרו בפרק ערבי פסחים (פסחים קיט, א) ובבא מציעא (נט, ב): נצחוני בני, ועיין שם. והגם כי מידת בשר ודם הוא שכשנוצחים אותו נעצב, מלבד כי לדברי תורה לא יתכן לומר כן כאמור.

זאת ועוד, דאין זה מיקרי "מתריז כנגדו" ומפקפק בדינו כלל. ועוד, דאם זה ד"מתריז כנגדו" הוא בדברי תורה דפסק להפך הדין, מאי חזית לומר על הטוען בדברי תורה דיקרא מתריז כנגדו ומפקפק בדינו בעבור כבודו, ולא לחוש על כבוד התורה ודברי הפוסקים שפוסק זה המתריז כנגדו? ומעשים בכל יום, דור דור ושופטיו מימי עולם וכשנים קדמוניות, דכמה מחלוקיות נמצאו בפוסקים דזה סותר דינו של זה וזה בונה, בין כששניהם יחד או כל אחד בפני עצמו ובין בזה אחר זה, ומעולם לא שמענו ולא ראינו דיהיה בזה זילזול חס וחלילה.

19. ערוך השולחן, חושן משפט, הקדמה

וכל מחלוקת התנאים והאמוראים והגאונים והפוסקים, באמת למבין דבר לאשורו, דברי אלהים חיים המה, ולכולם יש פנים בהלכה. ואדרבא, זוהי תפארת תורתנו הקדושה והטהורה וכל התורה כולה נקראת שירה, ותפארת השיר היא כשהקולות משונים זה מזה, וזהו עיקר הנעימות. ומי שמשוטט בים התלמוד יראה נעימות משונות בכל הקולות המשונות זה מזה.

20. שו"ת שרידי אש ג, ט

מה שכתב להקשות על סברתי ברוב וחזקה מדברי גדולי האחרונים הפני יהושע והגאון רבי עקיבא איגר, לא נעלם ממני שגדולי האחרונים תפסו בפשיטות שרוב עדיף מחזקה. אבל מה בכך? הלא כן היא דרכה של תורה, לפלפל ולחדש גם נגד גדולי האחרונים, ורק בנוגע להלכה למעשה אסור לנו להעלים עין מדברי הגאונים ז"ל, שדעתם רחבה מדעתנו והננו כולנו כקליפת השום נגדם. אבל בנוגע לסברא ולהסברת המושגים, יש לנו רשות לחדש ולאמר דברים שלא עמדו עליהם, כי כל איש מישראל שנשמתו היתה במעמד הר סיני קבל חלקו בתורה ובחידושי התורה ואין לערער נגד זה.

ורגיל אני לפרש מה שמנו חז"ל בפרקי אבות (ו, ה) בין ארבעים ושמונה דברים שהתורה נקנית בהם: פלפול התלמידים ואמונת חכמים. ולכאורה הם סותרים זה את זה. ובכלל, מה שייך אמונת חכמים לקנין התורה? אבל זהו הדבר: אם אינם מאמינים בחכמים, אז עוברים על דבריהם בקלות דעת ובזהירות של שטות, לומר בזחיחות הדעת הם לא הבינו, ונמצא שאין אדם יגע כלל להתעמק ולהעמיד דבריהם ז"ל, וסוף הדבר מתברר שאנחנו טעינו ולא הם. ולכן מדרכי החכמה הוא להאמין שהם לא טעו חס וחלילה, ורק אנחנו קצרי ראות ומעוטי דעת. אבל להאמין סתם ולא להוגיע את המוח בעיון ובמחשבה, אלא לומר סתם הם ידעו ויכולים אנחנו לסמוך עליהם בלא מחשבה - גם כן לא נכון, אלא צריך לפלפל בסתירה ובספיקות כאלו היו אנשים משלנו, ועל ידי זה באים להעמקה יתירה ולחדירה עיונית. נמצא ששתי המידות יחד, אמונת חכמים ופלפול עד קצה האחרון, מביאים לקנין התורה. והקב"ה חדי בפלפולא דאורייתא.

21. משנה, בבא בתרא ט, י

נפל הבית עליו ועל אמו, אלו ואלו מודים שיחלוקו. אמר רבי עקיבא, מודה אני בזה שהנכסים בחזקתן. אמר לו בן עזאי, על החלוקין אנו מצטערין, אלא שבאת לחלק עלינו את השוין.

22. השגות הראב״ד על הרי״ף, ברכות כד, א, מדפי הרי״ף

ואף על פי כן דברי הרב ז״ל הם מדוקדקים יותר ומיושבים מכמה טעמים. האחד, שכל מה שיוכל אדם למעט מחלוקות בין שני אמוראים, צריך למעט. וכמה היו משתדלים להסיר המחלוקות מביניהם, והדבר ידוע ואינו צריך לפנים.

23. ראב״ד, כתוב שם, ברכות מט, א (עמ' יב)

כתוב שם: ובראש חדש מפלג פליגי, דלרב הונא הדר ולרב נחמן לא הדר כלל. אמר אברהם: הקרחי הזה, מה ראה להחזיק במחלוקת ולשום מחלוקת בין כל האמוראים, וכמה יש לרבי שלמון שמשים שלום בין התלמידים, וזה משים ביניהם מחלוקת שאינו.

24. נמוקי יוסף, בבא מציעא סה, ב, מדפי הרי״ף

וכל שכן שאין סברא להרבות בפלוגתא בין רש״י והמפרשים ז״ל, אלא הפחות שנוכל.

25. שו״ת מהרי״ק, צד (עמ' קפד)

ויש להביא ראיה על זה מהא דגרסינן בכתובות פרק מציאת האשה (סט, א): תלה ליה רב לרבי ביני חטי: האחים ששעבדו מהו? כו', עד: ורבי יוחנן אומר: אחד זה ואחד זה אין מוציאין. איבעיא להו: לרבי יוחנן לא שמיע ליה הא דרבי, ואי שמיע ליה הוה מקבלה, או דלמא מישמע שמיע ליה ולא קבלה כו'. ושקיל וטרי למפשט דשמיע ליה, ודחי לה.

וכתב רב האי גאון בתשובה, וזה לשונו: עכשיו באנו לחקור דברי רבי יוחנן שהוא בתראה, מימר אמרינן ששמע דברי רבי מוציאין לפרנסה וראה בהם קושיא ודחם, וכיון שדחם רבי יוחנן שהוא בתראה לא עבדינן כרבי, או דלמא לא שמע אותם, שאלו שמעו לא היה חולק עליו, תא שמע וכו', עד: נמצא דלא אפשיט אי שמיע ליה אי לא שמיע ליה, הלכך מספיקא לא מחזיקין פלוגתא בין רבי ובין רבי יוחנן, עכ״ל. הרי לך בהדיא שכתב רב האי גאון ז״ל דאין להחזיק פלוגתא, ואם כן אית לן למימר דלא שמיע ליה רבי יוחנן דברי רבי, ואי הוה שמיע ליה לא הוה חולק עליו. ועל כרחך היינו טעמא, דכיון דלא מצינו בשום ברייתא או מימרא משמיה דרבי דלימא הכי דמוציאין לפרנסה וכו', אלא שהשיב כך בתשובה שאלה לרב דתלא ליה ביני חטי וכו', משום הכי איכא לספוקי דילמא לא שמיע ליה לרבי יוחנן, ומשום הכי פוסק רב האי דאין לנו להחזיק מחלוקת.

297

26. שו"ת מהרי"ק, קעו

גם מה שנראה מתוך דבריך היותו מפליג תנא דברייתא על תנא דמתניתין דכל הבשר (בבלי, חולין קד, א), אין נראה לעניות דעתי, דאין לנו להועיל מחלוקת בין התנאים כי אם כאשר ימצא בהדיא. ואדרבא, בכל מקום שימצא התלמוד שהמשנה והברייתא לא יכוונו דבריהם, פריך "ורמינהי" וכו', ומתוך כך דוחק התלמוד לתרץ כמה שנויי דחיקי בכמה מקומות בתלמוד, ולא בעי לשנויי דפליגי, אלא היכא דאשכחן פלוגתא בהדיא. וזה דבר פשוט.

27. הליכות עולם, שער ב (דף טז ע"א)

פעמים יש אמוראים חולקים, ואומר הגמרא שאינם חולקים, אלא מר אמר חדא ומר אמר חדא ולא פליגי, כלומר דכל חד וחד מודה לחבריה. בפרק קמא דמציעא (בבא מציעא י, ב): קטנה אין לה חצר ואין לה ארבע אמות, ורבי יוחנן אמר יש לה חצר ויש לה ארבע אמות. ואף על גב דמשמע דפליגי, אמר התם דחד מיירי בגיטין וחד מיירי במציאה ולא פליגי, כלומר מר מודה ליה בגיטין ומר מודה ליה במציאה. וכהאי גוונא איכא טובא. וכל היכא דאפשר לומר כן ושלא לעשות מחלוקת בין החכמים - שפיר דמי.

28. שארית יוסף, נתיב הפלוגתא, כלל א (עמ' 60)

כל מה שנוכל לקרב הדעות שלא לאפושי במחלוקת הוא הנכון. כמו שמצינו בכיצד מברכין (ברכות לט, ב) בההיא דפתיתין, שהקשו התוספות לרש"י דאין סברא דפליגי בהפוך סברות, דלרב הונא פתיתין שהם גדולים עדיפא ולרבי יוחנן שלמה עדיפא. וכן בתמורה (יב, א) וזה לשונם: סברת אמוראי הפוכה כזו לא מצינו, עד כאן. וגדולה מזו מצינו, שהגמרא מהפך לשון רבים ליחיד כדי למעט הסברות. אמרינן בפרק קמא דנדה (ח, ב): מאן חכמים? רבי אליעזר. וכתבו התוספות: אף על גב דתנא בלשון חכמים, ניחא ליה לאוקמה כרבי אליעזר ולא לימא שלשה מחלוקות בדבר.

29. שארית יוסף, נתיב הפלוגתא, כלל ג

כשיבואו אמוראים סתם, וסובל עניינם פירוש אשר ממנו יראה שחולקין ופירוש שאינם חולקין - יש לנו לפרש הפירוש אשר יראה שאינם חולקין, ואפילו שהוא פירוש דחוק מאד.

30. כללי שמואל, כלל שכד

מר אמר חדא ומר אמר חדא ולא פליגי... וכל היכא דאפשר לומר כן ושלא
לעשות פלוגתא בין החכמים שפיר דמי, דאורחא דגמרא בכל דוכתא קא
טרח להסיר פלוגתא בין המשניות ובין הברייתות ובין משניות וברייתות
ובין האמוראין. וזה הדרך הנכון להסכים הדעות ולא פליגי.

31. שו"ת הרדב"ז ב, תתל

דעתי הוא כדעת תלמידי הר"ר יונה ז"ל, וכן אני אומר שהוא דעת הטור בלי
מחלוקת, דכלל גדול בידינו אפושי פלוגתא לא מפשינן.

32. שו"ת התשב"ץ, חוט המשולש, הטור השני, יד

ועתה במה שכתבנו בהבנת דברי הרמ"ה ז"ל, עשינו אותו חולק על הרמב"ם
ז"ל... אבל מה נעשה, והרי דוחק לשון התשובה הכריחנו להבין אותה על
דרך שכתבנו, ולחלק בין הדין הראשון לדין האחרון, עד שיצאנו מדרך
הישרה, לעשות הרמ"ה חולק על הרמב"ם ז"ל. ודבר זה הוא דחוק למאד,
יותר מדוחק בילבול התשובה, דכלל גדול בידינו אפושי בפלוגתא לא
מפשינן, וכל היכא דמצינן לפרש הלשון אפילו בדוחק כדי להשוות דעות
הפוסקים מפרשינן ליה הכי אפילו בדוחק. לכן נראה ליישב דברי התשובה
באופן אחר, ואם הוא דחוק, כדי לתווך שלום בין הני רבוואתא ז"ל.

33. שו"ת גנת ורדים, אורח חיים, כלל א, מז

ואם כן מאחר דכל הפוסקים הנזכרים כתבו לדין זה בפירוש, ומסתמות
דברי הפוסקים הכי משמע, חובה מוטלת עלינו לעשות אוקמתא אפילו בדרך
רחוקה לתרץ דברי איזה פוסק דמשמע דפליג, כדי לעשות שלום בין
הפוסקים, דאפושי פלוגתא לא מפשינן, ואם כן על כרחינו לדחוק עצמינו
לפרש דבריו אף בדרך רחוקה, דשביק לקרא דאיהו דחיק ומוקי אנפשיה. כל
שכן שמה שכתבתי אין בו שום דוחק כלל.

34. פחד יצחק, ערך 'חתיכה הראויה להתכבד' (דף נט ע"ד)

כי כל עוד שיש לאל ידינו לפרש דברי כל מחבר בענין שלא יסתור את אמריו
הראשונים, אנו מחוייבים לעשות כן, אפילו להכניס פילא בקופא דמחטא,
ואם כן מה זה ועל מה זה אתה רוצה לפרש דברי הרב קארו בדרך סברתך
ולהוציא נפקותא ומשמעות מלבך כדי להקשות אחרי כן סברתו אסברתו,
והלא מוסכם הוא בכל הגמרא ובכל המפרשים ובכל פוסקי דוקני דאפושי

בפלוגתא לא מפשינן אפילו בין גברא לגברא, וקל וחומר בן של קל וחומר שחייבים אנחנו לחגור בעוז מותנינו לעשות כאלה בפוסק אחד, למען לא יהיה כסותר את דבריו הראשונים.

35. שדי חמד, מערכת מ, כלל טז

מחלוקת מן הקצה אל הקצה, דאחד מחייב חטאת ואחד מתיר לכתחלה, לא מצינו. עיין שבת (קלח, א): מי איכא מידי דרבי אליעזר שרי לכתחלה, ורבנן מחייבי חטאת? והיינו דוקא כשהחולקים הם שנים, האחד יחייב חטאת ואחד יתיר לכתחלה, זה לא יתכן. אבל אם אחד מחייב חטאת ואחד פוטר, יתכן שאחר יתיר לכתחלה והוא בא לחלוק על האומר פטור אבל אסור. עיין שם בגוף הסוגיא. והכי נמי איתא בשבת בפרק חבית (דף קמה ע"א) בשלקות שסחטן למימיהן, דלרב מותר ולשמואל פטור אבל אסור ולרבי יוחנן חייב חטאת. יש לומר דרבי יוחנן בא לחלוק על מה שאמר שמואל פטור ואמר איהו חייב. אבל בפלוגתא דתרי תנאי או אמוראי, לא יתכן דאחד יחייב ואחד יתיר לכתחלה, דזו מחלוקת מן הקצה אל הקצה. ...

ולא דוקא מחלוקת מן הקצה אל הקצה, אלא בכל ענין, כל שאין מחלוקת מפורש באותו דבר, אין לנו להמציא מחלוקת, וכל כמה דאפשר לקרב הסברות, עבדינן כל טצדקי דמצינן לקרב הדעות.

36. משנה, אבות ה, ז

שבעה דברים בגולם ושבעה בחכם. חכם אינו מדבר בפני מי שהוא גדול ממנו בחכמה, ואינו נכנס לתוך דברי חבירו, ואינו נבהל להשיב, שואל כענין ומשיב כהלכה, ואומר על ראשון ראשון ועל אחרון אחרון, ועל מה שלא שמע אומר "לא שמעתי", ומודה על האמת. וחלופיהן בגולם.

37. משנה, אבות ה, יז

כל מחלוקת שהיא לשם שמים, סופה להתקיים; ושאינה לשם שמים, אין סופה להתקיים. איזו היא מחלוקת שהיא לשם שמים? זו מחלוקת הלל ושמאי; ושאינה לשם שמים? זו מחלוקת קרח וכל עדתו.

38. ירושלמי סוכה פרק ב, ח (נג, 2)

מה זכו בית הלל שתיקבע הלכה כדבריהן? אמר רבי יהודה בר פזי: שהיו מקדימין דברי בית שמאי לדבריהן, ולא עוד אלא שהיו רואין דברי בית שמאי וחוזרין בהן. התיב רבי סימון בר זבדא קומי רבי אילא: או נאמר

תנייה חמתון סבון מינון ואקדמון? והא תני מעשה שהלכו זקני בית שמאי וזקני בית הלל לבקר את יוחנן בן החורוני, נאמר זקנינו וזקניכם.

39. בבלי, עירובין יג, ב

אמר רבי אבא אמר שמואל: שלש שנים נחלקו בית שמאי ובית הלל, הללו אומרים הלכה כמותנו והללו אומרים הלכה כמותנו. יצאה בת קול ואמרה: אלו ואלו דברי אלהים חיים הן והלכה כבית הלל.

וכי מאחר שאלו ואלו דברי אלהים חיים, מפני מה זכו בית הלל לקבוע הלכה כמותן? מפני שנוחין ועלובין היו ושונין דבריהן ודברי בית שמאי. ולא עוד אלא שמקדימין דברי בית שמאי לדבריהן, כאותה ששנינו (משנה, סוכה ב, ז): מי שהיה ראשו ורובו בסוכה ושלחנו בתוך הבית, בית שמאי פוסלין ובית הלל מכשירין. אמרו בית הלל לבית שמאי: לא כך היה מעשה, שהלכו זקני בית שמאי וזקני בית הלל לבקר את רבי יוחנן בן החורנית ומצאוהו יושב ראשו ורובו בסוכה ושלחנו בתוך הבית? אמרו להן בית שמאי: משם ראיה? אף הן אמרו לו, אם כך היית נוהג לא קיימת מצות סוכה מימיך. ללמדך, שכל המשפיל עצמו הקב"ה מגביהו, וכל המגביה עצמו הקב"ה משפילו, כל המחזר על הגדולה גדולה בורחת ממנו, וכל הבורח מן הגדולה גדולה מחזרת אחריו, וכל הדוחק את השעה שעה דוחקתו, וכל הנדחה מפני שעה שעה עומדת לו.

40. בבלי, שבת סג, א

אמר רבי ירמיה אמר רבי שמעון בן לקיש: שני תלמידי חכמים הנוחין זה לזה בהלכה הקב"ה מקשיב להן, שנאמר "אז נדברו יראי ה' וגו' (מלאכי ג, טז), אין דיבור אלא נחת, שנאמר "יַדְבֵּר עמים תחתינו" (תהלים מז, ד)...

אמר רבי אבא אמר רבי שמעון בן לקיש: שני תלמידי חכמים המקשיבים זה לזה בהלכה הקב"ה שומע לקולן, שנאמר "היושבת בגנים חברים מקשיבים לקולך השמיעני" (שיר השירים ח, יג), ואם אין עושין כן גורמין לשכינה שמסתלקת מישראל, שנאמר "ברח דודי ודמה" וגו' (שם שם, יד).

41. בבלי, תענית ח, א

רבא אמר: שני תלמידי חכמים שיושבין בעיר אחת ואין נוחין זה לזה בהלכה - מתקנאין באף ומעלין אותו, שנאמר "מִקְנֶה אַף עַל-עוֹלֶה" (איוב לו, לג).

42. בבלי, מגילה לב, א

כדרב משרשיא דאמר: שני תלמידי חכמים היושבים בעיר אחת ואין נוחין זה את זה בהלכה, עליהם הכתוב אומר "וגם אני נתתי להם חקים לא טובים ומשפטים לא יחיו בהם" (יחזקאל כ, כה).

43. בבלי, סוטה מט, א

אמר רבי אילעא בר יברכיה: שני תלמידי חכמים הדרים בעיר אחת ואין נוחין זה לזה בהלכה – אחד מת ואחד גולה, שנאמר "לנוס שמה רוצח אשר ירצח את רעהו בבלי דעת" (דברים ד, מב) – ואין דעת אלא תורה, שנאמר "נִדְמוּ עמי מבלי הדעת" (הושע ד, ו).

44. בבלי, תענית ד, א

אמר רבא: האי צורבא מרבנן דרתח – אורייתא הוא דקא מרתחא ליה, שנאמר "הלא כה דברי כאש נאום ה' " (ירמיה כג, כט). ואמר רב אשי: כל תלמיד חכם שאינו קשה כברזל אינו תלמיד חכם, שנאמר "וכפטיש יפוצץ סלע" (שם). אמר ליה רבי אבא לרב אשי: אתון מהתם מתניתו ליה, אנן מהכא מתנינן לה, דכתיב "ארץ אשר אבניה ברזל" (דברים ח, ט) – אל תקרי "אבניה" אלא "בוניה". אמר רבינא: אפילו הכי מיבעי ליה לאיניש למילף נפשיה בניחותא, שנאמר "והסר כעס מלבך" (קהלת יא, י).

45. בבלי, חגיגה כב, ב

תניא: אמר רבי יהושע: בושני מדבריכם בית שמאי... נטפל לו תלמיד אחד מתלמידי בית שמאי, אמר לו: אומר לך טעמן של בית שמאי? אמר לו: אמור. אמר לו... וזה טעמן של בית שמאי. מיד הלך רבי יהושע ונשתטח על קברי בית שמאי, אמר: נעניתי לכם עצמות בית שמאי, ומה סתומות שלכם כך, מפורשות על אחת כמה וכמה. אמרו: כל ימיו הושחרו שיניו מפני תעניותיו.

46. בבלי, יבמות צו, ב

אזל רבי אלעזר, אמר לשמעתא בי מדרשא ולא אמרה משמיה דרבי יוחנן. שמע רבי יוחנן, איקפד. עול לגביה רבי אמי ורבי אסי, אמרו ליה: לא כך היה המעשה בבית הכנסת של טבריא בנגר שיש בראשו גלוסטרא, שנחלקו בו רבי אלעזר ורבי יוסי עד שקרעו ספר תורה בחמתן. קרעו סלקא דעתך? אלא אימא שנקרע ספר תורה בחמתן. והיה שם רבי יוסי בן קיסמא, אמר:

תמיה אני אם לא יהיה בית הכנסת זו עבודת כוכבים. וכן הוה. הדר איקפד
טפי, אמר: חברותא נמי? עול לגביה ר' יעקב בר אידי, אמר ליה: "כאשר
צוה ה' את משה עבדו כן צוה משה את יהושע וכן עשה יהושע לא הסיר דבר
מכל אשר צוה ה' את משה" (יהושע יא, טו), וכי על כל דבר שאמר יהושע היה
אומר להם כך אמר לי משה? אלא, יהושע יושב ודורש סתם והכל יודעין
שתורתו של משה היא, אף רבי אלעזר תלמידך יושב ודורש סתם והכל
יודעין כי שלך היא. אמר להם: מפני מה אי אתם יודעין לפייס כבן אידי
חברינו?

47. בבלי, קידושין נב, ב

תנו רבנן: לאחר פטירתו של רבי מאיר אמר להם רבי יהודה לתלמידיו: אל
יכנסו תלמידי רבי מאיר לכאן מפני שקנתרנים הם ולא ללמוד תורה הם
באים אלא לקפחני בהלכות הם באים. דחק סומכוס ונכנס, אמר להם: כך
שנה לי רבי מאיר, המקדש בחלקו בין קדשי קדשים ובין קדשים קלים לא
קידש. כעס רבי יהודה עליהם, אמר להם: לא כך אמרתי לכם אל יכנסו
מתלמידי רבי מאיר לכאן מפני שקנתרנים הם ולא ללמוד תורה הם באים
אלא לקפחני בהלכות הם באים? וכי אשה בעזרה מנין? אמר רבי יוסי:
יאמרו מאיר שכב, יהודה כעס, יוסי שתק, דברי תורה מה תהא עליה? וכי
אין אדם עשוי לקבל קידושין לבתו בעזרה? ואין אשה עשויה לעשות לה
שליח לקבל קידושיה בעזרה? ועוד, דחקה ונכנסה מאי?

48. בבלי, סנהדרין כד, א

אמר רבי אושעיא: מאי דכתיב "ואקח לי שני מקלות לאחד קראתי נועם
ולאחד קראתי חובלים" (זכריה יא, ז)? "נועם" אלו תלמידי חכמים שבארץ
ישראל שמנעימין זה לזה בהלכה, "חובלים" אלו תלמידי חכמים שבבבל
שמחבלים זה לזה בהלכה.

"ויאמר אלה שני בני היצהר העומדים וגו' ושנים זיתים עליה" (זכריה ד, יד).
"יצהר", אמר רבי יצחק: אלו תלמידי חכמים שבארץ ישראל שנוחין זה לזה
בהלכה כשמן זית; "ושנים זיתים עליה" (שם שם, ג), אלו תלמידי חכמים
שבבבל שמרורין זה לזה בהלכה כזית.

49. בבלי, סנהדרין קי, א

"ויקם משה וילך אל דתן ואבירם" (במדבר טז, כה). אמר ריש לקיש: מכאן
שאין מחזיקין במחלוקת. דאמר רב: כל המחזיק במחלוקת עובר בלאו,

שנאמר "ולא יהיה כקרח וכעדתו" (במדבר יז, ה). רב אשי אמר: ראוי ליצטרע
– כתיב הכא "ביד משה לו" (שם) וכתיב התם "ויאמר ה' לו עוד הבא נא ידך
בחיקך" (שמות ד, ו). אמר רב יוסף: כל החולק על מלכות בית דוד ראוי
להכישו נחש – כתיב הכא "ויזבח אדניהו צאן ובקר ומריא עם אבן הזחלת"
(מלכים א א, ט), וכתיב התם "עם חמת זחלי עפר" (דברים לב, כד). אמר רב
חסדא: כל החולק על רבו כחולק על השכינה, שנאמר "בְּהַצֹּתָם על ה' "
(במדבר כו, ט). אמר רבי חמא ברבי חנינא: כל העושה מריבה עם רבו כעושה
עם שכינה, שנאמר "הֵמָּה מי מריבה אשר רבו בני ישראל את ה' " (במדבר כ,
יג). אמר רבי חנינא בר פפא: כל המתרעם על רבו כאילו מתרעם על השכינה,
שנאמר "לא עלינו תלֻנֹּתיכם כי (אם) על ה' " (שמות טז, ח). אמר רבי אבהו:
כל המהרהר אחר רבו כאילו מהרהר אחר שכינה, שנאמר "וידבר העם
באלהים ובמשה" (במדבר כא, ה).

50. מחזור ויטרי, פירוש למסכת אבות ה, יז (עמ' 547)

"כל מחלוקת שהיא לשם שמים סופה להתקיים" (אבות ה, יז). "לשם שמים"
– להעמיד דבר על אמיתו או להוכיח בני אדם על דבר עבירה, ולא להשתרר
ולקנות שם ולהתגאות בחינם איש על חבירו... "זו מחלוקת של קרח" –
שהיה מתכוין ליטול שררה, ראה שסופה לא נתקיימה המחלוקת ולא עמדה
לאורך ימים, אלא בא עליו פורענות, כדכתיב "ותפתח הארץ" וגו' (במדבר טז,
לב), נמצא בטל המחלוקת.

51. ספר חסידים, תתקעא

שנים שמתווכחים יחדיו, לא יאמר אדם לחבירו "חכם, מה אתה אומר",
כי משמע כמו שאומר לו "שוטה", אף על פי שחבירו אינו יכול להתקשט.

52. תשובות ופסקים לראב"ד, עמ' קיד

אל אלהים וישראל הוא ידע, אם באף אם בחמה אם לריב אם
למלחמה דברתי עד הנה, אל יושיעני היום הזה, אם לא מאשר ראיתיך בוחר
במנהגי הספרדים, שהם אוהבים זה לזה, ובהוכחם על דבר תורה נראים
כאויבים זה לזה, אמרתי גם אני אנסנו הילך בתורתם אם לא, ואכתוב
אליך אגרת אהבים ואמרי עגבים ואמרי שעשועים להשתעשע עמך, וחס
ושלום שלא היה בה דבר בזיון.

53. פירושי משנת אבות (ספר המוסר), לרבי יוסף בן יהודה תלמיד הרמב"ם, אבות ה, יז

"כל מחלוקת שהיא לשם שמים סופה להתקיים". פירוש, מחלוקת החכמים בענייני החכמה אינה כדי להראות כל אחד מהם שהוא גדול מחבירו או להטעות חבירו מדרך האמת אל השקר, אלא כולם לדרך אחת פונים, מהלכין בו עד שפוגעין האמת והיא מגמתם, ולא ימצא האמת בשני צדדים אלא בצד אחד. לפיכך אין אחד מהם מקנא בחבירו ולא מבקש רעתו מפני [מחלוקת] שנפלה ביניהם, שאותה המחלוקת היא לשום שמים ואינה לצורך מצרכי הגוף, אלא לדעת החכמה כלם מתכוונים להשיג האמת. כדאמרינן התם (משנה, יבמות א, ד): אף על פי שאלו פוסלין ואלו מכשירין אלו מטמאין ואלו מטהרין אלו אוסרין ואלו מתירין, לא נמנעו בית שמאי לישא נשים מבית הלל, ולא בית הלל לישא נשים מבית שמאי, וכל הטהרות והטמאות היו עושין אלו על גב אלו, לקיים מה שנאמר "והאמת והשלום אהבו" (זכריה ח, יט).

ומחלקת שאינה אלא לתאוות העולם הזה, כגון השררה והכבוד והקנייך והבנייך, אינה מתקיימת אלא בטלים הם ומחלקתם, מפני שזו המחלוקת על דברי תאוות העולם שאינן קיימין. והמחלוקת בחכמה אינה בטילה מפני שהחכמה קיימת לעד.

54. בית הבחירה, אבות ה, יט

כל מחלוקת שהיא לשם שמים סופה להתקיים כו'. יש לתמוה: איך ראוי לומר על מחלוקת שיתקיים, והרי על כל פנים לא יתקיים אלא אחת מן הדעות שחלקו עליהם, ומילת מחלוקת כוללת שני צדדים, ואין ראוי לומר דהמחלוקת יתקיים? ומכל מקום יראה לי שאין מחלוקת מיוחסת רק למשיב על הראשון, רוצה לומר כשהאחד מתעורר לעשות איזה דבר ואומר "ראוי שנעשה כך", או שישאלו לו איזה ענין ויורה עליו שהוא כך, אין זה מחלוקת. אבל כשהשני ישיב ויאמר "מה שאתה אומר שהוא ראוי שיעשה אינו ראוי", או "מה שהורית אינו כמו שהורית, אלא בהפך", זה מחלוקת. ונמצא שאין המחלוקת כולל אלא אחד מן הצדדים, והוא המשיב על הראשון. ואמר, שאם זה השני משיב וחולק שלא בדרך קנטור ונצוח אלא להודיע האמת, סופו שיתקיימו דבריו, כי האמת יעשה דרכו. אבל כשאינה לשם שמים אלא דמשיב וחולק דרך קנטור ונצוח, אין סופה להתקיים, אלא שיתקיימו דברי הראשון, וכל שכן מחלוקת שבדברים אחרים.

55. חיבור התשובה, מאמר א פרק ד (עמ' 106-107)

וממין הסבה החמישית גם כן החולק על דברי חכמים, והכונה בלשון "יחולקי" - מי שכוונתו לחלוק ולקנתר ולהעמיד דבריו כנגד האמת מצד הנצוח, כמו שיאמר תמיד לבעל המדה הזאת "פלגי", כאמרם (בבלי, גיטין לא, ב) על אחד מן היודעים, והוא בעל זאת המדה, עבר לפני חכמים אחרים ורצה האחד לעמוד לפניו ולהדרו כמצות "מפני שיבה תקום" (ויקרא יט, לב), והשיב לו האחר: מקמי פלג נקום?! כלומר: הנעמוד אנחנו מפניו אחר שהוא פלגי?! רצה בו בהשפיל מעלתו כל כך להיותו חולק על צד קנתור ונצוח.

ועל זה אמרו (משנה, אבות ה, יז): כל מחלוקת שהיא לשם שמים סופה להתקיים, וכל מחלוקת שאינה לשם שמים אין סופה להתקיים. אי זו היא מחלוקת שהיא לשם שמים? זו מחלוקת שמאי והלל, ואי זו היא מחלוקת שאינה לשם שמים? זו מחלוקת קרח ועדתו. קרא מחלוקת שמאי והלל "מחלוקת שהיא לשם שמים", שאין כונת אחד מהם לחלוק לכונת סתירת דברי חברו אלא לכונת ידיעת האמת, כאמרם בקצת מקומות (משנה, עדויות א, יב): "וחזרו בית הלל להורות כדברי בית שמאי". וקרא מחלוקת קרח ועדתו "מחלוקת שאינה לשם שמים", כמו שידוע היות ענינם לקנאתו על מעלת משה ואהרן, כאמרו בפרוש "ומדוע תתנשאו על קהל ה' " (במדבר טז, ג), והוא אמרו גם כן "כי כל העדה כלם קדושים" (שם), רצה בו שהם כולם על מדרגת מעלה ולא יצטרכו להנהגתו... ומצד מחלקתו לצד קנאה וקנתור קראוהו ז"ל "מחלוקת שאינה לשם שמים".

וכן בכל מה שיחלוק האדם על החכמים על צד קנאה וקנתור, לא על צד ידיעת האמת, יקרא "מחלוקת שאינה לשם שמים", וזה הענין המיוחס אליהם לגולם, רוצה לומר שהוא חולק עליהם לקנתר, ומפני זה אמרו עליו שאינו מודה על האמת, כאמרם ז"ל (משנה, אבות ה, ז): שבעה דברים בגלם ושבעה בחכם, חכם אינו מדבר בפני מי שגדול ממנו, ואינו נבהל להשיב ואינו נכנס לתוך דברי חברו, שואל כענין ומשיב כהלכה, אומר על ראשון ראשון ועל אחרון אחרון, ועל מה שלא שמע אומר לא שמעתי, ומודה על האמת, וחלופיהן בגלם. הורו בזה שאפילו היודע החולק על האמת, יקרא גולם כשלא יודה בו אחר שנודע לו אבל (ש)יחלוק בו על צד קנתור ומצד קנאתו באשר ינצחנו, כי הגולם לא יאמר על נעדר הידיעה לגמרי.

56. שו"ת הריב"ש החדשות, לג

ואף במחלוקתה של תורה מצינו שהשוה אותו למחלוקתו של קרח כמו שראיתי בהלכות נדוי הלכות ספרדיות על רבי אליעזר הגדול, וז"ל: רבי אליעזר

עשו לו מדת הדין אע"פ דחשוב טובא, שלא ירבו מחלוקות בישראל, שאין ראוי למחול על זה, ואפילו היה מופלג ואב בית דין. ואף על גב דאמר רב יוסף באושא התקינו אב בית דין שסרח אין מנדין אותו (מועד קטן יז, א), גרם מחלוקת שאני, דאמר מר שנאת חנם שקולה כנגד שלוש עבירות (ירושלמי יומא פ"א ה"א), אלמא אין לך חלול ה' גדול מזה. וראיה לדבר מחלוקת קרח וכל עדתו. לכן צריך להחרים ולשמת, עכ"ל.

ואם להזהיר שלא יעשו מחלוקת בישראל עשו כך במלאך ה' צבאות, אשר כל מעשיו לשם שמים ומלחמתו מלחמתה של תורה, ועל ידו נרעשו אשר בשמים ממעל ואשר בארץ מתחת והסכימו לדבריו כאשר נכתב בפרק הזהב (בבא מציעא נט, ב), אנחנו בני אדם השפלים והגרועים מן הבהמה בהיות יצרנו הרע מנצח את הטוב, וכל מחלוקתינו לשם הבלי עולם להתגאות ולנצח זה את זה, ורבים מעמי הארץ מתיחדים, זה מחלק אחד וזה מחלק אחד, להשמיד ולהרוג ולאבד גוף וממון, על אחת כמה וכמה כי כל ירא שמים יש לו להלחם מלחמתה של מצותיה ובנדוים וחרמות ושמתות ובכל טכסיסי המלחמה כנגד גורמי המחלוקת, ולהיות קנאים פוגעים בו.

57. מנורת המאור, נר ב, כלל ז, חלק א, פרק א

הכלל השביעי: שלא יחזיק במחלוקת. ונחלק לשני חלקים: החלק הראשון בדברי תורה, החלק השני במילי דעלמא. החלק הראשון בדברי תורה ויש בו שני פרקים.

לפי שטבע מציאות בני אדם מתחייב שישבו ביחד וישרתו אלו לאלו ויסייעו אלו לאלו בכל עבודתם ובכל צרכיהם, על כן ישובו של עולם הוא בקירוב דעות ואהבה ואחוה שיש ביניהם והסכמה ודעת אחד ומשפט אחד, לפיכך כל מחלוקת שיארע ביניהם היא השחתת הישוב. ובדברי תורה צריך חבורת תלמידים. ואם ישאו ויתנו בדבר ויחלקו בסברא לשם שמים להוציא הדבר לאמיתו זהו עבודת השם, כדי שלא תצא הלכה מוטעת, ויעמוד הדבר על בוריו. כדגרסינן בתעניות (תענית ז, א): אמר רבי אחא בר חנינא: מאי דכתיב "ברזל בברזל יחד" (משלי כז, יז)? לומר לך מה זה ברזל זה אחד מחדד את חבירו, אף שני תלמידי חכמים מחדדין זה את זה בהלכה. אמר רבה בר בר חנה: למה נמשלה דברי תורה באש, דכתיב "הלא כה דברי כאש נאם ה' " (ירמיה כג, כט)? לומר לך מה אש אינה דולקת יחידי אף דברי תורה אין מתקיימין ביחידי...

ואף על פי כן צריך שאם יארע חילוק דעות בין התלמידים שתהא כוונתם לשם שמים להוציא אמיתת ההלכה ולא לקנתר, כדגרסינן בקידושין (נב, ב)

ובנזיר (מט, ב): תנו רבנן, לאחר פטירתו של רבי מאיר אמר להם רבי יהודה לתלמידיו: אל יכנסו תלמידי רבי מאיר לכאן שקנתרנים הן ואינם באים ללמוד תורה אלא לקפחנו בהלכות הם באים. אבל אם יחלקו בהלכה לשם שמים כמחלוקת תלמידי הלל ושמאי הוא טוב ונאות, כמו ששנינו פרק ה מאבות (משנה יז): כל מחלוקת שהיא לשם שמים סופה להתקיים ושאינה לשם שמים אין סופה להתקיים. אי זו היא מחלוקת שהיא לשם שמים? זו מחלוקת הלל ושמאי. ושאינה לשם שמים זו מחלוקת קרח ועדתו....

וכן כל הדומה לזה מחלוקת מבית הלל ובית שמאי ומהתנאים והאמוראים והבאים אחריהם כלן הם דומים לזה שהם ענפי ענפים והכל היה לשם שמים, ומחלוקת כזה טוב הוא לברר אמיתת ההלכה. אבל יש להזהר שלא יבואו לידי קנאה וקטטה, כדגרסינן בפרק במה מדליקין (שבת לד, א) על ההוא עובדא דרבי שמעון בר יוחאי כד נפק ממערתיה, אמר ההוא סבא: טיהר בן יוחאי בית הקברות. אמר ליה: אלמלא (לא) היית עמנו, אי נמי היית עמנו ולא נמנית עמנו - יפה אתה אומר, ועכשיו שהיית עמנו ונמנית עמנו יאמרו זונות מפרכסות זו את זו, תלמידי חכמים לא כל שכן, יהב ביה עיניה ונח נפשיה. וגרסינן נמי בפרק קמא דתעניות (תענית ח, א): אמר רבא: שני תלמידי חכמים הדרים בעיר אחת ואין נוחין זה לזה בהלכה - מתקנאין באף ומעלין אותו, שנאמר "מקנה אף על עולה" (איוב לו, לג). אבל אם היו אהובין ונוחין זה לזה מעלין אף מן העולם ומקשיב הקב"ה תפילתן, כדגרסינן מסכת שבת (סג, א): אמר רבי ירמיה: שני תלמידי חכמים הנוחין זה לזה בהלכה - הקב"ה מקשיב להם, שנאמר "אז נדברו יראי ה' איש אל רעהו ויקשב ה' וישמע" (מלאכי ג, טז)...

ועל כל זה הקטן יכבד לגדול ממנו בחכמה ואל יהא בעיניו כחבירו, שכבר מצינו מה שאירע על זה לרב ענן עם רב הונא כדגרסינן בכתובות (סט, א): "שלח ליה רב ענן לרב הונא הונא חברין שלם, כי מטיא האי איתתא לקמך אגבה עשור נכסי. הוה יתיב רב ששת קמיה. אמר ליה: זיל אימא ליה, ובשמתא יהא מאן דלא אמר ליה ענן ענן ממקרקעי או ממטלטלי"...

ואף על פי כן אשרי הגדולים הסובלים לקטנים והקטנים הנשמעין לגדולים.

58.   פירוש ר' יוסף יעבץ הדורש ממגורשי ספרד, אבות ה, יט

הורה שהעיקר תלוי בכוונה, כי מי שכוונתו לשם שמים להוציא דבר לאמיתו, אפילו טעה בעיונו יחשב לו כאילו הסכים אל האמת. והטעם כי לא המדרש הוא העיקר אלא המעשה, וכיון שכל כונתו לא היתה אלא להוציא הלכה למעשה לזרז נפשו להתקרב אל השם יתברך הכונה ההיא משארת נפשו.

59. נועם וחובלים, עמ' 83

אמת שבמה שטענת נגדו שנתכבד בקלון האלוף מר חמיך ז"ל, זה היטב הרע לי, וחשבתי חי נפשי העלובה לכתוב לו בינו לביני תוכחת על זה. כי עם היות שלא הכרתי ולא ידעתי את מר חמיך, לשמע אזן שמעתי שמועתו, וריח שמו נודף למרחקים כצלוחית של פוליטון. ומאד אני מקנא בבזיון תלמידי חכמים, וכההיא דבמה מדליקין (צ"ל שבת קיט, ב) "לא נחרבה ירושלים עד שביזו בה תלמידי חכמים" כו'. ואף גם זאת אלו כתב נגד כבודו אחרי מותו כאשר טענת, דאית לן למימר גם אהבתם גם שנאתם כבר אבדה, וכההיא דרבי שמעון ברבי על רבי מאיר ורבי נתן, פרק כהן משוח (הוריות יד, א).

אלא שפה נמצא תלמיד אחד מונזיא"ה שראה את ספרו שהדפיס, וחקרתי ודרשתי מפיו, ונשבע שהוא נוהג כבוד גדול במר חמיך לקראו "גאון" ו"כהנה רבה" וכהנה רבות עמו. ואע"פ שכבוד כזה לחכמי זמנינו לא ערב לי, שהרי אפילו לאבות העולם, כגון הרמב"ם ורש"י והראב"ד ור"ת והרמב"ן והרשב"א וזולתם מן הפוסקים הגדולים, אין אנו נוהגין לקרא בשם גאון, קל וחומר בן קל וחומר לחכמי זמננו, ומשל למי שאין לו אלף דינרים כסף ומקלסין אותו באלף אלפים דיני זהב, הלא גנאי הוא לו, וכמו שהביאוהו בהיר ובמדרש רבות. ומפני זה לא נהגתי לתת את כל הכבוד הזה למי שהוא מגדולי דורנו, ואפילו לחכמי דורות שלפנינו שהיו טובים מאלה. מכל מקום כפי המסופר לי מפני התלמיד הנזכר, הוא נוהג במר חמיך את כל הכבוד הזה, ונראה ודאי שלא כיון רק לכבדו ביותר. ובכן משכתי את ידי מלהוכיחו, ועל משמרתי אעמודה. ואם יובא ספרו הנה ואראה שהקל בכבוד מר חמיך, תיתי לי אם לא אכתוב לו בני לביני ואוכיחנו, דהבט אל עמל לא אוכל... כל שכן קנאה כזאת שהיא חורבנו של עולם, שכשהתלמידי חכמים מבזים זה את זה התורה מתבזית על ידיהם, והרשעים ועמי הארץ שמחים ומתנשאים עליהם...

ואשר טענת שכתב על מר חמיך "מפני שהוא כהן מבית עלי". אין בזה בזיון אצלי. אדרבה מעלה וגדולה תחשב לו. ומי לנו גדולים מרבותינו בעלי התלמוד והיו מהם אומרים על עצמם "אנא מדבית עלי קאתינא" וכו'. ועוד אמרו: "רבה ואביי תרוייהו מדבית עלי קא אתו", כדאיתא בפרק קמא דראש השנה (יח, א). וחלילה שכיון בעל התלמוד לבזותם, אלא להעלותם ולהגדילם. וכבר לא נעלם מפניך ההיא דשלהי קדושין (ע, ב): "אמר רב יודא אמר רב שמואל: ארבע מאות עבדים, ואמרי לה ארבעת אלפים עבדים, היו לו לפשחור בן אמר, וכלם נטמעו בכהונה" כו'. על כן היו החכמים השלמים מפארים ייחסם שהם מבית עלי וזולתו מן מיוחסי כהונה, להודיע לעולם

שאינם חי"ו מאותם שנטמעו, ולא עבר זר בתוכם. ואם הוקשה בעיניך מפני הגזרה שנגזרה על בית עלי, מאי איכפת לן בהכי, הא אמר רבא (ראש השנה יח, א) "בזבח ומנחה הוא דאינו מתכפר, אבל מתכפר הוא בדברי תורה". וכיון דמר חמיך בעל תורה הוה, פשיטא שנתבטלה הגזרה לו, ולזרעו אחריו בגללו. לא תאונה אליו רעה ונגע לא יקרב באהלו.

ואם כתב על מר חמיך שי"דבריו בעלי מומין" וכו', ו"טעה", ו"חכמי הדור השיגוהו" וכו', ו"זיל קרי בפסקך ובפסקי וראה מי הוא הטועה" וכו', ו"צא מן המבוכה טרם יתפשט טעותך" כו', וכיוצא מאלה הדברים שהראיתני. אינם בזיון אצלי, שכך היא דרך המפלפלין והחולקין, ולא להבזות את מר חמיך נתכון בעצם ובראשונה, רק להשביח מקחו, ואישתבוחי הוא דקא משתבח בנפשיה. אף כי חמום התורה תביא המדברים לפעמים לידי כעס, וכהההיא דרבא (תענית ד, א): "האי צורבא מרבנן דרתח, אורייתיה היא דקא מרתחא ליה, שנאמר 'הלא כה דברי כאש' (ירמיה כג, כט)".

ומי הוא זה ואיזה הוא, ואפילו מגדולי המורים הראשונים הראשונים, המה הגבורים אשר מעולם אנשי השם, שלא השיגוהו ולא השיבוהו, אם יושר ואם בעול. וכמאמר החכם "כשם שהצורות משתנות כך הדעות" וכו'. כל שכן חלוקי התלמוד שהם רחבות מני ים. וכבר ידעת ההשגות שעשו חכמי המשנה והתלמוד והגאונים והפוסקים אלו על אלו, וההשגות שעשו לרבנו הגדול הרי"ם במז"ל. ולא יחוייב מפני שהיו גדולים יותר ממה שהפה יכל לומר, שלא תמצא להם איזו שגיאה קטנה או גדולה. ורז"ל אמרו (גיטין מג, א): "אין אדם עומד בדברי תורה אלא אם כן נכשל בהם, שנאמר 'והמכשלה הזאת תחת ידך' (ישעיה ג, ו)".

על כן אם אמר גם על מר חמיך שטעה ושחכמי הדור השיגוהו הדריכוהו, אל תתמה על החפץ, כבר היו לעולמים אשר היו מלפנינו. כל שכן דלא מפיו אנו חיין, ואם הוא אמר על מר חמיך שטעה וחכמי הדור השיגוהו, מר חמיך ישיב לו מיניה וביה שהוא נשתבש וגדולי עולם ישיגוהו מנוחה ידריכוהו עד נוכח הגבע"ה ממזרח שמ"ש. ואין אלו וכיוצא באלו אלא דברים בעלמא הפורחים באויר. ועל תשת לבך עליהם ועל כיוצא בהם. שלמה המלך עליו השלום בחכמתו צווח: "גם לכל הדברים אשר ידברו אל תתן לבך" (קהלת ז, כא).

60. שני לוחות הברית, תורה שבעל פה, כלל "פה קדוש"

ויש לתמוה דהרבה מקומות בתלמוד המקודש מזכיר איזה זילזול שדיבר אמורא אחד לחברו, וקשה קושיה אחת שהיא שתים: האחת איך דיבר לו

זלזול, והשניה איך כתבה הגמרא זה הלשון. ואביא לך קצת מהם: הרבה תימה איתא שהשיב לו "משום דממולאי קא אתיתו אמריתו מילי ממולאי" (יבמות עו, א), וביבמות (ט, א) "כמדומה שאין לו מוח בקדקדו", ובסנהדרין (כו, א) בעניין שביעית כהן וזמיר קראם "רועי בקר" כו' "רועי צאן" כו'.

דע, כי צריך לפרש להיות דבר טוב יוצא מהדיבור הזה, או להיפך הדבר על העניין אחר הבא לטעות. ומימי טרחתי תודה לאל כשמצאתי כן בגמרא, לפרש על דבר טוב, ועלתה בידי. והכל לפי העניין אשר מוזכר דבר זה שם. ואזכיר אחת מהנה: מה שאמר "משום דממולאי קאתיתו", לא אמר על דרך זילזול חס ושלום, אלא דרך חכמה ומוסר, והוא על דרך שאמרו רז"ל על בית עלי (ראש השנה יח, א): בזבח ובמנחה לא יכופר, אבל בתורה ובגמילות חסדים יכופר. ועל כן הוכיחו: מאחר שבאתם ממולאי, צריך אתם להתבונן בתורה ביתר שאת שלא יהא דברים ממולאים, ובזה תתכפר. וכל כהאי גוונא ישמע חכם ויוסיף לקח.

61. שו"ת פני יהושע ב, לד

כבר הלכה רווחת בישראל דחדש בזמן הזה אסור אף בשל גויים, ולא היה פוצה פה ומערער בדבר, כי הדברים יצאו מבטן הגאון הגדול רבינו יצחק הידוע, בעל התוספות ז"ל, והסכימו עמו כל הבאים אחריו... עד שקם חכם אחד, והוא הגאון בעל בית חדש, ונחלק על הר"י בעל התוספות כמבואר בספרו (ב"ח, יורה דעה, רצג). והנה יתבשר הגאון הזה במה שבישר הוא בכמה מקומות בספרו כי "שארי ליה מאריה" על אשר חלק על הר"י והנלווים אליו בחינם.

ולא על המחלוקת אני כועס, כי וודאי אין לך אלא שופט שבימיך, ורשאי כל אדם לחלוק בראיות ברורות אפילו על דברי הראשונים, וכמו שכתב הרא"ש ז"ל. אך על דבריו ועל רמות רוחא שנקיט ליה אני כועס, אשר סיים בדבריו כי איסור חדש בשל גויים אינו אלא חסידות ואסור לנהוג בו בפני רבים. והנה עשה את דברי הר"י בעל התוספות לאפס ותוהו, וכאלו דבריו נתונים מסיני עד שלא נחשבו דברי הר"י וכל הפוסקים אפילו לחוש להם לחומרא לכל הפחות. ובמקום אשר היה ראוי לומר "הגם שיש להשיב על דברי הר"י, מכל מקום אין לעבור עליהם הואיל ונפיק מפומיה", שכן דרך התלמוד והגאונים ז"ל, אבל לא לסמוך על דעתו ולגזור אומר שאסור לנהוג כדבריו. ועתה באתי להראות לפני העמים והשרים אשר אין בדבריו ממש, ואין גם אחד אשר יאמר עליו כי הוא זה תשובה על שיטת הר"י.

62. שו"ת חוט השני, יח

תשובה לגדול אחד, אלופי ומיודעי, אשר האשימני על השגתי על גדולי הקדמונים. קראת אחרי מלא איך נשאני רוחי ומלאני לבי להשיג על הקדמונים אחזו שער, אשר קטנם עבה ממתני, ומה גם לומר דאישתמיטתייהו דברי הש"ס והפוסקים. ואני תמה עליך בזה. הלא הלשון הזה בעצמו, רצוני לומר לשון "אשתמיטיה", הוא לקוח מהש"ס שאמר כך על גדולי האמוראים (ראש השנה יג, ב; יומא כז, ב; חולין קז, ב; בכורות קז, א, ובכמה דוכתי), והוא לשון נקיה ודרך כבוד לומר דבאותה שעה נשמט ממנו הדבר ההוא, כי השכחה הוא טבע אנושית כוללות כל האישים, ואם יש חילוק ביניהם בין רב למעט. ומי לנו גדול ממשה רבינו עליו השלום, מבחר הנביאים, דאישתמיטתיה שני דברים מתוך כעסו, כדרז"ל ופירוש רש"י בפרשת מטות (במדבר לא, כא). ומי לנו בפוסקים גדול מרמב"ם אשר כל תורה שבעל פה בספרו הגדול הכין ופעל פירוש על שיתא סדרי משנה מדברי הש"ס, וכתב בהקדמתו לסדר זרעים שהתנא חנינא בן חכינאי לא נזכר במשנה רק במסכת כלאים, ואשתמיטתיה שנזכר עוד במסכת מכות פ"ג, עיי"ש...

ורש"י שהיה אוצר בלום לתורה, וכתב בפירוש החומש על מה שמצא בשם ר' משה דרשן דרש על "ויקרא לה נובח" (במדבר לב, מב): "ולא ידעתי מה ידרוש בשני פסוקים הדומים לו" – וכתב עליו הרמב"ן (שם) שהיה נעלם ממנו מדרש רות אשר ממנה לקח ר' משה את דבריו. וכן רש"י בעצמו כתב בפירושו לחומש בששה מקומות: "איני יודע" וכו' "ולא ידעתי" וכו'... ראה בעיניך כי התוספות לא נמנעו מלגלות דבריהם נגד רש"י, הן במה שכתב שלא ידע הפירוש, או שלא ידע המקום, מלבד מה שהש"ס מלא וגדוש מהשגתם עליו בפירושי ההלכות והסוגיות.

63. שו"ת חוות יאיר, קנב

שאלה. נשאלתי אחר ד"דברי חכמים בנחת נשמעים" (קהלת ט, יז), ונאמר במשנה (אבות ב, י) "יהי כבוד חבירך חביב עליך כשלך", איך מצינו לפעמים קינטורים וזילזולים בש"ס, כעניין "כד נייס ושכיב רב אמר להא שמעתתא" הנאמר בכמה דוכתי (יבמות כד, ב ועוד), וכהנה רבים.

תשובה. יפה שאלת, כי וודאי אף על פי שנקראו תלמידי חכמים שבבבל "חובלים", במסכת בבא בתרא (צ"ל סנהדרין כד, א), לא מצד הריקודים והצעקות גדולות ומרות והכאת כף על כף כאלו נלחמים זה מול זה או מצד הקינטורים והזילזולים חלילה, כי לא על זה נאמר (קידושין לא, ב) "כי

312

ידברו את אויבים בשער" שאב ובנו רב ותלמידו נעשו אויבים, רק מצד שהם
מתנגדים בסברותיהם ובראיותיהם... והרי נוכל לפלפל בנחת ובטוב טעם
שישמע זה תחילה מה שחבירו מדבר ולא יכנס לתוך דבריו, כי זה אחד
משבע מידות, ואחר כך ישיב דבר. מי לא ידע מעלת הפילפול, שהרי שואלין
לאדם: פלפלת בחכמה? וכהאי גוונא היו קושיות ופירוש רשב"י ובנו רבי
אלעזר בפרק במה מדליקין (שבת לג, ב) ושל רבי יוחנן וריש לקיש בפרק
הפועלים (בבא מציעא פד, א). והיינו נמי מה שנאמר על רבה שעוקר הרים
(הוריות יד, א), וריש לקיש הרי הרים, בסנהדרין (כד, א), וחריפא סכינא (חולין
עז, א), וכך היא דרך חכמיהם המתווכחים וכן ויכוחי הפילוסופים
הקדמונים...

ונחזור למבוקשינו, שמה שאמר רב ללוי "כמדומה שאין לו מח בקדקדו",
ביבמות (ט, א) ובמנחות (פ, ב), לולי דמסתפינא לשלוח ידי במשיח ה', כי ידוע
שרב הוא רב אבא תלמיד המובהק והמובחר מתלמידי רשב"י מבעלי
חסידות... לכן יגורתי לומר עליו כי באמת שלא כהוגן דיבר ולכן שקלא
למטרפסיה באשר בכמה דוכתי אמר רב ששת עליו "כד נייס ושכיב אמר רב
להא שמעתתא" כמבואר במסכת יבמות (כד, ב; צא, א; קט, ב) ובבא קמא (מז,
ב; סה, א; סז, ב) ונדה (ס, א) ובכורות (כג, ב). מכל מקום האמת יעשה דרכו כי
מאמר "כד נייס ושכיב" אינו לגנאי רק שבח גדול ומופלג, שלפי מעלתו
ומדרגתו של רב אי אפשר לומר עליו שטעה בטעות כזה אם לא שאמרו כד
נייס ושכיב. ולא אמר "כד שכיב ונייס", כמו שאמרו התוספות בפרק ערבי
פסחים (פסחים קט, ב ד"ה אמר) שיש תרי גווני תנומה, אחד בתחילת השינה
ואחד בסופו, והנה זו שבסופה אע"פ שיטעה במאמרו, מאחר שמתעורר
והולך מרגיש אחר כך בטעותו וחוזר בו, מה שאין כן בדנייס ואחר כך שכיב.

ומה שאמר רב "כמדומה לי" וכו', היינו שמותר לרב להוכיח לתלמידו
בדברים קשים כדי לזרזם כדי שיעיינו וישגיחו וישמרו מן הטעות והשגיאה.
ולוי היה תלמיד רבי, כבגמרא סוף פרק קמא דסנהדרין (יז, ב): "למדים לפני
חכמים - לוי מדרבי". ולעניניות דעתי נראה שמדברי רבי אלו יצא להרמב"ם
(הלכות תלמוד תורה ד, ה) מה שכתב שחייב הרב לכעוס על תלמידיו אם רואה
שמתרשלים, הובא בשלחן ערוך, יורה דעה (רמו, יא). לכן מפני שרב ידע בלוי
שאדם גדול ומופלג הוא, ולא היה ראוי שיטעה אם לא ממיעוט עיון
והשגחה, לכן דיבר עליו קשות, חלילה לא מכעס או מגובה רוחו. והרי תניא
סוף סוטה (מט, ב): משמת רבי בטלה ענווה.

ולפעמים אמרו לשונות כאלו בדרך מליצה ובדיחא, כמו שאמר רבי יוחנן
לרב חייא בר אבא בבבא בתרא (קז, ב) ובכורות (יח, א): "עד דאכלית כפניתא

בבבל"... וכהאי גוונא מה שקראו אמוראי לחבריהם "תרדא", כמו רבה לרב
עמרם בבבא מציעא סוף פרק קמא (כ, ב), ורבי חייא בר אבא לרבי זירא
בזבחים (כה, ב), ואביי לאבא בן חנן בכריתות (יח, ב). וכהאי גוונא "תדורא",
פירש רש"י: "אין לב", רבא לרב עמרם בבבא קמא (קה, ב). כולם יש לומר
שהיו חבריהם וגדולים מהם ולא קפדי כלל. ולשון "משום שאתית ממלאי"
וכו' גם כן בכהאי גוונא. ובמסכת יבמות (עו, א) פירשו התוספות: שם מקום
ממלא. וכן כתב הערוך...

בכהאי גוונא מה שהשיב רבי ינאי לרבי יוחנן תלמידו "מה בין לי ולד",
מסכת שבת (קמ, א), אינו כדברי גאוה ורם לבו ומבזה זולתו, כי מותר לרב
לדבר אל תלמידו ולקנטרו על מיעוט הבנתו וסיבת התרשלותו. ומכל מקום
אפשר דרבי יוחנן שקיל למטרפסיה שכן השיב הוא לאיסי מסכת חולין (קלז,
ב), ובשניהם פירש רש"י: דידענא לפרש מתניתין טפי ממך. וזה צריך לי עיון
דבשניהם לא תלי בפירוש המשנה רק שכך קיבל. ולולי פה קדוש (דר"י)
[דרש"י] הייתי אומר שהם דברי ענוה, והגדיל מעלת תלמידו או חבירו, וכך
אמר ליה בתשובתו שכך קיבל ולולי ששימש רבותיו מאוד ועל כן רבתה
קבלתו מה בין לי ולד, כי מצד ההשגה ועיון וחכמה אין חילוק. אי נמי יש
לומר כי בין לי ולד כמובן לכל שודאי טובא יש, רק שמילת לי ולד עניינו
הבאת הדבר ממקום אחר אל האדם כנודע, ורצונו לומר שהרבה יותר
קבלתי ושמשתי רבותי מאסה (מאתה?) דאם כפשטיה להגדיל מעלתו על
מעלתן היה צריך לומר "מה ביני לבינך". וק"ל.

ויש עוד בכהאי גוונא לשונות קשות, ביארנום בספרי "מר קשישא", וכעת
לפי שאלתך יספיק תשובתי בדרך קצרה, ויערב נא שיחי עליך.

64. שו"ת גינת ורדים, יורה דעה, כלל ג, ג

עובדא הוה בחד צורבא מרבנן דהוה חריף טובא ואורייתיה מרתחא ליה,
וחיבר ספר על טור יורה דעה, הוא ספר פרי חדש, ויש בו חדושים רבים
מפלפול ובקיאות, ואע"פ שאין הכרעתו מכרעת לנו לענין פיסקא דדינא, מכל
מקום יועיל לנו הספר הלז להקל מעלינו טורח החיפוש, ולכל הפחות יועיל
להערה ואנחנו נדע מה נעשה. ובראותנו דבריו ומשפטיו ישרים נחזקם
ונאמצם, ואם לא ייטבו בעינינו - יהיו כלא היו. ויהי כבוא הספר הלז
למצרים, עברו מעברה על מקצת דבריו, ומצאו ששלח רסן לשונו לדבר תועה
על גדולי ישראל, אשר מימיהם אנו שותים ומפיהם אנו חיים, לא ישא פנים
לזקן שמורה הוראה, ועל רבינו הגדול בית יוסף אשר הוא לכל הוראתינו
יסוד ועמוד בכל התלמוד, וכתב עליו שטנה כדבר איש על תלמיד קטן

שלפניו ואפרוח שלא נפתחו עיניו "דלא ביש ליה שאסר את המותר" כו'. ויהי בהתפרסם הדברים, אזרו אנשי חיל בעוז מתנם, וקבצו חכמי ישראל מבני העיר, וגם גרים הנמצאים מארץ אחרת, ויבקשו לקעקע ביצתו, ועלתה הסכמת החכמים לפייס שני הצדדין לבלתי שלוח יד בחכם המחבר ולא לפגום בכבודו, חס וחלילה, לא בנגידא ולא בשמתא. אכן בינם לבינו בסתר דברו אתו תוכחות, והתנצל וידע אשר עשה, ובוש ממעשיו כבושת גנב כי ימצא. ולפייס את אנשי הצבא הרוזנים והסגנים, עלתה הסכמתם שספריו הנמצאים פה מצרים שישקעו בבנין. וגזרו והחרימו בכל תוקף ובכל אלות הברית על דעת המקום ברוך הוא, שלא יקרא אדם בספר הלז, לא קריאת עראי ולא קריאת קבע. וכתבו הסכמה זו למען תעמוד כל הימים, וחתמו בה כל חכמי העיר וגם הנמצאים מארץ אחרת. גם נקרו נקרו הנה רבני חברון תוב"ב, ושאלו מהם שיסכימו במעשה אשר נעשה, ואמרו שלרצון בני העיר הם חותמין בהסכמה זו, אכן אינם מקבלים הסכמה זו עליהם, שכצאתם חוץ לעיר יחזיקו בספר הלז וילמדו בו.

ולעת עתה שני רבנים שהיו גרים בארץ הלכו להם לארצם, והחכם המחבר נתבקש בישיבה של מעלה, ובכן כמה וכמה חכמים שלמים וכן רבים נכספה וגם כלתה נפשם להגות בספר הלז, כי יהיה להם מעיר לעזור, ומבקשים אולי תעלה תעלה למכה זו, ורמון זה שיעלה בידם - תוכו יאכלו כו'. ומה גם שהוא גם הוא בהקדמתו לספר הלז אמר שלא יסמוך שום אדם על הוראותיו ודחיותיו, רק יברר הטוב וההגון בעיניו וכן יעשה, גם התנצל על אשר דבר בגדולים. ועתה החרדים אל דבר ה' לשאול הגיעו אם אפשר להתיר חרם נזכר, כיון שנגע בכבוד גדולים, או לא?... וכשראיתי אני הצעיר קול הקריה הומה, וחפץ ורצון כמה תלמידי חכמים למצוא פתח תקוה, נתתי אל לבי להיות נדרש לדבר מצוה ולבדוק בזה עד מקום שידי יד כהה מגעת, מה גם שזה לי ימים והדבר הזה בלבי כאש בוערת, וחפץ הייתי שענין חמור כזה יפתח ויסתיים בגדולים, ועכשו יפתח בקטנים ויסתיים בגדולים, והם יבחרו ולא אני, וחפץ ה' בידינו יצלח, אמן כן יהי רצון.

תחלת כל דבר, מוצא שפתי אשנה, שכל פתגם אשר נעשה בתחלה שריר וקיים הוא. ואחר כך אבקש אם יש מחילה וכפרה לעון הלז אם לאו. ואחר כך אצדד בטענות המוצעיים למעלה. ואומר אני אף על פי שלכאורה נראה שהסכמה זו תמוהה הרבה, דכיצד יסכימו שלא לקרות בספר הלז שיש בו כמה חידושי דינים ולמנוע בר מן התלמידים, מכל מקום גדולה מזו מצינו שעושין מפני צורך השעה לגדר ולסייג לתורה. וכמו שאמרו בגמרא: פעמים שביטול התורה זהו יסודה. וכההוא עובדא דחנניה, שהיה מעבר שנים וקובע

חדשים, מצינו שעשו הפלגה גדולה לטהר את הטמא ולהתיר את האיסור, כי היכי דלא ליגררו אבתריה, כדאיתא בשלהי ברכות (סג, א-ב). ומשה רועה נאמן ואוהבן של ישראל שיבר לוחות מעשה אלהים, וגרם בזה רעות גדולות, שיהיו תלמידי חכמים לומדין ושוכחין ושיהיו לומדין תורה מתוך צער, אכן לצורך השעה עשה כן, שאמר מוטב שידונו כפנויה ולא ידונו כאשת איש, והסכים הקב"ה על ידו כדאיתא בפרק אמר רבי עקיבא (שבת פז, א). וכפי זה הדברים קל וחומר שהסכמה זו שרירא וקיימת, שחששו לכבודן של ראשונים ז"ל, ואין שם קום עשה רק גזרו בשב ואל תעשה, שלא ללמוד בספר הלז. וכל הסכמה דעלמא שאינה כל כך צורך השעה, אפילו שלא היו עושין אותה רק בית הדין שבעיר לבדו, הרי מעשיהם שריר וקיים, כל שכן בהתחבר לזה צורך השעה שחששו לפגם כבודם של ראשונים. אשר על כן המזלזל ומפקיר בהסכמה זאת הרי הוא כעובר על תורה חתומה שניתנה למשה מפי הגבורה, דקיימא לן דבית דין הממונה בעירו מינוהו אנשי העיר עליהם הרי הוא כבית דינו של משה רבינו ע"ה, דאמרינן (ראש השנה כה, א): כל שלשה ושלשה שנתמנו בית דין על ישראל הרי הוא כבית דינו של משה רבינו ע"ה, ע"כ... כללא דמלתא, דפתגם אשר נעשה הלכה קבועה היא, והמזלזל בה כמזלזל על דבריו של משה רבינו ע"ה.

ומעתה נראה אם יש רפואה למכתו דהאי צורבא מרבנן על שפגם וזלזל בכבוד גדולי ישראל. לזה אני אומר דאיתא בפרק יום הכפורים (יומא פו, א) ארבעה חלוקי כפרה שהיה ר' ישמעאל דורש, ואפילו עון גדול דחילול השם נתכפר ונתקנח העון לגמרי במיתה. והאי צורבא מרבנן, אף שנחמיר עליו שגדול עונו מנשוא, ומכשלה של חילול היתה תחת ידו שזלזל בכבודן של ראשונים, וירבו עבדים המתפרצים באדוניהם שהמון עם ירגילו עצמן לזלזל ולפקפק בדברי הראשונים, מכל מקום הרי נתכפר עון זה במיתה. וכיון שעונו נתכפר, יכולים בית דין להתיר החרם אשר נעשה בהסכמה.

אכן יש מקום עדיין לפקפק, דדלמא איכא למיחש דהמון עם ירגילו עצמן בכבודם של ראשונים. אמנם כיון דקיימא לן דמעשה בית דין אית ליה קלא, הרי נתפרסם בעיר מצרים ההסכמה הנעשית והחרם שהוטל בשביל עון שפגם בכבודם, ויקחו קל וחומר וידעו כי איסור גדול יש בדבר, ויזהרו הרבה מכאן ואילך בכבודן של ראשונים. ומה גם שנראה שחששא זו חששא רחוקה היא, שהרי מצינו שנתפשט ספרו זה בכל גבולי ישראל ולא מצינו שחששו לזה בשום מקום. ומכל מקום בית דין היפה שבמצרים יע"א יפה עשו שחששו אפילו לחששא רחוקה כזאת, מה גם שבזה שעשו נתרבה כבודן של ראשונים בעיני הבריות, וראוי והגון היה לעשות מה שעשו.

ובר מן דין כבר נודע שכל פותח ספר לא יחוש לדברי ספר הלז להתלמד ממנו
לזלזל ולפגום בכבודם של ראשונים, וקחזינא דכל ספר כיוצא בזה כל הוגה
בו אוכל תוכו וזורק קליפתו, וישראל קדושים הם שומעין להחמיר ולא
להקל ומכירין ויודעין בטיב ערכן של ראשונים ז"ל וצפרנס חביבה להם
מכריסן של אחרונים וקושטא מדיליה קאים, וכמה וכמה ספרים מצינו
שניתנו ליגנז ולית מאן דחש להון. אשר על כן, כיון דידענו דלא אהנו מעשיו
להביא תקלה על הצבור, ניתנה חטאתו לימחל.

ודברינו תלמוד ערוך הוא בפרק משוח מלחמה (צ"ל: פרק כהן משיח, הוריות יג, ב
- יד, א), בעובדא דרבי מאיר ורבי נתן שבקשו להכלים את הנשיא ולעקור
כבודו לירש את נשיאותו, וכשנודע הדבר לנשיא הוציאן מבית המדרש,
ולרוב חכמתם ולעוצם בינתם לימד עליהן זכות רבי יוסי והחזירן לבית
המדרש, וגזר הנשיא שלא יאמרו שמועה מפיהם, וגזרה זו היתה ממשמשת
ומלבטת אחריהם אפילו אחר מותם, עד שבא בן בנו של הנשיא ולימד
עליהם זכות, דכיון דהשתא כבר מתו שראוי להתיר מעליהם עונש זה.
ובספר עין יעקב מביא בזה פירוש הרמ"ה דמפרש שאפילו שכבר מתו לא
ניתן עונם לימחל, אלא משום דלא אהנו מעשייהו, אע"פ שהיתה כוונתם
לרעה, השתא מיהא ראוים הם לכפרה. ונראה דלא אהני טעמא דלא אהנו
מעשייהו אליבא דהרמ"ה, אלא בצירוף עוד לזה שכבר מתו.

נמצינו למדין לנדון הלז, דכיון דכבר האי צורבא מרבנן נפטר לבית עולמו
וגם נמי לא אהני מעשיו, שניתנה בבית דין של מטה להסיר העונש שענשוהו
שלא ללמוד בספרו. והדברים קל וחומר בנדון הלז, דחלילה לנו לומר
שהיתה לו כונה רעה לזלזל בכבודן של ראשונים, אלא דהוה ליה תרבות
בישא, והילדות עשתה את שלה.

65. משנת חכמים, סימן פה-פח

פה) והואיל וכן הוא בכלל אזהרה זו, יש להשמר הבעל תורה שלא לדבר
תועה על חבירו או חס וחלילה ליתכבד בקלונו, דכבר עונשו אמור מפי
סופרים, ועיין בזוהר ח"ג דף קסז ע"א, שמענה ואתה דע לך, בפרט בכתיבת
הפסקים, וכמה לעג וקלס הוא המחרף את חברו בפה וכל שכן בכתב. ועל
המדפיסים דברים כאלו קורא אני עליהם "ואשר לא טוב עשה בעמיו"
(יחזקאל יח, יח), שמא ישתו התלמידים ונמצא שם שמים מתחלל חלילה, ואם
באולי עברו ביניהם דברים קשים, מה תועלת בהדפסתם?! וה' יתברך הוא
העד והוא הדיין כמה עיכבתי את עצמי מלהדפיס הכתבים שהדפסתי נגד

ההוא נחש וסיעתו, תפח רוחם ונשמתם, לראות אולי יתקנו את אשר עיוותו
נגד ה׳ ותורתו, ולא נצטרך לפרסם הדבר דרך קנטור וזלזול.

אמנם כאשר חישבתי דרכי, וראיתי כתבי הצד המנגד וחירופיהן והמרד
והחוצפה שעמדו בה נגד כל חכמי ישראל כדי לקיים הטעות שיש בו מינות
שנפלו בו, והיה מעלה נחש זה, שכבר נפגר, תפח רוחו ונפשו, הדברים בכתב
ועשאם בדפוס למען יעמדו ימים רבים, הייתי מחוייב בעצמי להשיב להם גמול
בראשם ושלא לישא להם פנים, הואיל והם לא נשאו פנים לשמים לראות
את הנולד והקלקול שיוצא לכלל ישראל מהרס של עכנאי זה וכל כיוצאים
בו המתהווין בכל יום תמיד, כי היכי דלא להווי שתיקה כהודאה, מאחר
שרואה אני כל גדולי ישראל כובשין פניהם בקרקע ודנין את הדין על דרך מי
שיש לו אב יחיה ומי שאין לו אב ימות (בבלי, בבא מציעא פד, ב), קנא קינאתי
לה׳ צבאות ולתורתו ולעמו וגמרתי בדעתי ״ומתו גם שניהם״, דבמקום שיש
חילול ה׳ אין חולקין כבוד לרבים, וההכרח אם לא ישובח לא יגונה, מכל
שכן הכרח כזה שהיה בו ויש בו חיוב מן הדת ומן השכל המחייב, וכמו
שכתב האלוהי בשל״ה (דף תט) דכל דבר מגונה שנכתב מצד העונש לא שייך
לומר אל תספר בגנותו, כי זה הדין שלו, כמו שמעשים בכל יום להכריז על
אדם רשע דברי גנות, והיינו משום שהדין נותן ליענש בכך כדי לחייב את
החוטא שישוב מהחטא שבידו וכל העם ישמעו וייראו וגו׳ עיי״ש... ולכן כי
היכי דלא לגרירו עלמא אבתריי דנחש זה וכל כיוצאים בו, בהיותם רואין
שהיה מי שמחזיק בידם, עשיתי זאת כעין דרכה של תורה כמו שכתוב
״בראש הומיות תקרא בפתחי שערים אמריה תאמר״ (משלי א, כא).

והאלהים השופט תבל בצדק יעיד עלי כי הם פרצו את הגדר תחילה ושאני
לא הפרזתי על המדה, ומידת חכמים שנו כאן כי מידה כנגד מידה לא בטלה.
ואם הנחש וכל כיוצאין בו לא היו חוששין לכבוד שמים וכבוד הבריות, למה
זה היה לנו לחוש לכבודם ולכסותם כלילה, והם המגלים אשר גלו את
חרפתם ביום לעין השמש והירח בהיותם מחזיקים דברי מינות. ולכן מובטח
אני בה׳ יתברך לא יחשוב ה׳ לי עוון, כי אין ברוחי רמיה, ולא לכבודי ולא
לכבוד בית אבא וכל כיוצא בזה יוצא אני לקראת נשק ומשים עצמי אל מול
פני המלחמה, כי אם מהטעמים האמורים במכתבי ראשונים גם
אחרונים לעיני כל ישראל, וה׳ הטוב יכפר בעדי ובעד כל ישראל, ויתן בלב
הרחוקים יתמו חטאים וישמעו לדברי חכמים ויקרבום, אמן כן יהי רצון.

פו) אם ראית את חברך שעמל וטרח להוציא לאור איזה ספר להועיל בו את
הרבים, למה לך לגנות אותו, אשר לא עמלת בו ולא גדלתו, ולכתוב עליו
מרורות, כל זמן שאין טעותו דבר שיוצא נזק לכלל ישראל, או לתלמידים?

ואם נראה בעיניך שחכם גדול אתה ממנו, יבחנו נא דבריך ודבריו במשא
ומתן העיון והפלפול וכבוד כל אחד יהיה במקומו מונח. ואתה חשוב ותן
שבח והודאה ליוצר כל שחננך דעת צלולה ועמוקה מחברך, ועל זה הזהיר
שלמה החכם "ריבך ריב את רֵעֶךָ וסוד אחר אל תְּגָל" (משלי כה, ט). ומה מאוד
היה קשה בעיני איך הראב"ד ז"ל חסידא קדישא שבדורו היה גדול בתורה
וב—יראה, כמו שמעידין עליו שבזמנו של הרמב"ם היה כשהשיג עליו זקן
ומופלג בתורה ובחסידות, ובכדי בזיון וקצף סתר את קצת מדבריו והשיג
עליו, מאחר שהיה אפשר לו להשיגו באהבה ואחוה, וראה ערך מעלתו דהרי
על רובו ככולו קיים דבריו הואיל ולא סתר אותם, וכמו שכתבו בעלי
הכללים דכל מקום שאינו חולק הראב"ד ז"ל על הרמב"ם ז"ל הרי זה דעתו
של הרמב"ם ז"ל נחשב לשתי דעות, ובודאי עיניו ראו מה שכתב הרמב"ם
ז"ל בסוף פירושו למשנה, אשר בפה מלא כה אמר שמי שירצה לתופשו
ולהשיגו בחבורו אין ראוי לגנותו בתפיסתו, אבל הוא מושכר מן השמים על
זה ואהוב הוא אצלו, לפי שהיא מלאכת שמים, עכ"ד ז"ל. אם כן מה חרי
האף הגדול שהראה בהשגותיו כאילו חלילה אויב היה לו, וכאילו הוא
מחשיב להרמב"ם ז"ל לקטיל קניא באגמא?

פז) וכבר ראיתי להאלהי בעל שליה ז"ל בדף הנזכר לעיל, דתמה על כיוצא
בזה, דבהרבה מקומות מצינו ערוך בתלמוד שמביא איזה שפת יתר שדבר
אמורא אחד לחבירו, ומעיקרא הקשה על האמורא איך הוציא מפיו דבר
שאינו לפי כבוד חבירו, ואיך בעלי התלמוד כתבו דבריו על הספר הקדוש?
והביא קצת מהן, ההיא דעירובין (כה, ב) דהשיב חד לחבריה "משום
דממולאי קא אתיתו אמריתו מילי ממולאיי", וביבמות (ט, א) דאמרו
"כמדומה לי שאין לו מוח בקדקדו", ובסנהדרין פרק זה בורר (כו, א) בענין
החשוד על שביעית וכו' קראו "רועי בקר ורועי צאן" וכו'. והוא ז"ל יישב
ופירש הדבר, דחלילה להאמין דדרך זלזול קא אמר ליה אלא דרך חכמה
ומוסר ובלשון צחות דמשתמע לתרי אנפי, ע"ש דאין הספר לפני, כי האלהי
בעוצם בקיאותו וחסידותו לא הניח דבר שלא תקן. והביא ההיא דאמרו על
בנתיה דמר שמואל דאישתביין, ובנתיה דרב נחמן דהוו מבחשן קדרה
בכשפים, דבאמת נכתב כמו שהיה דאולי היה איזה עון על אביהם שלא
הוכיח אותן כראוי, לפיכך באו הבנות לכלל זה ועל צד העונש נכתב, ובכל
דבר שהוא על צד העונש אין איסור בדבר מכח התועלת היוצא מפרסום זה,
וכמו שכתבתי לעיל.

פח) ועוד נתישבה דעתי במה ששמעתי מפי מרן מר זקני ז"ל שהיה אומר
בשם אי"א ז"ל התנצלות נכון ואמתי, על דרך שאמרו בפרק הרואה (ברכות סג,

א) בענין חנניא בן אחי רבי יהושע שביזו אותו התלמידי חכמים ששלחו אחריו והיו אומרים להפך מדבריו כי היכי דלא ליגררו עלמא אבתריה. אם כן דהכא נמי ודאי כיון שראה הראב"ד ז"ל בחסידותו ובחכמתו החבור הגדול הזה שהוא נפלא מאד וטוב למאכל התלמידי חכמים בעלי ההוראה, אבל הוא סתום וחתום כאלו הלכה למשה נתנה לו מסיני, והאמת הוא כי יש בו מהדברים שחלקו וחולקים עליו גדולים מחכמי ישראל בכוונת השמועות, ולכן חשש שלא יגררו אחריו הדורות הבאים וייראו מגשת אליו לחלוק בחשבם שכך עלתה הסכמת חכמי ישראל כולם לדון כדבריו ככל אשר זמם ועשה בידיעתו ובכן לא יסורו ולא יטו מדבריו ימין ושמאל. לכן להרים המכשול מדרך חכמי ישראל הבאים אחריו סמך ידו עליו ועטרו בעטרת תפארת הסמיכה וקיים רוב דבריו אשר עלו בהסכמה, ולעומת זה הורה כי האמת אהובה אצלו ואזר כגבר חלציו וקם כגבור להתיר הרצועה לחכמים כמוהו לחלוק עליו. ולכן התיר את לשונו והוכיח בדברים קשים, כדי שידעו שלא צדק בכל דבריו, וכל איש חיל במלחמתה של תורה אשר בעיניו יבין ובאזניו ישמע פסק דינו יחקור עליו, ואם ימצא כי לא כן עלתה הסכמת רבים מחכמי ישראל הגדולים הרשות נתונה לחלוק עליו, כמו שעשה הוא ז"ל דהודה דטעה בפרטי דינים והמה מעטים. וכן מצינו שמליציו הישרים אוהביו וריעיו והאלהי המושלם הרמב"ן ז"ל והרב המגיד ז"ל הודו שיש קצת תפיסה על דבריו של הרמב"ם ז"ל. ואינו מן התימא לומר דטעה, דאשריו למי ששגגותיו ספורות, ומצינו בתלמוד ערוך דגם כן אמרו דטעו, כההיא דאמרו בשבת (כז, א) "הא דפלוני בדותא היא", "פלוני טעה בתרתי" (סנהדרין נב, ב), ובפרק השולח "נפק ודרש רב פפא דברים שאמרתי בפניכם טעות הם בידי", ובפרק כל הגט (גיטין כט, ב) "קפחינהו רב ספרא לתלתא סבי בטעותא".

66. צדקת הצדיק, אות קטו

כשמחדש דבר בתורה, צריך שלא יהא שום מצד נגיעה בלב שרוצה כך או להתפארות או לחלוק על דברי זולתו וכיוצא, רק מצד התשוקה לידע האמת. ואז אפילו טועה, נקרא דברי תורה ודברי אלהים חיים, שהרי נזכר בתלמוד דברי הטועים ושנדחו מהלכה, שגם ההוה אמינא הוא דברי תורה, שכך יסד השם יתברך מושכל ראשון ואחר כך הגעה לאמת, וגם המושכל ראשון הוא מהשם יתברך ודברי אלהים חיים. אבל כשהוא מצד הנגיעה, אז אינו נקרא דברי תורה כלל. כמו שכתוב בירבעם "החודש אשר בדא מלבו" (מלכים א יב, לג), ובודאי הוא דרש להם איזה דרוש ולימוד שחג האסיף הוא

בחשון, רק לפי שהיה מצד הנגיעה לעשות נגד בית דין שבירושלים, נקרא "אשר בדא מלבו", ולא נאמר בזה אלו ואלו דברי אלהים חיים. וכן דואג עשה הכל על פי התורה בדעתו, כי ראש הסנהדרין היה, והוא הורה "עמוני ואפילו עמונית" על פי הלכה שבדעתו שהרי אישתיקו נגדו (כמו שאמרו ביבמות עז, א), וממילא אי אפשר שיהיה דוד מלך, והוא מפסולי קהל, ודנו למורד במלכות וכן לאחימלך. ושאול אעפ"י שהיה סבור גם כן כך, הוא היה בטעות, ונקרא באמת בחיר ה', אבל דואג דברי תורה אלו נבעו מלבו מצד הקנאה, ואלולי נגיעה זו לא היה טועה. ובאופן זה נעשים דברי תורה סם המות, רוצה לומר שנאבדו מן העולם, כי אין זה נקרא דברי תורה באמת כלל, רק למראית העין.

67. שלום יהודה, לג (עמ' קה) (מכתב מבעל החזון-איש)

רצוני להעיר דחותבתנו ליזהר בלשוננו בדברנו נגד רבותינו, וקשה היה לי לשון כבוד תורתו שיחיה ששימש במלת "טעות" נגד הגאון מהרא"ז זצ"ל, ויש אפשרות לבאר הדברים בלשון נקיה ומכובדת כראוי לדבר בפני רבותינו. ולא עוד אלא שדורות הקודמים השתמשו בבקשת מחילה בעת שכתבו נגד החכם, מפני שכבוד רבם היה קבוע בלבבם, והיו מדברים ברתת ובזיע, לא כן אצלינו בקשת המחילה קובע את תקיפת הדעת שהשגתינו נכונה. ומאד מאד צריך התגברות בשעת השגה שלא ליהנות ממה שאינו צריך ליהנות, רק מגילוי התורה, ואם חובת הלב אין בידינו, אבל בלשוננו בידינו ליזהר.

68. שו"ת אגרות משה, יורה דעה ג, פח

בדבר שיש לך איזה חשש לקבוע מקומך בבני ברק מצד שבתוך דברי תורה איכא פעמים שאתה אומר שלא כדברי החזון איש זצ"ל, לא מובן שום חשש בזה, ואדרבה זהו כבודו אשר מזכירים שיטתו בדברי תורה ומעיינים בדבריו אף שהמסקנא דחכם המעיין הוא שלא כדבריו. ולא עלה כלל על דעת החזון איש זצ"ל שלא ימצאו תלמידי חכמים שיפלגו עליו ולא שייך שיקפיד על זה, דאדרבה "האמת והשלום אהבו" (זכריה ח, יט) כדאיתא ביבמות (יד, ב) על פלוגתא דבית שמאי ובית הלל. וענין "שפתותיו דובבות" הוא אף כשמזכירין דברי החכם וחולקין עליו.

אבל ודאי צריך להזכיר בדרך ארץ. ורבי יהושע (חגיגה כב, ב) שהושחרו שיניו מפני תעניותיו, לא היה משום שהקשה על דברי בית שמאי, אלא מפני שאמר בבטול: "בושני מדבריכם בית שמאי". אבל בלשון דרך ארץ ודאי שליכא שום קפידא, לא על מה שמקשין על דברי החכם ואף לא על מי

שחולקין עליו. ואדרבה מפורש בבבא בתרא (קל ע״ב), שאמר רבא לתלמידיו,
רב פפא ורב הונא בריה דרבי יהושע דאם יהיו להם קושיות על פסקא שלו
אסור להו לדון כדבריו, דאין לדיין אלא מה שעיניו רואות, והוא הדין
באיסורים, ורק אמר שלא יקרעו פסקא שלו לבטל דבריו, דאי הואי בחיים
דלמא אמינא לכו טעמא, ופירש רשב״ם: ושמא גם אתם תמצאו תירוץ
לקושיתכם. אבל כל זמן שלא מוצאין תירוץ אסור להם להורות כרבא אף
שהיה רבם. ואם כן כל שכן וכל שכן שאין לחוש מלהקשות ומלחלוק על
גדולי דורותינו אף הגדולים ביותר, אבל באופן דרך ארץ, שלכן ליכא שום
חשש ושום קפידא להשאר בבני ברק ולומר שיעורים, ואדרבה יהיה מליץ
יושר בעדך על שאתה מעיין בספריו.

69. תוספתא, סוטה ז, יא-יב (כתב יד ערפורט)

ועוד דרש: ״דברי חכמים כדרבונות״ (קהלת יב, יא), מה דרבן זה מכוין את
הפרה להביא חיים לעולם, כך דברי תורה מביאין חיים לעולם. או מה דרבן
זה מטלטל אף דברי תורה מיטלטלין? תלמוד לומר ״וכמסמרות נטועים״.
לא חסרין ולא יתרין? תלמוד לומר ״נטועים״. ״בעלי אסופות״ אלו תלמידי
חכמים שיושבין אסופות אסופות ואומרין על טמא טמא ועל טהור טהור.

לא יאמר אדם בעצמו: הואיל ואילו אוסרין ואילו מתירין למה אני למד?
תלמוד לומר ״ניתנו מרועה אחד״ (שם), רועה אחד קיבלן אל אחד בראן. אף
אתה עשה לבך כחדרי חדרים והכניס בו דברי מטמאין ואת דברי המטהרין.
אמר להם: אין דור יתום שרבי אלעזר בן עזריה שרוי בתוכו.

70. בבלי, חגיגה ג, ב

ואף הוא פתח ודרש: ״דברי חכמים כדרבונות וכמסמרות נטועים בעלי
אסופות נתנו מרועה אחד״ (קהלת יב, יא). למה נמשלו דברי תורה לדרבן?
לומר לך: מה דרבן זה מכוין את הפרה לתלמיה להוציא חיים לעולם, אף
דברי תורה מכוונין את לומדיהן מדרכי מיתה לדרכי חיים. אי מה דרבן זה
מטלטל אף דברי תורה מטלטלין? תלמוד לומר ״מסמרות״. אי מה מסמר
זה חסר ולא יתר אף דברי תורה חסירין ולא יתירין? תלמוד לומר
״נטועים״, מה נטיעה זו פרה ורבה אף דברי תורה פרין ורבין. ״בעלי
אסופות״ אלו תלמידי חכמים שיושבין אסופות אסופות ועוסקין בתורה,
הללו מטמאין והללו מטהרין הללו אוסרין והללו מתירין הללו פוסלין והללו
מכשירין. שמא יאמר אדם: היאך אני למד תורה מעתה? תלמוד לומר:
כולם ״נתנו מרועה אחד״ אל אחד נתן, פרנס אחד אמרן מפי אדון כל

המעשים ברוך הוא, דכתיב "וידבר אלהים את כל הדברים האלה" (שמות כ,
א). אף אתה עשה אזניך כאפרכסת, וקנה לך לב מבין לשמוע את דברי
מטמאים ואת דברי מטהרים, את דברי אוסרין ואת דברי מתירין, את דברי
פוסלין ואת דברי מכשירין.

71. פסיקתא רבתי, פרשה ג (מהדורת איש שלום, ח ע"א)

דבר אחר, מהו "כדרבונות" (קהלת יב, יא)? אמר רבי ברכיה : כדור של בנות,
כהדא ספירא דמינוקיתון שהן מקלטות בם, זו זורקת לכאן וזו זורקת
לכאן, כך הם חכמים נכנסים לתלמוד ועוסקים בתורה, זה אומר טעמו וזה
אומר טעמו, זה אומר טעם אחד וזה אומר טעם אחר, ודברים של אלו ואלו
נתנו ממשה הרועה ממה שקיבל מיחידו של עולם. מפני שזה אומר טעם
אחד וזה אומר טעם אחר, שמא דבריהן פורחין? תלמוד לומר "וכמסמרות
נטועים".

72. תנחומא, בהעלותך, פרשה טו

["בעלי אסופות" (קהלת יב, יא)], אלו הסנהדרין. ואם תאמר : הרי זה מתיר
וזה אוסר, זה פוסל וזה מכשיר, זה מטמא וזה מטהר, רבי אליעזר מחיב
ורבי יהושע פוטר, בית שמאי אוסרים ובית הלל מתירין, למי אשמע? אמר
הקב"ה : אף על פי כן כולם "נתנו מרועה אחד", זה משה שנאמר בו "ומשה
היה רועה" (שמות ג, א), שקיבל מיחידו של עולם, ודברים אחדים הם, אלא
זה אומר טעם אחד וזה אומר טעם אחר, לכך נאמר כולם "נתנו מרועה
אחד".

73. במדבר רבה, פרשה טו, כב

"אספה לי שבעים איש" (במדבר יא, טז), זה שאמר הכתוב (קהלת יב, יא) "דברי
חכמים כדורבנות וכמסמרות נטועים בעלי אסופות ניתנו מרועה אחד"...
"בעלי אסופות" אלו סנהדרין. ואם תאמר : זה מתיר וזה אוסר, זה פוסל וזה
מכשיר, זה מטמא וזה מטהר, רבי אליעזר מחייב ורבי יהושע פוטר, בית
שמאי פוסלין ובית הלל מכשירין - למי נשמע? אמר הקב"ה : אף על פי כן
כולם "נתנו מרועה אחד".

74. ירושלמי, ברכות פרק א, ד (ג, 2)

תני: יצאת בת קול ואמרה: אילו ואילו דברי אלהים חיים, אבל הלכה כדברי בית הלל. איכן יצאת בת קול? רבי ביבי אמר בשם רבי יוחנן: ביבנה יצאת בת קול.

75. בבלי, עירובין יג, ב

אמר רבי אבא אמר שמואל: שלש שנים נחלקו בית שמאי ובית הלל, הללו אומרים: הלכה כמותנו, והללו אומרים: הלכה כמותנו. יצאה בת קול ואמרה: אלו ואלו דברי אלהים חיים הן, והלכה כבית הלל. וכי מאחר שאלו ואלו דברי אלהים חיים, מפני מה זכו בית הלל לקבוע הלכה כמותן? מפני שנוחין ועלובין היו ושונין דבריהן ודברי בית שמאי. ולא עוד אלא שמקדימין דברי בית שמאי לדבריהן.

76. בבלי, גיטין ו, ב

כתיב "ותזנה עליו פילגשו" (שופטים יט, ב), רבי אביתר אמר: זבוב מצא לה; רבי יונתן אמר: נימא מצא. ואשכחיה רבי אביתר לאליהו, אמר ליה: מאי קא עביד הקב"ה? אמר ליה: עסיק בפילגש בגבעה. ומאי קאמר? אמר ליה: אביתר בני כך הוא אומר, יונתן בני כך הוא אומר. אמר ליה: חס ושלום, ומי איכא ספיקא קמי שמיא? אמר ליה: אלו ואלו דברי אלהים חיים הן, זבוב מצא ולא הקפיד נימא מצא והקפיד. אמר רב יהודה: זבוב בקערה ונימא באותו מקום. זבוב מאיסותא ונימא סכנתא. איכא דאמרי: אידי ואידי בקערה, זבוב אונסא ונימא פשיעותא.

77. ירושלמי, סנהדרין פרק ד, ב (כב, 1)

אמר רבי ינאי: אילו ניתנה התורה חתוכה, לא היתה לרגל עמידה. מה טעם? "וידבר ה' אל משה", אמר לפניו: רבונו של עולם, הודיעני היאך היא ההלכה, אמר לו: "אחרי רבים להטות" (שמות כג, ב), רבו המזכין זכו, רבו המחייבין חייבו, כדי שתהא התורה נדרשת מ"ט פנים טמא ומ"ט פנים טהור, מניין "ודגלו" (שיר השירים ב, ד). וכן הוא אומר (תהלים יב, ז): "אמרות ה' אמרות טהורות כסף צרוף בעליל לארץ מזוקק שבעתים". ואומר (שיר השירים א, ד): "מישרים אהבוך".

78. פסיקתא רבתי, פרשה כא (מהדורת איש שלום, קא ע״א)

[״פנים בפנים דיבר ה׳ עמכם״ (דברים ה, ד)]. אמר רבי תנחום ב״ר חנילאי:
אילו ניתנה תורה חתוכה לא היתה עמידת רגל למורה שיורה, שאם טימא
יש מטמאין כיוצא בו ואם טיהר יש מטהרין כיוצא בו.

אמר רבי ינאי: תורה שנתן הקב״ה למשה ניתנה לו ארבעים ותשע פנים
טהור וארבעים ותשע פנים טמא, מניין ״ודגלו עלי אהבה״ (שיר השירים ב, ד).
אמר לו: האיך עבידת? אמר לו: רבו המטמאין - טמא, רבו המטהרין -
טהור.

79. מדרש תהלים, יב

[״אמרות ה׳ אמרות טהרות כסף צרוף בעליל לארץ מזקק שבעתים״]. אמר
רבי ינאי: לא נתנה דברי תורה חתיכין, אלא על כל דבור שהיה אומר
הקב״ה למשה היה אומר לו מ״ט פנים טהור ומ״ט פנים טמא. אמר לפניו:
רבונו של עולם, עד מתי נעמוד על ביררו של דבר? אמר ליה ״אחרי רבים
להטות״ (שמות כג, ב), רבו המטמאין טמא, רבו המטהרין טהור. ר׳ אבהו
בשם ר׳ יונתן אמר: תלמיד וותיק היה לו לר׳ עקיבא, ור׳ מאיר שמו, והיה
מטהר את השרץ מן התורה במ״ט פנים טהור, ובמ״ט פנים טמא. ר׳ יהושע
בן לוי אמר: תינוקות שהיו בימי שאול ודוד ובימי שמואל, היו יודעין לדרוש
את התורה במ״ט פנים טהור, ובמ״ט פנים טמא.

80. בבלי, בבא מציעא נט, ב

וזה הוא תנור של עכנאי. מאי עכנאי? אמר רב יהודה אמר שמואל שהקיפו
דברים כעכנא זו וטמאוהו. תנא: באותו היום השיב רבי אליעזר כל תשובות
שבעולם ולא קיבלו הימנו, אמר להם: אם הלכה כמותי חרוב זה יוכיח.
נעקר חרוב ממקומו מאה אמה, ואמרי לה ארבע מאות אמה. אמרו לו: אין
מביאין ראיה מן החרוב. חזר ואמר להם: אם הלכה כמותי אמת המים
יוכיחו. חזרו אמת המים לאחוריהם. אמרו לו: אין מביאין ראיה מאמת
המים. חזר ואמר להם: אם הלכה כמותי כותלי בית המדרש יוכיחו. הטו
כותלי בית המדרש ליפול. גער בהם רבי יהושע, אמר להם: אם תלמידי
חכמים מנצחים זה את זה בהלכה, אתם מה טיבכם? לא נפלו מפני כבודו
של רבי יהושע ולא זקפו מפני כבודו של רבי אליעזר ועדיין מטין ועומדין.
חזר ואמר להם: אם הלכה כמותי מן השמים יוכיחו. יצאתה בת קול
ואמרה: מה לכם אצל רבי אליעזר שהלכה כמותו בכל מקום? עמד רבי
יהושע על רגליו ואמר: ״לא בשמים היא״ (דברים ל, יב). מאי ״לא בשמים

היא"? אמר רבי ירמיה: שכבר נתנה תורה מהר סיני אין אנו משגיחין בבת
קול, שכבר כתבת בהר סיני בתורה "אחרי רבים להטות" (שמות כג, ב).
אשכחיה רבי נתן לאליהו, אמר ליה: מאי עביד קוב"ה בההיא שעתא? אמר
ליה: קא חייך ואמר: נצחוני בני נצחוני בני.

81. בבלי, בבא מציעא פד, א

נח נפשיה דרבי שמעון בן לקיש, והוה קא מצטער רבי יוחנן בתריה טובא.
אמרו רבנן: מאן ליזיל ליתביה לדעתיה? ניזיל רבי אלעזר בן פדת דמחדדין
שמעתתיה. אזל יתיב קמיה. כל מילתא דהוה אמר רבי יוחנן אמר ליה: תנא
דמסייעא לך. אמר: את כבר לקישא? בר לקישא כי הוה אמינא מילתא, הוי
מקשי לי עשרין וארבע קושייתא ומפרקינא ליה עשרין וארבעה פרוקי
וממילא רווחא שמעתא ואת אמרת "תניא דמסייע לך", אטו לא ידענא
דשפיר קאמינא? הוה קא אזיל וקרע מאניה וקא בכי ואמר: היכא את בר
לקישא? היכא את בר לקישא? והוה קא צווח עד דשף דעתיה [מיניה]. בעו
רבנן רחמי עליה ונח נפשיה.

82. בבלי, בבא מציעא פו, א

אמר רב כהנא: אישתעי לי רב חמא בר ברתיה דחסא: רבה בר נחמני אגב
שמדא נח נפשיה. אכלו ביה קורצא בי מלכא, אמרו: איכא חד גברא
ביהודאי דקא מבטל תריסר אלפי גברי מישראל ירחא בקייטא וירחא
בסתוא מכרגא דמלכא. שדרו פריסתקא דמלכא בתריה ולא אשכחיה... ערק
ואזיל לאגמא. הוה יתיב אגירדא דדקולא וקא גריס. קא מיפלגי במתיבתא
דרקיעא: אם בהרת קודמת לשער לבן - טמא, ואם שער לבן קודם לבהרת -
טהור. ספק - הקב"ה אומר טהור, וכולהו מתיבתא דרקיעא אמרי טמא.
ואמרי: מאן נוכח? נוכח רבה בר נחמני. דאמר רבה בר נחמני: אני יחיד
בנגעים, אני יחיד באהלות. שדרו שליחא בתריה, לא הוה מצי מלאך המות
למקרב ליה, מדלא הוה קא פסיק פומיה מגרסיה. אדהכי נשב זיקא ואויש
ביני קני, סבר גונדא דפרשי הוא. אמר: תינח נפשיה דההוא גברא, ולא ימסר
בידא דמלכותא. כי הוה קא ניחא נפשיה אמר: טהור, טהור. יצאת בת קול
ואמרה: אשריך רבה בר נחמני שגופך טהור ויצאתה נשמתך בטהור.

83. בבלי בבא בתרא עה, א

"ושמתי כדכד שמשותיך" (ישעיה נד, יב), אמר רבי שמואל בר נחמני: פליגי
תרי מלאכי ברקיעא, גבריאל ומיכאל, ואמרי לה תרי אמוראי במערבא,

ומאן אינון? יהודה וחזקיה בני רבי חייא, חד אמר: שוהם, וחד אמר: ישפה.
אמר להו הקב״ה: להוי כדין וכדין.

84. בבלי, מנחות כט, ב

אמר רב יהודה אמר רב: בשעה שעלה משה למרום מצאו להקב״ה שיושב
וקושר כתרים לאותיות, אמר לפניו: רבונו של עולם, מי מעכב על ידך? אמר
לו: אדם אחד יש שעתיד להיות בסוף כמה דורות, ועקיבא בן יוסף שמו,
שעתיד לדרוש על כל קוץ וקוץ תילין תילין של הלכות. אמר לפניו: רבונו של
עולם, הראהו לי. אמר לו: חזור לאחורך. הלך וישב בסוף שמונה שורות ולא
היה יודע מה הן אומרים. תשש כוחו. כיון שהגיע לדבר אחד אמרו לו
תלמידיו: רבי מנין לך? אמר להן: הלכה למשה מסיני. נתיישבה דעתו.

חזר ובא לפני הקב״ה. אמר לפניו: רבונו של עולם, יש לך אדם כזה ואתה
נותן תורה על ידי? אמר לו: שתוק, כך עלה במחשבה לפני. אמר לפניו: רבונו
של עולם, הראיתני תורתו, הראני שכרו. אמר לו: חזור לאחורך. חזר
לאחוריו, ראה ששוקלין בשרו במקולין. אמר לפניו: רבונו של עולם, זו
תורה וזו שכרה? אמר ליה: שתוק, כך עלה במחשבה לפני.

85. פירושי רב סעדיה גאון לבראשית, פתיחה, עמ׳ 187-188

ואם ישאל אדם: כיצד נכנסו לתוך המשנה והתלמוד מחלוקות בין בעלי
הקבלה? נאמר: אין אלה מחלוקות באמת, אלא נראות כמחלוקת בתחילת
הגעת הדברים לשומע, ולאמיתו של דבר [המחלוקות שבתלמוד] הן משלושה
סוגים:

א. חכם הראה את עצמו כחולק על חברו והקניטו כדי שיוודע לו על ידי כך
טיב דעתו [של חברו], וכמו שהראה משה את עצמו ככועס על אהרן ובניו
ששרפו את שעיר החטאת, כדי שיגלו לו את דעתם הם, כי משה לא האמין
ששרפו [את שעיר החטאת] מחסרון ידיעה.

ב. הדבר נשמע מפי הנביא בשני אופנים שונים: באופן אחד הוא מותר ובשני
אסור. וקדם אחד מן החכמים והזכיר את האופן המותר ובא השני והזכיר
את האסור. ודברי שניהם צודקים, כי הדבר ההוא אמנם מותר באופן אחד
ואסור באופן אחר. ודוגמה לזה מה שאמר הכתוב ״לא תשחית את עצה״
(דברים כ, יט) ואמר ״רק עץ אשר תדע״ וגו׳ (שם שם, כ). ואמר ״בת כהן כי
תהיה לאיש זר לא תאכל״ (ויקרא כב, יב) ואחרי כן נאמר ״ובת כהן כי תהיה
אלמנה מלמה אביה תאכל״ (שם שם, יג). ואין הבדל [בין המקרים] שבהם

הכתוב מכריע בין שני הפסוקים המקבילים קרוב אליהם, ובין המקרים שהוא רחוק מהם מרחק פסוקים ומתברר אחר כך.

ג. אחד מן החכמים שמע דבר חלקי ודימה שהוא שלם, ואחרים שמעו סופו של דבר, וכשהזכיר הראשון מה שעלה על דעתו טענו נגדו ואמרו: אנו שמענו סופו של דבר והוא מצמצם את שמעותך אתה. ודוגמה לכך, אדם קורא בחומש השלישי שבתורה "ובגד כלאים שעטנז" (ויקרא יט, יט) והוא סובר שזה כולל הכל, וכשהוא אומר דבר זה לפני מי שקרא את כל התורה הלה, מודיעו שהכתוב צמצם את הכלל בחלק החמישי ועשאו פרט כאמור "צמר ופשתים" (דברים כב, יא), וכן כל כיוצא בזה.

86. אוצר הגאונים, ראש השנה לד, א

תשובת שאלה לרבינו האי גאון ז"ל על התקיעות שהתקין רבי אבהו (בבלי, ראש השנה לד, א). שאל רבינו הצדיק ז"ל מלפני אדונינו על התקיעות... ועוד, מקודם רבי אבהו מה היו עושין והוא חובה של כל שנה ושנה, ולא ייתכן מימות נביאים הראשונים ועד ימות רבי אבהו שהניחו שנה אחת בלא תקיעה, ואם החובה ידועה אצלם, מה תיקן להם רבי אבהו? והתיקון לא יהא אלא על דבר שנסתפק ונתערבב, ואנו אומרים שלא יתכן להיות אמת בשני דרכים, אלא אם התרועה היא האמת, השלושה שברים אינם חשובים, ואם השלושה שברים הם העקר התרועה לאו כלום היא...

תשובה: ...ומה שכתבתם: "אנו אומרים שלא ייתכן האמת בשני דברים", בודאי כן הוא, אלא מיהו זה רק בזמן שאותם שני דברים מכחישים זה את זה, אבל בזמן שזה כשר וזה כשר ייתכן להיות האמת בשני דרכים, השברים אמת ותרועה כשרה גם ביבבות.

87. רש"י, כתובות נז, א, ד"ה הא קמ"ל

דכי פליגי תרי אליבא דחד, מר אמר הכי אמר פלוני ומר אמר הכי אמר פלוני, חד מינייהו משקר. אבל כי פליגי תרי אמוראי בדין או באיסור והיתר, כל חד אמר הכי מיסתבר טעמא, אין כאן שקר, כל חד וחד סברא דידיה קאמר, מר יהיב טעמא להיתרא ומר יהיב טעמא לאיסורא, מר מדמי מילתא למילתא הכי ומר מדמי ליה בעניינא אחרינא, ואיכא למימר אלו ואלו דברי אלהים חיים הם, זימנין דשייך האי טעמא וזימנין דשייך האי טעמא, שהטעם מתהפך לפי שינוי הדברים בשינוי מועט.

88. מחברת הערוך, חלק הדיקדוק (דף ה ע״ד)

וכן נמי מקצרין בדברי רבותינו, כגון מה שאמרו בענין אילו ואילו דברי
אלהים חיים הן, פירוש הן דורשין, שלא יתכן שיהא בדברי אלהים חיים
חלוקה, אלא הלכה כאחד מהן ודברי השני נדחין ושכר דרשה יש לו.

89. ספר המנהיג, הקדמה

ויהי כאשר עוה הזמן נתיבותי, ויטרידני מרבצי ומארץ מושבותי, לעזוב
מחוז חפצי ונחלת אבותי, לשוט בארץ ולהתהלך בה... וימלך לבי עלי,
ברשיון רבותי ומשכילי, לשנס מתני שכלי וילדי רעיוני, להעיר ולהתבונן
במנהג כל מדינה ומדינה עיר ועיר, וארא והנה הנה דתיהם שונות, מתחלקות
לשבעים לשונות, המונים המונים, וכולם מכלים שונים. וגם אמנה כי כל
דתי עם אלוהינו ומנהגותם, ותורתם ויסודם ואשיותם וקירותם, בחצריהם
ובטירותם, כלם על יסוד האמת בנויים, ואלו ואלו דברי אלהים חיים, וכלם
חרדים לדברי יושב בשמים, ורצים ואצים להפיק רצונו, מדינה ומדינה
ככתבה ועם ועם כלשונו, איש רב ואיש צעיר, איש חלק ואיש שעיר, זה
יקריב פר וזה שעיר, זה ינסך דמעיו לצורו בכל עיר ועיר, וזה חלבו ודמו באש
דתו יבעיר, זה יקום חצות לילה וזה שחרים יעיר, וכולם ניתנו מרועה אחד,
ובין שאמרו להדליק ובין שאמרו שלא להדליק, שניהם לא נתכונו אלא
לדבר אחד.

90. שו״ת מן השמים, ג

ועוד שאלתי על סדר פרשיות שבתפילין וכך היתה שאלתי: אנא המלך הגדול
הגבור והנורא חכם הרזים מגלה נסתרות מגיד נעלמות שומר הברית
והחסד, הגדל נא חסדך עמנו היום וצוה למלאכיך הקדושים להודיעני את
אשר נסתפקנו בסדר פרשיות של תפלין, כי יש מהחכמים האומרים הויות
באמצע ואם החליף פסולות, ויש מחכמים האומרים הויות כסדרן ואם
החליף פסולות. ועתה מלך מלכים צוה למלאכיך הקדושים להודיעני הלכה
כדברי מי, ודברי מי אתה מחבב.

והשיבו: אלו ואלו דברי אלהים חיים, וכמחלוקת למטה כך מחלוקת
למעלה, הקב״ה אומר: הויות באמצע, וכל פמליא של מעלה אומרים: הויות
כסדרן. והוא אשר דיבר ה' ״בקרובי אקדש ועל פני כל העם אכבד״ (ויקרא י,
ג), וזה כבודו בהיות פרשת מלכות שמים תחילה.

91. תוספות רבינו פרץ, עירובין יג, ב

אלו ואלו דברי אלהים חיים, ואם תאמר: גבי איסור והיתר היכי שייך לומר "אלו ואלו דברי אלהים חיים", אם הוא אסור אינו מותר ואם הוא מותר אינו אסור? ואומר מורינו רבינו פרץ, נוחו עדן, דמצא בתוספות הר"ר יחיאל דאיתא במדרש דהקב"ה שנאה התורה למשה בארבעים ותשעה פנים מותר ובארבעים ותשעה פנים אסור, אמר משה להקב"ה: מה אעשה? אמר לו הקב"ה: הלך אחר רוב חכמי הדור, אם רוב חכמי הדור מסכימים להיתר יהא מותר.

ומכל מקום קשה ממעשים שכבר היו, כגון ממזבח, דחד מוכח מקרא שהיה ששים וחד מוכח מקרא דהיה עשרים (זבחים סב, א), והתם היכי שייך לומר "אלו ואלו דברי אלהים חיים", דהא ליכא למימר הלך אחר רוב חכמי הדור, דהא לא היה אלא בחד ענינא! ויש לומר דגם כולהו לא היה אלא בחד ענינא, אלא חד מוכח מקרא דבדין היה לו להיות הכי וחד מוכח מקרא דבדין היה לו להיות הכי, והא דקאמר "אלו ואלו דברי אלהים חיים", פירוש דמתוך הפסוקים יש משמעות למידרש כמר וכמר, אבל ודאי לא היה אלא בענין אחד.

92. פירושים ופסקים לרבינו אביגדור, פסקים במגילת שיר השירים, פסק תקפ, עמ' תעג

"אחת היא לְאִמָּהּ" (שיר השירים ו, ט) – בגמרא מפרש אע"פ שהללו אוסרין והללו מתירין, אילו ואילו דברי אלקים חיים הם (עירובין יג, ב). וקשה, איך ייתכן זה, אם הוא אסור אז אינו מותר, אם הוא טהור אז אינו טמא, דהתינח פילגש בגבעה אפשר דשניהם היו (טמא ו), זבוב שמצא בקערה ונימא קשורה באותו מקום, אבל גבי איסור והיתר קשה. ויש לומר כן העניין, אם רוב ישראל מסכימים לאיסור אף הקב"ה מסכים עמהם, שכן כתוב בתורה "אחרי רבים להטות" (שמות כג, ב), וכשיבא דור אחר שרובן מסכימים להיתר אז הקב"ה נמי מסכים עמהם. וראיה: מין במינו היה במשהו בדורו של רבינו הגאון רש"י, ועכשיו הסכימו לדברי רבינו תם ובטל בששים, הוי זה וזה "דברי אלהים חיים הם". בשם הקדוש רבינו ווירדימס.

93. מלחמות ה', הקדמה

ואחרי הודות את השם הנכבד והנורא הזה בכל לב ובכל נפש ובכל כח ובכל מאד, ושאלת הפיק רצון ממנו להדריכנו בדרך ישרה ובקשת המחילה מלפניו על שגיאות, אומר כי התנצלותי על החבור הזה מבואר משני פנים:

האחד, מצד החיוב המוטל עלינו לחפש בעניני התורה והמצות ולהוציא
לאור תעלומות מצפונים, ושאין אנחנו רשאין להתעצל בידיעתה ולהתרשל
בלמודה, ולא לירוא אדם בהוראותיה ומשפטיה, כמו שכתוב "לא תגורו
מפני איש" (דברים א, יז), וכאשר בא בביאור הכתוב הזה ויתר הכתובים
הדומים לו בדברי חכמי ישראל ז"ל. והשני, כי אין הספר הזה ברוב דבריו
מחדש דברים שלא נאמרו עד היותו...

ואתה המסתכל בספרי, אל תאמר בלבבך כי כל תשובתי על הרב רבי זרחיה
ז"ל כולן בעיני תשובות נצחות ומכריחות אותך להודות בהם על פני
עקשותך, ותתפאר בהיותך מספק אחת מהן על לומדיה, או תטריח על דעתך
להכנס בנקב המחט לדחות מעליך הכרח ראיותי. אין הדבר כן, כי יודע כל
לומד תלמודנו שאין במחלוקת מפרשיו ראיות גמורות ולא ברוב קושיות
חלוטות, שאין בחכמה הזאת מופת ברור כגון חשבוני התשבורות ונסיוני
התכונה. אבל נשים כל מאדנו ודיינו מכל מחלוקת בהרחיק אחת מן הדעות
בסברות מכריעות ונדחוק עליה השמועות, ונשים יתרון הכשר לבעל דינה
מפשטי ההלכות והוגן הסוגיות עם הסכמת השכל הנכון, וזאת תכלית
יכלתנו, וכוונת כל חכם וירא האלהים בחכמת הגמרא.

ויש אשר אנחנו מלמדים זכות על דברי רבינו, עם היותם עדיין רחוקים
בפשטי הסוגיא או הסוגיות, אבל כוונתנו בזה לגלות אוזן התלמידים במה
שיש בהם מן הזכות, ואין אנו מעלימים מהגיד לכל מסתכל בספרנו מה
שנשאר עליה מן הספק, וזה מותר לנו אנחנו מפני שאנו באים ללמד זכות על
הרב הגדול ודברי הראשונים. וכן חובתינו עמו, כמו שהורו חכמי ישראל ז"ל
לתלמידיהם, אמרו (בבא בתרא קל, ב): "כי אתי פסקא דדינא דידי לקמייכו
לאחר מיתה לא מקרע תקרעוניה ולא מגמר תגמורין מיניה. מקרע לא
תקרעוניה דלמא אי הואי אנא אית לי טעמא, מגמר לא תגמרון מיניה שאין
לדיין אלא מה שעיניו רואות". ויצא לנו מזה לחוש לדברי רבינו להחמיר ולא
להקל. וזה במיעוט המקומות. אבל ברובם מחשבתנו נכרת מתוך ספרנו,
שעיקרי הדברים מוכרעין כדברי רבינו, ואפילו בשקולין הרי הדין פסוק
עלינו בלי להטות מדבריו ימין ושמאל, כמו ששנו חכמים (עבודה זרה ז, א): היו
שנים, אחד מטמא ואחד מטהר אחד אוסר ואחד מתיר, אם היה אחד מהם
גדול מחבירו בחכמה ובמנין הלך אחריו. וכל שכן בהיותו קודם שהמחלוקת
מנועה מבעליה, שהיה לו לומר: כבר הורה זקן. וזאת אות הברית אשר
הקימותי בכל מחלוקתינו בענין ההלכות.

94. ספר הרימון, עמ' 131

אמנם כי כבר ידעת כי התורה נקראת עץ החיים... ואמנם כי האילן יש בו
ענפים ועלים וקליפה ומוח ושורש, וכל אחד מהם נקרא אילן ואין בו פירוד,
כך תמצא התורה יש בה כמה עניינים פנימיים וחיצוניים והכל תורה אחת
ואילן אחד ואין בו פירוד. והנה על אשר אמרנו כי בכמה מקומות תמצא
בתורה ענין אחד מבואר כך, ואחרי כן אותו הענין ממש מבואר בענין אחר,
ואחר כך בענין אחר הפך מכולם, אל יקשה בעיניך ואל יטה לבבך לצד אחר
להיות דעתך בחילוף אותם הדברים לומר שהם מתחלפים בעניינים
מופלגים, אלא כל התורה כולה עניינים נכונים ואין בהם פירוד, כי הכל ענין
אחד, כאשר דרשו (שבת פח, ב) "וכפטיש יפוצץ סלע" (ירמיה כג, כט), והכל
ממקום אחד והכל אחד.

ואף על פי שתמצא בדברי רז"ל זה אוסר וזה מכשיר, זה מחמיר וזה מתיר,
זה אומר כך וזה אומר כך, יש לך לדעת כי הכל אחד ואין זה מחליק דעתו
מזה, כי כולם אינם מתפרשים מדרך האילן חוצה, וכל הדעות נכונות. ועל כן
אף על פי שתמצא פירוש אחד לדבר זה ופירוש אחר ופירוש אחר עד כמה
פירושים, הכל הוא נכון, וכל אותם הדברים ניתן ונתהוה אותו הענין. ועל כן
אמרו ז"ל: הקול היה יוצא בשעת מתן תורה ומתחלק אותו הקול לשבעה
קולות, וכל אחד מהם מתחלק לעשרה פנים עד שנמצא הקול ההוא עולה
לשבעים פנים, והוא סוד קול אחד, וכל הפנים שהם שבעים הם בסוד אחד.
ולפי זה הסוד שבעים פנים לתורה, והכל אחד.

95. חידושי הריטב"א, עירובין יג, ב, ד"ה אלו ואלו

אלו ואלו דברי אלהים חיים. שאלו רבני צרפת ז"ל: האיך אפשר שיהו
שניהם דברי אלהים חיים, וזה אוסר וזה מתיר? ותירצו: כי כשעלה משה
למרום לקבל תורה, הראו לו על כל דבר מ"ט פנים לאיסור ומ"ט פנים
להיתר, ושאל להקב"ה על זה, ואמר שיהא זה מסור לחכמי ישראל שבכל
דור ודור, ויהיה ההכרעה כמותם. ונכון הוא לפי הדרש, ובדרך האמת יש טעם
סוד בדבר.

96. דרשות הר"ן, דרשה ה, נוסח ב

ואף אם יסכים היחיד לאמת יותר מן המרובים, יש לו לבטל דעתו אצלם...
וכבר אמרו בבבא מציעא (נט, ב) בענין רבי אליעזר ורבי יהושע: עמד רבי
יהושע על רגליו ואמר "לא בשמים היא" (דברים ל, יב), מאי "לא בשמים
היא"?! כבר נתנה לנו משה על הר סיני וכתוב בה "אחרי רבים להטות" (שמות

כג, ב). והפירוש אצלי הוא, כי החכם יתיר ספקות התורה שהוא יסוד הכל, וישמע אליו הנביא על כרחו, ואם הנביא יעיר לחכם דבר במשפטי התורה שיביאהו מצד נבואתו - לא ישמע אליו כלל. הנה ראו כלם שרבי אליעזר מסכים אל האמת יותר מהם, וכי אותותיו כלם אמתים צודקים, והכריעו מן השמים כדבריו ואף על פי כן עשו מעשה כהסכמתם, שאחר ששכלם נוטה לטמא, אף על פי שהיו יודעים שהיו מסכימים להפך מן האמת, לא רצו לטהר, והיו עוברים על דברי תורה אם היו מטהרים, כיון ששכלם חייב לטמא, שההכרעה נמסרה לחכמי הדורות, ואשר יסכימו הם, הוא אשר צוהו השם יתברך.

וזה נתברר בחגיגה, אמרו שם (ג, ב): ועוד פתח ודרש "דברי חכמים כדרבונות וכמסמרות נטועים בעלי אסופות נתנו מרועה אחד" (קהלת יב, יא). מה דרבן זה מכוין את הפרה לתלמיה להביא חיים לעולם, אף דברי תורה מכוונים לב לומדיהם מדרכי מיתה לדרכי חיים. רצה בזה, שכמו שהדרבן הוא מיישר את הפרה לעשות חרישתה ביושר ושלא תלך אנה ואנה, ומן היושר ההוא בא חיים לעולם והן התבואה והפירות, אף דברי תורה מכוונין לב האדם ומפקחין אותו, ולא פקחות שמגיע ממנו נזק או דעת נפסד, אלא השגת דעת אמתי יגיע בו האדם למה שהוא תכליתו. שיש חכמות מפקחות לב האדם אבל יטוהו מדרכי חיים לדרכי מות, ויגיעו מהן דעות נפסדות שבהן יהיה נטרד, אבל התורה לא תשאיר ללומדיה דעת נפסד ולא מדה מגונה. וכבר נרמז בקדושין, אמרו שם (ל, ב): "ושמתם" (דברים יא, יח) סם תם, נמשלה תורה לסם חיים. משל לאדם שהכה את בנו מכה גדולה והניח לו רטיה על מכתו ואמר לו: בני, כל זמן שרטיה זו על מכתך אכול מה שהנאתך ושתה מה שהנאתך ורחוץ בין בחמין בין בצונן ואי אתה מתיירא, ואם אתה מעבירה הרי היא מעלה רמה. כבר ביאר שלא יפחד בהיותו עוסק בתורה פן יתקפהו היצר, כי עסק התורה יצילהו מכל זה. וזהו מה שאמרו כאן מכוונין לב לומדיהם.

ואמרו עוד (חגיגה שם): "בעלי אסופות" אלו תלמידי חכמים שיושבין אסופות אסופות ועוסקין בתורה, הללו מטהרין והללו מטמאין הללו מכשירים והללו פוסלין הללו מתירים והללו אוסרין, שמא תאמר היאך אני למד תורה מעתה, כלומר אני יודע איזה מהם השיג האמת, תלמוד לומר כלם "נתנו מרועה אחד", כלן פרנס אחד אמרן מפי אדון כל המעשים ברוך הוא, שנאמר "וידבר אלהים את כל הדברים האלה לאמר" (שמות כ, א), דרשו מלת "כל", שאפילו דברי מי שלא השיג האמת.

וזה הענין צריך עיון, איך נאמר ששני כתות המחלוקות נאמרו מפי הגבורה,
הנה רבי אליעזר ורבי יהושע נחלקו, והאחד השיג האמת והשני לא השיגו,
ואיך נאמר שיצא מפי הגבורה דבר שאינו אמיתי? אבל הענין כך הוא: שכבר
ידוע שכל התורה שבכתב ושבעל פה נמסרה למשה, כמו שאמרו במגילה (יט,
ב): אמר רבי חייא בר אבא אמר רבי יוחנן, מאי דכתיב "ועליהם ככל
הדברים" (דברים ט, י) וגו'? מלמד שהראהו הקב"ה למשה דקדוקי תורה
ודקדוקי סופרים ומה שהסופרים עתידין לחדש. ומאי ניהו? מקרא מגלה.
דקדוקי סופרים הם המחלוקות וחלוקי הסברות שבין חכמי ישראל, וכולן
למדם משה מפי הגבורה. ומסר בו כלל אשר בו יודע האמת, והוא "אחרי
רבים להטות", וכן "לא תסור מן הדבר אשר יגידו לך" (דברים יז, יא). וכשרבו
המחלוקות בין החכמים, אם היה יחיד אצל רבים היו קובעים ההלכה
כדברי המרובים, ואם רבים אצל רבים או יחיד אצל יחיד - כפי הנראה
לחכמי הדור ההוא, שכבר נמסרה להם ההכרעה, כאמרו "ובאת אל הכהנים
הלוים או אל השופט אשר יהיה בימים ההם ודרשת והגידו לך את המשפט"
(שם שם, ט), וכן "לא תסור". הרי שנתן רשות לחכמי הדורות להכריע
במחלוקת החכמים כפי הנראה להם, ואפילו אם יהיו הקודמים מהם
גדולים מהם ורבים מהם, שכן נצטוינו ללכת אחרי הסכמת חכמי הדורות
שיסכימו לאמת או להפכו, וזה מבואר בהרבה מקומות.

ועל זה הדרך יתפרש מה שאמרו בפרק השוכר את הפועלים (בבא מציעא פו, א)
בעובדא דרבה בר נחמני הוה יתיב אגונדא דדקלא וקא גריס, שמע
במתיבתא דרקיעא אם בהרת קדמה לשער לבן טמא ואם שער לבן קדמה
לבהרת טהור, ספק - הקב"ה אמר טהור וכולהו מתיבתא דרקיעא אמרי
טמא. אמרי מאן נוכח, נוכח רבה בר נחמני דהוא יחיד באהלות, לא הוה מצי
מלאך המות למיקרב ליה מדלא הוי שתיק פומיה מגירסא, אזל אידמי ליה
לגונדא דפרשי, אמר תינח נפשיה דההוא גברא ולא תמסר בידא דמלכותא,
אשתיק ונח נפשיה, כי הוה ניחא נפשיה אמר: טהור טהור. יצתה בת קול
ואמרה: אשריך רבה בר נחמני שגופך טהור ויצתה נשמתך בטהרה.

וזו ההגדה צריכה ביאור. כי באמת לא היו משימים פקפוק במה שהשיגו
מהשם יתברך שהיה מטהר, וידעו בבירור שהוא האמת ולא זולתו, אם כן
היאך אמרו טמא עד שהוצרכו להכרעתו של רבה בר נחמני? אבל הגדה זו
מתפרשת על הדרך שכתבנו, כי עם היותם ש"ספק טהור" על דרך האמת,
היו אומרים טמא, שמאחר שהכרעת התורה נמסרה להם בחייהם, ושכלם
היה מחייב לטמא, היה מן הראוי שיהיה טמא אף על פי שהוא הפך מן
האמת, שכן מחייב השכל האנושי, והשאר אף על פי שהוא אמת, איננו ראוי

לעשות מעשה כן בדרכי התורה, כמו שלא טהרו בעלי מחלוקתו של רבי אליעזר אף על פי שנתנה עליהם בת קול מן השמים שהלכה כדבריו, ולא נסתפק להם שהענין מאת השם יתברך כמו שלא סופק על אלו, ואף על פי כן אמרו: אין תורה מן שמים. ולפיכך אמר "מאן נוכח? נוכח רבה בר נחמני", ולא באתה לו ההכרעה מן הנאות, כי לא נסתפקו בזה כמו שכתבתי, אלא שהכריע שׂכל האדם מחייב כפי התורה והמדות שהיא נדרשת בהן. ומה שהיו מטמאין, לא היה רק מקוצר שׂכלם בערך השׂכל האנושי, או מהתרשלם בלימוד תורה בחייהם.

97. אור ה', מאמר ג, כלל ה, פרק ב

הפרק השני, בהתר ספק שאפשר שיסופק בו בשורש הזה, והוא: אם - לפי שאיננו רחוק בחלק המקובל, והוא התורה שבעל פה, שיולדו בו ספקות ומחלוקות, ואף כי בתורה שבכתב כבר יהיה בה או דברים שאיפשר שיסופק בהם, ואיך לא?! וכבר קרה בתורה הזאת האלהית מחלוקת מכתות מודים היותה אלהית וחלוקים בשרשיה, מהם מאמינים שחלק ממנה נצחי וחלק בלתי נצחי, ומהם חולקים בפירוש חלק התורה שבכתב וברוב התורה שבעל פה ומחזיקין בטענותיהם באמרם שהם מקובלים מחכמי אומתם ומזקניהם, כצדוקין הנקראים היום בקצה המזרח והדרום קראים - היה שם דבר יוכל להתחזק בו ולהכריח בעל האמונה האמתית אמונתו? וזה, כי לכל אחד מבעלי הכתות מחשבה גוברת באמונתו ואולי שלא יכנס חשד ונדנוד באמתת דעתו ושקרות דעת זולתו. וכבר יראה שאין ההכרעה הזאת נתונה לכל אחד כפי בחינת ציורו, שאם היה זה השער הזה פתוח לבחור באמונות איש הישר בעיניו, לא ישאר בה כת קיימת באמונה, להיות הציור באנשים משתנה תמיד, וכאשר היה כן איך יבטח בעל האמונה האמתית באמונתו? מי יתן ואדע.

ואמנם התר ספק הזה איננו ממה שיקשה, עם מה שבא בתורה על זה ונתפרסם בקבלה. וזה, שהשורש שאצלנו כאשר יסופק או יפול מחלוקת בדבר מדברי התורה, שהמשפט ליושבים לפני השם יתברך במקום אשר יבחר, באומרו "כי יפלא ממך דבר" וגו' "וקמת ועלית אל הכהנים או אל השופט" (דברים יז, ח-ט). (ואולי) [ואולם] אם לא היו בהסכמה אחת אנו מחוייבים להמשך אחר הרוב, והיה החיוב זה לפי הקבלה "אפילו אומרין לך על ימין שהוא שמאל ועל שמאל שהוא ימין" (ספרי שופטים, קנד), וסמכו זה על אמרו "לא תסור מן הדבר אשר יגידו לך ימין ושמאל" (שם שם, יא), עד שבא בגמרא מציעא (בבא מציעא נט, ב) במחלוקת שבין ר' אליעזר וחכמים בתנורו של

עכנאי שיצאת בת קול אמרה: מה לכם אצל רבי [יהושע] [אליעזר]? עמד [רבי יהושע] על רגליו ואמר: "לא בשמים היא" (דברים ל, יב), ובא הפירוש שכבר נתן לנו התורה וכתוב בה "אחרי רבים להטות" (שמות כג, ב). בארו בזה שאף אם היה האמת בכונת התורה כרבי אליעזר, שאחר שרוב חכמי ישראל הסכימו בחלופו, אם שלא היה כן כוונת התורה, להם שומעים, אחר שהשורש התורריי לילך אחר הרוב אפילו אומר לך על ימין שהוא שמאל.

וכבר היה ראוי להיות כן, שאם לא היה החיוב הזה להמשך אחרי הכהנים או אחרי הסנהדרין אשר יהיה בימים ההם אלא בתנאי וקשר שיסכימו להלכה, הנה היה השער פתוח לחלוק עמהם ולמרות פיהם כל מי שיתעקש ויאמר שלא הסכימו להלכה. ויהיה גם כן סבה שירבו מחלוקות בישראל ותעשה תורה כאלף תורות. אבל עם החיוב הזה אי אפשר שישאר שום מחלוקות או ספק בדבר מדברי התורה, אם לא היה מסופק לכולם או לרובם, מה שהוא רחוק מאד. ואם היה נמצא הדבר הרחוק ההוא, הנה יש בו דרך ידוע לפי שרשי הקבלה איך נתנהג בספק ההוא. וכאשר היה זה כן, המחזיק באמונה על פי הסכמת השופטים או רובם בטוח הוא ומסולק מהחשד ומהערעור בתכלית מה שאפשר.

98. ספר הנצחון, סימן שכא (עמ' 176)

"בעלי אסופות" (קהלת יב, יא), פירשו רז"ל במסכת חגיגה (ג, ב): אילו תלמידי חכמים שיושבין אסופות ועוסקין בתורה, הללו מטמאין והללו מטהרין, ומסיק: ואם יאמר אדם איך אני לומד תורה מעתה? נתנו מרועה אחד, רועה אחד נתנם ומפרנס אחד אמרן, שנאמר "וידבר אלהים את כל הדברים האלה" וגו'. וגרסינן בעירובין (יג, ב): אמר רבי אבא אמר שמואל: שלש שנים נחלקו בית שמאי ובית הלל, הללו אומרים: הלכה כמותינו, והללו אומרים: הלכה כמותינו, ויצא בת קול ואמר: אילו ואילו דברי אלהים חיים הן והלכה כבית הלל. ומפני מה זכה בית הלל לקבוע הלכה כמותו? מפני שנוחין ועלובין היו וכו', עד: ללמדך שכל המשפיל את עצמו הקב"ה מגביהו וכו'.

והנה הדבר קשה להבין, בית שמאי מטהרין ובית הלל מטמאין, איככה איפשר לקיים שניהם שיהיו דברי אלהים ואיך קבל משה רבינו עליו השלום מאת הגבורה שניהם? אם קבל טהור לא קבל טמא ואי קבל טמא לא קבל טהור! ואי רצונו לומר שדברי שניהם נכונים, כלומר שכל אחד מראה פנים לדבריו, אבל בית הלל כיוונו כמו שקבל משה רבינו עליו השלום מאת הגבורה, איך אמר "רועה אחד נתנם" וכו'? ועוד איככה פריך "מפני מה זכו בית הלל לקבוע הלכה כמותם", הלא זה משום שכיוונו ההלכה? ומאי משנין

"מפני שנוחין" וכו', איך יועילו נוחים מעשיהם לאמת דבריהם? וכי תימא
שאמר השם יתברך למשה רבינו עליו השלום: "עתידים חכמי ישראל לחלוק
בדברי פלוני ופלוני", זה לא ייתכן, דאם כן מאי פריך בפרק קמא דגיטין (ו, ב)
אהא דאבייתר בני כך הוא אומר ויונתן בני כך הוא אמר, ופריך: ומי איכא
ספיקא קמיה קודשא בריך הוא? ועוד אם כן משה רבינו ע"ה וישראל לא
ידעו אי יטהרו או יטמאו עד שבא הבת קול ואמר הלכה כבית הלל. ואם
אמר למשה רבינו ע"ה לעשות כבית הלל, אם כן תחזור קושיותינו לדוכתיה,
מאי פריך "מפני מה זכה בית הלל לקבוע הלכה כמותו"?

על כן נראה שהשם יתברך נתן התורה ושלוש עשרה מדות לדרוש בהם
התורה כל חכם וחכם לפי השגת דעתו, ובלבד שיעסוק ויעיין בכל כחו בלי
התרשלות, ואם יראה לסנהדרין על פי התורה והמדות שדבר אחד הוא
טהור - יהיה טהור, ואם יעמדו הסנהדרין אחריהן ויראה להם שעל פי
התורה והמדות אותו דבר טמא - יהיה טמא. כי הוא השם יתברך שנתן לנו
התורה תלה אותה בדעת החכמים לפי ראות עיניהם, ועל זה נאמר "כי
מציון תצא תורה" (ישעיה ב, ג), רצונו לומר תצא דבר תורה היום שלא יצאת
אתמול. זה שאמר הכתוב "ושאבתם מים בששון ממעייני הישועה" (ישעיה יב,
ג) ותירגם יונתן "אולפן חדשה". לאפוקי מן הכופרים המפרשים על חידוש
תולדות יש, שהרי אמר "ושאבתם מים בששון" ואין לנו עצבון בחידוש
תורתו, אלא על חידוש תלמידי חכמים נאמר.

וגרסינן בסנהדרין (ו, ב): כתיב "ועמכם בדבר המשפט", אין לדיין אלא מה
שעיניו רואות. וכהאי גוונא במסכת ראש השנה (כה, א) על קידוש החודש,
נאמר שלושה פעמים "אתם" אפילו שוגגין, "אתם" אפילו מוטעין, "אתם"
אפילו מזידין. פירוש אפילו קבעו בית דין את החודש בטעות הכי אנו
צריכים לתקן המועדים לפי אותו החשבון. ועוד שמה שגזר רבן גמליאל על
רבי יהושע שבא אליו ביום הכיפורים שחל להיות לפי חשבונו במקלו
ובמעותיו. ועוד שהרי תדיר שאנו דוחין ראש השנה שחל להיות באד"ו
משום מיתייא וערבה (ראש השנה כ, א), ואם לא היה כדפירשתי, איככה יעקור
קביעות דאורייתא בשביל ערבה שהיא דרבנן? וכתיב "לא תסור מן הדבר
אשר יגידו לך ימין ושמאול" (דברים יז, יא), ופירשו רז"ל: אפילו אמרו לך על
ימין שהוא שמאול כו' (ספרי דברים, קנד). וגם זה מן הטעם שפירשו ואמרו
רז"ל (משנה, חולין ג, א): כל שאינה חיה - טריפה, שבהמה זו תמות ואין בה
אחת מכל מה שמנו בה חכמים היא כשירה, שנאמר "על פי התורה אשר
יורוך" (דברים יז, יא). וכן הא דזקן ממרא נהרג אפילו הוא אמר מן הקבלה

והן אומרין מסברת עצמן (סנהדרין פח, א), לפי שהתורה נתנה לפי הסכמת הרבים, שנאמר "אחרי רבים להטות" (שמות כג, ב).

וכן אמרינן בהדיא במסכת עדויות (ה, ז) שהדין משתנה לפי דעת הרבים, דתנן התם: אמר רבי (עקיבא) [עקביא] בן מהללאל לבנו בשעת מיתתו: בני חזור בך מארבע דברים (שהייתי אמר) שאמרתי, ואמר לו: ואתה למה לא חזרת בך? אמר לו: אני שמעתי מפי מרובים והם שמעו מפי מרובים, אני עמדתי בשמועתי והם עמדו בשמועתם, אבל אתה שמעת מפי יחיד והם שמעו מפי מרובים, מוטב להניח דברי היחיד ולאחוז בדברי המרובים. ומהאי טעמא אמר רבי יהושע (בבא מציעא נט, ב): "לא בשמים היא", כדפירשתי בסימן קמח. וכשם שדרשנו "החודש הזה לכם" (שמות יב, ב) שלכם יהיה, כך איכא לדרוש "ואתנה לך שני לוחות" (שמות כד, יב) וכתיב "תורתי נתתי לכם" (משלי ד, ב).

99. מעשה אפוד, הקדמה (עמ' 6)

ולאומר שיאמר, כי הוא בלתי אפשרי שיתייחד החיבור הזה התלמודיי בהקנאת ההצלחה האחרונה לאדם, לפי שהחיבור הזה כולל עניינים רבים שאי אפשר שיתחייב מהם ההצלחה לאדם, כמו שהוא העניין בהרבה מההגדות הנכללות בו וקצת מעשיות. וגם כי החיבור הזה כולל המחלוקות הגדולות אשר נפלו בין חכמי ישראל במשפטי התורה, אשר האחד מחלקי הסותר לבד הוא הצודק וזולתו בטל, ואי אפשר שתתחייב הצלחה נצחית מהבטל. וכבר אמרו על דבר המחלוקות האלה: משרבו תלמידי שמאי והלל שלא שמשו כל צרכן, רבו מחלוקות בישראל ונעשית תורה כשתי תורות (סוטה מז, ב). והחיבור הנזכר מלא כולו מהמחלוקות האלה והדומים להם.

ותשובת זה, כי המכוון בחכמת התלמוד אינו כל מה שבא בחיבור הזה. שאילו היה העניין כן, במה זכו דוד ושלמה וכל חכמי ישראל שהיו קודם חתימת החיבור הזה? התחשוב שתהיה חכמת שלמה השגת ידיעת החיבור הזה שחובר אחריו ביותר מאלף ושלש מאות שנה? וכבר אמרו על רבן יוחנן בן זכאי, שהיה קודם החורבן, שלא הניח מקרא ומשנה תלמוד הלכות... (סוכה כח, א), והחיבור הזה חובר ביותר מארבע מאות שנה אחרי החורבן. והתלמוד, זכרו אותו בהרבה מאד מקומות החכמים שהיו קודם החיבור הזה בכמה שנים.

הנה אם כן, המכוון בתלמוד הוא זולת זה, והוא החקירה האמתית במשפטי המצוות האלהיות מכח השכל, להוציא דבר מתוך דבר ולהבין בשלש עשרה מדות שהתורה נדרשת בהן, וההקפה במה שמקובל ממשה רבנו עליו השלום

מסיני מקצת משפטים התוריים שלא נזכרו בתורה האלהית, או שנזכרו אבל ברמז. וכבר כתב הרב מה שיובן ממנו זה בהלכות תלמוד תורה פרק א.

100. עקידת יצחק, שער יב (עמ' צ)

משל לשני חכמים העוברים לפני המלך, האחד יכסה את ראשו והשני יסיר את מצנפתו. כי עם שנתחלפו במעשיהם החלקיים כפי מה שחשב כל אחד מהם כי הוא דרך הכבוד, הנה נשתתפו בהסכמה אחת כי החלוק הכבוד למלך הוא הראוי והנאות. וכמה הפליגו חכמינו ז"ל להורות זה במה שאמרו פרק קמא דקדושין (ל, ב): "מאי 'כי ידברו את אויבים בשער'?! אמר רבי חייא בר אבא: אפילו האב ובנו הרב ותלמידו שעוסקים בתורה בשער אחד נעשו אויבים זה לזה, ואינם זזים משם עד שנעשו אוהבים זה לזה, שנאמר 'את והב בסופה', אהבה בסוף". וזה, כי בהתחלה כשיעשו דברים מתחלפים או יאמרו דעות מקבילות יראה שהם מתנגדים לגמרי, כמו שיהיה הענין באלו האנשים שאמרנו, שלכאורה יראה שהאחד חפץ ביקרו של מלך והשני לא כן ירצה. אמנם, כשישאו ויתנו בדבר ויודע טעם כל אחד מהם, ימצא לסוף כי הכבוד אשר ידרוש האחד, הוא עצמו מה שידרוש השני והוא הדבר אשר ייחדם. והוא טעם אמרם ז"ל (חגיגה ג, ב): "הללו מטהרין והללו מטמאין הללו מכשירין והללו פוסלין הללו מזכין והללו מחייבין, ואלו ואלו דברי אלהים חיים". כי כוונת כלם להעמיד התורה והמצוה על הצד היותר שלם שאפשר ולהפיק רצון האלהים שהנחילה לנו. ולזה היו כל הסברות ההם נכנסות תחת גדר ההגבלה ההיא ומקיימין אותה, כמו שאמר על זה: "כולם נתנו מרועה אחד". ומזה הטעם אמרו (אבות ה, יז): "כל מחלוקת שהיא לשם שמים סופה להתקיים" כו', והוא כאשר יהיה כמחלוקת בית שמאי ובית הלל, שהוא מזה האופן שהענין הכללי אשר ירצה האחד הוא אשר ירצה חברו, ולא יתחלפו כי אם בענינים החלקיים הפרטיים...

101. לב אבות, אבות ה, יז

קרוב למה שהורגלו המפרשים לפרש בכאן בחדשי על דבריהם חידוש נכון אומר, כי ידוע שהויכוח מן הצדדים ההפכיים בעיון ובלימוד הוא סיבת יציאת הדבר לאור והודע האמת והתבררו בזולת שום ספק, ולכן הספקות וההערות והקושיות הן מבוא גדול להשגת המבוקש, והחוקר עצמו אמר שהספקות עשו את האנשים חכמים, וזה הדבר ראוי שיהיה שמור ביד כל דורש ידיעת האמת בכל ספר וחכמה. ידוע שהספקות לא תשלמנה אלא בהמצא כת כנגד כת ושואל ומשיב להוציא לאור משפט.

והדבר הזה נעלם מעיני המלעיגים על מה שאמרו חז״ל (סנהדרין יז, א) שאם היו כל הסנהדרין מחייבין מיתה לאיש אחד לא היה מומת, ואם היו מיעוטם מזכים ורובם מחייבים היה מומת. שעם היות גזרת הכתוב מחייבת כן וכמו שדרשו בגמרא, הטעם אשר שמעתי בזה בשם הרמב״ם ז״ל הוא נכון מאד, והוא עצמו מה שכתבתי, להודיע ולהשמיע שכשאין כת מנגד על פי קושיות וטענות בחקירה מן החקירות אי אפשר שיצא הדבר לאור ואפשר שכלם יפלו בטעות, קרוב לטעם שזכרו (משנה עדויות א, ה-ו) למה הביא רבינו הקדוש סברת היחיד אצל סברת הרבים עם יודעו שאין הלכה כאותו יחיד לגביהן.

ואם כן יאמר התנא שכשהמחלוקת הוא לשם שמים, שכוונת החולקים הוא שעם אותו המחלוקת יתברר האמת ויצא לאור מה שלא היה יוצא זולתו, בודאי סוף אותו מחלוקת שיתקיים, כי עם היות שהאמת יתקיים וישאר אצל הצד האחד מהם, עם כל זה כל שני צדדי המחלוקת יתקיימו ויהיו נזכרים יחד, הואיל וכדי לדעת לברירת האמת צריך להאריך שתי כתות המחלוקת, ועם המחלוקת עצמו יתברר האמת, ולכן דין הוא שישארו כל כתות המחלוקת נזכרים ונעשים יחדיו, עם היות שאין האמת אלא כאחד מהם.

102. מדרש שמואל, אבות ה, יט

ואחר כך ביאר ענין המחלוקת ואמר : כל מחלוקת שהיא לשם שמים סופה להתקיים. והנה המפרשים הוקשה להם שראוי לעיין, כי מאחר שכל בעלי מחלוקת, אפילו שיהיה לשם שמים, מאמריהם סותרים זה לזה ויחלוקו בין האמת והשקר, הנה יתחייב שאם אחד מהם דעתו אמת הדעת האחר יהיה כוזב. ואיך יאמר ששום מחלוקת יתקיים שהרי לא יתקיים כי אם אחד משתי הדעות? ועוד, מה הפרש אם כן יש בין מחלוקת הלל ושמאי למחלוקת קרח ועדתו אחרי שהכת האחת בשתי המחלוקות כוזבת תמיד?

ואצלי ביאור הדברים הוא : כי ידוע כי מחלוקת הלל ושמאי היתה לשם שמים להוציא הדין לאמתו, ולכן לענין קיבול שכרו בעולם הבא שתי הכתות שוות, ואף אם לא צדקו בית שמאי בדבריהם ואין הלכה כמותם, עם כל זה על היות מחלוקתם לשם שמים, דבריהם חיים וקיימים לקבל שכר עליהם. וזהו אומרו סופה להתקיים. ושאינה לשם שמים כמחלוקת קרח ועדתו אין סופה להתקיים רק ירדו חיים שאולה.

והרב ר׳ מנחם לבית מאיר ז״ל כתב, יש לתמוה איך ראוי לומר על מחלוקת שתתקיים והרי אי אפשר להתקיים אלא אחת מן הדעות, ומלת מחלוקת

כוללת השני צדדים ואיך יתקיימו שניהם. ונראה לי שאין מלת מחלוקת מיוחסת רק על השני המשיב וחולק על האחד, רוצה לומר שכשהראשון מתעורר לעשות איזה דבר ואומר ראוי שיעשה כך ויורה לעשות כך עדיין אין כאן מחלוקת, אבל כשהשני ישיב עליו ויאמר אין ראוי לעשות כדבריך אלא בהפך, זהו המחלוקת, ונמצא שאין המחלוקת כוללת השני צדדים אלא האחד לבד שהוא השני המשיב על האחד. ואמר שזה השני אם משיב וחולק שלא בדרך קנטור ונצוח אלא להודיע האמת סופו שיתקיימו דבריו, ואם משיב דרך קנטור לא יתקיימו דברי השני אלא דברי הראשון, עכ"ל.

ולי נראה כי אפילו לפי דבריו לא תירץ ועדיין הקושיא במקומה עומדת, כי לפעמים אפשר כי זה השני המשיב על הראשון אפילו שיהיה לשם שמים, אפשר כי הראשון צדק בדבריו ודבריו עיקר והשני טעה במה שרצה להשיב ולחלוק עליו, והרי דברי השני שהוא החולק כוזבים ודברי הראשון עיקר, נמצא שהמחלוקת והם דברי השני אין סופה להתקיים כי הוא הדעת הכוזב, והדרא קושיין לדוכתין.

ואפשר לומר, כי מה שאמר כל מחלוקת שהיא לשם שמים סופה להתקיים, הכוונה שלעולם יתקיימו במחלוקתם והיום יחלקו בדבר אחד למחר בדבר אחר והמחלוקת תהיה קיימת ונמשכת ביניהם כל ימי חייהם, ולא עוד אלא שאורך ימים ושנות חיים יוסיפו להם, ושאינה לשם שמים אין סופה להתקיים, רק במחלוקת הראשון יסופו יתמו ושם ימותו כמחלוקתו של קורח.

ואפשר עוד לומר, כי במחלוקת הלל ושמאי וכיוצא בהם הללו פוסלין והללו מתירין וכו' ואלו ואלו דברי אלהים חיים כמאמרם ז"ל, וזה כי לכל הדברים יש להם שרשים יונקים מלמעלה והכל כפי הזמן וכפי המקום אשר הוא רומז למעלה באצילות. והלא תראה כי אברהם אבינו קיים אפילו ערובי תבשילין, ויעקב שהיה בחיר באבות נשא שתי אחיות אשר התורה אסרה אותן, וכן יהודה שבא על תמר כלתו אשר היא אסורה מן התורה וכל מלכות בית דוד לא יצאה אלא ממנו, אלא לאו שכל הדברים הם משתלשלים משרשם העליון כפי הצורך וכפי הזמן וכפי המקום, והכל על קו האמת. כן כל מחלוקת שהיא לשם שמים סופה להתקיים, כי יש לה שורש וקיום למעלה לשתי הסברות גם יחד, והדברים עתיקין ודי למבין.

103. עשרה מאמרות, מאמר חיקור הדין, חלק ב,יז-יח

כוליה עלמא ידעין ומשתבשין במאמר המפורסם לחכמים (חגיגה ג,ב) שהללו אוסרים והללו מתירים וכולם דברי אלהים חיים. והאמת הברור הוא, כי כל

מחלוקת שהוא לשם שמים סופה להתקיים ולאמת דבריה בכל חלקיה...
ואולם בפירוש אמרה תורה להטות הלכה למעשה אחרי רבים, כי "כל
נתיבותיה שלום" (משלי ג, יז). אבל לא יחשב שיהיה כזב בדעת היחידים
הנדחים, כי אין מדומה שקר חס ושלום במה שנאמר בסיני ובמה שהוא
חרות על הלוחות כפי מה שבארנוהו, אדרבה העיון ההוא הכולל השומר
אמת לעולם ישפוט לפעולות אדם הנאה והמגונה. והכל לפי מעשיו של אותה
שעה, כי מה שהיה נאה קודם נאה החטא - היות האדם ואשתו ערומים - שב
מגונה אחר החטא, והוא אם כן הנאה והמגונה בהיותם ערומים כל אחד
בזמנו דברי אלהים חיים, המושל על ההפכים על חילוף הזמנים. ומעולם לא
נחלק אדם מחכמי התורה להתיר את העורב ולאסור את היונה, על מה
נחלקו? בדבר שיש לו שני פנים אמיתיים וצודקים לכאן ולכאן, הללו
מסבירים פנים להיתר והללו לאיסור לפי מקומו ושעתו, נמצא ההיתר
והאיסור שניהם אמת, ולב בית דין מתנה עליהם איזה יכשר הלכה למעשה,
ומכאן אתה למד שיש הלכה ולא למעשה, ואינו אלא כדאמרן...

וכן מצינו שאכילת בשר נאסרה לאדם לגמרי, חוץ מבשר היורד מן השמים
שהיו מלאכי השרת צולין אותו לפניו (סנהדרין נט, ב), או בשר תמותת מידו לו
לצורך דמן ועורן (כדלקמן בחלק הרביעי פרק יח), והותרה אכילת הבשר לנח
ולבניו לגמרי, ולישראל הותרה קצתה מכלל האיסור שנתחדש בקצתה,
ולעתיד לבוא "ה' מתיר אסורים" שישלים לקצתה סימני טהרה...

הרי אלה ההפכין וחלופי ההוראה כמו היתר אכילת בשר ואסורו, בכל או
במקצת, בהשתנות העיתים, וכולם דברי אלהים חיים. ועד שלא נתמנה בית
דין של מטה היתה תורה יוצאה מבית דין של מעלה, "ודבר בעיתו מה טוב"
(משלי טו, כג), ועכשיו ניתנה תורה ונתחדשה הלכה "אחרי רבים להטות",
ואין לך אלא שופט שבימיך, שהרי בית דין מבטל דברי בית דין שקדמהו
בשנים, או אפילו קטן ממנו אם נפל מחלוקת בהבנת דרכי התורה שזה דורש
ומלמד במידה אחת וזה במידה אחרת, כגון רבויי ומיעוטי או כללי ופרטי.
ואילו היה שם יחיד בבית דין ראשון דורש כמו שעתיד לדרוש בית דין שני,
ובבית דין שני דורש אחד יחיד כמו היה דורש בית דין ראשון, זה וזה בדורו
נעשה "זקן ממרא" אם הורה לעשות כדבריו, אחרי שהסכימו על הפכו בית
דין שבימיו.

למדנו מזה אמות ההוראה בשני דרכים, ושהמעשה הנרצה ממנו הוא
המסכים לרבים לפי מקומו ושעתו, ובלבד בישביי לשכת הגזית ותלמידיהם
אחריהם מכוונים לבם למקום.

104. ים של שלמה, הקדמה למסכת בבא קמא

שלמה ע"ה אמר בחכמתו "ויותר מהמה בני הזהר עשות ספרים הרבה אין
קץ" (קהלת יב, יב). ודרשו רבותינו בפרק עושים פסים (עירובין כא, ב) שמחויב
הוא לשמוע לדברי חכמים שנקראו סופרים, במה שחידשו והוסיפו בקבלתם
בתורה שבעל פה הלכה למשה מסיני על תורה שבכתב שהוא בתכלית
הקיצור בכמות וארוך באיכות. אף הוסיפו וגזרו ועשו משמרת למשמרת,
כאשר הקדים החכם הזה שעשה אזנים לתורה, שנאמר "איזן וחיקר" (קהלת
יב,ט). וכל הנמצא בדברי חכמי התורה מימות משה רבינו ע"ה עד עתה, הן הן
החכמים שנאמר עליהן "דברי חכמים כדרבונות (כלם) נתנו מרועה אחד"
(קהלת יב, יא), ושלא לתמוה על מחלוקתם בריחוק הדעות שזה מטמא וזה
מטהר, זה אוסר וזה מתיר, זה פוסל וזה מכשיר, זה פוטר וזה מחייב, זה
מרחק וזה מקרב, אם דעתם לשם שמים, והראשונים אפילו בבת קול לא
היו משגיחים, וכולם דברי אלהים חיים כאילו קיבל כל אחד מפי הגבורה
ומפי משה. האף שלא יצא הדבר מפי משה לעולם להיות שני הפכים בנושא
אחד, ואעפ"כ דימהו החכם לרוב אישורו וחיזוקו, שאין בין דבר שהוציא
משכל הפועל אשר נתעוללו לו במושכלות שניות ושלישיות, לבין דבר שבא
אליו בכח חוש הדיבור בקבלה הלכה למשה מסיני, אף שלא ציירו במופת
שכלו להיות הכרח לולי צד הקבלה איש מפי איש.

והמקובלים כתבו טעם לדבר, לפי שכל הנשמות היו בהר סיני וקבלו דרך
מ"ט צינורות, והן שבעה פעמים שבעה "מזוקק שבעתיים" (תהלים יב, ז), והן
הקולות אשר שמעו וגם ראו, וכל ישראל רואים את הקולות, הן הדעות
המחלקות בצינור, כל אחד ראה דרך צינור שלו לפי השגתו וקיבל כפי כח
נשמת עליונו לרוב עילויה או פחיתותה, זה רחוק מזה, עד שאחד יגיע לטהור
והשני יגיע לקצה האחרון לטמא והשלישי לאמצעית רחוק מן הקצוות,
והכל אמת. והבן.

ולכן אמר החכם, מאחר שדברי החכמים האמתיים כולם דברי אלהים חיים
אפילו במחלוקתם, קל וחומר בהשוותם יחד, אם כן למה משה למה
לא כתב מפי הגבורה באר היטב כפי אשר ראוי מבלי שיפול בו שום ספק,
ויהיה פנים אחד לתורה ולא מ"ט? גם זולת זה מה שהיה ראוי להוסיף
ולגזור, ראוי היה למשה להודיע בספר, באם תגיע למקום שתתמצא בקעה
פרוצה גדור אותה ותוסיף בבנינה מה שראוי להוסיף, או מה שאינו ראוי
להוסיף בשום עניין, על דרך "אין גוזרין גזרה על הציבור אלא אם כן רוב
הציבור יכולים לעמוד בה" (עבודה זרה לו, א). על זה השיב החכם על תמיהתם
"עשות ספרים אין קץ", כלומר שאינו מן האפשרי לעשות ספרים בעניין זה,

כי אין קץ ותכלית לעניינו כמשמעו, כי אם כל רקיעי השמים גווילים וכל
הימים דיו לא יספיקו לכדי פרשה אחת עם כל הספקות שיפלו בה ומה
שיחודש ויוצא ממנה לרוב תועלותיה, עם כל מה שיכולים חכמים מישראל
להעמיק בשכל העיון להעמיק ולשנות ולהוסיף עליו. ועוד אדרבה, אם כל זה
היה כתוב בתורה, קל וחומר שהיה עליו יותר הוספה, רצוני לומר הוספה על
הוספה. רצוני לומר שאי אפשר שלא יפול ספיקות ושינוים ועומק הדעת
בהוספה הראשונה, עד שתגיע הוספה שניה לאלף אלפים כמותם. כלל הדבר,
אמר החכם והודיע שאינו בנמצא מן האפשרות להודיע ולבאר כל ספיקות
התורה מבלי חלוקת עד סוף, שתהא ידו של אדם מגעת אי אפשר, על כן
מסר התורה לחכמים השתולים בכל דור, כל אחד ואחד לפי חוצב מקור
שכלו לחלק לעילוי ולהוסיף כפי מה שיראו לו מן השמים, ואם בא לטהר
יסייעו לו. בריך רחמנא דיהיב חכמתא לחכימין.

105. דרך חיים, אבות ה, יז

כל מחלוקת שהיא לשם שמים וכו'. יש לשאול: מה ענין המאמר למאמרים
שלפניו? ועוד, שאמר איזה מחלוקת שהיא לשם שמים, מה שייך שאלה בזה
איזה מחלוקת היא לשם שמים, כל מחלוקת שיחלוק וכוונתו לשם שמים
היא המחלוקת שהיא לשם שמים, וכי לא היה מחלוקת רבי מאיר ורבי
יהודה ושאר תנאים לשם שמים חס וחלילה? ועוד, הלא הדברים נראים
סותרים, שאמר "איזהו מחלוקת שהיא לשם שמים זו מחלוקת הלל
ושמאי", ואם כן כל שאר מחלוקת היא שלא לשם שמים, ואם כן למה אמר
אחריו מיד: "איזהו מחלוקת שלא לשם שמים זו מחלוקת קרח ועדתו",
וידוע כי קרח ועדתו שהיו חולקים על השם יתברך, ומשמע אבל שאר
מחלוקת שאין חולקין על השם יתברך על עצמו סופו להתקיים, ואם כן קשיא
רישא לסיפא? ועוד קשיא, שאמר "מחלוקת שהיא לשם שמים סופה
להתקיים", והרי אי אפשר שיהיה שני חלקי הסותר אמת עד שאפשר שיהיו
מקויימים שניהם, ובודאי אחד תתבטל והשני תקוים, ולמה אמר אם כן
"סופה להתקיים"?!

ויש לפרש מה שנסמך מאמר זה לכאן מפני שאמר לפני זה: "ארבע מדות
ביושבים לפני חכמים", ופירשנו באותם שיושבים לפני חכמים ושומעים
הדעות מן החכמים, וכל המאמר של ארבע מדות הם על זה שיש מן
התלמידים מקבצים שתי הדעות שהם מחולקים וסותרין והם נקראים
"ספוג", ויש אין מקבל אפילו דעה אחת והם נקראים "משפך", ויש מקבלים
הדעת שאינו הלכה ומניחין הדעת שהוא הלכה והם נקראים "משמרת", ויש

מקבלים קבלת ההלכה ומניחין שאינו הלכה והם נקראים "נפה". ועל זה אמר שאם מחלוקת החכמים שהתלמידים מקבלים דעתם היא לשם שמים - סופה להתקיים, ופירוש הקיום הזה שסוף סוף בחיי החולקים לא יהיה בטול למחלוקת. ואפילו אם תאמר שלפעמים יש בטול אף בחייו של החולק, אין הפירוש סופה להתקיים שודאי תתקיים ומוכרח הוא להתקיים, אך פירושו סופה שתתקיים שאפשר למחלוקת הזאת הקיום. ורצה לומר אף כי המחלוקת היא שנואה לפני הקדוש ברוך הוא מאד, ומפני שהמחלוקת שנואה לפני הקדוש ברוך הוא אין קיום למחלוקת, מכל מקום המחלוקת שהיא לשם שמים אפשר שיהיה למחלוקת זה הקיום ואין השם יתברך מסבב ומבטל המחלוקת הזאת, כמו שהוא במחלוקת שאינה לשם שמים אשר השם יתברך מסבב ומבטל המחלוקת שלא יהיה נמצא המחלוקת, כי מרוחק המחלוקת מן השם יתברך, וכמו שאמרו (דרך ארץ זוטא, פרק ט) "אהוב השלום ושנא המחלוקת". ויותר מזה, שהשם יתברך מחזיק המחלוקת כאשר היא לשם שמים לגמרי, ולא אמר מחלוקת שהיא לשם שמים מקויימת, מפני שכך פירושו, שאל תאמר כי המחלוקת שהיא לשם שמים מקויימת היינו בתחילתה אבל לא בסופה, ועל זה אמר שאף סופה להתקיים. ומחלוקת שאינה לשם שמים אף כי בהתחלתה יש זמן שהיא מקויימת, שהרי כמה וכמה מחלוקת שהיו מקויימים זמן מה, ומכל מקום סופם בטלה שהשם יתברך מסבב בטול למחלוקת.

ואין להקשות איך אפשר שיהיו מקויימים שני חלקי הסותר, שאין זה קשיא. כי אף אם תתבטל המחלוקת מצד שעמדו בני אדם על הדעות ופסקו הלכה כאחד מן הדעות, אין זה בכלל ש"אין סופה להתקיים", כי השם יתברך לא ביטל מחלוקת זה, כי פירוש "אין סופה להתקיים" רוצה לומר שאין סופה להתקיים מן השם יתברך, ומחלוקת בית שמאי ובית הלל אע"ג שיצאה בת קול "הלכה כבית הלל" לא היה הבת קול מבטל המחלוקת מפני ששנואה המחלוקת, כי אהוב ואהוב היה המחלוקת הזה, רק כדי ללמד אותה הלכה שהיו חפצים לדעת ההלכה, ואדרבה בת קול היה אומר "אלו ואלו דברי אלהים חיים" והיה מחזיק את החולקים ולא היה מבטל המחלוקת. ולפיכך סמך המאמר הזה למה שלפניו, לומר שאם המחולקים היתה כונתם לשם שמים לא תתבטל דעות החולקים, ואותן תלמידים שהיו מקבלים דבריהם לא קבלו דעת שתתבטל. אבל אם לא היה מחלוקת לשם שמים רק לנצח - תתבטל מחלוקתם, ומה שקבלו תלמידים דבריהם הכל בטל ומבוטל, כך יש לפרש. ואמנם עוד יתבאר בסמוך.

ואמר: איזהו מחלוקת שהוא לשם שמים? זה מחלוקת שמאי והלל. שהמחלוקת שלהם היה לשם שמים לגמרי, שלא תוכל לומר עליהם שום צד שלא לשם שמים, שאי אפשר לומר שאם היו מטריחים עצמם בהלכה לעמוד על הדבר או ילכו לשאול לא היה צריך להם המחלוקת ואם כן אין כאן לשם שמים לגמרי, שדבר זה אינו, שהרי אלו ואלו דברי אלהים חיים ומאחר שאלו ואלו דברי אלהים חיים איך אפשר לומר שהיה אפשר להם לעמוד על האמת ולבטל דברי אלהים חיים? ומחלוקת כזה היא לשם שמים בודאי. אבל שאר מחלוקת אף על גב שהיה לשם שמים בודאי ימצא צד מה ובחינה מה שאינו לגמרי לשם שמים, שאפשר שהיה להם לבטל המחלוקת על ידי עיון רב ולשאול להרבה חכמים וכיוצא בזה, אף על גב שודאי הכונה היא לשם שמים, אמר בעצם המחלוקת אינו לשם שמים דבר שאפשר זולתו. ולא דמי למחלוקת הלל ושמאי שהיא בודאי לשם שמים, כי אדרבה השם יתברך רצה באותו מחלוקת שכל אחד ואחד מן הכתות היה מגלין דברי אלהים חיים, לפיכך מחלוקת זה בפרט היא לשם שמים מכל המחלוקות שהיו בעולם.

ואחר כך אמר: איזה מחלוקת שהוא שלא לשם שמים. פירוש שהוא שלא לשם שמים לגמרי עד שאין שם שמים בדבר כלל. כי לפעמים יש מחלוקת אף אם היה כונה לשם יוהרא, מכל מקום יש במחלוקת עצמה דבר לשם שמים שאומר שכך ראוי לעשות ויש צד מה שבו לשם שמים והוא טוב וכל אחד אומר לה' אני. אבל מחלוקת קרח ועדתו לא היה בזה שום צד בעולם לשם שמים, שהרי כתיב (במדבר כו, ט) "בהצותם על ה'", כי מה שהיו חולקים על משה ואהרן היה מחלוקת זו על השם יתברך, ולפיכך מחלוקת זו לגמרי שלא לשם שמים ולא היה קיום לאותה מחלוקת כלל.

ואין להקשות מעתה קשה רישא לסיפא, דודאי לא קשיא, כי מחלוקת קרח ועדתו מפני שהיתה מחלוקת שלו לגמרי שלא לשם שמים שלא היה לו קיום כלל, כמו שתראה שפצתה האדמה את פיה ובלעה אותם חיים, ודבר זה שהוא בליעה לגמרי ראוי למחלוקת שהיא שלא לשם שמים לגמרי, אבל שאר מחלוקת שיש בה צד בחינה לשם שמים ואינה שלא לשם שמים לגמרי, אף על גב שודאי אין סופה להתקיים מכל מקום אין הבטול בענין זה. כלל הדבר: לפי מה שהיא שלא לשם שמים המחלוקת הוא הבטול. וכן ברישא גם כן, הכל לפי לשם שמים הוא קיום במחלוקת, כי שאר מחלוקת שלא היה לשם שמים לגמרי לא היה הקיום כל כך כמו שהיה למחלוקת בית שמאי ובית הלל, כי בודאי השם יתברך היה מקיים את המחלוקת שלהם כי היה

אהוב המחלוקת הזה לפני השם יתברך כמו שיתבאר. ומעתה התבארו כל הקושיות, ואין ספק בפירוש הזה ואין צריך לדחוק דבר.

ויש לשאול עוד: מה טעם מחלוקת שהוא לשם שמים סופה להתקיים ומחלוקת שאינה לשם שמים אין סופה להתקיים? ואף כי בודאי שנואה המחלוקת מכל מקום קשיא, כי אף שאר דברים שהם שנואים לפני הקב״ה לא נאמר דבר זה עליהם. וכדי שתבין פירוש דברי חכמים, ומתוך דברים אלו יתבאר לך הפירוש הברור מה שנסמך מאמר זה אל מאמרים שלפניו, יש להאריך קצת שיובן המאמר הזה על אמתתו. דע כי המחלוקת אי אפשר להתקיים, וזה מפני כי המחלוקת היא אל אותן שהם הפכים. ובמציאות האש לא נמצא כלל דבר שהוא הפך לו הם המים, וכן במציאות המים אין מציאות לדבר שהוא הפך לו הוא האש. ולפיכך אי אפשר לשני דברים שהם מחולקים שיעמדו יחד, שאם כן היו שני הפכים בנושא אחד. ובאולי תאמר יהיה עומד כל אחד ואחד בעצמו, שהרי אש ומים שהם הפכים ויש להם קיום בעצמם, וכמו כן יהיו עומדים כל אחד במחלוקת כל אחד ואחד בפני עצמו? בודאי דבר זה אינו דומה, כי בודאי אש ומים הם שני הפכים בנושאים מתחלפים, וכיון שהם בנושאים מתחלפים לכך אפשר הקיום לכל אחד ואחד. אבל הבריות שהם בני אדם אף על גב שהם פרטים מחולקים הנה הם כלל אחד, ומכל שכן ישראל שהם עם אחד לגמרי ולא יתכן בזה שהם בנושאים מתחלפים, אם היה קיום למחלוקת שהאחד הפך לאחר היו שני הפכים בנושא אחד ולפיכך אין סופה להתקיים.

ויש לומר גם כן, כי אף (אם) אש ומים הם בנושא האחד שהוא העולם שהוא אחד, אמנם מה שיש קיום לאש ולמים אף שהם הפכים, זהו מה שאמר אחריו שכל מחלוקת שהיא לשם שמים סופה להתקיים, ופירוש דבר זה כי אש ומים חלוק שלהם לשם שמים, כי השם יתברך ברא כל אחד ואחד (וכל אחד ואחד) עושה רצונו, האש בפני עצמו והמים בפני עצמם, ובודאי דבר זה בגלל מחלוקת שהיא לשם שמים לכך יש לה קיום, כי לכך מחלוקת שהיא לשם שמים יש לה קיום אף כי הם הפכים, כי הוא יתעלה ויתברך הוא המאחד שני הפכים, כי אף אם מחולקים והפכים הם בעצמם מכל מקום מצד השם יתברך הם מתאחדים, כי הוא יתברך שהוא אחד הוא סבה לשני הפכים, ומה הוא סבה לשני הפכים דבר זה בעצמו אחדותו יתברך, שאם לא היה הוא סבה רק לדבר אחד כאלו תאמר שהוא סבה לאש, ואם כן חס ושלום יש עוד סבה להפך האש הם המים שהם הפך האש. ומפני כי הוא יתברך סבה להפכים, הוא יתברך אחד שהרי אין זולתו כי הוא סבה אל הכל אף אם הם הפכים, והרי בשביל ההפכים אשר הוא סבה להם הוא יתברך

אחד. ודבר זה בארנו במקומות הרבה בספר גבורת השם, כי השם יתברך
שהוא אחד הוא סבה להפכים ולפיכך המחלוקת שהוא לשם שמים, אף כי
המחלוקת מחולק מצד עצמו והם הפכים, וההפכים מצד עצמם אי אפשר
שימצאו יחד, אבל מצד השם יתברך אשר הוא סבה להפכים הנה אלו שני
הפכים הם אחד, כי הם אל השם יתברך שהוא אחד ובשניהם עושה ופועל
רצונו מה שירצה הוא יתברך. ולכן אותם הפכים אשר אי אפשר שיהו יחד,
מכל מקום מצד השם יתברך שהוא כולל הכל אם הם הפכים הם
מתאחדים. וזה אמרם כאן: כל מחלוקת שהיא לשם שמים סופה להתקיים,
ואמרו: איזהו מחלוקת שהיא לשם שמים? זה מחלוקת בית שמאי ובית
הלל, שהיתה לשם שמים, כי אף שהם הפכים מצד עצמם, שאלו פוסלין
ואלו מכשירין ואצל האדם הם שני דברים שהם הפכים, מכל מקום מצד
השם יתברך אשר המחלוקת הזה לשמו יתברך אשר הוא יתברך כולל
ההפכים ומן השם יתברך יצאו ההפכים, מצד הזה הם אחד.

וזה אמרם בפרק קמא דחגיגה (ג, ב): "בעלי אסופות" אלו תלמידי חכמים
שיושבין אסופות אסופות, הללו מטמאין והללו מטהרין הללו אוסרין והללו
מתירין הללו פוסלין והללו מכשירין, שמא יאמר האדם: הואיל והללו
מטמאין והללו מטהרין הללו אוסרין והללו מתירין הללו פוסלין והללו
מכשירין, היאך אני לומד תורה מעתה? תלמוד לומר "נתנו מרועה אחד"
כולם אל אחד נתן פרנס אחד אמרן מפי אדון כל המעשים שנאמר "וידבר
אלהים את כל הדברים האלה לאמר". עד כאן. והנה יש לך להתבונן: איך
אפשר לומר כי עם שהם הפכים לגמרי יאמר "אל אחד אמרם"? ועוד, למה
הוצרך לומר "מפי אדון כל המעשים" דאין ענינו לכאן? אבל פירושו שהוא
השם יתברך אל אחד, ומאחר שהוא אל אחד אי אפשר שלא יהיו ממנו כל
המעשים שהם הפכים כמו שבארנו. וכמו שהוא אדון כל המעשים שהם
הפכים, כי המים והאש הם שני הפכים מצד עצמם, מכל מקום שניהם הם
רצון השם יתברך שהוא רוצה באש ורוצה במים, וכך הם דברי חכמים אף
שהם הפכים כי אלו פוסלין ואלו מכשירין הנה שניהם מפי השם יתברך. כי
מצד זה, רוצה לומר מטעם זה, יש להכשיר, ומצד זה, רוצה לומר מטעם זה,
יש לפסול, ושני הצדדין האלו שהם הטעמים הן מן השם יתברך, שהרי
בזה טעם ובזה טעם והטעמים הם מן השם יתברך. כי מה שאמר: "כולם אל
אחד אמרם", אין הפירוש כלל פסול וכשר בלבד, רק פירושו בשביל טעם זה
הוא פסול ובשביל טעם זה הוא כשר, ושני הטעמים אמת מן הקדוש ברוך
הוא, שמצד זה הוא פסול ומצד זה הוא כשר שכל טעם הוא כשר בפני עצמו.

ולא שייך בזה ומי איכא ספיקא קמיה שמיא, דזה לא שייך להקשות רק גבי
פילגש בגבעה (גיטין ו, ב) משום שהיה על מעשה אחד שייך להקשות ומי איכא
ספיקא קמיה שמיא, אבל בכשר ופסול טמא וטהור שניהם מן השם יתברך,
כי הטעמים הם מן השם יתברך. ואף על גב דלענין הלכה איך יעשה האדם
הם הפכים ואי אפשר שיהיו שניהם למעשה, מכל מקום שני הדברים
והטעמים הם מן השם יתברך שהוא יתברך כולל ההפכים, ואם למד שתי הדעות
הרי למד התורה שהיא מפי השם יתברך, הן הפוסל והן המכשיר, וכאשר
אנו פוסקין הלכה אין זה רק הלכה למעשה איך יעשה האדם. דודאי אף על
גב ששני הדברים כל אחד ואחד יש לו טעם, אפשר שהאחד יותר הלכה. וכך
תמצא בנבראים שהם הפכים, אף על גב כי ההפכים שניהם מן השם יתברך,
מכל מקום האחד יותר קרוב אל השם יתברך מן האחר, מכל מקום בכל
אחד יש טעם אשר שני הטעמים ואם הם הפכים הם מן השם יתברך. ופסק
הלכה הוא מצד מדריגה שהיא למעלה מן המחלוקת. והכל הוא מן השם
יתברך, הן גוף המחלוקת שזה פוסל וזה מכשיר וכל אחד טעם בפני עצמו,
הן בירור המחלוקת דהיינו ההלכה והוא מצד השכל הפשוט שהוא שכל
גמור שלא שייך בשכל פשוט לגמרי מחלוקת, אף כי השכל הפשוט למעלה
משכל מכל מקום הכל הוא מן השם יתברך אשר מאתו הכל, ודבר זה פשוט.

ובאולי יקשה לך, אם כן למה היה בת קול אומר דוקא אצל בית שמאי
ובית הלל ״אלו ואלו דברי אלהים חיים״, הלא כל מחלוקת שבעולם של
חכמים כך הוא ששניהם מפי אדון כל המעשים? אין הדבר הזה קשיא, כי
הפרש יש, כי כאשר תבין לשון ״אלו ואלו דברי אלהים חיים״, מה שאמר
״אלהים חיים״, כי רמזו דבר גדול. כי שאר מחלוקת אף שהכל מן השם
יתברך כי כאשר שני חכמים חולקים בהלכה אף כי שני הדברים מן השם
יתברך, מכל מקום האחד יותר קרוב אל השם יתברך כמו שאמרנו, שאף
שגם זה מן השם יתברך מכל מקום האחד יותר קרוב אל השם יתברך מן
האחר, כמו שיש בנבראים גם כן שיש אחד מהם קרוב יתר אל השם יתברך,
אף שכולם הם נבראים שלו יתברך מכל מקום האחד קרוב יותר. וכך הם
בטעמים, אף ששניהם מן השם יתברך, מכל מקום האחד הוא יותר קרוב
אל השם יתברך מן האחר. אבל אצל בית שמאי ובית הלל שניהם דברי
אלהים חיים בשוה לגמרי, שלכך אמר דברי אלהים חיים. והמבין יבין כי
מה שאמר ״אלהים חיים״, רצה לומר ששניהם קרובים אל אמתת השם
יתברך, לכך אמר ״אלהים חיים״, כי החיות הוא אמתת המציאות שכאשר
יאמר ״זה חי״ רוצה לומר שהוא נמצא, והנעדר אין בו חיות, ולכך אמר כי
שניהם קרובים אל אמתת מציאותו. ועוד, תבין לשון ״חיים״ שהוא לשון

רבים על משקל שנים, בזה תבין מחלוקת הלל ושמאי, ואצל שאר חכמים אמרו "מפי אדון כל המעשים", כי החיים מתפשטים לימין ולשמאל ומזה היו מקבלים הלל ושמאי ולפיכך "אלו ואלו דברי אלהים חיים". והבן זה כי הוא ברור ונפלא בעיני מאוד, מה קשה בזה שאמרו אלו ואלו דברי אלהים חיים, עד שבזה רבו המפרשים, ויש שפירשו דבר זה על דרך הנסתר כי אין כאן הסתר, כי השם יתברך אשר אמר כשר או פסול אין זה רק מצד הטעם, כי אין דבר שבתורה שאין לו טעם, וכאשר הטעמים שום לגמרי שיש כאן טעם להכשיר וטעם לפסול עד שהטעמים שקולים שום, יאמר בזה "אלו ואלו דברי אלהים חיים" כמו שהתבאר, ואין כאן קושיא כלל, וכך היה מחלוקת בית שמאי ובית הלל, אבל שאר מחלוקת של חכמים אינה כך, אף שיש לכל אחד ואחד טעם הגון עד שמזה הצד יאמר כי גם דבר זה מן השם יתברך שכל טעם הגון הוא מן השם יתברך, מכל מקום כאשר יזדקק הדבר מצד השכל הפשוט אז גובר דעת האחד על השני, וזהו פסק הלכה. ומכל מקום בשניהם יש טעם, שכשם שהוא מן השם יתברך השכל הפשוט, כך מן השם יתברך השכל שאינו פשוט, רק כי השכל הפשוט הוא במדריגה העליונה. ומכל מקום התבאר לך הטעם שהמחלוקת שהיא לשם שמים מתקיימת, ושאינה לשם שמים אינה מתקיימת כי ההפכים אין להם עמידה ביחד כי האחד הוא הפך השני.

106. באר הגולה, באר א (עמ' יט)

ויש לך לדעת כי דוקא במחלוקת בית שמאי ובית הלל אמרו אלו ואלו דברי אלוהים חיים, כי הם היו תחלה במחלוקת התורה, שקודם שהיה מחלוקת בית שמאי ובית הלל לא היה מחלוקת בתורה כלל, וכאשר באו בית שמאי ובית הלל היה מחלוקת שלהם עד שדברי שניהם דברי אלהים חיים כמו שהתבאר למעלה. ואין ראוי שיבאו מישראל ממדריגה העליונה שלא היה בהם מחלוקת בתורה, אל מדריגה זאת שיהיה בהם מחלוקת ואחד מהם דבריו בטלים, ולכך היה המחלוקת אלו ואלו דברי אלהים חיים, ואחר כך נתחדש שאר מחלוקת, והבן זה מאוד. ובארנו עוד במקום אחר הלשון שאמר דברי אלהים חיים ואין כאן מקום להאריך.

107. דרשות מהר"ל, דרוש על התורה (עמ' מא)

ובאולי יעלה בדעתך, הרי אף למוד אחד או דין אחד מהתורה לא נמצא שלא יהיה בו מחלוקת תנאים ואמוראים או גאונים וקדושי עליון ודיעות שונות, זה אומר בכה וזה אומר בכה, וכי לכל מי שאין הלכה כמותו אין שכר על

תורתו, או כל שכן שיהיה חס ושלום בעונש הזה, והרי בית שמאי אין כל
דבריהם הלכה, וכי יהיו חס ושלום בכלל זה? לא מחכמה שאלת על זה. כי
על זה אמרו בפרק קמא דחגיגה (ג, ב): "בעלי אסופות" אלו תלמידי חכמים
שיושבין אסופות אסופות ועוסקין בתורה, הללו מטמאין והללו מטהרין
הללו אוסרין והללו מתירין הללו פוסלין והללו מכשירין. שמא יאמר
האדם: היאך אני לומד תורה מעתה? תלמוד לומר: כולם "נתנו מרועה
אחד", אל אחד נתן פרנס אחד אמרן מפי אדון כל המעשים ברוך הוא,
דכתיב "וידבר אלהים את כל הדברים האלה". אף אתה עשה אזנך
כאפרכסת וקנה לך לב מבין לשמוע את דברי מטמאין ואת דברי מטהרין את
דברי אוסרין ואת דברי מתירין את דברי פוסלין ואת דברי מכשירין. הלא
יש לפקפק: מה צורך לומר "מפי אדון כל המעשים", ומה ענין לשון זה
לכאן? אלא שבא לומר, שאל יקשה לך: מכיון שאינם הלכה איך נתנו מרועה
אחד ומה לנו ולהם? על זה אמר שהם מפי אדון כל המעשים, רוצה לומר
כמו שרבוי המעשים הם מאתו יתברך ככל הנבראים שעם שהם מחולקים,
ומהם הפכיים לגמרי, עם כל זה כלם מן השם יתברך שהוא אחד וכלם יש
בהם האמת מצד, כמו שאנו אומרים (ברכת קידוש הלבנה) "פועל אמת
שפעולתו אמת". כי המים בבחינת מה שנבראו עליו הם אמת, וכן האש
שהוא הפכם בבחינתו אשר הוא נברא עליו גם הוא אמת, ככה רבוי הדעות
בעצמם הם כולם מאתו יתברך. ואף אם הם הפכיות, מכל מקום כל אחת יש
לה בחינה אמתית מצד, כמו שיבא עדות וראיה ברורה כמשל ודמיון. וכמו
שהנמצאים הגם שכל אחד אמת מצד בחינתו, מכל מקום ימצא לפעמים
אחד מהם הקרוב אל האמת יותר מחבירו והוא האמת הגמור, כי אין ספק
שהאדם קרוב אליו בעצמו יותר מכל הבעלי חיים, כן הדעות המחולקות יש
קרובה אל האמת לגמרי והיא הלכה, אבל אעפ"כ אותה שאינה אמת גמור
עד שתהא הלכה, אין לדחותה מפני זה. כמו בנבראים שעל כל כל פנים האחרים
גם כן במציאות כאשר גם הם שלמים ואמיתיים מצד, וזה אמרם: "אף על
פי שזה אוסר וזה מתיר זה פוסל וזה מכשיר אל אחד אמרם", שכך אמר
הקב"ה שבבחינה אחת הדין כך, ומכל מקום האחד הוא אמת בעצמו לגמרי
לא בבחינת פרטית. אם כן אין לדחות השאר גם כן כאלו אין בו ממש, כמו
שאין לדחות מעשה השם יתברך, אף שיש מהם שהוא ישר ואמת יותר, ולכך
כל אחת מהדעות היא תורה ויש שכר טוב לפעולתם בכוונם לשם שמים לאל
אחד שאמרם.

108. לחם משנה, אבות ה, יז

כי ידוע שהנשמות חלוקות, יש מצד הדין ויש מצד החסד, והוא עניין שמאי
והלל, כי שמאי היה קפדן לפי שורש נשמתו ולכך היה בכל מקום לחומרא,
והלל ענותנותו מצד שורש נשמתו מצד הרחמים. והנה התורה נדרשת מ"ט
פנים לטהרה מצד הרחמים, ומ"ט פנים לטומאה ואיסור מצד הדין. והנה
הוצרכו בכל התורה המחלוקת, כי אין בהשגת איש אחד לדורשו לכאן
ולכאן, כי אם שורש נשמתו מדין – נוטה לעולם לחומרא, לאיסור ולטומאה
ולחיוב, וצריך מתנגדו לחדש להיפוך מצד שורש נשמתו להתיר ולטהר
ולזכאי, כעין מחלוקת שמאי והלל.

109. יערות דבש, חלק ב, דרוש ח

אבל העניין, אמרו במשנה (אבות ה, יז): "כל מחלוקת שהיא לשם שמים סופה
להתקיים, ואיזו היא? זו מחלוקת הלל ושמאי, ומחלוקת שאינה לשם
שמים, כגון מחלוקת קרח ועדתו, אין סופה להתקיים". ויש להבין מה זה
שסופה להתקיים, איך נתקיימו דברי בית שמאי, הלא במקום בית הלל
דברי בית שמאי אינם משנה כלל (בבלי, יבמות ט, א), ומה מעליותא יש
במחלוקת שתהיה סופה להתקיים?...

אך באמת בגוף הדבר, הוא הדבר שנאמר: "אל תהי מפליג לכל דבר, שאין
דבר שאין לו שעה ומקום" (אבות ד, ג). וכמו כן אמרו: "אלו אוסרים ואלו
מתירין" (חגיגה ג, ב), "אלו ואלו דברי אלהים חיים" (עירובין יג, ב). ולכאורה זר
הדבר, איך ייתכן שני הפכים בנושא אחד?

אבל העניין כך, כי זה העולם עולם תמורה, והכל בסוג עץ הדעת טוב ורע, כי
הוא תחת עולם הגלגל חוזר והולך, וכן למעלה בעולם עליון, כמבואר בפירוש
בספר יצירה (ב, ד): רל"א שערים פנים ואחור הולך הגלגל וחוזר, פעמים טוב
ופעמים רע, אין למעלה מעונג ואין למטה מנגע. תם מת, עשר רשע. וכן הכל
טוב ורע מתהפך פעמים זה ופעמים זה, ולכן הכל לפי עניין הגלגל העליון
ותחתון סובב והולך מתהפך, ואם כן מה שבזמן הזה טמא, בזמן אחר טהור,
וכן כולם. ולכן אלו ואלו דברי אלהים חיים, כי בזמן הזה טמא, בזמן אחר
לפי סיבוב הגלגל העליון - טהור.

וזהו אמרם "אל תהי מפליג לכל דבר", שאמר זה חכם טמא והוא טהור, כי
אין לך דבר שאין לו מקום וזמן שיגיע שיהיה באמת טמא. וכן מצינו במצבה
שהיתה אהובה בימי אבות והיתה מצווה וקדושה, ושנואה אחר כך שהיה
טמא ועבירה. וכן כולם מתהפך, פעם כה ופעם כה לפי מערכות כנ"ל, ואלו
ואלו דברי אלהים חיים, כי הכל משורש טוב ורע. ולכן אין ממנין בסנהדרין

רק מי שיודע לטמא הטהור וכן להיפך (סנהדרין יז, א), כי אין זו חריפות של
הבל ושקר כדעת התוספות (שם, ד"ה שיודע), רק אמת, והכל בזמנו, וצריך
להתחכם בענין החכם ההוא, אף שהוא טמא, אין החלט, ויש זמן שהוא
טהור, והכל לפי הזמן. וכמה פעמים מצינו בדברי חז"ל שאסרו ואחר כך
בזמן התירו, וחזרו אחר כך ואסרו, כי הכל יפה בעתו לפי עת הרל"א שערים
כמבואר בספר יצירה כנ"ל, והבן. כללו של דבר: אל תהי מפליג לכל דבר
לומר "זהו שקר הוא" כמו שבארנו, כי בזמנו הראוי יהיה אמת, ואין לך
שקר רק מה שהוא שקר בעצמותו...

וזו היא כוונת חכמי משנה ז"ל: "מחלוקת שמאי והלל סופה להתקיים", כי
אע"פ שהיום הלכה כבית הלל שדבר זה טהור, יהיה זמן שיהיה טמא כדעת
בית שמאי, כי אין לך דבר שאין לו זמן ומקום, וכן להיפך. ולכן זו היא
מחלוקת לשם שמים כי דבריהם סופם להתקיים ושניהם אמת, מה
שאין כן מחלוקת קרח ועדתו שחלק על משה בטלית שכולה תכלת וכדומה,
לא היה ויהיה מעולם והוא שקר מוחלט. ולכך אין סופה להתקיים כלל,
כעלה נובל וענן כלה, זו היא מחלוקת קרח. וזו היא שלא לשם שמים, והבן.

110. פתח עיניים, בבא מציעא נט, ב

אם הלכה כמותי חרוב זה יוכיח וכו' (בבא מציעא נט, ב). יש להבין בהני
הוכחות דרבי אליעזר חרוב ואמת המים וכתלי בית המדרש ושוב הוכיח
מבת קול, ולהבין אומרים (שם) "אין מביאין ראיה מן החרוב" וכו'.

ואפשר לומר דרך דרש וחידוד בעלמא, במה שאמרו (עירובין יג, ב): אלו ואלו
דברי אלהים חיים, והוו בה קמאי, איך יתכן דאלו ואלו דברי אלהים חיים
והלא מי שאין הלכה כמותו לא דיבר נכונה? ואמרו הראשונים דיען אין
האור ניכר אלא מתוך החשך והאמת לא ניכר אלא מתוך השקר, כן הדבר
הזה, דלא יובן ויתייישב מעצמותו אלא מהפכו. לכן אמר ה' אל משה דברי
המזכין והמחייבין וכיוצא, כי מתוך הסברא דחויה תבנה ותכונן האמיתית.
הא חדא. ועוד למדו מדברי רש"י בכתובות (נז, א) דזמנין דשייך האי טעמא
וזמנין דשייך האי טעמא, ונמצא דעל כל פנים הסברא דחויה במציאות אחר
תתקיים בשנוי מועט. ועוד בה בשלישיה ושבה והיתה לבאר מפום רבנן רבני
צרפת, כי הקב"ה אמר למשה מ"ט פנים טהור ומ"ט אשר איננו טהור
וכיוצא, ואמר לו שהלכה כפי הסכמת חכמי הדור, והן דברי אלהים חיים
ממש.

ובזה אפשר לפרש דרך חידוד דרבי אליעזר אמר "חרוב זה יוכיח" כלומר
שיעקר ממקומו כלומר שסברתו אמת ושלהם שקר, רק שמתוך השקר יובן

האמת, וזה רמז במה שיעקר החרוב לומר שסברתם נעקרת לגמרי ואין בה אמת ולא תועיל כי אם להבין סברתו, והיינו על דרך תירוץ ראשון שאמרו הראשונים.

והדר אמר "אמת המים תוכיח", כלומר הגם שתאמרו שאין סברתכם שקר, מכל מקום אינו אלא דזמנין דשייך טעמא דידהו ועל דרך תירוץ שני הנזכר, ולכן אמר "אמת המים תוכיח" שהיא תחזור לאחוריה, כלומר דאף דסברת החולקים אינה הלכה ואינה מתקיימת, דומה לאמת המים דחזרה ומים הוו מיהא אלא שנשתנו ממקומם, ואף סברת החולקים אמיתית היא, ובעניין אחר בשינוי הנדון מתקיימת, דטעמה נכון ואמת במקום אחר.

וחזר לומר "כתלי בית המדרש יוכיחו" דאפילו תאמרו דשני הסברות אמת וההכרעה ביד חכמי הדור, כתלי בית המדרש יוכיחו כי ברבים היו עמדי ולא קדמני אדם לבית המדרש ולא יצאתי והנחתי אדם, כמו שאמרו פרק הישן (סוכה כח, א).

111. שו"ת יוסף אומץ, נא

דאפשר לומר דעיקר תקנת הקדמונים לומר מימרת אביי הלזו היינו לזכות את ישראל ואמר כל העם משנה וגמרא, ובחרו במימרא זו שהיא מעניין קרבנות. וכבר ידוע מה שאמרו פרק קמא דעירובין (יג, ב) אלו ואלו דברי אלהים חיים, וכתב הריטב"א בחידושי עירובין משם רבני צרפת דשתי הסברות אמת, ואמר משה רבינו עליו השלום להקב"ה: הלכה כדברי מי? והשיבו דהדבר מסור ביד חכמי הדור. ואם כן כיון דהסברות אמת אהניא לן במקום לימוד גמרא. ואי אתיא מביניייא מידי דלאו הלכתא לא אכפת לן, דסברא זו גם כן אמת ואלו ואלו דברי אלהים חיים.

ומעין דוגמא אני אומר על אשר תקנו לשנות פרק "איזהו מקומן" (משנה זבחים, פרק ה), וכתב מרן בבית יוסף (אורח חיים, סימן נ) בשם הרא"ה שבחרו בפרק זה שאין בו מחלוקת, ע"ש. וכתב הרב מופת הדור מהר"ח אלפאנדארי ז"ל בהגהתו בספר בני חיי, דהכוונה שלא הוזכר בו מחלוקת, אבל יש דברים שנויים במשנת איזהו מקומן דאיכא בהו פלוגתא דתנאי, עכ"ל. וגדולה מזו כתב הריטב"א ז"ל בחידושיו לעבודה זרה (יט, ב) וזה לשונו: "וזה שבררו להם פרק איזהו מקומן יותר משאר פרקים, אומר מורי נר"ו (הוא הרא"ה ז"ל) מפני שכולו שנוי בלא שום מחלוקת כלל. ואעפ"י שאין כולו הלכה, דהא קתני הפסח אינו נאכל אלא עד חצות ואנן קיימא לן לדעת רבינו הרמב"ן כרבי עקיבא דסבירא ליה אכילת פסחים כל הלילה דהא איכא חדא סתמא כוותיה פרק ב דמגילה, מכל מקום אחר שנשנה כל הפרק כולו בלא מחלוקת

כלל, הוא ראוי לשנות יותר משאר פרקים", עכ"ל. הרי דמלבד דיש בו מחלוקת, עוד זאת יתירה דאיכא מידי דלאו הלכתא.

וכן ראיתי להרשב"ץ ז"ל, בסוף מאמר חמץ בפירוש איזהו מקומן ובברייתא דרבי ישמעאל, שכתב דיש תנאים חולקים על רבי ישמעאל בקצת מאלו המדות שאינן דברי הכל, ע"ש. ועם כל זה מאחר דמסורת בידינו דאלו ואלו דברי אלהים חיים, הכל הוא תורת אמת ויוצא אדם ידי חובתו ממקרא ומשנה וגמרא. ואף על פי שהטור והריטב"א וסיעתם כתבו דהתקינו לומר ברייתא דרבי ישמעאל במקום גמרא, מכל מקום אפשר דכיוונו גם במימרת "אביי הוה מסדר" וכו' ללמוד גמרא, ולענין לימוד מועיל אף דאיכא מידי דלא כהלכתא, דגם סברא זו אמת, דאלו ואלו דברי אלהים חיים כמדובר.

והגם דבלימוד גם הסברות שאינם כהלכה הוא לומד תורה דאלו ואלו דברי אלהים חיים, מכל מקום תנן פרק קמא דעדיות (א, ד-ה) : ולמה מזכירין דברי שמאי והלל לבטלה וכו' ולמה מזכירין דברי היחיד וכו', כי עם היות דגם סברות שאינם כהלכה הן הן תורה שלימה דאלו ואלו דברי אלהים חיים, מכל מקום כיון דרצה הקב"ה שההכרעה תהיה ביד חכמי הדור וכבר הלכה רווחת את כל ונוכחת כסברת החולקים, יש בצד מה דנראה דמזכיר דבריהם לבטלה והוי סרך זלזול, והשיב דנפקא מינה נמי צד לטובה כדמפרש ואזיל.

112. קדושת לוי, ליקוטים, ד"ה תיקו

תיקו, הראשי תיבות : **ת**שבי **י**תרץ **ק**ושיות **ו**אבעיות. ובהשקפה ראשונה יש לדקדק : הא זה יהיה הכל אחר ביאת הגואל במהרה בימינו אמן, ולמה יתרץ אליהו הקושיות והאבעיות, הא יעמוד משה רבינו עליו השלום שנתן לנו התורה והמצות, ולמה לא יתרץ הוא הקושיות והאבעיות? ונראה, דהנה כתיב בספר [סדר] הדורות בהפלוגתא דרש"י ור"ת עם התפילין, דרש"י ז"ל היה משה רבינו בסייעתו, והר"ת לא השגיח על זה ואמר לו שכבר נתון לנו התורה ובידינו להורות כפי הוראות שכלינו בהתורה הקדושה. ונראה להבין זאת, ונבאר זאת בקיצור, דהיינו לגבי פלוגתא דבית שמאי ובית הלל אמרינן : אלו ואלו דברי אלהים חיים, דהנה יש בחינה שאדם לומד הפשט בהתורה הקדושה כפי הבחינה שלו, אם הוא מעולם החסד אז הכל טהור ומותר וכשר כפי הוראות שכלו בהתורה הקדושה, וכן להיפך, כשהוא ממדות הגבורה אז הוא להיפך. והנה בית הלל מדתו היה מדת החסד ולכך בית הלל לקולא, ובית שמאי שהיה ממדת הגבורה לכך בית שמאי לחומרא,

אבל באמת כל אחד לפי מדרגתו דברי אלהים חיים, וזהו : אלו ואלו דברי אלהים חיים.

והנה חז"ל שהיו אחר הדור בית שמאי ובית הלל וראו שהעולם צריך להתנהג בחסד וקבעו הלכה כבית הלל בכל מקום לקולא כבית הלל. והנה מי יכול להבחין זאת באיזה מדה צריך זה העולם להנהג שיופסק הלכה כמותו? מי שהוא החיים והוא בזה העולם הוא יודע באיזה מדה צריך זה העולם להתנהג, אבל מי שאינו חי אינו יודע כלל באיזה מדה צריכים לזה העולם להתנהג בו. והנה אליהו הוא חי וקיים ולא טעם מיתה והוא תמיד בזה העולם ולכך הוא יפשוט הקושיות ואבעיות כי הוא יודע באיזה מדה צריך בעולם להתנהג. ובזה יובן מה שאמר ר"ת למשה רבינו ע"ה שכבר נתן לנו התורה ובידנו להורות.

113. שו"ת זבחי צדק, יורה דעה, כו

שאלה. מה ששאלת על ענין מחלוקת חכמים אחד אוסר ואחד מתיר, היאך ניתנו למשה בסיני.

תשובה. שאלה זו היא עמוקה עד מאד ואין אנחנו יכולים ליגע לתכליתה, שאפילו הראשונים ז"ל לא יכלו לעמוד עליה. והנה שאלה זו כבר הקשו אותה רבני צרפת ז"ל, גמרא דעירובין (יג, ב) : "אמר רבי אבא אמר שמואל : שלוש שנים נחלקו בית שמאי ובית הלל, הללו אומרים הלכה כמותן והללו אומרים הלכה כמותן, יצאה בת קול ואמרה : אלו ואלו דברי אלהים חיים והלכה כבית הלל וכו'. וכי מאחר שאלו ואלו דברי אלהים חיים מפני מה זכו בית הלל לקבוע הלכה כמותן? מפני שנוחים ועלובים היו". ע"כ.

וכתב הריטב"א בשיטתו לעירובין וז"ל : "שאלו רבני צרפת ז"ל היאך אפשר שיהיו שניהם דברי אלהים חיים זה אוסר וזה מתיר? ותירצו כי כשעלה משה למרום לקבל התורה הראו לו על כל דבר ודבר מ"ט פנים לאיסור ומ"ט פנים להיתר, ושאל להקב"ה על זה, ואמר שיהיה זה מסור לחכמי ישראל שבכל דור ודור ויהיה ההכרעה כמותם, ונכון הוא לפי הדרש ובדרך האמת יש טעם סוד בדברי". עכ"ל הריטב"א ז"ל.

וכן כמו זה הביא מהרי"ש אלגאזי בספר יבין שמועה (דף פא ע"ב), וז"ל שמביא בספר משפטי שמואל שמפרש בשם רבינו חננאל ז"ל, שמה שאמרו אלו ואלו דברי אלהים חיים הכי פירושה שהקב"ה אמר למשה בסיני מ"ט פנים טהור ומ"ט פנים טמא, ולא הכריע בדבר אלא נשארה ההכרעה כפי מה שיסכימו הרוב כמו שכתוב בתורה 'אחרי רבים להטות' וכו'. עכ"ל.

וכן משמע במסכת חגיגה (ג, ב) וז"ל הגמרא : " 'בעלי אסופות' אלו תלמידי
חכמים שיושבין אסופות אסופות ועוסקים בתורה, הללו מטמאין והללו
מטהרין הללו אוסרין והללו מתירין הללו פוסלין והללו מכשירין. שמא
יאמר אדם : איך אני לומד תורה מעתה? תלמוד לומר : כולם 'ניתנו מרועה
אחד' אל אחד נתנם פרנס אחד אמרם מפי אדון כל המעשים ברוך הוא"
וכו'. עכ"ל שם. הרי בהדיא מוכח בגמרא כתירוץ רבני צרפת ורבינו חננאל
ז"ל ששניהם ניתנו למשה מסיני. וכמו שכתב כן השל"ה ז"ל (בדף כה ע"ב)
שבתחלה הביא דבר דברי הריטב"א משם רבני צרפת הנזכרים ואחר כך
הביא גמרא דחגיגה הנ"ל, ואחר כך כתב וזה לשונו : "הנה העידו עליהם
השלום כי כל חלוקי הדעות והסברות הסותרות זו את זו אל אחד נתנם
ופרנס אחד אמרם" וכו', עכ"ל ועיי"ש.

והרב חיד"א ז"ל בספר פתח עינים במסכת מציעא (נט, ב ד"ה אם הלכה כמותי
וכו'), הביא שלושה תירוצים על זה, וזה לשונו שם : "מה שאמר אלו ואלו
דברי אלהים חיים והוו בה קמאי, איך יתכן דאלו ודאלו דברי אלהים חיים
והלא מי שאין הלכה כמותו לא דיבר נכונה, ואמרו הראשונים דיען דאין
האור ניכר אלא מתוך החשך והאמת אין ניכר אלא מתוך השקר, כן הדבר
הזה דלא יובן ויתייישב מעצמותו אלא מהפכו. לכן אמר ה' אל משה דברי
המזכין והמחייבין וכיוצא, כי מתוך הסברא דחויה תבנה ותכונן האמתית
הא חדא. ועוד למדו מדברי רש"י בכתובות דף נז דזמנין דשייך האי טעמא
וזמנין דשייך האי טעמא, ונמצא דעל כל פנים דסברא דחויה במציאות אחר
תתקיים בשנוי מועט. ועוד בא שלישיה ושבה והיתה לבאר מפום רבנן רבני
צרפת, כי הקב"ה אמר למשה מ"ט פנים טהור ומ"ט אשר איננו טהור
וכיוצא, ואמר לו שהלכה כפי הסכמת חכמי הדור והן דברי אלהים חיים
ממש" וכו'. עכ"ל עיי"ש.

ומה שכתב הרב חיד"א ז"ל בתירוץ השני משם רש"י ז"ל בכתובות וכו', כן
כתב רש"י ז"ל בכתובות (נז, א ד"ה הא קיי"ל וכו'), וזה לשונו בסוף הדבור :
"אבל כי פליגי תרי אמוראי בדין או באיסור והיתר כל אחד אמר הכי
מסתבר טעמא, אין כאן שקר, כל חד וחד סברא דידיה קאמר, מר יהיב
טעמא להתירא ומר יהיב טעמא לאיסורא, מר מדמי מילתא למילתא הכי
ומר מדמי לה בעניינא אחרינא, ואיכא למימר אלו ואלו דברי אלהים חיים
הן, זמנין דשייך האי טעמא וזמנין דשייך האי טעמא, שהטעם מתהפך לפי
שנוי הדברים בשנוי מועט", עכ"ל רש"י ז"ל. למדנו מזה דשפיר אמרו רז"ל
אלו ואלו דברי אלהים חיים, דאע"ג דחכם זה שאומר אסור או מותר בזה

הדין אין הדבר כן, מכל מקום הסברא היא אמת וישנה בעולם ונתקבלה למשה מסיני על דין אחר, ושפיר אומר דברי אלהים חיים.

ועוד יש לרבני האחרונים ז"ל תרוצים אחרים, ועל כל זה החקירה לא תתיישב היטב על הלב ולא יש לנו דעת להגיע לתכליתה, כי אפילו על תירוץ רבני צרפת ז"ל כתב הגאון של"ה שם וזה לשונו: "וזה הדבר רחוק מאד משכל האנושי נמנע מחקו להולמו אם לא ילווה אליו דרך ה' סלולה דרך ישכן אור האמת", עכ"ל. עוד כתב למעלה מזה וזה לשונו: "והדעת לא ינוח בדברי רבני צרפת ז"ל כי אינם מספיקים בזה, אבל ינוח בטעם וסוד שיש בו על דרך האמת המקובל כמו שרמז הרב"י וכו', עכ"ל. ואם כן בזה השאלה לא נוכל לרדת לעומקה ולהאריך עוד בה. כי לפי הפשט למען ינוח הדעת מעט ובפרט כדי להשיב להמון כתבנו שלושה תירוצים, ויש בהם די והותר בזאת החקירה תן לחכם וישיב לשואלים הלכו בו, ובפרט לתירוץ רבני צרפת יותר יתיישב על הלב. אבל העיקר הוא בזה דרך הסוד ואין לנו ולכם עסק בנסתרות.

114. ויעש אברהם, קונטרס פרי הארץ, עמ' תקו-תקי

והנה מה שמצינו הבדל בין הגמרא ופוסקים ובין המקובלים, הוא כמו דאיתא בבבא מציעא (פו, א): "ספק שער לבן קדמה לבהרת, הקב"ה אומר טהור וכלהו מתיבתא דרקיעא אומרים טמא, אמרי: מאן נוכח? רבה בר נחמני" וכו' "כי הוה קא נח נפשיה אמר טהור טהור", עיין שם. ודבר זה הוא פלוגתא דתנאי (בסוף פי"ד דנגעים) ותנא קמא סבירא ליה טמא וכן הוא סתמא דמתניתין (דראש פ"ה שם) עיין שם, ואנן קיימא לן כסתם מתניתין. וזה לכאורה דבר זר מאוד, וכי שייכא פלוגתא נגד הקב"ה? והוא אומר טהור וה' אלהים אמת.

ונראה על פי מה שכתבו המקובלים ז"ל דבשמים ממעל הלכה כבית שמאי, וכן לעתיד לבוא תהיה הלכה כבית שמאי שהם גבוהים הרבה מבית הלל, ורק בזמן הזה הלכה כבית הלל. והענין הוא כי הנהגת הקב"ה בעולם הוא כפי שהסכימו רוב חכמי ישראל בפירושי המצוות, שכן צוה הקב"ה בתורתו "כי יפלא ממך דבר למשפט וגו' ועשית על פי הדבר אשר יורוך" (דברים יז, ח). וכשיהיה בבית דין עצמו חלוקי דעות גזרה תורה ואמרה "אחרי רבים להטות" (שמות כג, ב), וניזל בתר רוב דעות. ואע"ג שאין זה אמת לאמתו, שהרי יכול להיות כי המיעוט כוונו אל האמת יותר מן הרוב, מכל מקום כן גזרה התורה דניזל בתר רוב דעות.

ומאחר שהוא מגזירת יוצר בראשית וכן הוא רצונו יתברך שמו, אם כן תהיה
ההנהגה בעולם רק כפי הסכמת רוב חכמי הדור בפירוש המצוה ההיא,
ואע"ג שבשורשה יכול להיות האמת עם המיעוט. וגם אפשר שיבוא אחר כך
בית דין אחר בדור הבא, ורובו של הבית דין יסתור דעת רובו של הבית דין
שבדור הקדום ודעתם יהיה נוטה אל דעת המיעוט, ואז תהיה ההלכה כפי
דעת הבית דין האחרון, כמו שכתב הרמב"ם ז"ל בראש פי"ב מהלכות
ממרים, עיין שם, הנה אז תהיה ההנהגה למעלה גם כן על פי דעת הבית דין
האחרון שכן הוא גזירת ורצון ה' שאין לך אלא שופט שבימיך. ועל כל כיוצא
בזה דרשו: "אפילו יאמר לך על ימין שהוא שמאל ועל שמאל שהוא ימין -
תשמע לו" (ספרי דברים, קנד). ואע"ג שאין אמת אלא אחת, מכל מקום כך הוא
מגזירת התורה שביאורי המצות שלא נתפרשו להדיא בתורה יהיו תלוים
בדעת חכמי הדור.

וזה שהמליצו חכמינו ז"ל שהקב"ה אומר טהור, כלומר בשורש ההלכה היא
טהור וכן הוא האמת בשורשה, אבל מתיבתא דרקיע, והוא כינוי לסדרי
המשפט בהנהגת העולם, אומרים טמא, כי לפי רוב דעות החכמים שבאותה
הדור שקבלו עליהם הלכה כסתם משנה היא טמא, וממילא הוא כן בהנהגת
העולם. וכן הוא בפלוגתת בית שמאי ובית הלל, אע"ג שבשורש האמת כבית
שמאי, ולעתיד לבא תהיה הלכה כדבריהם, מכל מקום השתא שקיימו חכמי
הדור עליהם הלכה כבית הלל - העושה כבית שמאי במקום בית הלל הרי זה
מתחייב בנפשו, כעובדא דרבי טרפון (משנה, ברכות א, ג) שקרא בלילה והטה
כדברי בית שמאי, וגזרו ואמרו "בית שמאי במקום בית הלל אינה משנה",
כדאיתא בברכות (לו, ב).

ונמצא דכל התיקונים הנעשים בעולמות העליונים על ידי עשיות המצות הוא
רק אם עושה על דעת בית הלל במצוה זו, שכן הוא רצון השם יתברך שנשמע
אל מה שקבעו חכמים בענין ההלכה ההיא, ונמצא דרק כשעושה על דעת
בית הלל הוא מעורר רצון העליון ומתלבשים העולמות ומזדווגים הספירות
בסדר המצוה ההיא רק בדרך ההלכה שקבעו חכמים כפי שיקול דעתם
שהוא רצונו יתברך שמו. והעובר על דבריהם מהפך הצינורות ומתחייב
בנפשו.

וזה הוא גם כן הענין מה שאמרו באגדה בבבא מציעא (נט, א) במחלוקותו של
רבי אליעזר וחכמים בתנורו של עכנאי. דלאחר שנעשו כל האותות להראות
שבשמים הלכה כרבי אליעזר וגם יצתה בת קול דהלכה כרבי אליעזר, עמד
רבי יהושע על רגליו ואמר: "אין משגיחין בבת קול, דלא בשמים היא, שכבר
נתנה תורה בסיני וכתוב בתורה 'אחרי רבים להטות'", עיין שם. וקשה:

והא האי מעשה הוה בשעה שנחלקו, ואם כן היו הרבים יכולים עדיין לחזור
מדבריהן ולהסכים לרבי אליעזר כשראו שהודיעו מן השמים דהלכה כרבי
אליעזר? וצריך לומר כיון דצווי הקב"ה היה להורות על פי מה שיורה דעות
רוב חכמי הדור בשכלם וסברתם, אם כן אם רוב חכמי הדור היתה סברתם
נוטה לטמא את התנור ההוא מחויבים להורות רק על פי סברתם, ואם היו
חוזרין מדעתם לא מצד הסברא, רק מצד שכך הראו להם משמים, הנה היו
עושין נגד רצונו יתברך שמו שגזר ואמר שיהא תלוי ברצון וסברת רוב חכמי
הדור, אע"ג שהאמת בשורשו הוא לא כסברתם.

וזה שאמרו שם בגמרא שאליהו זכור לטוב גילה להם שהקב"ה כביכול שמח
אז ואמר "נצחוני בני, נצחוני בני", כלומר ששמח על שלא רצו לשנות ממה
שהורה להם דעתם וסברתם בהלכות התורה, שחשבו שרק כך הוא רצונו
יתברך שמו לשמוע אליהם גם אם יאמרו על ימין שהוא שמאל ולהיפך. וזה
ענין "נצחוני בני", כי מעתה תהיה גם ההנהגה למעלה רק על פי אותה
ההוראה שהורו בתנור זה רוב חכמי ישראל מסברתם.

ונראה דזה עצמו ענין מחלוקת המקובלים עם הפוסקים, שהמקובלים כתבו
לפי מה שנראה להם שורש ההלכה לפי צרופים ויחודים הידוע להם בקבלה
לפי מעמד העולמות, אבל מכל מקום אם רוב דעות חכמי ישראל הסכימו
ההיפך, וכן אם נתפשט המנהג במדינה ההיא לפי הפוסק המפורסם שבה עד
שנעשה להם לחוב גמור שלא לסור מהמנהג, שכן הוזהרנו "שאל אביך
וְיַגֵּדְךָ, זְקֵנֶיךָ וְיאמרו לְךָ" (דברים לב, ז) וכתיב "אל תטוש תורת אמך" (משלי א,
ח), נעשים כל התיקונים רק על פי ההוראה הזאת שנתקבלה בישראל. וכל
העושים כהמקובלים נגד הפוסקים הרי זה כעושה כבית שמאי נגד בית
הלל...

ולהכי שפיר כתבו דכל היכי דמחולקים המקובלים והפוסקים אין לנו אלא
דברי הפוסקים. מיהו היכי שאין הכרע בפוסקים וכן אם לא נתפשט המנהג
כאחד מן הפוסקים, הקבלה תכריע, כמו שכתב הרדב"ז בתשובה מובא
בשערי תשובה (אורח חיים, סימן כה), עיי"ש. אבל אם כבר נהגו ישראל כדעת
הפוסק האחד נעשים כל התיקונים רק לפי דעה זו, ואם לאו הוא מהפך
הצנורות חס ושלום, וכמו שכתבתי לעיל.

ובדרך שכתבתי יש להבין מה דאיתא בעירובין (יג, ב) בפלוגתת בית שמאי
בית הלל: "יצתה בת קול ואמרה: 'אלו ואלו דברי אלהים חיים, והלכה
כבית הלל'". וצריך להבין איך שני הפכים שזה אוסר וזה מתיר יוכלו להיות
שניהם דברי אלהים חיים בענין אחד, ועיין בחידושי הריטב"א שם. ובגמרא

שם הקשו: "וכי מאחר ששניהם דברי אלהים חיים למה זכו בית הלל לקבוע הלכה כמותן?", ולא הקשו "וכי אפשר להיות שניהם דברי אלהים חיים בשני הפכים". תו קשיא: והא גם אי לא נימא דשניהם דברי אלהים חיים קשה למה זכו בית הלל לקבוע הלכה כמותן, מאחר שהרוב דידהו לאו רוב גמור הוא, כדאמרינן ביבמות (יד, א) משום דבית שמאי מחדדי טפי, ועיין תוספות בבא מציעא (נט, ב ד"ה לא בשמים), ולמה תלו הקושיא במה ששניהם דברי אלהים חיים?

אבל דע והבן כי אין האמת ההלכותי כהאמת החשבוני וההנדסיי שאין לו אלא פתרון אחד, אלא הוא אמת שכליי והסברותי, כלומר לפי שמבינים וסוברים בו בני האדם לפי אשר יורה להם רוח מבינתם. וצוה הקב"ה בתורתו שכאשר יפלא ממנו דבר במשפטי התורה נשמע אל דברי הבית דין שבאותו הדור שהם יגידו הפתרון על פי אשר יענה אותם רוח מבינתם. ולפי שאין דעת בני אדם שוות זו לזו ובהכרח ישתנו הדעות רוב פעמים גם אצל אותו הבית דין עצמו, צוה השם יתברך להטות אחרי דעת הרבים. וכיון שהסכימו דעת הרבים לומר אסור, הוא רצון השם יתברך שיהא אסור. ואם יבוא בית דין בדור שלאחריהם ויהא רובו נוטה בסברתו לדעת המיעוט הראשון ולהתיר הדבר, גם זה הוא רצון השם יתברך שנתירו לפי שאמרה תורה "אל השופט אשר יהיה בימים ההם" (דברים יז ט), וכמו שכתב הרמב"ם ז"ל (בראש פ"ב מהלכות ממרים) וזה לשונו: "בית דין הגדול שדרשו באחת מן המדות כפי מה שנראה בעיניהם שהדין כך ודנו כך, ועמד אחריהם בית דין אחר לסתור אותו, הרי זה סותר ודן כפי מה שהוא נראה בעיניו, שנאמר 'אל השופט אשר יהיה בימים ההם' – אין לך אלא שופט שבדורך". עכ"ל.

והכל מטעם זה, דמאחר שתלתה התורה פתרון זה בהאמת הסברותיי והדעות מתחלפות, וכל סברא וסברא יש לה קביעות בדעות בני אדם, ואפילו באדם אחד מתחלפות הסברות לפעמים, וכדאיתא בעירובין שם (יג, ב) ברבי מאיר שהיה אומר על טמא טהור ומראה לו פנים, כלומר שהסביר הדבר במדע שכלי והיה אומר על טהור טמא ומראה לו פנים שנתן גם לזה מקום בסברא, ונמצא שהטמא והטהור שניהם יש להם מקום בדעת וסברא. וכל דבר שיש לו מקום בדעת נקרא "דברי אלהים חיים", שהרי צוה האלהים שנשמע לדברי הסברא והדעת של הבית דין כפי שהם מבינים בפתרון הספקות הנופלות במצות התורה. אלא לפי שהדעות מתחלפות, צוה שנלך בתר רוב דעות. ואע"ג שיכול להיות שהמיעוט כיוון אל האמת יותר מהרוב, מכל מקום כדי שלא יתחלקו ישראל לכמה בעלי תורות היתה גזירת הכתוב שנקבל לאמת סברותי כפי שיאמר הרוב בסברתו. וכשיעמוד אחר כך בית

דין אחר והרוב שבו יבין אחרת ממה שהבין הבית דין הראשון, ידון כפי
סברתו באותו העת. ונמצא מה שהיה קודם טמא ברצון הקב"ה שנשפוט לפי
דעת וסברת הבית דין ההוא, נעשה עתה טהור ברצון הקב"ה שנשמע אל
סברת השופט שבדורנו, ונמצא ששניהם דברי אלהים חיים המה, ואנחנו
נשמע מגזירת הכתוב אל הרוב שבבית דין שבאותו הזמן.

וזה שלא שאלו בגמרא "אם אלו אוסרין ואלו מתירין אפשר ששניהם דברי
אלהים חיים", בתמיה, לפי שהיה דבר פשוט אצלם, שכל מה שהוא בסברת
השכל דברי אלהים חיים המה וכמו שביארתי למעלה. אבל שאלו מאחר
ששניהם דברי אלהים חיים ורוב ליכא וכמו שהבאנו לעיל מגמרא
דיבמות (יד, א), למה זכו בית הלל שנקבע הלכה כמותן שיצתה בת קול
ואמרה הלכה כבית הלל, והרי הדבר מסור לחכמים שבדור שישאו ויתנו
בדבריהם והרוב יכריע? ומשני: משום דנוחין וכו'.

כללו של דבר, סברת האוסר וסברת המתיר מאחר ששניהם יש להם מקום
בשכל האנושי שבו בחר ה' להיות הפותר בספקות התורה, אם כן עושה
שניהם ה', ולהכי נקראים שניהם דברי אלהים חיים. אלא שלמעשה צוה
הקב"ה דניזל בתר רוב דעות הבית דין שבדור ההוא, ויוכל להתחלף על
ידי בית דין אחר שבדור שאחריו. ואם כן שניהם הם אמת, לא כאמת
הנדסיי מציאות ממשיי, אלא אמת שכל מדעי סברותיי לפי הבנת בני אדם.

ומאחר שכל מצות התורה הוא ענין בחיריי שבהם בחר ה' ברצונו,
שבאמצעות קיום מצות אלה נזכה לחיים בגשם וברוח, הנה היה גם רצונו
שבספקות הנופלות באיכות קיום המצות נפתור על פי סברת אנושי שכלי על
פי חכמי התורה שבדור, וכפי פתרונם כן הוא רצון השם יתברך. וכל העובר
על דבריהם, כל זמן שלא עמד בית דין אחר בדור אחר וסתר דבריו, הוא
עובר על לאו שבתורה "ולא תסור מן הדבר אשר יגידו לך ימין ושמאל". ואף
שיוכל להיות שטעו בדבר משפט בשכלם, גזירת הכתוב הוא שנשמע להם גם
אם יאמרו על ימין שהוא שמאל ועל שמאל שהוא ימין כדאיתא בספרי
פרשת שופטים (שם). וכן הוא הדרך האהוב לפני המקום ברוך הוא בקיום
מצותיו יתברך שמו. ואם כן יש בו מן האמת הסברותיי לפי שכן חפץ הוא
יתברך שמו בדרכי המצוות.

ובדרך הזה שכתבתי יבואר עוד מה שקבעו חכמים בש"ס הלכה כאחד מן
החולקים בכל המקומות, כמו: רבי מאיר ורבי יהודה הלכה כרבי יהודה
(עירובין מו, ב), רבי מאיר ורבי יוסי הלכה כרבי יוסי, וכן בהאמוראים. וקשה
טובא, וכי אפשר לומר שרבי מאיר לא כוון מעולם אל האמת והחולקים

362

כוונו לעולם אל האמת? זה רחוק מאד בסברא. וכבר עמד בזה הגאון בעל שו"ת חוות יאיר ז"ל (סימן צד).

אבל כבר כתבתי שהאמת ההלכותיי אינו כאמת ההנדסיי שאין לו אלא פתרון אחד. וכל דבר שיש לו מקום בסברא ודעת נבונים שבאנשים, הוא אמת סברותיי והם מתחלפים לפי דעות בני אדם שבאותו הזמן. והיתה רצון נותן התורה למסור הדבר לחכמי הדור בכל הספקות הנולדות, כי לא היה אפשר לכתוב הכל בתורה ובהכרח יולדו ספיקות במשך הזמן. ועיין כל זה היטיב בלשונו הזהב של הרמב"ן ז"ל (פרשת שופטים יז, יא) עיי"ש, וצוה וגזר שנלך בתר רוב דעות. ומאחר שבימי חכמי התלמוד ז"ל כבר נתרבו מאוד חילוקי הדעות בכל הלכה והלכה וחששו שלא יתחלק חס ושלום ישראל לכמה תורות, וכבר לא היה אפשר בימיהם להכריע בין הראשונים בכל הלכה לעצמה ורוב ההלכות המסתעפות בכל מצוה ומצוה, וגם לא חשבו שהם כדאי להכריע מסברא בין הראשונים כמלאכים, סמכו עצמם על מה שכתוב בתורה שפתרון המצות תלוי בדעת בית הגדול. והתורה נתנה רשות לבית דין היותר גדול שבדור לבחור בהלכה כפי דעתם שבזה יתמעטו המחלוקת, כדי שלא יעשו ישראל לכמה תורות. והחמירה תורה כל כך לדון זקן ממרא במיתה כדי שלא ירבו המחלוקת, עיין ברמב"ם (פ"ג ממרים ה"ד).
ולכן המציאו להם כללים בדרכי ההוראה, וכשראו שאחד מן התנאים או האמוראים בהרבה פעמים באו ברוב פעמים סברתו יושר ישרה, קבעו הלכה כמותו בכל מקום. ואע"ג שבפרט אחד הסברה האמיתית נראה כהחולק, לא חשו לזה לפי שהסברות מתחלפות וכל שהוא נראה היום כנכון יוכל לראות מחר גם ההיפך. וכמו שהבאנו לעיל מגמרא עירובין מרבי מאיר שהיה אומר טמא ומראה לו פנים ואחר כך אומר טהור ומראה לו פנים. וכן קבעו הלכה כרב באיסורא וכשמואל בדינא (בכורות מט, ב), לפי שנראה להם אז שסברת שמואל בדינא יותר ערוכים בסברא וכן לרב באיסורא. לבד מה שראו להדיא שאין סברתם סובל כלל. וכדרך שאמרו (גיטין לח, א): "כל מקום ששנה רשב"ג במשנתיו הלכה כמותו לבר מערב וציידון וראיה אחרונה". וכן בכל מקום הלכתא כרבא לגבי אביי חוץ מיע"ל קג"ם, וכן בדוכתי טובי בש"ס. וכן מה שאמרו דעד אביי ורבא הלכתא כקדמאי ומאביי ורבא ואילך הלכתא כבתראי, יש לומר לפי שראו שההוויות דאביי ורבא ולאחר כך היתה רוב רוב ענינם לדקדק בדברי הראשונים, וכיון שהעלו הלכה מתוך סברתם נמצאו הם הבית דין האחרון והלכה כמותם, וכמו שהבאנו לעיל מדברי הרמב"ם (בראש פ"ב ממרים), עיין שם.

115. עין אי"ה, ברכות פרק ט, אות סח

"אמר רבי ביזנא בר זבדא אמר רבי עוקבא אמר רבי פנדא אמר רבי נחום אמר רבי בירים משום זקן אחד, ומנו? רבי בנאה: עשרים וארבעה פותרי חלומות היו בירושלים, פעם אחת חלמתי חלום והלכתי אצל כולם, מה שפתר לי זה לא פתר לי זה, וכולם נתקיימו בי" כו' (ברכות נה, ב). למדנו שישנם לפעמים דיעות מחולקות שבאמת אין בהם מחלוקת, אלא שכל אחד דן מצד השקפתו על הדבר ואין השקפה אחת שוללת את זולתה. ואפילו ההשקפות שנראות כסותרות זו את זו, אין להחליט שהם שניים במחלוקת כי יתכן שנראה הדבר כמחלוקת מפני חסרון ההעמקה וההרחבה בטיבו של ענין, אבל לכשיודע לו הענין על בוריו ימצא שיש פנים לכל אחד מהצדדים אפילו הנראין כסותרים.

116. מכתב מאליהו, חלק ג, עמ' 353

ומה ששאלתם ביאור הגמרא בברכות (לד, ב): "כל הנביאים כולן לא נתנבאו אלא לבעלי תשובה, אבל צדיקים גמורים - 'עין לא ראתה אלהים זולתך', ופליגי דרבי אבהו, דאמר מקום שבעלי תשובה עומדים צדיקים גמורים אינם עומדים". ושאלתם שהרי יש ליישב, דמצד גילוי חסדו יתברך מתגלה יותר בבעל תשובה, מה שאין כן העבודה העצמית מתגלית יותר בצדיק מעיקרו. צדקתם בדבריכם מאד. והנה באמת לא שייך מחלוקת אלא בדבר הלכה, וגם בזה רק בנוגע למעשה איך לעשות, אבל בעצם תוכן הענין לא שייך מחלוקת, כאמרם ז"ל: אלו ואלו דברי אלהים חיים (עירובין יג, ב). פירוש דשתי הדעות - שני מבטים אמת, ושניהם אמת. למשל, אם נקח גליון של ניר, והאחד יראנו אך מצד עביו, וצד השטחי נסתיר ממנו, והשני יראנו אך מצד השטחי, הלא תפרוץ מחלוקת ביניהם אם הניר הוא שטחי או חד, וכל אחד ואחד ידמה בשכלו כי חברו טועה לגמרי. ואיך הוא באמת? שניהם רואים אותו הגליון עצמו, אך משני מבטים, היינו משני צדדים. וגם זוהי בחינת מה שהזכרת במכתבך במחלוקת בית שמאי ובית הלל, דלעתיד לבא תהיה הלכה כבית שמאי, כי לעתיד לבא יהיה המבט להלכה בבחינת מדת הדין, ושניהם דברי אלהים חיים, וגדר מחלוקתם דכל אחד ראה את האמת מצד בחינת מדתו בעבודת ה'. ועיין מה שכתב בזה אדוני אבי זקני הגאון רבי ישראל סלנטר זצ"ל באור ישראל (סימן כח).

והנה מפורש בתקוני זהר דבעניני אגדה וקבלה לא שייך מחלוקת. והביאור הוא כנ"ל, משום דשני המבטים אמת כל אחד בבחינתו, ואינו חלוק למעשה. ועיין באבן שלמה להגר"א בעניני משיח, דשני גדרי משיח יש. האחד בגילוי

גדול ברוחניות - משיח בן דוד, והשני גאולה משיעבוד מלכויות לבד - משיח בן יוסף, ומאמרי חז"ל הסותרים בזה "לא פליגי". ולכאורה תמוה מאד שהרי ש"ס ערוך הוא בגמרא לעיל בברכות, בסנהדרין (צט, א) ובשבועות (צ"ל שבת סג, א), ועוד מקומות כמדומני, דכל הנביאים לא נתנבאו אלא לימות המשיח כו' "ופליגי דשמואל דאמר אין בין העולם הזה לימות המשיח אלא שיעבוד מלכויות בלבד". אלא על כרחך כנ"ל, דהאי "ופליגי" היינו דשתי בחינות חלוקות הן בגאולה, האחד "בן דוד" והשני "בן יוסף", ופירוש "פליגי" היינו שהוא מופרש וחלוק זה מזה. והנה בודאי החילוק שלכם בהא דבעל תשובה אמת וברור הוא, וכמדומני שכבר ראיתי גם החילוק הזה מכבר בספרים הקדושים, וחילוק זה עצמו היינו היינו ז"ל אמרם "ופליגי".

117. שעורי דעת, חלק א, דרכה של תורה, פרק ה

ומה שיש לדעת עוד בזה הוא, כי אף בין אלה הזוכין לכוון לאמתה של תורה, אפשר שתהיינה מחלוקות בהלכה, שאלה יטמאו ואלה יטהרו, אלה יאסרו ואלה יתירו, אלה יחייבו ואלה יפטרו, ו"אלה ואלה דברי אלהים חיים".

טעם הדבר הוא, כי התורה הקדושה, שהיא יסוד ושורש הבריאה, תלאה הקב"ה בבחיר היצורים, כמה שנאמר "תמשילהו במעשה ידיך" וגו' (תהלים ח, ז), וכשנתנה התורה לישראל, נמסרו חקי ענייניה לחכמי התורה, שמחשבתם, אם היא רק מכוונת לטעמה וסודה, קובעת את מציאותה ומציאות הבריאה התלויה בה. ולכן היא שונה משאר החכמות שהחוקרים בהן לא יקבעו את מציאותן אלא ימצאוה, כי במחשבתם והחלטתם לא תשתנה המציאות לעולם, לא כן היא דעת התורה שמציאות טומאה וטהרה, איסור והיתר, חיוב ופטור נקבעים בהחלטת חכמי התורה. וכבר עמד רבי יהושע על רגליו ואמר: לא בשמים היא ואין משגיחין בבת קול... וקודשא בריך הוא חייך ואמר: נצחוני בני נצחוני בני" (בבא מציעא נט, ב). כי גם בדעת תורה יש למצא צדדים לכאן ולכאן, ובכל דבר חכמה יש טעמים המטים לצד אחד וטעמים אחרים המתנגדים לו, כי לא רק עמוקה היא החכמה משאול אלא גם רחבה מני ים. והחכם באמת לא יסתפק בהבנת החכמה מצד אחד, אלא צריך הוא להקיף אותה מכל צדדיה, וכדמצינו בבית הלל שהיו שונים דבריהם ודברי בית שמאי (עירובין יג, ב), כי שני הצדדים תורה הם, וההכרעה נקבעת בין כל הצדדים הללו היא היא קביעת ההלכה המכרעת על המציאות לכל אחד, כל זמן שלא עמדו למנין וקבעוה לרבים. וכל אחד מוציא את הדין באמת לפי מעלת נפשו, מזגו ושורש נשמתו

והשפעת המחשבה ודרך החכמה שקבל מרבותיו אשר יצרו את הלך מחשבתם של תלמידיהם, וכמה שאמרו חז"ל: "כל המלמד את בן חברו תורה מעלה עליו הכתוב כאילו עשאו" (סנהדרין צט, ב). אבל כל הטעמים וכל ההכרעות, אלו ואלו דברי אלהים חיים הם.

118. פחד יצחק (הוטנר), חנוכה, ג

פעמים שביטולה של תורה זה הוא קיומה, שנאמר "אשר שברת" (שמות לד, א), "יישר כוחך ששברת" (סנהדרין סב, א). מעשה שבירת הלוחות הוא מעשה של קיום תורה על ידי ביטולה. והרי אמרו חכמים שאלמלא נשתברו הלוחות לא היתה תורה משתכחת מישראל (עירובין נד, א). נמצא אפוא, כי שבירת הלוחות היה בה גם משום השכחת התורה. למדים אנו מכאן חידוש נפלא, כי אפשר לה לתורה שתתרבה על ידי שכחת התורה, עד כי באופן זה יתכן לקבל "יישר כוח" עבור השכחת התורה. ופוק חזי מה שאמרו חכמים (תמורה טז, א) כי שלש מאות הלכות נשתכחו בימי אבלו של משה והחזירם עתניאל בן קנז בפלפולו. והרי דברי תורה הללו של פלפול החזרת ההלכות, הם הם דברי תורה שנתרבו רק על ידי שכחת התורה. ולא עוד אלא שכל ענין המחלוקת בהלכה אינו אלא מצד שכחת התורה, ואף על פי כן הלא כך אמרו חכמים: "אף על פי שהללו מטהרין והללו מטמאין הללו פוסלין והללו מכשירין הללו פוטרין והללו מחייבים" וגו' (חגיגה ג, ב), "אלו ואלו דברי אלהים חיים" (עירובין יג, ב). ונמצא דכל החילוקי דעות וחילופי שיטות הם הגדלת התורה והאדרתה, הנולדות דוקא בכוחה של שכחת התורה.

וחידוש עוד יותר גדול יוצא לנו מכאן, כי מרובה היא מדת הבלטת כוחה של תורה שבעל פה המתגלה במחלוקת הדעות, מאשר במקום הסכמת הדעות. כי הלא בהך דאלו ודאלו דברי אלהים חיים כלול הוא היסוד כי גם השיטה הנידחית מהלוקי דעת תורה היא, אם רק נאמרה לפי גדרי המשא ומתן של תורה שבעל פה. והיינו משום דתורה ניתנה על דעתם של חכמי התורה (לשונו של הרמב"ן, דברים יז, יא) ואם יעמדו למנין אחר כך ויכריעו כהדעה הנידחית, מכאן ואילך תשתנה ההלכה אליבא דאמת (יעוין אור ישראל פרק ל בהערה). ונמצא כי מחלוקתם של חכמי תורה מגלה את כוחה של תורה שבעל פה הרבה יותר מאשר הסכמתם. מלחמתה של תורה איננה אופן אחד בין האופנים של דברי תורה, אלא שמלחמתה של תורה היא יצירה חיובית של ערכי תורה חדשים, שאין למצוא דוגמתם בדברי תורה סתם. "על כן יאמר בספר מלחמות השם את והב בסופה" (במדבר כא, יד), ופירשו חכמים (קידושין ל, ב): "אפילו אב ובנו רב ותלמידו נעשים שונאים זה לזה, ואינם

זזים משם עד שנעשים אוהבים זה לזה". בהשקפה הראשונה הדברים הללו באים להשמיענו את הרבותא בגודל כוחו של חיבור האהבה הטמון בדברי תורה, דהיינו שכוחו של חיבור של אהבה זה גדול הוא עד כדי הבטחת הריעות הנאמנה אפילו לאלה שמקודם נעשו שונאים זה לזה. לפי הבנה זו הרבותא היא בכאן כי למרות השנאה של שעת המחלוקת, הרי לבסוף באה היא האהבה ומכריעה אותה, ואינם זזים משם עד שנעשו אוהבים. אבל מכיון שנתבהרה לנו הנקודה כי מלחמתה של תורה היא מדרגת יצירה חדשה נוספת על מדרגת דברי תורה סתם, הרי בהירות זו תלמדנו לדעת שאין העניין בכאן שהאהבה לבסוף באה היא למרות המחלוקת הקודמת, אלא שכך הוא דרך גידולה של אהבה זו, שהיא נולדת ומתגדלת דוקא על קרקע המחלוקת הקודמת. מפני שכל אהבה מגיעה למרום פסגתה בשעה ששני הצדדים יש להם שותפות של יצירה, ושני הצדדים המתנגחים בהלכה הרי הם שותפים ליצור של ערך תורה חדש, אשר שמו הוא מלחמתה של תורה.

וחוזרים אנו בזה להתחלת הדברים. מציאות של מחלוקת בדברי תורה ההולכת ונמשכת עד ימינו אלה נולדה אמנם בחושך יון, מכל מקום אין מציאות זו שיור בגאולת יון. אדרבה, פורקן החנוכה על ידי בית דין של חשמונאים הוא נצחון על חושך יון, על ידי הוצאת האור מתוך החושך עצמו. "יגדיל תורה ויאדיר" (ישעיה מב, כא) – על ידי שכחת התורה, ביטולה זה הוא קיומה. בעוד שמפלתן של בבל ושל מדי היתה אמנם רפואה לשעבודה של כנסת ישראל, הרי מפלתה של יון היה בה גם משום רטיה אשר הוכנה מתוך המכה עצמה. כשעמדה מלכות יון הרשעה על עמך ישראל להשכיחם תורתך, והנה בתוך השכחה עצמה פתחו פיהם מעיינות תורה חדשים על ידי פלפולה של תורה המתחדש לבקרים, לשם החזרת בירורה של תורה ההולכת ומשתכחת. חנוכה היא הקביעות האחרונה בסדרי זמנים של מועדי דורות. מכיון שגם בגוף החושך של השכחה יתכן למצא נצוצי אורה של ריבוי תורה, שוב אפשר הוא בכחה של סגולה זו לצעד במסילת השכחה הארוכה של גלות אדום המובילה עד אחרית הימים. אז אגמור בשיר מזמור חנכת המזבח.

119. שו"ת אגרות משה, אורח חיים א, הקדמה

אבל הוא מטעם שהנכון לעניות דעתי בזה, שהיו רשאין ומחוייבין חכמי דורות האחרונים להורות אף שלא היו נחשבין "הגיע להוראה" בדורות חכמי הגמרא, שיש ודאי לחוש אולי לא כיוונו אמיתות הדין כפי שהוא האמת כלפי שמיא. אבל האמת להוראה כבר נאמר "לא בשמים היא" (דברים

ל, יב), אלא כפי שנראה להחכם אחרי שעיין כראוי לברר ההלכה בש"ס
ובפוסקים כפי כחו בכובד ראש וביראה מהשם יתברך, ונראה לו שכן הוא
פסק הדין - הוא האמת להוראה, ומחוייב להורות כן אף אם בעצם גליא
כלפי שמיא שאינו כן הפירוש. ועל כזה נאמר שגם דבריו דברי אלהים חיים,
מאחר שלו נראה הפירוש כמו שפסק, ולא היה סתירה לדבריו, ויקבל שכר
על הוראתו, אף שהאמת אינו כפירושו. והוכחה גדולה לזה מהא דשבת (קל,
א) : "אמר רבי יצחק : עיר אחת היתה בארץ ישראל שהיו עושין כרבי אליעזר
ונתן להם הקב"ה שכר גדול שמתו בזמנן, וכשגזרה מלכות הרשעה גזירה על
המילה לא גזרו על אותה העיר". אף שהאמת אליבא דדינא נפסק שלא כרבי
אליעזר והוא חיוב סקילה במזיד וחטאת בשוגג. אלמא דהאמת להוראה
שמחוייב להורות וגם מקבל שכר הוא כפי שסובר החכם אחרי עיונו בכל
כחו, אף שהאמת ממש אינו כן. וזהו ענין כל מחלוקות רבותינו הראשונים
והאחרונים שזה אוסר וזה מתיר, שכל זמן שלא נפסק כחד יכול כל אחד
להורות במקומו כמו שסובר, אף שהדין האמתי הוא רק כאחד מהן, ושני
החכמים מקבלים שכר על הוראתם. ומטעם זה מצינו הרבה חלוקים גם
באיסורים חמורים בין מקומות הנוהגים להורות כהרמב"ם והב"י ובין
המקומות הנוהגים להורות כחכמי התוספות וכהרמ"א, ושניהם הם דברי
אלהים חיים, אף שהאמת האמתי גליא כלפי שמים שהוא רק כאחד מהם.

ומפורש כן בסנהדרין (ו, ב) אחר שאמר "ויהו הדיינים יודעין את מי הן דנין
ולפני מי הן דנין ומי עתיד ליפרע מהן, שמא יאמר הדיין : מה לי בצער
הזה?" ופירש רש"י : "שאם אטעה איענש", "תלמוד לומר 'ועמכם בדבר
המשפט' (דברי הימים ב יט, ו), אין לו לדיין אלא מה שעיניו רואות", ופירש
רש"י "דאין לו לדיין לירא ולמנוע עצמו מן הדין אלא לפי מה שעיניו רואות
לידון ויתכוין להוציא לצדקו ולאמתו ושוב לא יענש", עיי"ש. וכוונתו דזהו
האמת להוראה שמחוייב להזדקק ולהורות ולדון, אף שאינו האמת ממש.

ובזה ביארתי מה שאיתא במנחות (כט, ב) : "אמר רב יהודה אמר רב : בשעה
שעלה משה למרום מצאו להקב"ה שיושב וקושר כתרים לאותיות, אמר
לפניו : רבונו של עולם, מי מעכב על ידך? אמר לו : אדם אחד יש ועקיבא בן
יוסף שמו שעתיד לדרוש על כל קוץ וקוץ תילין תילין של הלכות". שלכאורה
לא מובן לשון "כתרים" שאמר, ועוד קשה שאלת משה "מי מעכב", מה
כוונתו בזה, דמה שפירש רש"י : "למה אתה צריך להוסיף עליהם", אין שייך
ללשון מעכב, דאף אם היה שייך כביכול להיות מעכב יקשה למה לו זה, ואם
כוונתו להקשות למה לא כתב בפירוש, לא מובן תירוצו בזה שרבי עקיבא
ידרוש תילין של הלכות.

אבל לפי מה שבארתי מדוייק לשון ״כתרים״, שנמצא שהשם יתברך עשה את אותיות התורה למלכים, היינו שיעשה החכם וידמה מלתא למלתא ויפסוק הדין כפי הבנתו טעם האותיות שבתורה, וכשיהיה מחלוקת יעשו כפי הבנת רוב חכמי התורה אף שאפשר שלא נתכוונו להאמת ולא היה דעת הקב״ה כן, דהקב״ה נתן את התורה לישראל שיעשו כפי שיבינו את הכתוב ואת המסור בעל פה בסיני לפי הבנתם, ויותר לא יפרש ולא יכריע השם יתברך בדיני התורה, ש״לא בשמים היא״, אלא הסכים מתחלה להבנת ופירוש חכמי התורה. ונמצא שאותיות התורה הם מלכים שעושין כפי מה שמשמע מהתורה לחכמי התורה, אף שאולי לא היה זה כהבנת השם יתברך. וניחא לשון ״אמרה תורה״ שמצינו בכמה דוכתי, משום דאנו דנין רק איך אומרת התורה. וכן ניחא מה שאיתא בעירובין (יג, ב) על בית שמאי ובית הלל אלו ואלו דברי אלהים חיים, דכיון שיכולין לפרש בתורה כבית שמאי וכבית הלל הרי נמצא שנאמר כתרוייהו, כל זמן שלא נתבטלו דעת אחד ברבים החולקין. וזהו פירוש ״מי מעכבי״, שמשה שאל למה עושה הקב״ה האותיות למלכים, שיעשו כפי משמעות החכמים בלשון הכתוב והמסור, דמי מעכב שתכתוב באופן שלא יהיה אפשר לפרש רק דרך אחד ככוונתך האמתית ולמה נתן כח מלוכה להאותיות שימצא שלפעמים יעשו שלא ככוונתך? והשיב הקב״ה משום שעל ידי זה ידרשו רבי עקיבא וכל החכמים תילין של הלכות שהוא הגדלת תורה ממעט הנכתב והנמסר, ולכתוב הרבה כל דבר בפרט אין קץ, שהתורה היא בלא קץ וגבול, עיין בעירובין דף כא, א.

120. מכילתא יתרו, מסכתא דבחודש, פרשה ז (עמ׳ 229)

״זכור״ (שמות כ, ח) ו״שמור״ (דברים ה, יב), שניהם נאמרו בדיבור אחד ; ״מחלליה מות יומת״ (שמות לא, יד) ״וביום השבת שני כבשים״ (במדבר כח, ט), שניהם בדיבור אחד נאמרו ; ״ערות אשת אחיך״ (ויקרא יח, טז) ו״יבמה יבוא עליה״ (דברים כה, ה), שניהם נאמרו בדיבור אחד ; ״לא תלבש שעטנז״ (דברים כב, יא) ו״גדילים תעשה לך״ (שם שם, יב), שניהם נאמרו בדיבור אחד ; מה שאי אפשר לאדם לומר כן, שנאמר (תהלים סב, יב) : ״אחת דיבר אלהים שתים זו שמענו״, ואומר (ירמיה כג, כט) : ״הלא כה דברי כאש נאום ה׳״.

121. בבלי, שבת פח, ב

אמר רבי יוחנן : מאי דכתיב ״ה׳ יתן אומר המבשרות צבא רב״ (תהלים סח, יב)? כל דיבור ודיבור שיצא מפי הגבורה נחלק לשבעים לשונות. תנא דבי ר׳

ישמעאל: "וכפטיש יפוצץ סלע" (ירמיה כג, כט), מה פטיש זה נחלק לכמה
ניצוצות אף כל דיבור ודיבור שיצא מפי הקב"ה נחלק לשבעים לשונות.

122. בבלי, סנהדרין לד, א

כדבעא מיניה רבי אסי מרבי יוחנן: אמרו שנים טעם אחד משני מקראות,
מהו? אמר ליה: אין מונין להן אלא אחד. מנהני מילי? אמר אביי: דאמר
קרא (תהלים סב, יב) "אחת דבר אלהים שתים זו שמעתי כי עז לאלהים",
מקרא אחד יוצא לכמה טעמים ואין טעם אחד יוצא מכמה מקראות. דבי
רבי ישמעאל תנא: "וכפטיש יפוצץ סלע" (ירמיה כג, כט), מה פטיש זה מתחלק
לכמה ניצוצות אף מקרא אחד יוצא לכמה טעמים.

123. במדבר רבה, פרשה יג, טו

"מזרק אחד כסף" (במדבר ז, יג), כנגד התורה המשולה ביין, שנאמר "ושתו
ביין מסכתי" (משלי ט, ה), ולפי שדרך היין לשתות במזרק כמה דתימא
"השותים במזרקי יין" (עמוס ו, ו) לכך הביא מזרק. "שבעים שקל בשקל
הקדש" (במדבר שם, שם), למה? כשם שיין חשבונו שבעים, כך יש שבעים פנים
בתורה.

124. זוהר, בראשית, מז, ב

"וכל צבאם" (בראשית ב, א), אלין פרטי דאורייתא, אפין דאורייתא, שבעים
פנים לתורה.

125. זוהר, ויקרא, כ, א

ומתמן הוו ידעין סנהדרין שבעים לשון דאינון שבעים פנים לתורה דאית
שבעים לשון מסיטרא דמלכות הרשעה וכו' כלא בפרודא. הדא הוא דכתיב
"מאלה נפרדו איי הגוים בארצותם ללשונתם", כלהו שבעים לשון בפירודא
דא מן דא. אבל דאורייתא שבעים פנים לתורה בלשון חד.

126. פירושי האגדות לרבי עזריאל, חגיגה ג, ב

"דברי חכמים כדרבונות וכמסמרות נטועים בעלי אסופות" (קהלת יב, יא),
אלו תלמידי חכמים שיושבים אסופות אסופות ועוסקין בתורה, הללו
מטמאין והללו מטהרין, הללו אוסרין והללו מתירין, הללו פוסלין והללו
מכשירין. ושמא תאמר כיון שהללו מטמאין וכו', היאך אני למד תורה
מעתה? תלמוד לומר: כולן "נתנו מרועה אחד", כולם אל אחד נתנם, פרנס

אחד אמרן מפי אדון כל המעשים ברוך הוא, שנאמר "וידבר אלהים את כל הדברים האלה לאמר".

שים לבך להבין שלוש מעלות אלו, אמרו חז"ל "שבעים פנים לתורה", והפנים משתנים זה מזה לטמא ולטהור לאיסור והיתר, ואמר חבר אחד: יכול אני לטהר את השרץ במ"ט פנים. וכל זה כי בדבור אחד היה, שנאמר "קול גדול ולא יסף" (דברים ה, יט), היו בו כל הפנים המשתנים והמתהפכים, לטמא ולטהור לאיסור והיתר לפסול וכשר, כי לא ייתכן להאמין שיהיה הקול ההוא חסר כלום, ולכן בקול ההוא היו הדברים מתהפכים לכל צד את זה לעומת זה. וכל אחד מן החכמים העתידים לעמוד בכל דור ודור קבל את שלו, כמו שאמרו (שמות רבה כח, ו): "ולא הנביאים בלבד קבלו מהר סיני אלא אף כל החכמים העומדים בכל דור ודור כל אחד ואחד קבל את שלו, שנאמר "את הדברים האלה דבר ה' אל כל קהלכם" (דברים ה, יט). וזהו שאמרו: אלו ואלו דברי אלהים חיים (עירובין יג, ב), ואמר: כולם אל אחד נתנם.

127. ספר החינוך, מצוה עז

כל אלה הדברים למדנו מ"לא תענה על ריב לנטות" (שמות כג, ב). וענין זה מכח חכמת התורה, שיש להבין מדבר אחד ממנה כמה דברים. זהו שאמרו זכרונם לברכה "שבעים פנים יש לתורה". ולפי שיודע אלהים כי העם מקבלי התורה בהתנהג על הדרך שנצטוו בה, יהיו נכונים אל החכמה ואל התבונה ויבינו בה כל הצריך להם אל הנהגת העולם, סתם להם הדברים במקומות, ומסר להם הפירוש על ידי הסרסור הגדול אשר ביניהם ובינו, ולא נתנה במלות רחבות יותר, לפי שכל מלותיה גזורות ומחויבות בחשבון ובצורתן להיות ככה, כי מלבד משמעות מצוותיה היקרות שאנו מבינין בה, נכללו בה חכמות גדולות ומפוארות, עד שהעלו רבותינו ז"ל גודל החכמה שהניח האל ברוך הוא בתוכה, שאמרו עליה שהביט הקב"ה בה וברא את העולם (בראשית רבה א, א).

128. שו"ת הרדב"ז ג, תרמג

שאלת ממני אודיעך דעתי למה אין כותבין הנקודה בספר תורה, כיון שהכל נתן למשה רבינו עליו השלום בסיני, וגם הטעמים היו ראוים שיכתבו אותם כדי שיקרא הקורא קריאה ישרה בלי שבוש, שהרי גם הטעמים מבארים טעם הכתובים לפעמים.

תשובה. שאלתך זו תלויה במה ששאלו המלאכים להקב"ה כשעלה משה רבינו ע"ה לקבל את התורה (שבת פח, ב): אמרו מלאכי השרת: מה לילוד

אשה ביניו? אמר להם הקב"ה: לקבל תורה בא. אמרו לו: תנה לנו. והיינו דכתיב "אשר תנה הודך על השמים" (תהלים ח, ב). אמר להם משה: תורה מה כתיב בה? "לא תרצח, לא תנאף" וכו', רציחה יש ביניכם וניאוף יש ביניכם? תורה למה לכם? והודו ואמרו: "ה' אדונינו מה אדיר שמך בכל הארץ" (שם). ויש להקשות: וכי המלאכים לא היו יודעים התשובה זו? אלא מאי אית לך למימר, שהם היו קורין בתורה קריאה אחרת רוחנית בלא פיסוק תיבות, על דרך שמותיו של הקב"ה. וכן אמרו רז"ל: כל התורה כולה שמותיו של הקב"ה. והודיעם הקב"ה שיש לתורה קריאה אחרת גשמית על דרך פיסוק תיבות בעניני בני אדם בטומאה וטהרה ואיסור והיתר ופטור וחייב וכן כל שאר דינים. ואחר שידעת זה תבין שאלתך, כי צוה האל יתעלה שיכתבו את התורה בלא נקודות וטעמים כאשר היתה באמנה אתו יתברך, כדי שיהיו בה שתי קריאות, רוחנית וגשמית, כדי שמי שיכול להשיג ישיג. וכן אמרו: "יודע היה בצלאל לצרף אותיות שנבראו בהם שמים וארץ" (בבלי, ברכות נה, א). ומסר הנקודות והטעמים כשאר תורה שבעל פה שהיא פירוש לתורה שבכתב, כן הנקודות והטעמים הם פירוש לתורה שבכתב. והדבר ידוע כי האותיות בלא נקודות וטעמים יש בהם משמעיות הרבה וצירופים שונים וקריאות הפכיות, ולכן לא נתנו הנקודות והטעמים ליכתב בספר תורה, ויכתבו בחומשים משום "עת לעשות לה'" (תהלים קיט, קכו), כדי שלא תשתכח תורת הקריאה, כשאר תורה שבעל פה.

ובמה שכתבתי לך תוכל לתרץ כמה ספיקות אחרות, כגון מה ששאלו הראשונים למה לא נכתב תורה שבעל פה, או למה נכתבו קצת ספורים שנראה לכאורה שאין בהם צורך, וכמה גופי תורה נרמזו ברמז כל שהוא. אלא שיש לך להאמין שאין לך (אלא) אפילו תיבה קטנה שאין בה סודות עמוקות וצירופים שלא נשיגם אנחנו, ואין לך בתורה אפילו אות אחת לא לצורך, ולא לתפארת הקריאה ולא בפה רפה כלשון ישמעאל כאשר חשבו רבים, ושים תמיד כל זה נגד עיניך ותצליח, ואני ערב. והנראה לעניות דעתי כתבתי.

מה שמצאתי כתוב בגליון וז"ל: מצאתי לאחד מן הראשונים ולא ידעתי שמו: דע כי מפני שהנקוד הוא צורה ונשמה לאותיות, לפיכך לא נעשה הספר תורה נקוד, לפי שהוא כולל כל הפנים וכל הדרכים העמוקים, וכולם נדרשים בכל אות ואות פנים לפנים מפנים ותעלומות לפנים מתעלומות, ואין (לך) [לה] גבול ידוע אצלנו, (ואמרו) [כאומרו] "תהום אמר לא בי היא" (איוב כח, יד). ואם ננקד הספר תורה היה לו גבול ושיעור כדמיון החומר שהגיעה לו צורה ידועה, ולא היה אפשר לו להיות נדרש כי אם לפי הניקוד המסויים

באותה תיבה. אבל מפני שספר תורה בלול ומובלל בכל מיני שלמות ובכל מלה ומלה נתלים בה תלי תלים, לא נעשה מנוקדים, כדי שיהיה נדרש בכל מיני שלמות. ולפיכך אמרו "אל תקרי כך אלא כך", ואלו היה מסויים לא נוכל לומר כך.

והנה חכמים ז"ל נתעוררו בכמה מקומות לזה על צד הדרש המעולה: "ויתד תהיה לך על אזנך" (דברים כג, יד), אל תיקרי "אזנך" אלא "אזנך", מלמד שכשישמע אדם דבר מגונה יתן אצבעו בתוך אזנו (בבלי, כתובות ה, א). ובמקום הזה העירו אותנו על סוד טעם היות הספר תורה בלתי נקוד, ונתנו לפתאים במדרש פסוק זה לחם סובין ולחכמים נתנו בזה [המדרש ממש] לחם אבירים, והכל מתוך פשטיה דקרא, וכל התורה נוהגת על דרך זה. ולפיכך אמרו חז"ל: שבעים פנים לתורה, והבן. עכ"ל.

129. בעלי ברית אברם, הקדמה

והנה נתבאר לך, שהחכמים הראשונים עם גודל מעלתם וקורבתם אל הנבואה, כמו שאמרו רז"ל בפרק כצד מערבין (עירובין נג, א): לבם של ראשונים כפתחו של אולם ושל אחרונים כנקב של מחט, וגם כן אמרו בפרק אלו קשרים (שבת קיב, ב) ובירושלמי דדמאי (פ"א ה"ג ושקלים פ"ה ה"א ובבראשית רבה, ס): אם הראשונים בני אדם אנו בני חמורים. ופרק קמא דיומא (ט, ב): טובה צפרן של ראשונים מכרסן של אחרונים. ואם הראשונים עם גודל חכמתם היו נשמרים מלומר דבר שלא שמעו, כנזכר למעלה, דאמר ליה: "לא שמענא ולא אימא" (זהר, שמות פו ע"ב), קל וחומר לאחרונים. ואם כן ראוי לחקור ולדעת מי התיר לאחרונים לחדש משכלם ולפרש פשטי הכתובים כל אחד ואחד כפי השערת שכלו בלי שיקבלנו מרבו ורבו מרבו, כי הנה זה יראה כמגלה פנים בתורה שלא כהלכה, כדמשמע ממאמרי הזוהר שהקדמנו, וראוי לעונש עצום.

והנה המשל בזה אצלי הוא: למלך שיצא דבר מלכות מלפניו, ויעבירו קול בעיר מטעם המלך וגדוליו לאמר להקהל כל יוצא צבא ולעמוד על נפשם כל איש בכלי מלחמתו בידו, ולעמוד על מעמדם לבלתי יבא האויב על העיר בטח להשמיד להרוג ולאבד, וכל העובר את מצות המלך אחת דתו להמית, ויכתב בשם המלך ונחתם בטבעת המלך. ויהי כאשר חדל הקול, ויבוא זקן אחד מזקני העיר ונכבדיה וידבר באזני אנשי העיר בסתר לאמר: לא הבנתם דברי הכרוז ואת מצות המלך לא ידעתם, כי באו דבריו באין מבין וכי דבריו הם סוד כמוס וחתום עמדי. ויפצרו האנשים בהזקן מאד להודיע להם כוונת המלך, ויאמר להם הזקן: ידוע תדעו כי האויב היושב במארב הוא יצר לב

האדם רע מנעוריו, כי אויב איש אנשי ביתו זה זה גופו, ומצות המלך הוא לאמר לו תענהו בסגופים ותעניות, כי הם כלי מלחמה כנגדו לשמור הנשמה מן האויב היושב במארב הנשמה, ואל תתנו שנת העצלה לעיניכם, ומה מאד מתוקה מדבש מליצת הכרוז ומשלו אשר דבר. וייטב דברי הזקן בעיני כל העדה, וישיאו קולם יחד ויאמרו לו: החייתנו, נמצא חן בעיני אדוני. וישמעו האנשים את דברי הזקן ויאמינו לדברו. ויתנצלו העם איש עדיו מעליו ויקראו צום ועצרה וילבשו שקים וישובו אל ה' בכל לבבם ובכל מאודם ויכניעו יצרם הזונה, כדבר הזקן. ויהי בלילה ויבא האויב על העיר בטח ואין איש עומד בפניו, וישלול שלל ויבז בז וילך לו לדרכו. ויהי ממחרת ויאמר המלך אל עבדיו: למה לא תקנתם למצותי ואותי השלכתם אחרי גוכם? וישאו כל העדה את קולם ויבכו ויתחננו למלך ויפלו לפני רגליו ויאמרו לו: ירא ה' על איש הזקן וישפוט, כי הוא אשר היה בעוכרינו. ויספרו לו את כל הקורות אותם עם האיש הזקן, ויקצוף עליהם המלך וגם על האיש הזקן היה הקצף.

והנה המשל בעיני דומה לנמשל, כי כאשר תהיה הכוונה האלהית בפסוק כוונה אחת, ויפרוש הפסוק בכוונה מתהפכת מכנגד כוונתו יתברך, בבלתי השמר פן ואל מלשנות את תפקידו, מה מאד גודל ענשו, כי הפשיט התורה מבגדי מלכות והלבישה שק. ואם כן מי יתן ידעתי אבוא עד תכונתו, איך מצאו חכמי ישראל הראשונים, וכל שכן האחרונים, לפרש התורה כל אחד כפי שכלו יהולל, ואיש אל עבר פניו ילכו, לא ראי זה כראי זה.

אמנם התשובה בזה אומר. הנה כאשר הסתכל קצת בדברי רז״ל נמצא כי זה דרכם במדרש ובאגדה, ושמא הוא יותר רחוק, כי לא כל דברי רז״ל הם מקובלים, אמנם יש בהם מה שחדשו הם ז״ל מצד עיונם הזך, לא על דרך אמונה ועיקר. אמנם כוונתם היתה להרבות טעמי המקרא לדורשו בכל פנים שאפשר, והנה רוב דבריהם על הכתובים לא נאמרו על צד הפירוש ככל דרכי הפשטנים אשר יכוונו להבנת עצם הענין כפי הוראת מצות הספור ההוא, אמנם כוונתם לעניינים ולימודים מן החוץ, אם להורות על דרכי טובו וגבורתו של אלהינו או לשבח איזו מעלה או לגנות איזה פחיתות או ללמד איזה מושכל להרחיק האדם מאיזה סכלות, אשר עם כל זה סמכו אותם העניינים על הפסוק ההוא לציון ולזכר. הלא תראה מה שכתב הרב המורה צדק הרמב״ם זללה״ה (מורה נבוכים ג, לד), וז״ל: ״נחלקו בני אדם בדרשות לשני חלקים, האחד ידמה שהם באור ענין הפסוק ונלחם ומתגבר לאמת הדרשות ולשמרם ושמשפטם כמשפט הדינים המקובלים, והשני מבזה אותם ויחשבם לשחוק אחר שהוא מבואר נגלה שאין זה ענין הכתוב. ולא

הבינה אחת משתי הכתות שהם על צד מליצת השיר אשר התפרסם דרכה בזמן ההוא, וכדרשה (כתובות ה, א): תני בר קפרא: 'ויתד תהיה לך על אזנך' (דברים כג, יד), אל תקרי אזנך אלא אוזנך, מלמד שאם ישמע אדם דבר מגונה יתן אצבעו בתוך אזנו. ואני תמיה אם זה התנא אצל אלו הסכלים כן יחשוב בפירוש זה הפסוק, וזאת הוא כוונת המצוה ושהיתד הוא האצבע ואזניך הם האזנים. איני חושב שאחד ממי ששכלו שלם יחשוב זה. אבל מליצת השיר טוב מאוד, הזהיר בה על מדה טובה, והוא כי כמו שאין לומר דבר מגונה כן אסור לשמוע. וסמכו זה לפסוק על צד המשל והשיר, וכל מה שיאמר במדרשות אל תקרי כך אלא כך זהו עניינו". עכ"ל... ולזה אין משיבין מן הדרוש ולא על הדרוש, כי אין הכוונה באותו הדרש לפרש לנו הכתוב, כי אם אסמכתא כמו שאמרנו.

אמנם דבריהם בהלכות, הנה אין לנטות ימין ושמאל ולא יחלוק עליהם, רחמנא ליצלן, היפך פירושם כי אם סכל ומתעקש, כי בזה יצדק המשל שהמשלנו לעובר על מצות המלך שחייב את ראשו למלך בלי ספק, כי הפירוש המקובל להם ז"ל בפירוש ההלכה אי אפשר שנפרש סותרו כנזכר. והנה הרמב"ן ז"ל נתן כלל זה ואמר, אם יש בהם נפקותא של דינים לא נסור מהגמרא. ומהמין האחד, רוצה לומר מין הדרשות, הוא ענין האחרונים שהורשו לפרש הכתובים כפי מה שיראה לכל אחד, ואם היות שאינם דרך אסמכתא הם כפי הכוונה השנית, כמו שראיתי כתוב בשם הרמב"ן ז"ל, כמו שימצא ממנה במקרא, ועל צד הכוונה השנית, דברים נחמדים מסתרי המציאה ממה שאפשר לעמוד עליהם, כן אפשר שיאמר שלא מהתועלת שמו קצת ממשכילי עמינו הספורים הם רמוזים בם אצל הכוונה השנית.

והנה זה הדרך הני"ל יחייביהו השכל גם כן, והענין: כמו שהתוכנים בחכמתם שיערו באומד שכלם שיש בשמים גלגלים יוצאי מרכז וגם כן גלגלי ההקפה וגם כן גלגלים נוטים מהמשוה, עם היות שהניחו יסודם על הקדמות יכחישם הטבע, על כל זה סמכנו על דבריהם אחר שהחוש והשכל יעידו עליהם. ולזה, כאשר הניח בטלמיוס גלגלי ההקפה ויוצאי מרכז, כתב בספר השלישי מהמגסטי, וז"ל: "הדבר הזה אם הוא אמת אם לא האלהים ידעו, אבל דיינו שמצאנו דרך אשר הנה אפשר לקיים כל המתראה לנו מצד תנועות המאורות והכוכבים בשמים", עכ"ל. וכן נאמר אנחנו: הפשט הזה, אם הוא אמת ואם לא האלהים ידעו, אבל דיינו שמצאנו דרך לדרוש ולתור איזה קוטב אשר עליו יסוב היתר ספיקות הנראים בכתובים או במאמרים, אם כולם בסגנון אחד או מחולפים כפי מה שיקבליהו השכל. וכל שכן שרז"ל פתחו לנו פתח השער באמרם (שבת פח, ב): " 'וכפטיש יפוצץ סלע', מה

הפטיש הזה נחלק לכמה נצוצות, כן דברי תורה יחלקו לכמה טעמים". הורו
לנו ז"ל, כי המוציא (רוצה לומר בדברים הנאמרים בנבואה וברוח הקודש)
כוונות מתחלפות, מה שלא ימצא זה הענין בדיבור אנושי, לא ירחיקהו
השכל. והענין, כמו שעשב אחד בראו האל יתברך ותעלותיו מתחלפות, על
דרך משל היין שביארו בו הרופאים שיש בו קרוב משישים תועלות ורפואות,
הנה אין לומר לאיזה תועלת מהם נברא, כל שכן הדבור האלוהי יסבול
הרבה פרושים ולא נאמר לאיזה מהם כוונה נאמר, וזה שאמרו רז"ל (מגילה
טו, ב) : "אשכחיה רבה בר אבוה לאליהו, אמר ליה : כמאן חזיא אסתר ועבדה
הכי? אמר ליה : ככולהו תנאי וככולהו אמוראיי". והכוונה כנזכר שרוצה
לומר כי גם בדבור האנושי יתכן שישפוט ויכוון אל כל חלקי הסותר שאפשר
לשערם השכל, וכל שכן וכל שכן בדבור האלהי כנ"ל.

ולזה אמרו רז"ל (ירושלמי פאה פ"ב ה"ד ; יג, 1) : כל מה שעתיד תלמיד ותיק
לחדש הכל נאמר למשה בסיני, וגם כן אמרו : שבעים פנים לתורה (במדבר רבה
יג, טו), וגם כן אמרו (סנהדרין נא, ב) : דרוש וקבל שכר. והכוונה לדעתי, כי איש
כזה הוא מוסיף כח בפמליא של מעלה ומראה שכל השלימות נרמזים
בתורה. ולזה לא ניתנה תורה שבעל פה עם תורה שבכתב, להודיע כי תורה
שבכתב הונחה מוכנת לקבל כל המושכלות והרשמים שיונחו כנגדה, כמו
המראה הספיריית, כל הצורות הנרשמים כנגדה תקבלם בלי שום שינוי, כן
התורה. וזהו שאמר בן בג בג (אבות ה, כב) : "הפך בה והפך בה דכולא בה",
רצונו לומר המושכלות ושלמויות הם רמוזים בתורה בלי ספק, וזאת
"דכולא בה". אמנם מה שאינם נראים הוא לחסרון השקידה וההפוך בה,
ולזאת "הפוך בה והפוך בה". ומה נחמד אומרים : "ובה תחזה", כפי המשל
שהנחנו, רוצה לומר שהתורה כמו המראה המזוככת שתראה בה פניך וכל
הפנים המתראים כנגדה כן התורה. ולזה חתם דבריו ואמר : "שאין לך מדה
טובה הימנה", רצונו לומר כי לא תמצא זאת הסגולה בזולתה מהתורות
הנמוסיות, כנ"ל.

130. דרך עץ חיים, פסקה ראשונה

ועל זה אמר התנא (אבות ה, כב) : "הפוך בה והפוך בה דכולה בה", כי צריכים
העוסקים להיות הופכים והופכים עד שתתלהב כמעשה האש ממש. והנה
בהיות השלהבת מתלהטת, כבר אמרתי שיש בה כמה גוונים מרוקמים, וכן
נמצאים כמה ענינים גדולים נכללים בשלהבת של האור הזה. אמנם עוד ענין
אחר נמצא, כי יש כמה פנים לתורה, וכבר קבלו הקדמונים שלכל שורש
מנשמות ישראל יש כלום בתורה, עד שיש ששים רבוא פירושים לכל התורה

מחולקים לששים רבוא נפשות של ישראל, וזה נקרא שהתורה מתפוצצת לכמה ניצוצות, כי מתחילה מתלהטת, ואז נראים בה כל האורות הראויים לענין ההוא, ואותם האורות עצמם מאירים בששים רבוא דרכים בששים רבוא של ישראל, וזה סוד (ירמיה כג, כט) "וכפטיש יפוצץ סלע".

131. ספרי דברים, פרשת ראה, פיסקה צו

"לא תתגודדו" (דברים יד, א), לא תעשו אגודות אלא היו כולכם אגודה אחת, וכן הוא אומר: "הבונה בשמים מעלותיו ואגודתו על ארץ יסדה" (עמוס ט, ו). דבר אחר: "לא תתגודדו", לא תתגודדו כדרך שאחרים מתגודדים, שנאמר "ויתגודדו כמשפטם" (מלכים א יח, כח).

132. ספרי דברים, פרשת וזאת הברכה, פיסקה שמו

"יחד שבטי ישראל" (דברים לג, ה), כשהם עשוים אגודה אחת ולא כשהם עשוים אגודות אגודות, וכן הוא אומר: "הבונה בשמים מעלותיו ואגודתו על ארץ יסדה" (עמוס ט, ו). רבי שמעון בן יוחי אומר: משל לאחד שהביא שתי ספינות וקשרם בהוגנים ובעשתות והעמידן בלב הים ובנה עליהם פלטרין. כל זמן שהספינות קשורות זו בזו פלטרין קיימים, פרשו ספינות אין פלטרין קיימים. כך ישראל כשעושים רצונו של מקום בונה עליותיו בשמים, וכשאין עושים רצונו כביכול אגודתו על ארץ יסדה. וכן הוא אומר: "זה אלי ואנוהו" (שמות טו, ב), כשאני מודה לו הוא נאה, וכשאין אני מודה לו כביכול בשמו הוא נאה. כיוצא בו: "כי שם ה' אקרא" (דברים לב, ג), כשאני קורא בשמו הוא גדול, ואם לאו כביכול וכו'. כיוצא בו: "ואתם עדי נאם ה' ואני אל" (ישעיה מג, יב), כשאתם עדיי אני אל, וכשאין אתם עדיי כביכול איני אל. כיוצא בו: "אליך נשאתי את עיני היושבי בשמים" (תהלים קכג, א), אילמלא אני כביכול לא היית יושב בשמים. ואף כאן אתה אומר "יחד שבטי ישראל", כשהם עשוים אגודה אחת ולא כשהם עשוים אגודות אגודות.

133. ירושלמי, פסחים פרק ד, א (ל, 4)

מתניתין: מקום שנהגו לעשות מלאכה בערבי פסחים עד חצות - עושין; מקום שנהגו שלא לעשות - אין עושין. ההולך ממקום שעושין למקום שאין עושין, או ממקום שאין עושין למקום שעושין - נותנין עליו חומרי המקום שיצא משם וחומרי המקום שהלך לשם. ואל ישנה אדם מפני המחלוקת.

...רבי שמעון בן לקיש שאל לרבי יוחנן: ואינו אסור משום בל תתגודדו? אמר ליה: בשעה שאילו עושין כבית שמאי ואילו עושין כבית הלל. בית

שמאי ובית הלל אין הלכה כבית הלל? אמר ליה: בשעה שאילו עושין כרבי
מאיר ואילו עושין כרבי יוסה. רבי מאיר ורבי יוסי אין הלכה כר' יוסי? אמר
ליה: תרי תנויי אינון על דרבי מאיר ותרין תנויין אינון על דרבי יוסי. אמר
ליה: הרי ראש השנה ויום הכיפורים ביהודה נהגו כרבי עקיבא ובגליל נהגו
כרבי יוחנן בן נורי? אמר (רבי) [ליה]: שנייה הוא, שאם עבר ועשה ביהודה
כגליל ובגליל כיהודה יצא. הרי פורים הרי אילו קורין בי"ד ואילו קורין
בט"ו? אמר ליה: מי שסידר את המשנה סמכה למקרא "משפחה ומשפחה
מדינה ומדינה ועיר ועיר" (אסתר ט, כח).

134. בבלי, יבמות יג, ב – יד, א

תנן התם (משנה, מגילה א, א): מגילה נקראת באחד עשר ובשנים עשר ובשלשה
עשר ובארבעה עשר ובחמשה עשר, לא פחות ולא יותר. אמר ליה ריש לקיש
לרבי יוחנן: איקרי כאן "לא תתגודדו" (דברים יד, א), לא תעשו אגודות
אגודות! האי "לא תתגודדו" מיבעי ליה לגופיה, דאמר רחמנא לא תעשו
חבורה על מת. אם כן לימא קרא "לא תגודדו", מאי "תתגודדו"? שמע מינה
להכי הוא דאתא. ואימא כוליה להכי הוא דאתא? אם כן לימא קרא "לא
תגודו", מאי "לא תתגודדו"? שמע מינה תרתי. אמר ליה: עד כאן לא שנית:
מקום שנהגו לעשות מלאכה בערבי פסחים עד חצות עושין, מקום שנהגו
שלא לעשות אין עושין (משנה, פסחים ד, א)? אמר ליה: אמינא לך אנא
איסורא, דאמר רב שמן בר אבא אמר רבי יוחנן: "לקיים את ימי הפורים
בזמניהם" (אסתר ט, לא), זמנים הרבה תיקנו להם חכמים, ואת אמרת לי
מנהגא? והתם לאו איסורא הויא? והתנן: בלילה בית שמאי אוסרין ובית
הלל מתירין (משנה, פסחים ד, ה)? אמר ליה: התם הרואה אומר מלאכה הוא
דלית ליה.

והא בית שמאי מתירין הצרות לאחים ובית הלל אוסרים (משנה, יבמות א, א)?
מי סברת עשו בית שמאי כדבריהם, לא עשו בית שמאי כדבריהם. ורבי יוחנן
אמר: עשו ועשו.

ובפלוגתא [דרב ושמואל], דרב אומר: לא עשו בית שמאי כדבריהם, ושמואל
אמר: עשו ועשו. אימת? אילימא קודם בת קול, מאי טעמא דמאן דאמר לא
עשו? ואלא לאחר בת קול, מאי טעמא דמאן דאמר עשו? אי בעית אימא
קודם בת קול ואי בעית אימא לאחר בת קול. אי בעית אימא קודם בת קול
וכגון דבית הלל רובא, למאן דאמר לא עשו דהא בית הלל רובא, ומאן דאמר
עשו כי אזלינן בתר רובא היכא דכי הדדי נינהו הכא בית שמאי מחדדי טפי.

ואי בעית אימא לאחר בת קול, מאן דאמר לא עשו דהא נפקא בת קול, ומאן דאמר עשו רבי יהושע הוא דאמר אין משגיחין בבת קול.

ומאן דאמר עשו, קרינן כאן "לא תתגודדו" לא תעשו אגודות אגודות! אמר אביי: כי אמרינן "לא תתגודדו" כגון שתי בתי דינים בעיר אחת הללו מורים כדברי בית שמאי והללו מורים כדברי בית הלל, אבל שתי בתי דינים בשתי עיירות לית לן בה. אמר ליה רבא: והא בית שמאי ובית הלל כשתי בתי דינים בעיר אחת דמי? אלא אמר רבא: כי אמרינן "לא תתגודדו" כגון בית דין אחת בעיר אחת פלג מורין כדברי בית שמאי ופלג מורין כדברי בית הלל, אבל שתי בתי דינין בעיר אחת לית לן בה.

תא שמע: במקומו של רבי אליעזר היו כורתים עצים לעשות פחמים בשבת לעשות ברזל, במקומו של רבי יוסי הגלילי היו אוכלים בשר עוף בחלב. במקומו של רבי אליעזר אין במקומו של רבי עקיבא לא, דתניא: כל אמר רבי עקיבא: כל מלאכה שאפשר לעשותה מערב שבת אין דוחה את השבת. והאי מאי תיובתא? מקומות מקומות שאני. ודקארי לה מאי קארי לה? סלקא דעתך אמינא משום חומרא דשבת כמקום אחד דמי, קמ״ל.

תא שמע: דרבי אבהו כי איקלע לאתריה דרבי יהושע בן לוי הוה מטלטל שרגא, וכי איקלע לאתריה דרבי יוחנן לא הוה מטלטל שרגא. והאי מאי קושיא, ולא אמרינן מקומות שאני? אנן הכי קאמרינן: רבי אבהו היכי עביד הכא הכי והיכי עביד הכא הכי? רבי אבהו כרבי יהושע בן לוי סבירא ליה, וכי מקלע לאתריה דרבי יוחנן לא הוה מטלטל משום כבודו דרבי יוחנן. והאיכא שמעא? דמודע ליה לשמעא.

135. חידושי הריטב״א, ראש השנה לד, א (תשובת רב האי גאון)

ונשאל רבינו ז״ל: וכי קודם שבא רבי אבהו לא יצאו ישראל ידי תקיעת שופר, שהרי נראה שהיה הדבר ספק ביניהם ענין התרועה, כדאמרן "בהא ודאי פליגי" (ראש השנה לג, ב), ואין ספק שהכרעה היתה להם בדבר, כי האיך אפשר שבמצוה כזו שהיתה בכל שנה לא ידעו אמתתה ולא ראו אלו לאלו איש מפי איש עד משה רבינו עליו השלום איך היה נוהג?

והשיב הוא ז״ל, כי בודאי תרועת תורה בכל אחת מאלו בין בגנוחי בין בילולי, שכוונת התורה בתרועה לעשותה מקולות ושברים. ובתחלה היה עושה זה שברים וזה יבבות כפי מה שנראה לו שהוא יותר יפה, והיו כולן יוצאין ידי חובה, והחכמים היו יודעין כן, אבל המון העם היו טועין שהיו סבורין שיש חילוק ביניהן ושלא יצאו אלו או אלו. וכדי להוציא מלבן של

הדיוטות וגם שלא תהא תורה כשתי תורות, בא רבי אבהו ותקן לעשות כל
אחד כדברי אלו ואלו. וגם הוסיף תרועה אחת משלו, כי נתן דעתו לתקן
התרועה בכל מיני קול נשבר שאפשר הנוהגין, ומפני שהיה הדבר נראה
להדיוטות שיש מחלוקת ביניהן נקיט ליה תלמודא על דרך מחלוקת ובדרך
קושיא ותירוץ.

136. רש"י, יבמות יג, ב, ד"ה לא תעשו

לא תעשו אגודות אגודות, דנראה כנוהגין שתי תורות, כשקורין כפרים את
המגילה ביום כניסה, ועיירות גדולות בי"ד, ומוקפין חומה בט"ו.

137. שו"ת רש"י, קכח

מעשה שהיה ואירע פורים באחד בשבת וקדמו להתענות בחמישי בשבת, וכן
עמא דבר. ובאתה אשה אחת לפני רבינו, שהיה לה לרכוב אחר השלטון.
ושאלה [אם] איפשר שתתענה למחר ותאכל היום מפני טורח הדרך. ואמר
רבינו: אעפ"י שאין [זה] תענית ציבור קבוע, לא מדברי תורה ולא מדברי
סופרים, אלא שנהגו העם כן... מכל מקום אסור לו לאדם להיות פורש מן
הציבור, כדאמרינן בפרק קמא דיבמות (יג, ב): "לא תתגודדו, לא תעשו מצות
אגודות אגודות". ויש פרושים שאע"פ שמתענין בחמישי עם הציבור חוזרין
ומתענין למחר, כדי לסמוך התענית לפורים, שכן הוא דינו, הואיל ואי
איפשר לו בשבת יעשה בערב שבת. ורבי קורא עליהם ["והכסיל] בחשך
הולך" (קהלת ב, יד). מפני שהוא עצמו אינו אלא מנהג [שעושין] זכר לדבר, והן
מחמירין לעשותו במקומו כאילו הוא קבוע מן התורה. וכיון שהורגלו רבים
בחמישי [דיו] בכך. ולכך נהגו בחמישי לפי שאין מתענין ערב שבת.

138. כוזרי, מאמר ג, מט

והנה אילו קיבלו הקראים עליהם את הזהירות מן הטומאות מצד הנקיות
ולא חשבוה למצוה - לא היה רע בדבר, אך הואיל ואין הדבר כך, יתפסו
להתחכמות מתוך בערותם וישנו את התורה, ובאים לידי מינות, זאת
אומרת, יתפלגו לכתות שונות אשר לכל אחת מהן שיטה משלה, והתפלגות
כזאת היא מקור לבטול אחדות האומה ויסוד ליציאה מכלל "תורה אחת
ומשפט אחד" (במדבר טו, טז).

139. ספר המצוות לרמב״ם, לאווין, מה (תרגום אבן תיבון)

שהזהירנו מעשות שרט לנפש בבשרינו כאשר יעשו עובדי עבודה זרה, והוא אמרו יתעלה ״לא תתגודדו״ (דברים יד, א)... והנה אמרו שבכלל זה האזהרה מחלוק דתי העיר במנהגם וחלוק הקיבוצים, ואמרו (ספרי ראה, פיסקה צו): ״׳לא תתגודדו׳ - לא תעשו אגודות אגודות״. אבל גופיה דקרא הנה הוא כמו שביארנו לא תעשו חבורה על מת, וזהו כמו דרש.

וכן אמרו (סנהדרין קי, א): ״המחזיק במחלוקת עובר בלאו שנאמר: ׳ולא יהיה כקרח וכעדתו׳ (במדבר יז, ה)״, הוא גם כן על צד הדרש, אמנם גופיה דקרא הוא להפחיד, ולפי מה שבארו החכמים הנה הוא שלילה, לא אזהרה, כי הם ביארו שעניין זה המאמר הוא שהאל יתעלה מגיד כי מי שיחלוק ויעורר על הכהונה במה שיבוא מן הזמן, לא יענש במה שנענש קרח, ואמנם יהיה ״כאשר דיבר ה׳ ביד משה לו״ (שם), רוצה לומר הצרעת, כאמרו למשה ״הבא נא ידך בחיקך״ (שמות ד, ו), וכמו שהתבאר בעזיהו המלך (דברי הימים ב כו, יט).

140. משנה תורה, הלכות עבודה זרה יב, יד

ובכלל אזהרה זו שלא יהיו שני בתי דינין בעיר אחת, זה נוהג כמנהג זה וזה נוהג כמנהג אחר, שדבר זה גורם למחלוקות גדולות, שנאמר: ״לא תתגודדו״ (דברים יד, א), לא תעשו אגודות אגודות.

141. שו״ת הרמב״ם, שכט (פריימן, קיא)

אבל אסור להם מענין אחר, משום ״לא תתגודדו״ משום לא תעשו אגודות אגודות, אלא כך חייבים כל ישראל הנקראין בשם יעקב, המחזיקים בדת משה רבינו עליו השלום, להיות כל עדה וקהל מישראל אגודה אחת, ולא תהיה ביניהם מחלוקת בשום דבר בעולם. ואתם חכמים ונבונים, ויודעים מהו עונש המחלוקת וכמה רעות גורמת.

142. שו״ת הרמב״ם, רסב (פריימן, לג)

מה יאמר אדונינו ירום הודו אור העולם יהי שמו לעולם, בדבר עיר שהנהיגו בה חכמיה לישב בקדושת היוצר, אחר כך בא לאותה העיר אחרי זמן ממונה כראש עליה, ונהג לעמוד בקדושת היוצר, ונמשכו אחריו מעט אנשים והתחילו עומדים...

תשובה: ...וזאת העמידה בקדושת היוצר הוא מנהג בורים בלא ספק, וזאת הישיבה שהנהיג בה זה החכם, הוא הראוי. אבל עמידת זה החכם הסומך על מנהג ארצו, היא טעות גמורה, לפי שאפילו בדברים אשר תלוי בהם דבר

איסור אמרו "אל ישנה מפני המחלוקת" (פסחים נ, ב), כל שכן במה שאין תלוי בו איסור בשום פנים. ועבר בזה משום "לא תתגודדו" - לא תעשו אגודות אגודות.

143. חידושי הרמב"ן, מגילה ב, א

מה ששנינו "כרכין המוקפין חומה מימות יהושע בן נון קורין בחמישה עשר, כפרים ועיירות גודלות בארבעה עשר" (משנה, מגילה א, א), אני תמה מאוד מה ראו על ככה ומה הגיע אליהם לעשות ישראל אגודות במצוה הזו, אע"פ דליכא הכא משום "לא תתגודדו" דהוו להו שני בתי דינים בשתי עיירות כדאיתא בפרק קמא (דיומא (דיומא [ד, א)] [דיבמות (יד, א)], מכל מקום לכתחילה למה חלקום לשתי כתות? ועוד היכן מצינו בתורה מצות חלוקה בכך? והתורה אמרה "תורה אחת ומשפט אחד יהיה לכם" (במדבר טו, טז), וכל דתקון רבנן כעין דאורייתא תקון?

144. חידושי הריטב"א, יבמות יג, ב

"מאי לא תתגודדו? שמע מינא להכי נמי הוא דאתא... ודילמא כולה להכי הוא דאתא"... ויש מרבותינו מקשים על זה, היכי מצי למימר דכולהו לאגודות בלחוד אתא, דהא גבי מת כתיב, והיכי עקרינן ליה מיניה?... והנכון בעיני כפירוש רש"י ז"ל, ודקשיא להו היכי עקרי ליה ממת דכתיב גביה, לא קשיא, דהא שקלא וטריא דתלמודא הוא לברורי מילתא כל היכא דאפשר טפי. ועוד דדלמא הכי קאמר קרא: "בנים אתם לה' אלהיכם" (דברים יד, א), וכיון שאתם בני אב אחד ואל אחד, ראוי הוא לכם שלא תעשה אגודות אגודות, וכאלו יש כאן שתי תורות ושני אלהות. וראוי הוא גם כן שלא תשימו קרחה בין עיניכם למת כיוון שאתם קדוש לה' אלהיכם.

145. הגהות הרמ"א, אורח חיים תצג, ג

מיהו בהרבה מקומות נוהגים להסתפר עד ראש חודש אייר, ואותן לא יספרו מל"ג בעומר ואילך, אף על פי שמותר להסתפר בל"ג בעומר בעצמו. ואותן מקומות שנוהגין להסתפר מל"ג בעומר ואילך לא יסתפרו כלל אחר פסח עד ל"ג בעומר. ולא ינהגו בעיר אחת מקצת מנהג זה ומקצת מנהג זה משום "לא תתגודדו". וכל שכן שאין לנהוג היתר בשתיהן.

146. שו״ת מהרשד״ם, יורה דעה, קנג (דף טו טור ד)

והואיל ואתא לידן, ראיתי לכתוב כאן מה שהקשה אחד מחשובי חברנו
בישיבה. דאמרינן בסוכה פרק לולב וערבה (מד, א), על ענין נטילה: "והא יום
טוב ראשון דלדידן לא דחי ולדידהו דחי"? ומשני: "אמרי: לדידהו נמי לא
דחי". ופירש רש״י: "שלא לעשות ישראל אגודות ונראה כשתי תורות,
דלדידן לא דחי לולב שבת". ע״כ. ותימה, שהרי אפילו לאביי (יבמות יד, א)
שתי בתי דינים בשתי עיירות לית ביה משום "לא תתגודדו", וכל שכן לרבא?
ונראה לי גם כן קושיה זו גם בתקיעת שופר שהתקין רבי אבהו (ראש השנה לד,
א), ולמה הוצרך, שאף על פי שעשו אלו כך ואלו כך כיון שהיו במקומות
מחולקים לית לן בה?!

ואני תירצתי פתאום, שענין לאו מ״לא תתגודדו" יש בו שתי בחינות: אחת
לעבור עליו מן התורה, וב׳ שאע״פ שאין איסור צריך לעשות מצוה מן
המובחר. ואם כן לענין איסורא פשיטא לכולי עלמא ליכא איסורא בשני
מקומות אפילו לאביי, מכל מקום להיות הדברים בלתי נאות, שנראה
כמצוה כוללת לכל ישראל יהיה חלוק ביניהם, בשב ואל תעשה אמרו שלא
ליטול לולב אפילו לדידהו דהוו ידעי בקבועה דירחא. וכן אמרתי שזה נראה
טעמא דרבי אבהו בתקיעת שופר.

147. שו״ת פסקי עזיאל בשאלות הזמן, ב

ונראה לי שדין זה תלוי במחלוקת עיקר הטעם של "לא תתגודדו — לא תעשו
אגודות אגודות". דרש״י מנמק משום שלא תהיה תורה כשתי תורות,
ולדידיה במנהגי מקומות לא נראה הדבר כשתי תורות, ולהרמב״ם טעם
האסור הוא משום שדבר זה גורם למחלוקות גדולות (הלכות עכו״ם פרק יב
הלכה יד). ולפי זה בכל אופן וענין צריך שכל בני העיר, וגם הקבוצים
שנמצאים בה מעיירות אחרות, חייבים לנהוג בכל עניני תורה ומצות מנהג
אחד, ולא תהיה מחלוקת בינם בשום דבר שבעולם, וכמו שכתב (הרמב״ם)
בתשובתו. ולדעתו צריכים אנו לומר, דמה שאמרו בתלמודין דבדבר
שבמנהג אין בו משום "לא תתגודדו", אינו אלא לענין זה שמותר לנהוג בכל
מקום כמנהגם, כגון מחלוקת רבי עקיבא ורבי יוחנן בן נורי דבגליל נהגו
כרבי יוחנן בן נורי וביהודה נהגו כרבי עקיבא. אבל לנהוג שני מנהגים שונים
זה מזה במקום אחד אסור משום "לא תתגודדו", אפילו בדבר שהוא מנהג,
דכיון דטעם אסור זה הוא משום מחלוקת אין לחלק בין איסורא למנהגא.
וכמו שכן כתבו התוספות בשם הירושלמי דבני הכפרים היו קורין המגילה
בי״א ובי״ב וכו׳ בעירם (יבמות יד, א תוספות ד״ה כי אמרינן).

148. רבינו ירוחם, ספר אדם וחוה, נתיב ב (דף כג ע"א)

וכתב רמ"ה: ואפילו בית דין אחד בעיר אחת דוקא כשמורין מקצתן להתר ומקצתן לאיסור, אבל אם אינם מורין - מותר, מאחר שאינם מורין הוראה להדיא. וכמו כן אותם המתירין יכולין לנהוג איסור בפני האוסרים ואין זה אגודות אגודות, וכן מוכח בכמה דוכתי.

149. חידושי הריטב"א, יבמות יד, א, ד"ה אמר ליה

אמר ליה רבא: והא בית שמאי ובית הלל כשתי בתי דינים בעיר אחת הם? כך הגרסא בכל הספרים. ותמיה לי מילתא: מאי "כשתי בתי דינים"?! הוה ליה למימר "שתי בתי דינים הם". ואביי נמי היכי טעי בהאי?

ויש לומר, דאביי סבר שאין אגודות אגודות בבעלי מחלוקת עצמן לעשות כפי מה שנראה שהוא אמת, שכן התירה לו התורה, וליכא למימר אגודות אלא באחרים הבאים לעשות כדבריהם, כי אע"פ שיכולים אלו לעשות כאלו ואלו כאלו, כיון שהן שקולים, מכל מקום משום אגודות אגודות יש לכולן לתפוס שיטה אחת לחומרא כשהן בעיר אחת, והאי לישנא דקאמר "שתי בתי דינים חד מורו כבית שמאי וחד מורו כבית הלל". ורבא אהדר ליה שאם יש לשני בתי דינים אלו שאתה אומר משום אגודות אגודות, אף לבית שמאי ובית הלל עצמה יש אגודות אגודות בשני בתי דינים, אלא דלא שאני לן בין הא להא.

150. פסקי ריא"ז, יבמות, פרק א, הלכה א, אותיות טז-יז

ובכל מקום שהיתה מחלוקת בין החכמים נקבעה הלכה כאחד מהן, שלא תיעשה [תורה] כשתי תורות. ועל דבר זה רמז הכתוב "לא תתגודדו" (דברים יד, א), לא תיעשו אגודות אגודות. גם בזמן הזה שיש ברוב מקומות מחלוקת בין החכמים ובין הגאונים, אסור להם לבני העיר ליחלק ולנהוג במנהג פשוט, קצתן כאחד וקצתן כאחד, אלא יעמדו על המנין ויעשו כולן על פי הרוב.

151. שו"ת המבי"ט א, כא

ולכן היה מן הדין שיתקבצו חכמי העיר ויעמדו למנין אחר העיון ומשא ומתן, וינהיגו את בני העיר על פי רובם בין להקל בין להחמיר, וכל עוד שאין עושים כך נראה אגודות אם מקצתן ינהיגו איסור וקצתם היתר.

אלא שמצאתי בספר אדם וחוה (נתיב ב) שכתב משם הרמ"ה ז"ל, שאפילו בית דין אחד בעיר אחת דוקא כשמורים מקצתם להיתר ומקצתן לאיסור,

אבל אם אינם מורים מותר, מאחר שאינם מורים הוראה להדיא, כמו כן אותם המתירים יכולים לנהוג היתר בפני האוסרים ואין זה אגודות אגודות, וכן מוכח בכמה דוכתיי. עכ"ל. ואם כן משמע דכל היכא דלא עמדו למנין ואין מורים קצתם להיתר וקצתם לאיסור, דיכול כל אחד לנהוג כפי סברתו בין לקולא בין לחומרא, אבל אם מורים לאחרים אלו להיתר ואלו לאיסור איכא משום אגודות לכולי עלמא.

וכתב רבנו ישעיה מטראני ז"ל בפירושו ליבמות (תוספות רי"ד, יבמות יג, ב), דכל היכא דאיכא משום "לא תתגודדו", לא יעשו אלו כדבריהם ואלו כדבריהם, אלא ישאו ויתנו אלו עם אלו עד שיושוו לדעת אחת או שיעמדו למנין ויגמרו הלכה להקל או להחמיר ולא יהו אלו מקילים ואלו מחמירים, ואם לא יוכלו לגמור הלכה, לא יוכלו לסמוך על דבריהם אלא יחמירו בדבר עד שיגמרו הלכה. ע"כ.

ואפילו הכי נראה דכל שלא הורו אלו להיתר ואלו לאיסור, אלא שהיה נוהג כל אחד כסברתו - ליכא אגודות. ואפשר נמי דאפילו רואים אחרים חכם אחד מחמיר או מקל ומחמירים או מקילים כמוהו - ליכא אגודות, כיון דליכא הוראה לרבים בפרהסיא, כל שכן אי לא הוו רבים הנמשכים אחר סברת חכם אחד, דכל שהיו רבים ורבים הוא דנראין כאגודות, כמו שכתב רבינו ישעיה ז"ל שם.

ועם כל זה, אינו עולה בדעתי עדיין שאהיה רשאי לסמוך על עצמי בסברא זו אפילו להחמיר, עד שיסכימו רוב חכמי העיר ואחריהם אלך אחר שיעמדו למנין בהסכמת מורינו הרב גדול בדורו כמה"ר יעקב בירב, ואני דן לפניו בקרקע ארץ ישראל להלכה אבל לא למעשה כו'.

152. שו"ת מהרשד"ם, יורה דעה, קנג

והואיל ואתא לידן, ראיתי לכתוב כאן מה שהקשה אחד מחשובי חברנו בישיבה. דאמרינן בסוכה פרק לולב וערבה (מד, א), על ענין נטילה: "והא יום טוב ראשון דלדידן לא דחי ולדידהו דחיי"? ומשני: "אמרי: לדידהו נמי לא דחיי". ופירש רש"י: "שלא לעשות ישראל אגודות ונראה כשתי תורות, דלדידן לא דחי לולב שבתי". ע"כ. ותימה, שהרי אפילו לאביי (יבמות יד, א) שתי בתי דינים בשתי עיירות לית ביה משום "לא תתגודדו", וכל שכן לרבא? ונראה לי גם כן קושיה זו גם בתקיעת שופר שהתקין רבי אבהו (ראש השנה לד, א), ולמה הוצרך, שאף על פי שעשו אלו כך ואלו כך כיון שהיו במקומות מחולקים לית לן בה?...

חזר והקשה משני ימים טובים שאנו עושים שני ימים ובני ארץ ישראל אינם עושים אלא אחד. גם מזה אינו תמיה, שהם בני ארץ ישראל מעולם לא עשו אלא יום אחד, ואלו בני חוץ לארץ היינו עושים שנים מן הדין הגמור, משום ספק, והיה טעם הדבר ידוע לכל. ונשאר הדבר כמו שהיה, אף על פי שעתה גם אנחנו יודעים כמו הם.

עוד אמרתי, שמה שאמר רש״י ז״ל (סוכה מד, א ד״ה לדידהו) משום ״לא תתגודדו״ היינו לחכמים שעמדו לתקן שלא ליטול לולב, לא היה איפשר להם לומר אלו יטלו ואלו לא יטלו, שאז נראה בית דין אחד פלג מורין כן ופלג מורין כן, אבל יום טוב לא היו צריכים לומר, אלא הם מעצמם בני חוץ לארץ עשו מספק ואלו לא עשו.

153. שו״ת פרשת מרדכי, אורח חיים, ד

וצריך לומר דדווקא ברבים המשנים שייך לא תתגודדו, אבל ביחיד המשנה ליכא ביה לא תתגודדו, דלא מיחזי כשתי תורות, דתלינן טפי שהיחיד טועה או שוגג בדין, אעפ״י דטעמא ד״אל ישנה (וגם) [אדם] מפני המחלוקת״ שייך ביחיד טפי, אבל הך דלא תחזי תורה כשתי תורות קיל טפי ביחיד. והא דלא חיישינן במגילה הנ״ל למחלוקת כבר כתבתי למעלה. ומכל מקום זהו דוחק.

154. שו״ת מהרש״ג ב, יב

אשיבהו דנראה לי דאיסור זה של ״לא תתגודדו״ לא נאמר אלא על מי שמורה לאחרים לנהוג כן, דהיינו דאם יש בעיר בית דין אחד, ודיין אחד מאותו בית דין יורה לכל להניח תפילין בחול המועד ודיין השני מאותו בית דין יורה לכל שאין להניח תפילין בחול המועד, בכהאי גוונא איכא האיסור של ״לא תתגודדו״ הנאמר בגמרא יבמות (יג, ב). והכי משמע לישנא דהגמרא שם במסקנא, דאיתא שם בלשון זה: ״אלא אמר רבא: כי אמרינן לא תתגודדו, כגון בית דין בעיר אחת פלג מורין כדברי בית שמאי ופלג מורין כדברי בית הלל, אבל שתי בתי דין בעיר אחת לית לן בה״, עכ״יל. ולמה לא אמר: ״כגון שני אנשים בעיר אחת, זה נוהג כבית שמאי וזה נוהג כבית הלל״? אלא ודאי משמע לי מזה, דעל אנשים דעלמא שעושין רק לעצמן ואין מורין לאחרים כלל, לא נאמר איסור זה כלל, כי כל אחד יוכל לעשות כפי חוות דעתו בדרכי התורה ובדרכי עבודת השם יתברך, והרי אמרינן בש״יס מנחות בפרק הקומץ (כט, ב) דמפני מה יו״ד ראשה כפוף? מפני מעשיהם של צדיקים שאינם דומים זה לזה. ולא נאמר האיסור הנ״ל אלא באותן שמורין לאחרים, שאם בעיר אחד נבחרו מבני העיר שלשה אנשים

להיות בית דין אחד להורות לבני העיר בעניני מצוה ורשות ואיסור והיתר וטומאה וטהרה, צריכין להשוות מדותיהן, אבל אדם לעצמו אינו בכלל איסור זה.

ונראה כקצת ראיה לדבר מברייתא דמייתי הש"ס ביבמות שם ובחולין פרק אלו טרפות (מג, ב), דאיתא התם: "לעולם הלכה כדברי בית הלל, והרוצה לעשות כדברי בית שמאי עושה, כדברי בית הלל עושה" וכו'. ומתרץ בש"ס שם הברייתא הנ"ל, דכאן קודם בת קול כאן לאחר בת קול. ואם כן יוצא לנו מדברי הברייתא הנ"ל, דקודם בת קול שלא נתברר עדיין הלכה כמאן, היתה הרשות ביד כל אדם לעשות או כבית שמאי כקוליהן וכחומריהן או כבית הלל כקוליהן וכחומריהן. והנה משמע מזה, דאפילו אם היו שני אנשים דרים בעיר אחת כן כן היתה גם הברירה ביד זה לעשות כבית הלל, דאם לא כן הוה ליה למימר "מקום שרוצין לעשות כבית שמאי עושין, מקום שרוצין לעשות כבית הלל עושין", ומדנקט "הרוצה" משמע אף ליחיד. ואם כן קשה, איך ניתן ברירה לכל יחיד לעשות כמו שירצה, הא איכא משום לא תתגודדו?... אלא וודאי יש להוכיח קצת מזה, דהלאו של לא תתגודדו לא נאמר אלא במורה לאחרים, שלא יפסוק אחד לאחרים כדברי בית שמאי והשני יפסוק לאחרים כבית הלל, אבל במה שכל יחיד עושה לעצמו ואינו מורה כן לאחרים - לית לן בה.

עוד היה נראה ראיה מתפילין דרבינו תם, שמבואר בשולחן ערוך (אורח חיים לד, ב) דראוי למי שמוחזק בחסידות להניח אותם. ואמאי לא נימא דשייך גם בזה לא תתגודדו? אלא וודאי לא נאמרו הדברים אלא במורה כן לאחרים. וכן נמצאים עוד יחידים המניחים גם תפילין של שימושא רבה ולא עלה על דעתם לחוש משום לא תתגודדו.

וגם הרמב"ם שכתב (הלכות עבודה זרה יב, יד) "שלא יהיו מקצתן נוהגין כן" וכו', גם כן יש לומר דכוונתו הוא שמנהיג אחרים לעשות כן. ואף על פי שבתשובות השיב משה הנ"ל (שו"ת השיב משה, יורה דעה, לא) שמביא מעלת כבוד תורתו, לא כתב כן, וגם בתשובת תשורת שי (סימן פט) לא הבין כן, מכל מקום נראה לעניות דעתי כמו שכתבתי. וגם ראיה דפוק חזי מאי עמא דבר, שכמה דברים יש שמקצתן מדקדקין בהם ומקצתן אין מדקדקין, זה נזהר מאיסור חדש וזה אינו נזהר, וכן זה נזהר מלאכול מבהמה שהיתה בה סירכא ועברה על ידי קילוף הנהוג וזה אינו נזהר, ולא נשמע משום אדם שבעולם לפקפק על זה מכח האיסור של "לא תתגודדו", אלא וודאי כל שהוא נזהר רק לעצמו ליכא חששא של לא תתגודדו.

ומה שטען בהשיב משה הנ"ל נגד סברא כיוצא בזו, דאם כן נפל האיסור של
לא תתגודדו בבירא, אין זה קושיא, דבאמת נפל ויפול כך ראוי לנו. ומהאי
טעמא אין העולם מדקדקים בו, משום דנפל על פי הרוב בבירא. ואדרבה,
לדבריו יש להפליא על הטור ושולחן ערוך שביארו לנו כל המעשה אשר
יעשון כל הדינים הנהוגים בזמן הזה, ובאיסור זה של לא תתגודדו, המבואר
בש"ס בפרק קמא דיבמות דקאי על הבית דין שלא יעשו אגודות אגודות,
קצרו ולא ביארו לנו כלל, לא האיסור ולא אופני האיסור, ולא נמצא מזה
האיסור כלל, רק במגן אברהם (אורח חיים, תצג ס"ק ו) ביאר לנו איזה דינים
בזה, וגם הוא לא ביאר כל הצורך. מזה נראה דסבירא להו כמו שכתבתי,
דבזמן הזה כמעט אין כאן איסור "לא תתגודדו" כלל, משום דרק כל אחד
עושה לעצמו, ושהבית דין בעצמם יפלוגו לא שכיח הדבר. וגם נראה לי
דדעתם דדרשה זו של אגודות אגודות אינה דרשה גמורה ואינה אלא
אסמכתא, ודלא כמו שכתב מעלת כבוד תורתו בשם שו"ת בית יצחק
דדרשה גמורה מדאורייתא הוא. ולכן אין מדקדקין באיסור זה כל כך.

155. שו"ת שרידי אש ב, נו (עמ' קמד)

ועל פי הנ"ל מצאנו שער בישוב דברי הרמב"ם (הלכות עבודה זרה יב, יד), שיש
כאן שני דינים: דין על אנשי העיר ודין על בית דין ומנהיגי העיר. שבודאי
מחוייבים אנשי העיר לכתחילה להושיב בית דין אחד שיורה הלכה אחת לכל
בני העיר וכן מחוייבים בית דין עצמם לשאת ולתת בידן עד שיבואו לדעה
אחת, אבל במקום שלא יכלו בית דין לבוא לדעה אחת ועל ידי זה נתהוו שני
בתי דין ואחד מורה כך והשני מורה כדעה אחרת, מחוייבים אנשי הקהילה
לעשות כדעת בית דין שלו כמו שנתבאר למעלה, וזוהי דעת רבא. אבל
הרמב"ם אינו מדבר מאנשי העיר אלא ממנהיגי העיר, שמחוייבים לכתחילה
להושיב בית דין שוה בדעות, וכן מחוייבים חברי הבית דין לטרוח ולבוא
לכלל דעה אחת. ומדוקדק לשון הרמב"ם שכתב (שם): "שלא יהיו שני בתי
דינין בעיר אחת זה נוהג כמנהג זה" וכו', שהרמב"ם מדבר ממינוי הבית דין
ע"י ראשי הקהל או מחיוב חברי הבית דין, והגמרא ביבמות (יד, א) מדברת
מחיוב אנשי העיר. ודו"ק.

156. בבלי, יבמות יד, א

ומאן דאמר עשו, קרינן כאן "לא תתגודדו" (דברים יד, א) לא תעשו אגודות
אגודות? אמר אביי: כי אמרינן "לא תתגודדו" כגון שתי בתי דינים בעיר
אחת הללו מורים כדברי בית שמאי והללו מורים כדברי בית הלל, אבל שתי

בתי דינים בשתי עיירות לית לן בה. אמר ליה רבא: והא בית שמאי ובית הלל כשתי בתי דינים בעיר אחת דמי? אלא אמר רבא: כי אמרינן "לא תתגודדו" כגון בית דין בעיר אחת פלג מורין כדברי בית שמאי ופלג מורין כדברי בית הלל, אבל שתי בתי דינין בעיר אחת לית לן בה.

תא שמע: במקומו של רבי אליעזר היו כורתים עצים לעשות פחמים בשבת לעשות ברזל, במקומו של רבי יוסי הגלילי היו אוכלים בשר עוף בחלב. במקומו של רבי אליעזר אין במקומו של רבי עקיבא לא, דתניא: כלל אמר רבי עקיבא: כל מלאכה שאפשר לעשותה מערב שבת אין דוחה את השבת. והאי מאי תיובתא! מקומות מקומות שאני. ודקארי לה מאי קארי לה? סלקא דעתך אמינא משום חומרא דשבת כמקום אחד דמי, קמ"ל.

תא שמע: דרבי אבהו כי איקלע לאתריה דרבי יהושע בן לוי הוה מטלטל שרגא, וכי איקלע לאתריה דרבי יוחנן לא הוה מטלטל שרגא. והאי מאי קושיא, ולא אמרינן מקומות שאני? אנן הכי קאמרינן: רבי אבהו היכי עביד הכא הכי והיכי עביד הכא הכי? רבי אבהו כרבי יהושע בן לוי סבירא ליה, וכי מקלע לאתריה דרבי יוחנן לא הוה מטלטל משום כבודו דרבי יוחנן. והאיכא שמעא? דמודע ליה לשמעא.

157. ראב"ן, אבן העזר, יבמות (קיח ע"א)

תנו התם (משנה מגילה א, א): מגילה נקראת באחד עשר ובשנים עשר ובשלושה עשר וכו', שבני הכפרים מקדימין לקרות ביום הכניסה כשבאין לכרך ביום הכניסה, לדין או לספר תורה, ופעמים דיום הכניסה היה בי"א באדר ופעמים בי"ב פעמים בי"ג כדמפרש התם במגילה. ואמר ליה ריש לקיש לר' יוחנן: קרי כאן לא תתגודדו לא תעשו אגודות אגודות חבורות חבורות לעשות אילו בענין אחד ואילו בענין אחר, ושקיל וטרי בה עד דאוקי רבא: כי אמרינן לא תתגודדו כגון בית דין בעיר אחת, כלומר רב אחד ותלמידיו, ונחלקו לחבורות דאילו אוסרין ואילו מתירין, דכיון דאדם אחד קבלו אין להם להתגודד, אבל אם יש שני חכמים בעיר ותלמידיו של זה אוסרים ותלמידיו של זה מתירין, אין זה אגודות, דאילו אמרי כמו שקיבלו מרבם, וכל שכן אם הם בשתי עיירות דאין כאן אגודות. אבל קריאת מגילה אין בה אגודות שאין חלוקין בדבר, אלא תקנת כל החכמים היא שהקילו על הכפרים כדי שיספקו מים ומזון ביום התענית לאחיהם שבכרכים ולא יהיו טרודין בקריאת מגילה, ואין [כאן] אגודות.

וסוגייא דשמעתין דשני חכמים הדרין בעיר אחת או בשני מקומות, ואילו אוסרין ואלו מתירין דבר אחד, שצריכין המתירין להודיע לאוסרין: "דבר

זה אתם אוסרין ולא תאכלו ממנו". הילכך בני מגנצא שנוהגין איסור בבועה בשיפולי ריאה ובמחובר לקרקע בשני ימים טובים של גלויות עד לערב של מוצאי יום טוב השני בכדי שיעשו, ואוסרין ריחא דמילתא היא וכיוצא בהן, ובוורמישא מתירין, כשבאין בני מגנצא לשם צריכין להודיעם "זה הבשר בועא היתה בשפולי ריאה, וזה הלחם נאפה עם בשר בתנור או עם הגבינה, ואילו פרות הובאו ביום טוב ראשון". ואם כשמודיעין לו היתה דעתו נוטה אחרי חכמי ווירמישא מותר הוא לנהוג עמהן אע"פ שאסור במקומו, כדאמרין (יבמות יד, א) : "ר' אבהו כי מיקלע לאתריה דר' יוחנן לא מטלטל שרגא, כי מיקלע לאתריה דר' יהושע בן לוי מטלטל שרגא". ואמרין : "ר' אבהו היכי עביד הכא הכי והכא הכי? ומשני : "ר' אבהו כדר' יהושע בן לוי סבירא ליה הילכתא, (דהוא) [ולפי שהוא] תלמידו של ר' יוחנן כי מיקלע למקומו של ר' יוחנן עביד כוותיה, ומודיע לשמעיה דסבירא ליה כר' יהושע שלא יתמה.

158.   משנה תורה, הלכות עבודה זרה יב, יד

ובכלל אזהרה זו שלא יהיו שני בתי דינין בעיר אחת, זה נוהג כמנהג זה וזה נוהג כמנהג אחר, שדבר זה גורם למחלוקות גדולות, שנאמר : "לא תתגודדו" (דברים יד, א), לא תעשו אגודות אגודות.

159.   בית הבחירה, יבמות יד, א, ד"ה זו

זו שאמרה תורה "לא תתגודדו" (דברים יד, א) גו', אע"פ שעיקרה בא שלא לעשות חבורה על המת, כמו שהתבאר במקומו, רמז יש בו שלא לעשות מצוות אגודות אגודות, רוצה לומר שיהו עושין אלו כדרך זה ואלו כדרך זה עד שיהו נראין כנוהגין שתי תורות. במה דברים אמורים? כשאין בעיר אלא בית דין אחד, ואף אותו בית דין בעצמו חלוקין לפסוק מקצתו כשיטה אחת ומקצתו כשיטה אחרת. אבל כל שהם שני בתי דינין אע"פ שהן בעיר אחת, ובית דין אחד נוהג לפסוק כשיטה זו ובית דין האחר כשיטה זו, אין כאן אגודות אגודות, שאי איפשר לעולם שיסכימו כלם על דעת אחת. וכל שכן בדברים התלויים במנהג שאין קפידא אם הללו נוהגים כך ואם הללו נוהגים כך. מעתה, מקום שנהגו לעשות מלאכה בערבי פסחים עד חצות עושים, מקום שנהגו שלא לעשות אין עושים, על הדרך שביארנו במקומו (מאירי, יבמות יד, א ד"ה מאחר שביארנו), שהרי יש כאן חלוק מקומות, ושאין בעשייתה או במניעתה אלא מנהג.

160. סמ"ג, לאוין, סב

ובכלל "לא תתגודדו" דרשינן בפרק קמא דיבמות (יג, ב - יד, א) אל תעשו
אגודות אגודות, שלא יהו שני בתי דינין בעיר אחת, זה נוהג מנהג אחד וזה
נוהג מנהג אחר.

161. ספר החינוך, מצוה תסז

וכתב הרמב"ם זכרונו לברכה (הלכות עבודה זרה יב, יד) כי עוד דרשו זכרונם
לברכה בכלל אזהרה זו שלא יהו שני בתי דינין בעיר אחת, זה נוהג במנהג
אחד וזה נוהג במנהג אחר, שדבר זה גורם למחלוקת; ולשון "לא תתגודדו",
כלומר לא תעשו אגודות אגודות, כלומר שתהיו חלוקין אלו על אלו.

וממורי, ישמרו אל, למדתי שאין זה אסור אלא בחבורה אחת שחולקין
קצתן על קצתן והן שוין בחכמה, שאסור לעשות כל כת מהן כדבריו שזה
גורם מחלוקת ביניהן, אלא ישאו ויתנו בדבר הרבה עד שיסכימו כלם לדעה
אחת. ואם אי אפשר בכך, יעשו הכל כדברי המחמירין אם המחלוקת הוא
על דבר שהוא מן התורה. אבל בשני בתי דינין חלוקין והן שוין בחכמה, לא
נאמר על זה "לא תתגודדו". והביאו ראיה ממעשה דמסכת עבודה זרה
שאמרו שם (מ, א) : נפקי שפורי דרב ואסרי ונפקי שפורי דשמואל ושרו.

162. פסקי ריא"ז, יבמות, פרק א, הלכה א, אותיות טז-יז

בימי החכמים הקדמונים היתה מחלוקת גדולה בצרות העריות בין חכמי
בית שמאי וחכמי בית הלל, והיו בית שמאי מתירין את הצרות לאחין,
ומרוב חכמתם היו מביאין ראיות גדולות לדבריהם, ולא היה כח בחכמי בית
הלל להשיב לרוב ראיותיהן, אלא שסמכו על הקבלה שקיבלו קדמוניהן
מחגי הנביא שצרות העריות אסורות על האחין כמו שביארנו, ופשט הדבר
לאיסור. ובכל מקום שהיתה מחלוקת בין החכמים נקבעה הלכה כאחד
מהן, שלא תיעשה [תורה] כשתי תורות. ועל דבר זה רמז הכתוב "לא
תתגודדו" (דברים יד, א), לא תיעשו אגודות אגודות.

גם בזמן הזה שיש ברוב מקומות מחלוקת בין החכמים ובין הגאונים, אסור
להם לבני העיר ליחלק במנהג ולנהוג במנהג פשוט, קצתן כאחד וקצתן כאחד, אלא
יעמדו על המנין ויעשו כולן על פי הרוב. במה דברים אמורים? בבית דין אחד
בעיר אחת, כגון אם היתה ישיבה אחת ומקצת החכמים נוהגין איסור
ומקצתן היתר, אבל אם היו שתי בתי דינין בעיר אחת, ונחלק בית דין זה
מבית דין זה, אין בהן משום לא תתגודדו. וכל שכן שתי עיירות הנחלקות זו
מזו.

163. שו״ת בנימין זאב, שג

ואם כן, לפי דרכינו דוקא שתי בתי דינין בשתי עיירות ליכא לאו דלא
תתגודדו, אבל שתי בתי דינין בעיר אחת, זה נוהג מנהג אחד וזה נוהג מנהג
אחר, איכא לאו דלא תתגודדו. והכי משמע מדברי הרמב״ם ז״ל (הלכות
עבודה זרה יב, יד) וזה לשונו : ״ובכלל אזהרה זו שלא יהו שתי בתי דינין בעיר
אחת זה נוהג במנהג אחד וזה נוהג במנהג אחר, שדבר זה גורם למחלוקת
גדולה, שנאמר לא תתגודדו לא תעשו אגודות אגודות״. וכן כתב סמ״ג (לאוין,
סימן סב), והיינו דפסקו כאביי. אמנם קשה לי בנימין אהאי פסקא דפסקו
כאביי, ואנן יש לנו כל היכא דנחלק אביי ורבא קיימא לן כרבא בר מהלכות
דסימניהן יע״ל קג״ם, כדאיתא בבבא מציעא פרק ב (כב, ב) ובפרק האיש
מקדש (קידושין נב, א)...

והשתא ניתן טעם למה פסקו הרמב״ם וסמ״ג נגד הכלל של יע״ל קג״ם,
והוא מה שנראה לעניות דעתי דמה שפסקו נגד הכלל משום דטפי מסתבר
מילתיה דאביי בהא מדרבא... כדאשכחן בעירובין פרק מי שהוציאוהו (מו,
ב) : ״אמר רבי אבא אמר רבי יוחנן : רבי יהודה ורבי שמעון - הלכה כרבי
יהודה״. וכן פסק אשירי שם. ואמר שם רב משרשיא : ״ליתנהו להני כללי״.
פירש רש״י (שם) : ״להני כללי דכללינן לעיל פלוני ופלוני הלכה כפלוני בכל
מקום, אלא היכא דמסתבר כמר - הלכתא כותיה, והיכא דמסתבר בדוכתא
אחרינא כאידך - עבדינן כותיה״...

אמנם כל זה יש לדחותה לפי מה שנראה לעניות דעתי דלעולם איכא למימר
דאית לן כלל דיע״ל קג״ם, והכא דפסקו הרמב״ם וסמ״ג כאביי ולא חשיבי
ליה בכלל יע״ל קג״ם, משום דהכא לא איפלגו אביי ורבא אליבא דנפשייהו
אלא פלוגתייהו הוא אליבא דתנאי כהתם, דאיכא ריש לקיש ורבי יוחנן
(יבמות יג, ב) אהא דתנן מגלה נקראת בי״א בי״ב בי״ג בי״ד ובט״ו לא פחות
ולא יותר, ואמר ליה ריש לקיש לרבי יוחנן : ״איקרי כאן לא תתגודדו לא
תעשו אגודות אגודות״, ופירש רש״י : ״לא תעשו אגודות אגודות דנראה
כנוהגין שתי תורות כשקורין את המגלה ביום הכניסה ועיירות
גדולות בי״ד ומוקפין בט״ו״. ועוד מקשה התם : ״והתם לאו איסורא היא?
והתניא : הלילה בית שמאי אוסרין״, פירוש לעשות מלאכה בליל בדיקת
חמץ, ״ובית הלל מתירין״, ואית דעבדי כבית הלל ואית דעבדי כבית שמאי,
והרי כאן אגודות? ועוד מקשה : ״בית שמאי מתירין הצרות לאחים ובית
הלל אוסרין״. ואהא אמר אביי התם, פרק קמא דיבמות (יד, א) : ״כי אמרין
לא תתגודדו כגון שתי בתי דינין בעיר אחת, הללו מורין כדברי בית שמאי
והללו מורין כדברי בית הלל, אבל שתי בתי דינין משני עיירות לית לן בה״.

ואסקה רבא ד"כי אמרן לא תתגודדו כגון בית דין בעיר אחת, פלג מורין כדברי בית שמאי ופלג מורין כדברי בית הלל, אבל שתי בתי דינין בעיר אחד לית לן בה". ומשום דהכא מסתבר טפי מילתא דאביי ממילתיה דרבא כדפרישית, פסקו כותיה, ולא נפקי מכלל יע"ל קג"ם, דפלוגתייהו אליבא דתנאי הוא כדפרישית ולא אליבא דנפשייהו.

164. שו"ת הרדב"ז ה, אלף שפד

שאלת ממני על מה שכתב הרמב"ם ז"ל (פרק יב מהלכות עכו"ם, הלכה יד), וזה לשונו: "ומכלל אזהרה זו שלא יהיו שתי דינין בעיר אחת, זה נוהג במנהג זה וזה נוהג במנהג אחר, שדבר זה גורם למחלוקת גדולה, שנאמר לא תתגודדו, לא תעשו אגודות אגודות", ע"כ. וקשיא לך דהיכי פסק כאביי לגבי רבא, דגרסינן פרק קמא דיבמות (יד, א): "ומאן דאמר עשו בית שמאי כדבריהם קרי כאן לא תעשו אגודות! אביי אמר : כי אמרינן לא תתגודדו כגון שתי בתי דינין בעיר אחת הללו מורין כדברי בית שמאי והללו מורין כדברי בית הלל אבל שתי בתי דינין בשתי עיירות לית לן בה. אמר ליה רבא : והא בית שמאי ובית הלל כשתי בתי דינין בעיר אחת דמי? אלא אמר רבא : כי אמרינן "לא תתגודדו" כגון בית דין בעיר אחת פלג מורין כבית שמאי ופלג מורין כדברי בית הלל אבל שתי בתי דינין בעיר אחת לית לן בה". ואילו אנן קיימא לן כל היכא דפליג אביי ורבא הלכתא כרבא בר מיע"ל קג"ם?

תשובה. אפשר לומר דפסק הרב ז"ל כאביי בהא, משום דמסתבר טעמיה שלא ירבו מחלוקת בישראל, דכיון שהם בעיר אחת אע"ג שהם שתי בתי דינין אי אפשר להנצל מן המחלוקת, שהרי הציבור הנגררים אחריהם זה מיקל וזה מחמיר זה פוטר וזה מחייב זה מטמא וזה מטהר, והעם פוסחים על שתי הסעיפים וירבה ביניהם השנאה והמחלוקת, וזה דבר נראה לחוש העין. אבל שתי בתי דינין בשתי עיירות לית לן בה, דכל עיר ועיר ימשך אחר בית דינו. ומה שהקשה רבא לאביי : "והא בית שמאי ובית הלל כשתי בתי דינין בעיר אחת דמי", לא קשיא ליה לאביי כולי האי, דשאני בית שמאי ובית הלל, כיון שיש בכל כת מהם כמה וכמה בישראל - כשתי בתי דינין בשתי עיירות דמי. וכל שכן שכבר היה מחלוקותם מפורסם, ואף על פי שכל כת היה עושה כסברתו דהכי מסקינן בגמרא "לא נמנעו אלו מאלו", מפני שחסידים גמורים היו והיו מודיעים לחבריהם, כדאיתא בגמרא גבי צרת הבת, שהרי כל מחלוקותם לשם שמים. תדע, שהרי כשהקשה רבא לאביי לא הקשה "והא בית שמאי ובית הלל בעיר אחת הוי", אלא "כשתי בתי דינין בעיר אחת דמי", משמע דאביי לא מדמי להו. ואפשר לתרץ נמי דבית

שמאי ובית הלל בשתי עיירות הוו דיירי, אבל בעיר אחת אפילו בתי דינין כבית שמאי ובית הלל קרינין בהו "לא תתגודדו" ויש לחוש למחלוקת.

ואף על גב דקיימא לן כרבא לגבי דאביי, הא אמרינן דהני מילי היכא דפליגו בסברא דנפשייהו אבל בסברא דאחריני לית לן האי כללא, והכא נמי איכא למימר דלא פליגי במימרא דנפשייהו אלא בתירוצא דקושיין אפליגו, ובכי האי סברא סבירא ליה לרב ז"ל דלא הדרין לכללין.

אי נמי יש לומר דאפילו לדעת רבא אמרינן דעד כאן לא אמר רבא (כו') "אבל שתי בתי דינין בעיר אחת לית לן בה" אלא בתי דינין חשובים כבית שמאי ובית הלל, שלא ימשך מהם מחלוקת מהטעמים שכתבתי למעלה, אבל שתי בתי דינין בעלמא, אפילו בעיר אחת, מודה רבא שיש לחוש למחלוקת וקרינן ביה "לא תתגודדו". והשתא ניחא ממה שהקשו בתוספות דמגילה, דבעיר אחת היו קורין לבני העיר בי"ד ולבני הכפרים מקדימין ליום הכניסה, ומתוך קושיא זו אמרו כי בעירם היו קורין בני הכפרים ובעירם היו מתכנסין, ובמה שכתבתי יתיישב שכיון שהיה הדבר מפורסם שבני הכפרים מקדימין ליום הכניסה ובני העיר קורין כדרכם בארבעה עשר, לא ימשך מזה מחלוקת ולא קרינן ביה "לא תתגודדו", כדאמרינן גבי פלוגתא דבית שמאי ובית הלל.

165. שו"ת הרדב"ז ח (מכתב יד), קמא

עוד כתב לפי שיטתו "ולא שייך למימר בהא לא תתגודדו כדאיתא בפרק קמא דיבמות (יד, א) דדוקא בעיר אחת ובית דין אחד פלג מורין כבית שמאי ופלג כבית הלל, אבל שתי בתי דינין בעיר אחת לית לן בה". עד כאן. ואני שמעתי ולא אדע, אם שמואל ואבוה הוו שתי בתי דינים, אם כן כל החולקים יהיו שתי בתי דינים, ואם כן לא משכחת לה לא תתגודדו! אלא אין הדברים אמורים אלא במחלוקת בית שמאי ובית הלל שהיו כמה אלפים בשיטת בית שמאי וכמה בשיטת בית הלל, ודכותה שתי בתי דינין קבועין להורות לרבים פלג כבית שמאי ופלג כבית הלל, אבל שני אמוראים החולקים אינם חשובים כשתי בתי דינים. ואם כן לדעתו שמקצתן היו נוהגין להקל כשמואל ומקצתן היו נוהגין להחמיר איכא משום לא תתגודדו.

166. שו"ת תשב"ץ ג, קעט

במקומות שיש קהלות חלוקות בתקנותיהם, שהם כמו שני בתי דינין בעיר אחת פלג מורין כבית שמאי ופלג מורין כבית הלל, דלית ביה משום לא תתגודדו לא תעשו אגודות אגודות, כדאיתא בפרק קמא דיבמות (יד, א),

ונשא איש מאנשי קהלה אחת אשה מאנשי קהלה אחרת, אין ספק שהאשה היא נכללת עם בעלה בכל חיובו, דאשתו כגופו בכל הדברים, ונפטרה מקהלת בית אביה. ודבר זה מלתא דפשיטא היא ואין בו ספק,שלא יהיו שנים מסובין על שולחן אחד חלוקין בעסותיהן, האסור לזה מותר לזה.

167. שו״ת הרד״ך, בית יא, חדר א

שאלה. במתא ארטא נתיישבו ארבעה קהלות, קורפייטי וסיסלייני וקאלברסי ופוייזי, וכל קהל בית הכנסת לעצמם נוהגים כמנהגם כאשר היותם במקומם. וקהל קאלבריסי הסכימו במעמד טובי קהלם שלא יורשה אחד מהם להפרד מהם וללכת להתפלל בשום אחד מבתי כנסיות האחרות, ואפילו אם יתקוטטו זה עם זה, הן יחיד והן רבים, ושלא יורשו להעריך דין כי אם לפני זקני קהלם, ושיקבלו עליהם המריבים, הן יחידים הן רבים, מה שיגזרו עליהם זקניהם. ועתה מחדש הלכו חלק מהם בבית הכנסת של סיסלייני, ושלחו זקני קהל קדוש קאלבריא לזקני קהל קדוש סיסילייאה שלא יתפללו עם אותם שיצאו מבית הכנסת שלהם להתפלל עמהם, רצוני בבית הכנסת של ק״ק סיסלייא, שהם עברויינים. והם לא אבו שמוע להם. גם מבית הכנסת של ק״ק פוליא הלכו בבית הכנסת של ק״ק סיסיליא להתפלל שמה, וכן גם כן מק״ק קורפו הלכו שמה להתפלל.

כאשר ראו טובי הקהלות ומנהיגיהם, נתקבצו בבית הכנסת של בני קורפו, ושלחו למנהיגי ק״ק סיסילייא ובאו שם. ואמרו להם בני קורפו : למה לא תעריכו דין עם אלו! והשיבו שהם פסולין לדון אותנו בהיות שגם מאנשי קהלכם באו להתפלל עמנו. וכראותם כן הסכימו השלושה קהלות קדושות, קורפו ופוליא וקאלבריא, שלא יורשה שום אחד מהשלשה הקהילות הנזכרים ללכת להתפלל בבית כנסת אחר דרך קבע, רק דרך עראי באקראי בעלמא. ואם יקפידו מנהיגי הבית הכנסת ההיא שהיה מתפלל שם על שהלך האיש ההוא בבית הכנסת אחר, שהחזן ומנהיגי הקהל ההוא שהלך זה להתפלל בבית הכנסת שלהם לא יתפללו עמו. וכל זה עשו שלא יתרבה המחלוקת בין הקהלות. ומנהיגי ק״ק סיסלייני לא רצו להכנס בהסכמתם ולא אבו שמוע לקולם.

ועתה יורינו המורה אם פסולים אנשי ק״ק קורפו וק״ק פוליא לדון בין ק״ק סיסיליא ובין ק״ק קאלבריא על אודות הסכמת ק״ק קאלבריא אשר כבר הסכימו כדלעיל. וכן אם ק״ק סיסילייא המועטים, מחוייבים לנהוג כמנהג הג׳ קהלות האחרות המרובים, ולהיות נגררים אחריהם, או לא? וכל שכן שבעוונותינו שרבו בינינו עניים ומסים וארנוניות, ואם לא ישוב

איש אל אחוזתו ואיש אל משפחתו יתקיים עלינו חס ושלום ״חלק לבם״
וגו׳. מצורף לזה, יש בינינו אנשים שאינם הגונים, ואם נפרד איש מחברו חס
ושלום יכלו כרם ה׳ צבאות.

תשובה. ...ולעניין ההסכמה אשר הסכימתם השלוש קהילות, נראה שאין
אנשי הקהל הרביעי חייבים להכנס בהסכמתכם, שאין בני הקהל אחד
כפופים לבני קהל אחר, גם כי בני הקהלות האחרות רבים מהם, שכל אחד
ואחד מן הקהל וקהל בעניין זה כעיר בפני עצמו, שאין בני העיר אחת
כפופים לבני עיר אחרת, ואין בני קהל אחד כפופים לבני הקהל האחר,
דהואיל וכל קהל נוהג כמנהגו הראשון הוו להו כשני בתי דינין בעיר אחת,
וקיימא לן כרבא דהיכא דאיכא שני בתי דינין בעיר אחת, אלו נוהגין לאסור
ואלו נוהגין להיתר, ואין כאן משום לא תתגודדו, כדאיתא בפרק קמא
דיבמות (יד, א).

ומה שכתב הרמב״ם ז״ל (הלכות עבודה זרה יב, יד) וכן בעל הסמ״ג ז״ל (ולא-
תעשה סב) שבכלל אזהרה לא תתגודדו הוא שלא יהיו שני בתי דינין בעיר
אחת, זה נוהג כמנהג זה וזה נוהג כמנהג אחר, נראה שהם ז״ל רוצים לומר
שכשיש בעיר חילוק מנהגים שחלק מהם נוהגים מנהג זה וחלק מהם נוהגים
מנהג אחר, שבזה הדבר הם נעשים שתי בתי דינין, אבל אינם שני בתי דינין
ממש בכל דבר ובכל עניין ככ״ש, וכמו שתמצא היום בשלוניקי העיר הגדולה
אשר היא אם בישראל, שהספרדים בית דין בפני עצמם והאשכנזים בית דין
בפני עצמם, אלו נוהגים מנהגיהם כמבראשונה ואלו נוהגים מנהגיהם
כמבראשונה. וכן בכל מקום שימצאו כיוצא בזה מודים הם שאין כאן לא
תתגודדו, דכרבא קיימא לן. ואפשר שלזה דקדקו בלשונם ולא כתב ש״שתי
בתי דינין בעיר אחת לא יהיו נוהגים זה שלא כמנהג זה״, אלא כתב ״שלא
יהיו שתי בתי דינין בעיר אחת״ וכו׳, פירוש שבבמה שנוהגים שני מנהגים הם
שתי בתי דינין. ואפשר נמי שנפל טעות בספרים והגירסא הנכונה היא ״שלא
יהיו כשני בתי דינין״ וכו׳, והסופרים חסרו הכף. והרמב״ם ז״ל בספר
המצוות הקצר שחיבר כתב (ספר המצוות, לאוין מה) וזה לשונו: והנה אמרו
שבכלל זה האזהרה מחלק דתי העיר במנהג וחלוק הקבוצים, עכ״ל. ולא
הזכיר הרב לומר שלא יהיו שני בתי דין בעיר אחת.

168. שו״ת הרד״ך, בית יב, חדרים א-ב

שאלה. יורונו רבינו אם שלושה בתי כנסיות בעיר אחת תקנו תקנה בעניין
הרקוד עם הנשים הנשואות משום הדברים המכוערים שהיו עוברים בכל
יום במחול, כמעט כאלו המחול היתה קובה של זנות, שהיה אומר הבחור

למסדר המחול "הביא לי את פלונית ואם לאו אינו מרקד", וגם כן היא
היתה אומרת כן. ובשבת אחד אירע בלבול בתוך המחול, כי בעלה של בחורה
אמר לאשתו אל תרקדי עם פלוני, ואחר כך מצאה בעלה מרקדת עמו, ונעשה
בלבול עד שהגיע הדבר בערכאות של גוים. ובראות כל הקהלות הפרצה
היוצאת מזה הרקוד, עמדו ותקנו ושמו חרם גמור ברוב מנין ורוב בנין עם
כל החומרות שאפשר, שלא ירקד אלא איש עם אשתו ואב עם בתו ואם עם
בנה ואח עם אחותו. ותתקיים תקנה זה קרוב לשלש שנים. ואחר כן בעבור
קטטה שעבר בין הקהילות הנזכרים מעניין המס, נפרד אלו מאלו, נתקבצו
קצתם לומר טענות של הבל: "מאחר שאנו קהל בפני עצמו, ואנו נפרדים
מהם במס, אנו רוצים להתיר ההסכמה של הרקוד בינינו". והאחרים
השיבו: "אין אתם יכולין לעשות כדבר הזה, כי הסכמה כזאת אין לה
התרה, כל שכן שאתם המעט ואנו הרוב". והם השיבו: "ההסכמה אינה
כתובה, ומאחר שאינה בכתב - ממש אין בה", וכו'. סוף דבר לא אבו שמוע,
ויתנו כתף סוררת, ועברו הסכמה ורקדו ביניהם. מה דינו? אם יכולים
המעוט לבטל בלי דעת הרוב בטוענם שהם קהל בפני עצמם? ועוד טוענים
שההסכמה היתה סתמית בלא זמן, אם כן הרשות בידינו לקיימה זמן מה
ולבטלה אחר כך כנראה בעינינו.

תשובה. ...ואף על גב דמשנעשו קהל בפני עצמם הוי כבני עיר אחרת, ובדבר
שאין בני עיר אחת כפופין לבני עיר אחרת אין בני קהל אחד כפופין לבני
קהל אחר, דכיון שכל קהל וקהל נוהג כמנהגו הוו להו כשני בתי דינין בעיר
אחת, וקיימא לן כרבא (יבמות יד, א) שהיכא דאיכא שני בתי דינין בעיר אחת,
אלו נוהגין לאסור ואלו נוהגין להתיר, ואין כאן משום לא תתגודדו. ומה
שכתב הרמב"ם ז"ל (הלכות עבודה זרה יב, יד) וכן בעל הסמ"ג ז"ל (לא-תעשה סב)
שי"בכלל אזהרה לא תתגודדו הוא שלא יהא שני בתי דינין בעיר אחת זה
נוהג כמנהג זה וזה נוהג כמנהג אחר", נראה שהם ז"ל רצו לומר שכשיש
בעיר אחת חלוק מנהגים שחלק מהם נוהגים כמנהג זה וחלק אחר נוהגים
מנהג אחר, שבזה הדבר הם נעשים שני בתי דינין אבל אינם שני בתי דינין
בעיר אחת ממש בכל דבר ובכל עניין כבית שמאי וכבית הלל - הם בכלל לא
תתגודדו. אבל היכא שהם שני בתי דינין בעיר אחת כבנדון סיסיליייאני
וקאלבריסי, וכל אחד בית הכנסת לעצמם, אלו נוהגים בכל דבר ובכל עניין
כמנהגם ואלו נוהגים וכו' - הוו להו כשני בתי דין בשתי עיירות, והיינו טעמא
דבני סלוניקי אשר היא עיר ואם בישראל.

ואפשר שלזה דקדק הרמב"ם ז"ל בלשונו, וכן בעל סמ"ג, ולא כתבו ששני
בתי דינין בעיר אחת לא יהיו נוהגין זה שלא כמנהג זה, אלא כתב "שלא יהיו

שני בתי דינין בעיר אחת" וכו', פירוש שבמה שנוהגים שני מנהגים הם שתי
בתי דינין. ואפשר נמי שנפל טעות בספרים והגירסא הנכונה היא "שלא יהיו
כשני בתי דינין" וכו', והסופרים חסרו הכף. והרמב"ם ז"ל בספר המצוות
הקצר שחיבר כתב (ספר המצוות, לאוין מה) וזה לשונו: "והנה אמרו שבכלל זה
האזהרה מחלק דתי העיר במנהגם וחלוק הקבוצים", עכ"ל. ולא הזכיר הרב
לומר שלא יהיו שני בתי דין בעיר אחת. ולפי זה אין כח לבני בית הכנסת
אחד לכוף לבני בית הכנסת אחר דהוו קהל לעצמם, הני מילי היכא דלאו
מגדר מלתא ותקנתם לכלם היא, אבל היכא דמגדר מלתא ותקנתם לכלם
היא - כופין, דברוב בני העיר תליא מלתא לענין להסיע על קצתם
וכדכתיבנא. ואף שהם בכמה מקומות בבתי כנסיות, כופין הרוב למיעוט,
כיון דבעיר אחת יושבין, כל שכן במה שכבר קבלו דפשיטא דחייבים לקיימו,
ולית דין צריך בשש.

169. שו"ת בנימין זאב, שג

בעיר ארטא נתיישבו ארבע קהלות שבאו מגרוש מלכות ספרד ופורטוגל:
ציצלייא וקלבריא ופוליייא וקהל תושבים היו שם מקדם קדמתא מיושבים
בטירותם ובחצרותם, כפי מנהג ק"ק קורפו היה כל מנהגם, ולכלם מנהג
אחד בדין איסור והיתר, גם בענייני מיסים וארנוניות כולם כו', איש לרעהו
יעזורו, ידובקו ולא יתפרדו. וקרה מקרה בין הקהלות הנ"ל שבאו מהגרוש,
שנמצאו שלש נשים מעוברות מארוסיהן בעודן ארוסות, בלא חופה ובלא
שבע ברכות ובלא טבילה. ונודע הדבר אצל הבית דין של הערכאות והוליכו
חלק מהן אצל שופט העיר וענש אותן כפי דיניהם. עוד רעה שנית העידו
לפנינו, איך חלק מפריצי בני עמינו בהיותם חלין במחולות, אנשים ונשים
יחד, שלחו ידיהם בחיק הנשים שהיו נשואות, ותהי זעקה גדולה ומרה על
הפועל הרע הזה. ובאו לפני חכמי העיר ומנהיגיה וסיפרו להם כל זאת.
וכאשר ראו חכמי העיר המעשים המגונים אשר נעשו, קראו לממוני הקהלות
והודיעו להם חומר האיסור הן בענין הרע שבעלו ארוסותיהן בלא טבילה
ובלא שבע ברכות וכן לא יעשה בישראל, הן בענין הרע השני כדמפורש לעיל.
והחכמים השלמים רצו לגדור למיגדר מילתא, והסכימו שלא יורשה שום
ארוס ליכנס בבית הארוסה אחר שיעשו ברכת אירוסין וסעודת שבת, עד זמן
הכנסתם לחופה. וכל זאת כדי להפרישם מאיסורא, שחשו שמא יבעלו
ארוסותיהם נדות כדלקמן. גם לא יחולו אנשים ונשים יחד בשביל הפועל
המגונה כדלעיל. והחכמים השלמים אשר בקהלות ארטא יצ"ו כתבו לגאוני
קושטדינא ושלוניקי המעשים הנזכרים. וחלק מעמינו מוחין באותו גדר

הנזכר שעשו השלושה חכמים. וגאוני שלוניקי וקושטדינא כתבו והסכימו
וגזרו בגזרת נח"ש על כל מי שיעבור על התקנה והגדר שעשו השלשה
החכמים למיגדר מילתא. וביום נועד עמדו השלשה החכמים השלמים אשר
בארטא וקראו לממוני הקהלות וגם לממוני קהילת פולייא ואסיפת עם רב,
והודיעו להם מה שהסכימו לאפרושי מאיסורא, והודיעו להם מה שכתבו
חכמי וגאוני קושטדינא ושלוניקי יצ"ו, והוציאו ספר תורה על הדוכן,
והחרימו בקנס נח"ש על כל מי שיעבור בתקנתם כנ"ל. ובעוד שהיו גוזרין עם
הספר תורה צעקו ממוני קהילת פולייא שאינם חפצים על ההוא תקנה
שתקנו השלושה חכמים, אלא מנהג אבותם בידם ליכנס הארוס בבית
הארוסה לאכול ולשתות יחד, ולכן אל יחרימו על זה, ויצאו מבית הכנסת
בזעקה גדולה. והחכמים השלמים שלחו להם בגזרת נח"ש שיבואו להכנס
בההוא חרם ותקנה שנעשה למיגדר מילתא, וקיימו וקבלו הממונים עליהם
ועל זרעם לקיים תקנת החכמים השלמים. ואף דממוני קהל פולייא יצאו
בבהלה, מכל מקום נהגו בההוא תקנה וגדר ארבע שנים כאשר נהגו כל
הקהלות. ועתה מקרוב באו, כתבו ובדו טעמים מלבם אנשים מורים להם
היתר ויצאו לערוך מלחמה בחנית ושריון להראות לשרים את יקרם, חשבו
לשלוח יד בשלשה החכמים השלמים, בדו וכתבו אל הגאון תפארת הרבנים
למהר"ר יוסף טייטצאק איך ההוא קהילת פולייא אינם חפצים על ההוא
תקנה דהוא הפרשת איסור, כיון דלא קבלוהו אז ברצונם, ואפילו שאחר כך
נהגו בו לאיסור, היה בשביל שלא יכלו להפרד מהקהלות יצ"ו. עתה יורינו
המורה אם יש יכולת ביד ההוא קהילה לסלק עצמו מההוא גדר או לא.

אומר אני, נכונו שופטים ללצים, לדון למנאצים, והיום רבו מתפרצים,
בכותבם להשתרר קופצים, על זאת יצאו פרוצים, על כן אתקנא בפורצים,
לבל יהיו קופצים, נגד העומדים בפורצים, ואם כי צעיר אני לימים, לא אירא
מהעמים, גם את הארי גם את הדוב הכתי היום מימים, ובמקום שיש משפט
אשפוט לעמים, נגד השרים והפרתמים... לפי הנראה לעניות דעתי, דהההוא
קהל פולייא אינם יכולין לפרוק עצמם ממגדר מילתא כי האי, כיון
שהסכימו והחרימו הרוב על הפרשת האיסור לעשות משמרת למשמרת,
דבאיסורא פשיטא דאזלינן בתר רובא. וכל שכן שהחכמים והגאונים
שבשלוניקי ובקושטדינא כתבו שהם מסכימים כאלו היו הם עמהם בההוא
תקנה וגדר, והעובר עליהם כעובר על הדת ויהיה מוחרם ומנודה לשמים
ולבריות בגזרת נח"ש...

ולא יהיה הכא אלא משום לאו דלא תתגודדו, ראוי לכל חכם שלא להטפל
להתיר להם, אפילו היה דבר הרשות, כל שכן דאיכא מיגדר מילתא דבא

מהתמרתו איסור דאורייתא. וכיון דשניהם בעיר אחת, אין לנהוג זה מנהג אחד וזה מנהג אחר, דבכהאי גוונא נראה כשתי תורות. ואין לומר הכא הא דאמר רבא פרק קמא דיבמות (יד, א) "דכי אמרינן לא תתגודדו כגון בית דין אחד בעיר אחת, פלג מורין כדברי בית שמאי ופלג מורין כדברי בית הלל, אבל שתי שתי דינין בעיר אחת לית לן בה", ולפי זה יהיה פתחון פה לבעל דין לחלוק עלי דשפיר דמי, דזה אינו, דהא קהל פוליא לא היה ביניהם בעל תורה דנחשיבם לבית דין אפילו אליבא דרבא. ודוק, דרבא "בית דין" קאמר, ובית דין לא יקראו אלא בעלי תורה ומומחים. כל שכן דאביי סבר שם ד"כי אמרינן לא תתגודדו כגון שתי דינין בעיר אחת, הללו מורין כדברי בית שמאי והללו מורין כדברי בית הלל, אבל שתי בתי דינין בשתי עיירות לית לן בה".

והשתא יש להקשות מקריאת המגלה דשרינן לבני הכפרים ומקדימין ליום הכניסה וקורין, דבשלמא לרבא דאמר דליכא משום לאו דלא תתגודדו אלא היכא דאיכא בעיר אחת בית דין אחד פלג מורין כדברי בית שמאי ופלג מורין כדברי בית הלל אבל שתי בתי דינין בעיר אחת אתי שפיר, דלדידיה ניחא דבני הכפרים ובני העיר דמיין כשתי בתי דינין בעיר אחת. אלא לאביי דאמר דאיכא לאו דלא תתגודדו כגון שני בתי דינין בעיר אחת, הללו מורין כדברי בית שמאי והללו מורין כדברי בית הלל, היכי שרינן לבני הכפרים לקרות בעיירות בי"א בי"ב בי"ג ולבני העיר בי"ד שהוא זמנה, הא הוו להו כשתי בתי דינין בעיר אחת, וקשה לאביי?!

ויש לומר דהכא נמי כשתי בתי דינין בשתי עיירות דמיין, שהרי בני הכפרים מצויינין הן לעצמן ודעתם לחזור לביתם, ובני העיר מצויינין הן לעצמן, והוו כשתי בתי דינין בשני עיירות ושפיר דמי. וליכא למימר דאם בן העיר מקרא להם המגלה ומוציאן ידי חובה, ולפי זה יהיו כשתי בתי דינין בעיר אחת, דזה אינו, דעל כורחינו לומר דלא היה בן העיר מקרא להם המגלה ומוציאן ידי חובתם, אלא אחד מבני הכפרים הוא דמוציאן, דהא בני העיר עדיין לא חל עליהם זמן חיוב קריאתה ולאו בני חיוב נינהו, וכל שאינו מחוייב בדבר אינו מוציא את חבירו ידי חובה כדאיתא בירושלמי דמגלה פרק הקורא תניין. וכיון דכן הוא, הוו בני הכפרים כבית דין אחד דהא דעתם לחזור לביתם, ובני העיר כבית דין אחר בעירם, ודמיין כשתי בתי דינין בשני עיירות, ושפיר דמי לאביי בין לרבא דבכהאי גוונא לא שייך לאו דלא תתגודדו אפילו לאביי. ומה שלא היו קורין המגלה בכפר שלהם לפי שלא היו מתקבצין יחד אלא בעיירות.

ואם כן, לפי דרכינו דוקא שתי בתי דינין בשתי עיירות ליכא לאו דלא
תתגודדו, אבל שתי בתי דינין בעיר אחת, זה נוהג מנהג אחד וזה נוהג מנהג
אחר, איכא לאו דלא תתגודדו. והכי משמע מדברי הרמב״ם ז״ל (הלכות
עבודה זרה יב, יד) וזה לשונו : ״ובכלל אזהרה זו שלא יהו שתי בתי דינין בעיר
אחת זה נוהג במנהג אחד וזה נוהג במנהג אחר, שדבר זה גורם למחלוקת
גדולה, שנאמר לא תתגודדו לא תעשו אגודות אגודות״. וכן כתב סמ״ג (לאוין,
סימן סב), והיינו דפסקו כאביי. אמנם קשה לי בנימין אהאי פסקא דפסקו
כאביי, ואנן יש לנו כלל כל היכא דנחלק אביי ורבא קיימא לן כרבא בר מהלכות
דסימניהן יע״ל קג״ם, כדאיתא בבבא מציעא פרק ב (כב, ב) ובפרק האיש
מקדש (קידושין נב, א).

170. שו״ת אבקת רוכל, לב

ילמדנו רבינו קהלות שנוהגים כהרמב״ם ז״ל בקולותיו ובחומרותיו דור
אחר דור מהו לכוף אותם לנהוג כהרי״י וזולתם מהאחרונים המביאים
הסברות או דילמא הזהרו מנהג מנהג אבותיכם ואם רב במלכיות רבים מהו?

מי הוא זה אשר ערב אל לבו לגשת לכוף קהלות שנוהגים כהרמב״ם ז״ל
לנהוג כשום אחד מן הפוסקים ראשונים ואחרונים? והא דאמרינן בפרק
קמא דעירובין (ו, ב): ״תני, לעולם הלכה כבית הלל והרוצה לעשות כבית
שמאי יעשה, מקולי בית שמאי ומקולי בית הלל מחומרי בית שמאי
ומחומרי בית הלל עליו הכתוב אומר ׳והכסיל בחשך הולך׳ (קהלת ב, יד), אלא
כבית שמאי כקוליהון וכחומריהון אי כבית הלל כקוליהון וכחומריהון״.
והלא דברים קל וחומר, ומה אם בית שמאי דאין הלכה כמותם אמרו אי
כבית שמאי כקוליהון וכחומריהן, הרמב״ם ז״ל אשר הוא גדול הפוסקים
וכל קהלות ארץ ישראל והאראביסטאן והמערב נוהגים על פיו וקבלוהו
עליהם לרבן, מי שינהוג כמוהו בקולותיו ובחומרותיו למה יכפוהו לזוז
ממנו? ומה גם אם נהגו אבותיהם ואבות אבותיהם, שאין לבניהם לנטות
ימין ושמאל מהרמב״ם ז״ל. ואפילו רבו באותה העיר קהלות שנוהגים
כהרא״ש וזולתו, אינם יכולים לכוף למעוט הקהלות שנוהגים כהרמב״ם ז״ל
לנהוג כמותם. וליכא משום ״לא תתגודדו״, דהואיל וכל קהל נוהג כמנהגו
הראשון הוה ליה כשתי בתי דינים בעיר אחת, וקיימא לן כרבא דהיכא
דאיכא שתי דיינים בעיר אחת אלו נוהגים לאסור ואלו נוהגים להתיר אין
כאן משום ״לא תתגודדו״ כדאיתא פרק קמא דיבמות (יד, א), וכל קהל וקהל
כעיר בפני עצמו שאין בני קהל אחד כופין לבני קהל אחר. וכן כתב מוהר״ר
דוד כהן ז״ל בתשובותיו (בית יא), והנראה לי כתבתי הצעיר.

171. שו"ת מהר"י בן לב ג, יד

במה שנהגו בקושטנדינא רבתי האומנים העומדים על הניקור על מה שכתב
רש"י ז"ל להקל על אותו הקרום החזק, וכל הפוסקים רובם או כלם
חולקים עליו, והמנקרים הנזכרים מחלקים בין הכבשים לשוורים ואומרים
שהקרום בשוורים הוא חזק והרי הוא אפוי בשר ולא כן בכבשים.

ויש לחקור בזה הנדון ארבע חקירות. האחת, אם באולי יסכימו כל הקהלות
אשר בקושטאנטינה, הרומאניוטיש והספרדים יצ"ו, כלם כאחד לבטל זה
המנהג ולקבל עליהם המנהג אשר נוהגים להחמיר לנקר אותו החלב
המכוסה באותו הקרום כסברת רוב הפוסקים, וכל הקהלות אשר שמענו את
שמעם נוהגים להחמיר זולתי האשכנזים אשר מימי קדם קדמתא החזיקו
כסברת רש"י להקל, וגם הקהל מהאשכנזים זה קצת שנים בשאלוניקי שנו
את מנהגם ונטו להחמיר, ויש מקום לשאול אם כל הקהלות יסכימו
לבטל המנהג שנהגו להקל אם יש בזה לעז וזלזול בראשונים שנהגו להקל או
נגיעה בכבוד החכמים הראשונים אשר קיימו המנהג ההוא ולא מיחו בידם.

עוד שנית צריך לחקור אם באולי לא יסכימו הקהלות הקדושות מרומנייא
להקל, אם יהיו הקהלות קדושות מספרד אשר אבותיהם בארצותם היו מן
המחמירים באותו החלב רשאים לעשות אגודה, ואם יהיו בזה עוברים על
מה שאומרים לא תתגודדו לא תעשה אגודות אגודות, וכמו שבא בסוף פרקא
קמא דיבמות (יג, ב). עוד צריך לחקור, דאפילו אם תמצי לומר דאמרינן דכגון
האי לא הוי אגודות, אם באולי יתחלקו קהל ספרד, שקצתם ירצו להחזיק
המנהג שנהגו כבני רומניא וקצתם לבטל זה המנהג ולהשיב המנהג שנהגו
אבותיהם לאיתנו, האם נאמר דהוי אגודות אגודות ואינם רשאים בכך?...

ועל החקירה השנית צריך לדעת אם קהלות רומאנייא וקהלות הפראנקוש
הם כשתי בתי דינין בעיר אחת ולא קרינן בהו לא תתגודדו, או דילמא הם
כבית דין בעיר אחת פלג מורים כב"ש ופלג מורים כב"ה. ובפרק קמא
דיבמות (יד, א) אמרינן: "ומאן דאמר עשו בית שמאי כדבריהם, קרי כאן לא
תעשו אגודות? אמר אביי: כי אמרינן לא תתגודדו כגון שני בתי דינין בעיר
אחת הללו מורין כב"ש והללו כב"ה אבל שתי בתי דינין בשתי עיירות לית לן
בה. אמר ליה רבא: והא ב"ש וב"ה כשתי בתי דינין בעיר אחת דמי? אלא
אמר רבא: כי אמרינן לא תתגודדו כגון ב"ד בעיר אחת פלג מורין כב"ש ופלג
מורין כב"ה, אבל שתי בתי דינין בעיר אחת לית לן בה".

וכתב סמ"ג (לאוין סב): "שלא יהו שתי בתי דינין בעיר אחת, זה נוהג מנהג
אחד וזה נוהג מנהג אחר", ע"כ. משמע שהוא פוסק כאביי, וקיימא לן דאביי

ורבא הלכה כרבא בר מיע"ל קג"ים. ומהר"ר דוד הכהן ז"ל בפסקיו (שו"ת הרד"ך, בית יא) הוקשה לו זאת הקושיא, ותירץ דכוונת הרמב"ם והסמ"ג הוא לומר שלא יהו שתי בתי דינין כו' כלומר בהיותם ב"ד אחד לא יעשו עצמם כשתי בתי דינין, פלג נוהגין מנהג אחד ופלג נוהגין מנהג אחר. וכתב הרב הנזכר וז"ל: "ואפשר שלזה דקדק הרמב"ם וכן סמ"ג שלא כתבו ששני בתי דינין בעיר אחת שלא יהיו נוהגים זה שלא כמנהג זה, אלא כתבו שלא יהו שתי בתי דינין בעיר אחת כו', פירוש שבמה שנוהגים שני מנהגים הם שתי בתי דינין, ואפשר נמי שטעות נפל בספרים והנוסחה הנכונה היא שלא יהיו כשתי בתי דינין כו' והסופרים חסרו הכ"ף". ע"כ.

והרב הנזכר כתב: "והיינו דבני שאלוניקי אשר היא עיר ואם בישראל", ע"כ. והאמת כן הוא, שקהל האשכנזים היו נוהגים שני מנהגים שלא כמנהג כל הקהלות, אחד לחומרא ואחד לקולא, האשכנזים היו נוהגים חומרא בכל אותם המקומות שאין הנקב פוסל בהם היכא דנסרכה הריאה להם זולתי במצר החזה כסברת רוב הפוסקים, והספרדים סמכו על ר"ת והרי"זה והרמב"ם והיו מכשירין בנפיחה. ועל אותו הקרום החזק היו האשכנזים נוהגים לקולא כדברי רש"י, והספרדים היו נוהגים כדברי רוב הפוסקים לחומרא. והיו מחזיקים עצמם כשתי בתי דינין בעיר אחת. ודי במה שכתבתי באלו השתי החקירות הראשונות.

172. שו"ת המביי"ט ג, עז

ולענין אם שלושה או ארבעה בתי כנסיות בעיר אחת, אם יכולים רוב מנין ורוב בנין הבתי כנסיות לכוף את המיעוט אפילו הם קהל אחד שיקבלו עליהם הסכמת רוב הקהלות, האריך בזה החכם נר"ו להכריח שיכולים לכוף רוב קהלות שבעיר אחת לקהל אחד שבעיר שיסכימו עמהם בכל מה שיש בו מגדר מלתא דאיסורא. ונראה לי שהדין עמו גם בזה.

ובתשובות של הרשב"א והריב"ש שכתבו שאין קהל אחד יכול להכריח את קהל אחר להסכים הסכמתם, נראה שהקהל אחד קורא כאן בני עיר אחת, כמו שכתב החכם נר"ו וכמו שנראה מלשון תשובתם, אבל בתי כנסיות של עיר אחת יכולים להכריח הרוב את המיעוט שיקבלו עליהם הם במה שהיא למגדר מלתא דאיסורא, כפשטה דברייתא פרק קמא דבתרא (בבא בתרא ח, ב) "רשאים בני העיר להתנות וכו' ולהסיע על קיצתן". וכן כל הפוסקים כתבו "רשאין בני העיר" וכו' סתם, דמשמע בני עיר אחת, בין שיהיה בה קהל אחד או כמה קהלות, כי אין פירודם בשני קהלות או שלוש או ארבע אלא מפני שאין מקום בית הכנסת המועט מחזיק את המרובים כמו בבית המקדש

שהיו עומדים צפופים ומשתחוים רווחים, וצריכין בכל עיירות ישראל שיש
בהם עם רב לעשות בתי תפלה, אם מפני שאין בית הכנסת יכול אותם כמו
שכתבתי, אם מפני שהעם רב והעיר רחבת ידים ואין כל אדם הדר בקצה
העיר יכול להשכים ולהעריב לבית הכנסת, ואין כולם זוכים לשכר פסיעות
וצריכין בית הכנסת בכל שכונה ושכונה. ולא מפני זה יהיו נפרדים
בתקנותיהם, אלא כולם הם אגודה אחת ולב אחד לכל מה שהוא למגדר
מלתא דאיסורא... וכן צריך שיהיה בכל ענייני העיר שיהיו כולם אגודה אחת
כמו שהם מיוחדים באל אחד ותורה אחת ומשפט אחד, כך יהיה גם כן
בתקנות שיש בהם מגדר מלתא דאיסורא שחייבים להיותם נגררים
אחרי הרוב בכל עניינים אלו, אפילו שיהיה כמה בתי כנסיות בעיר אחת, רוב
מנין גולגלתא או קרקפתא דגברי חשיבי שבעיר ורוב דבתי כנסיות
יכולים לכוף את המיעוט, בדבר שנראה להם לפי הזמן שצריך לעשות תקנה
וגדר שלא יגעו באיסור תורה, או אפילו דרבנן אם רואים שהוא קרוב או
מצוי לעבור עליו. ולא נאמר די לנו מה שאסרה תורה ומה שאסרו חכמים,
כי ההסכמה או התקנה מעמדת ומקיימת איסור תורה ודברי סופרים.

173. שו"ת מהרש"ג ב, יב

עוד אני חושב סברא אחת, דכמו דלענין בל תוסיף שהוא בוודאי לאו
דאורייתא גמור, והרי מבואר בפרק המוצא תפילין במסכת עירובין (צו, א)
דהמניח שני זוגות תפילין עובר על בל תוסיף, ועל כל זה מבואר בשולחן
ערוך (אורח חיים לד), דלענין תפילין של רש"י ושל ר"ת דמספק שפיר דמי
להניח שניהם יחד, ואין כאן שום חשש של בל תוסיף, כיון דעושה כן רק
מחמת ספק ולא מחמת ודאי אין כאן בל תוסיף. אם כן כמו כן לענין לאו
של "לא תתגודדו" גם כן לא נאמר אלא באם כל אחד מהנוהגים אומרים
שהם נוהגים כן מחמת ודאי, שברי לו שהדין הוא כן ושהדעת השניה הוא
טעות גמור. אבל במי שאומר שעל הדבר ספק ופלוגתא בין הפוסקים רוצה
הוא לחוש להחמיר דשמא הלכה כדברי המחמיר, הגם שהשני אינו רוצה
להחמיר מספק, מכל מקום כיון שגם העושה אינו עושה כן בתורת ודאי
אלא בתורת ספק להחמיר, לא שייך בזה "לא תתגודדו", דאם לא נימא כן,
אם כן לא יהיה שום אדם רשאי להחמיר באיזה דבר שיש בו נדנוד חשש
יותר מחבירו. ולמשל, אם הלה אוכל בפסח מצה מבושלת והלה אינו אוכל,
הכי יעלה על הדעת לומר דיש בזה איסור משום לא תתגודדו! אלא ודאי
משום דגם הנזהר מודה דאינו אסור מעיקר הדין, רק הוא רוצה לחוש
להחמיר שמא נשאר מעט קמח שלא נאפה ולא נקלה, ומחמיר רק מחמת

חשש ספק וחומרא, אין בזה משום לא תתגודדו. ובאמת זה נכלל בדברי מעלת כבוד תורתו, שכתב לי שאינו מברך על הנחת תפילין בחול המועד ושמהאי טעמא לא יהיה שייך בזה ״לא תתגודדו״, רק שמעלת כבוד תורתו לא ביאר היטב הטעם, ואני ביארתי דכיון דאינו מברך נראה שאינו עושה מחמת ודאי רק מחמת ספק וחומרא, לכן לא שייך בזה לא תתגודדו.

וזה לשון שולחן ערוך התניא (אורח חיים תצג, ז): ״אבל אם ידוע לו מנהג המקום, אין לו לשנות מן מנהג המקום להקל בימים שאנשי המקום מחמירין, או להחמיר בימים שהן מקילין, אם אינו עושה כן מחמת חומרא בעלמא שמחמיר על עצמו לחוש לדברי המחמירין בימים אלו, אלא הוא מתראה שעושה כן לפי שכן ראוי לעשות לכל אדם מפני שהעיקר הוא כמחמירין, שאז נראה הדבר כשתי תורות, שהוא מחמיר ואנשי המקום מקילין או להיפך, ויש בזה איסור לא תתגודדו כלומר לא תעשו אגודות אגודות״ וכו', עכ״ל. מלשון זה מבואר, דאם עושה כן מחמת חומרא שרוצה לחוש לספק אין בזה איסור של לא תתגודדו. והוא מוכרח לדעתי עוד, שהרי כל השולחן ערוך מלא לכתוב על כמה הלכות שהם קצת מפוקפקות ״וטוב להחמיר״ או ״המחמיר תבוא עליו ברכה״, והרי אם לא נימא כנ״ל, לכאורה אסור להחמיר אפילו לעצמו משום לא תתגודדו, אלא ודאי שמע מינה דכל שאינו מראה שהדבר אצלו כודאי הלכה אין כאן משום לא תתגודדו.

ויש להרכיב תירוץ זה עם התירוץ ראשון שכתבתי למעלה, ומשום דלכאורה מנא נדע אם כוונתו רק מחמת חומרא או כוונתו מחמת שסבירא ליה כן לעיקר דין? אבל יש לומר דנתברר ממה שמורה כן גם לאחרים וצועק על האחרים שאין עושין כמותו שהן עושין איסור או שלא כדין. ואם כן כיון שבנידון העניין של תפילין בחול המועד, לפי מה שכתב מעלת כבוד תורתו, הרי אינו צועק על אחרים שאין מניחים שהם מבטלים מצוות עשה של הנחת תפילין, רק עושה הדברים לעצמו, אם כן הרי נראה לכל שעושה כן רק מחמת חומרא, אם כן אין בזה משום לא תתגודדו, כנ״ל.

174. בית הבחירה, יבמות יד, א, ד״ה ומגלה

ומגילה שהיא נקראת בזמנים חלוקים לעיירות ולכפרים וכרכים כמו שהתבאר במקומו, אין כאן אגודות, שהרי כאן חלוק מקומות הם, שהרי אף בני הכפרים עצמם הם קורין כמו שהכרענו במקומו (בית הבחירה, מגילה ב, א). ועוד, שאף לדעת המפרשים שבעיירות היו קורין, הרי העניין כשתי בתי דינין בעיר אחת, או שאף בעיר אחת כשתי עיירות הם, שמצויינים הם בעיר, והם בעיר כבני עיר אחת.

ועוד אני אומר, שדין מגילה אינה בדין אגודות כלל, אף לדעת האומר כאן שאף בשני בתי דין בעיר אחת איכא משום אגודות עד שיהו שני בתי דינין בשתי עיירות. ואני מפרש "אמר אביי כי אמרינן לא תתגודדו" (יבמות יד, א), בדבר שהוא מצד מחלוקת והם שני בתי דינין בעיר אחת, ואצרות דמתניתין קא מהדר, אבל קריאת מגילה אינה בדין זה כלל, שאין הדבר מצד מחלוקת שיהו הללו עושין כדברי זה והללו עושין כדברי זה, שהרי הללו מודים לבני כפרים שזהו זמנם והללו מודים לבני עיירות שזהו זמנם, והרי הוא כענין קריאת שמע שזמנה בהנץ החמה והקל בו ביוצא לדרך משיעלה עמוד השחר. או שמא קריאת הכפרים אינה בכלל אגודות, ולא היתה עיקר הקושיא אלא מי"ד וט"ו שהם זמנים מובהקים, ושזה אסור לקרות בשל זה, וכמו שאמר כאן זמנו של זה אינו זמנו של זה, אבל כפרים אילו רצו לקרות בי"ד ניחא טפי, אלא שהקלו עליהם להקדים, ואיהו לא קשיא ליה אלא היכא דאיכא איסורא, וכמו שאמר (יבמות יג, ב) "אמינא לך איסורא" כו'.

175. חידושי הריטב"א, יבמות יד, א, ד"ה והקשו בתוספות

והקשו בתוספות: ואמאי לא פריך ממגילה ובני כפרים כשמקדימים לקרוא ביום הכניסה הרי בעיירות הם קורים והוו להו שני בתי דינים בעיר אחת, כי אלו קורין ביום הכניסה ואלו קורים בזמנם? ויש שתרצו בזה תירוצים הרבה. ובתוספות תירצו בכלל דבריהם, דמגילה לית בה משום אגודות כלל, דלא שייך אגודות ותורה כשתי תורות אלא בדבר של מחלוקת שאין אלו מודים, אבל בדבר שכולן מודים אלו לאלו ולכל אחד ואחד יש טעם לדבר לעשות כמו שעושה, אין בו משום אגודות, הא למה זה דומה, ללולב שניטל במקדש שבעה ובמדינה יום אחד ותקיעת שופר דהיתה במקדש בחצוצרות ובמדינה בלא חצוצרות. וכיוצא בזה תירץ בירושלמי בפרק מקום שנהגו, וטעם נכון הוא ומוסבר מאוד.

אלא דקשה לי דהא ריש לקיש פריך ממגילה ולא אדכר ליה שום גברא האי טעמא ואיהו נמי לא חזיא ליה. ויש לומר לפי שיטה זו, דרבי יוחנן ואמוראי מהאי טעמא לא חשו למיפרך מתניתין דמגילה ולא אדכרוה כלל, וריש לקיש סבר דאע"ג דאיכא טעמא לכפרים וכן לעיירות וכן לכרכים לעשות כל אחד לעצמו, אין הטעם הכרחי כל כך, וכיון שהדבר ביד אנשי כנסת הגדולה לתקן מוטב שיתקינו לכלם זמן אחד או שיעשו בי"ד ובט"ו. כך נראה לפרש לפי שיטת התוספות הזאת.

176. רא"ש, יבמות, פרק א, סימן ט

ומקשינן (יבמות יג, ב) אהא דתנן: "בית שמאי מתירין את הצרות לאחין ובית
הלל אוסרין", ותו אהא דתנן: "מגילה נקראת באחד עשר בשנים עשר
בשלשה עשר בארבעה עשר ובחמשה עשר", קרי כאן לא תתגודדו לא תעשו
אגודות אגודות. ואסקה רבא (שם יד, א): "כי אמרינן לא תתגודדו, כגון בית
דין אחד בעיר אחת, פלג מורין כבית שמאי ופלג מורין כבית הלל, אבל שתי
בתי דינין בעיר אחת לית לן בה", וכל שכן שתי בתי דינין בשתי עיירות.

ובמגילה, אף על פי שקורין לבני העיר בארבעה עשר ומקדימין לבני הכפרים,
והוי כמו בית דין אחד בעיר אחת פלג מורים כבית שמאי ופלג מורים כבית
הלל, לא קרינן ביה לא תתגודדו, כיון דלא עבדי הכי משום פלוגתא אלא
שהמקום גורם, ואם היה בן מקום זה הולך למקום אחר היה עושה כמותם
הלכך לא מיחזי כשתי תורות. ואף על פי שריש לקיש הקשה לרבי יוחנן
ממגילה, רבי יוחנן לא חש להשיבו משום דלא חשיב ליה כשתי תורות
מטעמא דפרישית, ואמר לו: "עד כאן לא שנית מקום שנהגו?!" מההיא היה
לך להקשות, כי מההיא דמגילה לא קשה מידי.

177. משנה, פסחים ד, א

מקום שנהגו לעשות מלאכה בערבי פסחים עד חצות - עושין; מקום שנהגו
שלא לעשות - אין עושין. ההולך ממקום שעושין למקום שאין עושין או
ממקום שאין עושין למקום שעושין - נותנין עליו חומרי מקום שיצא משם
וחומרי מקום שהלך לשם, ואל ישנה אדם מפני המחלוקת.

178. משנה, יבמות א, ד

בית שמאי מתירין הצרות לאחים, ובית הלל אוסרים. חלצו - בית שמאי
פוסלין מן הכהונה, ובית הלל מכשירים. נתיבמו - בית שמאי מכשירין, ובית
הלל פוסלין. אף על פי שאלו אוסרין ואלו מתירין, אלו פוסלין ואלו מכשירין
- לא נמנעו בית שמאי מלישא נשים מבית הלל, ולא בית הלל מבית שמאי.
כל הטהרות והטמאות שהיו אלו מטהרין ואלו מטמאין - לא נמנעו עושין
טהרות אלו על גבי אלו.

179. משנה, עדויות ח, ז

אמר רבי יהושע: מקובל אני מרבן יוחנן בן זכאי, ששמע מרבו ורבו מרבו,
הלכה למשה מסיני, שאין אליהו בא לטמא ולטהר, לרחק ולקרב, אלא
לרחק המקרבין בזרוע ולקרב המרחקין בזרוע. משפחת בית צריפה היתה

בעבר הירדן ורחקה בן ציון בזרוע. ועוד אחרת היתה שם וקרבה בן ציון בזרוע. כגון אלו - אליהו בא לטמא ולטהר, לרחק ולקרב. רבי יהודה אומר: לקרב, אבל לא לרחק. רבי שמעון אומר: להשוות המחלקת. וחכמים אומרים: לא לרחק ולא לקרב אלא לעשות שלום בעולם, שנאמר "הנני שלח לכם את אליה הנביא" וגומר "והשיב לב אבות על בנים ולב בנים על אבותם" (מלאכי ג, כד-כה).

180. תוספתא, יבמות א, י-יא

אף על פי שנחלקו בית שמאי כנגד בית הילל בצרות ובאחיות ובספק אשת איש ובגט ישן ובמקדש בשוה פרוטה ובמגרש את אשתו ולנה עמו בפונדקי - לא נמנעו בית שמאי לישא נשים מבית הילל, אלא נהגו אמת ושלום ביניהם, ולא בית הילל מבית שמאי, לקיים מה שנאמר "האמת והשלום אהבו" (זכריה ח, יט).

ואף על פי שאלו אוסרין ואילו מתירין, לא נמנעו עושין טהרות אילו על גבי אילו, לקיים מה שנאמר "כל דרך איש זך בעיניו ותכן לבות ה'" (משלי כא, ב – משלי טז,ב).

181. בראשית רבה ד, ו

למה אין כתיב בשני "כי טוב"?... רבי חנינא אומר: שבו נבראת מחלוקת, שנאמר "ויהי מבדיל בין מים למים" (בראשית א, ו). אמר רבי טביומי: אם מחלוקת שהיא לתקונו של עולם ולישובו אין בה "כי טוב", מחלוקת שהיא לערבובו על אחת כמה וכמה.

182. ויקרא רבה, פרשה ט, ט

חזקיה אמר: גדול שלום, שבכל מסעות כתיב "ויסעו ויחנו" (במדבר לג, ו), נוסעים במחלוקת וחונים במחלוקת. כיון שבאו לפני הר סיני נעשו כולם חנייה אחת: "ויחנו שם בני ישראל" אין כתיב כאן, אלא "ויחן שם ישראל" (שמות יט, ב). אמר הקב"ה: הרי שעה שאני נותן תורה לבניי...

בר קפרא אמר: גדול שלום, מה אם העליונים, שאין בהן לא קנאה ולא שנאה ולא תחרות ולא מצות ולא דבבות ולא מחלוקת ולא עין רעה, צריכין שלום - "עושה שלום במרומיו" (איוב כה, ב), התחתונים שיש בהן כל המידות הללו על אחת כמה וכמה.

183. בבלי, ברכות טז, ב

רב ספרא בתר צלותיה אמר הכי: "יהי רצון מלפניך ה' אלקינו שתשים שלום בפמליא של מעלה ובפמליא של מטה, ובין התלמידים העוסקים בתורתך, בין עוסקין לשמה ובין עוסקין שלא לשמה. וכל העוסקין שלא לשמה יהי רצון שיהו עוסקין לשמה".

184. בבלי, ברכות לט, ב

איתמר: הביאו לפניהם פתיתין ושלמין, אמר רב הונא: מברך על הפתיתין ופוטר את השלמין, ורבי יוחנן אמר: שלמה מצוה מן המובחר... תני תנא קמיה דרב נחמן בר יצחק: מניח הפרוסה בתוך השלמה ובוצע ומברך. אמר ליה: מה שמך? אמר ליה: שלמן. אמר ליה: שלום אתה ושלמה משנתך, ששמת שלום בין התלמידים.

185. בבלי, ברכות סד, א

אמר רבי אלעזר אמר רבי חנינא: תלמידי חכמים מרבים שלום בעולם, שנאמר "וכל בניך למודי ה' ורב שלום בניך" (ישעיהו נד, יג), אל תקרי בניך אלא בוניך. "שלום רב לאהבי תורתך ואין למו מכשול" (תהלים קיט, קסה), "יהי שלום בחילך שלוה בארמנותיך; למען אחי ורעי אדברה נא שלום בך; למען בית ה' אלהינו אבקשה טוב לך" (תהלים קכב, ז-ט), "ה' עז לעמו יתן ה' יברך את עמו בשלום" (תהלים כט, יא).

186. בבלי, קידושין ל, ב

ואומר "אשרי הגבר אשר מלא את אשפתו מהם לא יבושו כי ידברו את אויבים בשער" (תהלים קכז, ה). מאי "את אויבים בשער"? אמר רבי חייא בר אבא: אפילו האב ובנו, הרב ותלמידו, שעוסקין בתורה בשער אחד, נעשים אויבים זה את זה ואינם זזים משם עד שנעשים אוהבים זה את זה, שנאמר "את והב בסופה" (במדבר כא, יד), אל תקרי "בסופה" אלא "בסופה".

187. דרך ארץ זוטא ט, כה

וכן היה רבי אלעזר הקפר אומר: אהוב את השלום ושנוא את המחלוקת. גדול השלום, שאפילו עובדין עבודה זרה ויש שלום ביניהן, כביכול אין שכינה יכולה לנגוע בהן, שנאמר "חבור עצבים אפרים הנח לו" (הושע ד, יז). אם יש ביניהן מחלוקת, מה נאמר בהן? "חלק לבם עתה יאשמו" (שם י, ב). הא כיצד? בית שיש בו מחלוקת סופו ליחרב. וחכמים אומרים מחלוקת

בבית הכנסת סופה להתגזר. שני תלמידי חכמים הדרים בעיר אחת והם בתי דינין וביניהן מחלוקת, סופן למות. אבא שאול אומר: מחלוקת בתי דינין חורבן העולם.

188. שאילתות, קרח, שאילתא קלא

שאילתא. דאסיר להון לדבית ישראל למיעבד פלוגתא, דכיון דקיימי בפלוגתא אתו למיסנא אהדדי, ואמר רחמנא ״לא תשנא את אחיך בלבבך״ (ויקרא יט, יז). ולא מיבעיא דזוטר בעי למיכף לרבה, אלא אפילו רבה מיבעי ליה למיכף לזוטא, דלא תהוי פלוגתא, דכתיב ״ויקם משה וילך אל דתן ואבירם״ וגו' (במדבר טז, כה), ואמר ריש לקיש: מיכן שאין מחזיקין במחלוקת. ואמר רב יהודה אמר רב: כל המחזיק במחלוקת עובר בלאו, דכתיב ״ולא יהיה כקרח וכעדתו״ (במדבר יז, ה). רב אסי אמר: מיצטרע, כתיב הכא ״לי״ (שם) וכתיב התם ״ויאמר ה' לו עוד הבא נא ידך״ וגו' (שמות ד, ו). אמר ר' חמא בר חנינא: כל העושה מריבה עם רבו כעושה עם השכינה, דכתיב ״המה מי מריבה אשר רבו בני ישראל את ה'״ (במדבר כ, יג), וכי עם השכינה עשו מריבה? והלא עם משה עשו מריבה, שנאמר ״וירב העם עם משה״ (שם שם, ג)! אלא למדנו: כל העושה מריבה עם רבו כאילו עושה מריבה עם השכינה. אמר רב חנינא בר פפא: כל המתרעם על רבו כמתרעם על השכינה, שנאמר ״לא עלינו תלונותיכם כי עם על ה'״ (שמות טז, ח). אמר רבי אבהו: כל המהרהר אחר רבו כמהרהר אחר השכינה, שנאמר ״וידבר העם באלהים ובמשה״ (במדבר כא, ה). ואמר רב חסדא: כל החולק על רבו כחולק על השכינה, שנאמר ״בהצותם על ה'״ (במדבר כו, ט).

189. כד הקמח, ערך 'שנאת חינם'

שנאת חנם הוא חלוק הלבבות, שדעות בני אדם משתנים זה מזה ואינן מסכימין לדעת אחת, וכל אחד ואחד יש לו דעת בפני עצמו, ואין לחבירו יתרון עליו, ואין אחד מהם מכיר ערך מי שהוא גדול ממנו אלא שרוצים להיות כלם ראשים, ובכן דעותיהם ולבותיהם חלוקים, ואין השכינה שורה בעם שלבו חלוק, שכן דרשו ז״ל (במדבר רבה טו, יד): ״ויהי בישרון מלך בהתאסף ראשי עם״ (דברים לג, ה), כלומר כשהיו אגודה אחת. ואמר הנביא: ״חלק לבם עתה יאשמו״ (הושע י, ב), פירשו אותו חלוק הלב. אין צריך לומר שמועיל התאחד הלב בעבודת השם יתברך, שאף בעבודה זרה מועיל, והוא שכתוב: ״חבור עצבים אפרים״ וגו' (הושע ד, יז), כי אע״פ שהיה מן הראוי

לטרדן מן העולם מפני שהם עובדי עצבים, כיון שהם חבורה אחת ודעת אחת, הנח לו, כלומר אאריך אפי להם.

סיבת השלום ועיקרו הוא הייחוד, וסיבת המחלוקת ועיקרו הוא הפירוד, כלומר חלוק רצון והשתנות דבר מדבר. ומזה תמצא במעשה בראשית ביום ראשון שירמוז על היחוד לא תמצא בו שום קטרוג ולא שום חלוקה ופירוד דבר מדבר, אבל ביום שני שהוא תחלת שנוי, שבו היתה החלוקה בין מים למים, משם התחיל המחלוקת ופירוד הרצון והשתנות הענינים. והמחלוקת היתה סבת כל מחלוקת וכל חלוק רצון בעליונים וכל חלוק לבבות בתחתונים, וזהו שלא נאמר בו ״כי טוב״, כי הטוב נעדר מפני המחלוקת.

והנה יום שני היה סבה לכל החולקים שנמשכו אחריו מכחו, ועל כן תמצא בכולם קטרוג ופירוד הרצון. ביום שלישי נאמר בו: ״תוצא הארץ עץ פרי עושה פרי״ (בראשית א, יא), והיא לא עשתה כן, אלא: ״עץ עושה פרי״. ביום רביעי קטרגה הלבנה, ביום חמישי הרג את הנקבה וסירס את הזכר, ביום ששי חטאו אדם וחוה וגורשו מגן עדן. ומי היה סבת הקטרוג ופירוד הרצון בכל הימים האלה? יום שני, שהבאים אחריו משכו מכחו והוא היה תחלה להם וסבה לקטרוג. והרי לך מדה זו של שנאת חנם, שהיא חלוק לבבות, נמשכת מן היום השני שלא נאמר בו ״כי טוב״.

וידוע כי בעון מדה זו חרב בית שני, שכן דרשו ז״ל (יומא ט, ב): בית ראשון מפני מה חרב? מפני עבודה זרה. בית שני שאנו בקיאין בהן שהיו חסידים ואנשי מעשה מפני מה חרב? מפני שנאת חנם. ואמרו במדרש איכה (איכה רבתי א, כא): ולא עוד אלא שהיו שמחים במפלתם אלו על אלו, שנאמר: ״כי רעתכי אז תעלוזי״ (ירמיה יא, טו), וכתיב: ״שמח לאיד לא ינקה״ (משלי יז, ה).

190. יערות דבש, חלק ב, דרוש ח

אמרו במשנה (אבות ה, יז): ״כל מחלוקת שהיא לשם שמים סופה להתקיים, ואיזו היא? זו מחלוקת הלל ושמאי, ומחלוקת שאינה לשם שמים, כגון מחלוקת קרח ועדתו, אין סופה להתקיים״... והנה יש לדייק באמרו ״איזו היא מחלוקת שהיא לשם שמים״, ומה שאלה? הרבה מחלוקות שהם לשם שמים! וגם קשה הדיוקים, דקאמר ״כגון מחלוקת שמאי והלל״, משמע הא זולת דוגמא הלזו אינה לשם שמים, ואחר כך קאמר ״שלא לשם שמים - מחלוקת קרח ועדתו״, משמע זולת זה הכל לשם שמים, וקשיא אהדדי.

אבל בעוונותינו הרבים, כל מחלוקת, תהיה מה שתהיה, היצר הרע מפתה ואומר שהיא לשם שמים ולמצוה גדולה, להכניע בוגדים ולשבר זרוע רמה, וכהנה דברים רבים. כללו של דבר, אין לך מחלוקת שאין יצר הרע מפתהו

411

ואומר שכל הכוונה לשם שמים, וחס ושלום לומר על מחלוקת שהיא לא לשם שמים. רק אם כן במה יודע אפוא אם היא באמת לשם שמים או לא? בזאת יודע: אי המחולקים ובעלי ריבות, זולת הדבר שחלקו בו ומנגדים זה לזה, הם אוהבים גמורים בלב ונפש, זהו אות שמחלוקתם לשם שמים, אבל אם אויבים ונוטרים שנאה זה לזה על ידי מחלוקת, זהו שלא לשם שמים, ויתיצב השטן בתוכם. וזה הסימן מסרו לנו חכמי המשנה: "איזו היא מחלוקת שהיא לשם שמים", כי בכל מחלוקת אומרים שהיא לשם שמים, אמרו "כמחלוקת שמאי והלל", שאהבו זה את זה וכבדו זה את זה, הנאהבים ונעימים, זהו אות שמחלוקתם לשם שמים. אבל כמחלוקת קרח ועדתו, שהיו נוטרים איבה ושנאה וכמעט יסקלוהו למשה וכדומה, זו היא שלא לשם שמים, כי למעלה אהבה ואיש אל אחותו, וזהו לאות בכל מחלוקת להבין אם היא לשם שמים או לאו.

191. חידושי אגדות מהר"ם שיק, אבות ה, יז

כל מחלוקת שהיא לשם שמים וכו'. נראה הכוונה שלפעמים החיוב עלינו לעשות מחלוקת, דהיינו אם רואה אם שאחד אומר על טרפה כשר, אל תאמר: "מה לי לאמור לו ולעשות מחלוקת, דילמא באמת הדין עם המורה, ולמה לי לעשות מחלוקת? וגדול השלום", את זה אסור לאמר אלא מחויב לחלוק עליו ולאמר שהוא טרפה לדעתו. ואפשר באמת להמורה טעם נכון להוראתו ישמע טעמו ויקבל האמת. ויש שחולק על חברו או על מורה בעירו רק להראות כחו ועוצם ידו להתפאר על המורה נגד בני אדם שהוא יודע הדין טוב מהמורה, וזו עברה גדולה, שהוא אינו רוצה האמת כלל ועושה מחלוקת ומפיר שלום רק להראות לכולם כחו ועוצם ידו חריפתו טובו שכלו ותבונתו. וכן נמי אנו מצווין לחלוק מן הרשעים בגופנו ובמעשנו גם כן מצד האמת ודיני תורה כדי שלא יפסד האמת והתורה, כמו שהסכימו הרבנים הגדולים, שאם רואים שהעומדים בראשם הם רשעים צריכים להפרד מהם. כמו דכתיב בזכריה (ח, יט) "האמת והשלום אהבו", ונקט תחלה האמת ואחר כך השלום, כי האמת הוא התורה שאין אמת רק מה שאומרת התורה, והתורה היא עמוד שהעולם עומד עליו, והשלום הוא רק קיום העולם, תחלה צריך להיות חזק העמוד ואחר כך יש לקיימו, אבל אם אין כאן עמוד על מה שנשען עליו ממילא אינו יכול להתקיים, ולכן תחלה צריך להיות האמת ואחר כך השלום. ועבור האמת לא די שרשאים לעשות מחלוקת אלא אדרבה מחויבים אנו לעשות מחלוקת, כי על ידי שעושה מחלוקת עבור

האמת ומחזיק עמוד העולם ממילא עושה גם קיום העולם, ואם כן בזה המחלוקת עושה מה שהשלום עושה.

וזה נראה כונת תנא דמשנתנו שאמר "איזו היא מחלוקת שהיא לשם שמים", רוצה לומר שצריך להבין ולשאול איזו היא מחלוקת שהיא לשם שמים סופה להתקיים, היינו בסוף בא לקיים העולם כיון שהמחלוקת היא עבור התורה, ומחלוקת הלל ושמאי לשם שמים היתה ולהעמיד האמת. ושאינה לשם שמים אין סופה עומד לקיים העולם, אלא אדרבא על ידי הפרת שלום מפיר קיום העולם שעל השלום העולם קיים. ולפעמים עושים מחלוקת עוד כדי לחשוך האמת כדי שבני האדם שהולכים בדרך הישר ורוצים האמת יראו לעשות כחפצם, ועושים מחלוקת שלא יהיו יכולים לעשות כחפצם. וזה בודאי עברה כפולה היא, שלא די שמפירים השלום שהוא קיום העולם מפירים גם את האמת שהוא עמוד גדול לקיום העולם. והשקר אין לו רגלים ובסוף אמת מארץ תצמח ויבינו כל הרשעים עם מי היה האמת, ושכל כונת הרבנים שהסכימו על הפירוד היא לטובת הרשעים שישובו מדרכם וישמרו גם הם האמת היינו התורה כי היא האמת הנצחיי, וה' יתן שהשקר יתאבד מן העולם והאמת מארץ יצמח. אמן.

192. פרי צדיק, ספר במדבר, פרשת קרח, ה

בזוהר הקדוש (קרח, קעו ע"ב): "כד ברא קוב"ה עלמא לא יכול לאתקיימא עד דאתא ושרא עלייהו שלום, ומאי הוא? שבת, דאיהו שלמא דעלאי ותתאי, וכדין אתקיים עלמא" וכו'... ואמר עוד בזוהר הקדוש (שם): "צלפחד פליג על שבת דהוה מקושש עצים" וכו'. והיינו כמו שאמר בזוהר הקדוש (שלח קנז ע"א): "יהו"ה דייק על אילין אילנין הי מיניהו רב על אחרא וכו' תא חזי שני אילנין וכו' בדא חיין בדא מותא" וכו'. והיינו דתורה שבכתב נקרא "עץ חיים", וכמו שאמר בריש תנא דבי אליהו על עץ חיים דגן עדן: "ואין עץ חיים אלא תורה" וכו', ואלמלא חטאו ישראל לא ניתן להם אלא חמשה חומשי תורה וכו', כמו שאמרו (נדרים כב, ב), והיה די בזה לבד והיו יודעין הכל מתורה שבכתב, וכמו שיהיה לעתיד דכתיב: "ולא ילמדו עוד איש את רעהו וגו' כי כולם ידעו אותי" וכו' (ירמיה לא, לג). אבל התורה שבעל פה יש בה מסטרא דעץ הדעת טוב ורע דאיהו איסור והיתר וכו', וכמו שאמר בזוהר הקדוש (רעיא מהימנא, בהעלותך קנג ע"א), ויש בהם מ"ט פנים טהור ומ"ט פנים טמא, וזהו מחלוקת, אבל הוא לתיקונו של עולם. ואמר צלפחד דאפשר ד"עץ הדעת טוב ורע" מעולה מ"עץ החיים" כיון שמוציא אור מתוך החושך

דייקא, שהוא הרוב חכמה לתקן הרוב כעס, וזה שאמר דהוה פליג על שבת שהוא שלום.

ואמר אחר כך (זהר, קרח, שם): "אורייתא הוא שלום, דכתיב ׳וכל נתיבותיה שלום׳ (משלי ג, יז)". שכן כתיב "ויחן שם ישראל נגד ההר" (שמות יט, ב), כאיש אחד בלב אחד (כמו שדרשו במכילתא), ואז זכו למתן תורה שבכתב. ואף בתורה שבעל פה שיש בה מחלוקת, הוא לתיקונו של עולם ושלום בסופו, כמו שנאמר "ואת והב בסופה" כמו שאמרו (קידושין ל, ב): "אפילו האב ובנו וכו׳ נעשים אויבים זה את זה ואינם זזים משם עד שנעשין אוהבים זה את זה" וכו׳.

ואמר בזוהר הקדוש למעלה (קעו ע"א): "דקרח אזיל במחלוקת וכו׳ מחלוקת פלוגתא דשלום׳ וכו׳, שהוא טעה ואמר שלא יזיק המחלוקת, והיה סובר שהוא מכוין רק לשם שמים מפני שאין נראה בעיניו הנהגת רעהו וחולק עליו, לא יזיק בזה המחלוקת. ובאמת "אמת ושלום חד הוא" (ספר הבהיר), ד"אמת ושלום קשיר דא בדא" (זהר חדש ג, יב ע"ב) שאי אפשר להיות אמת רק כשיש שלום. ובמחלוקת שמאי והלל שהיה באמת לשם שמים, אף בשעת מחלוקתם חיבה וריעות נוהגין זה בזה לקיים מה שנאמר (זכריה ח, יט) "האמת והשלום אהבו" (כמו שאמרו יבמות יד, ב). וכן נקראו התלמידי חכמים "חברים", שהם יש ביניהם ההתחברות באמת, וכמו מלאכים שנקראו חברים לפי שאין בהם איבה וקנאה ושנאה ותחרות (כמו שאמרו שיר השירים רבה ח, ט). אבל כשיש תרעומות בלב וכעס על חבירו הוא סימן שהוא מחלוקת שאינו לתיקונו של עולם אלא לערבובו. וזה היה טעות קרח, וחלק על אהרן שהיה אוהב שלום ורודף שלום אוהב את הבריות ומקרבן לתורה, והיינו שכוחו להכניס הדברי תורה בלב ישראל, שהוא עיקר תורה שבעל פה. וכמו שנאמר (מלאכי ב, ז) "כי שפתי כהן ישמרו דעת ותורה יבקשו מפיהו", ואורייתא הוא שלום.

193. עולת ראי"ה, חלק א, עמ׳ של

"אמר רבי אלעזר אמר רבי חנינא: תלמידי חכמים מרבים שלום בעולם, שנאמר יוכל בניך למודי ה׳ ורב שלום בניך׳ (ישעיה נד, יג), אל תקרי בניך אלא בוניך" (ברכות סד, א).

יש טועים שחושבים, שהשלום העולמי לא יבנה כי אם על ידי צביון אחד בדיעות ותכונות, ואם כן כשרואים תלמידי חכמים חוקרים בחכמה ודעת תורה, ועל ידי המחקר מתרבים הצדדים והשיטות, חושבים שבזה הם גורמים למחלוקת והפך השלום. ובאמת אינו כן, כי השלום האמיתי אי אפשר שיבוא לעולם כי אם דוקא על ידי הערך של רבוי השלום. הרבוי של

השלום הוא שיתראו כל הצדדים וכל השיטות, ויתבררו איך כולם יש להם
מקום, כל אחד לפי ערכו מקומו וענינו. ואדרבא, גם העניינים הנראים
כמיותרים או כסותרים, יראו כשמתגלה אמתת החכמה לכל צדדיה, שרק
על ידי קיבוץ כל החלקים וכל הפרטים וכל הדעות הנראות שונות וכל
המקצועות החלוקים, דוקא על ידם יראה אור האמת והצדק ודעת ה'
יראתו ואהבתו, ואור תורת אמת. על כן תלמידי חכמים מרבים שלום, כי
במה שהם מרחיבים ומבארים ומילדים דברי חכמה חדשים, בפנים מפנים
שונים, שיש בהם רבוי וחילוק עניינים, בזה הם מרבים שלום, שנאמר "וכל
בניך למודי ה'". כי כולם יכירו שכולם, גם ההפכים בדרכיהם ושיטותיהם
כפי הנראה, המה כולם למודי ה', ובכל אחת מהנה יש צד שתתגלה על ידו
ידיעת ה' ואור אמתו.

"ורב שלום בניך", לא אמר גודל שלום בניך, שהיה מורה על ציור גוף אחד
גדול, שאז היו הדברים מתאימים לאותו הרעיון המדומה שהשלום הוא
צריך דוקא לדברים אחדים ושיווי רעיונות, שזה באמת מגרע כח החכמה
והרחבת הדעת, כי אור הדעת צריך לצאת לכל צדדיו, לכל הפנים של אורה
שיש בו, אבל הרבוי הוא "רב שלום בניך", אל תקרי "בניך" אלא "בוניך", כי
הבנין יבנה מחלקים שונים, והאמת של אור העולם תבנה מצדדים שונים
ומשיטות שונות, שאלו ואלו דברי אלהים חיים, מדרכי עבודה והדרכה
וחנוך שונים, שכל אחד תופס מקומו וערכו. ואין לאבד כל כשרון ושלמות,
כי אם להרחיבו ולמצא לו מקום. ואם תראה סתירה ממושג למושג, בזה
תבנה החכמה ביתה. וצריך לעיין בדברים איך למצוא את החוק הפנימי
שבמושגים, שבזה יתישרו הדברים ולא יהיו סותרים זה את זה. ורבוי
הדעות שבא על ידי השתנות הנפשות והחנוכים, דוקא הוא הוא המעשיר את
החכמה והגורם הרחבתה, שלסוף יובנו כל הדברים כראוי ויוכר שאי אפשר
היה לבנין השלום שיבנה כי אם על ידי כל אותן ההשפעות הנראות כמנצחות
זו את זו.

"יהי שלום בחילך" (תהלים קכב, ז). החיל, מקום החיל או הכחות העובדים,
הם מתברכים בברכת שלום. ומהו שלומם? לא שיהיו כולם כח שוה, כי
דוקא על ידי רבוי הכחות והתנגדותם תמצא פעולת החיים, אלא שערך
ההבדל וההתנגדות נערך בערך מתאים, שכולם מובילים למטרה אחת, על
כן נמצא "שלוה בארמנותיך", במקום הדרוש שקט ושלוה, במרכז התכלית.

"למען אחי ורעי" (תהלים קכב, ח), שלכולם יהיה מקום לעבודה, עבודת שכל
ועבודת נטיה ורגש. "אדברה נא שלום בך", המצב של ההתאחדות הבא
מקיבוץ כחות ודעות נפזרות. "למען בית ה' אלקינו", התכלית הנרצית,

הנקודה שכולם עובדים בעבודה, "אבקשה טוב לך", הטוב הנאסף מתוך כלי השלום, שהוא מחזיק הברכה.

"ה' עוז לעמו יתן" (תהלים כט, יא), יתן להם חיים מלאים ענין שהוא העוז, וכשהחיים מלאים ענין מלאים הם צדדים רבים, ונבנים מהרכבות של כחות רבים על כן זאת היא ברכת השלום האמתית הבאה מהעוז. "ה' יברך את עמו בשלום". וברכת השלום הבאה עם העוז, היא השלום של התאחדות כל ההפכים, אבל צריך שימצאו הפכים כדי שיהיה מי שיעובד ומה שיתאחד, ואז הברכה ניכרת על ידי הכח של אלו ואלו דברי אלהים חיים. ועל כן שלום הוא שמו של הקב"ה, שהוא בעל הכחות כולם, הכל יכול וכוללם יחד, יהי שמו הגדול מבורך מן העולם עד העולם.

194. עין אי"ה, ברכות פרק ו, טז

"מעשה ברבן גמליאל והזקנים שהיו מסובים בעלייה ביריחו, והביאו לפניהם כותבות ואכלו, ונתן רבן גמליאל רשות לרבי עקיבא לברך. קפץ וברך רבי עקיבא ברכה אחת מעין שלש. אמר לו רבן גמליאל: עקיבא, עד מתי אתה מכניס ראשך בין המחלוקת? אמר לו: אף על פי שאתה אומר כך וחבירך אומרים כך, למדתנו רבינו: יחיד ורבים הלכה כרבים (בבלי, ברכות לז, א).

יסוד ההכרעה בהלכות בנוי על פי האמת והשלום. לפעמים יכריע כח האמת ולפעמים יכריע כח השלום. ביאור הדבר, ודאי בכל מחלוקת וספק יש לחקור אחר האמת, אחר כל מי שהדעת והסברא והראיות נוטים לדבריו. אמנם כשכבר אין בידינו להכריע בראיות, אז יש על כל פנים צורך להכריע, ועל כן "אחרי רבים להטות" (שמות כג, ב), והיינו מפני השלום, שלא ירבו מחלוקת בישראל.

וזהו שאמר לו רבן גמליאל: "עד מתי אתה מכניס ראשך בין המחלוקת", כאילו הנך כדאי להכריע דברי מי נראים יותר. אמר לו שלא בא לידי מדה זו, כי אם בחר בנטיה אחרי רבים לא מצד ידיעתו שהם צדקו יותר, כי אם שאהבת השלום שהוא יסודו של עולם דורש כך. אם כן זה כלל הכנסת הראש, שהוא השכל שלו, בין המחלוקת באופן שיראה כמבטל שכל רבו, כי אם גם יהיו הדברים לעצמם מאומתים כדעת רבו ראוי להניח הכרעתו מפני השלום.

ויש לומר דמשום הכי לא אמר "אחרי רבים להטות" כלשון הכתוב. כי בזה יש לומר כמו שאמרו המפרשים שהוא דוקא כשהם במעמד אחד. וטעם הדבר יש לומר דגם בטעמא דקרא יש לדון, אם הוא מפני שהדעת נותנת

שהרבים מסכימים לאמת או מפני שחובת השלום דורשת כך. וכשהם
במעמד אחד יש לומר דהרבים ודאי הסכימו לאמת שהרי שמעו כל דברי
החולקים, אבל שלא במעמד אחד יש לומר אילו היו שומעים טענות
החולקים היו חוזרים בהם. ויש לומר דהונח הלכה כרבים אפילו שלא
במעמד אחד, מפני השלום, שלא ירבו מחלוקת בישראל. ויש לומר דבזה
פליגי בית הלל ובית שמאי (בבלי, יבמות יד, א). דבית שמאי סברי דטעם אחרי
רבים להטות הוא מפני האמת, אם כן כשמחדדי טפי אין שייך להטות אחרי
רבים להטות, דהגדולים בחכמה יורדים יותר לעומק האמת. ובית הלל
סברי שיסוד אחרי רבים להטות הוא מפני השלום, על כן אין להביט כי אם
על המספר המורגש ולא על המעלות של החכמים, שמשקל הערכים עצמו
יכול להביא מחלוקת. על כל פנים שכשנקבע דבר זה, שיחיד ורבים הלכה
כרבים גם כן בלא מעמד אחד, הוא מפני השלום, ואין גנות בזה לסברת הרב
היחיד שנדחת.

195. שו"ת אגרות משה, אורח חיים ד, כה

ביאור שאלת משה "ואמרו לי מה שמו" (שמות ג, יג) ותשובת הקב"ה... כי
לכאורה לא מובן שעל בקשת משה "ואמרו לי מה שמו מה אמר אלהם"
השיב השם יתברך בשני מאמרות, מאמר ראשון "אהיה אשר אהיה"
ובמאמר שני בפסוק זה עצמו "כה תאמר לבני ישראל אהיה שלחני אליכם",
ויותר לא הוזכר שם זה בתורה...

וצריך לומר דהנה זה ודאי שאף שכל יחיד ויחיד בכל מקום שנמצא הוא
תחת השגחת השי"ת לפי מעשיו ועושה עמו כל הטובות שעושה עמו, אבל
ענין הגאולה לא היה זה רק ענין להטיב עמם להסיר מהם השעבוד וליתן
להם מכל הטוב, כי זה היה אפשר גם שיעשה השי"ת במצרים, שיתן דעה
בלב פרעה ושריו שמעתה יתחילו אדרבה לכבדם כמו שהיו מכובדים ולא
חסר להם כל דבר כל זמן שחי יוסף והשבטים ועוד יותר, אבל עיקר הגאולה
הבינו כבר כל ישראל שצריך להגאל מכל דרך האומות שמתנהגים רק לפי
תאוותיהם ומדותיהם הרעים, אלא בדרך אחר לגמרי שילמדם השי"ת כאשר
עשה תיכף בנתינת התורה, שלזה אי אפשר להיות מעורב עם האומות אלא
כאשר הבטיח השי"ת להאבות שנהיה לגוי אחד עובדי השי"ת ושומרי
תורתו בקדושה במקום המקודש והנבחר לזה שנתן להם כבר. שלכן תיכף
כשאמר למשה ששולח אותו להציל מיד מצרים ולהעלותם משם, אמר לו
תיכף שהוא להעלותו אל ארץ טובה ורחבה, לא להיות עם הכנעני, אלא אל
מקום הכנעני, שהוא עם ישראל בעצמם שישבו תחתם אחרי שיכחידום מן

העולם, ושם יהיו עם סגולה וממלכת כהנים וגוי קדוש, שזה תהיה גאולה אמיתית להתנהג בדרך התורה וקיום המצות בלא קנאה ושנאה ומלחמות וגזל וחמס, כעיקר התכלית שהבינו כל ישראל.

אבל הא צריך לידע, איך אפשר להיות זה? כי אף שכל ישראל יקבלו התורה והמצות, הרי בעניני התורה והמצות שייך שיהיה יותר חלוקי דעות מבכל עניני העולם הגשמי, שבעצם אין שם אלא דבר אחד שיהיה קיום חיות הגשמי כפי הצורך, שהוא בעצם שוה לכל אדם, שכל אחד הוא צריך ורוצה ליהנות באותן הנאות עצמן ואיכא בעולם כפי הצורך לכל, ובידיעה אחת שהשם יתברך הוא הזן ומפרנס לכל ומכין מזון לכל בריותיו לא שייך כלל שיהיה מחלוקת לא בין אדם לחבירו ולא בין האומות, וכל הפרוד והמחלוקות והשנאה והקנאה והגזל והחמס היא מחסרון אמונה בה' אלהים אמת. אבל בעניני התורה והמצות הוא דוקא על ידי האמונה הגדולה והרצון הגדול שיש לכל אחד ואחד מישראל לידע ולהבין האמת, ולא רק בעצמו, אלא שגם ילמד לאחרים ולהשפיע עליהם שגם הם ידעו האמת ולעשות כרצון השם יתברך בתורה הקדושה, הא כמעט אי אפשר שיהיו כולם בשיטה אחת ובדעה אחת, שממילא יש לחוש שאף שלא יהיה להם חסרון אמונה חס ושלום ולא יהיה מחלוקת בשביל תאוות הגשמיות לגזול ולחמוס ולעשות מלחמות כפי שיש אצל האומות, הא יש לחוש שיהיה מחלוקת בדיני התורה איך לקיימם ויהיו חבורות פרודות, כל רב גדול ותלמידיו לבד, וכדחזינן בכל הש"ס שאיכא כמעט בכל דיני התורה כמה פלוגתא דרבוותא, וכן בכל זמן וזמן.

וזה כוונת השאלה שאמר משה שיאמרו לי "מה שמו" (שמות ג, יג). עיין ברמב"ן ואור החיים שעמדו בזה, כי לא יתכן שיהיה כלל שאלה בזאת... אבל שאלתם "מה שמו" הוא ביחוד על ענין שליחות גאולה זו, איך שתתקיים שתהיה גאולה זו גאולה אמיתית של שלום ושלוה אחוה ורעות.

והשיבו השם יתברך : "אהיה שלחני אליכם", היינו שהשם יתברך יהיה עם כל המתעסקים בתורה שירצו לדעת האמת, ולא איכפת כל צד בנצוח אלא בידיעת האמת, כמפורש ביבמות (יד, ב) בברייתא על מחלוקת בית שמאי ובית הלל : "ללמדך שחיבה וריעות נוהגים זה בזה מה שנאמר 'האמת ושלום אהבו' (זכריה ח, יט)", דאדרבה זה מרבה אהבה ושלום וחבה וריעות, וכמו שדרשו על הקרא "את והב בסופה" בקידושין (ל, ב) : "אמר רבי חייא ב"ר אבא : אפילו האב ובנו הרב ותלמידו שעוסקים בתורה בשער אחד נעשים אויבים זה לזה ואינם זזים משם עד שנעשים אוהבים זה את זה". וזהו האמירה השניה שאמר השם יתברך למשה שיאמר זה לבני ישראל.

אבל איכא עוד ענין גדול, שאף בתחלה השני דעות, ולפעמים עוד יותר, הם דברי תורה ממש, כהא דאיתא בערובין (יג, ב) על מחלוקת בית שמאי ובית הלל: "יצאה בת קול ואמרה אלו ואלו דברי אלהים חיים הן והלכה כבית הלל", הרי אף שהלכה כבית הלל, מכל מקום גם דעת בית שמאי הם דברי אלהים חיים. ומטעם זה פשוט על מי שקם בבקר ויודע שבהזמן שעד התפלה ילמוד רק דברי בית שמאי ולבאר דבריהם, צריך לברך ברכת התורה משום שהם כן דברי תורה ממש ותורת אמת, וכן הוא בכל המחלוקת שבמשנתין ובריתות ובשני התלמודים בבלי וירושלמי ואף דברי הגאונים, ואף בגדולים דבזמננו שייך זה שבחזקה דלומדים לשמה. וזה אמירה הראשונה "אהיה אשר אהיה", שבית שמאי ידעי ש"אהיה" הוא גם עם בית הלל, ובית הלל ידעי ד"אהיה" הוא גם עם בית שמאי, דלכן שנו בית הלל גם דברי בית שמאי, וברור שבית שמאי שנו גם דברי בית הלל אף בקביעות, אך החלוק היה מה שבית הלל היו מקדימין בלמודם דברי בית שמאי לדבריהן כמו שבית שמאי הקדימו. ואמירה ראשונה אמר רק למשה, שסתם אינשי לא יבינו דבר כזה ויהיה נדמה שהוא ענין סתירה שאי אפשר להיות כלפי שמיא, אבל למשה אמר השם יתברך שימסור זה ליהושע ולכל הגדולי תורה עד לעולם, שדבריו שניהם הם דברי אלהים חיים, שנמצא שגם מתחלה הוא אהבה ואחוה ורעות ולא היו אף לרגע כאויבים זה לזה ובעצם איכא תרוייהו, דכשלומד אב ובנו רב ותלמידו כשהאחד גדול הרבה מחברו כועס לפעמים האב על הבן והרב על תלמידו, אבל לבסוף שרואה שגם דעת הבן וגם דעת התלמיד הם דברים נכונים ובאים להשואה, ואף כשנשאר במחלוקתן, אבל האב והרבה גדולים הכירו שדעת הבן ותלמיד ראוי גם כן להאמר, נעשו אוהבים זה לזה כמו כן גדולי תורה גם מתחלתן היו באותה אהבה אף שחלוקין בדעותיהן.

196. תוספתא, סנהדרין ז, א

אמר רבי יוסי: בראשונה לא היו מחלוקות בישראל אלא בבית דין של שבעים בלשכת הגזית, ושאר בתי דינין של עשרים ושלשה היו בעיירות של ארץ ישראל, ושאר בתי דינין של שלשה שלשה היו בירושלם אחד בהר הבית ואחד בחיל. נצרך אחד מהן הלכה, הולך לבית דין שבעירו. אין בית דין בעירו, הולך לבית דין הסמוך לעירו. אם שמעו אמרו לו, אם לאו הוא ומופלא שבהם באין לבית דין שבהר הבית. אם שמעו אמרו להן, ואם לאו הן ומופלא שבהן באין לבית דין שבחיל. אם שמעו אמרו להן, ואם לאו אילו ואילו הולכין לבית דין הגדול שבלשכת הגזית. בית דין שבלשכת הגזית, אף

על פי שהוא של שבעים ואחד אין פחות מעשרים ושלשה. נצרך אחד מהם לצאת רואה אם יש שם עשרים ושלשה יוצא, ואם לאו לא יצא עד שיהו שם עשרים ושלשה. ושם היו יושבין מתמיד של שחר ועד תמיד של בין הערבים. בשבתות ובימים טובים לא היו נכנסין אלא בבית המדרש שבהר הבית. נשאלה שאילה, אם שמעו אמרו להם, ואם לאו עומדין למנין. רבו המטמאין טימאו, רבו המטהרין טהרו. משם היה יוצאת הלכה ורווחת בישראל. משרבו תלמידי שמאי והילל שלא שימשו כל צורכן הרבו מחלוקות בישראל.

197. ירושלמי, חגיגה פרק ב, ב (עז, 4)

בראשונה לא היתה מחלוקת בישראל אלא על הסמיכה בלבד, ועמדו שמאי והלל ועשו אותן ארבע. משרבו תלמידי בית שמאי ותלמידי בית הלל ולא שמשו את רביהן כל צורכן ורבו המחלוקות בישראל ונחלקו לשתי כתות, אילו מטמאין ואילו מטהרין, ועוד אינה עתידה לחזור למקומה עד שיבוא בן דוד.

198. בבלי, סוטה מז, ב

משרבו זחוחי הלב, רבו מחלוקת בישראל. משרבו תלמידי שמאי והילל שלא שימשו כל צורכן, רבו מחלוקת בישראל ונעשית תורה כשתי תורות.

199. בבלי, תמורה טו, ב - טז, א

תנן התם (משנה, סוטה ט, ט): "משמת יוסף בן יועזר איש צרידה ויוסף בן יוחנן איש ירושלים בטלו האשכולות", איש שהכל בו. ואמר רב יהודה אמר שמואל: "כל אשכולות שעמדו להן לישראל מימות משה עד שמת יוסף בן יועזר היו למדין תורה כמשה רבינו, מכאן ואילך לא היו למדין תורה כמשה רבינו". והאמר רב יהודה אמר שמואל: "שלשת אלפים הלכות נשתכחו בימי אבלו של משה"? דאישתכח להו אישתכח, ודגמירין להו הוו גמירי כמשה רבינו. והא תניא: "משמת משה אם רבו מטמאין טמאו אם רבו טהורין טיהרו"? ליבא דאימעיט, מיגמר הוו גמירי להו כמשה רבינו.

במתניתא תנא: "כל אשכולות שעמדו לישראל מימות משה עד שמת יוסף בן יועזר איש צרידה לא היה בהם שום דופי, מכאן ואילך היה בהן שום דופי". והתניא: "מעשה בחסיד אחד שהיה גונח מלבו, ושאלו לרופאים ואמרו אין לו תקנה עד שיינק חלב רותח שחרית, והביאו עז וקשרו לו בכרעי מיטתו, והיה יונק ממנה חלב. למחר נכנסו חביריו לבקרו, כיון שראו העז

אמרו: ליסטים מזויין בתוך ביתו, ואנו נכנסים לבקרו? ישבו ובדקו ולא
מצאו בו עוֹן אלא של אותה העז בלבד. ואף הוא בשעת מיתתו אמר: יודע
אני בעצמי שאין בי עוֹן, אלא של אותה העז בלבד, שעברתי על דברי חבירי,
שהרי אמרו חכמים: אין מגדלין בהמה דקה בארץ ישראלי. וקיימא לן: כל
היכא דאמר ״מעשה בחסיד אחד״ - או ר׳ יהודה בן בבא או ר׳ יהודה בר
אילעאי, ורבנן בתר יוסף בן יועזר איש צרידה דרי דרי הווי?! אמר רב יוסף:
״דופי של סמיכה קתני״. והא יוסף בן יועזר גופיה פליג בסמיכה? כי
אפליג בה בסוף שניה, דבצר ליבא.

גופא. ״אמר רב יהודה אמר שמואל: שלשת אלפים הלכות נשתכחו בימי
אבלו של משה. אמרו לו ליהושע: שאל. אמר להם: ׳לא בשמים היא׳ (דברים
ל, יב). אמרו לו לשמואל: שאל. אמר להם: ׳אלה המצות׳ (ויקרא כז, לד), שאין
הנביא רשאי לחדש דבר מעתה״. אמר ר׳ יצחק נפחא: ״אף חטאת שמתו
בעליה נשתכחה בימי אבלו של משה״. ״אמרו לפנחס: שאל. אמר להם: ׳לא
בשמים היא׳. אמר לו לאלעזר: שאל. אמר להם: ׳אלה המצות׳, שאין נביא
רשאי לחדש דבר מעתה״.

אמר רב יהודה אמר רב: ״בשעה שנפטר משה רבינו לגן עדן אמר לו
ליהושע: שאל ממני כל ספיקות שיש לך. אמר לו: רבי, כלום הנחתיך שעה
אחת והלכתי למקום אחר? לא כך כתבת בי ׳ומשרתו יהושע בן נון נער לא
ימוש מתוך האהל׳ (שמות לג, יא)? מיד תשש כחו של יהושע ונשתכחו ממנו
שלש מאות הלכות ונולדו לו שבע מאות ספיקות, ועמדו כל ישראל להרגו.
אמר לו הקב״ה: לומר לך אי אפשר, לך וטורדן במלחמה. שנאמר ׳ויהי
אחרי מות משה עבד ה׳ ויאמר ה׳ ׳ וגו׳ (יהושע א, א)״.

במתניתין תנא: אלף ושבע מאות קלין וחמורין וגזירות שוות ודקדוקי
סופרים נשתכחו בימי אבלו של משה. אמר רבי אבהו: אף על פי כן החזירן
עתניאל בן קנז מתוך פלפולו, שנאמר ״וילכדה עתניאל בן קנז אחי כלב״
(יהושע טו, יז).

200. שמות רבה, פרשה כח, ו

״וידבר אלהים את כל הדברים האלה לאמר״ (שמות כ, א), אמר רבי יצחק:
מה שהנביאים עתידים להתנבאות בכל דור ודור קבלו מהר סיני, שכן משה
אומר להם לישראל: ״כי את אשר ישנו פה עמנו עומד היום ואת אשר איננו
פה עמנו היום״ (דברים כט, יד), ׳עמנו עומד היום׳ אין כתיב כאן, אלא ״עמנו
היום״, אלו הנשמות העתידות להבראות שאין בהם ממש שלא נאמרה בהם
עמידה, שאף על פי שלא היו באותה שעה כל אחד ואחד קבל את שלו.

וכן הוא אומר "משא דבר ה' אל ישראל ביד מלאכי" (מלאכי א, א), 'בימי מלאכי' לא נאמר, אלא "ביד מלאכי", שכבר היתה הנבואה בידו מהר סיני, ועד אותה שעה לא נתנה לו רשות להתנבאות.

וכן ישעיה אמר: "מעת היותה שם אני" (ישעיה מח, טז), אמר ישעיה: מיום שנתנה תורה בסיני שם הייתי וקבלתי את הנבואה הזאת, אלא "ועתה אלהים שלחני ורוחו" (שם), עד עכשיו לא ניתן לו רשות להתנבאות. ולא כל הנביאים בלבד קבלו מסיני נבואתן, אלא אף החכמים העומדים בכל דור ודור - כל אחד ואחד קבל את שלו מסיני.

וכן הוא אומר: "את הדברים האלה דבר ה' אל כל קהלכם, קול גדול ולא יסף" (דברים ה, יט), רבי יוחנן אמר: קול אחד נחלק לשבעה קולות והם נחלקים לשבעים לשון. רבי שמעון בן לקיש אמר: שממנו נתנבאו כל הנביאים שעמדו.

201. אמונות ודעות, הקדמה (עמ' י)

ואמרו חכמי ישראל במי שלא השלים עניני החכמה: משרבו תלמידי שמאי והלל שלא שמשו כל צרכן רבתה מחלוקת (סוטה מז, ב). למדונו דבריהם אלה, שאם התלמידים השלימו למודיהם לא תהא ביניהם מחלוקת ולא ויכוחים. ולכן אל יפנה הסכל קצר הרוח הרות את חטאו כלפי הבורא יתרומם ויתהדר לומר שהוא אשר הציב לו את הספקות, אלא סכלותו או קוצר רוחו הפילוהו בהם, כמו שבארנו. כי לא יתכן שתהא פעולה חד פעמית מפעולותיו תסלק ממנו את הספקות, כי אז היה יוצא מחוק הנבראים והוא נברא. ומי שלא הטיל בזה את חטאו על אלוהיו, אלא רצה שישימהו ה' יודע מדע שאין בו ספקות, הרי אין בקשתו זו אלא שיעשהו אלוהיו כיוצא בו, כי היודע בלי סבה הוא בורא הכל יתברך ויתקדש, וכפי שנתבאר לקמן, אבל כל הנבראים לא תתכן ידיעתם אלא על ידי סבה והיא הלמוד והעיון, אשר לכך דרוש זמן כמו שבארנו, והרי הם מן הרגע הראשון של אותו הזמן עד סופו בספקות כפי שפירשנו. אבל המשובחים הם הממתינים עד אשר יזקקו את הכסף מן הסיגים, כאמרו "הגו סיגים מכסף ויצא לצורף כלי" (משלי כה, ד), ועד אשר יחבצו את המלאכה ויוציאו חמאתה, כאמרו "כי מיץ חלב יוציא חמאה ומיץ אף יוציא דם" (משלי ל, לג), ועד אשר תצמח זריעתם ואז יקצרוהו, כאמרו "זרעו לכם לצדקה קצרו לפי חסד" (הושע י, יב), ועד אשר יבשיל פרים באילנם ויכשר למזון, כאמרו "עץ חיים היא למחזיקים בה" (משלי ג, יח).

202. פירושי רב סעדיה גאון לבראשית, פתיחה (עמ' 187-188)

ואם ישאל אדם: כיצד נכנסו לתוך המשנה והתלמוד מחלוקות בין בעלי הקבלה? נאמר: אין אלה מחלוקות באמת, אלא נראות כמחלוקת בתחילת הגעת הדברים לשומע, ולאמיתו של דבר [המחלוקות שבתלמוד] הן משלושה סוגים:

א. חכם הראה את עצמו כחולק על חברו והקניטו כדי שיוודע לו על ידי כך טיב דעתו [של חברו], וכמו שהראה משה את עצמו ככועס על אהרן ובניו ששרפו את שעיר החטאת (ויקרא י, טז), כדי שיגלו לו את דעתם הם, כי משה לא האמין ששרפו [את שעיר החטאת] מחסרון ידיעה.

ב. הדבר נשמע מפי הנביא בשני אופנים שונים: באופן אחד הוא מותר ובשני אסור. וקדם אחד מן החכמים והזכיר את האופן המותר ובא השני והזכיר את האסור. ודברי שניהם צודקים, כי הדבר ההוא אמנם מותר באופן אחד ואסור באופן אחר. ודוגמה לזה מה שאמר הכתוב "לא תשחית את עצה" (דברים כ, יט) ואמר "רק עץ אשר תדע" וגו' (שם שם, כ). ואמר "בת כהן כי תהיה לאיש זר לא תאכל" (ויקרא כב, יב) ואחרי כן נאמר "ובת כהן כי תהיה אלמנה וגרושה אביה תאכל" (שם שם, יג). ואין הבדל [בין המקרים] שבהם הכתוב מכריע בין שני הפסוקים המקבילים קרוב אליהם, ובין המקרים שהוא רחוק מהם מרחק פסוקים ומתברר אחר כך.

ג. אחד מן החכמים שמע דבר חלקי ודימה בנפשו שהוא שלם, ואחרים שמעו סופו של דבר, וכשהזכיר הראשון מה שעלה על דעתו טענו נגדו ואמרו: אנו שמענו סופו של דבר והוא מצמצם את שמועתך אתה. ודוגמה לכך, אדם קורא בחומש השלישי שבתורה "ובגד כלאים שעטנז" (ויקרא יט, יט) והוא סובר שזה כולל הכל, וכשהוא אומר דבר זה לפני מי שקרא את כל התורה, הלה מודיעו שהכתוב צמצם את הכלל בחלק החמישי ועשאו פרט כאמור "צמר ופשתים" (דברים כב, יא), וכן כל כיוצא בזה.

203. מבוא התלמוד לרב שמואל בן חפני גאון, הקדמה

אבל המחלוקת בתורה שבעל פה, לפעמים באה המחלוקת לשני פנים אחד לשלילה ואחד לחיוב, שהאחד שמע באופן מסוים והשני באופן אחר, ואין שם סתירה כיון שהם על שני פנים, וזה כגון אמרם (בבא בתרא מו, ב): "אמר שמואל: אריס מעיד". ואמרו: "והתניא: אינו מעיד?" ותירצו שזה שאמר אריס מעיד אם לא היה בשדה שהוא בה פירות, ומה שאמר אינו מעיד אם היה בה פירות והוא אריס בה, ובזה ישבו שתי השמועות, והוא אמרם: "לא קשיא, הא דאיכא פירי בארעא הא דליכא פירי בארעא".

ויש ששתי השמועות אחת לשבח ואחת לגנאי והם בפנים שונים, כגון אמרם
(ברכות מו, ב): "העונה אמן אחר ברכותיו הרי זה [משובח. והתניא: הרי זה]
מגונה?!" ותירצו שמשובח בבונה ירושלים, והמגונה אחרי המוציא וכיוצא
בה מברכות הדומות לה.

ופעמים נחלקים השומעים מפני ששניהם שמעו מרבם דבר אחד, ואחר כך
חזר בו הרב, וידע אחד מהם בחזרתו והשני לא ידע, כגון אמרם (ביצה כד, ב):
"אין צדין דגים וכו', מותרין למאי? רב אמר: מותרין לקבל. ולוי אמר:
מותרין באכילה. אמר רב: לעולם אל ימנע אדם עצמו מבית המדרש אפילו
שעה אחת, דהא אנא ולוי הוה יתבינן במדרשא קמיה דרבי כד אמרה להא
שמעתא, באורתא אמר מותרין באכילה, בצפרא הדר ביה ואמר מותרין
לקבל, אנא דהואי בי מדרשא הדרי בי ולוי דלא הוה בי מדרשא לא הדר
ביה".

ופעמים שומע אחד השומעים את הענין באופן כללי והשני שומע בפרט,
ונחלקים בפשט, כגון אמרם באופן כללי (משנה, עירובין ג, א): "בכל מערבין
ומשתתפין חוץ מן המים ומן המלח". ואמרו בפרט (בבלי שם כז, א): "והא
איכא כמהין ופטריות דלא מערבין בהו?!" ועל זה אמר רבי יוחנן: "אין
למדין מן הכללות ואפילו במקום שנאמר חוץ". וכן גם כן באמרם באופן
כללי (משנה, קידושין א, ז): "כל מצות עשה שהזמן גרמה - אנשים חייבין
ונשים פטורות", ואמרו עוד (שם): "כל מצות עשה שלא הזמן גרמה - אחד
אנשים ואחד נשים חייבין". ואמרו בפרט ארישא (בבלי שם לד, א): "והרי מצה
ושמחה והקהל דמצות עשה שהזמן גרמה ונשים חייבות?!" ואמרו בפרט
אסיפא: "והלא תלמוד תורה ופריה ורביה ופדיון הבן דמצות עשה שלא
הזמן גרמה ונשים פטורות?!"

ופעמים ישבו תלמידים לפני רבם, והיה בידו שמועה ממי שאין הלכה כמותו
והזכיר אותה שמועה בתוך איזה נושא ושמע השומע והבין מכלל דבריו שכך
הלכה, והשני שמע את ביאור הענין, ולפיכך באין לידי מחלוקת. וזה הוא
שאמר ר' יהודה (משנה, עדויות א, ו): "אם כן למה מזכירין דברי היחיד בין
המרובים? שאם יאמר אדם: כך אני מקובל, אומרים לו: כדברי איש פלוני
קיבלת".

204. מבוא התלמוד לרבי שמואל בן חפני גאון, פרק ה

והפרק החמישי הדיבור בסיבות שבגללן נפלו הסתירות במה שיש בין
המוסרים במשנה ובתלמוד בהן. ואומר שיש לזה עשר סיבות.

והסיבה הראשונה היא שהמסורת הגיעה בשני פנים מתחלפים, אחד מהם בשלילה והשני בחיוב, וימסור אחד מן המוסרים לפי פן ידוע וימסור האחר לפי הפן האחר, והרי אין ביניהם סתירה אם היו במעשה פנים שונים. וזה כאומרם (בבא בתרא מו, ב): "אמר שמואל: עריס מעיד". ואמר: "תניא: עריס אינו מעיד?" והיה אמרם: עריס מעיד אם לא יהא בשדה שהוא מעיד עליה פירות, ומה שאמר עריס אינו מעיד אם יהיו בה פירות והוא אריס בה. ובזה יישרו את שתי אלו המסורות בעניין, אמרו: "לא קשיא, הא דאיכא פירי בארעא והא דליכא פירי בארעא".

ויש שהגיעו שתי מסורות, אחת מהן משובחת והאחרת מגונה, באופנים מוחלפים. וזה כאומרם (ברכות מו, ב): "העונה אמן אחר ברכותיו הרי זה משובח", ואמרם: "העונה אמן אחר ברכותיו הרי זה מגונה". ויהיו המשובח מסודר בברכת בונה ירושלים והמגונה בשאר הברכות, לאומרם: "לא קשיא, הא בבונה ירושלים הא בשאר ברכות".

ויש שתסתתור מסורת המוסר האחד בשני פנים שונים, ואינם סותרים זה את זה, כמו שאמרו בתלמוד (בבא בתרא קמט, א): "איבעיא להו: מכר כל נכסיו, מהו למיחזר? אמר רב יהודה אמר רב אסי: עמד חוזר. וזימנין אמר רב יהודה אמר רב: אינו חוזר. ולא פליגי, הא דאיתנהו לזוזי בעיניהו הא דפרעינהו בחובו." וההשלמה בזה תנהג בדרך ההשלמה בין שני כתובים המכחישים זה את זה.

ואם יאמר האומר: אני אמנם אקבל במה שהזכרת שני כתובים המכחישים זה את זה, משום שאני יודע שהם [שניהם] נכונים, ולא [כן] במסורת המשנה והתלמוד ולנו לא... אל קבלת מסורות המשנה והתלמוד אלא אחר הידיעה שהן נכונות. ו[אמנם] כבר הזכרנו ההוכחה על זה במה שקדם, ובמה שהזכרנו ישתתק בו השואל בזה.

והסיבה השניה הוא, חילוף מסורת המוסרים [שלא] שמעו כל שתי [—] מסורת מיוחדת [—] האחר, וזה כאמרם (ביצה כד, ב): "למאי? אמר רב מותרין [לקבל, ולוי אמר: מותרין לא]כילה. אמר רב: לעולם לימנע (=לא ימנע) אדם עצמו אפילו שעה [אחת מבית] המדרש, דהא אנא ולוי הוה יתבינן בבי מדרשא [קמיה דרבי] כי אמרה להא שמעתא, באורתא אמר מותרין באכילה, [בצפרא] הדר ביה ואמר מותרין לקבל, אנא דהואי בבי מדראשא [הדרי בי], לוי דלא הוה בבי מדראשא לא הדר ביה".

והסיבה השלישית היא, שתהא מתחלפת מסורת המוסר מפני הפירוש, לא מפני הנוסח בזה. ויפרש אחד המוסרים... כפי מה שיפול לו (שנראה לו),

והוא כמו שאמר בתלמוד מי שמת (בבא בתרא קנה, ב): "איבעיא להו: תוך זמן כלפני זמן או כלאחר זמן? רבא אמר רב נחמן: תוך זמן כלפני זמן. רבה בר בר שילא אמר רב נחמן: תוך זמן [כלאחר ז]מן. והא דרבא לאו בפירוש איתמר אילא מכללא איתמר, [דההוא] תוך זמן דזבין ניכסיה ואתא לקמיה דרבא, אמר להו: לא עשה ולא כלום. מאן דחזיא סבר משום דתוך זמן כלפני זמן, ולא היא, שטיותא יתירתא חזא ביה רבא דהוה קא משחרר להו לעבדיה". ומשום כך יאמר אחד לחברו: "בפירוש שמיעא לך או מיכללא שמיעא לך?" והוא כמו כן שאמרו בתלמוד מי שהוציאוהו גוים (עירובין מו, א): "אמר ליה רבי זירא לרבי יעקב בר אידי: בפירוש שמיעא לך או מיכללא שמיעא לך? אמר ליה: בפירוש שמיעא ליי".

והסיבה הרביעית היא, שישמע אחד מן המוסרים את המסורת הכללית וישמע האחר את המסורת המיוחדת ויחלקו בפירוש בדבר זה. כמו שאמרו בענין עירוב (משנה, עירובין ג, א): "...בכל מערבין ומשתתפין חוץ מן המים ומן המלח". ואמרם ב[תלמוד] (שם כז, א): "והא איכא כמהין ופטריות דאין מערבין בהם?" ולזה אמרו: "אמר רבי יוחנן: אין למדין מן הכללות ואפילו במקום שנאמר בהן חוץ". וכמות שאמרו גם כן במסורת הכלל (משנה, קידושין א, ז): "כל מצות עשה שהזמן גרמה האנשים חייבים והנשים פטורות". ואמרו במיוחד (בבלי שם לד, א): "הרי מצה ושמחה והקהל דמצות עשה שהזמן גרמה ונשים חייבות?" ואמרם עוד (משנה, שם): "וכל מצות עשה שלא הזמן גרמה אחד אנשים ואחד נשים חייבין". ואמרו במיוחד (בבלי, שם): "הרי תלמוד תורה ופריה ורביה ופדיון הבן דמצות עשה שלא הזמן גרמה ונשים פטורות?".

והסיבה החמישית היא, שמקצת מן בעלי המסורת זכרו את המסורות ומקצתם שכחוה ויחשוב בה דבר שלא מן העניין. הלא תראה מה שאמרו (פסחים נב, ב): "רב ספרא אפיק גראבא דחמרא דשביעית, אלו בהדיה רב כהנא ורב [הונ]א [בר איק]א, אמר להו: מי שמיע לכו מירבי אבהו הלכה כר' שמעון בן אלעזר אילא? אמר ליה רב הונא בר איקא: הכי אמר רבי אבהו: אין הלכה כר' שמעון בן אלעזר. אמר רב ספרא נקוט דרב הונא בר איקא לידך, דדייק וגמר כי רחבא מפום בדיתא".

והסיבה השישית, שנשתבשו בפירוש השמועות שפירשו והיו מחולקים בפירושיהן ובענייניהן. הלא תראה מה שאמרו (עירובין נג, א): "אמר רב יהודה אמר רב: בני יהודה שהקפידו על לשונם נתקיימה תורתן בידן, בני גלילא שלא הקפידו על לשונם לא נתקיימה תורתן בידן". ומקשינן: "מידי בקפידא תליא מילתא? אמר רבינא: אינו (=אינהו) דקפדי מתותב בהו סימאנא

ומקימא בידייהו, בני יהודה דדיקי לישאנא נתקיימה תורתן בידן בני גלילא דלא דיקי לישאנא לא נתקיימה תורתן בידן". וגם הועיל מה שהיו מזכירים זה לזה, והוא כאמרם (שם): "בני יהודה דגלו מסכתא נתקיימה תורתן בידן, בני גלילא דלא גלו מסכתא לא נתקיימה תורתן בידן".

והסיבה השביעית, קצת ממוסרי השמועות היו שמים לב לשמועתם וזוכרים אותה, ומקצתם לא נתנו לבם עליה מחמת טרדה, וסברו בה שלא כמו שאמר המוסר. והוא כאמרם (שבועות כו, א): "רב כהנא ורב אסה כי הוה קימי מקמיה דרב, מר אמר: הכי אמר רב, ומר אמר: הכי אמר רב. כי הוה אתו לקמיה דרב הוה אמר כחד מינייהו. אמר ליה אידך: אנא שיקרא דאמרית? אמר ליה: אנת לבך אנסך".

והסיבה השמינית, מקצת מבעלי השמועה ראו את מוסר השמועה פנים אל פנים וירדו לסוף דעתו, אבל במי שלא ראה (את מוסר השמועה) לא היה הדבר כך. הלא תראה מה שאמר אחד מהם (יבמות טז, ב): "מעיד אני עלי שמים וארץ שעל מדוכה זו ישב חגי הנביא ואמר שלשה דברים, צרת הבת אסורה" וגו'. והכוונה בזה מה שאמרו (אבות א, א): "ונביאים מסרוה לאנשי כנסת הגדולה".

ואם יאמר אדם: הרי החולק עליכם בנוגע לאמתות המסורות של הרבניים בדברים שהוא אינו מודה בהם, תובע מכם הוכחה לאמתותה, וכיצד יאות לכם להביא ראיה (לאמתות המסורת שלכם) מהמסורת שלהם? והלא תודו שכל ראיה לדבר מאותו דבר עצמו היא נפסדת ובלתי נכונה! נאמר לו: אין אנו מסתייעים במסורותיהם לאימות מסורותיהם, אלא אנו מוכיחים את אמתותן בזה שהן נמסרות באופנים המחייבים את אמתותה, והיא היותן מסורות מפה לפה ברציפות, ועל ידי רבים, והשכל מחייב שהרבים אי אפשר שכולם ישקרו. ואם כן, הרי אין כאן הבאת ראיה לדבר מהדבר עצמו.

205. אגרת רב שרירא גאון, עמ' 8-11 (נוסח ספרדי)

והכי הויא מילתא דראשונים לא אתידעו שמהתהון, אלא שמותם של נשיאים ושל אבות בית דין בלבד, משום דלא הוה מחלוקת ביניהון, אלא כל טעמי דאורייתא הוו ידעין להון ידיעה ברורה, ותלמודא נמי הוו ידעי להון ידיעה ברורה והויות ודיקדוקים במשנתן על כל דבר ודבר...

וכמה דהוה בית המקדש קיים כל חד וחד מרבוותא הוה מגמר להו לתלמידי טעמי אוריתא ודמשנה ודתלמוד במילי דמחבר להון בשעתיה ומורי לתלמידייהו כי היכי דחזי, והות נפישת חכמה ולא הוו צריכין לטרחי אחריני. וההיא פלוגתא דסמיכה בלחוד היא דהות ביניהון. וכד אתו שמאי

427

והלל נמי בתלת מילי בלחוד הוא דאפליגו, דאמרינן (שבת יד, ב): אמר רב הונא בג' מקומות נחלקו שמאי והלל.

וכיון דחרב בית המקדש ואזלו לביתר וחרב נמי ביתר ואתבדרו רבנן לכל צד, ומשום הנך מהומות ושמדים ושבושים שהיו באותו זמן לא שמשו התלמידים כל צרכן ונפישו מחלוקות.

206. חידושי הריטב"א, ראש השנה לד, א (תשובת רב האי גאון)

ונשאל רבינו ז"ל: וכי קודם שבא רבי אבהו לא יצאו ישראל ידי תקיעת שופר, שהרי נראה שהיה הדבר ספק ביניהם ענין התרועה, כדאמרן "בהא ודאי פליגי" (ראש השנה לג, ב), ואין ספק שהכרעה היתה להם בדבר, כי האיך אפשר שבמצוה כזו שהיתה בכל שנה לא ידעו אמתתה ולא ראו אלו לאלו איש מפי איש עד מפי משה רבינו עליו השלום איך היה נוהג?!

והשיב הוא ז"ל, כי בודאי תרועת תורה בכל אחת מאלו בין בגנוחי בין בילולי, שכוונת התורה בתרועה לעשותה מקולות ושברים. ובתחלה היה עושה זה שברים וזה יבבות כפי מה שנראה לו שהוא יותר יפה, והיו כולן יוצאין ידי חובה, והחכמים היו יודעין כן, אבל המון העם היו טועין שהיו סבורין שיש חילוק ביניהן ושלא יצאו אלו או אלו. וכדי להוציא מלבן של הדיוטות וגם שלא תהא תורה כשתי תורות, בא רבי אבהו ותקן לעשות כל אחד כדבריו אלו ואלו. וגם הוסיף תרועה אחת משלו, כי נתן דעתו לתקן התרועה בכל מיני קול נשבר שאפשר הנוהגין, ומפני שהיה הדבר נראה להדיוטות שיש מחלוקת ביניהן נקיט ליה תלמודא על דרך מחלוקת ובדרך קושיא ותירוץ.

207. רש"י, בבא מציעא לג, ב, ד"ה בימי רבי

בימי רבי נשנית משנה זו -- הא דקתני: "גמרא -- אין לך מדה גדולה מזו". לפי שמשרבו תלמידי שמאי והלל שהיו לפניו שלושה דורות רבו מחלוקות בתורה ונעשית כשתי תורות, מתוך עול שעבוד מלכויות וגזירות שהיו גוזרין עליהן ומתוך כך לא היו יכולים לתת לב לברר דברי החולקים, עד ימיו של רבי שנתן הקב"ה לו חן בעיני אנטונינוס מלך רומי כדאמרינן בעבודה זרה (י, ב), ונחו מצרה ושלח וקבץ כל תלמידי ארץ ישראל. ועד ימיו לא היו מסכתות סדורות, אלא כל תלמיד ששמע דבר מפי גדול הימנו גרסה ונתן סימנים: הלכה פלונית ופלונית שמעתי משם פלוני. וכשנתקבצו אמר כל אחד מה

ששמע, ונתנו לב לברר טעמי המחלוקת דברי מי ראויין לקיים, וסידרו המסכתות, דברי נזיקין לבדם ודברי יבמות לבדם ודברי קדשים לבדם. וסתם נמי במשנה דברי יחידים שראה רבי את דבריהם ושנאן סתם כדי לקבוע הלכה כמותם. לפיכך אמרו בגמרא אין לך מדה גדולה מזו, שיתנו לב לטעמי המשנה.

208. ספר הקבלה לראב"ד, עמ' 47

זה סדר הקבלה כתבנוהו להודיע לתלמידים כי כל דברי רבותינו ז"ל, חכמי המשנה והתלמוד, כולם מקובלים חכם גדול וצדיק מפי חכם גדול וצדיק, ראש ישיבה וסיעתו מפי ראש ישיבה וסיעתו, עד אנשי כנסת הגדולה שקבלו מהנביאים זכר כולם לברכה. ולעולם חכמי התלמוד, וכל שכן חכמי המשנה, אפילו דבר קטן לא אמרו מלבם, חוץ מן התקנות שתקנו בהסכמת כולם כדי לעשות סייג לתורה. ואם לחשך אדם שיש בו ריח מינות לומר: מפני שנחלקו בכמה מקומות לפיכך אני מסופק בדבריהם, אף אתה הקהה את שניו והודיעהו שהוא ממרה על פי בית דין, ושלא נחלקו רז"ל לעולם בעיקר מצוה אלא בתולדותיה, ששמעו עיקרה מרבותיהם ולא שאלום על תולדותיה מפני שלא שמשו כל צרכן. כיוצא בדבר לא נחלקו אם מדליקין נר בשבת אם לא. ועל מה נחלקו? במה מדליקין ובמה אין מדליקין. וכן לא נחלקו אם אנו חייבין לקרוא קריאת שמע ערבית ושחרית אם לא. על מה נחלקו? מאימתי קורין את שמע בערבית ומאימתי קורין את שמע בשחרית, וכן בכל דבריהם.

209. פירוש המשניות לרמב"ם, הקדמה לסדר זרעים (עמ' ח)

ועם מות יהושע מסר לזקנים מה שקיבל מהפירושים, ומה שנתחדש בזמנו ולא היה בו מחלוקת, ומה שהיה בו מחלוקת ונפסקה הלכה כדעת הרוב, והם שאמר בהם הכתוב "וכל ימי הזקנים אשר האריכו ימים אחרי יהושע" (יהושע כד, לא). ואותם הזקנים מסרו מה שקבלו לנביאים עליהם השלום, והנביאים מסרו זה לזה. ולא היה דור שלא היו בו דברי עיון וחדושים. וכל דור היה עושה דברי קודמיו ליסוד, ומהם לומד ומחדש. והיסודות המקובלים לא היה בהם שום מחלוקת. וכך נמשך הדבר עד אנשי כנסת הגדולה, והם חגי זכריה ומלאכי ודניאל וחנניה ומישאל ועזריה ועזרא הסופר ונחמיה בן חכליה ומרדכי וזרובבל בן שאלתיאל, ועם אלו הנביאים תשלום מאה ועשרים זקן מן החרש והמסגר ודומיהם. וגם הם עסקו בעיון כמו שעשו קודמיהם וגזרו גזרות ותקנו תקנות. ואחרון אותה החבורה

הטהורה הוא ראשון לחכמים שנזכרו במשנה, והוא שמעון הצדיק, והוא היה כהן גדול באותו הדור.

וכאשר עבר הזמן אחריהם עד רבינו הקדוש עליו השלום והיה יחיד בדורו ומיוחד בתקופתו, איש שכלל בו ה׳ מן המדות הטובות והחסידות מה שזכהו בעיני אנשי דורו לקרותו רבינו הקדוש, והיה שמו יהודה. והיה בתכלית החכמה ורום המעלה, כמו שאמרו (גיטין נט, א): מימי משה ועד רבי לא ראינו תורה וגדולה במקום אחד. והיה בתכלית הענוה ושפלות הרוח והרחקת התאוות, כמו שאמרו (סוטה מט, ב): משמת רבי בטלה ענוה ויראת חטא. והיה צח לשון ובקי בשפה העברית יותר מכל אדם, עד שהיו החכמים עליהם השלום לומדין ביאור מלים שנסתפקו להם בלשון המקרא מפי עבדיו ומשרתיו, וזה מן המפורסמות בתלמוד. והיה לו מהעושר וההון עד שאמרו עליו (שבת קיג, ב): אהרריריה דרבי עתיר משבור מלכא. ולכן היטיב לחכמים ולתלמידים, וריבץ תורה בישראל, ואסף כל הקבלות והשמועות והמחלוקות שנאמרו מימות משה רבינו ועד ימיו, והוא בעצמו היה מן המקבלים, שהוא קבל משמעון אביו, מגמליאל אביו, משמעון אביו, מגמליאל אביו, משמעון אביו, מהלל אביו, משמעיה ואבטליון רבותיו, מיהודה בן טבאי ושמעון בן שטח, מיהושע בן פרחיה ונתאי הארבלי, מיוסי בן יועזר ויוסי בן יוחנן, מאנטגנוס איש סוכו, משמעון הצדיק, שקבל מעזרא, לפי שהוא היה משיירי כנסת הגדולה, ועזרא מברוך בן נריה רבו, וברוך בן נריה מירמיה, וכך קבל ירמיה בלי ספק מן הנביאים שקדמוהו, נביא מפי נביא עד הזקנים שקבלו מיהושע, ממשה.

וכאשר אסף כל הסברות והשמועות, החל בחבור המשנה הכוללת ביאור כל המצות הכתובות בתורה, מהם קבלות מקובלות ממשה עליו השלום, ומהם למידיות שלמדום על פי הדין ואין בהן מחלוקת, ומהם למידיות שנפלה בהם מחלוקת בין שני הדנים, וקבעם כפי מחלוקתם: ״פלוני אומר כך ופלוני אומר כך״, ואפילו יחיד החולק על רבים קבע דברי היחיד ודברי הרבים. ועשה כן לכמה ענינים מועילים מאד נזכרו במשנה עדיות (א, ה-ו), והנני מזכירם, אבל אחרי שאזכיר כאן יסוד גדול שנראה לי להזכירו כאן. והוא, יש לטוען לומר: אם היו פירושי התורה מקובלים ממשה, כפי הכללים שאמרנו כשהזכרנו אמרם: ״כל התורה נאמרו כללותיה ופרטותיה ודקדוקיה מסיני״, אם כן מה הם אותם ההלכות המיוחדות שאמרו בהם שהם הלכה למשה מסיני? והנה זה יסוד צריך שתדעני. והוא, שהפירושים המקובלים ממשה אין בהם מחלוקת כלל, לפי שעד עכשיו לא מצאנו שנפלה מחלוקת בין החכמים בשום זמן מן הזמנים ממשה רבינו עד רב אשי שאחד

אמר שמי שסימא עין אדם מסמין את עינו כמאמר ה' יתעלה "עין בעין"
(דברים יט, כא) ואחר אמר דמים בלבד הוא חייב. גם לא מצאנו מחלוקת במה
שאמר הכתוב "פרי עץ הדר" (ויקרא כג, מ) שאחד אמר שהוא האתרוג ואחר
אמר שהוא הפריש או הרמון או זולתם. גם לא מצאנו מחלוקת ב"עץ עבות"
(שם) שהוא הדס. ולא מצאנו מחלוקת בפירוש אמרו יתעלה "וקצותה את
כפה" (דברים כה, יב) שהוא דמים. ולא במה שנאמר "ובת איש כהן כי תחל
לזנות את אביה היא מחללת באש תשרף" (ויקרא כא, ט) שאין מבצעין עונש
זה אלא אם היא אשת איש דוקא. וכן עונש מי שלא נמצאו לה בתולים
שנסקלת, לא שמענו בה חולק מימות משה ועד עכשיו שאינו אלא אם היא
אשת איש ונתברר בעדים והתראה שאחרי הקידושין זינתה. וכן כל כיוצא
בזה בכל המצות אין בהן מחלוקת, לפי שהם פירושים מקובלים ממשה,
ועליהם ועל כיוצא בהם אמרו: "כל התורה כולה נאמרו כללותיה ופרטותיה
ודקדוקיה מסיני". אבל עם היותן מקובלות ואין בהן מחלוקת, הרי מדקדוק
המקרא שניתן לנו אפשר ללמוד אלו הפירושים בדרכי הדין והאסמכתות
והרמזים וההוראות שיש במקרא.

וכשתראה בתלמוד נושאים ונותנים ונחלקים על דרך העיון ומביאים ראיה
על אחד מן הפירושים הללו ודומיהם כמו שאמרו (סוכה לה, א) על אמרו
יתעלה "פרי עץ הדר", ואולי הוא הרמון או הפריש או זולתן, עד שהביאו
ראיה מאמרו "פרי עץ" ואמרו: עץ שטעם עצו ופריו שוין, ואמר אחר: פרי
הדר באילנו משנה לשנה, ואמר אחר: פרי הדר על כל מים, אין זה מפני
שהדבר ספק אצלם עד שלמדו עליו בראיות אלו, אלא ראינו בלי ספק
מיהושע עד עכשיו שהאתרוג הוא הניטל עם הלולב בכל שנה ואין מחלוקת
בכך, ורק חקרו על ההוראה שיש במקרא לפירוש המקובל הזה. וכך
למידותם גם על ההדס. ולמידותם שהעונש ממון הוא שחייב לשלם מי
שאבד לחבירו אבר מן האיברים, וכך למידותם על בת כהן האמורה שם
שהיא אשת איש. וכל הדומה לזה אינו אלא אלא לפי היסוד הזה, וזהו ענין אמרם
"כללותיה ופרטותיה", כלומר העניינים שתראה אותנו למדים אותן בכלל
ופרט, וכן ביתר שלש עשרה מדות, הם קבלה ממשה מסיני, אלא שאע"פ
שהם קבלה ממשה לא אמרו בהן "הלכה למשה מסיני", שאין אנו אומרים
פרי עץ הדר הוא אתרוג הלכה למשה מסיני, או חובל בחברו משלם לו ממון
הלכה למשה מסיני, לפי שכבר קדם שהכלל אצלינו שכל הפירושים כולם
קבלה ממשה ויש להם כמו שאמרנו רמזים במקרא, או שנלמדים באחת
המדות כמו שאמרנו. וכל ענין שאין לו רמז במקרא ולא אסמכתא ואי אפשר
ללמדו באחת המדות, באלה בלבד אומרים "הלכה למשה מסיני". ולפיכך

כשאמרנו (עירובין ד, א) "שיעורין הלכה למשה מסיני" הקשינו על זה ואמרנו :
איך תאמר עליהם שהם הלכה למשה מסיני, והרי השיעורים רמוזים בפסוק
"ארץ חיטה ושעורה" (דברים ח, ח). והיתה התשובה על זה שהם הלכה למשה
מסיני, ואין להם שום יסוד שילמדו ממנו באחת המדות, ואין להם רמז בכל
התורה, אלא הסמיכום לפסוק זה כעין סימן כדי שישמרום ויזכרום, ואין
זה מענין הפסוק, וזהו ענין אמרם "קרא אסמכתא בעלמא", בכל מקום
שנזכר...

נמצא לפי הכללים שהקדמנו, שכל הדינים הקבועים בתורה נחלקים
לחמשה חלקים :

החלק הראשון, הפירושים המקובלים ממשה שיש להם רמז בכתוב או
שאפשר ללמדם באחת המדות, וזה אין בו מחלוקת כלל, אלא כל זמן
שיאמר אדם : קבלתי כך וכך - מסתלק כל כוח.

החלק השני, הם הדינים שבהם אמרו שהם "הלכה למשה מסיני", ואין
עליהם ראיה כמו שאמרנו, וגם זה ממה שאין בו מחלוקת.

החלק השלישי, הם הדינים שנלמדו באחת המדות, ובהם נופלת מחלוקת
כמו שאמרנו, ונפסק בהם הדין כדעת הרוב לפי הכללים שהקדמנו. במה
דברים אמורים? כשהדבר שקול, ולכן אומרים : "אם הלכה נקבל ואם לדין
יש תשובה" (משנה יבמות ח, ג ; משנה כריתות ג, ט). ולא תפול מחלוקת ומשא
ומתן אלא בכל מה שלא שמענו בו קבלה, ותמצאם בכל התלמוד חוקרים על
דרכי הדין שבגללם נפלה מחלוקת בין החלקים ואומרים: "במאי קא
מיפלגיי?", או : "מאי טעמא דר' פלוני?", או : "מאי ביניהו?", כי יש שהם
הולכים בדרך זו בענין זה במקצת מקומות ומבארים סבת המחלוקת,
ואומרים שפלוני סומך על דבר פלוני ופלוני סומך על דבר פלוני, וכיוצא בזה.

אבל סברת מי שחשב שגם הדינים שיש בהם מחלוקת קבלה ממשה, ונפלה
בהם מחלוקת מחמת טעות בקבלה או שכחה, ושהאחד צודק בקבלתו והשני
טעה בקבלתו, או ששכח, או שלא שמע כל מה שצריך לשמוע, ומביא
ראיה לכך מה שאמרו (סנהדרין פח, ב): "משרבו תלמידי שמאי והלל שלא
שמשו כל צרכן רבתה מחלוקת בישראל ונעשית תורה כשתי תורות" - הנה
זה, חי ה', דבר מגונה ומוזר מאד, והוא דבר בלתי נכון ולא מתאים לכללים,
וחושד באנשים שמהם קבלנו את התורה, וכל זה בטל. והביא אותם לידי
השקפה נפסדת זו מיעוט ידיעת דברי חכמים הנמצאים בתלמוד. לפי
שמצאו שהפירוש מקובל ממשה, וזה נכון לפי הכללים שהקדמנו, אבל הם
לא הבדילו בין הכללים המקובלים והחדושים שנלמדו בדרכי העיון. אבל

אתה אם תסתפק במשהו, ודאי לא תסתפק במחלוקת בית שמאי ובית הלל באמרם (ברכות נא, ב) "מכבדין את הבית ואחר כך נוטלין לידים" או "נוטלין לידים ואחר כך מכבדין את הבית", שאין אחת משתי הסברות מקובלת ממשה ולא שמעה מסיני. וסבת מחלוקתם כמו שאמרו, שאחד מהם אוסר להשתמש בעם הארץ והשני ומתיר. וכן כל הדומה למחלוקות אלו, שהם סעיפי סעיפים.

אבל אמרם: "משרבו תלמידי שמאי והלל שלא שמשו כל צרכן רבתה מחלוקת בישראל", ענין זה דבר ברור מאד, כי שני אנשים שהם שווים בהבנה ובעיון ובידיעת הכללים שלמדים מהם, לא תהיה ביניהם מחלוקת במה שלומדים באחת המדות בשום פנים, ואם תהיה - תהיה מועטת, כמו שלא מצאנו מחלוקת בין שמאי והלל אלא בהלכות אחדות, לפי שדרכי למודם בכל מה שהיו לומדים אותו באחת המדות היו קרובים זה לזה, וגם הכללים הנכונים שהיו אצל זה היו אצל השני. וכאשר נתמעט למוד תלמידיהם ונחלשו אצלם דרכי הדין בהשואה לשמאי והלל רבותיהם, נפלה מחלוקת ביניהם בשעת המשא ומתן בהרבה ענינים, לפי שכל אחד מהם דן לפי כח שכלו ולפי הכללים הידועים לו. ואין להאשימם בכך, כי לא נוכל אנחנו להכריח שני בני אדם המתוכחים שיתוכחו לפי רמת שכלם של יהושע ופינחס, וגם אין אנחנו רשאים לפקפק במה שנחלקו בו מפני שאינם כשמאי והלל או למעלה מהם, כי לא חייב אותנו בכך ה' יתעלה אלא חייב אותנו לשמוע מן החכמים חכמי איזה דור שיהיה, כמו שאמר "(או) אל השופט אשר יהיה בימים ההם ודרשת" (דברים יז, ט). ועל אופן זה נפלה מחלוקת, לא שטעו בקבלתם וקבלת האחד אמת והשני בטלה. וכמה ברורים דברים אלה למי שמתבונן בהם, וכמה גדול היסוד הזה בתורה.

והחלק הרביעי, הם הדינים שקבעום הנביאים והחכמים שבכל דור ודור על דרך הגדר והסייג לתורה, והם שצוה ה' לעשותם באופן כללי באמרו "ושמרתם את משמרתי" (ויקרא יח, ל), ובא בקבלה: "עשו משמרת למשמרתי" (יבמות כא, א), והם שקוראים אותם חז"ל גזרות. וגם בהם יש שתהיה מחלוקת, כגון שייראה לאדם לאסור כך משום כך ואחר לא ייראה לו, וזה הרבה בתלמוד, ר' פלוני גזר משום כך וכך ור' פלוני לא גזר, וזוהי אחת מסיבות המחלוקת. הלא תראה שבשר עוף בחלב הוא גזרה מדרבנן להרחיק מן העבירה, ואינו אסור מן התורה אלא בשר בהמה טהורה, ואסרו חכמים בשר עוף כדי להרחיק מן הדבר האסור, ומהם מי שלא נראית לו גזרה זו, לפי שר' יוסי הגלילי היה מתיר אכילת בשר עוף בחלב, והיו אנשי מקומו כולם אוכלים אותו כמו שנתבאר בתלמוד (שבת קל, א). וכשהיה

הסכמת הכל על אחת מגזרות אלו אין לעבור עליה בשום פנים. וכל זמן שפשט איסורה בישראל אין דרך לבטל אותה גזרה, ואפילו נביאים לא יוכלו להתירה, ואמרו בתלמוד שאפילו אליהו לא יכול להתיר אחד משמונה עשר דבר שגזרו עליהן בית שמאי ובית הלל, ונתנו טעם לזה ואמרו לפי שאיסורן פשוט בכל ישראל.

והחלק החמישי, הם הדינים שנעשו בדרך העיון להסדרת העניינים שבין בני אדם, דבר שאין בו הוספה על דברי תורה ולא גרעון, או בעניינים שהם מפני תיקון העולם בעניני הדת, והם שקוראים אותם חכמים תקנות ומנהגות.

210. מורה נבוכים, חלק א, לא

ויש שם דברים שהאדם מרגיש תשוקתו גדולה להשגתם והשלטת שיכלו על דרישת אמיתתם, והחקירה בהם מצויה בכל כת מבעלי העיון בבני אדם ובכל זמן, ובאותם הדברים מתרבות ההשקפות ותארע המחלוקת בין החוקרים, וימצאו השיבושים מחמת שאיפת השכל להשיג אותם הדברים, כלומר התשוקה אליהם, והיות כל אחד חושב שהוא כבר מצא דרך לדעת בו אמיתת הדברים, ואין בכח השכל האנושי להביא על כך הוכחה, לפי שכל דבר שנודעה אמיתתו בהוכחה אין בו מחלוקת ולא ויכוחים ולא התנצחויות, זולתי מצד סכל המתעקש עקשות הנקראת העקשות המופתית, כדרך שתמצא אנשים שיתעקשו נגד כדוריות הארץ והיות הגלגל עגול וכיוצא בכך, אלה אין להביאם בחשבון בענין זה. ודברים אלה אשר אירעה בהם מבוכה זו רבים מאוד בעניינים האלוהיים, ומעטים בעניינים הטבעיים, ונעדרים בעניינים הלימודיים.

אמר אלאסכנדר אלאפרודיסי כי גורמי המחלוקת בעניינים שלושה: האחד אהבת ההתנשאות והנצוח המטין את האדם מהשיג את האמת כפי שהוא, והשני עדינות הדבר המושג כשלעצמו ועמקו וקושי השגתו, והשלישי סכלות המשיג וקוצר יכולתו להשיג מה שאפשר להשיג, כך אמר אלאסכנדר. ובזמננו גורם רביעי שלא הזכירו מפני שלא היה אצלם, והוא ההרגל והחנוך, לפי שיש לאדם בטבעו אהבה להרגלו ונטיה כלפיו, עד שהנך רואה אנשי הכפרים כפי שהם מן הנוול והעדר התענוגות ודחקות המזון, מתעבים את הכרכים ואינם נהנים בתענוגותיהם ומעדיפים המצבים הגרועים שהורגלו בהם על המצבים התקינים שלא הורגלו בהם, ואין נפשם ניווחת במגורי הארמונות ולא בלבישת המשי ולא בהתעדנות במרחץ ובשמנים ובמיני הבשם. כך יארע לאדם בהשקפות אשר הורגל להם ונתחנך בהם, שהוא

434

מחבבן ומגן עליהם ומתרחק מזולתם. וגם גורם זה מעוור את האדם מהשגת האמת ויטה כלפי הרגליו...

ואל תחשוב כי זה שאמרנו על קוצר השכל האנושי והיות לו גבול שהוא נעצר אצלו הוא דבר שנאמר על פי התורה, אלא הוא דבר שכבר אמרוהו הפילוסופים והשיגוהו השגה נכונה בלי שום קשר עם דת או השקפה, והוא דבר הנכון, לא יסתפק בו אלא מי ששכל במה שכבר הוכח מן העניינים.

211. מורה נבוכים חלק א, עא

דע כי המדעים הרבים שהיו באומתינו באמיתת דברים הללו אבדו במשך הזמן ובשלטון העמים הסכלים עלינו, ומפני שלא היו אותם הדברים מסורים לכל בני אדם כמו שביארנו, ולא היה הדבר המסור לכל בני אדם אלא מקראות הכתובים בלבד. וכבר ידעת כי אפילו תורה שבעל פה המקובלת לא היתה כתובה לפנים, כפי הציווי המפורסם באומה "דברים שאמרתי לך על פה אי אתה רשאי לאמרם בכתב" (גיטין ס, א-ב), והרי זו היא תכלית החכמה בתורה, לפי שהיתה הרחקה ממה שאירע בה בסופו של דבר, כלומר ריבוי הסברות והסתעפות השטות, ומשפטים בלתי ברורים שיארעו בהסברת המחבר, ושיכחה שתארע לו, ויתחדשו מחלוקות בין בני אדם ונעשים כתות ונבוכים במעשה. אלא נמסר הדבר בכל זה לבית דין הגדול כמו שבארנו בחיבורינו התורתיים, וכפי שמורה על כך לשון התורה. ואם במשפטי ההלכה חשו לקבעם בספר שיהיה מסור לכל אדם, מחמת מה שיארע בסופו של דבר מן ההפסד, קל וחומר לחבר ספר בדבר מסתרי תורה הללו שימסר לכל אדם, אלא היו נמסרים מיחידי סגולה ליחידי סגולה, כמו שבארתי לך באמרם "אין מוסרים סתרי תורה אלא ליועץ חכם חרשים" (חגיגה יג, א).

212. משנה תורה, הלכות ממרים א, ג-ד

דברי קבלה אין בהם מחלוקת לעולם, וכל דבר שתמצא בו מחלוקת בידוע שאינו קבלה ממשה רבינו. ודברים שלמדין מן הדין, אם הסכימו עליהם בית דין הגדול כלם הרי הסכימו, ואם נחלקו בהם - הולכין אחר הרוב ומוציאין הדין אחר הרבים. וכן הגזרות והתקנות והמנהגות, אם ראו מקצתן שראוי לגזור גזרה או לתקן תקנה או שיניחו העם המנהג הזה, וראו מקצתן שאין ראוי לגזור גזרה זו ולא לתקן תקנה זו ולא להניח מנהג זה - נושאין ונותנין אלו כנגד אלו והולכין אחר רובן ומוציאין הדבר אחר הרבים.

כשהיה בית דין הגדול קיים לא היתה מחלוקת בישראל, אלא כל דין שנולד
בו ספק לאחד מישראל שואל לבית דין שבעירו. אם ידעו - אמרו לו, אם לאו
- הרי השואל עם אותו בית דין או עם שלוחיו עולין לירושלים ושואלין לבית
דין שבהר הבית. אם ידעו - אמרו לו, אם לאו - הכל באין לבית דין שעל פתח
העזרה. אם ידעו - אמרו להם, ואם לאו - הכל באין ללשכת הגזית לבית דין
הגדול ושואלין. אם היה הדבר שנולד בו הספק לכל ידוע אצל בית דין הגדול
בין מפי הקבלה בין מפי המדה שדנו בה - אומרים מיד, אם לא היה הדבר
ברור אצל בית דין הגדול - דנין בו בשעתן ונושאין ונותנין בדבר עד שיסכימו
כלם, או יעמדו למנין וילכו אחר הרוב ויאמרו לכל השואלים: כך הלכה,
והולכין להם. משבטל בית דין הגדול רבתה מחלוקת בישראל, זה מטמא
ונותן טעם לדבריו וזה מטהר ונותן טעם לדבריו, זה אוסר וזה מתיר.

213. בית הבחירה, אבות, פתיחה (הבלין עמ׳ 43)

ודע שכל הזמנים שהוזכרו עד סוף זמן הנביאים, והוא זמן חורבן בית
ראשון, לא ראו עצמן צריכין לכתוב דבר שראוי להיותו נמסר על פה. ולא
היה להם כתוב רק התורה והנבואות, כי כל הצריך להם מביאורי המצוות
התלמודים הכל היה נמסר להם על פה מפי איש לאיש בשלימות.

ומה שהיה מתחדש להם והצטרכו בו להתבוננות לפי חידוש העניינים, נמסרו
להם העקרים והמדות שמהם היו מוציאים תעלומותיהם לאור ומבררים כל
דיניהם, ומה שלא הספיק להם בו ההקש והסברא, לפעמים היו הולכים בו
אחר הרוב, כאומרו ״אחרי רבים להטות״ (שמות כג, ב). ולפעמים היתה
הנבואה מבררת להם כל תעלומה, כמו שידעת מדברי קצת חכמינו השלמים
שהנבואה תגיד השגות עיוניות, לא יוכל העיון להשיגם, כל שכן הסברא. כי
כמו שיגיע לכח המדמה השגת מה שלא יגיע אליו מן החושים, כן יגיע לכח
השכלי השגת מה שלא ישיגהו בעיון ובהקדמות ובהקש וסברא. אבל מכל
מקום, הם היו נושאים ונותנים בדרכי ההקש והמדות והסברא להוציא
לאור תעלומותיהם, וכל זה לא באין מחלוקת ביניהם כלל, כי היו אז נמסרים
לנביאים וסרים למשמעתם ונשמעים אליהם.

ולפעמים היו סומכין על עניינים ודברים שהיה עניינם מקובל אצלם שכך
הלכה למשה מסיני, והוא בדבר שאין העיון ולא הסברא ולא אחת מן
המדות שהתורה נדרשת בהם שולטות בו. ולפעמים גם כן היו סומכין
קבלותיהם במקראות דרך אסמכתא בעלמא, והכל היה נשאר להם דרך
קבלה מאיש לאיש, עם מה שיחדשו להם מנהיגיהם לפי הזמן ולפי הצורך
המתחדש בלא מחלוקת.

214. בית הבחירה, אבות, פתיחה (הבלין עמ' 52)

ואחריו הגיע זמן אנטיגנוס, והיה ראשון לישיבת החכמים בזמן בית שני ולא היה לישיבתו בן זוג, ומתוך כך לא נפלה מחלוקת בישיבות בזמנו, אלא שכל חבריו ותלמידיו וחכמי דורו היו נמשכים אחר דבריו, ולכן לא הוזכרו מן החכמים שבימיו אחד מני אלף. ואחריו היה נשיא הממונה בדור, וראש ישיבה, רוצה לומר אב בית דין, זוג אחד ממונה לכל עניני הנהגת הישיבות וההוראות שבהם, ואז הוחל זמן המחלוקת. ונתמנו בתחלת הנהגה זו אחר אנטיגנוס יוסי בן יועזר ויוסף בן חנן שקבלו ממנו עם הרבה חכמים שבדורם...

והתרחב בזמנם המחלוקת מעט מצד שהיו הנשיא וראש הישיבה חולקין זה עם זה והיו תלמידים נמשכים אחריהם, זה בכה וזה בכה. ומה שנתפרסם ממחלוקותם בתלמוד הוא בקרבן הבא ביום טוב אם סומכין עליו אם לא (משנה, חגיגה ב, ב), שבכל אלו הזוגות היה האחד וסיעתו אומרים שלא לסמוך... והאחר הוא וסיעתו גם כן היו מתירין.

215. בית הבחירה, אבות, פתיחה (הבלין עמ' 62)

וסוף הדברים, אחר שנפטר הלל הזקן נחלקו הישיבות, והיו קצתם נגררות אחר הלל ונקראו בית הלל, וקצתם אחר שמאי ונקראו בית שמאי. אז פרח מטה המחלוקת ויוצא פרח ויצץ ציץ, גבהה קומתו ותארכנה פארותיו ותרבנה סרעפותיו, ונחלקו הדעות ברוב הענינים. וזהו שאמרו בברייתא של חגיגה (תוספתא חגיגה ב, ט): בתחילה לא היתה מחלוקת בישראל... משרבו תלמידי שמאי והלל שלא שמשו כל צרכן רבו מחלוקת בישראל ונעשית תורה כשתי תורות.

216. מגן אבות, הקדמה (עמ' ה)

ועם היות התורה משלמת זה ומאחדת הדעות, וכל שכן בעזר הנביא או המנהיג החכם בהודעת דרכיה ואפני סודותיה, עד שכל מניחי הנמוס הבאים אחר תורת ה' התמימה יתחקו על שרשנו, לאחד ולהסכים לבותיהם לדעת אחת, עם כל זה יקרה בכמה ענינים, שהתורה וכח ההנהגה לא תקיף פרטיהם לאחד הדעות בהם מכל צד, ולא עוד אלא שכמה פעמים יקרה המחלוקת בביאור דרכי התורה, וכל שכן בדברי החכמים הקדומים אשר בצל דבריהם והנהגתם חמדנו וישבנו, ומפיהם אנו חיים ומתמידים בעבודת האל יתברך שמו ויתברך זכרו, וכל שכן בכמה דברים יתחלקו הדעות מכח מנהיגים חלוקים לפי ריחוק המקומות וריחוק דעות המנהיגים האחרונים,

שכל אחד ינהיג במקומו כפי הנראה לו והישר בעיניו, והבאים אחריו יחזיקו במנהג ההוא, וידמה בעיניהם כי כל היוצא מגדרו כאלו החטיא את כונת התורה או כונת החכמים ז"ל.

וכבר ידעת כי סבות המחלוקת ארבע. האחת בקשת הניצוח, והשנית דקות הענין ועמקו, והשלישית סכלות האחד וגסותו וקשוי הבנתו, הרביעית החברה והגידול, כי טבע האדם לאהוב מי שנתחבר עמו או שנתגדל עמו, וידמה בעיניו היות דבריו ועניני הנהגתו כאלו הם כתובים על ספר, ויקשה בעיניו מאד סור מן הדרך ההוא כל רב או במעט.

217. ספר העיקרים, מאמר ג, פרק כג

הדבר השלם הוא אשר לא ידומה עליו תוספת ולא חסרון. ואחר שנמצא דוד יתאר תורת השם בשהיא תמימה (תהלים יט, ח), הנה אי אפשר שיהיה בה שום חסרון להגעת שלמותה ותכליתה. ומאשר כל דבר הנכתב מאיזה מין שיהיה כבר אפשר שיובן בשתי הבנות מתחלפות, עד שאפשר שתהיה ההבנה האחת מסכמת לכונת האומר והשנית מתחלפת לה מכל וכל, כמו שכתב הרמב"ם ז"ל באגרת תחית המתים כי "שמע ישראל ה' אלהינו ה' אחד" (דברים ו, ד) העברים יבינו ממנו האחדות הגמורה ואחרים יפרשו אותו על כונה אחרת, בעבור זה היה מחוייב כדי שתהיה תורת השם יתברך תמימה ותובן על הכונה הראויה שבתת השם יתברך אותה אל משה בכתב יפרש אותה לו על הכונה הראויה, וכן משה ליהושע וכן יהושע לזקנים וזקנים לנביאים וכן דור אחר דור, כדי שלא יפול שום ספק בהבנת הכתב כפי מה שראוי.

והפירוש הזה מהתורה שבכתב שמסר משה ליהושע ויהושע לבאים אחריו הוא שקראו "תורה שבעל פה", לפי שאי אפשר שיבא הפירוש הזה בכתב, כי בכתב ההוא יפול גם כן הספק שאמרנו שיפול במכתב הראשון, ויצטרך פירוש לפירוש וכן לבלתי תכלית, כמו שקרה לחבור המשניות שהוא פירוש תורה שבכתב שנפל בו מן הספק והמבוכה עד שהוצרך לפירוש אחר והוא חבור הגמרא שעשה רב אשי לפרש המשניות, וכן הגמרא שהוא פירוש המשניות הוצרך לפירוש גם כן, ורבו עליו הפירושים וחלוקי הסברות, וכן על הפירושים גם כן. ולזה הוא מבואר שאי אפשר שתהיה התורה שבכתב שלמה אם לא בהמצא עמה הפירוש הזה על פה וזהו הנקרא "תורה שבעל פה", ועל זה הוא שאמרו רז"ל (גיטין ס, ב): "לא כרת הקב"ה ברית עם ישראל אלא בשביל תורה שבעל פה", וזה לפי שאין מציאות להבנת התורה שבכתב אלא עם תורה שבעל פה.

ועוד, לפי שאי אפשר שתהיה תורת השם יתברך שלמה באופן שתספיק בכל
הזמנים, לפי שהפרטים המתחדשים תמיד בעניני האנשים כמשפטים
והדברים הנפעלים הם רבים מאד משיכללם ספר, על כן נתנו למשה בסיני
על פה דברים כוללים נרמזו בתורה בקצרה, כדי שעל ידם יוציאו החכמים
שבכל דור ודור הפרטים המתחדשים, והם הדרכים שנזכרו בתורת כהנים
בתחילתו באותה ברייתא המתחלת: "רבי ישמעאל אומר: בשלש עשרה
מדות התורה נדרשת מקל וחומר ומגזרה שוה" וכו'. ועל ידי אותן הדרכים
או אחד מהן יודע כל מה שלא נמצא בתורה בפירוש. אבל מה שנמצא בתורה
בפירוש או בקבלה אין היוצא באותן הדרכים מועיל ולא מעלה ולא מוריד
לבטל הכתוב או הקבלה. ובעבור זה תמצא פעמים הרבה בגמרא שיאמרו:
"זו מנין לך?" ויאמר המשיב: "הלכה למשה מסיני". וכן יאמר המקשה:
"אם קבלה נקבל, ואם לדין יש תשובה".

ולפי שאפשר שיפול מחלוקת בין חכמי ישראל בדבר שלא באה הקבלה בו
אלא שיוצא באחת מהי"ג מדות או באחת משאר דרכי ההבנה, הסכימה
החכמה האלהית - כדי שתהיה תורת השם יתברך תמימה - לסלק
המחלוקת במה שאפשר. וזה בשנתנה ההכרעה בכל דור ודור לרוב החכמים
ואמרה "אחרי רבים להטות" (שמות כג, ב) ואמר גם כן "לא תסור מן הדבר
אשר יגידו לך ימין ושמאל" (דברים יז, יא), ובארו רז"ל: אפילו יאמרו לך על
ימין שהוא שמאל ועל שמאל שהוא ימין (ספרי שופטים, קנד). וכוונתם בזה
לומר, כי לפי שכל אדם מדרכו לחשוב מחשבות וליחס לעצמו ההתבוננות
והסברא והשכל יותר מכל מה שזולתו, עד שתמצא כמה פתאים ונשים ועמי
הארץ מדברים תועה על החכמים ויחשבו עצמם משכילים יותר מהם, אמר
הכתוב כי אף אם יראה לחלוק שהחכמים אומרים על ימין שהוא שמאל ועל
שמאל שהוא ימין, לא יזח מדבריהם לעולם, אבל תהיה ההכרעה מסורה
תמיד אל רוב החכמים. ואף אם אפשר שיהיה היחיד יותר חכם מכל אחד
מהם ויהיה יותר מסכים אל האמת מכולם, תהיה ההלכה כהכרע הרוב ואין
היחיד רשאי לחלוק עליהם לעשות מעשה כדבריו כלל.

וזהו ענין רבי יהושע עם רבי אליעזר (בבא מציעא נט, ב), כי אף על פי שרבי
אליעזר היה מופלג בחכמה יותר מכולם עד שיצתה בת קול ואמרה: "מה
לכם אצל רבי אליעזר שהלכה כמותו בכל מקום"? עמד רבי יהושע על רגליו
ואמר: "לא בשמים היא" (דברים ל, יב), שאף על פי שהאמת יהיה כדברי רבי
אליעזר אין ראוי שנניח דברי המרובין לעשות כדברי היחיד, כי כבר נתנה
תורה על הר סיני שכתוב בה "אחרי רבים להטות" (שמות כג, ב). ואם בדבר
אחד נעשה כדברי היחיד ונניח דברי המרובין, יתחדש מחלוקת גדול בישראל

439

בכל דור ודור, כי כל יחיד יבא לחשוב שהאמת אתו ויעשה כדבריו הלכה
למעשה, ובזה תפול התורה בכללה.

218. בית אלהים, שער היסודות, פרק לו

יש מקום לקטני אמנה להרהר על אמונת עיקר זה, על דבר המחלוקות
שנחלקו חכמי ישראל משנים קדמוניות, מזמן הסמיכה נשיא ואב בית דין,
זה אומר: לסמוך, זה אומר: שלא לסמוך (משנה, חגיגה ב, ב), עד שרבו תלמידי
שמאי והלל וחס וחלילה נעשית התורה כשתי תורות. וכן האמוראים
והגאונים והחכמים הבאים אחריהם עד היום חולקים, זה מתיר וזה אוסר,
זה פוטר וזה מחייב, זה מטמא וזה מטהר בדבר אחד. ואם האמת הוא כמי
שמתיר או מטהר או פוטר, יהיה שכנגדו מוסיף על מה שכתוב בתורה, ואם
הוא כדברי אחר יהיה שכנגדו גורע ממה שכתוב בתורה, וכמו שאמרו זה
לזה במשנת זבחים (ח, י): "אם כן אתה מוסיף על מה שכתוב בתורה, אם כן
אתה גורע" וכו'. ואם נחפש, נמצא מחלוקת זה ברוב דיני התורה. ועם מה
שכתבתי בפרק שלפני זה שעיקר האזהרה בבל תוסיף ובל תגרע הוא בתורה
שבעל פה יקשה יותר, כי רוב המחלוקת שנפלו בין החכמים הם בתורה
שבעל פה.

ותשובת דבר זה כפי דיני התורה היא, כי התורה צותה "אחרי רבים
להטות" (שמות כג, ב), והוא, כי אחר שמסר האל יתברך למשה רבינו כללות
פירוש התורה ופרטותיה בסיני, מה שאי אפשר בטבע שכל אנושי לקבל
לריבויים ועמקם כדכתיב "ארוכה מארץ מדה" (איוב יא, ט) והוא ריבוי
אריכות דיני התורה, "ורחבה מני ים" (שם) והוא רוחב עומק דיני התורה
כעמקה של ים, ולא למדה משה אלא מפי הגבורה שהיה נותן בו כח לקבל
כל אורך ורוחב דיני התורה בפרטות, אפילו מה שתלמיד עתיד לומר בפני
רבו, והוא לא היה יכול ללמוד לאהרן ולבניו ולזקני ישראל ולכל ישראל כל
מה שלמד, כי מה שלמד מפי הגבורה ביום אחד מן הארבעים יום לא היה
מספיק ללמדה להם בשנה אחת מן הארבעים שנה שנתעכבו במדבר, ואם
הספיק ללמד להם מה שלמד ביום אחד ונמצא שלמדו כל
התורה בארבעים שנה כמו שלמדה הוא בארבעים יום, היה מפני שישראל
שבאותו הדור היו מוכנים ששמעו כולם מפי הגבורה "אנכי" ו"לא יהיה לך",
והיו דור שכולו דור דעה, ולא ניתנה תורה שלמה כמו שלמדה משה רבינו
מפי הגבורה אלא להם, שהיו אוכלי המן, לחם אבירים, לחם שמלאכי
השרת ניזונין ממנו. ומשם והלאה בדורות הבאים זה מוסרין זה לזה כללי
התורה וקצת פרטות, כי לא היו מספיקים הדורות הבאים ללמוד כל התורה

כמו שלמדוה יוצאי מצרים, אלא שהיו דורשים התורה במדות שהיא נדרשת בהם כפי מה שנמסרו בידם ללמוד מהם פרטי דיני התורה, כל אחד כפי חכמתו וכפי השגתו לדרוש וללמוד הרבה בדיני התורה בלי שום מחלוקת, כי כל זמן שהיתה נבואה בישראל היו מוכנים ללמוד דיני התורה על ידי המדות שנדרשת בהם בלי שום מחלוקת כנתינתן מסיני.

ואחר אנשי כנסת הגדולה שפסקה הנבואה לא היו מוכנים ללמוד כל הדברים בבירור, והיו נופלים להם ספקות בעניני הלמידות עד שהיו באים לידי מחלוקת מצד קבלתם, זה מתיר וזה אוסר וכו', ולזה אמרה המשנה (אבות א, א): "משה קבל תורה מסיניי", כי לא היה כח והכנה בידו ללמדה כי אם מסיני מפי הגבורה, וכן למדה לכל ישראל כמו שבארנו, אלא מפני שיהושע היה נכנס לארץ והיה מלמדה הוא ובית דינו לדור אחר שלא שמעו בסיני "אנכיי" וי"לא יהיה לך" ולא היו מוכנים ללמוד כולה אלא כללותיה וקצת פרטותיה, לכן אמר שמסרה ליהושע, כלומר שמסר לו שילמדה דרך כללות על ידי המדות, דרך מסירה שיוכלו ללמוד פרטיה מן כללותיה, וכן עד אנשי כנסת הגדולה שמסרוה הנביאים להם. ואחריהם שפסקה הנבואה נולדו הספקות והמחלוקת כמו שנתבאר, ועל זה אמרה תורה "אחרי רבים להטותי", במה שיחלקו בו בדיני התורה בדורות הבאים. ואחר שיטו אחרי רבים, הרי זה כמו הלכה למשה מסיני, עליו אין להוסיף וממנו אין לגרוע, והמיעוט נגררים אחר הרוב, והרי שאין בכל דיני התורה לא תוספת ולא גרעון, כי הכל הולך אחר הרוב.

ומה שאמרו על מחלוקת צרת הבת (יבמות יד, א): "איכא מאן דאמר לא עשו בית שמאי כדבריהם ואיכא מאן דאמר עשוי וכו', אפילו הכי אחר שנפסקה הלכה כבית הלל הרי היא כהלכה למשה מסיני ועליו אין להוסיף וממנו אין לגרוע, וכן בשאר התנאים והאמוראים החולקים בדיני התורה אחר שנפסק הלכה כאחד מהם.

ולא לבד בענין המחלוקות עשה רושם הפסק הנבואה, אלא גם לענין השמטת חלק מישראל מתורה שבעל פה, והם הצדוקים וחבריהם, כי תורה שבכתב לא יכלו להכחישה להיותה כתובה וחתומה מזמן נתינתה והיה ספר תורה ביד כל שבט ושבט מכתיבת משה רבינו עליו השלום. ותורה שבעל פה גם כן כל זמן היות נבואה בישראל לא יכלו להכחישה, כי כמו שהיו רואים שניתנה למשה בנבואתו בפירוש התורה גם כן לא נכתבה. אבל אחר שנפסקה השפעת הנבואה הכחישו גם כן מה שהיה להם מקובל בפירוש התורה מנבואת משה, כיון שלא היה כתוב בפירוש מאז עד עתה.

219. מגלה עמוקות אופן עד

ואלו נכנס משה לארץ ישראל לא היה מחלוקת בעולם, אבל משהכה משה
בסלע רבו המחלוקת בישראל, והוא סוד "סלע המחלוקת", רוצה לומר מן
הסלע בא המחלוקת בישראל. וזה סוד "המה מי מריבה אשר רבו בני
ישראל" (במדבר כ, יג), רוצה לומר בהכאות הסלע גרם משה שהתורה יורדת
טיפין טיפין ובא המחלוקת. וזה סוד הפסוק "הלא כה דברי כאש נאם ה'"
(ירמיה כג , כט), דמי גרם הניצוצין שמתחלקין לכמה גווונין? זה בא לנו מן
"פטיש יפוצץ סלע" (שם), הפטיש שהכה משה בסלע גרם שמתפוצצין ורבין
המחלוקת בישראל. "פטיש" בגימטריא "מטה משה", שזה גרם הכאת
המטה... ולכן רצה משה לכנס לארץ ישראל שלא יהיה מחלוקת שמאי והלל
בעולם, שישתמשו תלמידים כל צרכם ויהיה תורה אחת ומשפט אחד לכל
ישראל (במדבר טו, טז), על זה אמר "אשר מי אל בשמים ובארץ", אל אחד
בראנו כן יהיה אב אחד, כשיהיה משה בארץ ישראל יתקיים קרא "כולם
נתנו מרועה אחד" (קהלת יב, יא)... ולכן רצה משה להיות בארץ ישראל לקיים
משפט אחד יהיה לנו, לקיים קרא "מי כעמך ישראל גוי אחד בארץ" (שמואל
ב ז כג) דייקא, כי אב אחד יהיה לכולנו... השיב הקב"ה: "רב לך", אתה הוא
הגורם שרבו מחלוקת בישראל על שהכית בסלע, ואני אמרתי שנה עליו
פרשה אחד או הלכה אחת, וזה סוד "אל תוסף דבר אלי עוד", לפי שפגמת
בדבר הזה, רוצה לומר בדיבור הזה, שפגמת שלא דברת לסלע.

220. הכוזרי השני, ויכוח שלישי, אותיות א-יב

אמר הכוזרי: ראיתי ונתון אל לבי, שכל מה שאמרת לזכות חז"ל ואמתתם
הוא אמת ויציב. אמנם עדיין יש מקום למכחישים לרדות. שהרי יאמרו:
דאם איתא שכל דברי חז"ל הן קבלה, איך ראינו אותם חולקין מן הקצה אל
הקצה: זה מכשיר וזה פוסל, זה מטהר וזה מטמא, זה אוסר וזה מתיר, זה
מחייב וזה פוטר, וסוף דבר זה אומר בכה וזה אומר בכה?

אמר החבר: דע אדוני המלך, שמעולם לא נפל מחלוקת בין חז"ל על
העיקרים המקובלים, אלא על פירוש קצתם. כגון תקיעת שופר בראש השנה
נכתבה בתורה ברמז, שנאמר "יום תרועה יהיה לכם" (במדבר כט, א), ונזכרה
במשנה כדבר ידוע לכל ישראל, כדאיתא בפרק שלישי דראש השנה (משנה ב):
כל השופרות כשרין חוץ משל פרה. ואף על גב דנאמרה תקיעה ותרועה
בחצוצרות, מעולם לא עלה על לב איש ישראל לומר, שתרועה של ראש
השנה תעשה בחצוצרות או בכלי אחר שלא יהיה שופר. וכן בפרק שלישי
דסוכה (משנה ד) מזכיר האתרוג כדבר ידוע אף על פי שלא מצינו בתורה אלא

"פרי עץ הדר" (ויקרא כג, מ), דתנן: "רבי ישמעאל אומר: שלושה הדסים ושתי ערבות, לולב אחד ואתרוג אחד". ואין חולק על זה, מפני שהוא עיקר מקובל בכל ישראל ש"פרי עץ הדר" האמור בתורה הוא אתרוג, והמכחיש זה כאילו מכחיש בתורת משה, וכן בשופר.

אמנם המחלוקת היא על פירוש קצת העיקר. כגון רבי יוסי שמכשיר של פרה, שסובר שגם הוא בכלל שופר, והמחלוקת הזאת אינה נוגעת בעיקר בשום פנים. וכן ב"ענף עץ עבות", כולי עלמא לא פליגי שהוא הדס מפני שזה עיקר מקובל, אבל יחלקו אם צריך שיהיה אחד שלם לפחות או לא איכפת לן אם אפילו שלשתן קטומים, וזו אינה מחלוקת בעיקר המקובל כלל. וכן במלאכות של שבת כולי עלמא לא פליגי שהן שלושים ותשע, מפני שזה קבלה. וכן בטרפיות. וכן כמעט בכל הדינים שכולם עיקרים מקובלים ואין חולק עליהם....

אמר החבר: כתוב בתורה: "ראשית בכורי אדמתך תביא בית ה' אלהיך" (שמות כג, יט) וכתיב בהבאת הביכורים: "וענית ואמרת וגו' ועתה הנה הבאתי את ראשית פרי האדמה אשר נתת לי ה'" (דברים כו, י), והנה אין ספק שהקדוש ברוך הוא הורה למשה בסיני כל הדינים העיקריים הנוגעים לביכורים, אבל הדינים שאינם עיקריים, אף על פי שנוגעים בהם, עזבם לסנהדרין ונכללו תחת "כי יפלא" (דברים יז, ח). כגון הא דאיתא פרק רביעי דגיטין (מז, ב): "המוכר שדהו לפירות, דפליגי רבי יוחנן וריש לקיש, רבי יוחנן אמר: מביא וקורא, קנין פירות כקנין הגוף דמי. ריש לקיש אמר: מביא ואינו קורא, קנין פירות לאו כקנין הגוף דמי"...

אמר הכוזרי: ... אמנם, כיון דמילתא דשכיחא היא שימכור אדם שדהו לפירותיו, איך שכחו הדין עד שהוכרחו לחלוק בו ריש לקיש ורבי יוחנן?

אמר החבר: דע אדוני המלך, שהביכורים לא היו נוהגין אלא בפני הבית, ובית שני נחרב לפי חשבון ה"צמח דוד" בשנת ג' אלפים תתכ"ח. ורבי יוחנן וריש לקיש היו בג' אלפים תתק"ץ. הרי שעברו יותר ממאה וששים שנים אחר החרבן. נמצא שאינו דבר תימא ששכחו דין זה, כיון שלא היה נוהג בימיהם, ובבואם לעיין בהלכות ביכורים נסתפקו מה יהיה משפט הלוקח שדה לפירותיו ובקשו לפסוק אותו בדרך סברא. ואין ספק אצלי שהיה פשוט בזמן שבית המקדש קיים, מפני שהיה אז דבר מצוי בין לגבי מכירת שדה לפירותיו בין לגבי הביכורים.

221. שו״ת חוות יאיר, קצב

הנה הרב בנה חומה בצורה סביב תורה שבעל פה במה שכתב שלא שייך בה שכחה, הלואי שנוכל לחזקה ולהעמידה, מה שאי אפשר לדעתי (אף כי יצא שכר בהפסד במה שאמר שכל שאר מחלוקת חז״ל, שהם רובא דרובא מתורה שבעל פה וכמעט כל סדרי משנה, אינם כלל מסיני). ודמיא למה שכתב הרמב״ן (השגות לספר המצוות, שורש א) על הרב במנין המצות על מה שכתב בלאו תסור שכולל גם טלטול מחט בשבת וכל מילי דרבנן שהעובר לוקה מלא בזה (עיין בקונטרסים כרך א דף כח ע״ב וסוף כרך ב זכרונם בהשגות מגילת אסתר במ״ש שם ד״ח ע״ג). כי כל דבריו הם תמוהים, ואי אפשר לעניית דעתי וקלושת שכלי להולמם ולקרבם אל דעת נוטה ודעת תורה בש״ס. (ואין דברי דרך מי שמשיג ודוחה דברי מי שקדמו, רק כמודיע צערו לרבים במה שלא ירד לפלגות חקרי לב ודעת קדושים).

ונחקרה ונשובה על האחרון ראשון, כי יאמר שכל מחלוקת שאינה בפירוש כתובים או על פי י״ג מידות אינו ענין לומר שאחת משני דעות שנחלקו בו הלכה למשה מסיני, ועל כרחך עליהם אמרו רז״ל שלא היה מחלוקת בישראל עד הזוגות ומשם נתרבה והלך. איך יקבל השכל אם לא היה להם קבלה עד משה רבינו עליו השלום איש מפי איש, איך השוו כל חכמי ישראל לדעת אחת בדברים הבנויים על פי השכל ויש פנים לכאן ולכאן?

שנית, לימודים הנלמדים מי״ג מידות הם מסיני כמו שנתבאר, ואם כן לא שייך בהם שכחה, והרי התלמוד מלא במחלוקת בהם?! והרי גזירה שוה שלכולי עלמא צריך שיהיה ללמוד בקבלה עד משה רבינו עליו השלום, ובלי ספק שמשה רבינו עליו השלום ביאר הגזירה שוה ביאור היטיב, והרי נחלקו בה מהיכן יליף גזירה שוה או מדבר פלוני או מדבר אחר, שעל כן כתבו שלפעמים היו מקובלים המלות לבד לא המקומות ולפעמים בהיפך, וזה בא על ידי שכחות המלות או המקומות, כי חלילה לומר כי קבלת משה רבינו עליו השלום מסיני או מסירתו ליהושע היה חסר הבנה. ואפילו האומר כל התורה מן השמים חוץ מקל וחומר הרי זה אפיקורס. ועיין מה שכתבתי כרך ד דף מח ע״א בזה גם בספרי מר קשישא.

שלישית, דפרק קמא דברכות (ה, א) דריש מקרא ״ואתנה לך את לחות האבן״ וגו' (שמות כד, יב) שגם משנה ותלמוד ניתן למשה רבינו עליו השלום מסיני. ולפי דעת הרב לא ניתן רק פירוש המקראות ודברים הנדרשים במידות שהם חלק פחות מאחד ממאה מדינים הנזכרים במשנה וגמרא. גם על כל אמר (אבות א, א): ״משה קיבל תורה מסיני ומסרה ליהושע״...

רביעית, מה יאמר בשבע מאות, ויש אומרים אלף ושבע מאות או שלושת אלפים, קלין וחמורין וגזירות שוות שנשתכחו בימי אבלו של משה רבינו עליו השלום (בבלי, תמורה טו, ב), ואיך נשכחו והרי הם מקובלים מסיני?

חמישית, במה שכתב שאין מחלוקת בשום פנים וכו'. ולעניות דעתי כי אי אפשר בשום צד להימלט מלומר שיש שכחה, הן בפירוש הכתובים, הן במידות הנדרשים, הן בדברים שקראו חז"ל הלכה למשה מסיני, הן בשאר פרטי דינים בכל סדרי זמ"ן נק"ט, אף כי כולם הלכה למשה מסיני (וכפירוש רש"י פרשת תולדות (כו, ה) "תורתי" - תורה שבעל פה הלכה למשה מסיני. והכי מוכח בגמרא מסכת סוטה פרק ב (טז ע"א), ורש"י ז"ל על פלוגתתם בפרק ה דגיטין (ס, ב), אם רוב התורה בעל פה או בכתב, שפירש רש"י: תורה שבעל פה - שאין רמז ללמוד לה בתורה, ועל כרחינו צריך לפרש כן, דאי סלקא דעתך דכל הש"ס והנדרש בי"ג מידות קרי תורה שבעל פה, וכן הפירושים והמדרשים, איך יאמר מאן דאמר רובו בכתב? אלא על כרחך שם פירוש "רובו בכתב" כל פירושי תורה שבכתב ודרשות רז"ל על ידי י"ג מידות, אף כי בכל דוכתי זולת פלוגתתם זו, וגם שם במימראות דבתרה, קרי כל דרשות רז"ל זולת תנ"ך - "דברים שבעל פה". נקוט מיהא דאיכא למאן דאמר רובה הלכה למשה מסיני שאין רמז בכתוב, ועל כרחינו רצונו לומר פרטי הדינים במצוות עשה ומצוות לא תעשה, על דרך משל דיני שבת חגיגות ומעילות, כדתנן סוף פרק קמא דחגיגה, וכן כמעט כל דיני ממונות וטריפות גיטין וקדושין. נקוט מיהא דיש שכחה ופלוגתא בהלכה למשה מסיני).

אף כי אמר כי אמר היודע נסתרות יתברך, שסוף שיולדו ספיקות על ידי שכחה והתרשלות ועון "כי יפלא ממך" וגו' "לא תסור" ו"אחרי רבים להטות", ומצד זה שעלה במחשבתו יתברך דעת החולקים נגד האמת וגם להם ראיה וסברא מן התורה והשכל לשם שמים כמו שאמרו "בין שאמרו להדליק" וכו' (פסחים נג, ב), לכן שפיר אלו ואלו דברי אלהים חיים הם, ודוחק הוא לפרש כך. ואין לנו עסק במדרשים שונים או חלוקים בזה, כי במדרש חזית (שיר השירים רבה, א, ד) תיכף כשאמרו ישראל "דבר אתה עמנו" (שמות כ, טז) נולדה השכחה, ויש מדרש שמהכאת הסלע נולדו המחלוקת.

ודרך המלך הוא הש"ס נלך, כי בפרק אין דורשין (חגיגה טז, א) שיוסי בן יועזר אומר שלא לסמוך, ופירש רש"י (שם) שהיתה מחלוקת הראשונה בישראל. ובפרק ב דתמורה (טו ע"ב): "מימות משה עד שמת יוסף בן יועזר היו למדים תורה כמשה רבינו עליו השלום", ומפרש שם: "אותן דגמירין", משמע דאותן שלושת אלפים שנשתכחו באבלו של משה, לא היו מסכימים

445

להחזירם מתוך פלפולם, רק היו חלוקים. ונראה לי שמכל מקום מפני שלא היו שני כיתות זו מול זו, רק היו חלוקים בדעות ולמעשה הלכו אחר הרוב, לא היה נקרא מחלוקת עד זמן יוסי הנ״ל, שהתחילו לחלוק מערכה מול מערכה, אב בית דין ונשיא יחד. ובזה מתורץ קושיית התוספות פרק אין דורשין (חגיגה טז, א ד״ה יוסי) משאול ודוד שנחלקו במקדש במלוה ופרוטה.

222. מבוא התלמוד (מהר״ץ חיות) פרק יד

וכן מצינו גם כן (סנהדרין פ״ז ע״ב) דמתחלה לא היו מחלוקת בישראל, משום דעל כל הדבר המסופק, והיו דיעות שונות, עמדו למנין והכריעו כדעת המרובין. ורק מזמן יוסי בן יועזר שהיה בזמן החשמונאים, שנתפזרו חכמי הדור בשעת גזירות אנטיכוס למקומות שונות, ולא היו יכולים להתאסף במקום אחד ולא היה אפשרות לעמוד על הדברים למנין להיות נמנים וגומרים, ומפני זה נשארה ענין הסמיכה מני אז במחלוקת (חגיגה י״ז ע״ב), ובכל זאת אחר כך הטיב ה׳ לעמו ושבו הסנהדרין למקומם שוב, לא שמענו מחלוקת בשאר דברים, רק בסמיכה לבד נחלקו, מפני שכל נשיא או אב״ד החזיק בדעת הנשיא הקודם, ולא רצו לגמור הדבר במנין, ובימי שמאי והלל נחלקו עוד בשלשה דברים המנויים (שבת ט״ו ע״א). והנה מצינו עוד בימים הראשונים מחלוקת באיזה דברים בין חכמי הדור, כמו שראינו שנחלקו עוד דוד ושמואל, אם מקדש אשה במלוה ופרוטה, אם דעתו על מלוה או פרוטה, (סנהדרין כ״א ע״ב). וכן ראינו דנחלק חזקיה מלך יהודה וחכמי דורו, אם מעברין ניסן בניסן, ולא הודו לו חכמים (סנהדרין י״ב ע״א). ועוד נחלקו שני כהנים גדולים, אשר נשתיירו מן מקדש ראשון, זה אומר בידי הקפתי וזה אומר ברגלי הקפתי (יומא נ״ט ע״א). ובאמת התוספות (חגיגה י״ז ע״א) התעוררו על זה, דהרי שם בחגיגה אמרו דרק סמיכה לבדה היא מחלוקת ראשונה בישראל, וכן בתוספות ישנים יומא בהך דשני כהנים גדולים. אכן המעיין היטב יראה דלא קשיא מידי, דלא נחשב מחלוקת בסמיכה, רק מפני שהתמידה המחלוקת זמן ארוך והיתה מחלוקת קיימת בישראל, שלא נכרעה בישיבות הקודמות מזמן יוסי בן יועזר עד זמן אחרון תלמידי שמאי והלל, מה שאין כן אלו אשר הזכרנו למעלה, לא עמדו במחלוקתן רק לשעתן בלבד מפני איזו סיבה, ומיד בנפול הסיבה בטל המסובב, ועמדו למנין ונכרעו אלו המחלוקת על פי דעת המרובין כמו שכתבתי בספרי משפט ההוראה.

223. אור ישראל, סימן ל, הערה (עמ' פה)

ובזה יתבאר ענין בית שמאי ובית הלל. ובל נשתומם על המראה, איך נולד הדבר ומה סיבתה, מדוע תלמידי בית שמאי ובית הלל יסכימו לרוב כל חבורה לדעה אחת, ומה ענין חבורה לזה? כי סיבת מחלקותם היתה משינוי מזג כוחות נפשם, אשר אין ביד האדם להפרישם משכלו (כנ״ל) ואין לכל חוקר בתורת ה' אלא מה שעיניו רואות, לאחר היכולת ושמירת ערכו לבל יפרץ גבולו, ובטהרת שכלו לפי כח האנושי, אשר על פי רוב בני החבורה כוחות נפשם יצעדו במצעד שוה. והוא מאמר רז״ל: ״אלו ואלו דברי אלהים חיים הס״, כי אין סתירה בכוחות הנפשיות (כנ״ל), ואם כי כוחות נפש האדם ישתנו בכל עת, לא יפול שני בדעת שכל האדם (המטהר שכלו בדרך הישר) מצד כוחות נפשו, כי שינוי בכוחות הנפש יבוא מפאת התעוררות ענין או רעיון מה.

וזאת תורת האדם וחובתו, לחתור בכל עוז להיות כחות נפשו נחים ושקטים בעת עיונו בדבר שכלי, ובמצב שקיטת הכחות כמעט שוים המה בכל עת, ופרט לאדם השלם השומר נפשו מהתעוררות חזקות אשר ישרשו בנפשו כחות עלולים להתחלף תמיד.

224. רסיסי לילה, טז

בכל חדושין דאורייתא אי אפשר להיות דבר מבורר שלא יהיה נטייה לכאן ולכאן, כמו שאמרו (חגיגה ג, ב) : ״הללו מטמאין״ כו' ו״אלו ואלו דברי אלהים חיים״ (עירובין יג, ב), פירוש אלהים בעל הכוחות כולם הנפרדים שבעולם, וזהו לשון רבים, וכן ״חיים״ לשון רבים, דדברי תורה הוא חיות הבריאה כולה. ויש חלוקות של חיים, ועל זה נאמר ״פלגי מים לב מלך ביד [ה']״ וגו' (משלי כא, א), ״מאן מלכי? רבנן״ (כמו שאמרו גיטין סב, א), ואין מים אלא תורה (בבא קמא יז, א), והם נפלגים למעיינות שונים לאסור ולהיתר, וכסבורים אנו דהוא בדעתו של חכם, ואינו כן, אלא גם זה ביד ה' שמאיר עיניו ומטה לבבו כפי החפץ ורצון אלהי לבד.

ולכך נקרא ״דברי אלהים חיים״ דבאמת הן דברי השם יתברך. וכמו שאמרו (בבא בתרא יב, א) דמן החכמים לא ניטלה נבואה. דבאמת הוא מהשם יתברך כנבואה, רק החילוק דנבואה הוא ״כה אמר ה'״ היינו כזה ממש ואין בו הטיה וחילוק, ושני נביאים המכחישים זה את זה האחד נביא שקר, כי נביא מלשון ניב, כמו שפירש רש״י בחומש (שמות ז, א), והיינו דבורו דהשם יתברך, דהדבור דהשם יתברך ממש בגרונו של נביא, והדבור הוא התגלות לפועל, ובהתגלות אי אפשר להיות שני הפכים בנושא אחד כידוע, דשכל בני אדם

מכחיש זה, כנודע מדברי רמב"ם (מורה נבוכים ג, טו). אבל חכם הוא דבוק
בחכמתו של השם יתברך שהוא במחשבה שבמוח, שם אפשר להיות שני
הפכים בנושא אחד. ולא עוד אלא שהוא כמעט מוכרח, כפי מה שיסד השם
יתברך כל הבריאה דבר והפכו, כידוע מספר יצירה, ואין לך דבר בעולם שלא
יהיה היפוכו ממש גם כן, ובודאי יש לזה רשימו בחכמתו יתברך שהוא שורש
הרצון המוציא לפועל. רק שבפועל שני ההפכים אינם בנושא אחד, כשהוא
יום אינו לילה וכשהוא לילה אינו יום, מה שאין כן במקור שם כולא חד.
ולכך כל חידוש דברי תורה שיוצא לעולם על ידי איזה חכם, בהכרח יוצא אז
גם כן ההיפך.

וזה טעם "פוטר מים ראשית מדון" (משלי יז, יד), מים היינו תורה, מי שפותח
איזה שער ודבר, הוא ראשית מדון ומחלוקת. ואמרו ז"ל פרק קמא
דסנהדרין (ז, א): "ריש מאה דיני", פירוש כי יש חמישים שערי בינה, וזה
טעם "מ"ט פנים טמא ומ"ט פנים טהור", כי שער החמישים אין מושג,
והיינו ד"פנים" פירוש גילויים מה שהחכם מראה פנים מפני מה אומר כן.
וידוע מ"ט הם שבע פעמים שבע, נגד שבע מדות הבנין של כח ההתגלות,
ושער החמישים נגד הבינה שבלב, שזה אי אפשר לגלות כלל לחבירו הרגשת
הלב מה שהוא מרגיש בלבו הטעם לדבר, דטעם אי אפשר להסביר ולגלות
כלל, וכדרך שאמרו בסנהדרין (לה, א) "ליבא דאינשי אינשי", שאי אפשר
לגלותו בכתב, וכן בדבור אי אפשר, רק הרשימו שבלב מתלבש בדבור, שכפי
הרגשת הטעם שלו בלב, כך הוא כח הדבור, וניכר על הדבור הרגשת הלב,
אבל אמיתות טעם שהוא מרגיש זה אי אפשר לגלות.

225. מכתב מאליהו, חלק ד, עמ' 56-57

מדרש הש"ס לומר "אמר ר' פלוני אמר ר' פלוני" וגם "איכא דאמרי בשם ר'
פלוני" וכדומה. ענין הדייקנות הזאת הוא, שלא יחול שום שינוי וחילוף
במסירת התורה שבעל פה מדור לדור. וכן אמרו "חייב אדם לומר בלשון
רבו" (משנה, עדיות א, ג. ועיין ביאור הגר"א שם למה דייק הלל לומר "מלא
הין מים שאובים"). כי הדייקנות הכי גדולה באה מהההערכה הכי גדולה.
ציור לזה: במשקל היהלומים מדקדקים בכחוט השערה.

כשנתמעטו הלבבות והוזל ערך התורה בלב, נתמעטה הדייקנות ורבתה
השכחה. ואמרו ז"ל (שיר השירים רבה א, ד) שאילו שמעו ישראל את כל התורה
מפי הקב"ה לא היתה שייכת אצלם שכחה, והיינו כנ"ל. באמת כל לימוד
האדם הוא בבחינת נס, כי "אתה חונן לאדם דעת", אלא שהוא בבחינת נס
נסתר. אבל לימוד מפי הגבורה הוא בבחינת נס נגלה, ורואים בבהירות

נפלאה את ערכו הגדול של הנלמד, ואז לא שייכת שכחה. ואם במשנה ובתלמוד וגם בעניינים מחודשים מדברי סופרים דייקו כל כך במסורת קבלתם, כל שכן במסורת המקרא, שגם היא מעיקר תורה שבעל פה מפי משה מפי הגבורה.

יש אשר נתעלמו הלכות במשך הזמן, היינו נתעלם בירור דיוקי הדברים, אף שכמה עיקרי ופרטי הדין ההוא עדיין היו ידועים להם, והיו יכולים להסיק גם את החלק שנתעלם, מכל מקום פנו אז חז"ל לדרוש מתורה שבכתב, כי כיון שכבר בטלה במדת מה הדייקנות בזכירת העניין שוב אין לזה דין תורה שבעל פה, ואין פוסקים הלכה על פי זה בלי ראיות מן הכתוב.

ואף שהרבה פעמים ודאי היה בידם מנהג, איך נהגו בעניין זה מדורות שקדמו, מכל מקום אין לזה אלא דין מנהג ולא דין תורה שבעל פה, ואין סומכים על המנהג אלא בבחינת מנהג ולא בגדר הלכה. ואף שאמרו מנהג ישראל תורה הוא, היינו שהוא תורת מנהג ולא בבחינת תורת הלכה.

וזהו הביאור הנכון בכל ענייני המחלוקות בחז"ל ובראשונים, בדברים שבהכרח היה להם איזה אופן שהיו עושים כן מאז מעולם - למשל, מחלוקת בית שמאי ובית הלל בצרת ערוה, וכן רש"י ורבנו תם בתפילין - שבודאי היה אופן שנהגו כך דור דור, אבל מכיון שלא היתה להם מסורת גמורה מדוייקת לפי תנאי הדיוק הנדרשים, לא נחשב זה אלא מנהג, ועל פי דין תורה יש הכרח לשוב ולברר את הדין על פי דרכי הבירור, התנאים והאמוראים בדרכי הדרשות מתורה שבכתב, והראשונים על פי ראיות מש"ס בבלי וירושלמי ועוד. וכיון שעל פי בירור זה היה מתברר להם היפך הנהוג, דחו את הנהוג מפני בירור ההלכה על פי הגדרים שפסקה התורה, ואין לדיין אלא מה שעיניו רואות.

וגדרי אופני הדרשות הללו מתוך תורה שבכתב הם מדוייקים בתכלית הדיוק, והם הלכה ממש, ככל ההלכות שנתקבלו מסיני, ונמסרו בתכלית הדיוק. אבל מאז שנאבד ממנו דיוק גדרי הלימודים של ל"ב מדות שהתורה נדרשת בהן, אין לנו רשות לעשות דרשות לעצמנו שנסמוך עליהן להלכה. ואף שלכאורה ידענו את אופני הדרשות לפי מה שנמצאו כל כך הרבה מהן בדברי חז"ל, ונוכל אולי לדמות מילתא למילתא, אולם אפילו אם הגאון היותר גדול בתורה ידרוש על פי השואותיו והכרעות שכלו, אין לזה שום בחינת הלכה אלא הוא פלפולא בעלמא. ולפעמים אנו תמהים למה סמכו חז"ל כל כך בודאות על פירוש אחד בדרש הכתוב שדרשו, מאחר שלפי דעתנו המקרא סובל כמה פירושים אחרים. אבל הביאור הוא שהם קבלו

את הדרך המדויקת איך לדרוש ולפרש את הכתובים, ורק דרך זו בלבד זו היא ההלכה ולא הדרכים האחרות.

226. מכתב מאליהו, חלק ד, עמ' 355

וצריך לדעת שגם על פי דברי הרד"ק ברור הוא שלא בהזדמנות בעלמא נתרבו הנוסחאות. אין מקרה אפילו בגשמיות, אלא רק במשפט וצדק על פי דעתו יתברך אשר גילה. אם כן כל שכן במחלוקת בדברי תורה, מחלוקת לשם שמים, בודאי לא במקרה באו, ו"ה' נצב בעדת אל" והיה יכול להטות הכרעת כולם לצד אחד, אלא כך היה ברצונו יתברך, שתהיה מחלוקת זו, ואלו ואלו דברי אלהים חיים. ולצורך סיבב השם יתברך שתהיה המחלוקת וכו' וכו'. וכן הוא בהכרח בנוסחאות שבתורה ובנביאים שהרי מיד ה' נסתבב, ולא שייך מקרה על פי האמונה הטהורה. ולפי זה, גם אם נאמר למען הנבוכים שאפשר לפרש דקרי וכתיב תלוי בנוסחאות, אבל על כל פנים מיד ה' הוא, ובכוונה גדולה במשקל ובמשפט (ויש עוד דברים בזה בפרטי התועליות שאפשר לראות בענינים הללו), וכיון דאתינן להכי הרי הגענו לנקודה ששניהם, הן הקרי והן הכתיב, אמת הם.

227. שעורים לזכר אבא מרי, שני סוגי מסורות, עמ' רכח-רלא

שתי מסורות ישנן: א) מסורת המתייחסת כולה למסורה של לימוד, ויכוח, משא ומתן והוראה שכלית, זה אומר כך וזה אומר כך, זה נותן טעם לדבריו וזה נותן טעם לדבריו, ועומדים למנין, כמו שהתורה מציירת לנו בפרשת זקן ממרא. ב) מסורת מעשית של הנהגת כלל ישראל בקיום מצוות, וזו מיוסדת על הפסוק "שאל אביך ויגדך זקניך ויאמרו לך" (דברים לב, ז).

ידוע מה שאירע בין זקני, הגאון רבי יוסף דב הלוי, ובין האדמו"ר הגאון מראדזין בנוגע לתכלת שבציצית, שהרבי מראדזין חידשה וציוה לכל חסידיו להטיל תכלת בציציותיהן. האדמו"ר ניסה להוכיח על יסוד הרבה ראיות כי הצבע הזה הוא באמת התכלת. רב יוסף דוב טען כנגד, ואמר שאין ראיות וסברות יכולות להוכיח שום דבר במילי דשייכי למסורת של "שאל אביך ויגדך". שם אין הסברה מכריעה כי אם המסורה עצמה. כך ראו אבות וכך היו נוהגים וכך צריכים לנהוג הבנים...

והנה מחלוקת שייכת רק למסורה של לימוד. אם, למשל, ההלכה נמסרת על ידי לימוד והבנה, וקיומה מתבצע רק כשהתלמיד תופס את ההלכה ומשיגה בשכלו, אז שייכת חלות מחלוקת. אם אחד החכמים אינו תופס הלכה פלונית או אלמונית, ודעתו מכריעה בניגוד לה, הרשות בידו לחלוק ולאמר:

אני פוסק אחרת ואינני מסכים. וזאת מפאת העיקרון של "אלו ואלו דברי אלהים חיים" (עירובין יג, ב), הקובע ששני הפנים בתורה מהווים חפצא של תורה, אע"פ שהלכה כדברי פלוני. חילוקי דעות המה מגופה של מסורה וקבלה, והרי נכללים הם בכלל מה שתלמיד ותיק עתיד לחדש שאמר לו הקב"ה למשה בסיני.

ברם מסורת של מעשה והידמות, שבה אין הכרעה שכלית מעלה ולא מורידה, אינה נתפסת במחלוקת כלל וכלל. למשל, אם יבוא אדם ויאמר: אין מצה זו של חטה אלא של אורז, או שיאמר על צבע זה שאינו שחור אלא ירוק, או על יום השביעי המקובל שאין זה יום השבת, בודאי שדבריו בטלים ומבוטלים לא שרירין ולא קיימין. ולא עוד אלא שהוא נקרא כופר במסורה של מעשה המקובל בידינו מדור דור. ולפיכך כתב הרמב"ם, בהקדמה לפירוש המשנה, שאין מחלוקת חלה בין החכמים בפירושי התורה המקובלים ממשה מסיני - שלא מצינו מימות יהושע ועד רב אשי שיבוא אחד ויאמר ש"עין תחת עין" הוא ממש או "פרי עץ הדר" זהו תפוח - משום שקבלות אלו נמסרו על ידי שימוש ומעשה, לא על ידי לימוד והסבר גרידא (אם כי הגמרא יליף זה פשט זה גם מפסוקים). העיקר הקובע אותן הוא מעשה שנתקבל מדור דור. וכך הוא לשון הרמב"ם בהקדמתו: "אלו הראיות לא הביאו מפני שנשתבש עליהם העניין עד שנודע להם מהראיות האלה, אבל ראינו בלא ספק מיהושע עד עתה שהאתרוג היו לוקחים עם הלולב בכל שנה ואין בו מחלוקת". הדגש מוטל כאן על ראיית המתבצע למעשה ולא על שמיעה הגיונית ומילולית. ומעין זה כתב, בפרק א מהלכות חובל ומזיק הלכה ו, ביחס לפירוש הכתוב "עין תחת עין": "ואע"פ שדברים אלו נראין מעניין תורה שבכתב וכולן מפורשין הן מפי משה רבינו מהר סיני, כולן הלכה למעשה הן בידינו, וכזה ראו אבותינו דנין בבית דינו של יהושע ובבית דינו של שמואל הרמתי ובכל בית דין ובית דין שעמדו מימות משה ועד עכשיו". הרמב"ם מדגיש כאן כי הפירוש מבוסס על "הלכה למעשה", על מסורה וקבלה של שימוש ומעשה: "וכזה ראינו עושים בכל בתי דין מימות משה ועד עכשיו". אמנם הסוגיא בריש החובל (בבא קמא פג, ב - פד, א) טרחה לבאר את זה במסורה של לימוד ולהסיק כך מדברי הכתובים וממדרכי הסברא ההלכתית. אבל תוקף ההלכה מיוסד על מעשה, על הלכה למעשה, ולפיכך מופקעת מחלוקת, שהרי היא היתה, אדרבה, כוללת כפירה בסמכות המעשה שהוא העיקר הגדול.

INDEX

References are to passage numbers.

As a rule, topics to which sections of the book are devoted are not indexed. Where found, entries for such topics list references to the said topics in other sections. The Table of Contents should therefore be consulted in conjunction with this index. Topics discussed in the Interpretive Essay are not indexed.